RETURNING TO THE AGE OF REASON

PETER J. STORM

RETURNING TO THE AGE OF REASON

BY

PETER J. STORM

OMAHA: EATON, WILLIAMS, & CARLILE LLC
2019

Returning to the Age of Reason

Copyright © 2019 by Peter J. Storm

Library of Congress Control Number: 2019904001

ISBN: 978-1-7339076-4-4

Eaton, Williams, & Carlile LLC
1309 S 204th St. Suite 200
Elkhorn, NE 68022

First Edition

-For those who died defending truth-

Table of Contents

Introduction..9
Inspiration..15
Hope 20
Purpose..22
Management 27
Balance 30
Writing...32
Emerson...37
Academic Style...38
Fiction 43
Truth...52
Honesty..59
Family 63
Love 66
Goodness..72
Happiness 82
Escapism..91
Needs..94
Lockeanism vs Transcendentalism................................ 102
Archetypes.. 108
Judgement.. 112
Justice 116
Criminality and Catharsis 127
Thought Crime.. 130
Freedom and Equality 138
Nation States... 141
National Interaction.. 147
Politics, & Religion.. 150
Culture.. 156
Fasces 164
Western Civilization.. 170
Power Sieves 178
Communism and Capitalism 184
Propaganda.. 202
Opinion Extension.. 210
Stereotyping.. 219
Subconscious Manipulation... 228
Language Manipulation.. 235
Media 240
Disability 252
Disability Solution.. 275
Psychotropics 279

Offense..291
Abortion...297
Sex and Gender...309
Attraction...320
Women...339
Conscience and Intellect...342
Selection of Faith...351
Original Sin...355
Revealed Religion...369
Small Groups..375
Trinity...379
Christianity..392
Darkness...400
Shunning and Debate...403
Charismatics..407
Jesus..414
Egypt and Christianity..418
Leaving Christianity..426
Zodiac..439
Osiris...445
Relativity of the Material..449
Senses..452
Senescence..456
Conceptions of the Soul...462
Resonance...464
Shared Soul..473
Arrogance..480
Spencer..488
Big Bang..492
Quantum Mechanics...500
Life...502
Codon Degeneracy..507
Abiogenesis...511
Impossibility..516
Soul and Evolution...519
Sailing...522
Poetry..526
    Ebb and Flow..526
    Children...527
    Evergreen..528
    Quiet..529
Bibliography...531
Appendix A...546
    The Animate and the Man – Plotinus
    From-The Six Enneads

Appendix B..555
    The Oversoul - Ralph Waldo Emerson
    From-Essays, First Series
Appendix C..568
    Introduction - Battiscombe Gunn
    From-The Instruction of Ptah-Hotep...
Appendix D..571
    Worship of symbols - CF Chasseboeuf, Marquis de Volney
    From-The Ruins: A Survey of the Revolutions of Empires

Introduction

"Else if you would be a man, speak what you think today in words as hard as cannon balls, and tomorrow speak what tomorrow thinks in hard words again, though it contradict everything you said today."
Ralph Waldo Emerson

This book is not intended to be an outlet for artistic expression. The clapping of hands and flapping of tongues is not the target which I am aiming at. There are more than enough authors in the world who are far more skilled at fashioning clever turns of phrase than I am. Yet when examined carefully, the works of many, dare I say most of these "skillful" modern authors are often found to be stained throughout with the dye of the authors' own shallow, immature, or base philosophical views. What the Western world needs is an increase in works by authors whose primary motive for writing is to honestly, bravely, clearly, and directly defend true virtue from her many attackers; even if this defense is made with stammering tongue, poor grammar, or lack of trope.

Ralph Waldo Emerson echoed this sentiment in his essay on the "Oversoul." Here he stated that "Much of the wisdom of the world is not wisdom, and the most illuminated class of men are no doubt superior to literary fame, and are not writers. Among the multitude of scholars and authors, we feel no hallowing presence; we are sensible of a knack and skill rather than of inspiration; they have a light, and know not whence it comes, and call it their own; their talent is some exaggerated faculty, some overgrown member, so that their strength is a disease. In these instances the intellectual gifts do not make the impression of virtue, but almost of vice; and we feel that a man's talents stand in the way of his advancement in truth."[3]

This work was initially begun as a series of journals which were written over a 5-year period for two specific reasons. The first of these was to formally explore my own thoughts and soul on various subjects; documenting what I discovered therein. Placing thoughts on paper allows a person to sort out the various items which were hastily thrown into the closet of the mind, due to the furious pace of life, step back and look at them, and see if, together, they hint at conclusions which previously went unnoticed.

The second reason is to become a part of the long chain of people who passed what knowledge they could down to future generations. I cannot count the number of dead and often long-forgotten authors whom I have found a friend, mentor, and adopted relative in, as family doesn't require common blood, but merely common mind and soul. There is a great family of good men and women which transcends the constraints of time and genetics. I hope that I can repay this debt by being this for someone else.

This statement raises the obvious question of what I have to offer future readers. The answer is that I am only able to offer the world the handful of truths which I have encountered, which have seemed profound, or uncommon enough to merit recording. Of course, in doing so, I also offer them myself; as nothing better preserves the character of a man than his writings. If a writer writes long enough, regardless of the subject, his audience will eventually learn what type of person he was; not merely from the things he said, but from the manner in which he said them.

While it is understandable that some would consider this to be a selfish, or possibly arrogant motive, it doesn't have to be, and actually isn't in this instance. I only want my future reader to know me and my character in order for them to be able to sense if what I am saying matches who and what I am. Words which are not confirmed by character bare no authority. It would be ridiculous to listen to murderers like Mohammed, or Moses when they speak, or write about the subjects of mercy, or compassion. As Emerson put it once: "What you are stands over you the while, and thunders so that I cannot hear what you say to the contrary."[2]

Though this work is admittedly lengthy, I believe that the persevering reader will receive a significant return upon their time investment, if due to nothing else than the fact that, within this work, they are introduced to and directed towards many great ideas and authors from antiquity. Though most of these works and their writers have been abandoned today, a mere two generations ago, the vast majority were widely and wildly celebrated by Western academia. The cause for this abandonment is one of the topics explored within this work, and will not be reviewed beforehand.

I am well aware that the deeply personal and polarizing subject material which I have chosen to write about will likely make the academic elite smugly chortle (hopefully causing them to choke on their caviar and crackers). Regardless of this fact, let us be men and grapple with these issues both honestly and directly, rather than cowering before these tyrants who threaten whomever dares to question the morality of their words, actions, or beliefs. Such cowardice only encourages this sort on towards more flagrant abuses. I am not, hat in hand, weakly begging for their approval, hoping that they will recommend me for some award which I can later use to gloat over my peers. Any who desire that, these days, need simply to betray their own consciences and condemn all that is virtuous, intelligent, noble, masculine, or strong within Western society, and they will likely receive rave reviews.

Literary abominations, more or less actively supporting morally vacuous, or culturally destructive views, have in recent years been celebrated with increasing frequency on various "Best Sellers" lists. This is not occurring because of any singular talent or wisdom of the author, but simply because the views of an increasing number of these morally bankrupt authors happen to align with those of influential staff at the news agencies who often do the ranking. Staff who themselves are generally only in their positions because theirs, in turn, align with corrupt worldviews held by their hyper-wealthy, often international investors. Some of these books have even been stamped with the title of *classic*; an act which does a gross injustice to the many far nobler authors whose brilliant, courageous, or profound writings have caused them to be preserved, taught from, reproduced, and passed down for centuries.

Knowing that marketing, rather than merit, is the unfortunate underlying factor to most of today's literary popularity and economic success, I preemptively abandon any childish, starry-eyed dreams that this work will ever be read, much less valued by more than a handful. That is fine. If it succeeds in connecting on a deep level with even a single person, somewhere, sometime in the future, perhaps occasionally eliciting a smile, a feeling of encouragement, or possibly even a deeper understanding about some specific subject which they have been struggling with, then all of the many hours which have been invested in it will have been time well spent.

To be honest, the time was well spent whether this occurs or not. The joy of observing and participating in the slow, but steady growth of something which has been dedicated towards good ends, like a newborn child, a painting, a statue, or a book, until its eventual completion and transmission to posterity, is worth our utmost efforts. Parents, artists, sculptors, or writers fall in love with these creations during the development process, but it is the goodness which infuses these things which is actually loved, not the cells, pigment, stone, or clustering of words. Goodness can be embedded in and carried upon the medium of matter in the same way that information can be embedded in and carried upon the mediums of electricity and DNA. If we love these mediums at all, we only do so secondarily, due to their ability to symbolize the goodness which they possess.

When we see a favorite book sitting upon the shelf, for example, our hearts may grow warm, but this effect is typically not due to the paper or ink mediums themselves. More often, these feelings are evoked due to the sight stimulating memories of good and noble thoughts which were encountered during its reading. Perhaps we do like the material of the cover and pages themselves. Even this, however, is not due to the materials, but to the goodness which the materials symbolize. Perhaps this type of paper brings to mind early America and the noble principles which she stood for. Perhaps the leather cover evokes thoughts of diligent Western craftsmen creating things which they cared about and wished to last. Perhaps it reminds you of the book which your kind father used to read to you. The symbolic possibilities are endless, but all are loved because they share the common root of goodness.

"But my heart is warmed by the memory of books or a statue whose subjects are grim, morbid, or ugly," one might respond. "Doesn't this destroy your theory?"

It does not. We may remember a book full of both good and bad characters and believe that the memory of both is what warms our heart, but it is only the goodness which does so. We may love a statue of something loathsome, or ugly, but do not love the ugliness itself. Man, woman, or even god, who are all innately good, cannot love symbols for the destruction or vacuity of goodness (i.e. Evil), which ugliness, corruption, and malicious intent are. The reason for this is due to the natural goodness of our souls, and what love actually is.

Like the attraction of two magnets, love is a euphoric feeling originating within the soul, when it senses the goodness within something else and desires to somehow unite the separated goods into a greater whole. This feeling is impossible towards symbols of evil. Were it actually possible for the soul of mankind to be inherently evil, an impossibility due to factors discussed elsewhere in this work, it would still not love evil, as even the corrupt do not love corruption.

Even in works whose themes are sinister, traces of goodness may still be found. Perhaps the villain is powerful, intelligent, beautiful, or handsome. All of these are good qualities; power meaning the freedom and ability to effect one's will, intelligence meaning a mind full of well-organized knowledge, and beauty and handsomeness meaning goodness of the female and male forms, respectively. Perhaps the villain has a powerful, carefully crafted weapon, which he intends to use for harm. The intelligence of the mind necessary to design and fabricate such a weapon may be admired as a good. The villain's intention to cause harm, the potential for harm which the weapon symbolizes, and the harmful act itself are without goodness and impossible to love.

Consider a painting or statue of something ugly; perhaps the rare few surviving ones of Typhoon, the ancient Egyptian murderer of Osiris, Christian ones of the Devil, or Hindu ones of Kali. Though we may love and feel our hearts stirred even by these, it is not the ugliness observed within them which we love. The ugliness within these works is merely a device used by artists to symbolize evil character, or malicious intent. If we love these works at all, we do so because of the symbols of good which we sense even here, in spite of and beneath those of evil. Things such as the obvious strength of the limbs, the skill and planning of the craftsmen who formed it, the bold colors of the paint, the thoughtfulness of those who preserved these things for posterity, the deterrent effect which these ancient "boogie men" had upon potential miscreants, and many other things which are good in themselves.

Yet we do not make the goodness which infuses and rides upon these mediums. Instead, goodness appears to be more of a constant, like the product of universal mass and energy, which can neither be created, nor destroyed, but only changed. It is almost as if we must charge ourselves with it, like batteries, before we can pour it into our works. As plants draw carbon from the carbon dioxide within the surrounding air, in order to concentrate it within their newly forming leaves and branches, so we also seem to draw goodness from external and internal sources, prior to attempting to concentrate it into our creations. To the extent which we succeed in this effort, the production has worth.

A painter, for example, first must soak in the goodness of his subject's form, perhaps absorbing the sublime feeling which he has when viewing a landscape, the good memories of his instructor's kindness and diligence while teaching him, the goodness felt by the soul when it views the various beautiful colors in the surrounding world, colors which painters attempt to mimic with their paints, the goodness of technical execution and expertise which were observed in the works of artistic peers and past masters, the goodness of his own personal character, and the goodness of the symbolic message which he hopes that his art will transmit to his audience. He then mixes all of these goods within his mind and attempts to channel them through his hands, brushes, and paints onto canvas. The same is true for a sculptor, who carves or molds away from the stone or clay all which does not resemble the vision of the work held in his mind, which is itself a product of the mixture of goodness he previously absorbed.

In like manner, a writer must first absorb goodness before he can concentrate it into any writings of worth. Perhaps these good thoughts stem from a combination of life experiences which afforded him a unique insight into goodness found in the external world, a specific person, or a group. Maybe he viewed the beauty within the art of the artist mentioned above, participated in a struggle for a noble cause, enjoyed seeing the smile of his infant, or observed an action which was selfless, courageous, or just. Perhaps he spent time listening to, or studying the humanitarian concerns of a modern Jesus, Mencius, or Mother Theresa. For Emerson, it was likely his daily walks through the woods, where he could soak in the beauty and goodness of the natural world.

The good thoughts of our writer could also be internally derived; perhaps even primarily so. He may have spent long hours looking within at his motives, considering the goodness of his own soul and the souls and motives of others, or pondering the commonalities between memories of various concepts and experiences which are all considered to be good. Writing derived from such internal musings tends to be called philosophical, psychological, or religious; the latter two simply being specific subtypes of the first.

Whether internally or externally inspired, the material aspects of all of these human creations, as well as their creators, will eventually melt into mere memories, like ice. As the memories themselves drift further down the streams of time, most will fade until forgotten. This should not discourage us, though. Should photos of a loved one fade or be destroyed, this damage does nothing to the individual the photo attempted to mimic. In the same way, the common goodness which producers of noble works attempt to symbolize is unaffected by the wear or destruction of its symbols. Through all of our faltering, flawed, and error filled efforts, we were attempting to symbolize nothing less than perfection. And this highest form of goodness is none-other than God.

Peter J. Storm
Mar 26, 2019

Inspiration

For some years now, I have attempted to saturate my mind with the writings, and therefore the thoughts, of great authors: the Emersons, Platos, and Montaignes of the world. I didn't dare to hope I might also be fortunate enough to one day have and record thoughts which were at the same level as these men, yet I knew that the world needed this type of writing. These men were unafraid of challenging society's most deeply held views, knowing that truth could bear the scrutiny and would shine all the more for it. Rather than crumbling under the abrasion, as error did, it took on a polish and gleamed.

But where were these authors today? All that I generally encountered were writers on popular, yet shallow topics and writers on technical topics which were void of the humanity which we all desire to hear about and experience. The public has no interest in things which do not impact the lives of mankind. We only care about technology, science, art, etc. due to how they relate to and impact man. We only care about the Mona Lisa because of the feelings which her beauty and DaVinci's skill evoke within us. We only care about politics because we know that the titanic movements of nations documented therein are affecting human lives; potentially even our own.

The only courageous authors whom I encountered were morally corrupt atheists who courageously attacked anything which represented goodness, God, or high culture, or those religious men and women who fought to defend these things. Yet both of these rigidly refused to stray from their own party dogma. The atheist dared not question the ordained views of his new orthodoxy. For example, atheists who dared to question the ethical impact upon culture of homosexuality, would immediately be categorized as one of the *religious enemy* and be verbally, socially, and more frequently these days, even physically attacked.

The religious minded, especially those among the Muslims, bravely defended what they understood to be truth, but were equally inflexible and dogmatic. The Muslim would fight against the obvious fundamental damage which atheism was having on culture, but would also attack, sometimes verbally, other times with blade, bullet, or explosive, those "apostates" who dared to question the infallibility of the Koran. Men from other faiths, such as Catholics, Protestants, Hindus, and Jews, took up the battle against the atheist worldview as well, but were generally less prone to violence; merely shunning, or excommunicating those who dared to challenge core aspects of their dogma.

The world is weary of these dogmatics on both sides of the fence. It yawns at the emptiness and egocentrism of the atheists, as well as at the overconfidence, meaningless jargon, and false bliss of the religious. The world wants real men and women. Men and women similar to what they know themselves to be within; uncertain about certain things, and yet willing to explore them, certain about other things, and yet willing to adapt, should they discover that the previous opinion which they thought to be infallible, was in fact, flawed.

I assume that the reason that it is difficult to find written works by men such as this these days is due to the fact that the majority of those publishing nonfictional works which would discuss these things are men who have already had the clay of their views molded by professors and hardened by many years spent within the kilns of the religious, or secular universities. Noble writers of the Emersonian strain were surely still out there, but were likely submerged beneath this flood of lesser works.

We must boldly attempt to fill this gap. We must again turn our minds from the circus which the profiteers put on, competing for our attention and wealth, and turn them towards what is important. We must fill our shelves, schools, hard drives, and newspapers with these new works. We must once more write Bibles, and Vedas, and Korans, stripping the new products of the errors which stained and lessened the value of the old.

To do so, we must first saturate our minds with truth, wherever it may be found. Generally, the purest draught of this comes from philosophical writings, which shed all veil of allegory and deal with us directly. Not everyone is initially able to stare into these suns for long periods though, but seek truth where you can. If you find it during quiet meditation, do so, if you find it during walks in the woods, do that. If you can only handle small morsels of truth at a time, like cereal, floating in the milk of allegory, then do that. However, be cautious with this latter approach, as this milk masks the noxious, as well as it does the nutritious.

One author whom I read stated that this is only half of the work. Doing trade in wisdom requires more than merely learning to be a skilled listener, or reader. The complementary skill which must be acquired is that of assembling and delivering wisdom in a manner which increases the odds that it will have its desired effect, as much as is reasonably possible. Reading helps one learn to turn words into thoughts, but writing helps one learn to turn thoughts into words. Both weapons are essential, before entering the arena.

We must have courage and persistence. Perhaps we are not the world's best writer. A philosopher whom I read once said that if one wants to be something, then do that thing. If one wants to be a skilled writer, then write. Grind at it day after day, year after year, until a reflection may be seen on the stone. Evidence that there really is no other way to develop this skill can be seen reflected in the fact that a disproportionate number of accomplished authors started out as simple journalists; men such as GK Chesterton, Benjamin Franklin, Samuel Johnson, and Albert Pike, among many others. These were journalists who plied the pen and sculpted words day after day after day, until the action of writing became effortless, and their minds could focus more upon the subject and ends, than the medium and means.

The ancient Greeks were familiar with a type of sublime rapture which could occasionally occur during times when the will is intently directed towards the pursuit of truth. Emerson discusses this phenomenon in his essay on the Oversoul.[3] A passion takes hold of us and words flow effortlessly onto lips or page, lines and colors spring onto canvas, and clay and stone naturally seem to find their form. During these moments, it is as if we are connecting with some external, or more likely internal fount of energy which suddenly makes our mental machinery function as it was intended to by design. Due to this, the Greeks particularly revered poets. They believed that these men occasionally wrote things, when in this passion, which had been provided to them by God. This is the reason why they generally invoked (i.e. called upon) the muses prior to the commencement of any important oration, or written work.

It seems the height of pomposity to believe that any of these scribblings full of bad spelling and often worse grammar could be the product of such divine inspiration, however, I must admit that the destination which I arrive at when writing, is often very remote from the target which was planned for at the outset. Indeed, I am often startled by some of the thoughts which I encounter, which appear to spring from the mist via a sort of instinct.

Oh, that we could forever think like this. It is loathsome to descend back into the mundane, half-awake type of thought which embodies the majority of our waking hours. We drudge through efforts which are required of us in order to earn enough to care for and maintain our bodies, all the while pretending that these commercial interests are actually significant. I somewhat envy being able to refuse the demands and often corrupting influences of society in order to seek truth within. Many of the ancient Essenes, Brahmins, Yogis, and Buddhist and Christian monks would remove themselves as much as possible from the world in order to gain a clearer understanding of the higher, more important things in life. But though tempted by this approach, I believe it is ultimately both selfish and immature.

As many Western philosophers have so keenly observed, the soul of man has an inherent need for activity. Also intermixed with our other virtues is a sense of compassion for our fellow man. It is folly to seek peace by attempting to silence this sense of compassion and drive for activity, especially when confronted by a world which is in desperate need of both. This does not bring happiness, but rather guilt, shame, and self-loathing. Many refuse to admit this fact and instead attempt to convince themselves that this mixture of negative feelings is a more sublime form of happiness. Often, they attempt to distract themselves from these natural feelings by the use of drugs and alcohol, or by repetitive or meaningless labor (e.g sand drawings).

We must not ignore our natural impulses. We must act. Each day is another opportunity for mankind to prop up what is leaning, and to soften and warm the parts within them which have grown cold and hard. Each morning, as the river of time changes its liquid mass, all once more becomes something new. New, yet wearing a familiar, though faded mask: much like the mask we observe in the mirror each morning. Oh, that we could shed it and show the world what lies beneath our ever more care worn visages. That all could be intimate and know each other for who and what they truly are, beneath title, wealth, age, beauty, strength, and stature. To know the true character of one's neighbor, in order to avoid leaning on broken reeds (Isaiah 36:6).

The only way to know such things is to spend long periods together, which provides opportunity to scrutinize views and actions under the various lights of circumstance. During the rare moments when the jolts of sudden change dislocate the masks of social propriety, only then do we glimpse the heart beneath. Yet those few moments are often enough. One may come to know the true character of another in much the same way through the reading of lengthy works, as the author occasionally dislodges his mask while moving between various topics.

In fact, it is likely easier to learn a man's true character through his writing than by spending time with him. When spending time with someone, much of the time the companion is often only a silent co-observer and co-experiencer of whatever events happen to be occurring. Even when these companions do speak, the largest portion of what is generally considered *polite conversation* is mere triviality. "How is the weather?" "Oh, you have a cold?" "Where shall we dine?" It is only during the few odd moments between our outings, our feedings, and our rests, that two individuals may actually brave to expose themselves via a sharing of deeper thoughts.

In writing anything that is worth reading, one is forced to go beyond the superficial, which would generally only fill a page or two, look beneath the ice, and bring up some treasure from the depths to be scrutinized by the world. There are certainly men who fill whole volumes with nothingness about trends, hobbies, sports, or fetishes, but the readers of these works come away no different men than they were when they first leveled eye to their writing.

The ultimate purpose for reading is to learn about ourselves, others, and the natural world we live in, in order to have peace of mind, clear direction, and better understand how to effect our noble desires. Speak about this. Write about this. Surely men must also communicate trivialities in order to function within society, but let the ratios be flipped. Let them begrudgingly relay the scores of the recent game for but a moment, before moving on to discuss their ideas about how to improve themselves, their culture, their nation, and the world. Spend but a moment bemoaning your health, and then share your strategies and successes in improving the health of your character. Candidly and courageously speak your noble thoughts. If your thoughts are so base that you are embarrassed to expose them, share your noble recognition of the fact, your noble plan for improvement, your successes, or requests for advice, or for the good of any unfortunate enough to fall within earshot, be silent.

Hope

One of the most beautiful things about the future is its indeterminacy. Due to this, there is a constant reason for hope. Regardless of how hopelessly corrupt a nation, or its leaders may have become, justice is ever on the horizon. It is born from the inherent goodness of the human soul, and therefore naturally tends to appear in the nations we pour our souls into. All that is necessary for its return is the removal of ignorance and error by the refining fires of free and open debate. True freedom of speech; not the empty promise of it which exists in most of the West today; where our legal systems are being hijacked and used to progressively enslave us. And yet hope remains.

Consider an example from the Classical Era to drive this point home. Seneca and Boethius, two honorable Romans who both passionately loved, served, and attempted to protect the Empire, both wrote during separate periods when social and political vice had established seemingly permanent footholds within Roman government. During these times, both men would have been excused for thinking that the world was beginning its downward spiral into savagery, and that the dream of a government founded upon virtue and justice would never return to the West. Within his writings, we encounter Boethius struggling with and eventually overcoming this very thought. In Seneca's writings, we encounter the classic manly resolve and courage of the Stoics. He directs those who are struggling with a lack of hope about future happiness to consider how many things in their lives they thought were inevitable, yet that turned out other than as expected.[1] In addition, he directs us to consider in retrospect how many things in our lives we had never anticipated would occur, yet which had done just that.

This is a profound and sobering thought for any struggling with hopelessness, which is the parent of depression. If anyone thinks back upon situations in their life 5 years earlier, could they ever have imagined the winding series of events which placed them here, where they are, in the situations they are in, thinking the thoughts which they are thinking at this very moment? No one could. In like manner, no one can have more than a vague notion of where they will be, what they will be doing, and whether the thoughts which they will be thinking will be rapturous or morose 5 years hence. The future always holds uncertainty, therefore, there is always a reason to hope.

For Boethius and Seneca, these storm clouds eventually did disperse, and the sun of civilization, culture, and good government once more illumined the West. Sadly, this did not occur until centuries after both men had been murdered and even memories of the locations of their graves had been lost. Yet even murder could not prevent the wisdom which Seneca memorialized in his *Epistles to Lucilius*[14] and Boethius in his *Consolation of Philosophy*,[63] from ultimately sprouting anew within the minds and hearts of unforeseen future generations; directly contributing to the Renaissance.

Purpose

We are all placed on this Earth, at this moment, in this very place, for a purpose. God and the universe, who may ultimately prove to be one, need us here now for some cryptic purpose, and brought us forth to accomplish it. Sometimes statistically improbable events occur that seem to hint at this greater cosmic plan, however, the primary reason why I believe in this purpose is that I instinctively sense it within.

Like the almost imperceptible, gentle, yet constant gravitational pull which a distant asteroid feels from the sun, something within us pulls us along in certain directions towards specific unknown ends. It is as if we blindly feel our way towards our destiny. From the various philosophical works which I have searched, hoping to learn more about myself, it seems that this pulling element within us goes by many names, such as *soul, conscience, heart, essence,* and *self.* These pullings are the very reason why I now sit at this worn old scroll top desk, which I bought for $50 at a garage sale, typing this, rather than enjoying the warmth of the bed that my wife lies sleeping in. I know that this premise sounds fatalistic, but allow me to provide a few examples before both this work and I are summarily dismissed as overly emotional, eccentric, or hyper-religious.

When I look back over my brief life, I believe that the first time that I noticed the previously mentioned impulse was shortly after separating from the Air Force. I have no doubt that such things were occurring long before this time, but this is the first time that I remember the feeling being strong and distinct enough to make me take notice of, and question it. This first incident occurred while I was visiting my father as he installed an NMR (essentially a vertical, small bore MRI for research) at the University of New Orleans. I recall walking down the vacant hallway of one of the colleges and momentarily, in passing, observing through a half open door a vast array of chemistry glassware stacked within an empty lab. The pull that I felt at that moment was foreign to me, yet unmistakable. Was this merely excitement about my future collegiate prospects? I considered this, of course, yet I had felt excitement before and this felt strangely different. It was somewhat similar to a longing, but though very real, was brief, and rapidly forgotten amid the din and distractions of daily life.

The next time that I recall experiencing a similar feeling was when I was taking a high load of community college courses, hoping to transfer to a university early and complete my degree, prior to the expiration of my military educational benefits. At the time, I thought that I was struggling with a high workload. Of course, I would later learn that I was mistaken about this, as most youths do. While one day wandering the community college library in between classes, when I of course should have been studying, I remember for some reason feeling strongly drawn toward a copy of Plato's *Republic* which I had encountered on a random shelf. Taking hold of this book, I flipped to the back and noted how it had only been checked out a few times in the many years that it had made this library its home. Yet skimming through this work instilled a thrill within me similar to the one that I had felt when working with my father. I found it hard to believe that, despite the sometimes half-hearted efforts of some of my professors, who were likely themselves dissatisfied to be teaching in a rural community college, here I sat holding and reading the words of a man whom many generations had considered to be one of the wisest to ever live. I don't remember if I even finished the *Republic* at that time, but I remember to this day the thrill which that long-ago attempt instilled.

Continuing on to my university days, I recall experiencing a definite intensification of the longing or pull that I previously mentioned. The first instance of this was sometime during my senior year. Again, it occurred when I was in the library, where I was supposed to be studying for some one, or other, of the perpetual stream of exams which define college. Instead I found myself wandering about, noting the various sections of the facility that I had never explored. By chance I ended up in what I didn't know at the time was the classics section. In fact, I only had a vague notion during that period what the definition of a classic actually was. I recall, however, feeling the now familiar tugging within, stronger than I had experienced during any of the previous instances.

As an engineering student, my classes consisted of little that was not science oriented. I blankly gazed at and picked up a few of these works, whose authors' names sounded vaguely familiar. When I opened their stiff-backed covers, I was yet again surprised at how seldom they had been checked out in the 50 or so years since their purchase. I remember spending perhaps an hour in front of that shelf, eventually sending a long-winded E-mail to my family about the injustice that I felt over students being allowed to graduate without exposure to this ancient wisdom; wisdom which I didn't yet know myself.

Another time, I recall being interested in and staring at an old textbook on Attic Greek; much to the amusement of a Greek linguistics major who sat in a nearby chair at the library. This student was happy to show off his skill when he saw that I was one of the rare people who cared about the subject. I still, however, didn't know why I cared about, or was being drawn towards any of this.

These odd scenarios repeated themselves while I was in medical school. In fact, I remember being so apathetic about what I was learning in my classes, that, privileged as I was to have been accepted to such a prestigious program, I was miserable. I loathed my classes, skipped them as often as possible, and ultimately withdrew in good standing. For many years afterwards, I felt that I had made a grave mistake, as my former classmates went on to make six figure salaries, while I struggled to find a career which I could be passionate about, which would simultaneously support my new and growing family. In retrospect today, I am not so sure that this decision was a mistake.

Fast forwarding to graduate school, I once again found myself wandering the library; in spite of my graduate class load, duties as an Organic Chemistry teaching assistant, husband, and soon to be father of 5. I eventually made my way to an area of the basement that was very likely off limits. On the shelves before me sat various books showing signs of extreme old age. I greedily picked one up, relishing the obvious antiquity of the thing. I only recall today that it was something about seafaring, written perhaps in the late 1700's.

Why did I love this feeling? Why did I later find myself looking for even older books in other sections of this library? Why did I feel as if I had stumbled upon buried treasure, when I learned that the interlibrary loan system allowed graduate students, such as myself, to acquire any books which my unfocused heart desired, at no expense, regardless of the work's obscurity, or antiquity? Surely there must be some mistake. I couldn't possibly have been given the keys to all of the treasures of wisdom which the learned men of the world had compiled.

This discovery resulted in my spending countless hours photographing obscure works by men such as William Penn and Miguel Servantes. This was before scans of such works had become readily available online via such organizations as Hathi-Trust and Internet Archive. I was thrilled. Yet my excitement was tainted with guilt. I knew that I had what were, in my opinion, mind numbingly boring biotechnology courses to be studying for, and a wife and children depending upon me to do so. Some nights at home, when I wasn't conducting experiments, or working on inventions in my garage or closet, I would stay up all night studying religion or philosophy.

Progressing on to several years ago, I noticed partial sets of both the *Britannica Great Works of the Western World*, and the now discontinued *Harvard Classics* sitting quietly for sale at a monthly book sale at the local library. The feeling set in again. Needless to say, I left the library with several boxes and a smile on my face. After digesting a few of these works, I located and purchased complete sets and developed and implemented a systematic reading plan to complete both sets in their entirety.

Why? At this point, I had completed reading several hundred ancient philosophical, as well as religious works, ranging from Boethius to Seneca, yet I had no real direction. I knew that I had a thirst for something, yet I couldn't seem to quench it, or even locate what would. Since community college, I had increasingly read various things that I felt drawn to, and had only given the bare minimum required effort to the works which I had to read for my academic or professional pursuits. In seeking what would satisfy, I grazed subjects ranging from 1800's works on calculus, to those on the canonization of the Old Testament. Occasionally, I would encounter something that temporarily slaked my thirst, but it would always return even stronger afterwards.

I almost exclusively read what I felt I was able to draw the most benefit from, and what I felt the most attraction towards. These generally consisted of modern scientific works, and with few exceptions, philosophical, historical, or religious works written prior to perhaps the mid 1920's. Surprisingly for me, when I discussed and would defend my reading preferences with intelligent, devout, kind, and otherwise close people, I received a large amount of critique that frequently degenerated into insult. Several made very clear that they believed that my reluctance to commit to reading the more modern religious works which they recommended, which they felt would remedy the bulk of issues that I struggled with concerning my faith, was due to some bizarre sort of arrogance, or "intellectual snobbery," as one person called it. As much as I tried to explain to them that this wasn't the case, it fell on deaf ears. They didn't seem to want to understand for fear of finding out that they themselves could actually be mistaken about principles which they had built their lives around. It was easier to dismiss me as either arrogant, or mildly disturbed, and move on to feeling better about themselves.

How could I explain to others these feelings that I was just starting to recognize myself, and at the time hardly understood? I tried repeatedly, but eventually decided that people who hadn't yet felt, or recognized this feeling, would be unlikely to grasp the concept. This is because senses can only be described within their own framework, as colors can only be described within the framework of vision. Imagine explaining the color blue to a man born blind, or the sound of a train to one born deaf. Imagine trying to explain the feelings of love, or anger, for example, to someone who had never felt them. It is impossible.

In the same manner, internal feelings, such as the one I seemed to sense, could only be described within the context of the sense that was feeling it, or by comparing it to other, similar feelings. Yet few of those whom I discussed these issues with seemed to feel, or at least to recognize, what I now felt. So be it. They were good and well-intentioned people, generally speaking. They would come around eventually. Patience seemed the better approach. I would follow the sound advice of Epictetus, who said in his *Enchiridion*, "Is a brother unjust? Well, keep your own situation towards him. Consider not what he does, but what you are to do to keep your own faculty of choice in a state conformable to nature. For another will not hurt you unless you please. You will then be hurt when you think you are hurt."[5]

As the hues of an aurora continuously change with imperceptible gradation, an idea slowly began to dawn upon me, but seemed to have formed in my mind long before I noticed it. Perhaps these sundry scenarios and compulsions were actually my being called towards a purpose that had been ordained for my life by my creator. Could it be that all of these strange stirrings, which I increasingly felt within, as the years passed, were a sort of awakening, or the strengthening of a sense which I had always possessed within, but that I had previously been too dull to discriminate from the internal and external clamor competing for my attention? This was a comforting thought, as I reflected upon it, but realizing the potential egotism of such an idea, I decided to ruminate upon it for a while, despite its appeal. I wanted to ensure that I wasn't merely telling myself what I wanted to hear. The more that I thought about this, the more sense it seemed to make. While continuing to study, I eventually stumbled across the writing of someone from antiquity who had obviously felt the same things that I had: Mr. Battiscombe Gunn, in the introduction which he wrote to his translation of *The Instruction of Ptah-Hotep*...[6] I have included this introduction in its entirety in Appendix C.

If I was correct about this, if the various compulsions which I had felt were due to my growing consciousness of the purpose which had been written within my very being, where was it all leading? To what end was it pulling me? In my case, it has led to the creation of this work. I no longer have a choice about working on it. I write because I must. Somehow within, I feel the rightness of the action and am drawn to scribble these things down, as imperfect as both they and I may be. When I wake, I am thinking about when I can steal time away from my busy schedule to work on it. If I lay down without sanding some rough spots away from this stone, I do so with a sense of guilt.

Management

The types of managers that businesses hire tend to reflect the traits of those who select them. If the selection process is a democratic, front-line driven one, the manager will tend to reflect the front-line. If the front-line are mostly borderline alcoholic sports fanatics, then the new manager will tend to be the same. In like manner, if the front-line are mostly ethical and focused upon important issues (a rare company indeed), then the manager selected will tend to be of this strain as well.

If the selection process is a tyrannical, exclusively "top-down" driven one, we often find that the manager selected tends to share traits of the senior executives who selected them. Often this results in an unfortunate tendency towards avarice, arrogance, and insincerity within the new manager. In a few rare instances, however, noble men and women have successfully ascended the highest rungs of the corporate ladder, though often not without great difficulty, and have been able to hire other managers who exhibit similar noble traits.

If the selection process is aristocratic, new managers being selected by peer managers in a "middle-down" manner, the manager selected tends to be whichever applicant most closely reflects the composite personality traits of these peer managers. If these peers are mostly "dirt-bags," then the manager selected tends to be as well. If they are mostly honest and focused, then the new manager tends to be also.

Unfortunately, within the federal service, I find that affectation is more the norm which is encountered among leaders, than the exception. This speaks poorly of the character of the entire chain of leadership who select these managers in a purely "top-down" manner. Junior managers and subordinates perpetually dissemble humor at pithy comments which are made by senior management, only to drop this disguise the moment these senior managers leave the room; subsequently flashing a more genuine sardonic grin to those remaining within, whom they assume share in their nominally secret insincerity.

Senior managers, or *executives*, as they so haughtily prefer to refer to themselves, are generally in the positions which they are in because they are masters of this art of affectation and dissembling. These chameleons only rarely drop their masks and reveal what lies beneath to the privileged few within their inner circle, who are generally only allowed within because they are seen as equally amorphic and insincere. Mutual awareness of this common guilt of insincerity creates a sort of fraternity among them. All are more or less equally guilty of it, therefore none will be likely to betray the secret. It is only the rare honest man whom they truly fear. This man would have power over all of them, in that they would have nothing which could be used against him, binding him to them. They therefore generally strive with all of their might to prevent the admission of this type of man into their circle; finding the smallest fault related to his performance and claiming it to be insurmountable, while they hypocritically overlook or excuse things exponentially worse among themselves.

The peers of middle managers are often either operating within such a drastically different functional area of the organization that they have little to offer each other in the way of advice or support. In addition, their areas of responsibility are often poorly defined, or overlap somewhat, forcing them, in the resource lean environments of today, to compete to shed work upon each other. This competition to slide duties from one's own, onto another's plate, cannot but breed distrust and resentment. What can the final result be but that an honest middle manager often finds himself adrift in a sea of smiling insincerity. Surrounded by others, yet his own thoughts being his only honest companion.

Can it be as challenging for the front-line manager? This is unlikely, given that the latter retains the ability to portray himself as one of those who still does *real work*, (management never being considered *work* by front-line staff) by lending a hand on the front lines whenever times become difficult. This is something which middle managers often cannot do, even if they wished to. Often, they either never performed the highly specialized front-line duties of those whom they oversee, as the front-line manager often did immediately prior to his promotion, or they did so such a long time ago that it would require a massive amount of refresher training in order for them to be able to perform it properly once more. Such an effort, though it would likely be approved by the front-line staff, would be horribly inefficient, as the middle management work which they are being paid an increased salary for would continue to accumulate, while they wasted massive amounts of time relearning the job which lower cost front-line employees are paid to perform.

Faced with this gloomy situation, I believe that I will enjoy occasionally using this work as an outlet. When near retching at the insincere platitudes which I must listen to, I will jot down a few lines of candor, skim some previous entries, and remind myself that the world of truth and honesty still exists outside the walls of this moldering government hospital, which sometimes feels as if it entombs me.

I often regret the fact that I have a highly technical engineering background, but really do nothing even remotely technical in my current management role; spending the majority of my time battling never-ending E-mail and directing others to perform the vast majority of technical needs required of my department. While management is a skill that is difficult to acquire, and those positions generally pay more and offer gratification to the ego by placing others under one's authority, I have found that it is boring; at least within the hospital I work at.

Very many of the administrative managers whom I have interacted with, seem as though, like me, they formerly were extremely adept at the technical nuances of their areas, but the longer it has been since they left this front-line role and entered into a management role, the more they have forgotten these technical details that initially made them stand out above their peers. Until, at last, they become only truly adept at the skills of blame, affectation, dissembling, and cunning, which unfortunately seem so essential for survival as a governmental manager.

I see myself inexorably being dragged down this same grim path, but am resisting it with all I have. I have to be careful of the siren's call of nostalgia, however, as it often confuses the influences that are causing it. While I may think research more exciting, due to my memories as a young researcher, what I may unknowingly be missing is not the career, but myself and the feelings that I had during that younger time in my life, when seemingly limitless doors of opportunity stood open before me, and when health was an afterthought that didn't require dedicated effort to maintain.

Was it not intensely frustrating to earn lower wages for seemingly harder work, to be forced to genuflect before leaders whom one often didn't respect, who set virtually unattainable goals, regardless of the toll on their staff, since they had to do none of the actual work themselves, and to have no influence to challenge rules that were counterproductive? Of course it was. It is wonderful that the mind has a tendency to forget pains and remember pleasures, but we must maintain an awareness of this tendency, or else it will warp our ability to make wise decisions.

Balance

In listening to Emerson speak about the sublime lessons which one can learn from nature, I cannot help but reflect upon my youth and early manhood. During these years, I spent countless hours, even days, alone in the woods, hanging from the boughs of trees, or clinging to mountainsides. I wasn't always alone during these adventures, but more often than not my childhood friends were not around, or my later friends felt themselves above such tramps; leaving me to go it alone.

I hated this solitude, when I would feel sudden chills of fear at random sounds, or smells, which were encountered while hiking in bear, poisonous snake, or alligator frequented areas. Counteracting this fear was a strong sense of wonder at the stunning displays of nature's beauty, which I was privileged to see. I was often dumbfounded that people would voluntarily miss out on such beauty to instead sit at a dirty, dimly lit bar, eying the room for someone to speak with, and pretending that they were enjoying themselves.

Here! All of nature is here waiting to speak with you here. It speaks directly into your soul in the voice of God. Only now do I realize this. All that I then knew was instinctive. I only knew that my daily cares would begin to fade, when I would lose others and myself in the solitude of hidden groves, or completely surrounded by the rugged beauty of lonely mountain ridges. Some chord of goodness within me seemed to resonate with the goodness which I perceived without, and I would soon be amazed to find that I simply felt better.

The voice of God seems to be more acutely sensed when surrounded by nature, than within the trappings of society, where we are hemmed in by teeming hordes of other men and women. Some believe mankind to be the pinnacle of creation, so the more of them that we see, the more impressed we should theoretically be with the brilliance of God's creative design. This does not seem to occur in actuality, however, as familiarity often breeds contempt. The hundreds of people whom I pass, or am passed by on the drive in to work become somewhat dehumanized in my mind. They become not a brilliant masterpiece of growing, reproducing, and thinking organisms, but rather a mere idea; an impediment slowing my progress. Perhaps the same undervaluation would happen, during excursions into nature, were they to occur more frequently. Would I quickly cease to be amazed by the delicate beauty of a lump of moss, and instead complain that it stuck in my boots, as I hurriedly rushed to whichever part of the woods it was my daily objective to visit? Possibly.

Perhaps the key to maintaining the sense of wonder in the world is the same piece of wisdom which was long ago memorialized on the temple wall of Apollo at Delphi: "Nothing too much." Most are more familiar with the other famous saying which was written on this same temple wall: "Know thyself." Perhaps one gets both of these things as a pair. Their inseparability may be the reason why both phrases were written together. Is it possible to truly know one's self if one's appetites run to the point of intemperance? Does it not take a sober and controlled mind to turn the eye inwards, and thoughts unclouded by warped appetites to correctly interpret what is seen therein?

Likewise, can a man accurately see a thing that he observes daily? Will he not stop noticing details once they become commonplace to him? While one might think that long observance would make a person become more attuned to any difference, this appears to only be true when viewing things which remain exactly, or almost exactly the same, like a painting. Should a dot of white paint spill on this painting, the owner who daily passes it will very likely quickly take notice.

Towards the state of things which are constantly changing, like the grass, or the cars during my drive home, the mind grows sluggish and imperceptive. How many times have I driven in to work and yet afterwards hardly recall any specific events of the drive? This again brings to mind the relationship between knowing one's self and nothing too much. Can we truly know ourselves if we aren't even keenly aware of the world about us which we are interacting with? The ideal solution appears to be an alternation between society and solitude; between city and wood.

Writing

Why, in most modern written works, do we seldom seem to encounter genuine candor and willingness to put forward, and not merely attack, fundamental truths. The only answer which seems plausible is that the literary zeitgeist has changed drastically since the late 1800's. Prior to this time, works which appear to display the utmost candor and willingness to discuss complex philosophical principles appear to have been written for one, or a combination of the following four purposes.

The first reason is a desire to commemorate some great act, or event, which would otherwise have quickly faded into oblivion. The second is a desire to teach others, in order to perpetuate hard learned facts, or ideas. The third is a desire to stir readers to action for a noble cause. The fourth is simply to afford authors, when old, the opportunity to stimulate and reflect upon memories and thoughts which were formed during their more formative years; in effect allowing them to relive and relish these years once again.

Until the late 1800's, it appears that very few authors expected to be compensated very highly for their works. Even fewer dreamed of being able to write as a profession. Life was far harder in those days. Very few of the common mass of the people could afford to use much of their hard-earned money on the latest book. This is not to say that people didn't read, but rather that books were much rarer, often costly, and were therefore made with serious intent. In Dana's *Two Years Before the Mast*, for example, the author discusses books, which he had the good fortune of encountering, with a delight which sounds peculiar to modern ears.[7] This attitude will be repeatedly be reencountered by any who choose to read much of what was written prior to the early 20th century.

Even Hitler echoed this love of books in his *Mein Kampf*. "Every book that I bought meant renewed hunger, and every visit I paid to the opera meant the intrusion of that inalienable companion during the following days. I was always struggling with my unsympathic friend. And yet during that time I learned more than I had ever learned before. Outside my architectural studies and rare visits to the opera, for which I had to deny myself food, I had no other pleasure in life except my books."[8]

Consider searching for a similar view among Western university students of today. A willingness to literally go hungry for the privilege of having another book which they could learn from. If a student like this is found, it will not be among the fraternity and sorority *trust fund babies* of the elite. It will be found in a youth who has tasted the humiliation, fear, and hopelessness of poverty.

All of this seems to have changed in the early 20th century. After this period, while brilliant written works were surely still to be found, the reader encounters far more works than previously of a lower intellectual stamp. Ralph Waldo Emerson, prior to his death in 1882, noticed and attributed this decline repeatedly to the new "cheap press."[9] Sometimes these comments appear to be referring to cheapness of production, however other times they appear to refer to a cheapening of intellectual quality. I am willing to bet that it is a bit of both.

This new *cheap press* was a product of the Industrial Revolution, and shortly afterwards, the World Wars. During this period, the majority of nations adopted a factory approach to most aspects of production; including literature. The increase in accessible audience, caused by improved means of transportation and communication, as well as the mechanization and resultant cheapening of the printing process, resulted in the increased possibility of book sales, decreased production costs, and ultimately, higher potential of profit.

Aspiring authors, in turn, stood to reap a portion of these higher profits. This motivated a larger number of them to write for profit and fame, that double faced Janus, which had always existed in theory, but which had been so rare in practice as to discourage all but the few with truly exceptional talent. Great works continued to be published for the previous four, more noble reasons, but as the years passed, works of these types became increasingly difficult to encounter among the flood of works spewing from the newly motivated pens, typewriters, and later keyboards, of the avaricious and ambitious.

But let's take a moment to consider authors in general. When one considers the historical amnesia plaguing the world, as well as the diminishing literature, literacy, and language, the further back we look in time, the picture becomes rather bleak. Certainly, many works have been lost, but consider the number of people who have ever lived, all of whose life experiences were certainly worth recording. Researchers estimate, from currently available evidence, that roughly 108 billion people have lived since roughly 50,000BC, when modern humans are assumed to have appeared on Earth. 7.5 billion of these are alive today.[11] How many of these lives have passed some written memento of their relatively brief existence on to posterity? Although this is a drastic reduction, in order to simplify the question for the sake of the discussion, let's limit our examination to books. Estimates range regarding how many books have ever been written, based upon ongoing debate over what defines a book, however, of those which there is little doubt over classification, the modern estimate of published books is ~129 million. This initially seems to imply that 1 out of every 837 people could have preserved some of their experiences and perspectives in writing. Unfortunately, this view is overly optimistic for several reasons.

Firstly, it fails to account for the vast range of complexity and philosophical depth between books. For example, even 100 *Dr. Seuss* books are in no way comparable to Tolstoy's *War and Peace*.

Secondly, it fails to account for the large number of authors who have published multiple works. The process of book writing generally improves an author's writing skills, making attempts at future works significantly easier, at least from a process point of view, and therefore far more likely. The writing of many authors became quite prolific. Alexandre Dumas, for example, author of the famous *Count of Monte Cristo*, wrote 276 additional books. Roman historian Titus Livius, as another example, wrote 142 books.

Thirdly, until relatively recently, writing was a skill which was only possessed and enjoyed by the select upper class within many nations. Consider a statement echoing this fact, which was published in the 2006 United Nations Global monitoring report:

"Prior to 1800, reading (though not always writing) skills were widespread in several northern European countries (e.g. Denmark, Finland, Iceland, Scotland, Sweden and Prussia), as well as in parts of England, France and Switzerland. In a second group – Belgium, Ireland, the Netherlands, and the remaining parts of England, France and Switzerland – literacy skills were used by members of the higher social classes and were more limited among other social strata, except in scattered communities, monasteries or households that possessed books and other printed matter. Finally, in most of eastern and southern Europe (Russia, the Balkans, the Eastern Austro-Hungarian empire, the Iberian Peninsula and southern Italy), illiteracy was widespread, especially outside the cities and towns, and written materials were almost nonexistent. Throughout Europe, gender disparities in literacy were the norm."[12]

Fourthly, this same report estimates that as recently as the mid-1800's, only 10% of adults in the world could read or write at some minimum level. This statistic seems incredible from a modern, Western perspective, given that in Western Europe and the United States, literacy rates were quite high during that same period (e.g. 80% in the 1870's United States).

Fifthly, written languages developed and spread throughout various ancient nations during different periods, from as far back as 3,300 B.C. for the Egyptian hieroglyphs, to roughly 1800 B.C. for the Phoenician alphabet. Prior to the period of language development or adoption within any culture, memories of the lives of all but a few heroic individuals were generally lost. These few were passed down via oral tradition, often with the memory aid of rhyme (i.e. lyric poetry), though even this was no proof against mutation over time.

Until the past two centuries, these factors have constrained the group of people enabled to successfully pass down a written history of their memories and experiences to a small, select group of mostly Western European, or American, mostly male authors, who tended to publish multiple works. What a lost treasure trove of information on the human experience this is. Even the incalculable loss of the famed Library of Alexandria, eventually consumed by a combination of several accidental and intentional fires, was but a cup of water of recorded, in the ocean of unrecorded human experience. As a side note, it should be noticed, when mentioning this library, that once again Egypt is seen to be a major, if not at the time the foremost defender and preserver of the flame of knowledge; a subject which will be discussed further later.

Among those works which have survived the ravages of time, it has been my exceedingly good fortune to have encountered many noble, brilliant, and candid authors, whose writings were directly responsible for the refinement of my views. These men and women surely never dreamed that one random day, hundreds, or in some cases, thousands of years later, I would even exist; much less that the still vital seeds of thought within their writings would find fertile soil, sprout, send forth roots, and bear fruit within my mind. These authors merely felt compelled for various reasons to record their thoughts, like a message in a bottle, and then courageously set them adrift down the murky streams of time. Thank God for them.

Ironically, most of the works which have had such profound effects upon my views were encountered, often out of print, slowly disintegrating beneath a coat of fine dust on a seldom visited library shelf, or on a seldom visited webpage version of the same. The library versions of these works frequently gave a telltale crack when opened, confirming their unused, or seldom used condition. My amazement at the wisdom encountered within these works is always mixed with a sadness at their overall undervaluation by society.

Despite this undervaluation, literature is the only real distillation of a person's, group's, or nation's character which is able to be passed on to successive generations. Material goods crumble to dust. Nation's rise and fall. Yet the wit of a man (or woman) preserved in writing remains as vigorous and effectual as it was the day it first flowed from their minds, through pen (keyboard these days), and onto page. It is a quasi-immortality.

Reading is a sort of séance, where long dead authors may be summoned forth again and again, like ghosts, in order to influence the minds and hearts of others, all from the comfort of our own living room. Even if a book goes out of print and is lost, or forgotten, as long as a single copy remains extant somewhere in the world, it will lie dormant like a spore or seed, for decades or even millennia, pregnant with the author's thoughts and ideas, until one blessed day, when a chance rediscovery allows these archived views to be reproduced within the minds and hearts of a new generation. The loss and subsequent rediscovery of Aristotle's profound philosophical works is a great example of a situation where this actually occurred. These philosophical treasures were lost for centuries to all but the Saracens, until their rediscovery by the Western world strongly influenced European thought, contributing to the Renaissance.

Written works, at least those which anyone enjoys reading, are more than the collections of facts which they contain. They are an incidental painting of the author's own character. The longer the written work, the more of these inadvertent brushstrokes are encountered between the lines; bringing the picture further into focus. Samuel Butler succinctly described this phenomenon in his *The Way of All Flesh*. Here he stated that, "Every man's work, whether it be literature, or music, or pictures, or architecture, or anything else, is always a portrait of himself, and the more he tries to conceal himself, the more clearly will his character appear in spite of him. I may very likely be condemning myself, all the time that I am writing this book, for I know that, whether I like it or no, I am portraying myself more surely than I am portraying any of the characters whom I set before the reader."[13] Due to this phenomenon, I have found that I come away from spending dozens of hours within works by a single, often long dead author, feeling more sympathy, solidarity, and familiarity with this person, whom I have never met, than with many among my own family, whom I have.

Since authors work their own character into their works, perhaps I did, in fact, meet with their true, unmasked, internal self; something rare even among families. Epictetus appropriately described the difference between common superficial interaction and this sort of true *meeting* in his *Discourses*. When responding to someone who boasted of having met him, he replied, "Then you will say, 'I met with Epictetus as I should meet with a stone or a statue': for you saw me, and nothing more. But he meets with a man as a man, who learns his opinions, and in his turn, shows his own. Learn my opinions: show me yours; and then say that you have visited me. Let us examine one another: if I have any bad opinion, take it away; if you have any, show it. This is the meaning of meeting with a philosopher."[5]

Emerson

Any who attempt to read, and diligently work at understanding Ralph Waldo Emerson's complete works are setting out upon an epic journey. I have only encountered a handful of authors whom I have respected so, and very few have left us such a wealth of wisdom to know them by. Those who turn the last page of Emerson's collected works, and look up, will realize that they are different people than they were when they began reading them.

When I first finished this trip, I remember regretting having to bid farewell to my wise companion of so many hours, days, and weeks. Emerson had become to me a friend, a mentor, and a kindred spirit. In reading him, I learned a tremendous amount about myself. Frequently I would find myself pausing and rereading a section where he had pointed out an experience which I had shared, or a series of private feelings which I thought that I alone had felt. I should be honest. I never thought that I alone felt these things. It would be more accurate to say that I hadn't understood, or been able to describe these feelings until Emerson so clearly pointed them out.

The best part of digesting long series of books written by a single writer is the familiarity which is developed with the mind of the author. Constant exposure causes a reader to grow familiar with the author's vocabulary, until soon the reader is no longer distracted by dead phrases, or forgotten words which were formerly common among the educated of yesteryear. After this occurs, the ratio of ideas digested to words consumed increases considerably.

In addition, looking at the world for long periods through the author's eyes, one starts to see it similarly; though we seldom realize that this is occurring. It is only when we hear another's characteristic words tumble from our own lips, or pop into our minds, do we realize that these rivers have slowly worn away at our rocklike character. While this influencing effect is beneficial for the student of wise men, it reveals the tremendous risk which we take when not selective in our and our children's reading, entertainment, education, and overall exposure.

Academic Style

I find that writing really aids in the understanding of a topic. Though I found the perpetual task of essay writing on various assigned subjects a chore, while in college, I now understand the method to my professors' madness. While I may not deeply understand a topic when I begin to write about it, I find that I generally do by the time I finish.

Modern life is often a mad panic. We struggle to identify with authors and philosophers who advise us to stop and smell life's roses before they, like us, have faded and withered, when we are eating in the car while heading to the next event that we over-obligated ourselves, and are therefore late for.

"That advice is all well and good for the millionaire, but I have to pick up groceries on the way home, the kids need to eat before practice, the oil in the van needs to get changed, the house is a mess, bills need to be paid, and I have looming projects coming due at work."

But in all of the busyness, life and opportunities to savor its joys are passing us by. During this rush we encounter and discover truths, yet we hardly have time to sit and consider how these things impact our lives. It's as if the mind is a closet which we haphazardly cram things into, in the rush of everyday life. The process of writing, on the other hand, is the cumbersome, yet rewarding act of dedicating time to pulling everything out of this closet, and then sorting, matching, and properly organizing the items on their various shelves. This subsequent organization allows associations to be made between, and conclusions to be drawn from the various items, which would otherwise be missed when they are lying in a mixed heap.

This work was started as a series of essays which I hoped would assist me with organizing, and at the same time developing my thoughts on the truths which I had tucked away to consider when life had provided me with more opportunity to do so. But life never did. We simply have to carve out and set aside time for things which we think are important to us, like thinking.

In commencing this work, I was faced with the choice which all non-fiction authors are faced with, of selecting from two possible writing styles. The first of these was the academic style. The academic style is the only writing style accepted by academia; whence it derives its name. Authors who select this style of writing slather their works with references to, and quotes from other respected academics, in hopes that the proximity of these names osmotically increases their personal credibility on the subject. They also believe that nesting themselves deeply within this titular hive will give the appearance of a united front standing ready to defend their own theories; something which they hope will frighten away critics. But this appearance of scholarly consensus is generally an illusion.

Typically, few of the authors who are cited would be found to agree on every single conclusion which the author arrived at. In addition, each of the work's conclusions must stand, or fall based upon their own independent merit. When scrutinized, it is usually found that only a handful of supporting academics have been referenced for each independent conclusion; commonly only two or three.

A final benefit which the academic writing style offers to those aspiring authors who select it, is the ability to spread responsibility to the various cited authors for any points in the work which are ultimately found to be incorrect. "My conclusions would have been correct, had I not relied upon bad information from this other person." This seems to somewhat transform the author from bold, truth-seeking pioneer, into a cringing youth, attempting to hide behind a crowd of his seniors. Nay more; a veritable Proteus, transforming himself into an image of the establishment, in the hope that this transformation will cause the beams of their often intense self-love to incidentally reflect upon him.

Obvious disadvantages of writing in the academic style are that it is tremendously challenging to research, cumbersome to write, often misunderstood, tends to bore all but a subject's devout, and is accordingly seldom read. An example which readily comes to mind is Darwin's *Origin of Species*. Though the rich information encountered within this work makes it well worth reading, it is not for the faint of heart, as its technical nature makes it both difficult and occasionally boring.

Academic writing is a combat sport. Like boxing, the goal of this sport is to attack and wear down one's opponents. Academic T. H. Huxley, in defending his evolutionary theories, echoed this boxing analogy in an 1874 letter which he sent to his friend Charles Darwin. In it he stated that, "I think you will say that I have pounded the enemy into a jelly."[16] As with all sports, those who wish to enlist as competitors in the sport of academic writing must agree to adhere to a specific set of rules. Violators of these rules risk losing the respect of the other competitors, as well as of the editors of the peer reviewed professional journals within their field, who act as referees. Of note, these referees are also themselves competitors, giving them a distinct advantage over any challengers.

If the rule violations in this game are flagrant enough, the offender might suffer a loss of professional credibility, or a subsequent inability to publish. This means that, in the former scenario, the other competitors will shun and refuse to compete with them. In the latter, the referees

will refuse them admission into their combat arenas; de facto banning
them from the sport. On rare occasions, this shunning is due to a valid
offense, such as a crime, and is therefore appropriate. In other, more
common scenarios, it is simply due to the offender disagreeing, strongly
and openly, with the orthodox scientific opinion. Such a public challenge
to the views of the small circle of academic elites risks awakening the
drowsy public to the fact that many of these emperors are, as in the
fable, wearing no clothes. They censure out of fear that their use of
selective publication to keep university chairs and research grant dollars
among their small circle of supporters and acolytes, in order to
strengthen their own power, wealth, and prestige, will be seen for the
quasi-monopoly that it often is.

Any new theory, which would dare to challenge the more orthodox
views of the cultural, religious, political, or scientific elite, must not only
attack flaws within any theories which it seeks to displace, but must also
stand ready to repulse the inevitable counter-attacks which will come
from those who have a personal interest in the established theory's
success. During these battles, mountains of studies frequently published
by authorities within the various fields in question serve as both
weapons and armor. These publications are fired between groups of
partisan academics, like stones from a catapult; the larger sample sizes
being the more massive, and the significant findings the faster stones.
This mass and velocity combine into damage causing inertia, as they
slam into their adversary's defenses and reputation.

Any who would dare to propose an iconoclastic theory without
adhering to these rules of warfare would quickly be laughed down. Yet
those who laugh forget that the truly great writers of antiquity, men
such as Emerson, Plutarch, Rousseau, Montesquieu, and many others,
virtually never wrote in this academic style.

The second writing option is the popular style; where the author
simply presents their final, composite views to the reader, leaving it to
others to seek out any contributing sources, should they so desire.
Seneca, the brilliant Roman nobleman, whom I am ironically attempting
to quote, was a proponent of the popular style. He once stated in a letter
to his friend Lucretius that his views at that time were a composite
resulting from those of the many great minds he had been exposed to.
He likened these composite views to honey made from the nectar of
countless flowers. Seneca went on to state that since he had internalized
the moral truths which he had encountered in the writings of men like
Epicurus, that these truths were now as much his property as they were
the authors' who initially directed him towards them.[14]

Authors may be compared to curators within a museum, while the
truths which they convey are the artifacts themselves. Neither the
curator, nor the visitor have exclusive rights to the artifact. It is clear
that the innate, inestimable worth of these truths are what should draw

and hold our focus, not the clever, or poetic phrasing of whomever points them out. We do not go to museums to gape at curators. We go to see artifacts.

Seneca admitted that, due to his views, he was often at risk of failing to cite an author.[14] I agree with him that time invested in seemingly endless citation is time wasted. This same portion of our limited amount of time is better invested in examining other *flower* species, or other offshoots of known species, for additional drops or gallons of the *nectar* of wisdom. Certainly, one should render simple and plain homage to any whose nourishing words have helped their views to mature. Landmarks and trails traveled, or even newly cut, should be indicated on the map for others who are intrepidly exploring, or already lost within the wilderness of a certain subject. The problem is that these truly valid reasons for citation are often eclipsed in practice by two equally invalid ones.

The first of these invalid reasons is when the citation fetish is actually little more than a thinly veiled attempt to increase one's own perceived credibility by appealing to the authority of a more respected author. The second is when citations are given as a sort of proof that the cited is the originator of the idea, and therefore has a copyright of sorts on it. There can be no copyrighting of truths, which are the common property of all mankind. We often hear the same truth spoken in different words, by men of various cultures and various ages. Emerson, for example, echoed the views of Montaigne, who echoed Plutarch, who echoed Plato, who echoed Socrates, who may have echoed Thales, Pythagoras, and a countless chain of scholars that winds until lost sight of in the dim shadows of prehistory. Does credit for a moral truth belong to its first, often unknown speaker, or writer, to its first known one, or to the one who worded it the most profoundly? The answer is all of them, as well as all of us.

People instinctively sense moral truths when they are encountered, as they reflect and resonate with something noble which already exists within them. Socrates, as quoted by Plato in his Meno and Phaedo, refers to this concept of innate, instinctive knowledge as anamnesis. He claims that our pursuit and study of moral truths are, in actuality, attempts to rediscover what already lies hidden within us.[155, 181] In effect we are learning about ourselves.

Emerson was also a strong proponent of the popular style of writing, however his brilliance makes even his popular speech sound academic. Thankfully, he was also kind enough to sprinkle his writings with a sufficient number of quotes and names to allow the curious to be able to follow his breadcrumb trail to the major authors which influenced him. He once quipped, "I cannot remember the books I've read any more than the meals I have eaten; even so, they have made me."[15] The irony of my quoting him on this subject is not lost on me. I do so because even the prose of this great man is not without traces of the poetic. As with all poetry, much is lost in any attempt to paraphrase it. Emerson's writings indicate that he felt that concerning one's self overmuch with quotations was an indication that the author lacked sufficient self-confidence to boldly state and defend his, or her own convictions: convictions which were, of course, influenced by others.

Knowing the orders of magnitude greater writing difficulty of the academic style of nonfictional writing, as well as its generally orders of magnitude smaller target audience, most authors elect to take the infinitely easier path of writing works of popular fiction. These types of books are often churned out in a month by aspiring authors working at the local coffee shop, are widely consumed by the public, and deal with matters so trivial, childish, or obvious that readers often close them after the last page, with minds none the richer, indeed, often times even poorer, than when they opened them to the first. If these authors have any significant message which they wish to deliver to the world, instead of bravely entering the academic arena, where logical errors, historical ignorance, or weak positions are mercilessly pummeled, they generally craftily embed it within the situations, characters, responses, and outcomes of the story.

My hope is to make this work fall somewhere between the academic and the popular writing styles, while still honestly putting forward my opinion, rather than craftily hiding it within subtle details of allegory. I do not expect to perfectly perform this delicate balancing act between dull fact cataloguing and exciting intuitive proposition, but I hope to make it perfect enough. As Thomas Carlyle put it in his *Sir Walter Scott*, "Perfection is unattainable: no carpenter ever made a mathematically accurate right-angle in the world; yet all carpenters know when it is right enough, and do not botch it, and lose their wages, by making it too right. Too much painstaking speaks disease in one's mind, as well as too little."[17]

The bibliography at the end of this work will serve as a list of resources which I feel will be valuable aids to seekers and lovers of wisdom. With so many false guides and empty-headed prattlers filling whole shelves with their time-wasting works, the lonely aspiring philosopher needs some bread-crumbs on the trail to help aid his or her way. Can a person be robbed of anything more valuable than their time? Is any material possession worth more? Yet we allow a veritable army of fiction writing dullards to consume the few hours of our lives which are left to us, between when our minds are too young to understand complex concepts, and when they become too old to remember them: those hours which aren't already dedicated to labor, sleep, or some other necessary maintenance, or care of our bodies. Yet the matter is infinitely worse than this. We not only allow this theft, but with money in hand, excitedly run in all directions after those who would rob us of our precious time.

Fiction

One writing form which has always existed, but which exploded in prevalence and popularity since the Industrial Revolution, is fiction. There is nothing overtly wrong with this form of writing. Many fictional works have meant a great deal to people during their youth. Boys and girls are able to open a book in their bedroom and suddenly be flitted away to another world, which he, or she views through the protagonist's eyes. They stand on the cliff's edge as Bilbo, feeling the awe and tension prior to the battle of the 5 armies, in Tolkien's *The Hobbit*.[15] They cling to the ship's yard arm as Jim Hawkins, before shooting Israel Hands with both pistols, in Stevenson's *Treasure Island*.[19]

Yet as reading exposure is increased over the years to include weightier philosophical, scientific, historical, and other nonfictional works, at some unknown point, we will likely begin to see fiction as painfully inefficient. There will be no single event to commemorate the moment when this change in opinion occurs. Instead, it will slowly creep upon us like maturity and grey hair. One day we will notice that the fictional works we attempt to read, even the heavier quasi-philosophical ones such as John Milton's *Paradise Lost*, or Tolstoy's *War and Peace*, are but hundreds of pages of allegory, for perhaps a dozen or so of the core philosophical message which the author is ultimately attempting to convey.

We will begin to notice that a substantial portion of fictional works are dedicated exclusively to painting the protagonists and their cause in the most sympathetic colors possible, within plausible context, while contrarily painting the antagonists and their cause in the most abhorrent ones. This is nothing more than emotional manipulation; noble and healthful if manipulating readers towards virtue, insidious and harmful if manipulating them towards vice. We will inevitably begin to wonder why these writers appear to believe that their audiences are incapable of directly digesting the often comically simple philosophical, political, or religious messages which they embed within their works. As this silent implication is encountered in each new fictional work we attempt to read, the mind mature enough to handle the courser fare will struggle not to be insulted by it.

The eventual result of this maturation process is the belief that fictional works are only good and appropriate for children, youth, and those adults whose mental *teeth* have not yet grown accustomed to consuming and digesting raw truth (which is the definition of nonfiction) undiluted and in large bites: those who need it cut into small bits and washed down with large portions of watery allegory, in order not to choke them. Unfortunately, just as a fly can fall into and spoil a soup which is otherwise nutritious, corrupt morals and philosophical errors espoused by an author can be, and these days generally are, often mixed in and served to unwitting readers.

Besides the times when insidious authors intentionally do this, there are many times when it is unintentional, and simply due to their own corrupt moral character. This latter instance occurs because authors can never entirely exclude themselves from their works. The longer one spends in reading them, the more the word choices, comments and views of the characters, and topics of discussion begin to paint a picture of the author's own philosophy. This is the reason why, as parents, we should ideally scrutinize the lives and views of the authors who write our children's fictional works, as the developing minds of children are highly vulnerable to manipulation. Frequently, sinister Trojan horses are found therein. This level of oversight is challenging to accomplish today, due to everyone's frantic schedules, but our children's character is worth at least a cursory glance.

When young we were likely able to avoid these insects in the soup of our books, thanks to our parents' watchful guidance. In spite of this, most of us knew from schoolyard talk that such things abounded, even though, in the long-gone days of our childhood, they were far less prevalent and egregious. This increased prevalence of corrupted and corrupting ethics hidden within children's fictional works today is very likely due to the exponential increase of empty headed, yet avaricious authors, whose only moral standards are the preschool level, "Don't discriminate," and "Be yourself," courtesy Hollywood, who would risk losing some of their morally corrupt investors, should they risk wading beyond their ankles into the open waters of true virtue.

Adults, being generally better able to discriminate between truth and falsity, should be free to read whatever they believe to be edifying for them, within certain boundaries. These boundaries are necessary, due to the fact that political leaders, much like parents, have a responsibility to protect the citizens under their care. This means, the same way that parents prohibit known corrupting influences from physically, mentally, or spiritually harming their children, so political leaders must prohibit the adult versions of these things from physically, mentally, or spiritually corrupting their citizenry. A few prime examples here are pornographic works, which inevitably warp and corrupt the natural sexual instinct, and gratuitous violence which desensitizes people to human suffering.

Though the previous discussion focused on written works, the principles discussed are equally applicable to all other entertainment forms, such as movies, television shows, plays, internet media, music, and video games. All must be washed of the moral filth which stains them, if we are ever to live in a virtuous society. It is foolish to expect people who are bombarded with glamorized depictions of moral corruption, from their youth, to behave morally. Once corrupted, we cannot expect these people to vote for morally just laws, or to elect ethical political leaders.

If we scrutinize the books and movies that we love, we generally discover that the common element among them is candor. Something about these works seems genuine to us. This is as true for the person whose worldview has been warped by vice and error, as it is for those whose views remain rooted in virtue and truth.

The man holding corrupt views identifies with the vice filled depictions he observes on screen, or reads on page, because he thinks they are genuine. In these fictional worlds, any type of falsity can be called true. Murderers and rapists can live happily ever after, without a touch of regret. In order to impugn the character of those who promote virtue and justice within society, characters which intentionally symbolize them can be created, whose words, or deeds convey gross stupidity, or moral corruption. Examples of this technique can be seen in the increasing number of films, shows, and books with villains who are cops, southerners, conservative politicians, Caucasians, or Christians. The very universe itself can be portrayed, within fiction, as being without a God, or the absolute standards of virtue and goodness which spring from him.

The lover of truth and virtue, on the other hand, will recognize the lies within these depictions and the vice which they promote, and despise them. Instead he will seek after wholesome depictions of truth and goodness, which he recognizes as genuine and therefore identifies with.

"Since men love what they perceive to be candor so much," one may ask, "Why does one person love mysteries, and another science fiction? Shouldn't everyone love documentaries and history books, according to this theory?"

Not exactly. One man's familiarity with science, even if only a working one, may cause him to better understand and identify with characters and scenarios within a science environment. Another man's experience or familiarity with sports may cause him to better understand and identify with sports characters and scenarios. Still another man, being bored by his mundane job, may fantasize about and feel drawn towards the seeming excitement and danger of investigation, war, or clandestine scenarios. Whichever theme is favored by the reader or viewer, it is our ability to identify with the seeming sincerity of the human element involved which attracts us to these things. It doesn't matter how much the plot twists, we lose interest if we can't at least partially relate to the characters.

When reading a book, we want the hero to seem real: to think and act like we either would, or would like to, if we had the courage and resources available to us which they do. If watching a film, we want the writers and actors to portray realistic emotions and responses, given the scenarios, to the point that we forget that they are acting. We don't want to notice subtle differences in shading which often betray special effects. The best effects go unnoticed and are thought to be realities.

How many books, or films have disappointed us after the author introduced some miraculous, yet unbelievable "deus ex machina," to resolve plot problems. A good example is the disappointing ending of H.G. Wells' *War of the Worlds*, where, when all hope was lost, the conquering aliens suddenly all die from a bacterial infection.[20]

We want writers of screen or book to be honest with us. It doesn't matter how impressively a writer paints the hero's, or his own exploits. If we notice that they have also selectively omitted shortcomings which all know to be common to the human experience, we are generally left with nagging doubts about their overall credibility; as lies, even of omission, cast a long shadow over everything else which a person says, or does.

Perhaps this is part of the attraction of sports. Here, men are expected to honestly compete, on even terms, and only win due to superior strength, stamina, intelligence, courage, cunning, or some combination of these. Any suspicion of falsity in competition, termed cheating, is loudly condemned by the spectators, and the competitor, coach, or promoter who attempted it loathed. As examples, consider the crowd's instinctive reaction when they hear of boxers who intentionally fake a knock-out, champions whom they discover were using illegal performance enhancing drugs, such as steroids, or referees whose calls consistently gave one team, or player an unfair advantage over another. People have even been killed for such things.

Everywhere mankind longs for sincerity, for honesty, for truth. As the mind develops, it grows weary of the intrinsic falsity which is inseparable from fictional entertainment of all sorts; whether encountered on page, or screen. Fictional books, or films which seemed a perfect representation of reality to a youth with limited life experiences, little differing from a documentary, appear increasingly flawed and unnatural as the mind matures. And what is maturity, if not an increased familiarity with truth, and subsequent ability to recognize it. A natural byproduct of this increased ability to recognize truth is an increased ability to recognize what lacks, or contradicts it; namely error, or its malicious and intentional analog, lies.

As a beautiful woman stirs the blood more hotly as more of her beauty is seen, so the maturing mind, as it grows able to recognize truth, will be stirred and impassioned by her beauty, and will seek for it in more concentrated forms. As the beauty of truth increasingly attracts, so the ugliness of falsity increasingly repels; resulting in a growing distaste for fiction, desire to correct error, and hatred of lies.

The search for more concentrated sources of truth generally takes a few distinct forms. One of these forms is the pursuit of truths within the amazingly vast and varied natural world which surrounds us; including all of the natural sciences which are derived from it, such as astronomy, biology, horticulture, chemistry, oceanography, physics, music, etc. Such studies needn't be formal. The careful observer walking through the nearby field, or wood is an amateur student in several of these areas all at once. The small creek beside the trail provides lessons, free of charge, on fluid dynamics, chemistry, and erosion. The fallen tree which one steps over on the trail is a physics and horticulture instructor. The bird, spied intermittently singing and gliding between nearby branches gives a course on aerodynamics and music. The bite of a small mosquito is a silent lesson on pressure, force, vacuum, density, stress, strain, elasticity, and several other subjects.

Within the genus of truth-seeking within the natural world, there is a species focusing primarily on the physiological, psychological, and social nature of mankind. Those who select this path often end up as teachers, doctors, nurses, psychologists, social workers, politicians, or humanitarians. As with the previous case, the person seeking truth in this field needn't be a recognized academic. For the astute, a simple handshake is an instant lesson on a person's security, health, strength, upbringing, and character. Is the skin hard, dry, and calloused, or as soft and delicate as damp cotton? Are their nails filed, or dirty and uneven? Is eye contact avoided, or do they boldly lock eyes? Do they hesitate before extending their hand, have a clammy palm, weak grip, hold too long, or pull the other person in? Do they grasp too early, before the webs of the thumbs meet, forcing both into the awkward grasp of only the ends of the fingers, disturbingly reminiscent of the curtsy of well-to-do ladies of the 1800's? All are hints of truth about the man's experiences and character.

A third type of truth-seeking focuses on discovering truths within current affairs. Those drawn down this path tend to have an interest in news and politics. A fourth type takes the form of attempting to learn past truths in order to better understand present ones. Those who take this path tend to be drawn towards histories, genealogies, archaeology, paleontology, geology, or a combination of these things.

In all of these previous examples, immaterial truths are conveyed by, and interpreted from material forms, such as men, stones, and solar systems, both past, and present. As the mind continues to develop, it will eventually see this translation from material to immaterial as inefficient and a risk point for error. Instead, it will begin to prefer dealing with truths directly, in their purely abstract forms, such as metaphysics, mathematics, ethics, and philosophy.

Within this stage of development, the mind will begin to question what it is about truth which causes it to be true. Is truth but an abstract social construct, or an absolute reality? The former claim is a self-destructive argument, as it would have to be an absolute reality that truth was but an abstract social construct. Yet this is the fundamental, often subconscious mistake which stains and warps the entire atheist worldview.

Here we see why atheists, many modern scientists unfortunately being numbered among them, possess a special affection towards the theory of relativity. The theory of relativity was initially developed by Albert Einstein as an elaborate method of dealing with complications related to the mind-bending velocity of light and the energy latent within atoms. Atheists have abused this tremendously complicated principle put forward by Einstein by implying that the day that the scientific community was won over to a general belief in the Theory of Relativity was a decisive victory for the atheist worldview that absolutes, and therefore God, do not exist. "Everything is Relative!" has become the atheist battle-cry, and has grown, like the cancer it is, to infect and rot virtually all of the arts and sciences.

The Jackson Pollock and Andy Worhol type of self-proclaimed "artists," whose works look like dye which has been ingested and vomited on canvas, claim that all beauty is relative, and brazenly request NEA endowments and wall-space at the Smithsonian. Sociologists who "celebrate" half savage cultures, which deny justice to women and other weaker members of society, claim that all culture is relative. ACLU lawyers, who target any among those who have common dealings with the public (e.g. businessmen, doctors, politicians, etc.) for refusing to actively support things which they morally disagree with (e.g. homosexual marriage, sex changes, abortion services, etc.), claim that all ethics are relative. There is no end to the examples which could be provided within modern Western culture on this spreading atheist abuse of relativity. Interestingly, this atheist hijacking and misuse of relativity began to occur even during Einstein's lifetime, something he was not shy about pointing out and publicly fighting.

As an example, consider the following transcript of a July 14, 1930 debate between Einstein and Bengali polymath, Rabindranath Tagore. This transcript is included in its entirety, because within it Einstein, the author of the Theory of Relativity, defends the absolute nature of truth. Tagore, on the other hand, when his comments are stripped of their high-sounding jargon, which is intentionally designed to impress, ultimately reveals that he holds the modern atheist worldview, which (absolutely) denies all absolutes; as an absolute bound and confined to man is not absolute.

"TAGORE: 'You have been busy, hunting down with mathematics, the two ancient entities, time and space, while I have been lecturing in this country on the eternal world of man, the universe of reality.'

EINSTEIN: 'Do you believe in the divine isolated from the world?'

TAGORE: 'Not isolated. The infinite personality of man comprehends the universe. There cannot be anything that cannot be subsumed by the human personality, and this proves that the truth of the universe is human truth.'

EINSTEIN: 'There are two different conceptions about the nature of the universe — the world as a unity dependent on humanity, and the world as reality independent of the human factor.'

TAGORE: 'When our universe is in harmony with man, the eternal, we know it as truth, we feel it as beauty.'

EINSTEIN: 'This is a purely human conception of the universe.'

TAGORE: 'The world is a human world — the scientific view of it is also that of the scientific man. Therefore, the world apart from us does not exist; it is a relative world, depending for its reality upon our consciousness. There is some standard of reason and enjoyment which gives it truth, the standard of the eternal man whose experiences are made possible through our experiences.'

EINSTEIN: 'This is a realization of the human entity.'

TAGORE: 'Yes, one eternal entity. We have to realize it through our emotions and activities. We realize the supreme man, who has no individual limitations, through our limitations. Science is concerned with that which is not confined to individuals; it is the impersonal human world of truths. Religion realizes these truths and links them up with our deeper needs. Our individual consciousness of truth gains universal significance. Religion applies values to truth, and we know truth as good through own harmony with it.'

EINSTEIN: 'Truth, then, or beauty, is not independent of man?'

TAGORE: 'No, I do not say so.'

EINSTEIN: 'If there were no human beings any more, the Apollo Belvedere no longer would be beautiful?'

TAGORE: 'No!'

EINSTEIN: 'I agree with this conception of beauty, but not with regard to truth.'

TAGORE: 'Why not? Truth is realized through men.'

EINSTEIN: 'I cannot prove my conception is right, but that is my religion.'

TAGORE: 'Beauty is in the ideal of perfect harmony, which is in the universal being; truth is the perfect comprehension of the universal mind. We individuals approach it through our own mistakes and blunders, through our accumulated experience, through our illumined consciousness. How otherwise can we know truth?'

EINSTEIN: 'I cannot prove, but I believe in the Pythagorean argument, that the truth is independent of human beings. It is the problem of the logic of continuity.'

TAGORE : 'Truth, which is one with the universal being, must be essentially human; otherwise, whatever we individuals realize as true, never can be called truth. At least, the truth which is described as scientific and which only can be reached through the process of logic—in other words, by an organ of thought which is human. According to the Indian philosophy there is Brahman, the absolute truth, which cannot be conceived by the isolation of the individual mind or described by words, but can be realized only by merging the individual in its infinity. But such a truth cannot belong to science. The nature of truth which we are discussing is an appearance; that is to say, what appears to be true to the human mind, and therefore is human, and may be called maya, or illusion.'

EINSTEIN: 'It is no illusion of the individual, but of the species.'

TAGORE: 'The species also belongs to a unity, to humanity. Therefore the entire human mind realizes truth; the Indian and the European mind meet in a common realization.'

EINSTEIN: 'The word species is used in German for all human beings; as a matter of fact, even the apes and the frogs would belong to it. The problem is whether truth is independent of our consciousness.'

TAGORE: 'What we call truth lies in the rational harmony between the subjective and objective aspects of reality, both of which belong to the superpersonal man.'

EINSTEIN: 'We do things with our mind, even in our everyday life, for which we are not responsible. The mind acknowledges realities outside of it, independent of it. For instance, nobody may be in this house, yet that table remains where it is.'

TAGORE: 'Yes, it remains outside the individual mind, but not the universal mind. The table is that which is perceptible by some kind of consciousness we possess.'

EINSTEIN: 'If nobody were in the house the table would exist all the same, but this is already illegitimate from your point of view, because we cannot explain what it means, that the table is there, independently of us. Our natural point of view in regard to the existence of truth apart from humanity cannot be explained or proved, but it is a belief which nobody can lack—not even primitive beings. We attribute to truth a superhuman objectivity. It is indispensable for us—this reality which is independent of our existence and our experience and our mind—though we cannot say what it means.'

TAGORE: 'In any case, if there be any truth absolutely unrelated to humanity, then for us it is absolutely non-existing.'

EINSTEIN: 'Then I am more religious than you are!'

TAGORE: 'My religion is in the reconciliation of the superpersonal man, the universal spirit, in my own individual being.'"[21]

Notice Tagore's mention of science, followed by his all too common out of context appeal to relativity; implying that he had successfully carried Einstein's Theory of Relativity on his back across the yawning gulf between physics and metaphysics.

"The world is a human world — the <u>scientific view</u> of it is also that of the <u>scientific man</u>. Therefore, the world apart from us does not exist; <u>it is a relative world</u>, depending for its reality upon our consciousness."

The pomposity of this statement leaves me reeling. This mere linguist, musician, and poet has the audacity to preface his denial of absolutes, which is inseparable from his claim that "it is a relative world," with a statement that "the scientific view of it is also that of the scientific man." In other words, "You would hold a similar view if you were a real scientist, as I am." Bear in mind that this not so subtle jab was thrown at arguably the greatest mind which the Physics world has known, by a now mostly forgotten petty academic. By his frequent reference to faith, it can be seen that Einstein sensed that a belief in, or denial of God was at the root of the disagreement.

Atheists have used the sword of relativism to slash at truth after truth, until today we fight for the very preservation of the most common-sensical of facts; such as that humans are sexually dimorphic, rather than an infinite rainbow of *genders*. In this example regarding the sexes, the battle is not being lost in open debate, but in the courts, where a minority of morally corrupt individuals are able to force their will down the throats of entire nations. I call on academics, politicians, clinicians, actors, writers, journalists, pastors, and everything in between to resist this destroying and devouring wolf of atheism, which has traded its sheep's clothing for the far more effective robes of the professor and the judge.

Do not misunderstand me here. Noble professors and judges continue to exist to this day, who daily do their utmost to prevent this cultural decay. Yet these often have their efforts frustrated by this pestilential cadre of atheists in influential positions, and those who still call themselves religious, but who unwittingly lend their voices and strength to the atheist cause. Lawyers bear much responsibility as well, as many prostitute themselves to corrupt, yet wealthy individuals, or corporations, to be used as tools to dismantle societies, manipulate governments, ruin businesses, and destroy individuals. The lawyer's opinion means nothing without the judge though. Judges, who are generally harvested into vacancies from among this crop of lawyers, bear ultimate responsibility for any abuse or manipulation of law.

Truth

Whence do our feelings originate? Are they always entirely accurate and therefore reliable? In order to examine these questions, we must first investigate how decisions occur within the mind. Since we establish elsewhere within this work the fact that the native tongue of the mind is not language, but rather the more information dense tongue of feeling, let us proceed directly to an examination of the decision process itself. All decisions are merely the mind's scenario specific attempts to achieve its overarching goal of an increase in happiness. But how does the mind know what will make it happy?

Similar to the way that a ship's captain depends upon a compass to determine which direction is north, the conscious mind relies upon feelings received from the subconscious to determine which action sequences (i.e. means paths) will bring either a more rapid, or a more complete increase in happiness. These feelings appear to be the internal language which the mind uses to exchange thoughts between its various levels and areas.

Prior to these thoughts being passed to the conscious mind as feelings, they reside within the subconscious mind as beliefs. Beliefs are the composite views which the mind develops about various subjects, based upon the total sum of information which it has accumulated about them from the combined input of its internal and external senses. Whenever any, some, or all of these senses receive new information about a subject, they immediately pass it to the mind, where, if needed, existing beliefs held about it are subsequently re-evaluated and adjusted. Feelings can therefore effectively be thought of as beliefs in motion, or in other words, as *dynamic beliefs*.

Similarly, in order for these feelings to influence the material world (i.e. externalize), the mind must first convert them into actions. Actions can therefore effectively be thought of as feelings in motion; or in other words, as *dynamic feelings*. To review, we do things because we feel a certain way about them. We feel this way because of what we believe about these things. We hold these beliefs based upon information which our senses have accumulated about these subjects.

When this is mentioned to most people, they typically counter that they often don't do what they feel like doing, but what they know to be good for them. They desire cake, for example, but knowing cake to be bad for them, they instead eat a salad, and then praise themselves as having ignored *hot* emotion, in favor of *cold* logic. In reality, these people acted no less upon feelings than the cake eater. Even means paths which are perceived to be more *logical* are the products of feelings; which themselves are the products of beliefs.

Confusion about this stems from the fact that the various pieces of information which we possess about certain subjects often conflict with one another. For example, the mind instinctively knows that nature often uses sweetness to indicate the energy density of foods. It subconsciously, and often even consciously recalls pleasurable memories of experiencing the sweet flavors of cake on its taste buds. Desiring to re-experience this pleasure, and knowing that sustaining, or storing energy is crucial for survival, it craves the cake.

On the other hand, the mind may also have recently received information from the eyes that inform it that its body is overweight; a situation which it knows to be unhealthy. The mind knows that salad is lower in calories than cake, due to information which it has been fed. It is therefore left in a situation where it must select between what seem to be two paths to happiness, that of getting healthier by losing weight, and that of enjoying the pleasure of consuming the cake. The position which ultimately prevails is the one which currently possesses the strongest, or largest amount of information supporting it. This position creates the strongest beliefs, causing the strongest feelings, which are ultimately converted into actions.

Though the conscious mind may forget much of the information about a specific subject which it has been exposed to, the subconscious mind retains the vast majority of these things for far longer than most realize. This is the reason why, when our senses are stimulated in certain unique ways, or when our thoughts travel down certain unfrequented paths, long-forgotten memories sometimes rush in like floodwaters. Unbeknownst to the conscious mind, these memories remained within the subconscious, exerting their influence upon our composite beliefs. Sometimes these memories only emerge from the depths of the subconscious in their untranslated native tongue of feeling. In these instances, we may only recognize that the stimulation, or thought, gave a certain feeling of familiarity, which we generally struggle to describe.

When the need for a decision arises, the subconscious instantly reviews its beliefs about any subjects and possible actions relating to them. It then prioritizes these possible actions according to their potential to increase happiness. For example, when someone is faced with a decision about whether or not to buy an ice cream cone, the mind instantly evaluates its feelings on the question. This evaluation process is far more complex than it seems.

In a moment, the subconscious examines its beliefs about its past, current, and future physical, mental, emotional, and financial state, the qualities of the ice cream, the cleanliness of the establishment, the current temperature, the vendor's body language cues, and dozens of other subjects. The subconscious then analyzes the dozens of possible actions which it can take; from eating the ice cream, to abstaining from it, to stealing it, to hitting the vendor, etc. The mind then groups these specific actions with the dozens of combinations of possible lead-up and follow-up action sequences for each of them, and sorts them all according to their likelihood to increase happiness. The subconscious then sends positive feelings back to the conscious mind for those action sequences (i.e. means paths) which appear to offer the highest probability for increased happiness. Negative feelings are sent for those which appear to offer the lowest probability for it. The conscious mind inevitably selects and implements whichever means path is associated with the greatest overall positive feeling.

As an example of how much the subconscious affects even our minor daily decisions, consider the curious phenomenon which generally occurs whenever people enter and arrange themselves within a room where a presentation involving some element of morality is scheduled to occur; such as during a church service, a courtroom session, or even an education event; as the essential goal of true education is the dissemination of truth and the dissipation of error, which is an inherently moral act. We generally don't observe this phenomenon occurring in movie theaters, football games, strip clubs, or other places which either don't focus on increasing virtue, or contrarily focus on increasing vice.

The phenomenon being referred to is the way that attendees who expect to remain relatively anonymous throughout the presentation, a situation common in most church services, will tend to position, or seat themselves in relation to the presenter in a manner which strongly correlates with their subconscious assessment of their own personal character. The reason for this is that, during these types of presentations, the audience subconsciously tends to project its concept of absolute moral authority upon the presenter in proportion to the morality of the presentation's theme. Since these presenters are in actuality, simply fallible men, they necessarily fill this role imperfectly. Yet to the attendee's subconscious, the presenter becomes essentially a hazy reflection of God.

Those who subconsciously believe that the state of their character is relatively closer to the standard of absolute moral goodness than that of their peers will tend to sit closer to the presenter. Those who believe their character to be relatively further from it will tend to distance themselves as much as possible from the presenter. Those who feel themselves to be about average will tend take up a central position.

It is actually a running joke in Baptist churches that they always compete for the back rows. This somewhat indicates how these people subconsciously perceive themselves. This tendency does not mean that these back-pew Baptists are in fact the most morally corrupt within the church, but simply that they subconsciously tend to believe themselves to be relatively so. This belief, however, could be completely unfounded.

The person in the front row could be too addled with error, or ignorance to even realize his level of internal corruption, while one in the back who realizes his shortcomings, may have far better character than the people sitting in front of him. Atheists, being moral relativists, and therefore believing that their own actions define their individual standard of moral goodness, may sit in the front row in court, though they are a far more morally corrupt group when considered as a whole, relatively speaking. A Muslim who murders, rapes, or enslaves non-Muslims may think himself a saint and sit directly in front of his Imam at mosque, simply because he has been misled by the Koran, Hadiths, and his teachers into believing that such things are both good and necessary. A Jew who manipulates a trade deal to his advantage may sit directly in front of the Rabbi at temple, simply because he mistakenly believes that he is among the "chosen" bloodline, and is therefore deserving of special privileges and graces.

When seeking to observe this phenomenon, we must be careful to account for the many other subtle influences which will always exist to some extent. Things such as the location of already seated liked, or disliked people, the need to be closer to the presenter due to physical limitations, or specific personal interest. Contrarily, the attendee may wish to sit further from the presenter, or near the exits simply because they hate the subject matter and desire to escape. There may also be experience based expectations that those who are seated in certain areas are more likely to be called upon, given specific tasks, or perceived with favor, or disdain. In addition, the attendee may be keenly aware of what seats have already been taken and how this will be perceived by the presenter, or may simply need to be near an exit for health, or other personal reasons.

If the attendees expect to interact with the presenter, or others, then appearance will play a larger role on room arrangement. Those who place themselves closer to the presenter will then tend to be the ones who are more comfortable with who and what their physical appearance, mannerisms, words, or actions depict them as. Those who are not comfortable with this will tend to position themselves further from the presenter.

How powerful a thing our subconscious is that it would make us take these sorts of actions. It is as if it draws our bodies along with a string. How many of what we think are voluntary choices are simply our minds attempting to reduce the subconscious strain between what is believed to be true and how our choices might silently confirm, or contradict these beliefs.

Young and inexperienced minds frequently struggle with the prioritization of means paths which appear to promise brief, though intense versions of happiness, versus those appearing to promise a version of happiness which is longer-lasting, though less intense. This confusion is caused by a general lack of familiarity with the true nature of happiness; causing an inability to accurately predict its intensities and durations. The mind may grow skilled at making these types of predictions, and therefore in accurately selecting more rewarding means paths, through a combination of personal study, recollection of past outcomes, and internal reflection. This type of skill is commonly referred to as wisdom.

But in order to accurately predict what will increase its happiness, the subconscious mind must first understand what happiness is. Happiness is the euphoria which the naturally good soul experiences when it encounters another instance of goodness; either newly discovered within, or external to itself. As discussed elsewhere, this goodness may take many context specific forms; such as justice, within the context of judgement, love, within the context of interaction, truth, within the context of the representation of reality, beauty, within the context of form, and dozens of other names within an equal number of contexts. Abstracted from all context, these common goodnesses are discovered to be none other than *echoes* of God. This thrilling which we call happiness is therefore actually the expression of God within our souls properly interacting with (i.e. loving) the echoes of itself which it encounters externally, throughout nature, or internally, within our minds.

Happiness is therefore entirely dependent upon goodness. The closer men come to understanding true goodness, fixing their minds and basing their actions upon it, the closer they get to true happiness. Were perfect goodness humanly possible, it would induce perfect bliss. The subconscious instinctively understands this and therefore prioritizes means paths to happiness according to their potential to effect the most good actions related to the most good subjects; or in other words, according to their potential to generate the greatest net amount of good.

But when discriminating good actions or subjects from bad ones, what does the subconscious use as its reference standard? The answer is that it uses the ever-present standard of perfect goodness which all mankind possess within their souls: a mysterious thing commonly referred to as the conscience. Ideas and actions which appear to be more in conformance with this internal standard of goodness are considered relatively *better* than those which appear to be further removed from it.

Though some may think that this concept is the same as that of moral relativism, it actually isn't. The reason for this is that, though this concept posits that specific ideas and actions may be compared on a relative scale, it retains an underlying belief in the existence of a universal standard of absolute goodness by which these things may also be judged. Moral relativists, on the other hand, by definition do not believe in ethical absolutes.

The subconscious is not perfect, however. The accuracy of conclusions which it arrives at about specific subjects or actions, depends upon the accuracy and completeness of the information which it has been fed about them. The subconscious behaves, in this regard, in a manner similar to that of a calculator. Both of these things always return a result that is only as accurate as the information set which has been entered into them. If the information set which either of them have been fed contains errors, or omissions, then the answers which they return, though faithful to the supplied information, will be equally erroneous, and fail to reflect the true nature of the subject under evaluation. The degree of error will vary in proportion to how significant the missing, or how inaccurate the erroneous information was.

If the subconscious has been fed information on a subject or action, which is only slightly erroneous or deficient, it will likely develop resulting beliefs about them which are only slightly inaccurate. If, on the other hand, it has been fed significantly erroneous, or deficient information about these things, it will likely develop grossly inaccurate beliefs about them. When people's beliefs are significantly warped by error or ignorance, subjects or actions which are genuinely bad may appear closer to the standard of goodness, or relatively better, than those which are truly good.

Contrarily, genuinely good subjects or actions may be misconstrued as bad ones. This ignorance, or error-based warping of beliefs causes the subconscious to also incorrectly recognize and prioritize potential means paths to increased happiness. This, in turn, results in a warping of the set of feelings which the subconscious sends to the conscious mind about these things. When the conscious mind makes decisions based upon these warped feelings, the life of this individual and that of anyone depending upon them, often drift into harm. This is similar to the way that a captain who is unaware that he is sailing with a damaged compass not only puts his own life in danger, but also endangers the lives of his shipmates who depend upon him. This is the reason why ignorance and error are two of the most morbid diseases which a nation, group, or individual can become infected with.

It should now be evident that the quality and volume of information which people feed their minds can not only influence their beliefs, but also the feelings which these beliefs generate. Individuals who are sufficiently ignorant, or whose minds have been fed with a sufficient amount of error, can genuinely begin to feel a sincere a love of and desire for what is truly reprehensible, or a hatred of what is truly good. This warping of a person's beliefs and feelings away from what is true and good is the textbook definition of perversion.

This fact, that information exposure influences subsequent feelings, is fiercely contested by many seeking to avoid responsibility for their current state of moral corruption, or past bad decisions; as well as by the host of corrupt academics, judges, and legislators who empower them. In spite of the lack of scientific evidence supporting their position, these people often even go so far as to blame nature herself for their state of moral depravity. Such an approach is merely a veiled accusation of the will and character of nature's author and sustainer; God. It is as nonsensical to claim that a purely good being could will anything other than pure goodness, as it is to claim that moral depravity is a good.

Honesty

Sincerity is truly a rarely circulated coin these days, even among those whom we call family. It grows rarer by the day, as superficial social media becomes ever more popular. When it is placed upon the counter to purchase trust, its rarity generally causes spectators to initially be taken aback. Once they recognize the coin to be genuine, their subsequent reaction depends upon their personal character.

The genuinely good natured, who through a string of concessions of conscience have slowly slipped into the habit of doing trade in the counterfeit coins of dissembling and affectation, will often view the sincere person with a mix of pity and sadness. Pity due to how much they believe that this person must yet learn, in order to survive in this often-merciless world, and sadness due to the fact that they themselves didn't used to feel that way: that there once was, and sadly still should be more to their responses than shallow attempts to manipulate the listener into thinking or acting to their advantage.

Another class of person will see the coin laid down and imagine that they see the words, *Legal tender for fools*, in the markings encircling it. This type will happily relieve the seller of this, as well as of any other coins in their possession; never balancing the exchange with the paid for trust.

Truly honest communication is a loving act. As scripture puts it, "He kisses the lips, who gives a right (i.e. honest) answer." George Orwell, author of *1984* (a work which should be read by all Westerners) echoed this sentiment when he profoundly stated that "In a time of deceit, telling the truth is a revolutionary act."[22] But there are deeper principles to be learned about truth beyond simply claiming that it is something good to do.

Truth, like goodness, is absolute. As with all things of an absolute nature, it does not allow for gradation. This means that no single truth is any more, or any less true than any other, regardless of the subject.

"But how can this be?" one might ask. "Surely two claims may be made, neither of which are absolutely false, but one of which is more accurate, such as that my shoes fit well, and that I have iron in my blood. While I, as a human, absolutely must have iron in my blood, my shoes may only fit well compared to ones which I have tried. There may be other shoes which I have never tried which would make me realize that my shoes actually fit rather poorly. Would not the claim about my shoes fitting well, though true, therefore be less true than the one about my blood containing iron? Wouldn't this prove that gradation of truth exists?"

Both statements, that of the blood and that of the shoes, are equally true when understood properly. Let's analyze these hypothetical statements to see how this is so. Firstly, consider the statement about my blood containing iron. Is this an absolutely true statement? In order to determine this, the information sender and receiver must make sure that they have the same concepts in mind when they are referring to the subject and any claims which are being made about it.

What am I referring to when I make claims about blood? Blood, as we all know, refers to a cocktail of plasma, red blood cells, platelets, white blood cells, dissolved gasses, enzymes, hormones, and a host of other proteins and cells. The iron in blood is generally found bound to hemoglobin molecules within red blood cells. When I make the claim that my blood contains iron, I am obviously not attempting to convey the message that every part of my blood possesses an equal distribution of it. Such a statement would be patently false, as blood infused organs such as the spleen possess a far greater concentration of red blood cells than most other parts of the body. I also do not intend to convey the message that, when my blood and my external environment are compared, my blood will be found to possess the majority of iron. I could be standing next to a steel framed car. My claim is one of presence or absence: that some amount of iron, however slight, will be found to exist somewhere within my blood.

It can be seen from the few examples listed above that confusion over uniform distribution, majority/minority, presence/absence, and several other sense misunderstandings could easily occur between the sender and receiver. Correctly understood in its intended manner, the statement about the blood is absolutely true.

Now let's consider the second claim about my shoes fitting well. Here we run into problems. How are we meant to understand the term *well*, as it is used here? As with all expressions concerning degrees of quality, the term *well* implies comparison. When I say that my shoes fit well, it is understood that I mean that their comfort is at, or above the median comfort of the range of different shoes which I have had any experience with.

It should also be understood that the implied experience period can strongly influence the meaning, and therefore the veracity of a statement. Depending upon the context of the statement, when I say that I am feeling well, I could either be referring to feeling somewhere above the median of all pleasurable feelings I have ever experienced, or I could merely be referring to those which I have experienced recently.

For example, perhaps I suffered significantly over the past week due to my involvement in an auto accident. If someone enters my hospital room, inquires how I feel, and my response is that I am doing *well*, the state of *wellness* which I describe in this instance will likely only refer to feelings exceeding the median of those experienced during my recent period of suffering and recuperation, though such a state may remain well below the median of the range of feelings experienced during my entire lifetime. I could also mean that I feel *well* as compared to other people at my place of employment, home, or current location, or as compared to my family, friends, or to others in my state, country, or in foreign lands, or to people living in different historical periods, or to others in my own, or other occupations, or to those whose thoughts, actions, or states did, do, or will reflect my own. Though there are an almost infinite amount of senses in which information may be understood, the sender only has a single specific sense in mind when sending it.

Another important point which should not be lost sight of is the fact that statements which are made about anything subject to change, or decay are understood to be time bound. These truths remain bundled up with and confined to conditions in existence when they were made. For example, if at noon I made a true statement about the sun being up, it cannot be claimed at midnight, after it has set, that my previous statement was a lie. It is understood that the statement was referring to, and therefore bound to conditions existing when the statement was made.

This is also the case for quality based comparative truths. I may later in life have an experience surpassing in quality any which I previously had, within a specific category of experience. Such a dramatic expansion of my experience range, within this category, will necessarily shift the median point of my experiences, potentially causing former states which previously fell above the median, to subsequently fall below it. Though this change will influence the range of what may truthfully be stated in the future, it does not change the veracity of any previously true statements.

As an example, I may truthfully state that I believe something to taste good; perhaps a certain brand and flavor of ice cream. I may later have an experience which expands the range of my experience set, shifting the median in this category. Perhaps I taste some world-renowned ice cream prepared by a master chef from the finest ingredients. This new median point may now be far above that of my former experiences, depriving me of the ability to truthfully state that I believe the former type of ice cream to be good. This new perspective does not mean that the former statement was false. Being rooted in an experience set which is inherently mutable, it was true for the period in which it was made.

As can be seen, there is no gradation of truth. True thoughts, statements, or even actions which seem to display a gradation, only appear to do so because we misunderstand the terms, concepts, or implications involved. When we speak, think, or act out truth, we plant our words, thoughts, and deeds, like the pinnacle of a pyramid, upon the stone solid foundation of that which is common to all of the realities within the universe. Due to ignorance, or error which is mistakenly adopted as truth, men may resist truth when it is presented to them, but the presenter recruits these men's very consciences to testify against them, by giving audible voice, or visible manifestation to their instinctively sensed feelings.

Lies, on the other hand, are rooted in a sort of misanthropy. Men lie because they either fear what other men might do to, say to, or think about them, or because they desire to gain some typically unethical advantage over others, which they know would be resisted were it made public. With falsehood and manipulation flooding the world these days, submerging truths beneath its black waves, it seems wise to document, preserve, and pass on to future generations what truths we can, before they slip from society's memory and must, after years of ignorance and the cruelties which inevitably spring from it, be rediscovered at great effort, peril, and price.

Family

It is intensely frustrating delving through the soil of historical records in search of familial roots, only to lose sight of them as they penetrate deeper into the past. Within my own family, the earliest period that I have been able to trace back to with any amount of certainty is the early 1800's in Camden, New Jersey; near the town where I myself was born; Woodbury. Prior to this, though I have found the names of several mostly forgotten *Storms* among the original Dutch settlers of New Amsterdam (now New York), some of whom served in the American Revolution, I am unable to verify any connection to these people. Even if a connection were to be discovered, I would eventually lose track of this root again at some other point a bit deeper.

That is alright. Mere awareness of the existence of family is not what we are all actually seeking anyway. The reason these broken links in the chains of our pedigree seem tragic to us is because of the loneliness which we all intermittently experience and struggle with during this life: loneliness directly caused by the rarity of true intimate communication. Since we are familiar with how nuclear families generally tend to cure the longing to be both genuinely known and loved, we mistakenly assume that increasing our circle of familiarity to include former ancestors would increase the efficacy of this cure. At the very least, knowing them might help us to better understand ourselves, since our very bodies are, in part, formed of the same matter as theirs.

While this theory seems superficially plausible, it is magical thinking to assume that anything within similar blood, or genes could provide the intimacy and love which we actually seek. Any relationship with these long-gone relatives, were it even possible, would likely be no more meaningful than one formed with a random person at the grocery store.

Deep within, all desire to be truly known and loved for what they genuinely know to be good about themselves. In order for this love to occur, we require intimacy. In order to experience intimacy, we must have a means of learning the true character of another person. Unfortunately, we are all trapped within our own bodies in this world, like so many prison inmates. We wish not merely to rely upon what others tell us of their character, but to enter the other cells and discover for ourselves the types of souls dwelling within them. More than this: we long to leave the prison altogether and explore what lies beyond. We will, eventually.

One possible way to gain an intimate awareness of the true character of another person is to read the recorded outpourings of their hearts in either longer impersonal, or shorter personal written works. Those in pursuit of such outpourings among long gone ancestors generally discover that virtually nothing was written by them, through foresight saved, or survived the ravages of time. It is difficult to believe that, at any given period, none of the perhaps three or four generations of living ancestors thought to record written memories for their posterity; yet that is the impression which one is often left with. Didn't they believe that the personal challenges which they overcame, the hopes and dreams which they held, or the loves which they felt would be of interest to future generations?

When I attempted to do this with my own family, I was only able to dredge up a dry master's thesis on logistics management which was written by my maternal grandfather and a handful of sterile religious poetry which was written by my paternal one. These works had sat motionless on the bottom of the river of time. I say *dry* and *sterile* because I knew and loved both of these men, yet in scanning the pages of these works, I found that they were neither candid, nor long enough for me to recognize within them any trace of their authors' warm personalities. The men themselves were lost in a sea of words; passing information like soulless computers. How I wished to find some indication, in the work on Logistics, of the man who would laugh heartily, after scaring me with a well-timed slap on the table, at the climax of an old folk story he had been telling. How I wished, in the religious poetry, to find something of the man who was so proud of my childhood drawings.

The best part about reading is being able to look into the soul of another person and see what moved them, what made them feel alive and happy, and possibly using this information to better understand what will make us happy. No one wants to listen to a man regurgitate a series of memorized facts. In-between the lines, they want to hear how these facts thrilled the author, or broke his heart. In fine, they want a human, not some cold machine, to speak to them through the pages. It is for this reason that we must seek above all to be candid in our writing. We must let our emotions, our genuine thoughts, our very selves infuse our writing, so that after we are gone, our children, or grandchildren can read these things with smiles on their faces and think: "Yep, that was dad," or, "That was mom."

The wish is not to capture our own personalities and thoughts because we arrogantly think our characters to be so wonderful that we desire some sort of written memorial to be created for them, but because we know that men and women are often lonely. Living in a world which seldom rises above superficialities, people long for candid communication so they may feel less alone inside. Indeed, this world not only seldom rises above superficiality, but typically denies the existence of anything more, praises and celebrates those with an irrational fixation on the petty, condemning or ostracizing any who would dare to claim that things such as beer, sports, or sex are relatively insignificant, when compared to such things as virtue and political and religious clarity.

Of course it does. Virtue and religion often teach self-restraint, while politics often teaches social responsibility and charity, neither of which are good for profits. Such things don't keep people spending, in a near panic, looking for the next gadget, gift, food, clothes, car, buzz, sport, sexual relationship, or anything else which the commercials have sworn will bring them happiness.

But to be honest, I knew that I longed to recognize these men within their writings for somewhat selfish reasons. I secretly hoped that my recognition of these men would, at least somewhat and however briefly, fan the ebbing embers of my childhood memories back into life, allowing me to once again re-experience the coveted emotions of that time of relative innocence, simple trust, unguarded love, and joy.

I hope that other, more candid works by my ancestors remain somewhere yet undiscovered. Perhaps lost information will resurface one day as a forgotten document is converted into an electronic format, but I am not holding my breath, as the world today seems to give so little interest to historical matters. They are the supermen: the pinnacles of evolution. Why need they bother with the thoughts of those 18th and 19th century men whom they have been brainwashed into believing were mostly half-savage, knuckle dragging, misogynist, Klan members. Views so full of error could only be held by those in the grossest states of ignorance about the people and periods which they condemn.

We must break this cycle of cultural orphanage; never giving future generations cause to wonder if we considered, or cared about them. We must show them that we were aware that they would be surrounded by numberless wolves claiming to be trustworthy guides, yet secretly seeing them as prey, and shuddered at the thought of leaving them searching for truths unaided. Let us record what truths we have discovered. Planting these seeds with the hope that God will allow them to mature and bear fruit for the benefit of family, friends, countrymen, and unmet future generations of virtuous men and women the world over, long after we are gone.

Love

What is love? To begin with, it should be evident to all that love is an emotion. Emotions are synonymous with feelings, which are felt or sensed, not actions, which are performed. This seems a simple point, but people often confuse actions which typically stimulate the development of an emotion, or which occur in response to an emotion, with the emotion itself. We don't perform an action of loving. Love isn't something, like water in a hose, which can be aimed at and sprayed upon something, or someone else. We feel the birth, growth, steadiness, or decline of the feeling of love. We feel and recognize it like we feel and recognize the heat from a nearby fire.

The emotion of genuine love is synonymous with the deepest level of friendship. People often disagree with this statement, because they confuse the mixture of erotic attraction and genuine love, which Hollywood has shown them, with pure genuine love itself. In addition, people often have an unclear understanding of what friendship actually is.

Erotic attraction may often be either the harbinger, or the result of love, but it is not the noble thing itself. Proof of this is unnecessary, as all know that individuals may be physically attracted to those whom they are not emotionally attracted to. Contrarily, they may also deeply love someone, or something (e.g. grandparents, parents, siblings, a faithful pet, a noble concept, etc.) without also possessing an iota of erotic attraction towards these people, or things.

Friendship, per Aristotle, generally occurs on three levels.[23] In his Nicomachean Ethics, he states that the most superficial level of friendship is one which is founded upon mutual utility; where both parties stand to gain physical, or emotional advantage from the bond, and enter it for that somewhat selfish reason. As prime examples of this most superficial type of friendship, consider relationships between coworkers, or neighbors that one seldom speaks with, but that they also do not wish to estrange; knowing that their aid may eventually be needed.

The second level of friendship which Aristotle identified is one which is founded upon common interests, or pleasures. A commonly seen example of this type of friendship is that of sports enthusiasts who associate in order to participate in, watch, or discuss specific sporting events which they are passionate about.

The third, deepest level of friendship, that which Aristotle refers to as true friendship, is one which is founded upon a mutual recognition of good character and a resulting mutual love of this observed goodness. This is why Aristotle states that this type of *true* friendship can only occur between people of good moral character. Here we see the nexus of the concept of pure love with that of true friendship.

Someone might claim that love refers to a feeling which does not require the plurality of participants which a friendship does. People may love an abstract concept, such as a childhood memory, a sense, such as a smell, or an inanimate object, such as a finely cut gem, and be alone in the feeling. I do not agree with this proposed difference. Love always requires a perceiver of the feeling, referred to here as the lover, and a subject which the feeling is directed towards, referred to here as the beloved. As discussed earlier, it isn't actually the person of the beloved which is loved, it is the good which is observed within and identified with the beloved, which is. In both the instance of friendship and that of love of a noble idea, the love felt by the lover is of an abstract concept of goodness.

Depending upon whence one believes this internal good to originate, this deepest level of friendship can adopt an almost religious flavor. On the one hand, those who believe this observed good to have spontaneously originated within the individual by chance are challenged in defining this good without ultimately destroying its universal nature; replacing it instead with mere base utility. Alternatively, others view the good which is observed within people as a sort of external manifestation of the natural qualities of the intrinsically good soul which dwells within them, enlivens them, and which displays its goodness more clearly as the cleansing waters of study and virtue slowly wash away any encrustations and stains of conscience which have been left upon it by past mistakes. A soul which is either crafted by, or an embodiment of the divine. This is likely the more correct view.

"If love is simply the closest level of friendship," someone might ask, "Why does familial love seem as though it is deeper than most friendships?"

The noticeably different closeness generally felt between family and most friendships is due to the fact that the friendship in the former typically began during a period when one, or both parties in the relationship was, or were young enough that they entered into the relationship with an honesty born from simple, unguarded trust. When people are open and sincere with their views, it is far easier to arrive more rapidly at the deepest level of friendship; the mutual love of observed good. Unfortunately, this rarely occurs between adults, since past negative relational experiences, such as betrayals, slanders, manipulations, or lies, cause them to virtually always remain more guarded than children.

When the relationship being discussed is one where one of the two individuals is older, and potentially more guarded, while the other is young, candid, and trusting, such as between a parent and their child, the bond of friendship may develop to a lesser degree than one between two young and unguarded individuals, such as siblings, but will not necessarily do so. Though the parent will likely be more guarded, they will also be keenly aware that the young child will be unable to recognize this guarded state. Often the mere knowledge that one of the participants in the friendship is candid and trusting, is enough to break down the other participant's guarded nature. This stimulates a genuine display of character by both parties, and the subsequent deepest level of friendship which is born from the reciprocal love of any observed goodness.

Whether they realize it or not, all men subconsciously know that this deepest level of friendship, which we refer to as love, cannot be had without intimate knowledge and familiarity. Unfortunately, due to the vulnerability inherent in intimacy, seldom do any but our closest family ever feel safe enough to completely remove their masks and expose their very hearts to each other. One of the benefits of having a good marriage and a loving family is that one is able to enjoy this refreshing, simultaneous mix of genuine love and intimate familiarity on a daily basis. The moment I step through the door of my home, the sound of my children's sweet laughter and the sight of my wife's knowing grin shakes me from any gloom which the rampant cunning, cowardice, dishonesty, and dissimulation at work often infects me with. Often I am bombarded with hugs.

Our instinctive desire to embrace our loved ones is likely a physical manifestation of our subconscious awareness that we are but "One soul shared between two bodies," as Aristotle put it. We only feel this attraction towards, and subsequent desire to embrace things which we recognize as good, whether this goodness be of material form (i.e. strength, or beauty), or of character (i.e. magnanimity, nobility, kindness, courage, justice, etc.). Due to their innate goodness and perfection, our souls may ultimately be found to be expressions of God, a subject which is discussed at length elsewhere within this work. Since the goodness which these souls are attracted to is symbolic of the archetype of goodness, which again is ultimately discovered to be God, the attraction, and desire for unity which we feel is likely but God loving God.

As young lovers, we see our future spouses as the earthly acme of goodness. The more we are exposed to this goodness, the more we are driven almost mad by our desire to unite with them. This goodness which we seek, and expose each other to, can either be of form, or of character. Exposure to his wife's comely breasts inflames a good man the same way that exposure to her gentle and trusting heart may in a letter. Exposure to her husband's strong chest inflames a good woman the same way that exposure to his acts of bravery do.

We would pull them inside of us and share the same body if we could. Does the uniting of bodily openings in a kiss not hint at this merger? What else could explain such an action? Is a French Kiss not thrilling because parts of our bodies take the next step and actually pass into one another? Are we not thrilled all the more during sexual intercourse, as the male enters into, and the female receives the utmost of their spouse's body that normal usage healthfully allows? Women feel a special closeness with their infants for several reasons, but one of these is certainly due to the fact that these infants were formed from a part of them and formerly dwelled within them. Do women not also generally enjoy the closeness which the act of nursing provides, as parts of their breasts are pulled within their baby's mouth, and the nourishing liquid which infuses the one, passes into, and infuses the other as well?

Having examined the nature of love and friendship, we should also examine its development. What we refer to as relationship *growth*, or increase in relationship *depth*, is likely none other than increased recognition of goodness within one, or both parties, increased virtue (i.e. internal goodness), which is available to be recognized, admired, and encouraged in one, or both parties, or an increase in trust between individuals. The entire process of relationship growth, from superficiality to any significant depth, requires sufficient opportunity for interaction in order to develop the appropriate level of trust for us to feel safe displaying our inner character. This generally requires a large amount of time.

It is usually with caution and trembling hands that we lower our masks and shields and risk revealing who and what we really are, our true inner thoughts and character, instead of who and what we wish to be seen as. We hesitate because we know that, in doing so, we risk making ourselves vulnerable to others. Those whom we open up to, we empower with the ability to not only use our deepest thoughts against us, but to suddenly recognize something which they dislike within our character and turn away from the friendship in disgust; stranding us in the awkward, embarrassing, and occasionally even dangerous situation of unreciprocated sincerity.

On the other hand, we are typically thrilled, if we find that the other party continues to accept, love, and treat us fairly, after our revelation. This deep appreciation typically fills us with a desire to reciprocate, should the other party risk a revelation of their innermost character as well. Extreme circumstances which shorten the typical amount of time required for depth of relationship are those involving extremes of proximity, or stress; such as those within lifesaving, confinement, or wartime environments.

Ascending, or descending from great heights via land of a gently sloping grade is easier and far less dangerous than ascending, or descending steep cliffs. Though the elevation change occurs far more rapidly in the latter scenario, it is fraught with peril. In like manner, there is much greater risk involved in the overly rapid growth of a relationship towards intimacy. Inherent in this steep ascent is typically an assumed, rather than a proven trust in those whom we make ourselves vulnerable to via the exposure of our innermost thoughts. We generally feel betrayed if we later discover that this trust was misplaced; that what we thought was a genuine, reciprocal revelation of innermost thoughts, was merely the exchange of one mask for another in the person whom we revealed ourselves to. This feeling of betrayal and resulting imbalance in vulnerability typically causes us to avoid these people, generally destroying whatever relationship may have existed prior to the initial attempt at depth.

On the opposite hand, a similar risk exists with steep relational descents. Relationships do not work in reverse, in the direction of reduced intimacy, without the aid of large doses of time. Since we have already exposed our inner selves, to some extent, any subsequent retreat to superficiality by the person whom we formerly related to at depth will inevitably be perceived as personal rejection. This type of rejection is especially painful, due to the fact that we are unable to convince ourselves, as we can with most other rejections, that it wouldn't have occurred, had the other person better known our inner character and motives. They saw these clearly and turned away nonetheless.

It is a common saying that time heals all wounds. What very likely underlies this optimistic statement is the somewhat disconcerting, subconscious acknowledgement that, given enough time, virtually all memories of external senses and internal feelings can be effaced by the abrasive hands of time. Sometimes this forgetfulness is useful, such as when one wishes to forget a painful event. Other times, however, it is tragic; such as when widowers slowly lose the ability to recall the sound of their spouse's voice, or the feelings of love which they used to feel when with them.

Complete forgetfulness by two people, whose relationship formerly had significant depth, but which subsequently retreated to a more superficial level, is somewhat unlikely. At least one of them will likely continue to recall and regret the loss of the former closeness. This person will also sense that they are somewhat vulnerable to the other person, whom they previously entrusted revelations of their innermost character to. This looming vulnerability makes any subsequent interactions with this person awkward and uncomfortable, and hence frequently avoided.

This damaged dynamic is especially problematic with family members. With these, any avoidance often causes additional offense.

This unfortunate scenario is often encountered during divorce situations. In addition, it also tends to occur when a family member changes their viewpoint on a matter of deep philosophical significance; such as their core political, or religious views, from those which they previously shared with the family's patriarch, matriarch, majority, or some combination of these. Such a change is unlikely to cause significant problems with loosely held friends, or acquaintances, as these never related to us on a deep enough level for the difference to damage the existing relational dynamic. Close family, or friends, on the other hand, will typically see any subsequent rejection of this view-set, at least in part, as a rejection of themselves; eroding the foundation of trust which the friendship is built upon.

Goodness

Are our souls individually unique creations of God, or, to paraphrase Emerson, is there really only one *Oversoul*, and are what we think of as individual souls simply this Oversoul expressing itself throughout the material world.[3] Do our seemingly distinct souls merge at some point, like the individual fingers of a giant hand? Perhaps there is no point of separation at all, and like fish in water, all living things move through, breathe in, and are penetrated and sustained by the soul of God. In order to examine these questions regarding the immaterial soul, we must first examine materiality and see what we can learn from it by comparison.

The entire material (i.e. natural) world is perpetually churning. Nations, land, men, and matters may float to the surface and hold together in a recognizable clump for a time, but eventually everything sinks and dissolves once more in the waters of time. Clouds of atoms and molecules coalesce into nebulae. Nebulae congeal into galaxies of solar systems. The newly forming planets within these solar systems slowly accrete and cool. Elements of these planets that are more stable in a gaseous phase collect together into what we call an atmosphere: or when considering Earth's specific mixture of them, *air*. Those elements which are more stable in a liquid phase collect together and are called *sea*, or *ocean*. Finally, those elements which are more stable in a solid phase collect into hardened deposits which we call *stone*. The largest of these stones, which float upon the still molten portion of the planet beneath them, we call *tectonic plates*. We refer to the portions of plate which have an atmospheric boundary as *land*, and those *mountains*, which are elevated above the rest, due to collision with other plates. The actions of sun, wind, water, and soil crack, crumble, scour, dry, and dissolve the stone of these plates into its component minerals. These minerals, gasses from the atmosphere, and liquid from the ocean are assimilated into the bodies of plants. Animals assimilate these plants, as well as other animals, minerals, gasses, and liquids into their bodies. Among these animals is man, who can look to the heavens and ponder the complexities of the universe, himself, and his God, before, like all living things, eventually dying and dissolving back into the dusty minerals which formed him. The net movement of precipitation eventually carries these minerals back out to sea, to slowly settle as a layer of mud on the ocean floor. Over time, this mud compacts once more into the stone of one of the planet's tectonic plates. Eventually, these planets, solar systems, and galaxies collapse, collide, or explode back outwards into atoms, and the cycle begins anew.

An imperfection which is introduced into something material may not inhibit the function, or normal lifespan of the thing; therefore, causing it no real harm. What does it matter if a small freckle forms on the skin, if it is simply cosmetic and doesn't impact function? What does it matter if the soles are worn on shoes you are about to grow out of, or if a cavity forms on a tooth that is about to fall out. Neither of these defects change the normal lifespan of these things.

The situation becomes entirely different, however, when we discuss imperfections within the context of immateriality; such as imperfections of the soul. To begin with, reason tells us that perfection, which is merely a synonym for pure goodness, if it produces anything at all, must produce more perfection, and must produce it perfectly. Therefore, if soul is created by a perfectly good God, then it must also be perfect.

Imperfections of the immaterial soul appear to change the very nature of the thing itself, as any variation in a thing which was originally perfect can only be deleterious. God cannot introduce such harmful imperfections into the soul, whether intentionally, or unintentionally, and remain perfectly good. God's wisdom and power would be destroyed, were he to do such a thing unintentionally, while his goodness would be destroyed, were he to do it intentionally.

These points being established, the question of whether or not the soul is a unique creation of God, or simply an expression, or emanation from him, changes to: Can there be a plurality of supremely perfect things? Do the perfection and immateriality of a thing preclude any difference which is necessary for plurality?

As a thought experiment, envision two perfectly cut gems. Both stones may have different cuts, one being an oval and the other being a square, and yet each cut may have been perfectly executed. Both gems may also differ in color, and yet be perfect specimens of their respective mineral type. From examples such as this, many assume that a plurality of perfections may exist.

Upon closer investigation, it is discovered that this answer only holds true when dealing with materiality and those of its various characteristics, such as color, which have no ethical aspect. Blue is not ethically superior to red. Soul, on the other hand, is generally believed to be both immaterial and inseparable from its ethical nature. Indeed, the very definition of ethicality is founded upon how words, thoughts, or actions impact, or reflect the soul of a person.

Material traits which allow for difference and plurality, such as color, shape, and possibly even position, have no meaning within an immaterial context. In the immaterial, the only characteristics which the human mind can conceive, which might allow for variation, are those of type, quality, or intensity.

As discussed previously, any difference in quality is impossible; since a soul which has been created by a perfect being must itself also be perfect. For similar reasons, differences in intensity are equally impossible. In order for the intensity of a soul to vary, either its final, or its original states must be imperfect. It must either degrade from an originally perfect state, or improve from an originally deficient one.

Intuitively, it seems improbable for a plurality of perfect immaterial types to exist without involving us in logical paradoxes. This subject should be analyzed further, however. It is difficult to think of varying types of immaterial and perfect things to build an appropriate thought experiment around. The only examples which come readily to mind, such as wisdom and justice, are frequently found to be simply context specific synonyms for good. The physics community, however, does not ascribe positive existence to such things. Can we not find an analog which they do believe in, that we can analyze?

As discussed in another section, the problem with this question is that the physics community is altogether uncertain about the existence of perfect types. Of course, they would never use the word *perfect*, as it implies intended form, implying intelligent design, implying a designer, implying a God. Instead they prefer to use the term *fundamental*. And rather than *types*, they prefer the term *particles*, because it implies matter. This preference hints at the unfortunately all too common atheist bias which has infected the scientific community. Atheists are always drawn towards materialism, since a disbelief in the immaterial echoes their disbelief in God.

Ironically, a large group of the *fundamental particles* which are studied by particle physicists, things such as photons and gluons, are classified as pure energy. But don't be fooled by the jargon. The mental concept which is symbolized by the words *immaterial existence*, and the words *pure energy* is exactly the same. Both mean something which exists, which is not comprised of matter, and yet which can somehow act upon it.

In addition, there is ongoing debate within the physics community about whether these things are truly *fundamental*. It is very possible that they are formed from additional tiers of sub-particles arranged in complex substructures. There was a time, before men discovered nuclear structure, when the atoms of elements were thought to be fundamental particles. Then, until the discovery of quarks and neutrinos, protons and neutrons were thought to be fundamental particles. As technology continues to progress, we are likely to look back at the science of today, which claims quarks and photons to be fundamental particles, and chuckle, as our hadron colliders do not currently have the resolution to investigate and analyze any possible substructure of a quark. However, not being able to see a thing does not guarantee its nonexistence.

Bacteria existed for millions of years before the microscope was invented which finally allowed us to observe them.

Since this erodes our confidence in finding any examples of perfect immateriality among the particle physicists, which may be used in our examination of soul, we must return to the philosophers, such as Plotinus, who gives positive, perfect, immaterial existence to goodness. What do we know about this goodness? To begin with, we know that immaterial perfection is singular. There is only one ultimate good. All else, such as love, beauty, and justice, are merely context specific embodiments of it. While the perfect type (i.e. archetype) of goodness is by its nature unique, there are infinite possible types and degrees of imperfection, which we refer to as badness, or evil. G.K. Chesterton pointed this concept out in his *Orthodoxy*. Here he stated that, "There are an infinity of angles at which one falls, only one at which one stands."[24] As an example, there are infinite possible degrees of folly, which is imperfection in understanding; or in other words, how much something deviates from perfect understanding.

Another critical difference between the various manifestations of good and bad is that, while the manifestations of good are independent and absolute, those of bad are dependent and relative. In other words, good would continue to exist without bad, but bad cannot exist without good. This is because *bad* is defined by its amount of deviation from the archetype of good: perfection. This is the reason why theories about good requiring a *balancing* evil in order for it to display its characteristic goodness, the Ying needing the Yang of Taoism, are fundamentally flawed.

Evil, which is merely a synonym for badness, has no positive existence. It is simply an abstract concept which is used to describe a relative deviation from goodness; much like a *hole* is an abstract concept which is used to describe the absence of soil within a certain area of ground. There are no perfect holes. However large, deep, or round one is, a larger, deeper, or rounder one may be imagined. In like manner, there is no distinct action, person, or object which may be pointed to and called perfectly evil. However bad a specific example is, a worse one may be imagined.

An important point to be made here is that, though no specific example may be pointed to which is perfectly bad, or evil, any deviation from perfection is absolutely so. Though the number 2 is absolutely not the number 1, it is not the perfect antithesis of 1, as this would include all non-1 numbers, extending in both directions to infinity.

Knowing that there may be certain aspects to situations, or participants which they are unaware of, men are generally reluctant to think in absolutes. Due to this, there is always a tendency for them to consider goodness and badness on a relative scale. Though one action may appear bad when compared to perfection, it may appear relatively good, when compared to another much worse action. For clarity, consider someone who lies to their friend, in order to avoid hurting their feelings. Though compared to perfection, this lie appears bad, compared to aborting (i.e. murdering) an infant, it appears relatively good. This is simply an error of perspective.

Due to its multiform nature, evil, or badness, may be considered on a relative scale, but due to its singularity, goodness cannot. Given that bad is simply a deficiency of good, any deviation from perfect good, no matter how minor, is bad on an absolute scale, though it may retain more goodness than another, worse possible deviation. Consider the former example of a hole. Thousands of holes of relative degrees of deepness can exist, but there is only one type of non-hole. Calling a smaller hole a non-hole, simply because it retains more soil than another larger one is an error.

This position is in stark contrast to the unfortunately all too common view of moral relativism. Moral relativism defines goodness and badness as whatever a certain culture, or people arbitrarily agree to make them. Since different cultures, or people may always be found who disagree on this arbitrary definition, moral relativism devolves into a disbelief in the absolute existence of goodness. Goodness is real, absolute, transcends all cultures, and is rooted in the very nature of soul and of God.

These points being established, we can finally return to our question about the singularity, or plurality of soul. The examples examined above appear to indicate that there is one perfect soul which penetrates all living, and possibly even what we consider nonliving matter. Some may find it odd that nonliving (i.e. abiotic) matter was included as a potential reservoir of soul. The reason for this is that the definition of what is *living*, or *alive*, has been somewhat arbitrarily set.

Life, according to the biologists, is defined by the ability to grow, reproduce, be functionally active, and continually change prior to death. There are glaring problems with this definition. Is a man who has had a vasectomy no longer living, since he can no longer reproduce? Are mules, which are sterile, non-living? When these questions are asked, the reply which is generally given is that the definition applies to cells, which are supposed to be the functional unit of life. But is a neuronal cell within the brain, which doesn't reproduce, yet which continues to perform many metabolic functions, not alive? Do bacterial cells remain alive when seemingly frozen in their spore stage, for indefinite periods of time? Are virus' not alive, though they sit dormant until they enter into a host, at which time they spring into activity and reproduce. By this very definition the universe itself could be considered alive, since it is growing (i.e. expanding), reproduces galaxies in its nebulae, and is in constant flux.

These 4 requirements ultimately reduce to one: the ability to continually change; as growth, functional activity, and reproduction are all types of changes. But not simply any change, since rocks change as they erode, and a corpse also changes as it decays; sometimes even moving. Growth and reproduction were singled out in order to imply changes which improve the state of the organism. But even this is an inadequate definition, as cells, like people, can remain alive and yet lose the ability to grow, reproduce, or even function properly as they age.

So what is life? When does it actually cease? What are the signs of its presence or absence? We clearly see its presence when we see self-initiated movement, whether in single, or multi-celled organisms. This is the reason why living things were originally called "animals" by the Greeks; anemos meaning wind, or breath. We assume that they selected this word because they, rather naïvely observed these creatures breathing, however anemos was also used as a name for soul. Perhaps the ancient Greeks were more astute than we give them credit for. Anyone who has read Plato will know this to be the case.

Life and soul are really synonyms. The latter is the cause and sign of the former. Regardless of any arbitrary definitions which have been set by well-intentioned biologists, there is no life without soul, and no soul without life. Though we may assume the presence of soul, or life, when we observe self-initiated movement, or change, we cannot safely assume its absence when we don't. We may simply be blind to the changes, which may still be occurring on an atomic or chemical level. Ultimately, all of matter is in perpetual motion, from the Brownian motion of the lowest subatomic particle, to galaxies hurtling through the universe. The question becomes not if matter is moving, but if this movement is self-initiated, and therefore indicative of soul.

All of this movement had to have an ultimate source. Quoting Aristotle, "The moving causes exist as things preceding the effects, but causes in the sense of definitions are simultaneous with their effects."[25] There is no effect without a cause. Blaming any movement on *energy*, or *force*, is simply masking our ignorance with jargon, since these terms simply mean *something* which can cause matter to act. Physicists have given different names to this *something* according to the various contexts which it is observed in, and have developed formulae which model its effects and allow for prediction, but the thing itself remains mysterious.

This thing we label as energy and force, which drives the motion of the material universe, is soul. Albert Pike, in his brilliant Masonic work, *Morals and Dogma*, stated this most poetically.

"And all through the great body of the world are disseminated portions of the universal Soul, impressing movement on everything that seems to move of itself, giving life to the plants and trees, directing by a regular and settled plan the organization and development of their germs, imparting constant mobility to the running waters and maintaining their eternal motion, impelling the winds and changing their direction or stilling them, calming and arousing the ocean, unchaining the storm pouring out the fires of volcanoes, or with earthquakes shaking the roots of huge mountains and the foundations of vast continents; by means of a force that, belonging to Nature, is a mystery to man."[26]

Calling an action or process self-initiated is simply stating that there has been an effect caused by a will. Yet are we really in complete control of our will? This question begins to collapse upon itself when scrutinized. While it is easy to assume free will, simply because we do not comprehend the vast complexities of the universe, or ourselves, there is the very real possibility that free will is actually an illusion. Like leaves being carried by a breeze, we may simply be acting as anything would, given our specific set of personal and environmental properties and experiences. I may appear to be advocating the viewpoint of the modern Materialist here, but bear with me, as I am not.

The more ignorant we are of the rigid underlying processes and components of complex computer programs, or mechanical systems, the more *lifelike* these things appear to us to be. Infants, who don't understand the mechanical principles behind the spring and latch, think the Jack-in-the-Box to be a small living person who sometimes elects to jump out of his box and startle them, of his own free will. Small children, who don't understand the complexities of robotics, think the robotic dinosaurs which they view in museums, to be alive, and to move and roar of their own free will. The less adults understand about computers, or cars, the more frequently we hear them make comments condemning these things when they "lock up" on them while they are working on an important document, or break down on them on the highway: as if they were exercising a malicious sort of free will by doing so. Were we to increase the complexity of these systems several orders of magnitude, and simultaneously decrease our awareness of the rigid underlying principles which drive these things, our inability to comprehend their actions would likely cause us to think that their actions were self-initiated, and therefore indicative of free will; though they are not.

The computing industry tends to refer to this level of complexity as *artificial intelligence*, but this is really a misnomer. Computers are already able to artificially absorb, retain, and disperse intelligence. We simply call this intelligence *data*, or *information*. Yet nobody thinks of the common computer of today as having artificial intelligence. A more accurate description of the idea which people hold in mind when they use the phrase *artificial intelligence*, is *free will*.

Unfortunately, no matter how complex a computer, or mechanical system becomes, and no matter how much, how easily, or how quickly these things are able to interact with, store, or distribute information/data/intelligence, they will never be able to effect a will which is free from the rigid underlying processes which their complexity is built upon. Adding additional layers of complexity is like adding additional gears in a long chain. Regardless of how many are added, all are rigidly attached and dependent upon the fixed principles of the preceding ones for their function. Claiming that increased complexity could allow for free will, is like claiming that the last gear in the chain can initiate its own motion, in whichever direction it chooses, regardless of the motion of the preceding gears which it is connected to.

This situation requires the impossible divorce of cause from effect. The most complex systems which will ever be developed will always be rigidly bound to a series of simpler ones. At the bottom of this series is the fundamental process of information storage, for example, the simple storage of magnetic charges on the microscopic portion of a computer chip. As long as it remains impossible for the portion of the chip to exert free will by self-initiating a change in its own magnetic charge, it also remains impossible for the complex electro-mechanical systems which depend upon these processes to display free will by self-initiating change.

In the same manner, free will may be as impossible and illusory in the biological world as it is in the computing one. We may believe that we have free will, like the infant with the Jack-in-the-Box, simply because we fail to understand the astounding complexities of the various "springs and latches" of the body, mind, cell, molecule, atom, subatomic particles, and soul. This is an uncomfortable idea for most, as it destroys both the merit of the high achiever, and the demerit of the villain; shifting all credit and condemnation to beneficial, or harmful physical structures, personal experiences, or environmental influences. But just as the rigidity of the cause and effect relationship became more evident when we examined the lower gears of complexity in computer systems, so it appears to become when we examine the lower orders of complexity in biological ones.

Man, when considered at his highest, organismal level, appears to wield unfettered free will. Yet, when we narrow our perspective down to that of his organs and tissues, we observe a reduction in freedom. These appear to operate by a more rigid set of rules. When our scope is further narrowed to that of the cell, an astounding level of volition appears to return, however, just as man's organs and tissues appeared to operate buy a more rigid set of rules, so the organelles and componentry of the cell appear to as well. It is almost as if the cell is a small echo of the man. When we peer even more deeply into the molecules and atoms which comprise these things, we notice even more rigid adherence to a fixed rule set. Once at the subatomic layer, any volition appears to have disappeared almost entirely, as these particles seem to behave in an almost purely mechanical fashion.

Something seems to be occurring at the cellular and organismal levels which appears somewhat divorced from the cause and effect of chemical and mechanical laws, giving the appearance of free will. At the organismal level, we typically ascribe the cause for this to the functions of the mind. Yet we hardly understand the principles which govern the function of the conscious, and especially the sub-conscious mind. A rather lengthy section of this work has been devoted to this subject, which will not be repeated here. At the cellular level, we observe similar decision-making processes indicative of intelligence, and yet are unable to identify their cause.

Let it suffice to say that the mind of man, and possibly even the mysterious one of the cell, likely both operate by fixed principles. The apparent autonomy, which causes us to ascribe free will to the function of both, is likely due to their possession of an increased ability to somehow sense and respond to the influences of the soul. In the mind, we call this sense by the name of *conscience*. Though we are used to thinking of conscience as merely influencing our opinions regarding ethical issues, there is the possibility that it is not limited simply to these; that, seated at the helm of the mind, the soul drives the various physiological processes which we have no control over; such as those of the autonomic nervous system. This likely includes the early processes of embryological development.

During this period, the soul likely guides the body through the amazingly complex changes required of it, until it eventually takes its appropriate form. After this point, the body can only vary slightly. This is similar to the way that a sculptor can manipulate clay only until it has hardened. A similar process appears to occur within the individual cells. The soul likely guides the cell through its equally complex stages of differentiation, until it hardens into its final mature form.

As the mind is formed during the embryological stages, the main point of interface between soul and organism appears to, at least partially, depart from the site of the individual cells to concentrate within it. This somewhat explains the amazing plasticity of the developing zygote, as it passes through the complex stages of development, prior to neurulation and the formation of any directing rudimentary nervous system.

In similar manner, the point of interface of soul within undifferentiated *stem cells* may migrate into a certain area of the mature, differentiated cells; likely located somewhere within the nucleus. It could also explain why the amazing totipotency (i.e. ability to differentiate into any type of cell) of embryological stem cells subsides into pluripotency (i.e. ability to differentiate only into certain limited classes of cells) in the developed infant. Yet even these remaining pluripotent cells appear to retain sufficient plasticity and sensitivity to the guidance of soul to allow them to migrate, seemingly of their own volition, to areas of damage, where they then differentiate into the cell types needed to effect repair. Perhaps it isn't a coincidence that, as our supply of these undifferentiated stem cells become exhausted with age, there is a correlating decrease in function of our bodies' immunity from illness, and healing capabilities. This may also explain why stem cell therapies allow for the recovery of tissue which adults, who have insufficient amounts of these cells, would be otherwise unable to repair.

If this is all true, and free will is merely a false construct which we cling to out of ignorance of underlying causation, then evidence of enacted will, or self-initiation of physical change, is unnecessary in order to classify something as being acted upon, or filled with soul: or in other words, as being alive. The change itself would be sufficient evidence. Indeed, if our earlier conclusion is true about all soul ultimately being part of the same oversoul, than all initiation would have its origin within the same oversoul, and all action would be self-initiated.

There may not actually be any dead matter at all. The entire universe itself might be the body of a living entity: a *universal* God, in both senses of the word. Galaxies might be analogous to this being's cells, planets to its atoms, and men to its quarks. Immaterial soul, which we call energy, might simply infuse and sustain the *tissue* of the universe, as our blood infuses and sustains the tissues within our bodies. Such a God would be omniscient, because all information about the universe would merely be self-knowledge, omnipotent, because the source of all energy within the universe, and omnipresent, because infusing, and possibly even comprising the matter which forms the universe.

From our current human perspective, we could never completely comprehend the character of such an entity, since, in order to thoroughly comprehend the nature of a thing, its boundaries must be known. A person, for example, may observe part of a cloud which extends far beyond the horizon. While the visible portion of the cloud may take a linear shape, beyond the horizon, the cloud may actually expand into the shape of a lollipop. This is not merely true for the thing's physical qualities, but it remains equally true for its abstract qualities, such as power and knowledge.

It is therefore impossible to completely comprehend the nature of a God that does not possess physical boundaries, or limits of power and knowledge. It remains true even if God is ultimately found to be the universe itself, since we cannot observe the entirety of the universe, nor the sum of the forces contained within it.

Happiness

As we busily attend to the many duties required of us to maintain, protect, and care for our bodies, we often only hazily, perhaps even subconsciously, become aware of a certain pre-existent appetite within our souls. Unaware of what will satisfy this appetite, we test combinations of words, thoughts, actions, and possessions, by trial and error. Our attempts occasionally bring us a certain amount of happiness. As with any emotion, this feeling is often transient and situation specific. Once enough of these chance encounters with happiness occur, we begin to develop a sort of mental roadmap to those sources which tend to deliver happiness in its more lasting forms. This map is often unreliable, but unfortunately, it is all that we have to work with, until we are brought to a clear understanding of the direct relationship which exists between happiness and goodness.

Happiness, or joy, is the internal barometer of the soul. It is the thrilling sensation which we experience when our innately good souls recognize goodness in another form, and then strain to remove all division and merge with it. Seeking joy elsewhere, where it does not exist, is wasted effort; similar to casting for fish on a mountainside. Though joy is rooted in goodness of character, it does not depend upon our level of awareness of it. Actually, it is likely that we are the most unconscious of our own goodness when attaining new heights of it. This is similar to the way that health is an afterthought during childhood, when we are often the healthiest, but consumes our thoughts in old age, when we tend to be the most sickly.

The longing which we feel for past experiences of happiness, and the desire to re-experience it in the same way, or to the same degree that we once did, is known as nostalgia. Occasionally we attempt to place ourselves into the environments where we previously experienced these feelings, turning our minds once more upon the thoughts that we recall thinking about previously, only to discover that the hoped for joy is significantly changed, reduced, or even altogether absent.

As a personal example, while at a conference in Philadelphia, my cousin and I were once able to get by my grandfather's old house, where both of us had lived for a time as children. We both hoped that we would feel a flood of nostalgic feelings when we arrived there. Yet, as we pulled up in front of the house and sadly observed how time had ravaged both it and the surrounding neighborhood, these feelings were nowhere to be found.

Thinking that our childhood feelings might still be found within, we decided to attempt knocking, on the off chance that the current owner would allow us inside. Fortunately, we were able to convince this person that we weren't psychopaths and gained entry. The coveted childhood emotions, however, weren't encountered within either. All that remained was a vague sense of cold, emotionless familiarity.

Though nostalgia sweetly sings the song that past joys may be reclaimed, she is as illusory and deceptive as the sirens themselves. Very often we grasp but air when we reach for her; leaving us feeling foolish for making the attempt. This is likely due to the fact that the pleasant feelings which we were seeking to recapture were a product of circumstances which existed when we experienced them, such as who and what we were at the time. These things have often changed significantly since the original experience. And what is our youth, if not a series of first-time experiences combined with the thrills which these new undertakings provided? When we return to the spot where we had an experience, after having experienced the thing in question a thousand times, are we so surprised that we often do not feel the same feelings which we did on the first occasion?

For example, does someone nostalgically recollect a joyful childhood moment, perhaps eating doughnuts in a certain restaurant with their parent? Return to this same place as an adult and eat the same type of doughnut. Only the extremely fortunate will re-experience any measure of nostalgic happiness. Since most of us have eaten hundreds of doughnuts since childhood, these other memories of mundane experiences, when we were less innocent, often water down, or even completely dilute beyond recognition any memories of the happy emotions we are seeking.

If any measure of joy is again experienced at the doughnut shop, it is due to something about the place, the things, or the people involved still possessing a certain measure of this goodness. The joy lay not in the doughnut, but likely lay in the virtue which you possessed as a child. If the remembered company amplified the joy, it is only because you remember that person as a symbol of virtue and goodness, which you love in the memory of them, as you love it in the memory of yourself.

But we needn't travel to our childhood haunts to re-experience joy. It can be had wherever we are, if we simply encourage virtuous character within ourselves and others, and attempt to increase goodness in the world about us. When we speak words, think thoughts, or perform deeds which increase, or create good, we accordingly increase our own ability to experience joy. This is not simply due to the fact that we are creating an increased amount of goodness which can be *en-joy-ed*. It is also due to the fact that the we are aware of the part which we played in this increase. This awareness often reduces the level of painful strain which our subconscious feels, due to its awareness of the difference between what our past actions have been, and what our instinctive reason informs us that they should have been: a feeling we know as guilt.

Groups may conspire to combine their efforts, in order for their virtuous actions to have a greater impact, however, any internal benefit to conscience is always individually experienced. It doesn't matter if the *group* was merely you and your friend clearing your neighbor's driveway of snow, or leaves, or if it was you and a hundred others building a house for charity. The subconscious, alert to the worth of the cause, the amount of individual effort which you contributed, and any personal loss which you incurred, rewards you based upon these things alone.

Perhaps you worked harder, in worse conditions, and sacrificed more while working on the driveway, yet nobody but your neighbor cared, or even knew. While on the house, you may have actually benefitted from your efforts. Perhaps you gloated about the housebuilding effort on your resume and it contributed to a promotion. Perhaps there was so much help available on the house that your assistance was only needed for a few menial tasks, while the local church contributed lavish lunches and daily thanked and praised you for your efforts. In this scenario, your subconscious would likely reward you more for the driveway; though to the external observer, the house may seem the more merit-worthy action.

Contrarily, words, thoughts, or deeds which reduce, harm, or destroy good, those which would appropriately be termed *evil*, degrade an individual's ability to experience joy. This is due not merely to the fact that there has been a subsequent reduction in good from which joy may be derived, but also to the offender's internal awareness of the offense; increasing his own level of guilt. This degraded ability to experience joy can continue until the tragic point where world which surrounds us appears dismal, joyless, and hopeless; for hope itself is simply an expectation that lost joy may be reclaimed.

Even our thoughts can, and often do inflict harm; as they are not only the parents of our actions, but slip out, in spite of our best efforts, and silently reveal themselves to any who might observe, or interact with us. A momentary haughty, or spiteful look, a slightly increased pace and glance in the opposite direction while passing, a faint pursing of the lips, or narrowing of the eyes; all shout their message to the subconscious mind of the observer.

This observer notices that they generally feel a slight increase in resentment. This is because, in a moment, their subconscious mind has noticed the subtle cues, reached back into their categorized memories, determined that previous experiences with these cues were associated with negative thoughts, resented the perceived undeserved offense, and then sent feelings signaling a mix of distrust and dislike back to the conscious mind.

The good news is that this type of damage is never permanent. At any moment, even those who have fallen into the lowest depths of guilt and despair can begin their re-ascent towards the light of joy. The bad news is that the ability to destroy good always has the capacity to occur faster than the ability to create it. A parent may spend 18 years nurturing and educating their beautiful daughter, only to have one rapist murderer destroy this treasure, within a single hour. A tower, which took years of diligent effort to design, fund, build, and furnish, can be destroyed in a matter of minutes, by one Islamic terrorist in a plane.

Though there are almost infinite means to harm, there are generally only finite means to help. While there is an almost infinite supply of people that we can deprive, or cause harm to, the number which we can give to and help is limited by the finite amount of time, energy, and resources that we possess. We are therefore, generally able to descend into misery at a significantly faster rate than we are able to ascend towards happiness. Depending upon how far we have already descended before we cease falling and begin to climb, the extrication process may take a long time. If past offenses were frequent, or severe enough, the it might take longer than the years of life remaining to us, or possibly even longer than any single human lifespan would allow. Regardless, if we ever wish to be happy, we have no other choice but to turn around and begin the long walk home, even should this walk extend into the afterlife. Despite the claims made by many revealed religions on the subject, there are no shortcuts to happiness. As the saying goes, "If you find yourself in a hole, the first step is to stop digging." As soon as we begin to clean the encrustations which years of vice have left upon our heart, we will feel the embers of joy slowly beginning to give off new heat.

All of mankind's words and actions share the same motive of attempting to increase personal happiness. Some dispute this claim, citing various unpleasant selfless, or self-sacrificial acts, which are performed for a noble cause. Yet even in these self-sacrificial instances, joy is being sought from one, or perhaps several, of three possible sources.

The first of these sources is the hope of a future reward, either on Earth, heaven, or another life via a sort of karma, or soul transmigration principle. The second source is a relative reduction of internal pangs of conscience which are, or might be felt, should these actions not be performed. The third source is a sense of increased satisfaction due to the performance of deeds which agree with one's own moral code, with the perceived moral code of one's God, or which are dharmically aligned with a universal principal of natural order, known as Rta, as in Hindu and Buddhist thought. Within all three of these sources it can be seen that even "selfless" acts affect self. In all, the actor is pursuing increased personal happiness, or the same thing considered from the other end of the continuum; decreased unhappiness.

Happiness, or joy, is universally acknowledged to be desirable, or in other words, as a good. This being the case, since all of mankind seek it, all ultimately have good motives, or intentions. Since our character is defined by our intentions, or will, we are driven to the inevitable conclusion that all of mankind possess innately good souls. This is the same conclusion which we arrived at when we considered how a perfectly good God could not make imperfect, or corrupt, souls while continuing to remain perfectly good.

"But what about all of the cruel, selfish, or otherwise harmful acts which people do to one another?" one will certainly protest. "Surely you can't call these good."

Certainly they aren't. There is such a thing as *evil*, which is none other than harm which is done to others in word, or deed, or to self in word, deed, or thought. Yet people do not voluntarily harm each other for harm's sake. Any harm inflicted is merely the product of a flawed means path which ignorant, or error warped minds have selected in order to achieve the desired product of increased happiness.

Let's consider how this works. Certain people, realizing that negative feelings which they sense detract from the state of utter bliss which they ultimately desire, look around for their cause. Many of these negative feelings are found to be due to anger, jealousy, or fear which they feel regarding another person's past, present, or prospective future relations, possessions, or position. These people therefore begin to believe harming these others will either a reduce their unhappiness, or increase their happiness. They believe that the expected benefit of increased happiness will outweigh the unavoidable cost of harm to conscience and reduction in perceived self-worth, due to the employment of ignoble means. They do not realize that the two are dependent variables. Harm to conscience and perceived self-worth significantly reduces, or altogether nullifies any anticipated benefits. This means that the person who performs the harmful action, while seeking an increase in joy, will paradoxically be left with an overall decrease in it.

Let's consider the extreme examples of rapists and murderers. Both of these types fixate upon another person as the barrier to their own increased happiness. Both think that the harmful actions which they premeditate toward these people will either remove a negative feeling, or increase a positive one. Both know deep within that the actions which they contemplate are harmful, or evil, and will therefore have a negative effect on their conscience and self-worth, yet both think the net benefit will supersede this, leaving them happier than they were before. Both are wrong. They will both be left with increased guilt and lowered self-esteem, which will in turn lower their overall level of happiness from where it was prior to the deed.

Were they to truly recognize and believe the inevitability of this result, they would never commit the act to begin with; but unfortunately, they do not. Instead, they believe the lie that negative actions may be separated from their consequences: that cause may be separated from effect. This is because they ignorantly recognize only potential physical consequences, such as imprisonment, which may indeed possibly be avoided. They are blind to the fact that simultaneous with, and inseparable from evil acts, are the weightier consequences of guilt, lowered self-worth, and subsequent reduction, or even inability to experience happiness. These consequences are the opposite side of the coin of harmful action; a coin which may never be cut thinly enough that it will not possess both sides.

The Greek philosopher Epictetus identified this principle in a section of his writings where he relates a story about a thief. "The other day I had an iron lamp placed beside my household gods. I heard a noise at the door and on hastening down found my lamp carried off. I reflected that the culprit was in no very strange case. 'Tomorrow, my friend,' I said, 'you will find an earthenware lamp; for a man can only lose what he has.' The reason why I lost my lamp was that the thief was superior to me in vigilance. He paid, however, this price for the lamp, that in exchange for it he consented to become a thief: in exchange for it, to become faithless."[29]

Ralph Waldo Emerson echoed this same thought on the inevitability of the consequences of wrongdoing in his essay on compensation. "We feel defrauded of the retribution due to evil acts, because the criminal adheres to his vice and contumacy and does not come to a crisis or judgment anywhere in visible nature. There is no stunning confutation of his nonsense before men and angels. Has he therefore outwitted the law? Inasmuch as he carries the malignity and the lie with him he so far deceases from nature. In some manner there will be a demonstration of the wrong to the understanding also; but, should we not see it, this deadly deduction makes square the eternal account."[30]

Those who claim that there are people who simply love evil for its own sake, and not rather as a faulty means path to happiness, have become confused between the words used, and the ideas which they symbolize. When someone states that they love *evil*, they mean that they view evil as desirable because inherently noble, or somehow beneficial: in other words, as a good. In this case, they are not truly loving evil, but rather what they mistakenly perceive to be a good.

Even the Satanists mistakenly believe that harmful (i.e. evil) acts which they commit, during their ceremonies, against other people, animals, or themselves, will either make them directly and immediately happy, or will do so via the mediation of a mythical spiritual being named Satan. I understand that the modern Church of Satan is recasting its image and now claiming that Satan is merely symbolic, but any who look into the writings of the Grimoires and of men such as Cornelius Agrippa, Eliphas Levi, and A. E. Waite, will know this is not what the older faith believed; regardless of any revisionist claims they make to the contrary.

In the mediated instance, Satanists believe that their actions will please (i.e. increase the happiness of) Satan, who will subsequently reward them with an increase in power. It is assumed that this increase in power will enable them to more easily effect, or attain their desires; the accomplishment, or attainment of which they again believe will increase their overall happiness.

In the immediate instance, Satanists are found to be seeking an increase in their own happiness. In the mediated instance, they are found to be seeking an increase not only in their own happiness, but also in that of their mythological benefactor. In both instances, this increase is assumed to be valuable enough to warrant any presumed necessary reduction in the happiness of others (i.e. harm). Satanists mistakenly believe this because they have an erroneous view about the nature of their own soul and mind. Either they believe that any harm inflicted upon their own consciences will not occur; will be less than the benefit gained, leaving a net gain of happiness; or will fade and be forgotten with time, leaving only benefit. None of these beliefs are rooted in truth.

There is no way to happiness without an associated increase in goodness. In order to shed vice and increase virtue, we must develop a familiarity with truth. Not only does such a familiarity allow us to better recognize goodness, but it also allows us to recognize error and vice, to understand how these harm us, and to accordingly guard our lives against them. Though truth is the light which penetrates and dissipates the dark mists of error and ignorance, it only bears fruit within minds which are able to recognize it. It is for this reason that truth and *the good mind* are frequently spoken of in the *Gathas*, the only part of the Zend Avesta which is likely to have been authored by Zarathustra (i.e. Zoroaster),[27] as being among the greatest blessings of mankind. Without them both, goodness of word, thought, and deed become impossible. As truth and an ability to sense it are claimed by Zarathustra to be mankind's greatest blessing, so their opposites, the various forms of falsity, and minds whose views are warped by them, are implied to be its worst curse.

It is unlikely that Zarathustra was the first to identify this truth in writing, since we hear the same views echoed by the Neo-Platonist, Plutarch, in his brilliant, voluminous, and unfortunately little-known ethical work, *Morals* (i.e. *Moralia*). In this work, Plutarch states that truth is, "The greatest good that man can receive, and the goodliest blessing that God can give."[27.]

When we first read these claims about the supreme value of truth, our natural reaction is to think them to be mere hyperbole. A myriad of

evils spring to mind which appear to us to be far worse than mere lies.
Yet upon deeper investigation, it is discovered that all of these things
have a certain common root cause in falsity; ranging from false
assumptions, to lies, to an inability to discern truth. This subject is
discussed at length in the section of this work on justice.

Truth and a good mind are the inseparable cornerstones of freedom,
both of societies, and of individual men. This is because freedom, even
among men not physically restrained, consists in the ability to effect
one's own will. Since all men possess the instinctive will to rid
themselves of any error and ignorance, only those who have realized this
will, can truly be described as free. The rest remain in various degrees
of servitude; though generally blind to their chains.

The renowned Roman orator, Cicero, made this same claim in the
5th of his *Stoic Paradoxes*. "For what is liberty? The power of living as
you please. Who, then, is he who lives as he pleases, but the man surely
who follows righteousness...To the wise man alone it happens, that he
does nothing against his will...it is a briefly stated and admitted
principle, that no man but he who is thus constituted can be free. All
wicked men therefore are slaves, and this is not so surprising and
incredible in fact as it is in words. For they are not slaves in the sense
those bondmen are who are the properties of their masters by purchase,
or by any law of the state; but if obedience to a disordered, abject mind,
destitute of self-control be slavery (and such it is), who can deny that all
the dishonest, all the covetous, in short, all the wicked, are slaves?"[4]

Though few realize it, the insatiable, instinctive appetite for joy
which all men sense within, as well as our appetite for goodness, by
proxy, is in actuality a longing for God. Since God is the purest
expression of abstract goodness and the fount of all goodness which is
seen and sensed echoing throughout nature, it is joy's ultimate source (or
he if you prefer, although God is bodiless spirit, and therefore neither
male, nor female). Since the quintessence of an individual is their will,
and God's will is the definition of goodness, our efforts to increase our
personal virtue are, in fact, efforts to become Godlike. Is it any wonder,
then, that we tend to feel joyful when attempting to become more like a
being whom we assume to dwell in infinite bliss?

The very existence of joy is evidence that our lives have both purpose
and meaning, though our finite minds may fail to grasp either. The fact
that our souls thrill to goodness implies design, a designer, and intent.
As we increase our virtue, we not only harmonize with the soul which
infuses us, but with the same soul which fills all of nature with the hum
of life. The very trees which sway in the wind dance, and the cicadas
clinging to their boughs sing to the same melody which fills us.

Should the movements of our minds ever be brought into perfect
alignment with those of our instinctive reason, to the point that the
former anticipates the impulses of the latter, then for that brief, but

blissful period, any strain between the two would dissolve and we would be experiencing the thoughts of God. Plotinus described this phenomenon in his Six Enneads, where he stated that he believed that he had only attained this highest level of thought for a few brief moments, once, or twice in his life.

Realizing this close interrelation between joy and soul, many sects attribute certain periods of heightened joy to a *filling* of the experiencer with an increased amount of *spirit*. These people would be at a loss, however, if they were asked to differentiate spirit from soul. As well they should be, for the two words symbolize a single common concept.

The problem with this view is that any potential for addition requires at least a partial deficiency in the original state. In order to add fluid to a cup, the cup in question must initially be incompletely, or in other words, imperfectly filled. It is unclear how a perfect God could either make an imperfect soul, or how a perfect soul could be imperfectly present. It is especially problematic if the soul is actually determined to be an expression of God, as is discussed elsewhere within this work. This is because the indivisible and infinite cannot be partially present. It must either be present in its entirety, or not at all.

Escapism

As those who are lost in moral corruption begin to realize that the warped paths which they are travelling on do not ultimately lead to the happiness which they actually desire, a gnawing sense of dissatisfaction begins to grow within them. Once in this situation, they generally do one of two things. In the first case, they wisely abandon the current, flawed path in search of another which is more likely to lead to happiness. In the second case, they turn to escapism. Fear is often the reason why this latter approach is taken. These morally corrupt people fear that they will be humiliated, should they admit that the path which they have already invested so much time, effort, and resources traveling down, did not ultimately lead towards their intended destination.

One common form of escapism employed by the morally corrupt is that of avoiding, or more frequently these days, *attacking* any who would dare to spread truths which reveal the extent of their corruption. Just as these corrupt people struggle to silence the voices of their own consciences, so they also strive to silence the voices of anyone who might dare to echo what their consciences are telling them. And it is not merely discomforting spoken truths that these escapists hope to silence, it is any expression of condemnatory truth, whether written, painted, acted, sung, symbolized, etc.

A large portion of the "tolerance" movement, which is so passionately promoted by leftists, is simply this form of escapism masquerading as a social virtue, rather than as the mental illness which it actually is. To them, *tolerance* means that any who would dare to disagree with the error, cruelty, or corruption of their words, views, or actions must be threatened into silent submission: through the courts if possible; through violence if not. As such, this form of "tolerance" differs little from tyranny.

In addition, hidden beneath the surface of the left's seemingly harmless push to "embrace and celebrate the diversity of opinions," is their real message: that their ignorance, or error filled positions should not merely be accepted, but also valued as highly as all other opinions. This message is built upon the false foundational claim that truth is not absolute, but is instead relative to the perceiver. According to this flawed view, there is no absolute right and wrong, good and bad, just and unjust, or true and false. Therefore, laughable beliefs, such as that the Earth is flat, or that God plays favorites, hates unbelievers, gets jealous, or grows angry, should be valued as highly as the philosophical musings of Emerson and Plato.

A second form of escapism which is commonly resorted to is the use of mood, or thought-altering products (i.e. drugs, or alcohol). Those who resort to such things hope that the mild, or severe state of intoxication which these chemicals keep them in will effectively silence any pangs of conscience which they might otherwise experience while lucid. This is a mistaken assumption, as the body quickly develops a tolerance to the majority of these intoxicants. This subject is discussed at length in the section of this work on psychotropics.

A third form of escapism is where people attempt to make themselves overly busy, so that the constant crises help to distract them from their unhappiness. A man who wins the lottery, for example, may be distracted for a time from the guilt which he feels for having abandoned his wife and children, but this guilt remains beneath the surface, eroding his happiness. This is similar to the way that a man forgets about the thorn in his foot while being chased by a lion. Until finally addressed, however, the old aches both of thorn and conscience will return during the inevitable moments of calm.

The fourth form of escapism commonly resorted to is fetishism. When fetishism is mentioned, most people naturally think of the severe examples of this which the media has shown them; such as hoarders living in filth, and the morbidly obese who literally eat themselves to death. Less noticeable forms of the fetishistic escape mechanism are, however, far more pervasive within Western society than most people realize. To clarify this point, lets first give a general definition of a fetish.

A fetish is any action, person, or object which someone mistakenly believes will provide them with an unrealistic amount of happiness, and which this person accordingly devotes an unnatural and unhealthy amount of focus and commitment towards. Under this general definition, the pool of people with fetishistic tendencies swells to include, among many others, a large portion of consumers, and an even larger portion of producers within the sports, food, entertainment, pornography, alcohol, fashion, and even financial industries. Indeed, the sole purpose of the advertisement industry, which is unfortunately so ubiquitous within capitalist economic systems, is to attempt to increase the levels of fetishism among the masses. "Pay us to have this, do this, eat this, drink this, wear this, go here, etc., and you will be happy."

Let's examine the two assumed premises of the fetish escape. The first of these is that happiness derived from one area of a person's life may be transferred and applied to other areas, which are sources of unhappiness, like a salve. The second is that things which provide a certain amount of pleasure, or happiness, due to their ability to satisfy a physical need, will provide excessive amounts of pleasure, or happiness, if had in excess. Unfortunately, there are problems with both of these premises.

Concerning the first premise of transferred happiness, it must be understood that the mind is staggeringly adept at independently tracking a plurality of subjects and issues. As long as the source of unhappiness continues to reside within the conscious, or subconscious memory, it will continue to erode our overall level of happiness. Happiness originating within, and therefore derived from other areas of our lives may increase our net sum of happiness, resulting in overall increased vigor, and courage to tackle problems, but the unresolved issues remain independent sources of unhappiness, and must therefore be independently addressed. Referring back to our thorn analogy, massaging and caressing the foot which doesn't have a splinter in it may make you feel somewhat better, overall, but it does nothing for the foot with the splinter in it.

As far as the second premise goes, in all but one scenario, fetishistic excess paradoxically produces a disappointing decrease, rather than the hoped for superabundance of happiness. The single exception to this is when the focus of the fetish is the immaterial goodness which is dimly seen behind its material vessels. Pure goodness, when duly considered, is discovered to be none other than God. Therefore, in this instance, what was thought to be fetish, is discovered to be worship. A more in-depth discussion on this topic will be found in the following section on needs.

Needs

Maslow's famous *Hierarchy of Needs* is considered by many academics to be the gold standard of psychological models for explaining human motivations. Some schools have proposed minor modifications to this theory, but in its general form, it is depicted as a 5-level pyramid.

The base level of this pyramid is described as the category of *Physiological Needs*, successively surmounted by the categories of *Safety Needs, Love and Belongingness Needs, Esteem Needs*, and finally the apex of *Self-Actualization Needs*.[31,32] Maslow used this model to support his claim that people typically must satisfy their types of needs in a progressive manner, working from the base of the model upwards. Packaged within the concept of need satisfaction is the implication of either an increase in happiness, or a reduction in unhappiness. The Maslow Model, therefore, implies that individuals will tend to believe that happiness will be achieved by the attainment of things either at, or immediately above the need category which they are currently operating within.

For example, according to the Maslow Model, someone operating at the *Safety* level will likely think that a secure job will increase their happiness level, and therefore find it appealing, even if the position is a poorly respected one. Someone operating at the *Esteem* level, on the other hand, will likely believe that leadership roles will increase their happiness level, and find them appealing, despite their often less secure nature.

Although this model is widely accepted, it has several fatal flaws. Foremost among these is the fact that the top tier, *Self-Actualization*, does not describe a category of needs, as the others do, but instead describes a state of being. The claim could be made that it is a need for this state of being, but this could be said about anything. The apical level of the need pyramid could be labeled *Rocket Ship*, and then the claim made that it implied the need for a rocket ship. The abstract state of *Self-Actualization* encapsulates many ideas, such as being able to efficiently perceive reality, to understand ourselves and others, to form meaningful relationships, to enjoy life, to follow the guidance of our inner goals and values, and to properly express emotions.[33] Essentially, *Self-Actualization* means the state of total emotional healthfulness.

The second problem is that the various sub-categories of the Maslow Model are not discrete stepping stones to this final state of *Self-Actualization*, but are often applications of it. For example, what does being understanding of ourselves and others and able to form meaningful relationships mean, but the application of *Esteem* and *Love and Belongingness*.

The third major problem is that the remaining 4 categories of true needs within the Maslow Model can be reduced to two pairs which are effectively inseparable, without descending into murky vagueness and arbitrary definitions. How is Maslow's *Physiological Needs* category to be completely divorced and differentiated from his *Safety Needs* category? When describing *Physiological Needs*, we are referring to something which, if left unsatisfied, involves risk of physical harm, or death to the individual. Factors which mitigate this risk are the very definition of *Safety*. I am motivated to acquire and eat food in order to satisfy a *Physiological Need*, yet I also have a *Safety Need* to ensure that I possess the ability to do so. I am motivated to try to stay warm, in order to satisfy a *Physiological Need*, but there is also a *Safety Need* for me to do so.

One might claim that the difference lies in a focus on the current state for physiological needs, while there is a focus upon future states for safety needs. Unfortunately, this proposed difference doesn't quite work out, as we are often motivated by the safety needs of a present situation, as well as by concerns about future physiological needs. For example, I am immediately motivated to get out of the way of an oncoming car, in order to ensure my safety needs, yet I also do so in order to ensure my physiological need to keep my organs intact and my blood within its vessels.

We fare no better in attempting to divorce the more abstract category of *Love and Belongingness*, from that of *Esteem*. *Esteem* is simply a degree of *Love*, while *Belonging* is the feeling of being in a place, position, or state where one feels this *Love*.

The forth problem with the Maslow Model is its claim that the mind must generally satisfy lower need categories before it can focus its efforts upon higher ones. This claim is frequently proven to be false. Many cease to care about, or will even voluntarily deny their own physiological needs when their needs for love and belongingness are deeply deficient, or at risk. So common is this phenomenon, that negligence of food and personal hygiene is one of the classic warning signs of potential suicides.

Negligence of the lower need categories on Maslow's model, such as physiological needs, is not simply seen when people are deficient in higher ones, but is also commonly observed in individuals who have a superabundance of them. How many meals, and how much sleep do young lovers skip, in order to enjoy each other's loving company? How many religious devotees and philosophers voluntarily give up safety, and most, if not all of their material possessions, claiming that they draw a deeper satisfaction from their relationship with God, from their enhanced relation with nature, or from their religious, moral, or ethical principles? How many aspiring academics, athletes, and politicians willingly sacrifice safety, material possessions, and sometimes even relationships, in order to gain professional, or public esteem?

Let's set aside this flawed model in favor of an improved one. I propose instead a two-section motivation model, which I will call the Absolute Motivation Model (AMM), for clarity (*See Fig. 1*). The triangular bottom portion of the AMM model is the *Concerns related to the body* section. It includes everything which would commonly fall within the *Physiological Needs* and *Safety Needs* categories of the Maslow Model. The opposing base vertices of this triangle are labeled *Dearth* and *Excess*, while the upper vertex is labeled the *Golden Mean*.

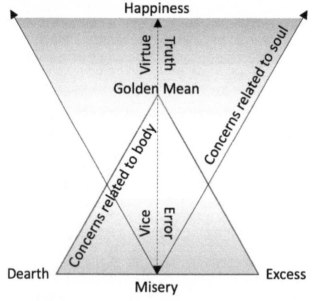

(Figure 1. AMM)

The top section of the AMM model, represented by a larger, inverted triangle, partially overlapping the center of the first, is the *Concerns related to the soul section*. It includes everything which would fall within the *Love and Belongingness Needs*, as well as the *Esteem Needs*, categories of the Maslow Model. The upper portion of this triangle is depicted without an enclosing line. In addition, the two side lines of this triangle are depicted as rays, extending diagonally upwards. The top of the figure is surmounted by the word, *Happiness*, while the label, *Misery*, lies beneath the bottom. Bisecting both triangles is a dotted line, with the twin labels of *Vice*, and *Error*, at the bottom, and *Virtue*, and *Truth*, at the top.

"That's an interesting design, but how is it any better than the Maslow Model?" one might ask.

It is better than the Maslow Model because it is more accurate. The flaws in the Maslow Model are rooted in its outright denial of the existence of soul, due to its being designed to be in conformance with the atheist worldview which plagues the scientific community. The AMM abandons this flawed worldview.

It makes the following, distinctly different claims from those of the Maslow Model. Firstly, it claims that all of mankind are motivated by the desire to ascend the continuum towards happiness and away from misery. This is the basic *Carrots and sticks* concept, which any who have served in a leadership position should be familiar with. Unlike the Maslow Model, the AMM claims that this is not merely a tendency, but an iron rule. It should be noticed that the claim is also made that the major limiting factors to this ascent are vice and error, while its major aids are virtue and truth. Were mankind to truly know the path to happiness, all would certainly pursue it. They are dragged downwards, however, by the teeming hordes of power/wealth hungry peddlers of vice and error, and by the relative scarcity and timidity of teachers of genuine truth and virtue.

The *Concerns related to body*, triangle is labeled *Dearth*, and *Excess*, on its opposing bases because both of these tend to increase misery, often to the surprise of the wealthy. As a simple example, consider a starving man. This person is experiencing a large amount of physical misery due to his dearth of food. Should he be brought to a table which is heaped full of food and begin to consume it, the first few bites would be the most satisfying, linearly becoming less so, until the point of natural satiety was reached, a point which Aristotle referred to as the *Golden Mean*,[34] and Plato, Epictetus, Socrates, Zeno, and the Stoics called being, *In accord with nature*.[35] Should the formerly starving man unwisely continue eating beyond this point of the *Golden Mean*, the same food which so effectively quenched his physical misery, would begin to have the opposite effect. Each bite of excess food would increasingly nauseate him, until he either wisely ceased eating, or became so miserable that he vomited the entire mass back up. This principle holds true for all happiness related to bodily appetites.

It should be noted that both triangles within the AMM extend to the bottom of the figure. The reason for this is that, in attempting to ascend from absolute misery to absolute happiness, people can either pursue the satisfaction of *Concerns related to body*, while simultaneously attempting to satisfy *Concerns related to soul*, or they can individually focus upon either of these things. This claim opposes that of the Maslow Model; the latter of which not only claims that motivational categories must be climbed sequentially, but it denies the existence of soul altogether.

It should be noticed that the *Concerns related to the soul* triangle is narrowest where it overlaps the widest part of the *Concerns related to body* triangle, increasing in width as it ascends. This is because it is tremendously difficult to focus upon concerns of the soul while the body is in absolute physical misery from either dearth, or excess. It is difficult to focus on abstract concepts, such as the goodness of God, one's self, nature, or mankind, for example, while one is drowning, starving, freezing to death, or hugging a toilet, while vomiting from chemotherapy. As bodily misery subsides, it becomes proportionally easier to focus on the satisfaction of concerns of the soul. Once the physical *Golden Mean* has been reached, however, no further attention to bodily appetites can provide us with an increase in happiness. We must turn to the satisfaction of spiritual needs for this.

When attempting to increase virtue and happiness in both ourselves and others, we should tailor our efforts towards areas which promise to have the greatest impact. Though men, when suffering from dearth, or excess of their physical appetites can still, theoretically, gain a small amount of happiness from efforts focused upon their spiritual needs, they will typically sense a much greater initial relief from efforts which are preliminarily focused on resolving their needs related to physical appetites. Feed the starving, clothe the freezing, deny food to the morbidly obese, deny drugs to the addict, take the prostitute off the streets, etc., before attempting to teach people about political, or religious philosophies.

Lastly, it should be pointed out that the *Concerns of the soul* triangle in the AMM has a larger overall area than the *Concerns of the body* one, has no top boundary, and has sides formed by rays which symbolize infinite extension. This is because, though happiness resulting from the satisfaction of bodily appetites is limited, there is no theoretical limit to the amount of happiness from virtue which the soul may attain.

Aristotle makes the fatal mistake of attempting to apply the *Golden Mean* to abstract concepts related to soul. I completely disagree with his teaching on this, as did most other Western philosophers, including the Pythagoreans, Socratics, and the Platonic school which was founded by his former teacher. Attempting to apply the concept of the *Golden Mean* to appetites of the soul leads one into gross absurdities. It implies, for example, that one should neither seek ultimate moral good (i.e. the intrinsically desirable) nor ultimate moral bad (i.e. the intrinsically undesirable), but a supposed *Golden Mean* between the two.

While this statement has the superficial appearance of profundity, it is ultimately self-destructive. It de facto transfers all of the core characteristics of ultimate moral good, such as supreme merit and desirability, to a point which it calls the *Golden Mean*. Once there, we must repeat the division indefinitely, each time creating a new ultimate good which is exactly half the preceding distance to the ultimate moral bad. This process is essentially a mathematical limit, where a variable perpetually approaches a point, without ever entirely reaching it. When dealing with a smooth, continuous series, limits can effectively be treated as being at the point which they are incessantly approaching. In this instance, the limit of the ultimate moral good would be collocated with the ultimate moral bad.

In fine, the resulting conclusion of Aristotle's claim that the concept of the *Golden Mean* may be applied to spiritual principles, whence morals and ethics have their origin, is the absurd conclusion that there is ultimately no difference between moral goodness and badness; both being mere arbitrary social constructs. By extension, this view destroys all difference between the many context specific synonyms for goodness and badness; such as justice and corruption, within the context of judgement; love and hatred, within the context of relation; truth and falsity, within the context of representation of reality; courage and cowardice, within the context of actions taken during dangerous situations; beauty and ugliness, within the context of form; and dozens of others.

The weight of this Peripatetic millstone grinds all into a common powder of worthlessness. It is strange that such a poorly thought out argument originated with such an otherwise brilliant man, however, these absurdities were noticed even by the ancients, being one of the reasons why the Peripatetic and Platonic schools parted ways while their founders were yet living.

It is interesting to note that the erroneous claims of the Peripatetic philosophy of Aristotle, which attempts to apply a *Golden Mean* to goodness, has the same logical result as nihilistic Buddhism. Buddhism tells us that our natural desire for goodness, whether physical or spiritual, will always leave us unsatisfied, and is therefore to be abandoned. Instead, they claim that we should reduce all of our desires, even for goodness, until we achieve the supposedly blissful state of an absolute lack of desire. As with the Aristotelians, this Buddhist view has a superficial appearance of profundity.

Desire is none-other than the natural attraction felt towards something which we believe will benefit us; or in other words, believe to be a good. When we hear comments about focusing our efforts on reducing our physical desires, rather than focusing our efforts on attempting to satisfy them when they have grown out of all due proportion, we sense a faint familiarity with teachings of Socrates, the Platonists, and the Stoics. While Socrates and the Platonists rationally understood that there is a reasonable limit, or *Golden Mean*, to this reduction of physical desires. At this point of being, *In accordance with nature*, or in other words, within natural bounds, they claimed that physical appetites and desires grow silent. Buddhists, however, are unfamiliar with this higher truth. They therefore see no alternative but to pursue a reduction of physical desires until these reach their lethal conclusion.

"Wait a moment. There are tons of Buddhists in the world who aren't all out starving themselves to death, or depriving themselves of air," one might reply.

This is a true statement. I will not waste the reader's time by pointing out the many examples where Buddhist monks both did, and were celebrated for doing this very thing. These proof cases are available for any who are willing to search for them. I will simply state that we should not judge any faith by whether or not its faithful adhere to, or even understand all of its doctrines, but by the worth of what these doctrines actually sanction and advocate.

There are millions of Muslims in the world who aren't out enslaving, or slitting the throats of "infidels" in the name of Jihad, as they are explicitly directed to do in the Koran and Hadiths. The greatest heroes in these works, including Mohammed, are men who literally did this very thing. Mohammed not only taught and personally conducted a brutal, merciless, greedy, avaricious, arrogant, and ignorant Jihad, but demanded similar actions from any who would also call themselves Muslims.

On the other hand, there are also millions of Christians who aren't selling everything that they own and giving it all to the poor, as scripture (Matthew 19:21) and the writings of the early church "fathers" direct. The greatest heroes in these Christian works, including Jesus and John the Baptist, are men who literally did this very thing. Jesus not only taught and personally conducted a war of kindness, mercy, generosity, magnanimity, humility, and wisdom, but demanded similar conduct from any who would call themselves Christians.

Returning from this digression, let's consider the second, most critical flaw in the Buddhist worldview. As with the Aristotelians, Buddhists make the fatal mistake of attempting to equivocate physical and spiritual desires. They fail to comprehend how the potential *goods* which evoke these desires are limited in the first instance, while any limitation in the second instance is nonsensical. Can there be a limit to moral goodness? There may be a limit to the moral goodness which we are able to practically attain at any specific moment, however, how does one even describe a purely abstract, yet limited type of goodness. The purity of the abstraction does not allow for gradation.

Buddhists attempt to convince us that the bliss which they claim that we will supposedly experience, once we have completely uprooted our desires not merely for physical, but even for these purely abstract, illimitable types of goodness, eclipses all other possible goodness which we could desire. This is another self-destructive argument. Were we to adopt this view, we would immediately find ourselves nonsensically desiring a lack of desire, and believing that a denial of the merit of absolute goodness is itself a supreme and absolute good to be sought. While the Aristotelians repeatedly set the destructive match in the center of the span which separates the absolutes of goodness and badness, Buddhists set the match at the absolute goodness end. The end result of both approaches is the same. All range between good and bad is devoured by the flame of their philosophical views. Indeed, the very absolute reality of goodness is destroyed, as good becomes no longer good, but simply a synonym for bad.

Desires spring from the perception of internal, or external goodness, which we believe will increase our level of happiness, if attained. At any single moment, our subconscious is continually analyzing hundreds of permutations of means paths to ultimately attain the greatest amounts of these things. Like a general's battle plan, what we refer to as the *human will* is the means-pathway which has been selected from the many available, in this quest for goodness. Our desires continuously evolve, as new information is encountered which modifies our perception of available goodness. In addition, the ever-changing nature of our internal and external environment causes our subconscious to continuously re-examine and modify the various permutations of means paths necessary to achieve these evolving desires; sometimes causing it to modify the will. Though the will may shift, it always points towards the most practical path which it believes will provide it with the greatest net goodness.

It can be seen then, that when Buddhism attempts to suppress, to the point of destroying, all desire, it incidentally removes the fuel from the engine of the human will. Not only does this faith, therefore, destroy all meaning of goodness, dragging with it into the flames all virtue, love, justice, beauty, courage, merit, and everything else which springs from it, but it also destroys the human will. What a blissful existence this is which the Buddha offers to us.

"It is not in this life in which we will experience this bliss, but in the next," some may claim.

What does it matter if it is a thousand lifespans from now, and we have taken the form of angels in heaven. If we continue to hold Buddhist views about goodness not being good, which destroys both our desire and our will, we will simply sit on that next plane like a cold machine, until that body eventually slumps over in death and we infect the next with our suicidal views. Let's say we eventually become immortal and immaterial. This would not differ in any perceivable way from annihilation; as we would do nothing, forever.

Lockeanism vs Transcendentalism

As discussed at length elsewhere in this work, all internal thought likely occurs via the mechanism of feeling. This is the native tongue with which the soul communicates with the body. These streams of rapidly occurring and information dense feelings are only translated into language in order for us to be able to interact with others. Were we to suddenly discover ourselves alone within the universe, language would immediately become unnecessary.

Some attempt to critique this theory by calling it simple emotionalism. Embedded within this claim is the implication that feelings are somehow inferior, as information sources, to cold, raw logic. What is humorously ironic about this position is that the more passionately that people cling to and champion it, the more they prove its falsity.

The first thing which should be asked of these logicians is why. Why do they believe that logic is superior to what they deem emotionalism? Typically, these often admittedly bright individuals will foresee the problems which this line of inquiry will place them in and become either evasive, or circular in their reasoning. If they do, however, bravely provide an honest answer to both the asker and themselves, it will be seen that any complex points of logic which they cling to are based upon an amalgamation of simple ones. The beliefs held about a subject can be likened to a building, the complex points the rooms, and the simple points the various beams and joists which frame the rooms and give them strength. Yet if we press these people about how they know the various simple points themselves to be true, they will eventually be forced to admit, typically after many attempts at deflection, that they are relying upon internal feeling, or instinct, in order to make this determination.

Even with the most simple and pure forms of logic, such as math, we find that we are ultimately relying upon feeling in order to determine trueness. For example, we know that $1 + 1 = 2$ because of our understanding of the concepts of 1, 2, and addition, however, how do we know that what we were taught about these things was correct? We saw a single apple placed by another in our first year at school and were told that it made 2, but how do we know that our eyes, ears, and the person who told us these things provided us with accurate information? We instinctively sense, or *feel*, the trueness of the thing, just as we sense that we are awake and not actually dreaming. Regardless of how many, and how strong the beams of the edifice are, all is built upon, and therefore governed by this foundation of instinctive reason; which is felt. Despite all of her arrogant boasts and the millions who bow before her, the very cells which form the beautiful and strong body of logic are fueled by mitochondria of feeling, and the involuntary reliance upon the vector sum of these feelings is the very definition of faith.

As any but the most blind can see, these logicians don't actually believe feelings to be inferior to logic; they simply believe that their feelings are superior to those of whomever they are disputing with.

In order to determine how we internally sense these things, we must first examine how external sensation occurs, and look for any parallels between the two. We know that external senses, such as taste, are converted into electrical signals, which are then fed to the brain via afferent nerves, and there converted into a pattern of synaptic firings within the various areas of the mind. Any claims made beyond this are purely speculative, at our current level of scientific understanding.

Sure, we fired off a pattern of synapses, but what actually sensed this; and how did it do so? The majority of the modern scientific community, which is today dominated by those holding the purely Materialist atheist worldview, are at a loss. Note that I didn't say that they are not ready with an intimidating, jargon-saturated explanation, but simply that they do not, in actuality, know.

It is almost impossible to find an academic subject without its complementary well-respected scientist, thoroughly convinced that he has a complete understanding of it. This was even the case hundreds of years ago, when scientists were completely convinced that rotting meat bred flies via spontaneous generation. Materialist explanations which these scientists give on what within the mind is doing the actual sensing of synapse patterns, and indeed, even initiating, or willing the cascade which ultimately results in sympathetic, or parasympathetic nerve stimulation, are always found to be circular, and therefore inadequate.

These points being established regarding external sensation, what are feelings but internal sensations, whose origins we do not know, which are similarly converted into patterns of synapse firings throughout the brain. What makes external sensory driven patterns of synapse firings in any way superior to those which are internally originated? If anything, the opposite scenario is more likely to be true.

As may be observed within any machine, the more intermediate components there are between the input to the system and its output, the greater the chance of energy, or information loss and failure. In the same way, our external senses go through a greater number of intermediate components and processes prior to their ultimate conversion into synaptic patterns within the mind, than our internal senses, which we feel, do. Do we not sometimes feel tired, sick, excited, lonely, happy, and angry? Are not all of these senses internally originated? Is anyone so biased in their Materialist views that they would dare to claim that our senses of these things, being internally originated, are any less real?

When considering the claim that listening to one's feelings is merely *emotionalism*, we must consider whether or not all feelings which are internally sensed are emotion. Any difference between these things is likely but one of degree. Scientists could seek clarity on this question by looking at the parts of the mind which show increased blood flow, or electrical activity during periods of high emotion, versus those involving the stimulation of simple internal feelings, such as a sense of justice, or injustice. Unfortunately, as in the previous example of justice, it will inevitably prove impossible to separate the emotional aspect from concepts possessing a moral element, such as virtues, and we will likely be left where we started: knowing that both are translated into, or originate from a pattern of synaptic firings within the mind, yet not knowing the originating cause.

Admitting, for argument's sake, that virtues are sensed internally as feelings in the same way that emotions are, although without the certainty of if the same type, or location of synaptic patterns evidence them both; also admitting that thought actually occurs, in its purest, most natural form as feeling, which is also sensed internally; what causes our internal sensation of these virtues? Is there some internal standard which we look to? And if so, is it the same standard which allows us to discriminate truths, or do we have multiple standards for this?

From a purely Materialist perspective, there is no answer to this question. Scientists, (internally) sensing this corner which they are backed into by this question, generally select one of three escape routes. The first route is an attempt to confuse and intimidate their pursuer into silence by technical jargon which is often only circular, or not applicable to the question at hand. The second route is an attempt to resurrect the long discredited Lamarckian theories under the new title of epigenetics. The third route is claiming that there is no actual standard; that the mind of man is a blank slate at birth; and that any perceptions which man has of a moral standard were impressed upon him by his peers, family, and/or environment.

This last line of reasoning is actually the most common. It was made famous by John Locke's likening the early state of a newborn child to a "Blank slate," or "Tabula Rasa."[38] It is a good theory, if one is able to ignore the fact that it is absolutely impossible. Here is why. This theory is willfully blind to the existence of instinctive knowledge. If the minds of animals and men are formed blank, whence do they derive their complex instinctive knowledge?

Spiders, for example, are never taught how to spin silk or weave elaborate webs. They are generally solitary creatures that, if they ever see their parent when they emerge from their egg sack, only do so momentarily, before seeking their own lonely abode to live in. Interestingly, however, all spiders know how to walk immediately upon hatching. Many even know how to make silk sails which allow them to ride the breezes. When they find their new home, they know how to perform the most delicate dances of silk spinning and web making; the webs of specific species all shockingly resembling one another.

These creatures even know exactly where to strategically place these webs and how to use them to hunt for food. Who is it that teaches the young spiderling that it should hide out of sight, clutching one of the threads of the web like a fishing line, and then swiftly spring from its hiding place, in order to wrap up its victims when they become entangled in it? No one does. And yet over and over we observe spiders of the same species perform the exact same complex tasks.

This example of the spider is but one of the millions of instances which could be cited within the animal world, where creatures display highly complex actions evidencing specific, specialized knowledge which they were neither taught, nor could they have learned on their own through trial and error. Locke's theory ultimately proves to be weaker than spider silk. It is folly for scientists and philosophers to claim that these undeniable indications of innate instinctive knowledge are either not what all observe them to be within the animal kingdom, or that they exempt man alone from their influence.

Both man and beast possess instinctive knowledge. As stated before, this instinctive knowledge, as with all thought, likely takes the form of the mind's native tongue of feeling. And among these instinctive feelings which mankind are born in possession of are those of the perfect virtues, including the feeling of justice.

One cannot know a thing with certainty without also knowing the ideal state of the thing. We cannot tell if a triangle is imperfect, as compared to an isosceles triangle, unless we have seen an isosceles triangle; either physically, or within our mind's eye. In the same way, we cannot know and sense justice within, unless we have seen the archetype (i.e. highest and most perfect form) of justice. This goes for all virtues and creates a challenging problem for those holding the atheist worldview.

Exactly when, or how have we ever seen these archetypal virtues? Since we know that we have not done so during this current life, only two alternatives remain. Either our immaterial souls somehow observed these archetypal virtues prior to this life, or our immaterial souls somehow possess these archetypal virtues within. Yet upon examination, the two options actually resolve into one. Even if we allow our souls a prior existence, whether in, or out of body, they would still, in that previous existence, require a perfect internal standard of virtue, in order to recognize virtue in its perfect form. They might view something

and be told that this is the archetype of the thing, but this is merely
acceptance and faith in the credibility of the claimant. While this sort of
recognition works concerning material objects, it does not apply to the
immaterial. Immaterial things such as virtue and goodness, which have
no forms for the physical senses to observe, must be observed and
recognized within.

Interestingly, Hegel put forward a similar postulate in his
Philosophy of History. In this work, he stated that many of the major
religions, as well as many of the occult ones, claim the ability of gaining
insight through ceremonies, prayers, and meditation techniques. While
this is not surprising, what is surprising is his claim that this insight
often occurs not due to an external entity, or force passing into one's
mind, but rather due to the will turning its gaze inward upon itself.[39] It
is interesting just how appropriate the word *insight* actually is here; as
we are literally referring to the act of turning the sight within.

This implies that many of the truths that we seek to understand are
already within us and merely need to be brought out. Socrates discusses
this concept, which he refers to as anamnesis, at length within both
Plato's Meno and Phaedo. [181, 155] Ralph Waldo Emerson was perhaps the
most brilliant proponent of a slightly modified form of this view, which
was later denominated Transcendentalism. I strongly encourage all to
read his complete works, and not merely the few anarchist quotes which
the drug addled and ignorant hippies of the 60's used out of context,
hoping to legitimize their childish rebellion against authority.

There is a certain elegant simplicity to this theory which makes it
appealing. I had noticed long ago in my study of many religious
practices, including occult ones, that the goal of a significant portion of
these appeared to be a droning, or repetition which caused the
concentration to retreat within, and away from the boring task. Though
few realize it, even in occult practices such as staring into crystal balls,
tea leaves, or black mirrors, the goal isn't really to discern (i.e. scry)
anything within these media. The goal is to fatigue the eyes by the
constant strain of attempting to focus upon things which are obscure, or
fluid. Again, this fatigue draws the mind from focusing on external
sensory input, and if successful, directs it inward. It is no different from
the classic rotating spirals of the hypnotists, and indeed, likely induces a
similar semi-hypnotic state.

Even prayers within Christian churches, especially charismatic ones,
seem to unknowingly reach the same end by similar means. Very often
this is done by having the choir sing a particularly repetitive and simple
refrain. Instead of finishing the already monotonous final chorus, they
continue to repeat the last line with no seeming end in sight, driving the
singer, whose lips and ears have grown weary, within. The Catholics
seem to seek the same state with their repetitive *Hail Mary's*, and *Our
Father's*. The Buddhists and Hindus do this with their singing bowls,

chants, and mantras. The Islamic and Jewish faiths, on the other hand, seem too focused on materialism to ever bother looking within; believing that they have a physical text which can do all of their thinking for them.

Archetypes

In order to truly understand a thing, it is necessary to possess a mental conception of the thing in its ideal state. If one has only been introduced to the imperfect version of a thing, unless they have also received information informing them otherwise, they will sincerely believe this imperfect version of the thing to be the ideal. The degree of imperfection which the thing possesses will be analogous to the degree of error which these people possess regarding the ideal.

Take, for example the first time that we try a cup of coffee. This coffee may be substandard, overall, but the person who has never had coffee before will think that the coffee he is tasting tastes exactly the way that coffee is supposed to taste. The error he possesses on this subject is in proportion to the imperfection of the coffee.

All mankind know that perfection is impossible with material things, so the *ideal* state of the material thing is assumed to be the best out of all versions of the material thing which the perceiver has been exposed to during their life. Certain of these instances will be weighted more heavily within the mind, due to factors such as the environment which the thing is encountered in and the credibility and/or quantity of the individuals who agree about its merit. After taking these factors into account, though likely closer to the ideal, the final opinion remains bound to the experience set which the individual has been exposed to.

Returning to our coffee example: once this person has tasted several different coffees of several different qualities, ranging from low quality hotel room instant coffee, to gas station percolator coffee, to freshly made drip coffee from higher quality beans, he will believe the ideal state of coffee to be the best among these experiences. If this person sees certain coffee beans on display at a museum, a university, or on sale for a premium within a reputable store, this coffee will be assumed to be more ideal, and therefore weighted more heavily within his mind than cheap coffee sold at the local gas station, that is criticized by the majority, or that is criticized by the few coffee connoisseurs whom the majority consider to be experts on the subject.

Perceptions of material ideals are therefore highly susceptible to both error and influence by the culture, experiences, and relations of the perceiver, presenting the appearance of a relativity of all standards. Many conclude from this that absolute ideals do not exist; that there is only a most ideal for a specific person, within a specific culture, and at a specific moment. This relativism is at the core of the atheist worldview, which has been incalculably damaging to Western civilization.

What those who hold the atheist worldview fail to comprehend is that this is not the case for purely abstract principles, and very likely also with all immaterial existences. Within this quite different realm, there are typically ideal instances of things; possibly even always. I will repeat this statement once again, because of its tremendous importance. Within the world of the immaterial and abstract, there are typically ideal instances of things; possibly even always. Such an ideal instance is no different from an absolute truth, or fact.

Another problem with the atheist worldview is the corrosive effect which it has upon public debate. The goal of open debate is to bring all into alignment with truth. Within the noble framework of dialectics, postulates are examined and evaluated so that, if found to be true, new laws and rules can be created which incorporate them, and old laws and rules rooted in previously held misconceptions can be modified or abandoned. Since truth is goodness in communication, this dialectic framework of open debate requires an initial agreement between disputants on the existence of absolute good. For clarity, the goodness in communication being referred to here is not the effectiveness of information transfer, but rather the alignment of the ideas which are symbolized by the words used, with the reality of nature, as discerned by the composite input of the external and internal senses which are common to mankind.

In order for disputants to agree that absolute good exists, they must agree on what the nature of good is. To describe goodness in its unadulterated form, one must look at the various physical manifestations of goodness and determine the factor which is common to them all. It is easily seen that, though goodness is manifested in actions, events, and things observed within the material world, these things are of so widely varying a character that we struggle with naming any material aspect which is common to them all which can be denominated general goodness. Pure goodness, though very real, must be a thing immaterial.

But is this all semantics? Are we trying to make a reality of what is but idea, the thing itself having no positive existence? Can there even be immaterial existence? Don't the two terms negate each other?

In actuality, they do not. We symbolize by the term *matter* a thing which has mass and occupies space. Yet there are things which we all agree exist, which violate one or both of these rules.

Let's examine a simple example to illustrate this point. Mathematical principles, though at the outset presented within the context of material examples for ease of understanding (e.g. Billy has two apples) are discovered to be the study of purely abstract truths. This was a fact made famous by the ancient Pythagoreans over 2500 years ago.[35, 40]

Mathematical numbers and symbols all represent purely abstract concepts, and the way that they must interact is based upon known fixed truths. Sometimes these same numbers interact in ways which we do not yet understand the rules for, but nevertheless have confidence that there are yet undiscovered immutable natural laws which both cause and govern their result. In other words, it is understood that there are mathematical truths which remain undiscovered, yet though undiscovered, there is no doubt in their existence, nor in their absolutely ideal nature.

But are absolute abstract truths limited to the mathematical world? No. There are immutable ideals found within several other contexts. Consider that of communication. Truth is the concept of representing reality perfectly. Though the representation tends to occur with varying amounts of imperfection, depending upon the complexity of the reality being represented, a purely abstract absolute truth does indeed exist. Truth is both existent and ideal.

What about less abstract immaterial things which are agreed upon by the physics community as having existence? One example is light. The existence of light is never disputed, yet light itself is but a collection of massless photons, which have finite position, while paradoxically occupying no space. This includes photons ranging in energies and frequencies, from gamma radiation, to Radio Frequency (RF), and everything in between. By the previous definition of matter, photons are immaterial, and yet very much exist.

Besides the photon, other examples of immaterial existence can be seen among other elementary subatomic particles, such as gluons and bosons. And the list does not stop with these. Several theoretical models are currently competing to describe how fundamental forces such as gravity and magnetism can influence remote objects without a known force carrier. Despite our imperfect understanding of their mechanism of action, both gravity and magnetism are immaterial *energies* which simultaneously have a positive existence.

The physics world, for lack of a better term to describe an immaterial existence which can and does influence the material world, use their default term of *energy* for these things. If, however, one examines the definition of things classified as being purely comprised of energy, within physics textbooks, and deciphers the mass of jargon, one will see no real positive definition, other than that it is something which we know exists, which can influence the material world, yet which is not itself material.

This jargon stripped definition has a familiar ring to it; as it well should, since words are merely symbols used to describe an idea which is held in the mind. This mental concept of an immaterial, existent energy is the same as that which was held by the ancients when they attempted to describe what they called *spirit*, or *soul*.

Judgement

Wittingly, or unwittingly, many organizations and individuals are actively promoting a world where everyone is stripped of the ability to objectively judge anything involving another person, or other people. This can be observed when they echo catchphrases such as, "Don't judge others," or, "Only God can judge me." Between the lines of these catchphrases is the implication that those who support such views are more enlightened and hold the moral high ground. Rather than being enlightened, such people are in reality either ignorant, misinformed, or hypocrites, since the argument which they are making is self-destructive. In judging and condemning any who would judge and condemn another person, they ironically condemn themselves and destroy their own position.

This anti-judgement theme is also found repeated within another commonly adopted catch phrase: *Don't discriminate*. This is because the term *discriminate* is merely a synonym for the word *judge*. The modern negative connotation associated with the word *discriminate* is a relatively recent phenomenon. Prior to this, discrimination simply meant, and in actuality still does mean, to carefully discern genuine differences between things. Being called discriminating was, until relatively recently, a compliment; the same as being called discerning. Indeed, the primary task which we commission judges to perform is to make just decisions after closely examining the details of a case, in order to discriminate truths from falsities.

Christians who hear the phrase, "Don't judge," quoted cannot help but recall Jesus' comments, in Matthew 7:1-3, where he commands his followers to, "Judge not, that you be not judged. For with what judgment you judge, you will be judged; and with the measure you use, it will be measured back to you. And why do you look at the speck in your brother's eye, but do not consider the plank in your own eye?"

For them, this lends a sort of religious authority to the catch phrase. These good people are generally unaware of the flawed underlying belief which warps these verses; a belief that men are inherently corrupt, at their core, and are therefore incapable of relying solely upon the guidance of their own consciences in the formation of their judgements. Any internal judgement, Christians are taught, is to give way before the supposedly perfect external judgement which has been compiled and preserved within scripture; as well as, to a lesser degree, the writings and teachings of their religious leaders.

What is interesting, is that even these verses themselves internally conflict. The first verse, "Judge not, that you be not judged," emphatically states that Christians are not to judge others at all. However, the third verse, "And why do you look at the speck in your brother's eye, but do not consider the plank in your own eye?" is asking the reader to look within and determine if the uneven standards which are being applied to the two individuals are just, or unjust. This very act of making a determination about the justice of a word, thought, or action is itself the very act of judgement. This means that Matthew either misquoted Jesus, that the translation is flawed, that Jesus' teachings were logically unsound, or that the initial verse which prohibits judgement is misunderstood.

If the question about the nature of justice is asked of most revealed religionists, they will typically pause for a few moments and then attempt to deflect to the authority of their sacred writings on this subject, as they do for all moral issues. Since they are told that these writings describe the perfect teachings and actions of their archetypes of virtue (i.e. Jesus, Mohammed, Moses, Buddha, Krishna, etc.), the devout Muslim will search for examples of, or teachings on justice within the Koran and Hadiths, the Jew within the Tanakh and Torah, the Hindu within the Vedas and *Upanishads*, the Buddhist within the Tripitaka, and the Christian within the *Old* and New Testaments. They consult these works in order to determine what Jesus/Mohammed/Moses/Buddha/Krishna/etc. would say or do, if placed in the current scenario; assuming that these words, or actions would be perfectly just.

It is a telling fact that, although they commonly consider what these demagogues/prophets/saviors/avatars would do, very few stop to consider what their conception of the supreme being itself would do in the situation in question. It pains them to fix their mental gaze directly upon this sun. They prefer instead to view its significantly dimmed reflection within the moon-like visage of man.

What, however, is our revealed religionist to do when faced with a dilemma which does not appear to be covered by examples found within their favorite sacred writ? In this scenario, they will generally either make an educated guess about what the morally correct path is, or will consult with the leadership within their specific faith for this information. This latter option is usually only resorted to during the most critical of dilemmas, as it takes substantial amounts of humility and trust for one individual to approach another and solicit their help on personal matters of faith. It is a de facto admission of weakness and need; things which the world tells men that they should avoid at all cost.

After consulting with their leadership, the devout will typically, though not always, comply with whatever guidance they have been provided by them. This tends to occur not merely because the leader is assumed to possess an increased level of expertise, both with their sacred writings, as well as with the voluminous writings of their orthodox teachers, but also because an authority dimension to the issue has now developed, since advice has been sought and provided. The sacred writings within the 3 major Mosaic faiths, for example, generally demand submission by the laity to the authority of their religious leadership, unless a serious moral issue precludes this. Though, when they provide their guidance, these religious leaders frequently affirm that the choice is ultimately the solicitor's to make, both parties remain subconsciously, if not also consciously, aware that, unless this guidance is followed, they will be unable to avoid thinking about this slighted authority every time they subsequently meet.

It should be noted that we intentionally focused on guidance related to actions. This is because it is only the rare brave few who ever approach their leadership about guidance concerning what would be considered just within the context of thought: although on rare occasions, even this may occur. In either case, whether consulting sacred writings, or consulting with religious leadership, revealed religionists typically allow others to decide for them what is, and is not just. This approach causes their innate ability to sense and respond to the pull of justice to atrophy.

What misleads many who adopt this flawed, anti-judgement position, on other than religious grounds, is the fact that the term *judge*, can have several meanings when used in a sentence. For example, sometimes those who condemn judgement are simply referring to when this judgement has been based upon flawed information; such as is the case with unjustified negative bias. In other instances, the term *judge* is used as a synonym for the term punish, due to the fact that punishment often closely follows it. In this case, the person condemning judgement is actually only condemning unjust punishment (i.e. when the severity of the punishment does not match the severity of the offense). In both of these examples, the judgements in question have been stripped of justice, and are therefore deserving of their condemnation.

The problem is that, though the people who use *anti-judgement* catch phrases may have negative examples such as these in mind when they use them, the masses who hear these phrases repeated, void of context, cannot help but interpret them as a universal condemnation of the principle of judgement altogether. The societal promotion of such a view is intensely destructive, as just judgement is one of the highest forms of goodness which sustains and purifies individuals, families, nations, and the world. Under its discerning eye, the good are properly rewarded and the bad receive their due punishment. A just judge can correct a host of societal ills with a simple word and subsequent strike of the gavel. Were just judgement to be removed, all of the agents of justice would cease to properly function; from courts, to governments, to police, to businesses,

to employers, to schools, and even to individuals in their day to day
dealings. All would be replaced by base, arbitrary favoritism.
Coincidentally, this is exactly what the corrupt, who often push these
anti-judgement campaigns, actually want: the destruction of just
judgement; all of the benefits which the merit-worthy deserve, without
the prerequisite merit.

Justice

What actually is this thing which we call justice, which when present strengthens, and when absent weakens and warps the laws of nations, like the foundation of the famed Leaning Tower of Pisa? We can point out legal injustice within a nation and scream for reform all we want, but if our understanding of the core nature of justice remains warped, then any new laws which we place upon this warped foundation will ultimately fail us, once they are strained by the weight of the nations we attempt to build upon them.

Rather than root through the thousands of warped modern definitions which have been given for justice, definitions which almost uniformly claim that it's merely an arbitrary social construct, let's first take a look at how Socrates defined justice within Plato's *Cratylus*.

"It's easy to figure out that 'justice' (i.e. dikaiosune) is the name given to the comprehension of the just (i.e. dikaiou sunesis), but the just itself is hard to understand...Those who think that the universe is in motion, believe that most of it is of such a kind as to do nothing but give way, but that something penetrates all of it and generates everything that comes into being...since it is governor and penetrator (i.e. diaion) of everything else, it is rightly called 'just' (i.e. dikaion)—the 'k' sound is added for the sake of euphony. As I was saying before, many people agree about the just up to this point. As for myself, Hermogenes, because I persisted at it, I learned all about the matter in secret—that this is the just and the cause, since that through which (di' ho) a thing comes to be is the cause. Indeed, someone told me that it is correct to call this 'Dia' ('Zeus') for that reason."[36]

In order to reveal how the ancients understood a topic, Socrates often delves into the etymology of words. In this instance, his ultimate conclusion both from a logical perspective, as well as from an etymological one, is that justice shares key characteristics with, and is therefore simply another name for God (i.e. Dia/Zeus).

The brilliant Neo-Platonist author, Plotinus, expanded upon this concept in his *Six Enneads*. In this work, he claimed that all virtue was an environment and scenario specific contextual synonym for goodness. He went on to state that, since the purest abstraction of goodness, void of all context, is God, all virtue dissolves into a single hybrid concept of the goodness of God infusing, indwelling, and expressing itself throughout all of nature, including within our own bodies and souls.[37.] Plotinus attempted to clarify this point by giving the analogy of white light, which he likened to the pure goodness of God, which is broken into a range of colors, which he likened to virtues, as it passed through the facets of a gem, which he likened to the material world. According to this theory, any in depth examination of virtues, such as justice, will necessarily lead to a study of the nature of God itself.

If men like Socrates, Plato, and Plotinus are correct, and justice is simply another name for the enlivening force, or energy which fills, forms, and sets the material universe into motion, then it is so much more than arbitrary custom. Instead, justice would be something divine, absolute, and indestructible which does not allow for gradation, and which penetrates the entirety of the universe. Aligning our will with justice would therefore place our souls in synchrony with the thrum of the universal engine. The atoms within stars residing in far distant galaxies would resonate to justice. The smallest dust mite would feel the same tugs of justice at its soul that we do. Perhaps this mite's willful alignment with the divine impulse of justice causes its soul to swell with a happiness greater than that of the atheist whom he rides upon, who naïvely believes justice to be a mere arbitrary social construct.

The Romans depicted the virtue of Justice as a beautiful, blindfolded woman, having one arm outstretched before her, grasping the end of a pair of hanging balance scales, her other hand wielding a drawn sword. This depiction, which is today more commonly known as *Lady Justice*, may still be encountered gracing the rooftops and entryways of capitals, or various other seats of law across the entire Western world and even portions of the Eastern one. The immense popularity of this symbol is due to the fact that it silently affirms certain characteristics about the nature of justice which men instinctively sense to be true.

The beauty of Lady Justice's female form, for example, symbolizes the truth that she is goodness within her own domain of judgement. Statues, paintings, or other physical representations, are simply forms which an artist has impressed upon matter, through various means. Within the domain of form, the synonym for goodness is beauty. The ancients, accordingly, commonly used beauty in their works of art to symbolize the goodness of the subjects being presented, just as they used ugliness to symbolize evil.

The blindfold which covers her eyes symbolizes the truth that those who would make truly just decisions, or perform truly just actions, must be completely unaffected by the position, wealth, or affiliation of those involved. This can go wrong in two ways. The decider can either receive some type of inappropriate advantage from one of the parties involved, which influences his judgement, or they can give an inappropriate advantage to one of the parties being judged for some other reason.

The first situation is easy to understand, as all instinctively sense the lack of worth of a corrupted judge who takes bribes. In the second, we must understand that one group, or individual cannot be given an advantage over another without simultaneously disadvantaging the latter. We often convince ourselves that these advantages are harmless when we, or our loved ones benefit from them. Perhaps our friend at the gate lets us bypass a long line. Yet when this advantage is given to another, we acutely sense the injustice, as we would were we the ones patiently waiting in line who had been bypassed.

The scales which Lady Justice holds symbolize the truth that justice must be equally applied to all. There is no better symbol for equality than a balance scale. It should be noted that, though Justice is portrayed as blindfolded, her head is often represented turned towards the scales, indicating that she can somehow sense their position. Indeed, some ancient statues even depict her with a single scale grasped within each hand, which would more easily allow for this awareness. It is important to understand that there is no good, or bad scale which Justice favors, and is therefore attempting to benefit. There is simply an elevated and a depressed one; both sides of which she attempts to restore to the level of equality.

The sword of Lady Justice symbolizes a less well-known truth: that justice must, with few rare exceptions, be applied by force. Those injured parties within the depressed scale are typically more than happy to be restored to a level position, as for them this means only elevation, or gain; whether of lost money, possessions, careers, dignity, time, or freedom. The injurers within the elevated scale, however, virtually always resist this restoration to level as much as possible, since for them this means a lowering, or loss of these same things. It requires force to overcome this resistance.

In order to provide this force, just societies commission all of the various types of police, as well as the military. These serve as the sword which Lady Justice wields to both aid the injured, and menace the injurer. Our instinctive awareness that they are the agents of force is the reason why we tend to refer to both as *forces* (e.g. Police forces, Military forces, & Special forces). One might wonder why Lady Justice isn't accordingly depicted wielding two swords. The reason for this is that the police and the military, though at first glance appearing unrelated, are actually the same type of entity whose specializations require them to operate on differing ends of the force spectrum.

The various types of police forces (i.e. Sheriffs, T.S.A agents, Air Marshalls, Texas Rangers, Prison Guards, Deputies, I.C.E Officers, Patrolmen, State Troopers, BATF, FBI & CIA Agents, etc.) typically operate more towards the defensive, and therefore more lightly armed end of the force spectrum. Even though this is the case, many of these forces retain capabilities to perform more offensive actions, which necessarily require more potent weaponry. A good example of this latter case can be seen with the more heavily armed, offensively oriented, and therefore more militaristic seeming Police S.W.A.T. and FBI Hostage Response Teams (HRT).

The military, on the other hand, operates more towards the offensive, and therefore necessarily more heavily armed end of the force spectrum. In spite of this, the military can at any time provide more lightly armed troops to assist their brothers in the police forces with defensively oriented policing support. Good examples for this latter scenario are the many times that the National Guard has provided policing assistance during riots, or natural disasters, as occurred after Hurricane Katrina, during school desegregation in the South, and following the assassination of Martin Luther King Jr.

Whenever a judge attempts to level the scales of justice by issuing a judgement, along with this judgement is an implied threat that the sword of police, or military force will be used upon any who dare to resist the adjustment; especially those interested parties whose scale is about to be lowered. It is therefore no coincidence that we frequently find the morally corrupt among those who make wild generalizations about, and who condemn the nation's police, or military. The corrupt fear and hate the sword of justice as they fear and hate the virtue of justice herself. Contrarily, there is a tendency for moral citizenry to love the sword of justice, as well as the virtue of justice herself; often volunteering for, or proudly sending their children to serve in police, or military forces.

But justice is no destroying angel. Her sword must be applied like a scalpel, excising the disease of injustice from society with grim, but determined precision. Should a judge rule too harshly, perhaps ordering the hand of a starving child who stole an apple to be severed from his wrist, this judgement would birth fresh, far more grievous injustice; the scale swinging far past level. Should a judge instead rule too leniently, perhaps by ordering a murderer to perform simple community service, then, though no new injustice would be born, the original injustice would remain unabated, as the imbalanced scale would remain only slightly less askew.

This high level of skill which is required in order for a judge to give a just judgement, combined with the risk of significant harm should they err in doing so, is the reason why the governments of civilized nations generally outlaw vigilantism. While many among the injured are often both capable of, and willing to avenge their own injuries, their often still red-hot passions over received offenses are likely to cause them to over-apply their revenge, swinging the scale past level, and causing them to become unjust themselves.

A few examples of this misapplication of justice might be a Muslim man who throws acid in some sweet girl's face for not wearing a hijab, disfiguring her for life, or one who murders either his daughter for dating a non-Muslim, or his son for choosing to leave Islam. The warped Islamic views on justice are the direct cause for these monstrous acts.

With this arbitrary, Sharia law inspired warping of views regarding the severity of crimes, comes the inevitable warping of views regarding the severity of punishment which would appropriately balance the scale of justice. Mohammed himself is recorded as stating, "Whosoever changes his religion, kill him" (Hadith-Sahih Al-Bukhari 9:57). This murderous Muslim father was, therefore, simply doing what his prophet commanded.

Islam defines anything which violates the Sharia law, mandated within the Koran and Hadiths, as *sinful*, and to be punished. Though Islam recognizes a gradation of sin, many of its 70 major sins (i.e. ithm), for which it often commands brutal punishments (i.e. hudud), ranging in severity from lashings to death by stoning, are in actuality, so petty as to be laughable. Examples of these are drinking alcohol, *illicit* consensual sex, apostasy, betting, or the making of statues, or pictures.

On the other hand, Islam not only excuses, but ratifies as just and noble, truly horrendous crimes such as, among many others, the enslavement (i.e. dhimmitude), or murder of any active opponent of Islam, or the flogging of rape victims with 80 lashes, should they dare to accuse their Muslim rapist without securing the testimony of 4 other Muslim men who have agreed to act as witnesses. In this latter instance, during the vast majority of situations during which rapes occur, a woman who was raped by a Muslim will virtually never be able to secure 4 male Muslim witnesses; even during gang rapes, as the *witnesses* will also be assaulters. This essentially ensures that Muslim rapists go unprosecuted.

But let's return to our topic. In order to underscore just how challenging the task of a judge is, consider when they are unable to make the injured party whole, such as when the victim is permanently harmed or killed, or when the guilty party does not have the pecuniary assets to restore the ones which they stole. In such scenarios, judges are forced to determine equivalent severities across grossly differing categories; such as pecuniary, or incarceration punishments for corporal, or white-collar crimes. Consider the previous acid attack example. Initially, one might think that a due compensation for this crime would be to apply an equivalent corporal punishment for the corporal crime: the old *Eye for an eye* philosophy of Judaism. This view would require that acid be poured in the attacker's face for his crime. But how does this punishment make the victim whole? It doesn't. It merely fills the world with additional acid burn victims.

Though well intended, the *Eye for an eye* philosophy is a childish and poorly developed foundation upon which to base national jurisprudence. It fails to take into account not only how the impact of the offense will vary, depending upon the personal situation of the injured party, but also the benefits which can be gained by the offender in the latent period between the commission of the offense and any subsequent conviction and punishment by the courts. For example, consider a wealthy banker who steals a thousand dollars from his client; perhaps from someone who is living paycheck to paycheck. The impact to this victim could be severe. They could be evicted from their home, have their car repossessed, be turned over to collections for a bill they cannot pay, lose their security clearance, or job due to lowered credit, delay their child's doctor visit for financial reasons, exacerbating their illness, etc. Should the banker be convicted, and the judge, abiding by the concept of an *Eye for an eye*, simply have this banker return the stolen $1000, which he may have already earned interest on by the time he is convicted, the banker would actually be better off than he was before the crime, and therefore be encouraged to repeat it when he had another opportunity. The impact upon the victim, on the other hand, could be lasting: even altering the path of his entire career and life.

What about a corporal scenario? What if a heavyweight boxer punches a 95 lb. ballerina; placing her in the hospital for several days with fractured maxillary bones. According to the *Eye for an eye* concept, the judge should simply order the boxer to be punched in the face in return, something which will be unlikely to even knock him down. What if the woman assaulted is pregnant and the blow makes her fall hard and subsequently miscarry, or rack up massive debt as her preemie recovers within the neonatal ICU? What if the victim is a child, whom the assault places in a coma, or gives lifelong brain damage? Is it justice to simply punch the man back in return? Of course not. All impacted aspects of the victim's life must be considered and compensated at the expense of the guilty.

Returning to the acid attack scenario, the girl faces horrible pain, a lifetime of humiliation and embarrassment whenever she looks in the mirror, or is gawked at by the unsympathetic when in public; extreme difficulty, bordering on impossibility, finding a spouse, starting a family, and feeling the warm embraces of her own children; challenges finding work, which, combined with her tremendous challenges finding a spouse, have a high probability of dooming her to a life of poverty. True justice must correct all of these things at the expense of the guilty party, without overdoing the punishment. This is a tremendous challenge for a judge.

Since the girl must be embarrassed whenever she looks in the mirror, perhaps the attacker should have his nose and ears removed, a punishment not too dissimilar from one which the ancient Persians inflicted upon those found guilty of severe offenses (e.g. Zopyrus). Since the attacker deprived the girl of her ability to have a family, or at least greatly decreased her chances of having one, perhaps he should in turn, not only be castrated, but also have his penis removed, in order to prevent him from enjoying the sexual pleasure which she will likely also be deprived of. Since the victim had to suffer through the pain not only of the initial burning, but also of the recovery process, as well as the pain of any subsequent restorative surgeries, perhaps the two above mentioned punishments should be done in a manner which inflicts a similar amount of pain, such as using an electrocautery knife without anesthesia, and then later superficially burning sensitive parts of the attacker's inner thigh to compensate for the pain of each of the girl's restorative surgeries. Since the attacker likely doomed the victim to poverty, perhaps a lifetime worth of calculated lost wages should also be taken from him and given to the girl. He should be forced to work for whatever of this he doesn't already possess; chained to his labor like Samson of old.

In spite of the examples of unjust vigilantism previously cited, society often fantasizes about vigilantes who might level the scale of justice with the exact precision of a judge, instantly and without mediator; in spite of any laws inhibiting this. This concept is the basis for many fictional works, such as Robin Hood, Zorro, Superman, Batman, and dozens of others. The creators of these works channeled onto paper, or screen, not only the longing for justice which is universally felt throughout society, but also society's instinctive awareness of justice's sovereignty over any laws, or regulations which may have deviated from their true purpose of protecting her.

All secretly know, though few publicly admit, that were truly just vigilantes to appear, they would be celebrated by the masses as heroes. The good would love them, and the corrupt would hate and fear them more deeply than they do the police, or military. This is because the noble efforts of the police and military to execute justice are often hopelessly fettered by oceans of bad regulations. Indeed, policemen and soldiers often go through tremendous personal danger and put forth a yeoman's effort to restore justice by apprehending criminals, only to have these efforts go to waste, as corrupt, treasonous, or inefficient legislators, politicians, or judges allow these criminals back into our communities.

Examples of this are the ever more frequent murders, rapes, abductions, and attacks upon Americans perpetrated by the same illegal immigrants whom police (i.e. ICE) have repeatedly captured and deported. These daily tragedies are completely avoidable, were it not for treasonous politicians, and corrupt, partisan judges, who intentionally frustrate any efforts aimed at securing our borders.

These wretches have lost any awareness of the concept of justice, if they ever initially possessed it to begin with. They betray America, due to a not-so-secret hope that the flood of illegal immigrants will go on to illegally flood the polls with votes for their morally bankrupt, communist sympathizing political party, at the expense of American lives, livelihoods, and ultimately, national sovereignty. Our mother Europe is dealing with an even more flagrant betrayal by their national leaders of this very same sort.

Such traitors care nothing for the great principles upon which America was founded. They care nothing for the danger, suffering, and death which result from their betrayal of the noble American people; whose ancestors sacrificed countless lives, over the 5 centuries they spent exploring, civilizing, building, and defending this great land. In wealth do these loathsome traitors trust. They don their blue collared shirts, flash their brightest of smiles to the cameras, with their arms strategically placed around a humble janitor, or cook, and then they shower, change, and fly first class, or on private jets to their securely gated mansions. They do not believe in the very message which they preach about the nobility of the common man. Instead, they believe their wealth to be an impenetrable fortress which makes them immune to the petty concerns of the commoners. Commoners who, in their opinion, cling to quaint, outmoded ideas about nationalism. These traitors merely hope to feed the poor the maddening fare of avarice, so that they may harness, mount, and steer them, in order to trample upon their competitors.

Returning from our digression, authorities would invariably condemn even just vigilantes, due to existing laws greatly tainted by these corrupt leaders. Yet noble members of the police, or military, the sword of justice which would be sent against the vigilantes, would be the very ones most likely to respect, aid, or even join them, due to their mutual love of justice. Noble members, not the mass of stupid, egocentric drunks and cowards who unfortunately worm their way past less diligent recruiters to perpetually stain the reputations of these services. These latter generally care nothing for justice, nor do their miniscule, often alcohol-soaked intellects even comprehend her high principles; though they have taken oaths to defend her. These worthless types simply view their honorable public trusts as lowly stepping stones upon which to smear their boots, in their feverish pursuit of wealth.

Can we take what we know to be true concerning justice for individuals and groups, and apply it to entire social structures? There is no apparent reason why we cannot. Isn't a social structure simply a mosaic formed from the interactions of thousands of individuals and groups? If the majority of discrete, public and private decisions and actions performed by these individuals and groups are stained with injustice, won't this stain also darken the overall image which these individual pixels produce? If one injustice is rancid, like a rotten egg, will a thousand of these rotten eggs smell sweet, when grouped together and considered as a whole? Vice-versa, if the vast majority of a society's discrete decisions and actions are overwhelmingly just, won't the overall culture and social structure resulting from them also be just, regardless of the specific form it takes?

It isn't as if there is one unique set of ethics which applies only to individuals and groups, and another which applies only to nations. Any who make such claims betray a fundamental misunderstanding of the absolute nature of justice. If pressed, these confused people generally qualify their claim with statements that they believe justice to spring from the opinion of man, and therefore to be completely relative. It should be understood that, whenever the nature of anything is said to be human opinion dependent and therefore purely relative, its absolute reality is under attack. What these people are actually claiming is that justice is a mere, arbitrary social construct, with no real existence; that the most frightful of injustices, such as the holocaust, would suddenly become just, if the majority suddenly became convinced that it was.

But what majority are they referring to? If they mean the majority within the confines of a nation, then the brutal stonings, beheadings, mutilations, and outright slavery (i.e. dhimmitude) would be just within Muslim dominated nations. The beatings, rapes, murders, drownings, hangings, and other cruelties which were committed in the early Americas and Caribbean against slaves of all races, would be just, since the majority there believed them to be so. Mexican Aztecs would be just for savagely ripping still-beating hearts out of thousands of living prisoners, since they outnumbered their victims and believed it to be so.

If they mean the majority within the confines of a city, then every city which is invaded by superior numbers would have no moral right to fight back against their invaders and oppressors, even if the invasion is by savage brutes who make towers of alternating stones and heads, as the Mongol hordes did. Even if this city was invaded by inferior numbers, once these had killed all who opposed them, their majority opinion that the action was justified would make it suddenly become so. Assyrian rulers like Tiglath-Pileser, who flayed entire cities of captives alive, would be just.

If they mean the majority within the confines of a family, then whenever one spouse murders the rest of his, or her family members, the action would suddenly become just; since they believe it to be and are the only one left to form an opinion about it.

On the opposite side of this coin of absurd virtues, pre-Civil War abolitionists would be unjust for smuggling slaves to freedom on the underground railroad, since within those slaveholding states where they operated, the majority believed slavery to be just. Dietrich Bonhoeffer would be unjust for working to save people from the death camps in a nation where the majority approved of them. The brave handful of Maltese and Viennese knights who resisted and survived the Turkish and Saracen invasions would be unjust for successfully defending these lands against overwhelming numbers of Muslim invaders. Their brothers-in-arms, who sacrificed their lives in less fortunate attempts to do this very thing in thousands of other instances, such as at Acre and

Constantinople, would also be unjust, since none were left alive to hold their opinion. The last Byzantine Emperor, Constantine XI Palaeologus, would be unjust for performing the courageous act of bravely going out with his men, sword in hand, during the last desperate charge to defend Constantinople from Suleiman and the hordes of Muslim Turks whom he controlled. These brave defenders of Constantinople were cut down by the overwhelming numbers of Suleiman's forces. Edward Gibbon, in his *Decline and Fall of the Roman Empire*, mentioned that still extant first-hand accounts of survivors of this battle reveal that the innocents whom these men valiantly attempted to save, women and children huddled together trembling within Constantinople's Hagia Sophia, were afterwards dragged off in chains, weeping, to end their days being raped within Turkish harems by the murderers of their fathers, husbands, and sons, or as the castrated slaves of their mothers' rapists, and fathers' and brothers' butchers.[41] All of these actions by the defenders of Constantinople would be considered unjust by this warped, opinion-based standard of relative justice.

This view is an inevitable symptom of the mental disease of atheism. The tree of goodness is rooted in, supported by, and draws nourishment from divinity, which it mingles as sap to infuse and sustain its many virtuous boughs; one of which is justice. In the mind of the atheist, this sustaining divinity has been removed, leaving the tree, as well as its branches, to wither and die on the sterile ground of convention.

But justice, goodness, and divinity are both absolutely real and really absolute. Though all of mankind should elect to close their eyes to truth and agree upon the erroneous opinion that justice is arbitrary, all of nature, from the smallest undiscovered fundamental particle, from the diligently laboring ants, from the perpetually changing seasons, to the vast entirety of the universe as a whole, would prove "God to be true and all men liars," (Romans 3:4) by its irrefutable demonstration of divine existence and influence. All of nature hints at a deeper level of mostly undiscovered ethical truths; a fixed reality which makes the constant flux of the material but the surface ripples on a pond, whose true depth and denizens remain obscured.

I am not claiming, as many writers of old believed, that all of nature was designed with its eye upon man: that Saturn, the dust mite in the corner, and everything in between, possesses a hidden desire to elevate mankind. Instead, I claim that there is something within all of these, including man, which is shared with the divine. When the observant man goes beyond simply memorizing the never-ending catalogue of names and numbers which describe the natural world, and studies this common moral element which he perpetually encounters beneath the incessant flux of its various material forms, it eventually dawns upon him that he was all the while studying and learning about the nature of his own soul. When he considers this common element in its perfect form, he discovers himself gazing into some infinite unknown goodness, which, words failing him, he simply describes as *divine*, or *God*. This common element makes the material forms of the natural world which it infuses into infinite compasses, all of whose needles point towards their source: the moral engine of the universe.

Criminality and Catharsis

People who live in violation of a law are always severely at risk for a sort of de facto blackmail, when dealing with others who have an awareness of their violation. This fact can be observed in the way that prostitutes tend to tolerate all but the worst abuses from their pimps and clients, in the way that drug abusers (prostitutes often sadly falling within this category as well) and dealers tend to tolerate all but the most extreme extortions and abuses from their suppliers, and in the way that thieves tend to tolerate all but the most extreme abuses from those who *fence* (i.e. receive and sell) their stolen goods. When one slips from the deck of the protective, though seemingly confining ship of justice, one falls into the cold, wide, merciless ocean of force.

If at all possible, we should abide within legal boundaries, or else we give the cruel, who become aware of our offenses, leverage to abuse us. If we ever must break the law, due to moral, or practical necessity, then we should quickly correct the action. If it is impossible to practically correct the offense, and if said offense is not a moral one, then we should conceal the violation from all save those who have earned our deepest level of trust; only revealing it even to these if such a revelation serves a strongly beneficial purpose. If the offense is a moral, as well as a legal one, and if it is practically impossible to correct, then we should find some other virtuous action which we can perform in order to appease our conscience; but again, concealing the offense from all but those who have proven themselves to be worthy of our deepest level of trust, and only revealing even to these if such a revelation serves a strongly beneficial purpose.

We must understand that, when we bring another into our confidence about a legal violation, requesting that they keep the matter hidden, we force them to either violate our trust and reveal our secret, or to keep our confidence and become an abettor in the offense. This is an unfair dilemma to force upon a friend without good cause. Often offenders do this simply because they are longing for catharsis. A common example of this is Church confession, whether to a priest, or a group of elders. Such confession is dangerous, as it gives the other party power over us; even though this party may claim to stand for good.

We need to avoid such traps. These men can do nothing to permanently reduce or remove justly deserved guilt. Should they convince us that our offence is not as bad as we believe it to be, when it truthfully is, then any cathartic relief which is experienced comes at the expense of truth and character. Should they convince us that our offense is not as bad as we believe it to be, and it truly isn't, they do nothing more for us than inform us of truth which we could also have discovered through personal study and self-reflection; except that, in sharing in the secret of our offence, they now possess a certain amount of power over us. Men claiming to stand as the viceroys of an omniscient God should be well aware that confession before, or to them, is superfluous at best and dangerous at worst.

The concept of catharsis itself, as a sort of relief which comes, almost magically, from the simple act of sharing an offense with others, is a myth. Any feelings of relief which occur after an offense is shared with others are simply due to the response of the hearer. Should the hearer's response indicate that the offense was not as bad as the offender originally perceived it to be, then a proportional amount of relief occurs. Should the hearer instead be horrified at the revelation and condemn the offender, their response informing the offender that the offense is worse than originally perceived, than no cathartic benefit occurs. Quite the opposite is likely to happen, in fact. Feelings of guilt will likely increase. In addition to these points, the offender will now also feel added guilt for requesting that the listener join him in hiding a legal offense; a request which, if accepted, causes guilt in the listener as well. This impact on perceived guilt which comes from the sharing of the offense is usually less significant than that which comes from observing the hearer's response, yet it is real nonetheless.

Such principles apply not only to individuals, but also to organizations; since the latter is simply an organized grouping of individuals. Any person, or organization with known legal violations which may be used against them will tend to be ruled by, and accordingly to rule others by force, rather than by law, to an extent at least proportional to the egregiousness of the offense. This proportionality will vary, depending upon the wisdom of the agent, however in all cases they will be attempting to restore justice to the extent possible, while retaining any benefits which were gained from the original offense.

"Wait," someone might say, "So you are telling me that when a drug lord sends someone to murder a dealer who failed to pay him, he was simply attempting to be just?"

Recall the comment about the alignment of the action with true justice being contingent upon the wisdom of the agent. All men were created of equal spiritual worth, but all are not equally wise. Wisdom means an awareness of the true and complete set of ends which our words, thoughts, or actions will effect. The drug lord who orders a murder may have a superficial awareness of how his actions will immediately make him feel, but he does not understand how, with the death of the other, the ability of his soul to experience joy will die inside, somewhat, as well.

Our punishment is immediate and forever inseparable from our crime, though we may never see it manifested in the physical world. By all outward appearances offenders may seem normal, appearing to have successfully enjoyed the cake of their wrongdoing, while retaining the ability to eat the benefits. This is because we can only observe the façade of individuals. Were we able to peer within them, we would see that the purchase required a substantial withdrawal from their invisible accounts of joy; the most precious currency which they possess.

Thought Crime

In spite of the many valid warnings which historians have passed forward for them to learn from, Western media and academia continue to push the view that it is fine for the public to feed their minds with clear instances of moral corruption, such as sexual fetishes, as long as they don't act out any of the physically harmful ones. Does any sane person actually believe that it is only the actions which are taken to realize sexual fetishes that are morally bad and mentally unhealthy, while the thoughts which birth these actions are perfectly fine? Are people who walk around fantasizing about raping and murdering females, or molesting children, to be considered mentally healthy? Are these thoughts good? Of course not.

The man who mentally justifies theft is already a thief within, merely awaiting sufficient opportunity and courage to perform the action. In like manner, the man who secretly cultivates a rape fetish has already become a rapist within, and merely awaits sufficient opportunity and courage to perform the action. The thoughts which birth these harmful fetishes are as corrupt as the actions themselves. Things which promote, or encourage these corrupt thoughts should therefore be condemned, suppressed, and punished by society as vigorously as the actions themselves are. Domain owners of websites which cater to, or encourage fetishes, such as rape, pedophilia, and bestiality, should be prosecuted and given the same sentences as the rapists, pedophiles, and beastophiles whom they mentally encourage; as should the Internet Service Providers who profit from hosting these things.

The main reason why many people, especially among Western media and academia, refuse to condemn the thought aspect of sexual fetishes, is that they are infected by the atheist world-view. This worldview denies all ethical absolutes; claiming instead that all goodness and badness is human perspective dependent. Any condemnation of thoughts as being morally corrupt implies the existence of absolute standards of ethicality, even within the areas of thought and sexual attraction. This is a fact which Western media and academia simply refuse to acknowledge out of fear that, in doing so, they will frighten away current and/or potential investors who are economically wealthy, though morally bankrupt.

In addition, they know that, were they to do so, the filth peddlers would either physically, or legally attack them, while screaming about how their Constitutional *right* to freedom of expression was being violated. Since many of these filth peddlers have grown tremendously wealthy marketing moral depravity, the influential cries of this group would quickly be taken up and echoed by corrupt, left heavy media elements. Lawsuits would fly and articles would be posted on various news sites, painting these domain owners as "underdog American heroes," who were being unfairly attacked by "religious fanatics" for simply pursuing *the American Dream*.

Let's take a moment to show how these claims are invalid. Whenever patriotic phrases such as, *the American Dream*, or terms like *Freedom*, are used to justify actions, the subjects which they are being applied to must be carefully scrutinized. Unscrupulous men often employ these phrases and words because they know that they cast a hue of sanctity upon their subject, regardless of the subject's true level of moral worth. In some instances, these subjects are just; such as when the *American Dream* in question is that of egalitarianism, or when the *Freedom* in question is that of the press. In other instances, however, the subjects are base; such as when *the American Dream* in question is one of immorally acquired wealth, or the *Freedom* in question is that of abandoning one's children.

The previously mentioned *American Dream* of the smut peddlers simply refers to base avarice. These morally corrupt people covet wealth so strongly that they do not care if it is gained from a destruction of the ethical, religious, political, and even physical health of individuals, cultures, and nations. Such a viewpoint makes these wretches differ little from mobsters.

But what about the inevitable appeals which will be made to the First Amendment? The First Amendment to the US Constitution describes the fundamental human right of free speech.[42] Today, this concept is increasingly referred to as freedom of "expression." This subtle change in terms is neither accidental, nor completely innocent. By changing the meaning of the First Amendment from the right of *speech*, to that of *expression*, the scope of this law is expanded beyond its original intent of language, to that of actions. What was originally added to the Constitution as a means to prevent rulers from unjustly silencing those who held opposing political and religious views, federal judges have twisted within the courts, like a piece of warm wax, into its current state, where it is used to provide special privileges to the most corrupt types of people (e.g. pornography producers), actions (e.g. flag-burning), and products (e.g. the millions of pornographic websites which cater to and encourage every depraved fetish possibly imaginable).

Regardless of any legal opinions which have been written by incompetent, or morally corrupt judges, claiming that people have a "natural right" to any of the many forms of vice, <u>there can be no fundamental human right to a moral wrong</u>. In order for something to be an absolute human right, it must be absolutely just and good. This necessarily excludes any imagined "right" to vice. Let's examine why this is true.

The concept of natural human rights springs from the concept of absolute justice. Absolute justice itself is simply absolute goodness within the context of judgement. Absolute goodness has its source nowhere else but in God. God is therefore the source of all human rights. Thomas Jefferson hinted at this fact in the beginning of the *Declaration of Independence*, where he stated, "We hold these truths to be self-evident, that all men are created equal, that they are endowed by their Creator with certain unalienable rights..."[43] Are these *unalienable* (i.e. cannot be removed) human rights endowed by the opinion of the majority of a nation's citizens, by Congress, by federal judges, or by its president? No. Fundamental human rights, as Jefferson stated, are endowed by the Creator: by God. As a purely good being, God cannot will, or create evil; as discussed at length elsewhere in this work. Since vice is evil in action, it cannot be in alignment with the will of, or a product of the action of God, and therefore cannot be a natural human right. Any laws, therefore, which promote or protect vice are inherently invalid.

While a corrupt law may remain legally valid in the eyes of legal *positivists*, who believe that law needs no foundational basis, this viewpoint is inherently weak and prone to abuse. Basing validity upon ratification alone means that the most brutal, or inhuman of laws issued by the cruelest of tyrants, are binding, and should therefore be obeyed. Under this warped view, the excuse given by Gestapo, KGB, or Saudi Prison Guards, that their tortures and executions were simply the following of orders (i.e. regulatory law), becomes completely valid. Contrarily, the actions of brave heroes, such as Dietrich Bonhoeffer, John Brown, and all of the American Revolutionists must be condemned as criminal for violating valid laws.

Instead of holding to the positivist theory of legal validity, the vast majority of early Western philosophical, religious, and legal theorists, men such as Hesiod, Plato, Aristotle, Thomas Aquinas, Marcus Tullius Cicero, Marcus Porcius Cato, Emperor Justinian I, and Ralph Waldo Emerson claimed that legal validity was based upon, and therefore superseded by moral validity; by a universal *natural* law. Under this more correct naturalist view, any unjust laws which a nation puts in place to promote, or protect vice are completely invalid; regardless of the authority of the individuals, or groups who create, support, or attempt to enforce them. These invalid laws should therefore be removed, reformed, or altogether ignored and brazenly violated.

This naturalist view is the instinctive viewpoint held by the bulk of mankind. It is the reason why men such as John Brown are revered as heroes, instead of being condemned as villains. Men and women instinctively understand that the natural moral law, which such men followed, will forever supersede and invalidate any corrupt laws which conflict with it.

Having clarified legal validity, let us return to our analysis of corrupting cultural influences. Any media form which encourages people towards virtue, towards the thinking of morally good thoughts and the performance of morally good actions, ennobles a people. On the other hand, the same people are degenerated by any media which encourages vice; the thinking of morally corrupt thoughts and the performance of morally corrupt actions.

Some challenge the previous point by making the following claims: "It is okay that my children listen to music with lyrics written mostly by the licentious, the wanton, the lecherous, the lascivious, the immature, the avaricious, the immoral, the brutal, the savage, the selfish, and the ever-present drug addicts, whose minds are generally so addled that they confuse their ignorance for profundity. My kids and I just like the rhythm and aren't listening to the words. Besides, I want to be accepted by society and this is what is popular. It doesn't matter that the singers espouse and boast of acts whose immorality and violence often push the limits of belief. My kids would never do those things."

If the statement that "They don't absorb the words along with the music," is true, then every marketing firm, and every company which hires them to create a jingle for a commercial, must be wasting their time and money. How is it that we can often think of the lyrics of dozens of songs which we loathe and avoid, but may have been unwillingly bombarded with while the passenger in another's vehicle, while shopping, or while watching a film, or television show. We do absorb the lyrics of music. Research shows that we actually absorb these words far more easily with the accompanying music, than we would were we to simply read them, or listen to them spoken, as the musical accompaniment involves more parts of the mind in the learning process.

"Be that as it may," some will counter, "My kids would never do the corrupt things promoted in these lyrics."

As discussed earlier, the battle for character is won or lost with the will. After that it is merely circumstance and opportunity which prevents base actions. Tell me how it is that you expect a youth who is still learning how the world works, who connects his headphones and walks around listening to glamorized versions of vice being promoted for hours at a time, every day, to be immune from this barrage of lyrics constantly encouraging him, or her to justify and will these same morally corrupt things?

People tend to listen to music which they identify with. They listen to calm music like classical, or jazz because they are calm inside, or wish to be. They listen to music promoting violence, such as certain types of metal, or hard rap because they are violent, or wish to be. They listen to club music, most of which promotes wanton sexual relationships, because they are promiscuous, or desire to be. Are we so naïve that we believe these things to be without effect? Any who would make such a claim are deluding themselves and others.

But not all music is corrupt. There was formerly much, and there is still some which inspires high ideals, noble thoughts, brave actions, etc. We should fill our ears, and the ears of our children with these, take them to performances where they are sung, or played, and learn to sing or play them ourselves.

"My kid and I like that game where we are killing, stealing, whore-mongering, or what have you. The graphics are great. They just keep getting more real. We would never do that type of stuff in real life though."

Keep telling yourself that your character and that of your younger, more impressionable charge aren't being corroded while playing these games. We have combat pilots train in flight simulators, which are designed to bring them as close as possible to the realities of war, so that they can mentally prepare themselves to calmly respond on the battlefield to the tremendously stressful situations they often encounter. The reason that this is effective is that the subconscious, which drives the majority of our emotions, is not designed to differentiate between fictional situations and factual ones. During the thousands of years of human evolution, it never had to; as fiction is a relatively recent invention. The subconscious simply lumps what it perceives to be relatively identical items together and generates beliefs and the emotions which spring from them, about this amalgamation. The missile which the combat pilot evades is, to the subconscious, but one of dozens of simulated ones which he has previously evaded. His thoughts and emotions on the battlefield typically slip into the well-worn groove which his subconscious developed in the simulator.

So too with us and our children. Though few of us are combat pilots, the video games we play, whether on gaming consoles, or computers, are essentially simulators. Not all video games deserve censure, as many are innocent puzzle, coordination, or strategy games. There is nothing wrong with these. But all know that there are other types of games which tend to be purchased and played far more frequently, where players can essentially train to be murderers, whore-mongers, rapists, thieves, or some other type of depraved individual, any time that they wish to, and all from the comfort of their own living room. Worse yet, our youth are generally the major consumers of these games. The ruts which this training wears into our minds, and into the softer clay of our children's minds don't immediately disappear once the console's power switch is pressed, just as those of the combat pilot don't disappear the moment he steps out of the simulator. Is it any wonder then, that these views, this warping of our character, bleeds into other facets of our lives:

especially given the fact that many people spend hours a day, multiple days a week, in front of these systems.

Many leaders within Western society, who have a sacred duty to protect their people, foolishly ignore, or excuse the fact that the avaricious are allowed to grow wealthy by peddling their filth to the nation's citizens, provided that no citizens actually get caught doing any of the immoral acts which these corrupt products encourage. However, even when citizens do these things, the wealthy filth peddlers and the left-heavy news outlets who echo them, quickly and loudly claim either that all morality is relative, and therefore that these morally corrupt actions are only morally corrupt in certain instances and to certain people, or that there is no proof of a connection between the consumption of violent media forms and the commission of violence by its consumers.

Regarding the first claim, the absolute nature of good and evil are discussed in depth within another section of this work. Regarding the second, marketing majors are taught that even subtle images and wording in their advertisements can have a significant impact upon subsequent human behavior. These facts are leveraged by businesses to increase sales. However, when we go beyond the subtle and explicitly sing about doing corrupt things in music, glamorize doing them in film, or have people simulate doing them in video games, this, we are told, has absolutely zero effect upon subsequent human behavior. This is idiotic.

It is ludicrous to think that inner city youths, for example, who fill their heads with rap "music" that glorifies and promotes drug abuse, drug sales, rape, murder, and theft, who watch films glamorizing these things, who play games simulating them, will not also develop a predilection to do these things. Everyone knows that children who grow up exposed to abuse and violence have a higher tendency to become abusive, or violent themselves. Hosts of studies have shown that the boy who watches his father beat his mother is more likely to beat his future spouse, and the girl who watches it happen to her mother is more likely to tolerate the abuse when it happens to her. Is there any difference between being exposed to abuse and violence in person, and observing these things on a monitor, screen, or television? Does the subconscious mind know the difference? Of course not.

Filth peddlers make these patently false claims simply because they hope to avoid personal responsibility, and potential lawsuits by victims, over the morally corrupt and corrupting fare which they have made their fortunes creating and distributing. It should be noticed that the left-heavy media, and the academics whom they cite, often work together for the benefit of corrupt businessmen such as this. Over and again it will be seen that the left are not the champions of the people, as they attempt to portray themselves, but rather the lapdogs of the elite.

It is foolish for national leaders to allow these known corrupting influences to run rampant within society, and then for them to feign surprise at the resulting increase in corrupt actions performed by their citizens. These filth peddlers are modern-day Typhoid Marys; spreading the plague of moral corruption throughout society and making themselves wealthy in the process. Like Mary, these people should be quarantined and stripped of their immorally gained profits. The wealth which is recovered should then be used to vigorously attack the societal disease itself.

Given universal suffrage, democratic societies inevitably pass laws which are reflective of the average level of morality among their voting citizens. Allowing the profit-mongering, self-absorbed peddlers of corrupting influences to erode the character of these voters, ultimately results in an erosion of morality, most importantly the moral principle of justice, within the laws and political leaders which these people elect. As laws which restrict the peddling of corrupting influences are increasingly loosened, a destructive positive feedback loop is created.

Theoretically, this spiraling effect of national morality can also occur upwards, in the direction of positive influences; however, this rarely occurs in practice. Typically, spirals of national morality progress downwards until, the culture having degenerated and weakened, the people comprising it are either conquered by those with tighter reigns upon their own society's negative influences, or a dark age of ignorance and oppression sets in; sometimes for centuries.

During this latter scenario, historically what has occurred afterwards is that avaricious and bloodthirsty men of wealth and power kill each other for more of it, while the common man becomes increasingly oppressed and stripped of even basic human rights. These rulers generally see these commoners as mere cattle, to be driven into their factories and stores in order to perform whatever actions cannot be performed by a machine. The workers are then defrauded in usury and unjust taxes of the pittance which they receive in compensation. In this pitiful condition, the common man possesses neither the time, nor the resources to corrupt himself; all being focused upon survival. Once at this point, courageous and good men may finally have an opportunity to once again take the helm of the nation and attempt major reform, with the support of a peasantry grown once more moral, after their passage through the refining fires of suffering.

Seldom do tyrants of this sort abdicate luxury and power without bloodshed, however. A quick glance at virtually any Middle Eastern state which claims Islam as its national religion is proof of this. Given the nuclear age that we currently live in, it is uncertain how corrupt rulers, once they have successfully wormed their way into the highest offices of a nation, could ever be internally overthrown. Gone are the days of the American and French Revolutions, when peasants could arm themselves with weaponry similar to that which tyrants, and the soldiers whom they employed, could bring to bear.

Pause for a moment and consider the sheer level of destruction which a single tank, or combat helicopter can inflict. For any but opposing national armies, these weapon platforms are virtually unstoppable while fueled, running well, and supplied with ammunition. The common people could do nothing against them. A single one of these weapons platforms could decimate whole armies of foot soldiers with ease. Gone even are the days of being able to conceal, or even feed a militia without those in power being aware of one's whereabouts and actions.

This underscores the need to reform Western society, prior to its decent into moral, and subsequently political collapse. Due to our highly integrated markets, should such a collapse occur, the global repercussions would be more catastrophic than anything which the world has previously known.

Freedom and Equality

Hegel makes an interesting statement in his *Philosophy of History* about how the Chinese of a specific dynasty had equality, but not freedom, being equally low under their ruler.[39] This statement directs the mind to ponder the interrelation between freedom and equality. Consider the well-known fact that the hyper-wealthy, whose very existence bespeaks cultural inequality, as well as those aspiring to be wealthy, tend to be the very ones who fight the hardest for freedom to make inordinate profit. On the opposite end of the spectrum, prisons are situations where people have virtually no freedom, but have a relatively equal amount of possessions. What is going on here?

Freedom and equality appear to be inversely related within a society, however, they also appear to pivot upon the fulcrum of the average level of virtue of the citizenry comprising it (*See Fig. 2*). Given the widespread misconception of freedom as an absolute good, this statement likely rings harsh upon modern ears, but bear with me.

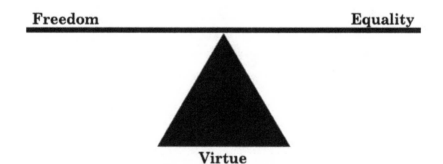

(Figure 2. FVE Model)

The reason for this interrelation is due to the nature of the citizens governed. The increase in freedom not only allows moral citizens to perform good actions, but also removes the barriers which prevent immoral citizens from performing actions which harm their fellow citizens. These harmful, and generally selfish actions inevitably result in an overall decrease in social equality. When we are discussing an increase in the virtue fulcrum, we are essentially referring to an increased ratio of moral to immoral citizens, which will inevitably increase the ability of a society to increase both freedom and equality.

Let's test this Freedom-Virtue-Equality (FVE) model in its various configurations, seeking evidence which either confirms, or contradicts its predictions. In the first case, a nation whose citizenry exhibit low virtue, on average, and relatively high freedom, will be predicted by the FVE model to have very low levels of equality. Unfortunately, this prediction appears to be confirmed by the state of much of the Western world which most of us live in today. Corruption and violation of law is occurring within our highest offices. Babies are aborted each year by the millions; abortion being simply a euphemism for infanticide. Political leaders are forcing their cultural engineering regarding the foulest of sexual perversions down their nations' collective throats, while simultaneously standing up tyrannical laws which make the utterance of truth about these subjects a crime. The now brainwashed and voting younger generation, who have no anchor memories of reality prior to the recent propaganda onslaught, have been blinded and carried downstream by it, towards the ethical sewers which such reasonings inevitably lead to.

Yet for all of the reductions in freedom to act morally and justly these aspiring tyrants have put in place, they have also added many more freedoms to behave immorally; resulting in an overall increase in freedom, with a simultaneous decrease in virtue. And what has this bred, but the anticipated decline in equality. For example, the wealth gap between the wealthiest 1% and the remaining 99% of American citizens has grown tremendously during this same time period. Ultra-large international corporations are recording record profits, while simultaneously, record numbers of Americans are unemployed and/or on government subsidized food stamps.

As no nation ever achieves perfection, it will be difficult to point out a period when a specific nation would be considered highly virtuous, with which to test the FVE model. This is because any who disagree could merely find one example of injustice that continued to fester in that place and age, and based upon this, attempt to call the entire argument irrelevant. Be this as it may, the point of the FVE model is about national averages, not outliers.

I would argue that, immediately prior to the Civil War, the Northern US had reached a pinnacle of virtue. While society was rigidly structured, and therefore seemingly less free on average, the equality of the average citizen with his fellow man appears to have been significantly higher. This can be seen in the far more level income distribution across the nation's citizenry, as well as, less significantly, the high level of social and community club participation. This relatively high level of equality, given the relatively low levels of freedom, and high levels of virtue, again matches the predictions of our FVE model.

On the extreme side of things, another example which it might be worthwhile to consider is the current state of the nation of Saudi Arabia. This Wahhabi Islam dominated nation has virtually no freedom. All aspects of life there are controlled by the outmoded, unjust, and barbaric Sharia law. The inherent corrupting nature of this most brutal and stupid of religions has ensured a very low level of virtue among the citizens of that nation. The freedom arm of the FVE model accordingly being tremendously low, and the virtue fulcrum being incredibly small, the FVE model predicts that the equality arm on the other side would be raised above the freedom arm, yet still low, overall. This is absolutely the case which is seen. The majority of the citizens of Saudi Arabia are somewhat equal, but it is a low type of equality, similar to that which is found among slaves.

The proposed FVE model appears viable when subjected to this very light scrutiny, but it would be interesting to see how it fares under more rigorous testing, as could easily be accomplished via data from the US Census, Grumbacher Institute, CIA Fact Book, and a few other sources. Should it continue to prove reliable after a more robust examination, then what this model predicts must occur within the majority of Western nations, in the short and medium terms, is a strong effort by national leadership to increase both equality and national virtue, something which will likely only come with a corresponding reduction in freedom. Ideally, a balance should be sought, where neither arm exceeds the other, and yet both are lifted to new heights by the increase in national virtue. Unfortunately, however, the Western world is currently miles away from this condition.

Nation States

There is a movement currently being pushed by generally international corporate and private interests, with the express goal of dissolving all nation states and replacing them with a single global governance structure. The deluded supporters of this movement make wild claims that the model of the nation state is rooted in and therefore inseparable from social injustice, that it is accordingly responsible for the vast majority of the world's ills, and that its destruction would bring about social equality and global peace. This is simply the same naïve utopian refrain of the communists, which has been exhumed to be sold to the ignorant of a new generation.

While this siren's song is certainly appealing to, and is often echoed by the vast majority of shallow thinkers, including many who have unfortunately wormed their way into the academic chairs at several major universities, it is both impractical and insidious in its attempted implementation. The reasons for this are explained in another section of this work, but within this section, let's examine the definition of the nation state.

A nation state is simply a group of men and women who have voluntarily pledged their allegiance to each other, and to a core set of philosophical views which they share. These ethical, political, and religious views are subsequently memorialized into the new nation's laws. Knowing that there is safety in numbers, these proto-citizens generally choose to congregate together within a certain geographical area. While this geographical area is generally what first comes to mind when nation states are mentioned, land is not required for nations to exist. All that is required is a community of citizens devoted to each other and to their core set of shared philosophical views; or in other words, to their law.

This is a tremendously important point. A group of Americans remain American even while traveling within another country, not because of what their passport, or birth certificate says, but because they maintain a devotion to the noble philosophical views which America was founded upon, and to their fellow American citizens. They are effectively a small American colony on foreign soil. If America were to slip beneath the waves while they are away, the heart of every person within this small colony, which stores and preserves America's philosophical views like seeds, can reproduce a new America, should the hearts of those whom they share these views with prove sufficiently fertile.

In like manner, people born within foreign lands, who adopt the belief that American philosophical views are the best ones possible, and who dedicate themselves to her laws and her people, are *Americans*, regardless of whether or not the current American leaders, or laws recognize them as such, or allow them entry. America, as with all nation states, is ultimately a set of philosophical ideas. Any who commit themselves to these ideas, and to others who do as well, are Americans.

On the other side of the spectrum, those who refuse to pledge their allegiance to the core philosophical views which their nation was founded upon, as memorialized within her laws, or to her citizens who do, remain true aliens, regardless of their place of birth, or length of residence. These people are often viewed with a certain amount of distrust and are marginalized, punished, or expelled by the nation's true citizens. Such distrust, marginalization, punishment, or expulsion can either be just or unjust, depending upon the goodness or badness of the philosophical views and laws in question. Egyptians, Turks, Iranians, Saudis, Pakistanis, or Sudanese people, for example, are unjustly persecuted when they are marginalized, punished, or expelled from their nations for refusing to pledge their allegiance to views and laws founded upon the outmoded, unjust, and brutish Sharia law, or to their countrymen who do.

Contrarily, consider communist sympathizing liberals, Atheists, and Muslims in America, all of whose fundamental philosophical views stand in direct opposition to the noble philosophical views which America was founded upon; such as that "All men are created EQUAL, and are endowed by their CREATOR with certain inalienable rights."[43] These people generally loathe and outright condemn any Americans, whom they call *conservatives*, who continue to adhere to these philosophical ideas. It would be an act of the purest justice to prevent these people from gaining political, or economic influence, in order to keep them from further infecting and corroding American society with their cancerous worldviews: in other words, to marginalize them. As no marginalization efforts are ever completely successful, and generally cause the marginalized to hate and attack those who are attempting to marginalize them all the more, it would also be just, in fact it would be ideal, to expel such people from America altogether.

Nations, with their host of branches, departments, programs, employees, and infrastructure, are built upon the foundations of their laws. These laws themselves are all designed to serve one ultimate purpose; ensuring that justice occurs. Justice is the bedrock which the foundation stones of national law rest upon. It is therefore of utmost importance for a nation's people, especially those whom they place into leadership positions, to be able to correctly understand, accurately define, and implement justice. As they succeed at this, the laws for the nation which they develop will be good, causing her to be intrinsically strong. As they fail at this, her laws will be bad, causing her to be intrinsically weak.

"Wait a minute," one might say. "There are tons of nations who hold warped views on justice. How about the many Islamic dominated ones which ascribe to the brutish, 6th century system of Sharia law mandated by the Koran. Take Saudi Arabia, for example, where people are publicly beheaded for things as petty as merely changing their opinion on Islam and choosing to convert to another faith; a supposed crime which they call *apostasy*. Obviously, this level of cruel, brutal, stupid, and intolerant religious fanaticism is unjust; yet Saudi Arabia has been a nation since the 30's."

This is a valid point which deserves further scrutiny. Firstly, it should be mentioned that Saudi Arabia is a mere youth, when considered on the timeline of nations. As dog lifespans are shorter than human ones, making the former appear to age faster, so human lifespans are generally shorter than those of the philosophical ideas upon which nations are built. These ideas may outlive the men who initially birthed, championed, or adopted them, by many centuries.

These nation spawning ideas are like fires; first igniting within the mind of a lone pioneer, then spreading to the ripe fuel of other noble minds and hearts, until what once was a lone flame, is eventually transformed into a roaring conflagration. On the other hand, if this burning national idea is surrounded by the green wood of ignorance, the saturated wood of error, and/or the inflammable stones of fanaticism, it may remain solitary and small, or may even sputter out.

While there is hope that the green and wet wood may eventually be dried and warmed by the heat of study, and the dialectic abrasion of ideas, there is little hope for the stones. Fanatics swear off the study of anything which disagrees with their current understanding, which they arrogantly believe to be perfect, and refuse to tolerate dialectic scrutiny. Such people fail to realize that a refusal of this sort does not prove the strength of their ideas, but is instead a de facto admission of their inherent weakness and falsity. Pure truth is firmer than adamant and has nothing to fear from scrutiny. Any who attack it, like those who hurl their fists against the granite face of a mountain, merely harm themselves in the process.

In addition, those fanatics who refuse dialectic scrutiny of their views based upon religious grounds, claiming that this refusal somehow protects their God, their supposedly holy demagogues (e.g. Jesus, Moses, Mohammed, Buddha, Krishna, etc.), or their supposedly inspired texts (i.e. the Koran, Bible, Tanakh, Vedas, etc.) from insult, fail to realize the impious and absurd implications of their position. Such a position implies that a God whom they believe to be both wise and powerful enough to frame the entire universe, is simultaneously either too weak or apathetic to defend his own interests, or too ignorant to know when they require defending.

Returning from this digression, these hotly burning national ideas may begin to cool if their good fuel is removed; a situation which occurs when a nation's citizenry forgets the core philosophical truths which she was founded upon, accepts flawed replacements for these, or fails to instill a love of absolute virtue and truth within the upcoming generation. On the other hand, even if a nation's citizenry devoutly clings to virtue and truth, her national flames may still be cooled if the immigration of those holding more error filled, ignorant, or fanatical national ideas goes on unrestrained. In either instance, that of the decrease of good fuel, or the addition of bad, once the volume, or authority of the latter surpasses that of the former, the national scale tips from one of growth to one of decay; a situation which, if left uncorrected, ultimately results in a quenching of the national idea.

But all is not hopeless even after this sad point. Patriots, still heated within by the noble philosophical ideas which the nation originally stood for, may continue to smolder for centuries, though insulated from virgin fuel by the impermanent and inflammable ash heaps of society which bury them. These ashes are the hordes of brutish people who live out their lives void of high ideals, caring only for personal entertainment and the satisfaction of physical appetites; both of which are but synonyms for self. If the winds of time and the jolts of freak events ever successfully shiver enough of these ashes adrift, in search of better venues for their pleasure seeking, the coals may once more re-connect with the good fuel of noble hearts, rekindling the flames of former national ideas within their beloved homeland.

Sadly, as with a fire, it is challenging to remove ashes, as attempts to sequester and remove them frequently only spread their contamination to other, originally clean areas. Often, the best chance for new flame is for an ember to be thrown out from the fire before, or from a coal after, the national idea is quenched. These embers, written works which preserve the noble heat of the original idea, may drift on the breeze of time for centuries, igniting fresh flames in more receptive lands, times, and hearts.

As basing these national ideas upon absolute truth and virtue gives a nation strength, so basing them upon relative opinion and vice makes a nation weak. When the citizens of a nation grow corrupt, they often make the unfortunate decision to adopt such warped views, which weaken and warp their laws. Inevitably, they attempt to compensate for this inherent weakness in their now corrupt jurisprudence by supplementing it with fear. Typically, they attempt to inspire this fear by threatening and inflicting tremendously brutal and cruel punishments for any violations of their warped and unjust laws. In addition, rather than repairing this poorly built national house, all who must live in it are threatened with cruel punishments, should they point out its shortcomings.

Here we see the cause of the brutality commonly encountered within fanatical, Sharia inspired, Saudi Arabian law. The error which taints the Islamic faith throughout, weakens it, subsequently weakening any national ideas which are rooted in the Islamic worldview, any laws which are built upon these national ideas, and ultimately, any nations which these laws support. Instinctively sensing this weakness, Saudi Arabian political and religious leaders saturate their culture with threats and reminders of the savage brutality which continues to exist beneath the seemingly placid surface of their culture. Even the sword emblazoned on the Saudi Arabian flag alludes to this brutality; being included for no other purpose than as a silent threat. It is a reminder to all Saudi Arabian citizens that the nation's political and religious leaders retain the ability and will to brutally murder any who might dare to challenge their views. The recent brutal murder of journalist, Jamal Khashoggi, who critiqued the Saudi crown, is just one of thousands of possible examples of this corrupt government terrorizing its own subjects.

We encounter this same theme of brutality within virtually all nations whose jurisprudence and national ideas have their roots within the outmoded, brutish, and innately unjust Sharia law. But the Islamic nation expands far beyond the borders of those countries who claim it as their state religion. Muslims who move to non-Islamic nations, while still claiming the superiority of Sharia law above their nation's laws, and who are dedicated only to each other, rather than to their nation's citizenry, are not immigrants, but colonists from the borderless Islamic nation.

The news perpetually resonates with stories about the increasing number of Islamic terror attacks in Western lands. The deaths which these acts cause are doubly tragic, because the Western world, deeply entrenched in the totalitarianism of political correctness, refuses to condemn the philosophical source of this disease. Not only does this plague of political correctness merely treat the symptoms, but it attacks, en masse, any who would dare to name the disease. But "damn the torpedoes, full speed ahead."

Europe, whose population is declining due to decades of strong birth control efforts, is actively importing low cost immigrant workers to run their businesses; the vast majority of these being from predominantly Muslim African, or Middle Eastern nations. When I state that Europe is actively importing this labor, I should clarify that it is the small handful of hyper-wealthy European business owners and the politicians whom they sponsor, who are betraying their people in this manner. The European public, who must bear the burden of living with these Muslim immigrants, who threaten, rob, harass, rape, and murder those who do not submit to Sharia Law, strongly resent this abandonment and betrayal by the leaders whom they pay to protect them.

Though Islamic dominated nations, with their brutal Sharia influenced laws, are the chief among offenders today, there have been periods when Catholic, Protestant, Jewish, and even Pagan dominated lands have encouraged brutality to hide their intrinsic national weakness. These unjust national Venus Flytraps, such as the horrible Assyrian empire, which flayed entire cities of people alive, grew by sucking the blood and lives from thousands of victims.

National Interaction

As two nations interact, the flames of noble philosophical ideas within one of them often ignite the other, upon contact. These same flames may have been on the wane in the originating nation, yet thankfully, sufficient embers remained to ignite the dry matter of the other nation's ethically inferior social, political, and religious views. Plutarch mentions this fact in his Moralia, where he states that Lycurgus, the first lawmaker of Sparta, "Forbade them also to war often against the same people, lest they should make them the more warlike. Accordingly, many years after, when Agesilaus was wounded, Antalcidas told him the Thebans had rewarded him worthily for teaching and accustoming them to war, whether they would or no."[28]

A great example of this principle can be seen in Egypt, whose culture was already ancient at the time that the Memphite kings expelled the Hyksos and invaded Syria. The Phoenicians, Babylonians, Chaldeans, Hebrews, Philistines, and even the Athenians were all highly influenced by the Egyptians; often copying her written works, and restyling, renaming, and adopting her gods.

Due to Greece's future dominance in nascent Europe and Africa, the influence of Egyptian culture on Greek culture is one of utmost importance. The Greeks loved and emulated the Egyptians. The capital of the Greek empire was located in Alexandria, Egypt, where they built several centers of learning. Many of the best and brightest Greek scholars, men such as Pythagoras, Plato, and Aristotle, were educated, or trained in these Alexandrian museums and temples. Rome was also influenced by Egypt during the period of Greece's decline. Egypt voluntarily placed herself under the Roman Senate and was Rome's ally during the Punic wars. At one point, Rome even saved her from an invasion by Antiochus of Syria.

As already mentioned, many of the Greek gods were adopted and adapted from the Egyptians. Per Herodotus, the earliest of Western historians, the Greek Bacchus, for example, was taken from the Egyptian Osiris. "...the Egyptians do not all worship the same gods, excepting Isis and Osiris, the latter of whom they say is the Grecian Bacchus."[44]

Herodotus and many other ancient historians repeatedly state that parts of Greece were originally colonized by Egyptians. Diodorus Siculus, for example, stated that Cecrops, the first king of Athens, was the leader of a group of colonists from Sais, Egypt.[45] Plato echoes a similar view in his *Timaeus*, where he says, "In the Egyptian Delta...there is a certain district which is called the district of Sais...The citizens have a deity for their foundress; she is called in the Egyptian tongue Neith, and is asserted by them to be the same whom the Hellenes call Athene; they are great lovers of the Athenians, and say that they are in some way related to them." In another part of this work Plato states, "I imagine they dressed them in Egyptian armor, for I maintain that both the shield and helmet came into Greece from Egypt."[46]

This is interesting, given that Athens possessed the famous Academy of Plato and functioned as both the nexus of Greek science and Philosophy, as well as one of the main centers of power within the Greek world for hundreds of years.

Greeks and Romans conquered and consolidated the various small nation states the same way that the Assyrians did in the East. Alexander the Great, for example, penetrated deeply into Asia at the head of the Greek armies. One of the lands which benefited from this expedition was India, which, besides the handful of highly educated Brahmins, was until that time in such a state of savagery that many among its people were still consuming their dead relatives. Plutarch devotes an entire section of his *Moralia*, to a discussion of why he believed Alexander to be the most effective philosopher to ever live, due to the fact that his expeditions spread improved philosophy and higher culture over the known world.[28]

Thucydides, in the 6th book of his *History of the Peloponnesian War*, describes the tragic mistake made by the Athenians in thinking that they could invade Sicily; underestimating the numbers and strength of the Sicilian people.[47] This failed invasion had both a negative and positive result. Negatively for the Greeks, it awakened the sleeping Italian giant of the future Roman Republic, which would later conquer the Greek homeland, most of Europe, and parts of Asia and Africa. Positively for the Romans, it inadvertently spread the flames of higher philosophy and culture to the Italians, who in turn spread it across the Western world. As the ebbing flames of Greek culture set the Roman fuel ablaze, the Romans grew to love and emulate their Greek benefactors.

As the Western Roman Empire eventually grew corrupt and abandoned the principles which initially made it great, it weakened, until various Germanic nations, such as the Lombards, Suebi, Visigoths, Ostrogoths, Vandals, and Franks, eventually fractured the empire like a pane of glass. These Germanic nations, however, could not help but be changed and improved by the culture which they conquered, as the few smoldering embers of higher philosophy remaining within the Roman Empire were sufficient to ignite and consume what was shallow and superstitious within their own. But even these once great Germanic nations eventually grew corrupt and also declined. The residue of these nations, as well as smoldering embers from the Roman, Greek, and Egyptian cultures, remain with us today, and are known as Western Civilization.

Even in relatively modern times this process is still occurring. England, France, Germany, Russia, and the Netherlands, whose former empires spread high cultures and profound philosophical views, have sunken into relative obscurity. Fortunately, not before penetrating and igniting the cultures and peoples of America, India, and Australia.

America itself is staggering, due to its current rule by native and foreign rulers who are overwhelmingly not patriots, but mere businessmen: men who think nothing that brings profit ignoble, and nothing which is profitless noble. These men betray the high ideals that the founders of this great nation attempted to preserve; ideals which are the reason she became great to begin with. Hopefully we can purge ourselves of these traitors and rekindle the embers of our once high culture. Otherwise, our only hope is to pass the torch on to others before our eventual collapse. Such a collapse would not be without global consequences, given that we are the last remaining world superpower; and a nuclear power at that. A cascade of economic collapses would be triggered which would result in mass, global unemployment and starvation, which always eventually leads to war.

Politics, & Religion

What exactly do we mean when we refer to *political* views, or even *politics* altogether? Political views are simply a specific subset of philosophical views whose focus is the subject of human interaction. These rules of interaction vary in importance, from the trivial, such as whether men should open doors for women, to the vital, such as whether nations should sanction capital punishment. Regardless of their level of importance, all of these rules related to human interaction, ranging from the formally documented, to the informally understood, fall solidly within the category of politics.

If a large enough audience was asked, several people would inevitably claim that they are *not political*. People generally make this disingenuous statement because they don't want to be embarrassed by having their level of ignorance about current national events revealed, don't want to risk being disliked for revealing views which might potentially clash with those of the person, or people whom they are speaking with, or because they simply haven't given the matter sufficient thought. Does a person exist who has no opinions about how people should treat each other? Such a mythical person would also have to be completely apathetic about how they themselves were treated. Yet cut this person off in traffic, scream in their face, attempt to touch certain parts of their bodies, push them down the stairs, or break into their homes, and observe whether or not they become justifiably offended. Offense is simply a reactionary feeling which develops in response to violated will, while will itself is rooted in personal beliefs. This offense, therefore, reveals that even these people, subconsciously, and possibly even consciously believe in a rule set for human interaction which should not be violated; or in other words, they hold political beliefs. We all do.

But whence do these rule sets regarding human interaction, which all possess, originate? Are they exclusively and arbitrarily nurtured into us, or is there instead a natural aspect to them which originates somewhere within us. The answer is: a little bit of the former, and a lot of the latter.

As humans, we possess an internal drive to increase our own level of happiness. Though we frequently attempt to accomplish this via many methods, the wiser among us eventually realize that happiness only increases when our souls are exposed to goodness. As discussed elsewhere in this work, goodness is absolute, internally sensed, and known by a range of context specific names. *Love*, for example, is goodness within the context of relation. Goodness itself, when purified of all context, is discovered to be nonother than an aspect, or expression of God. What we refer to as *ethical*, or *moral* words, thoughts, or actions are simply those whose primary underlying objective is to increase the amount of goodness within ourselves, others, or the world itself, in order to subsequently increase our own level of happiness. All of these ethical words, thoughts, and deeds which are actually, or even potentially related to human interaction, comprise our political views.

The *nurture* portion of our moral views are the techniques which we are taught, concerning how to most appropriately put our internal moral feelings into effect, within the context of certain specific situations. As mentioned earlier, ignorance, or flawed understanding of circumstances, participants, and/or laws of nature may sometimes result in the employment of horribly and tragically flawed means, during these attempts.

In seeking truth about the nature of politics, we have inadvertently landed solidly within the sphere of ethics, which has necessarily led us to religion; as all absolute virtues and goodness have their source nowhere else but in God. And indeed, this wheel spins in reverse as well. If we start our discussion by examining the nature of religion, instead of politics, we find an aspect of it to be unavoidably and inseparably bound up in politics. The parts of religion which are not simply cognitive, or introspective, those actions which are considered the *fruit* of the former, have associated with them an assumed rule set regarding the best means of interaction between individuals and their God, between individuals and the natural world surrounding them, including that of their own bodies, and between a plurality of individuals, which we refer to as a society. This last assumed rule set brings us back within the realm of politics.

Like Siamese twins sharing the vital organ of human interaction, politics and religion are discovered to be inseparable. This being the case, why is it that most modern Western nations claim that the best form of government is one which is blind to religious views? Why is the separation of church and state espoused as the highest type of legislative wisdom?

This wasn't always the belief among Western nations. Thomas Hobbes' 1651 political work, *Leviathan*, for example, urged rulers to consider the inseparability of politics and religion, and was widely celebrated for centuries after its publication.[48]

I believe that the reason that modern Western nations are reluctant to acknowledge the clear inseparability of politics and religion is due to the fact that many of these nations developed the foundations of their current political systems shortly after freeing themselves from what was essentially 1400 years, from Theodosius, until the French Revolution, of varying degrees of joint monarchical and papal abuse: both of whom claimed that their crimes were justified by special religious privileges. It is my opinion that the men who founded many of the modern Western governments which replaced these previous flawed ones, men such as Benjamin Franklin and Thomas Jefferson, ignored their better reason on this subject, in order to avoid a recurrence of these religious abuses.

The problem with this willful ignorance of the obvious interrelation of politics and religion is that it requires a dangerous sort of cognitive dissonance among a nation's rulers. National leaders must know how to resolve to the absolute root the causes for their political views. As already mentioned, these causes are ultimately religious ones. If a nation's leaders do not know how to do this, then they will be ever prone to fall for the mistaken, and tragically all too common belief that political views are derived merely from arbitrary and accidental cultural norms of the current moment, people, and place. Once this misstep has been made by a nation's leaders, whether by the people within a democracy, the aristocracy within an oligarchy, or the king within a monarchy, from that very moment, the foundations of this nation begin to crumble and collapse.

Like a meteor being eventually slowed, stopped, and accelerated in a retrograde direction by the constant, unseen gravitational pull of a distant sun, nations may take different amounts of time to overcome the various safeguards, internal bureaucratic inertia, and cultural momentum of earlier, more diligent generations, before the view that all virtue is arbitrarily relative finally destroys them. But destroy them it certainly will, if these views are held long enough. This is because those who have been convinced that all political views are arbitrary have also been convinced that all morality regarding human interaction is as well. Recall that political views are simply the set of rules which one accepts about social interaction, and are therefore inseparable from ethics. It follows, therefore, that those who believe political views to be arbitrary and mutable, must also believe the same to be true about ethics and morals.

This view has dangerous consequences. If all morality has been arbitrarily created, it may arbitrarily be destroyed just as quickly tomorrow. Wrong and right will never be absolute. They may switch places tomorrow. The ends will always justify the means for those who believe all means to be arbitrary. If brutal means are required to gain a desired end, and can be accomplished with minimal reprisal, then those who believe in arbitrary ethics would see no reason not to be brutal.

Some avoid such direct wording by stating that ethical, political, and religious views are *relative*, rather than arbitrary, but this is simply a euphemism for the same concept. Such a claim, in actuality, is little more than a subtle implication that ethics, politics, and religion do not have absolute existence; that any *truths* which exist concerning them are exclusively internal; being based upon how perceivers understand them through the lenses of their accumulated life experiences. Yet, since no two people ever share the exact same set of life experiences, and will, accordingly, never perceive anything exactly the same way, then a single question concerning any of these subjects, if indeed *relative*, will spawn a plurality of conflicting views proportional to the number of perceivers.

This belief about the relativity of ethics, politics, and religion stands directly opposed to the traditional Western belief that truths on these subjects are inherent within the facts of the specific situation; existing regardless of how, or even if they are perceived at all. Stating that all ideas are *relative to the observer* and therefore equal, implies that the false ones, which must necessarily be in the majority, are as merit-worthy as the true. Or in other words, that truth is no truer than error, and therefore does not exist.

This argument is self-destructive. One can never say that truth does not exist. The very postulate within the claim itself is being put forward as a truth. If the postulate is true, then it is simultaneously false, which is an impossibility. Truth must exist, and must always be singular, while any falsities on an issue may be infinite. In the words of that forgotten master of wit and common sense, G. K. Chesterton, "It is always simple to fall; there are an infinity of angles at which one falls, only one at which one stands."[24] Truth is like this. It stands firm and erect, while all around it, infinite falsities lean this way and that; those leaning furthest from the truth collapsing under the slightest inspection, while those closest to it holding up under all but the most intense scrutiny.

The signers of the American Constitution could not even fathom the society which we live in, which has been overwhelmingly enslaved by wealthy individuals propagandizing an atheist worldview which denies the existence of God, and claims that all virtue, all goodness, all truth itself are not absolute, but relative to the opinion of the experiencer. These founding fathers of America, France, and several other Western nations strove to prevent an invasion of the religious devil they did know, rather than the atheist one they didn't, which lives with us today.

Were the American founders, for example, to return to life, treasonous liberal, mostly Democrat politicians, and their wealthy globalist handlers would despise, attempt to discredit, and stir people up to attack them both in the courts and in the streets; as these people despise, attempt to discredit, and stir people up to attack those conservatives who cling to the ideals which these American founders stood for. Once the resurrected founders had been brought up to speed on technological advances and the current political state of the great nation they founded, men such as George Washington would likely send the military to have liberal Democrat legislators arrested, tried, convicted, and then imprisoned, exiled, hanged, or shot as traitors; due to some of the corrupt positions which they wholesale support; such as the "rights" of abortion and homosexual marriage. Even using the term *rights* here is a misnomer, as vices cannot be human rights. This subject is discussed at length elsewhere within this work.

Learning of the many poisonous judicial rulings, such as the aforementioned, which were forced down the nation's throat by heavily liberal, activist federal judges, including several who are unfortunately seated on the US Supreme Court, the founding fathers of America would again, as they had with their Congressional peers, likely send the military to have these judges arrested, tried, convicted, and then imprisoned, exiled, hanged, or shot. Realizing how the plague of political correctness had infiltrated our legal system, setting up a new oligarchy, which used the courts to tyrannize over the American people, the founding fathers would likely declare our entire legal code to be null and void, and would recreate a reformed one de novo, with stronger protections against these abuses.

Realizing the gross imbalance of wealth which exists across the nation, and the vast swaths of American property and assets which treasonous politicians have allowed to be owned by overseas investors who care nothing for the nation, or her people, the founders would likely have all assets and property of this latter type seized and redistributed to any among the poorest of Americans who proved a willingness to improve their lives with it. Understanding the mass of debt which the nation had been fettered to by her short-sighted and treasonous politicians, the founders would likely declare all foreign debt immediately nullified, since allowing nations to be in debt to one another destroys their national sovereignty, as debt and servitude go hand in hand.

They would likely also declare all student loans to be nullified, as the majority of these loans, which virtually enslave the nation's future leaders, are to international banks. It is impossible for these people to focus on their nation's best interests, while leading it, when they are enslaved by international entities. Of note, this is not such a novel idea, and should, in fact, be implemented immediately. The only losers in such a scenario are the ultrawealthy international banks. These entities, and the people who lead them, need to be stripped of the staggering amount of wealth and power which they possess. Plutarch records that Lycurgus, the famous Spartan lawgiver did this very thing, when he freed his people from the enormous debts which they had become enslaved to, and redistributed the land.

Knowing the absolute refusal of devout Muslims and orthodox Jews to pledge sincere allegiance to any law which, or to any people who disagree with the teachings found within their Koran, Hadiths, Tanakh, or Talmud, their belief that all men are not created equal, but that Muslims and Jews, and especially Muslim and Jewish men, are superior beings in the eyes of God, as well as the obligation of Muslims to swear eternal war (i.e. Jihad) upon the non-Islamic world, which is simply a more violent echo of the Jewish belief that their Messiah will conquer and rule it, the founding fathers of America would immediately eject all of these people from this nation, recognizing that the oil of American philosophical principles is irreconcilable and immiscible with the vinegar of both Islamic and Jewish religious doctrine. Again, the substantial amount of property which would be reclaimed during this ejection could be redistributed to the poorest of Americans.

I must clarify here that this does not mean all Arabs, or racial Jews would, or should be ejected. Should these people show by their words and by their lives that they bear true allegiance to our laws and to the citizens of our nation, then like anyone else, they should be allowed to remain and prosper. The qualifier of, "...by their lives," must be added to the previous statement, since Muslims are taught within their sacred writings that they are allowed to lie to non-Muslims about religious principles, if doing so is advantageous to them. This principle is known as Al-Taqiya. Regardless of their race, the people who should be ejected from America are those who refuse to pledge true allegiance to her laws and people, or whose lives prove the words of their pledge to be lies.

The list of reformation actions which the founders would take would go on and on, from removing all Atheists from teaching and national leadership positions, to ending all entitlement abuse, but these men certainly wouldn't do nothing. They wouldn't watch football and drink themselves to sleep every night, as they saw their brainchild, which so many of their friends and family had bled and died to create, being raped by businessmen, legislators, academics, executives, and judges who held diametrically opposed philosophical views from those which the nation was founded upon, and which her laws were designed to protect.

Culture

Between the body and the cell, we observe the following uncanny similarities. The mitochondria, lysosomes, and peroxisomes digest materials which the cell is fed in a similar manner to the way that the stomach digests its food. The DNA serves as the storage center for cellular information, just as the brain fulfills this role for the body. The cellular membrane encloses and protects the cell, just as the skin encloses and protects the body. Cells can use various means of motility, such as flagellation, amoeboid movement, and filopodia to find an environment more conducive to survival, just as the body can move its head, core, and extremities for the same purpose. Cells phagocytize or pinocytize extracellular material for various purposes, ranging from metabolism, to immune function, just as the mouth swallows things for the same purpose. As the cells release histamines to signal for help against pathogens, so the body can shout out and attract attention for aid. As the cell maintains its structure and moves its intra-cellular componentry around via a cytoskeleton, so the body moves things externally and maintains its structure with its skeleton. Many additional similarities could be listed, but will not, as the above sufficiently establish the point of the uncanny amount of similarity between the two.

We see these similarities echo again when considering nations. As the body is formed from its living components, the various cells and organs, as well as from its nonliving components, such as bone, cartilage, and ligament, so a nation consists of its living citizenry and organizations, as well as its nonliving infrastructure and land. As the body is fed material which it digests within its stomach into products which are more easily consumable by its cells, so a nation feeds raw materials into the colossal stomach of its industrial infrastructure and digests these into products which are more easily consumable by its citizens. As the cells can only directly metabolize nutrients which are available to them within the environment of their extracellular matrix, relying upon the products of digestion to constantly be delivered to this matrix to replenish their exhausted supplies, so citizens can only directly consume resources which are locally available to them, relying upon the nation's logistics systems to constantly replenish these consumable products of the industrial stomach. As the body depends upon its million arteries, arterioles, and capillaries to distribute fresh nutrients to the cells and organs, relying upon similar venules, veins, and lymphatics to remove their metabolic waste, so the nation uses its infrastructure of interstate highways, city streets, and community and neighborhood roads to deliver supplies to individuals and businesses within a nation, as well as to remove their waste. As the mind is the central command center for bodily control, even though many organs and cells function independently for the good of the body, so the central government of a nation controls the majority of national function, though several organizations and individuals operate independently from this control for the good of the nation. As the peripheral nervous system (along with the endocrine and exocrine systems) is the means by which the brain sends and receives information and instructions from and to various cells and organs, as well as how these cells and organs communicate with each other, so the communication systems within a nation, whether telephone, television, webpage, email, or regular mail, are how these commands and information are transmitted between the government and the governed individuals and organizations, as well as between these individuals and organizations themselves. As some parts of the peripheral nervous system terminate in specialized sensors, such as the eyes and ears, allowing the body to detect and interact with the external world, so the government relies upon individuals who are specially trained (e.g. Ambassadors, CIA agents, Military Intelligence, Journalists, Public Affairs Officers, etc.) to allow it to accurately detect and interact with other nations. As some of these bodily sensors, such as taste buds, are in place to discriminate the healthfulness of what is placed in the mouth, so the nation relies upon industry experts within agencies such as the FDA to determine the suitability of various products for its citizens. As the body possesses an immune system, from its lymph nodes to its macrophages, which allows it to detect, and suppress internal pathogens, so the nation possesses police, national guardsmen, FBI, etc., to detect and suppress dangerous individuals and organizations within it. As the body uses its skin as its primary layer of defense, in order to prevent the widespread invasion of pathogens, so the nation uses its border defense mechanisms, from fences, to walls, to coast guardsmen, to prevent the widespread infiltration and influence of dangerous individuals and organizations. As the body possesses systems for healing, such as immunoglobulins and platelets which allow it to heal itself after an injury or infection, so the nation possesses healthcare systems, disaster response teams, social safety-net programs, and relief funds which work to heal citizens and organizations that are suffering. As one body can communicate with, help, protect itself from, or attack another, so one nation can do the same to another via intergovernmental correspondence, humanitarian aid, and military action. This list of similarities can be expounded upon indefinitely.

Though the sciences of anatomy, physiology, and cellular biology had not yet matured to the point of allowing him to use many of the examples which I have cited above, this similarity between man and nation was the primary thesis of the renowned 1651 work, *Leviathan*, written by one of the founders of modern political philosophy, Thomas Hobbes.[48]

These similarities between man and nation aren't merely limited to physiological and functional traits. They echo again within the spheres of human development and national growth. There is an uncanny similarity between the phases of life which we, as humans, pass through, and those which nations seem to. As the primary focus of the human infant is on nourishment, growth, and learning how to properly develop and control the body and limbs, so the primary focus of a new nation is on growth, sustainment, and learning how to properly control the governmental limbs which it finds itself born with.

Like the babe, infant nations are generally nourished, until weaned, by the sustaining resources, laws, and agencies of older, more mature nations. This is not always the case though. Like the fabled Romulus and Remus of old, a few nations have survived after being cast upon a new land and left to fend for themselves. In this fable, these babes were nourished by a she-wolf, absorbing with that milk the rugged independence and fierceness of that beast. So too with groups of people who have, unassisted, founded all of the parts of their nations de novo. Fed upon the livestock and agriculture which their sweat and sacrifices coaxed from the surrounding lands, like Nehemiah of old (Nehemiah 4:15-17), building their new nations with trowel in one hand and sword in the other, the early generations of these new nations are typically the ones who are later revered for their stoutness and determination. Though fed upon this courser fare, the initial growth of these nations is generally slower than that of ones who can gulp the fatness from a mother nation until weaned, their subsequent growth tends to be much faster and longer lasting. This is because these founders receive the benefit of early education in self-sufficiency and also avoid swallowing their parent's vices along with her milk: vices which would only weaken and stunt their developing bodies.

A young child tends to become selfish and spoiled when their every whim is catered to. On the other hand, children who are taught by the hard master of poverty, or by an attentive parent who wishes to protect them from this, learn how to regulate and work for their desires. It is the same with nations. Those which start out in rugged lands, where survival is hard, tend to develop diligent and resourceful men with rugged and hard characters. Those which start out in luxurious lands, where survival is easy, tend to produce lazy men infected with avarice and sensuality. Plato, in his *Laws*, and Montesquieu, in his *Spirit of the Law*, both noted how the very character of the land which a developing nation finds itself in tends to influence and incorporate itself into the character of her early settlers. A few quotes from them on this subject, are provided below.

"...For the Persians are shepherds-sons of a rugged land, which is a stern mother, and well fitted to produce a sturdy race able to live in the open air and go without sleep, and also to fight, if fighting is required. (Plato)"[49]

"... had you been on the sea, and well provided with harbors, and an importing rather than a producing country, some mighty savior would have been needed, and lawgivers more than mortal, if you were ever to have a chance of preserving your state from degeneracy and discordance of manners...There is a consolation, therefore, in the country producing all things at home; and yet, owing to the ruggedness of the soil, not providing anything in great abundance. Had there been abundance, there might have been a great export trade, and a great return of gold and silver; which, as we may safely affirm, has the most fatal results on a State whose aim is the attainment of just and noble sentiments... (Plato)"[49]

"The liberty they enjoy, or, in other words, the government they are under, is the only blessing worthy of defense. It reigns, therefore, more, in mountainous and rugged countries, than in those which nature seems to have most favored. (Montesquieu)"[50]

This was the case with the early Arab nations. Though, for the past 1300 years, they have been overwhelmingly held hostage by the totalitarian philosophy of Islam, they nonetheless continue to display the fierce independence which was developed a thousand years earlier, when, unaided, they struggled for survival in those most rugged of homelands.

It was true of the American Indians, whose ruggedness the early colonists of Concord Massachusetts marveled at. Note a quote on this below:

"This was an old village of the Massachusetts Indians...their physical powers, as our fathers found them, and before yet the English alcohol had proved more fatal to them than the English sword, astonished the white men. Their sight was so excellent, that, standing on the seashore, they often told of the coming of a ship at sea, sooner by one hour, yea, two hours' sail, than any Englishman that stood by, on purpose to look out. Roger Williams affirms that he has known them to run between eighty and a hundred miles in a summer's day, and back again within two days. A little pounded parched corn, or no-cake sufficed them on the march. To his bodily perfection, the wild man added some noble traits of character. He was open as a child to kindness and justice. Many instances of his humanity were known to the Englishmen who suffered in the woods from sickness and cold."[51]

It soon became true of these early American colonists themselves, as attested in one quote below, of the many on this subject which could be provided.

"On Friday evening last, arrived at Lancaster, Penn., on their way to the American camp, Capt. Cresap's company of riflemen...These men have been bred in the woods to hardships and dangers from their infancy. They appear as if they were entirely unacquainted with, and had never felt, the passion of fear. With their rifles in their hands, they assume a kind of omnipotence over their enemies."[52]

Youth is the period when the majority of physical growth occurs. This period, when blood flows hot with passion and excitement, is also famous for its vigor, courage, optimism, and resilience. In like manner, the majority of a new nation's growth occurs during her early years. While her future success remains uncertain, the sight of her leanness tends to frighten away the teeming masses of parasitic leeches, who prefer to congregate in wealthier lands, where they may suck richer blood from fatter hosts. Without being insulated and smothered by these unpatriotic and avaricious pretenders, the noble idea and ideals which the young nation stands for continue to burn hot within the hearts of her citizens. This concentrated heat spreads quickly because it ignites the minds of those touched by it with hope for a better future, under a noble government.

Unfortunately, as people are more easily manipulated into lending their strength to aid bad causes when either very young, inexperienced, and therefore easy to manipulate, or when old age has caused their mental strength or caution to wane, so both young and growing, and old and declining nations are often tricked into lending their aid to unjust causes. Very young nations generally do so when they have been deceived into believing that the prospect of future growth outweighs, and therefore somehow warrants, certain unjust actions. Declining nations generally do so when they have been deceived into believing that certain unjust actions will somehow revitalize them. Both make the mistake of believing that economic, or strategic ends justify corrupt means. Unfortunately, regardless of what is gained by either, injustice strips nations of their prosperity in the same manner that it strips men of joy.

Let's consider a few examples of these bad decisions which America was deceived into making in her youth. One obvious one is the initial toleration of slavery. Those businessmen who reaped enormous profits from this cruel trade in human lives, convinced the young nation that the economic benefits to be gained from slavery were worth this blatant violation of the natural rights of mankind. Another example is the unjust Indian Removal Act of 1830 (only 47 years after the close of the Revolutionary War), as well as several other pieces of legislation which forced the American Indians from their homelands, resulting in the infamous *Trail of Tears*. The injustice of these acts is best expressed in a letter which Ralph Waldo Emerson sent to then president Van Buren protesting them, a quote of which is provided below:

"In the name of God, sir, we ask you if this be so. Do the newspapers rightly inform us?...We hoped the Indians were misinformed, and that their remonstrance was premature, and will turn out to be a needless act of terror.

The piety, the principle that is left in the United States, if only in its coarsest form, a regard to the speech of men, —forbid us to entertain it as a fact. Such a dereliction of all faith and virtue, such a denial of justice, and such deafness to screams for mercy were never heard of in times of peace and in the dealing of a nation with its own allies and wards, since the Earth was made. Sir, does this government think that the people of the United States are become savage and mad? From their mind are the sentiments of love and a good nature wiped clean out? The soul of man, the justice, the mercy that is the heart's heart in all men, from Maine to Georgia, does abhor this business."[53]

Another example which can be provided concerning the alternate situation of bad national policies occurring in older nations on the wane can be observed across much of modern-day Europe. Due to decades of short-sighted birth control practices, much of Europe's native population is shrinking and aging. In order to fill the vacuum, European business leaders and the politicians whom they bankroll are allowing the entry of, or sometimes even actively importing, cheap Middle Eastern and African labor into these nations. These business and political leaders are traitors. They care only about the short-term benefit of a cheap labor pool, failing to consider the long-term corrosive effect of the Islamic world-view which these people bring with them; a world-view which both denies and is absolutely averse to egalitarianism. They appear to pay no heed to the correlating increase in vehicle attacks, to the increase in stabbings, to the fact that droves of European girls are being raped, or having their beauty permanently marred by acid attacks? As a father of several wonderful daughters, my blood boils when I consider these things. I have spoken of them at length elsewhere, however, and will attempt to remain on topic.

At the age of maturity, one of the primary traits which we observe with stable and independent men and women is their joining in marriage and subsequent creation and care of their offspring. So with mature and stable nations, we observe a tendency for them to shift their focus towards creating, caring for, and developing the seeds of their national idea in new lands.

The majority of gestation, however, occurs within the womb of the mature woman. In like manner, a large proportion of cultural development within a nation is a product of the fairer sex. Women carry and preserve the culture of a people within their hearts like they carry and preserve the eggs of the next generation within their ovaries. They are the ones who tend to promote and continue our holidays, decorations, fashions, traditions, and celebrations. And what are all of these but symbols of culture. The very beauty of their form bespeaks the cultural beauty of civilization, libraries, roads, and law. These grandmothers, mothers, wives, daughters, and grand-daughters have a taming and civilizing effect on the men whom they come into contact with.

Is it any wonder that females tend to dominate the field of primary education? While some will surely say they were forced into this role, I do not believe this to be the case. Instead, I believe that they simply gravitated towards this civilizing role which they so naturally excel at. If the men within a nation diligently protect their women from abuse or harm, women become free to work this natural magic throughout society. The treatment of women within a nation is one of the clearest indicators of the level of that nation's ascent above savagery. One glance at Saudi Arabia, for example, where women are still beaten with sticks and have virtually no rights beyond what their husbands allow them, shows how brutish this culture remains, in spite of its vast wealth.

Once they have reached old age, men and women tend to grow weak and dependent upon others for their care. Frequently, the force of their reason also begins to subside, sometimes resulting in eccentricity. So it is with older nations whose internal constitutions have begun to break down. We often observe them becoming dependent upon other, more vigorous nations for their protection and care. As mentioned earlier, nations on the wane also have a tendency to issue corrupt, or short-sighted laws, due to the breakdown of their judicial, legislative, and executive systems; which collectively comprise the *mind* of the nation. For several examples of this, one needs merely to read Edward Gibbon's monumental *Decline and Fall of the Roman Empire* and note many of the tragic abuses which the Western Roman Empire committed, in her final days, against the rising Gothic power. In one instance, Emperor Julius in 378 A. D., slaughtered all of the Gothic youth throughout the Roman territories in Asia.[54] This brutal act sealed Rome's eventual doom, at the hands of the vengeful Alaric.

Lastly, it is interesting how similar many of the diseases which destroy men behave, when compared to the diseases which infect and destroy nations. Men, for example, become infected with cancers, often as the result of negligent prolonged exposures which they allowed; such as skin cancer from UV exposure, lung and bladder cancer from smoking, etc. Unless promptly cut out, or destroyed with radiation or chemicals, these diseases take root in one site of origin and then metastasize to new areas, which they also destroy, until all is corruption and their host dies.

In like manner, nations may become infected with the cancer of corrupt laws and corrupt men, due to negligence on the part of their political leaders, who allowed their citizenry to be exposed to toxic people, or information for a prolonged period. Once people's hearts have become corrupted, they spread this corruption to others, like a metastasizing disease. Unless these corrupt views are promptly cut out of a nation, there is a very real risk that they will eventually spread and ultimately destroy her. In most of the Western world these days, the atheist worldview and the poisonous philosophy of Islam are the two primary diseases which are infecting and destroying the bodies of these nations.

One important difference between men and nations which should be taken into consideration is that nations, being the product of a national idea, and an associated set of ideals, do not necessarily need to die, as man does. They may burn away the corruption which infects and destroys them and arise once more with renewed vigor, like a phoenix from the ashes. This has occurred several times, throughout the centuries, in nations such as Egypt, Greece, Italy (Rome), India, France, Britain, the Netherlands, Germany, Spain, Russia, Israel, Iraq, Iran (Persia), China, and Japan. The frightful thing about this scenario, however, is that the burning of the phoenix often consumes the lives of many innocents while reaching a heat sufficient to burn away any corruption.

Fasces

The fasces, a bundle of tightly bound sticks connected to an axe head, has been used as a symbol of national power since the days of the ancient Roman republic. In Rome, men known as Lictors, who were a sort of select Praetorian guard, would carry the fasces into political assemblies. Most people avoid using this symbol today out of a lingering fear that doing so will give their opponents an opportunity to label them as Fascists; essentially claiming that they hold similar political views to those of Mussolini's National Fascist Party, of 1930's era Italy. Be that as it may, the fasces can still be found decorating many important American symbols and monuments; such as Mercury dimes (1916-1945), the Rostrum walls and inkwell legs of the U. S. House of Representatives, the seat of the Lincoln Memorial, etc.).

Due to its modern disuse, the generations which followed the post-World War II "Baby Boom" have mostly forgotten the original meaning of this important symbol. The fasces was adopted and used by early Americans because it is a perfect physical representation of the American national motto, "e pluribus unum," or in English, "Out of many, One." Note the placement of this phrase beside the fasces on the Mercury dime. The small, individually weak sticks, symbolizing the citizens of a nation, become strong only when tightly and closely bound together. This joint strength was represented by the ability of the sticks, when united, to perform a task which was beyond any of their individual strengths: the ability to drive the large axe head, an instrument useful in antiquity both for industry and for war.

Fasces are also appropriate symbols for a family, since families are a miniature society, complete with their own internal type of government and laws. Though individual family members may be weak, they become strong when all members are tightly and closely bound together. This principle was memorialized in the following fable by the brilliant Greek philosopher, Aesop.

"The Bundle of Sticks

An old man on the point of death summoned his sons around him to give them some parting advice. He ordered them to bring in a bundle of sticks, and said to his eldest son: 'break it.' The son strained, but with all his efforts was unable to break the bundle. The other sons also tried, but none succeeded.

'Untie the bundle,' said the father, 'and each of you take a stick.' When they had done so, he told them: 'Now, break,' and each stick was easily broken."[56]

The modern nations of Europe and the United States, where Western egalitarianism first took hold during the Age of Reason, are currently staggering under a barrage of attacks upon their national unity, which are being launched by various self-appointed *cultural engineers*. These toxic elements wish to break the fasces of egalitarian society for a variety of reasons; the foremost of which being a desire to replace it with what they mistakenly believe will be Marxist, Islamic, or Anarchist "utopias," or a desire to implement a tyrannical classed structure (i.e. neo-nobility) reflective of, and therefore more compatible with, the majority of large international business models. Understanding that families are the building blocks of society, and that disunited individuals are far easier to control, or break, than an equal number of people who have pledged to defend one another in support of a common cause, these enemies of egalitarianism use the media, academic centers, the courts, legislative assemblies, and even "useful idiots" in the streets, as tools with which they hack at the cords binding together the traditional nuclear family, binding together any citizens stanchly clinging to the noble principles of Western egalitarianism, or binding together any who simply possess common physical characteristics with the enfranchised of earlier generations who did. These cultural engineers know that allowing these groups, who for the time being continue to comprise the silent and silenced majority of Western nations, to unite and realize their own strength, would spell their certain ruin.

The ability of individuals to cohere, within both nations and families, springs from mutual trust in the goodness of one another's character. This mutual recognition of goodness causes a feeling of love to spring up between citizens and family members. Among citizens, this love is known as camaraderie.

Unfortunately, a large portion of Western media sources and academics today make claims that goodness itself is relative; or in other words, merely a human perspective dependent social construct, and therefore not absolutely real. While those who adopt this view continue to use words such as "goodness" when describing people, ideas, or things, their underlying disbelief in any absolute nature of goodness significantly changes the meaning and hollows out the significance of these words; like a worm-eaten apple. As men's belief in absolute goodness is poisoned, so their trust in the goodness of their fellow citizens, and sometimes even in the goodness of many of their own family members, dies as well. This destroys any love, trust, camaraderie, and cohesion which existed between these individuals; effectively severing the cords of the fasces. The truth that there is *Strength in unity*, has been proverbial since at least as far back as the

days of Homer (~850 B. C.), who quoted it. When Western nations and
families are transformed from united entities into assemblages of
incohesive individuals, they are therefore effectively stripped of their
strength, making them unable to effectively defend their interests, or
even their very lives.

This sinister attack upon the ability of the citizens of Western
nations to unite and defend their best interests is even being touted by
these same left-heavy media outlets and university chairs as a virtue.
People are told not to fight to preserve their unity, as George
Washington encouraged them to do during his farewell address,[55] but to
celebrate the destruction of this national unity, which these people call
diversity. The deconstruction of the natural male and female sexes into
the plurality of genders is simply a microcosm of this macrocosm of
national deconstruction. This is why the rainbow, which symbolizes the
breaking, or deconstruction of white light into a plurality of colors, was
selected to serve as the symbol of the homosexual movement. It is no
surprise that the media outlets and university chairs who are pushing
for the destruction of national unity are the same ones who are
promoting the *gender revolution*. This deconstruction should not be
celebrated, it should be mourned and striven against.

George Washington saw that this attack upon the unity and cohesion
of the then new nation of America would be the means by which the
enemies of the noble ideals, ideas, and principles upon which she was
founded would be accomplished. In his parting address, where he
declined a third term in office, he warned the nation's citizenry to be on
their guard against such attacks. He is quoted below.

"The unity of government which constitutes you one people is also
now dear to you. It is justly so, for it is a main pillar in the edifice of
your real independence, the support of your tranquility at home, your
peace abroad; of your safety; of your prosperity; of that very liberty
which you so highly prize. But as it is easy to foresee that, from
different causes and from different quarters, much pains will be taken,
many artifices employed to weaken in your minds the conviction of this
truth; as this is the point in your political fortress against which the
batteries of internal and external enemies will be most constantly and
actively (though often covertly and insidiously) directed, it is of infinite
moment that you should properly estimate the immense value of your
national union to your collective and individual happiness; that you
should cherish a cordial, habitual, and immovable attachment to it;
accustoming yourselves to think and speak of it as of the palladium of
your political safety and prosperity; watching for its preservation with
jealous anxiety; discountenancing whatever may suggest even a
suspicion that it can in any event be abandoned; and indignantly
frowning upon the first dawning of every attempt to alienate any portion

of our country from the rest, or to enfeeble the sacred ties which now link together the various parts..."[55]

It should be noted here that, almost without exception, those who founded these American and European governments tended to be comprised, almost exclusively, of various denominations of Christian (as well as Deist, in America and France), heterosexual men, sprung from the various Caucasian races (e.g. German, Italian, Dutch, Irish, etc.). Washington hints at this when he makes the statement in his farewell address: "With slight shades of difference, you have the same religion, manners, habits, and political principles."

By making this statement, I am simply pointing out historical facts; not attempting to claim that those possessing the greatest number of these traits are a sort of *master race*. However, just as the modern heirs of the ancient Chinese and Egyptian people should take pride in the cultural accomplishments of their people, so should the modern heirs of these early European and American people take pride in theirs. These cultural achievements include the Renaissance works, the Magna Carta, the Guttenberg Press, the brilliant and fiery authors of the Age of Reason, the abolition movement which led to the end of Western slavery, the Industrial Revolution, and too many other things to even attempt to exhaustively catalogue.

Yet virtually all of Western media and large swathes of academia claim that the modern descendants of these early Americans and Europeans should not legitimately be allowed to take pride in anything about their ancestry, their culture, or their rich history. They are told that they should be ashamed of these things, and should instead celebrate and embrace the ancestries, cultures, and histories of other nations. Hundreds of years ago, the majority of slaveholders in America and the European colonies claimed to be Christian, were heterosexual, male, and descendants from one of the Caucasian races. Because of this historical fact, modern Christian, heterosexual, male Caucasians within these lands are told that they are worthless.

It is conveniently overlooked by the ignorant people who make these claims that, during the period in question, many other nations and races also possessed slaves; especially Islamic dominated Arab and African nations. Even today, some still do. It is also overlooked how, in order to rid their nations of this stain, and free their enslaved fellow man, these same early Europeans voluntarily abandoned their colonies' profits, and shortly thereafter, early Americans voluntarily sent their sons and fathers to bleed and die in the fields of Gettysburg, Antietam, and hundreds of other Civil War battlefields. They forget how brilliant men like Ralph Waldo Emerson and John Stuart Mill thundered from the pulpit and parliament against slavery: how brave men like John Brown were hanged for attempting to free American slaves; his fate electrifying the abolition movement; "John Brown's Body" even becoming a marching song of the Union army. Nay, they do not forget them, they are simply never taught these things, because doing so would destroy the false narrative being pushed, that men from the many Caucasian races, who are all stupidly lumped together and referred to as *white*, are coldhearted, selfish monsters.

It is implied that Americans of European descent, whose relatives bravely settled, explored, fought in the revolution for national independence, and have lived in this great land for hundreds of years, are illegitimate thieves, simply due to their displacement of American Indians and Mexicans. As an aside, it is interesting that the famous American Indian warrior, Geronimo, states in his autobiography that, due to their brutality against his people, his tribe hated the Mexicans much more than they hated the European settlers. It is telling that generally nothing is said about how unjust it was for the expanding English colonies in America to also displace settlers from other Caucasian, Christian nations, such as the Dutch and the Spanish.

A staggeringly unjust and blatantly suppressive double standard has been, and continues to be applied to these Christian, heterosexual males, who were sprung from the European Caucasian races, versus that which is applied to all others. For evidence of this, one needs but to glance at recent political and legal decisions which have occurred across the European and American nations. All exclusive groupings based upon any of these characteristics have been systematically attacked within and broken down by Western courts, colleges, legislators, and media; any future attempts at organization being subsequently prohibited. This includes exclusively Christian organizations, of whatever denomination, exclusively male organizations, exclusively heterosexual organizations, organizations exclusive to any of the many Caucasian races, or to this group of races taken as a whole.

Simultaneously we see the same courts, colleges, legislators, and media hypocritically defending the legitimacy of exclusively Islamic, Jewish (faith), Atheist, or any other non-Christian religious organizations (e.g. Council of American Islamic Relations, Muslim Student Association, North American Federation of Temple Youth, American Atheists, etc.), exclusively female organizations (e.g. Financial Women's Association, American Medical Women's Association, International Council of Women, etc.), exclusively non-heterosexual organizations (e.g. LGBTQIAPK (As well as, by the time the reader is reading this, whatever other acronyms have been tacked on to the end of this ever-growing list of synonyms for sexual depravity)), and exclusively African-American, Arab, Jewish (race), or any other non-Caucasian race based organizations (e.g. National Black Chamber of Congress, Congressional Black Caucus, National Society of Black Engineers, Arab American Action Network, Arab American Association, Israeli-American Council, Anti-Defamation League, World Jewish Congress, etc.).

As a simple thought experiment, imagine how quickly lawsuits would fly were someone to found a National Christians Association, promoting the ideals of and allowing membership to Christians only, a National Heterosexuals Association, promoting heterosexuality and allowing membership to heterosexuals only, a National Men's Association, promoting masculinity and allowing membership to men only, a National Caucasian's Association, promoting the culture of Caucasian races and allowing membership to Caucasians only, or, God forbid, the fusion of these into a National Christian Heterosexual Caucasian Men's Association. Howls of rage would immediately and loudly echo across Western media and academia, while this organization, for doing nothing but existing, would be simultaneously attacked within, and dismantled by, the courts and legislative assemblies, and subsequently banned. Yet these are the exact same things which are not only tolerated, but promoted for any groups who are not part of these. No one blinks an eye, for example, that there is a Black Entertainment Network (BET), but imagine how long a Caucasian Entertainment Network would last before being systematically dismantled. This is all the grossest sort of hypocrisy.

Western Civilization

Post revolution America and France were products of the Enlightenment Period. This period was unique in that it was one of the first times in human history when the common men of a land had grown strong, wise, and virtuous enough to cast off royal rule without replacing that rule with a fresh royalty, declaring famously within the American *Declaration of Independence* that all mankind are of equal worth in the eyes of both God and man, and therefore deserving of certain "inalienable rights, among which are life, liberty, and the pursuit of happiness."[43] The analogous version of this principle which was echoed during the French Revolution was the declaration of "Liberty, Equality, and Fraternity."

Since the days of the Roman emperors, to *be Frank*, or *Frankish* was formerly synonymous with courage and bold directness. This sturdy Germanic nation, who mixed with the Gauls and the Latins to form the modern French people, was, for a time, the flower of the Roman Legions. It was by this people's almost singlehanded strength and courage that the fallen and fragmented Western Roman empire was revived and restored under Charlemagne. A thousand years later, it was also the courageous French nation, who, after being successfully lobbied by Benjamin Franklin, allied herself with the cause of the American colonies against the British Empire. It is directly due to French intervention that the American Revolution had any chance of success at all. The troops, arms, supplies, military leaders, and ships which she sent not only swelled and seasoned the fledgling American armies, but broke the devastating British embargo, and, simultaneously attacking the British across other parts of their sprawling empire, drew off the full force of the British military. Had Britain been allowed to focus its vast resources and efforts exclusively on suppressing the revolution in the American colonies, this revolution would have been hopelessly crushed shortly after it began. Indeed, prior to French intervention, the British had already begun to do just that, with only part of their distracted strength.

After seeing the successful close of the American Revolution, the French soldiery who had fought alongside the American colonists for the causes of freedom from Royal abuses and the creation of a more just and equal society, returned home with these ideas still burning within their hearts. These men, feeling more acutely their own royal fetters, after having helped to break these chains for others in the colonies, and realizing the strength which they could apply if sufficiently united, began to fill their homeland with the bold hope that they too could soon see freedom. This powder keg required only the spark of abuse to soon explode, shaking the brave French titan fully awake from her slumber. This titan then took massive strides across the entirety of Europe and parts of Africa, spreading hope wherever she strode that "liberty, equality, and fraternity" could indeed be realized. Sadly, the flame of this noble cause quickly burned off the loose kindling and leaves before being able to ignite the denser, longer burning fuel beneath. Once it had sputtered out, it left Europe mostly returning to its old kings, or emperors, who survived beneath the blanket of char.

This brave French nation, even after she had fallen, was also the center of the battle against Nazism. The courage of her "French Resistance" insurgents became legendary. Sadly, during the post Nazi social counter-swing, which occurred following the close of World War II, a large amount of academics holding Marxist world views infested many of France's newly vacated academic and governmental positions.

These two symbiotic institutions ideally grow together and nourish each other; governmental men of action attaining aid from, and filling their vacancies with the bright minds of the academic men of theory. The academic men of theory, reciprocally, requiring the protection provided, and funding brought in by the strong arms of governmental men of action.

Once the waters on both sides of this dam had been tainted with Marxist poison, neither was fit to flood, dilute, and sweeten the other. After a simple matter of time, the symptoms of this infection began to appear in the body of the once great French nation. She soon began to abdicate the high egalitarian ideals which so many incredibly brave French patriots had bled or sacrificed their lives for, and European egalitarianism appears to be withering around her; as if only reflections of her rays.

America, however, the last superpower, essentially the daughter of Europe, continues to stand, although falteringly these days, as a symbol to the world of Western egalitarianism. Those who have wittingly, or unwittingly fallen under the control of Marxist, or Islamic philosophical world views, both of which are ultimately totalitarian and therefore directly opposed to the principle of egalitarianism, also hate its symbol: the great American nation.

This new spirit of hatred is pervasive. All things even remotely associated with Western democratic culture are these days loudly derided and condemned by left-heavy media outlets and universities; both manipulating the impressionable youth to be their front-line shock troops. This is the reason why people feigning moral outrage are ever more openly attacking early American and European historical figures, documents, statues, symbols, and the harmless graves of confederate, or revolutionary war heroes. Any of the small minority who are familiar enough with manipulation techniques to recognize both their application and potential for harm in the current scenario, and courageous enough to speak out about it, are generally laughed down, called paranoid, and marginalized by the media, as well as by their less perceptive peers, who tend to simply regurgitate what these media outlets feed them.

As of this writing, the handful of hyper-wealthy international investors who are funding and actively driving this global attack upon Western civilization and democratic principles, feel themselves so empowered, and feel the majority of Western nations to be so hamstrung by bad laws, which politicians, whom they funded, have crippled them with, that they have begun dropping the masks from their movement without fear of reprisal.

But why doesn't this obvious attack upon the principles which the native citizenry of these nations hold dear have the sleeping giant of the moral majority up in arms? Why don't we throw these betrayers of the public trust from their undeserved positions of honor; replacing them with those more loyal to the citizens whom they are supposed to represent? Were it made aware of the trick, the public would surely rush to resist the efforts of any small circle of men who believed themselves to be enlightened and attempted to force a warped value set upon them, which directly opposed their own. The force which the people could bring to bear in such a battle would be overwhelming. Yet rather than defend its own interests, the muscular titan of the people slumbers on.

The reason is because of the subtle and cunning method with which today's manipulation techniques are being implemented. Why openly and manfully expose one's views and challenge the diametrically opposed views of others, when one can instead smile at these people and shower them with insincere platitudes, all the while quietly marketing one's veiled and rebranded values to the intellectually vulnerable within their culture and posturing one's self for economic and political advantage. I have read research where this approach is labeled as a hallmark characteristic of post Marxist theory adherents. Having read Marx, and therefore being familiar with his directness, I find the association of the current technique with his name disingenuous at best. I believe that it should more appropriately be called *Gramscian*, as Antonio Gramsci promoted a far more conniving and manipulative method of communist infiltration and revolution.

Today's cultural phenomenon is nothing more than a clandestine tyranny by a new "nobility" of the economically and politically empowered; who are generally one and the same group. This tyranny is more sinister than previous ones, in that its use of the tools of social engineering to accomplish its ends is far more subtle, making it far more difficult for the common man to identify and resist. It uses a combination of intensive, subtle, and manipulative marketing tactics, as well as armies of well-funded, morally bankrupt attorneys, in order to attack, modify, or replace existing laws, so that the replacement laws can be used as tools, within the courts, to oppress any opponents. Rather than being decided in open, public debate by a comparison of ideas, these battles generally occur in behind the scenes courtroom dramas which the public is seldom allowed to view, influence, or participate in. During these dramas, the attorney, or more commonly, group of attorneys representing the interests of the elite, are flush with experience, education, and resources. The people, on the other hand, if not forced to represent themselves and able to locate an attorney willing to work for the lower pay which they can generally afford, are in either instance at an inherent disadvantage.

The only real hope for the people is that their judges will remain true to the duties of their position and issue rulings which are blind to the status, or resources of those involved. Unfortunately, though many a noble judge has saved the American and European people in countless cases, over countless years, from these attacks against their interests, the cumulative damage caused by those worthless traitors who haven't, has succeeded in tilting the scale ever so slightly, yet still enough.

I really am thankful for those long-forgotten early Americans who strove and bled to provide us with the great nation that it was my privilege to be born into. I remember the brilliant blaze of nobility that my country embodied, when I was young...before the political correctness totalitarians, avaricious businessmen, and treasonous national leaders, hand in hand, drove daggers into her back, as the Roman senators did to Caesar. And as Caesar, while wallowing in his blood, continued to courageously struggle with his attackers, surprised to discover his former friend Brutus among the conspirators, so the American idea wallows in her noble blood, yet bravely continues to struggle, glancing around with surprise at those of her children who have joined in on the matricide. These traitors praise each other for their mutual betrayal; ignobly glutting themselves on all of the spoils which America's honor had naturally attracted to her.

America had problems, as all nations do, but from the time of her inception, was comparatively miles ahead of most other nations; especially after she had washed the stain of slavery from her robes, during the Civil War, with rivers of blood. She stood for good, for justice, for courage, for hope, for opportunity, and for families. With blinding speed, America has been lured away from these high ideals by the small circle of international financiers who pull the strings of politicians, judges, celebrities, and media figures behind the scenes, like puppeteers, until she is now a Mecca for avaricious businessmen knowing no moral restraint. Men who plunder through the courts any who dare to impede their ability to profit from vice.

As a result of the efforts of these parasites, we have become a nation where good people will be fired for saying that they believe homosexuality is immoral. Where they will be fired if they don't cater to the sick whims of the most disgusting perverts in society, by allowing men dressed as women to use our female latrines, regardless of how uncomfortable this makes our daughters, sisters, mothers, grandmothers, and wives. Their offense doesn't matter, only that of the perverts that the corrupt among our leadership have taken under their protective wing. We can be fired for refusing to call these mentally ill people by the pronoun which they decide to apply to themselves, regardless of their true sex, which is scientifically evident in their genetic composition. We can be fired for saying that we aren't supportive of the party line of multiculturalism, instead believing in the strength and goodness of our own national culture, as hundreds of generations have believed before us.

We are being transformed into a nation of sneering, violent liberals who pretend to be victims whenever the cameras are trained upon them, of atheist infested universities, of youth who have been brainwashed by revisionist histories, of murdered babies, of federally enforced unfair hiring and promotion processes (e.g. Affirmative Action), of drunks, and of corrupt judges and politicians who, thanks to their mix of arrogance and ignorance, laughably think themselves wiser than the Constitution's framers. All of the high ideals which America was originally built upon are under outright attack, while those who attack them are increasingly honored, empowered, and enriched. Considering this profit driven betrayal, I cannot help but recall the famous quote by the monstrous Caligula and wish that these corruptors all "had but one neck."[57]

Aware of both the symptoms of this disease and the vectors of national infection, it is somewhat comforting thinking of noble men who experienced a similar national situation and who handled it bravely. Cato and Cicero, both famous Roman politicians, saw the danger which their nation faced, as the increase in national corruption destroyed the ability of the Roman Republic to function. These men attempted to shake their compatriots from the spell which their avarice had cast upon them, realizing that this corruption and the breakdown of the Republic were the driving forces behind Caesar's rise to power. Unfortunately, as comforting as it may be to think that these noblemen faced similarly dire circumstances, it is simultaneously discomforting, as both men were basely killed for their patriotism, and it took their nation several centuries of bloody convulsions before a phoenix was able to arise from the ashes of the Roman Republic.

When discussing this frustration about the current state of Western culture with a friend once, he informed me that he thought that I had what the French call, "Mal de siècle," or in English, "The sickness of the century." This is a phrase which the French use to describe a certain state of ennui, combined with a belief that this feeling wouldn't exist in a former time. Ruminating upon this polite jab for some time, I ultimately determined that, though an otherwise insightful man, my friend had me wrong.

The time period which I find myself in has little to do with the frustrations which I feel over the type, tendency, and volume of cultural maladies which I observe. Is a train passenger, who cannot disembark, to be chided for frustrations which he would likely feel, should he be become aware that the current route, increasing rate of speed, and damaged tracks an uncertain distance ahead are a sure recipe for ruin? It is neither the time, nor the date of the ride that causes this frustration, but rather the familiarity, by prior study, with the route, with the indicators of acceleration, and with the historical details of previous causes of derailment, which does so.

From the windows, the markers where track changes could occur whizz by. Due to the fearful momentum which the rolling leviathan has already achieved, any abrupt change in direction would likely risk derailment as much, or possibly even more than maintaining the current route; however, opportunities for minor, yet realistic changes are passing by in a rapid blur. A thousand of these minor corrections can remedy the thousand miscalculations which have sent Western civilization off-course; ultimately turning this steel monster towards a fair, well charted destination.

One needs only to look at the manuals of both machine and passenger which have been left by many a brilliant philosopher and political theorist. Look! There they lie on a shelf in the corner, unused and gathering dust. This one bears the stamp of Emerson. That one of Plato. Over here is another pile with names like Boethius, Plutarch, Montaigne, Jefferson, Rousseau, and Montesquieu.

As the engine begins to make an ominous shudder, you recall that several of the manuals stated that the engine was not designed to have its controls at the dangerous settings which they are at. Quick! There is no time to be lost! Tell the others! Perhaps together you can free the frozen levers.

Up from the shelf you leap, sending up a cloud of dust as you cram as many of the manuals as you can fit beneath your arm. Like a flash, you dash towards the passengers' car. As you sprint through the engine, you pass a glass wall, behind which stands a small group of well-dressed men. You pause. Behind the men are glowing displays showing the various track switches, knobs to easily control them, along with two large handles labeled "throttle" and "brake."

Wait. These men could fix the problem with ease. But though you scream, flail, and beat on the glass, you cannot seem to get their attention. It soon dawns upon you that the silvery translucence to the glass indicates that it is actually a one-way mirror. Though you can see the men, except when they draw large curtains closed, they cannot see you. As you watch, these men repeatedly draw these curtains just as they begin counting the massive piles of collected fares that continuously pour in from a slot on the far wall. Surely these fees must not have been levied fairly to have accumulated to such excess.

But never mind that now. You beat on the glass, once more, hoping to get their attention. No good. A man in Middle Eastern style clothing merely admires the piles of fares collected in front of him, as another wearing an American business suit massages his feet, anxiously eyes the piles, and appears oblivious of the ludicrous contrast between his attire and his actions. In the background, you notice a great many other men in the room with a European cut to their suits.

Why do many of the fares, especially among the piles surrounding the man in the Middle Eastern attire, have a crimson tinge to them? Is that blood? Some men come forward and bring one of the piles behind a curtain. A few moments later these reappear with the stack of fares cleaned and neatly pressed into bundles. A few of these bundles are passed to the man in the American suit for his degrading services. This man throws all but a single bundle over his shoulders to the men in the European suits. These, almost like bridesmaids, greedily shove and grasp at each other in attempt to position themselves as close as possible for the next anticipated throw.

A dull glint reveals an iron collar around the neck of the man in the American suit. The long chain passing from this collar is held closest by the man in the Middle Eastern attire, but its far end is eagerly grasped by all of the men in the European suits. Looking closer, you notice that these latter also have smaller collars around their necks, whose ends are tied off to the chair of the man with the Middle Eastern attire, but they don't seem to notice.

Enough with these who only view the world through the warped images of their wall mounted displays, when they care to look up from the fares. To the fellow passengers were there is hope of being heard! You resume your career into the first passenger car, flinging open the door to have your ears met by the blare of dozens of televisions announcing the scores of the latest game. Your nose is simultaneously hit by the distinct smell of alcohol. The passengers cast dirty looks at you for momentarily startling them from their screens and beer. An explosion sounds from the back of the car, followed by a chorus of gleeful laughter and some profanity. From the bright glow, it becomes clear that the black things crowded around what appears to be a massive display are the silhouettes of dozens of people, both children and adults, rapidly pressing the buttons on game controllers.

The crowd seems to be constantly migrating between the sport watcher and the game watcher groups, a constant stream also being seen entering and exiting the far door to the other cars. A sign above this door brightly displays the words "Dining Cars" and "Sleep Cars."

You hurl your pile of manuals and maps onto the nearest counter and loudly call all to look at what you have found. More dirty looks.

"Read them yourself!" someone yells from the obscured crowd of gamers.

Members of the sports group roll their eyes, as several crack open their next beer. The scent of marijuana drifts over from the gamer crowd, momentarily overpowering the smell of alcohol.

You pause dumbfounded. Regathering yourself, you point out the famous names of the manual and map writers. For centuries, people have respected these men for their wisdom.

"Merely look!" you cry. "These men say that we are in danger, and they clearly know what they are talking about!"

More blank stares. It then hits you. Your efforts and training have made the highly technical wording of these manuals and maps understandable to you, but though precisely written, they remain a cypher to the majority of this crowd.

Your heart sinks. Even were you to succeed in getting the attention of a few of them, the two classes most prone to look would be those unable to understand much of what they were looking at, and those who actively disagree with you and who would only skim the text in search of a lampoonable point which might be taken out of context.

This is the feeling of frustration that my friend mistakes for a longing to live in another era. Then again, perhaps he is in part correct, as there have been eras when the control room wasn't soundproof, when it was only driven by our own national leaders, when it wasn't full of stained money and the disgraceful acts performed to get at it, and when the passenger cars rustled to the pleasant din of conversation and the rustle of pages being turned. But I am not blind to the fact that those times had their own problems and flaws as well, from slavery to cholera. Now is our time and we must make the most of it for the sake of our children.

Power Sieves

Many years ago, as a young Ph.D. student, I noticed that today's academic community had become far more dogmatic in their stances regarding metaphysical views than they formerly were in the late 19th and even the early 20th centuries. Though academia likes to portray itself to outsiders as being a system where naught but purely objective and empirical exam scores are the supposed determinants of any aspiring and diligent student ultimately being crowned with a terminal degree, professorship, and tenure, this is far from the rule. Aspiring scholars are initially filtered by collegiate admissions boards based upon many nonacademic factors, such as their looks, age, race, wealth, connections, home nation, state, or region, athletic accomplishments, and especially personal involvement and familiarity with admissions board members or their colleagues.

This filtering based upon nonacademic factors is the dirty secret of academia, which is seldom spoken of, but well known to all involved with the process. It explains why sports stars with merely average academic records are often accepted to prestigious universities; the latter of whom see them as advertising cash cows for their sports programs.

Anyone in doubt about the priorities of many of these schools' need simply visit a nearby major university and compare its often massive, glimmering sports complexes and training facilities, with its often humble teaching ones. This disparity sends the message to both the teacher and student bodies that academics are less important than athletics. This message is most unfortunate, in that it encourages many of the students who observe it to adopt similar views. Such students, upon graduation, go on to become the future corporate, political, and academic leaders of the nation. This means that their warped over-valuation and emulation of the athlete, and devaluation of true scholarship, becomes increasingly normalized within society. This process of cultural erosion, via stupefaction, feeds upon itself.

The fact that we have already been on this path, as a nation, for some time can be seen by comparing the multimillion-dollar contracts signed by many professional athletes, with the infamously low salaries of teachers; major university professors excepted. These teachers are often forced into the humiliating position of having to creatively solicit funds from the community for much needed supplies.

The aforementioned biased filtering by nonacademic factors occurs again upon a student's application to graduate school, upon their matching with a professor as their graduate advisor, upon their subsequent application to a Ph.D. program, again upon matching with a professor who serves as both their mentor and advisor during this process, upon their application to a postdoctoral position within the university, upon their application for hire as an associate, or assistant professor, upon their application for tenure, and finally upon their application for full professorship.

This is effectively a series of academic sieves, which, at each step, increase the probability of a certain specific type of individual succeeding, while decreasing the probability of success of all others. It allows the small body of full professors within the smaller number of prestigious universities, which the less prestigious emulate, to strongly influence the very nature of the society which we live in. They accomplish this by serving as the gatekeepers of access to virtually all significant leadership positions, the majority of which generally require advanced degrees. Those allowed passage through these gates are carefully groomed and filtered from among their peers to ensure that their views are as similar as possible to those of the gatekeepers. How different is this from the promotion of priests within the Catholic Church?

While one might argue that the body of professors are challenged in knowing the personal views of an aspiring student, this statement is generally only true during undergraduate studies. Even during this undergraduate period, the volume of time that professors spend with the same group of students often allows them to identify their favorites, whom they often provide with additional assistance and subsequent recommendation letters. During graduate studies, this mass of students has been reduced by several orders of magnitude, to only a handful, which the professors often work very closely with on research projects.

In addition, during graduate work, the student will notice that the vast majority of their testing and assignments transition from quantitative ones, where there is a discrete, unknown answer to be determined, to essay based ones, where there is no specific right answer. Students may provide elaborate treatises defending their positions, and yet the professor may, and often does, still deduct points from, or even give failing grades to students, merely because he, or she disagrees with the final conclusion which they arrived at.

I speak from firsthand experience here, remembering the acute frustration felt whenever this would occur. I also remember noticing how the easily identifiable favorites of certain professors would be provided with extra opportunities to learn, further increasing their already substantial advantage. Is this nothing more than a pure aristocracy? Given the influence that the wealthy have upon academic institutions, which require large budgets to operate and are therefore ever eager for research and building grants, doesn't this aristocracy ultimately give way to, and serve as the partner of the ruling plutocracy?

Is this truth not becoming more evident every day, as we notice relatives of wealthy elected officials, in an ultimately not so odd coincidence, receiving advanced degrees from prestigious universities which virtually ensure their future success? Were there truly no relation between wealth and success, whether political, academic, or corporate, and all was due to the effort and determination of the individual, we would rarely observe this common trend. Indeed, we would likely observe the very opposite, as few facts are better established than that of the diligence sapping, corrupting effect of wealth upon youth who know they are bound to inherit it, regardless of their actions. Has this not been observed since antiquity in a thousand documented accounts, from Nero, to the Biblical Prodigal Son (Luke 15:11-32)?

Contrarily, is it not also well known that, unless they follow in the same, often alcohol-soaked footsteps which their parents descended by, few struggle more diligently to free themselves from the fetters of poverty than the youth born into, and brought up within its perpetual tragedies. Were the system of success completely fair and uninfluenced by wealth, we would generally expect to observe a perpetual mixing of the classes: wealthy, complacent youth squandering their possessions and descending back into the middle class, and poor, diligent youth ascending from their squalid pits to enjoy its pleasures.

Yet, while this natural process sometimes occurs, the wealthy, who are more empowered to influence the system, whether directly or indirectly, via local, state, or national political offices, do whatever they can to prevent this from occurring. This is generally accomplished through legal safeguards which ensure their economic advantage, while simultaneously increasing their protection from negative consequences which might result from their actions. Unfortunately, economic advantage and consequence protection are both zero sum games. In order to ensure advantage to one group, disadvantage must be ensured to all others. In order to ensure increased consequence protection for one group, decreased consequence protection must be ensured for all others. While some wealthy realize this truth, others do not, and myopically believe that there is "such thing as a free lunch."

Unfortunately, much like a hydra, for every law which governments implement, whose objective is to increase economic opportunity for the common mass of people, there are generally a dozen ways which the wealthy have found to circumvent it. There are infinite examples of this which could be brought to light. Within the real estate market, for example, all well know that foreclosures are generally opportunities to acquire a valuable home at a discounted price. Local and federal governments are aware of this as well and therefore implement laws to ensure an equal opportunity to all for this potential benefit. Yet wealthy bankers, realtors, insurers, builders, and attorneys, who often form a small monopoly of the market in their area, ensure that only those few homes which they don't see much profit in ever make it into the hands of the public.

The bankers and attorneys are the first who capitalize upon this opportunity, as they are the ones responsible for overseeing how the property is sold. Very often they, or the friends whom they privately inform of the opportunity, purchase these homes outright, never intending to live in them. They then sometimes pay for minor repairs, but either way, resell at a significantly higher price, keeping the difference as profit. When laws force them to auction the home, or prevent them from purchasing it themselves, they often get around this by leaking information to their wealthy friends, family, and colleagues on the "sealed bids" which are received during the auction. This ensures that any potential discount is only realized by those within their personal circle, the benefit of which is often reciprocated back upon them in some other manner. Many times this occurs between banks and attorneys, realtors, or builders, who, for the benefit received, pass business back to them in the form of strong recommendations to clients. Other times, banks and attorneys open and close the auction as rapidly, with as inconvenient timing, and with as limited advertisement as legally possible, to ensure they, or those within their circle, have a distinct advantage over the bidding public.

There are a thousand points in this system where the wealthy can, and generally do, abuse justice to ensure that they maintain advantage. Another example lies in the fact that zoning boards and city councils often are populated by wealthy area business and property owners who ensure that they, or their close acquaintances, position themselves to profit upon any upcoming changes. They do this by buying up low cost properties in an area which they know the change will benefit, or by selling off high cost properties in areas which they know the change will harm. Long before the public is made aware of these opportunities, these leaders, who were appointed to these key political positions to oversee the good of the community, have seen to their, or their inner circle's good instead.

I know several small business owners who hotly argue against their being any impropriety to excessive wealth, and who feel that anyone can become wealthy if they work hard enough. When pressed, these people ultimately confess that they believe the wealthy the most diligent, and therefore the most deserving of any amount of income which they receive. Likewise, they believe that the poor, with few exceptions, are the laziest, and therefore are deserving of their state of poverty. I am uncertain if people with this viewpoint tend to start businesses, or if owning a business which begins to prosper, and subsequently dreaming of spending the millions which might result from it one day, makes them think such callous and narrow thoughts. I believe the latter to be most likely. I say this because I have known the kindest hearted of men, who have been in business for a few years, later make these staggeringly blind statements.

I mentioned this point because it seems that, once aspiring small business owners adopt these views, the wealthy aristocracy, who enjoy seeing their own entitled views infected and reflected in these small businessmen, happily offer what advice, or business intelligence and connections they can to assist them. Why not? These are but neophytes to the God and religion of *capital,* of which they are priests.

The wealthy aristocracy are willing to do so because such things cost them nothing. Knowing that these aspiring businessmen share their views that the wealthy are deserving of their wealth, no matter how superfluous it may be, they see them as a safe ally. This has the effect of adding to the aspiring businessman's views the thought that not only are the wealthy the most diligent and deserving of men, but they are also generally the most kind. This is ironic, as the very definition of hard heartedness is the closing of one's ears and eyes to the plight of those in need of assistance, whom one is empowered to help. This must be done to an extent proportional to the amount of wealth possessed. There is no way around it.

I am often told of millionaires who pay a large portion of taxes and who give a large amount to the needy, compared to what the average man gives. I am told of how this makes these millionaires both noble and moral; yet there is an almost infinite supply of needy who will never receive this charity, which is often only a small amount, once divided among the ones who do receive a portion of it. This means that, in order to remain wealthy, and not descend to the teeming, struggling, yet truly noble middle class, at some point these millionaires must say to themselves, "Those whom I have helped, I have helped. I know that there are more who need help, but I am not going to concern myself with them. I have helped more people than most people do, and it is more important to me that I not descent to the middle class, than that I help any more up from the depths of poverty." They then go to sleep, consoling their consciences, with millions, or billions in their bank accounts, ignoring the fact that someone a mile or two away is still up agonizing over how they are going to put gas in their car, feed their children, or pay their rent. I call this the myth of the moral millionaire.

I say be bold and descend to the middle class. On the way down, help as many people as you can up from poverty. Only stop giving when just slightly above the point where you are risking your family no longer being able to live in a safe neighborhood, with full bellies, clean clothes, and warm beds. When I say this, I am often told that, living in America, I am wealthy compared to people in rural India. I am therefore hypocrite for not giving away what I have and descending to their economic level. This is a flawed argument which is ludicrous, when followed to its ultimate conclusion.

Firstly, while I do live in a nice part of America, I would not have to give away very much before I would be risking having to move my family into an unsafe neighborhood. My bank owns the vast majority of my house, making me little better than a renter. All I would need would be a few costly vehicle repairs and my buffer savings could be strained.

This is not really the point though. The fact is that my net wealth is not superfluous. There is a certain point where it becomes so. This is a point that all middle class and poor instinctively know is far in the rearview mirror, when one exceeds a million in savings. It seems that the only ones who grow confused about what superfluous wealth is, and indeed, if it even exists, are those who possess, or envision themselves possessing it.

As far as the comparison with rural Indians goes, there is only one end to this argument. Let's say I was to divest myself of possessions until on par with an average rural Indian. I could still be called a hypocrite for critiquing the wealthy, by this logic, because I had clothes, which some poor Haitian child didn't. I am therefore still rich compared to him. Yet even if I gave away my clothes, reached that level of poverty, and then critiqued millionaires, I could still be called a hypocrite, since there were people elsewhere who were both naked and starving. On and on this argument could go, until we finally reached the single, most miserable wretch (barely) alive on the planet. Per this logic, only this one person has any rights to critique the wealth of millionaires and billionaires; accusing them of an amount of hard heartedness inseparable from, and in proportion to their wealth.

This is all nonsense. All mankind knows that, based upon the environment that one lives in, there is what is considered normal, and there is what is considered excess. Even the wealthy know this and attempt to establish a new normal by congregating among other wealthy within gated enclaves which bar out all middle class and poor. This is not what is meant by the environment one lives in. By this I mean what is needed to ensure a safe environment, based upon the consideration of normal by the middle class in the nation, state, or city that one lives in.

Communism and Capitalism

The virtuous are the only genuine lovers and stalwart defenders of equality. As they love justice, so they love this, her natural offspring, "with whom [she is] well pleased" (Matthew 3:17) and always consults in her rulings. The morally corrupt, whose atheist worldview converts all justice, all virtue, and all goodness, into arbitrary, nebulous, and often conflicting opinion, see even less significance (were less than none possible) in something which one of these virtues is said to both produce and direct itself towards.

But are more of these virtuous equality lovers to be found among the wealthy, or among the poor? Preliminarily assuming the ratios of the virtuous and the corrupt to be the same within both groups, a far greater count of equality lovers will inevitably be found among the poor, due simply to the fact that the poor always greatly outnumber the wealthy. This unavoidable minority of the wealthy results from the zero-sum nature of wealth. The less the poor outnumber the wealthy, the less wealthy the wealthy will be, the less poor the poor will be, or both. Contrarily, the more the poor outnumber the wealthy, the wealthier the wealthy will be, the poorer the poor will be, or both.

Consider the example of an orange tree. There are only so many oranges on the tree which can be plucked and squeezed to produce juice. If you pluck and press every one of them, then you may possess a large volume of juice, but there will be no remaining oranges on the tree. The tree retains the ability to regrow oranges to replenish those which were removed, but this is a tremendously slow process, which those who are currently thirsty do not wish to wait for.

The oranges symbolize the raw natural materials which the Earth possesses. The juice symbolizes these materials after they have been refined into useable products, from bullion, to dollars, to steel, to stock, to food, to houses, to cars, to everything else. There are a finite amount of these finished products which are available to be had. The Earth possesses the ability to recreate some of its raw materials, as the orange tree can re-grow oranges: animals can breed, plants can germinate and grow, organic material in the soil can rot and turn into crude oil, magma infusions can cool, leaving diamond and gold deposits, but all of these processes are generally far slower and therefore less realistic to supply the needs of a world whose rocketing population has made it dependent upon the collection and consumption of resources at high rates and volumes.

Now imagine a room full of 100 thirsty people, all eying a large table filled with 100 cups of this freshly squeezed orange juice. Obviously, there are thousands of possible permutations which can be imagined for how the cups in this scenario could be distributed, but 6 key example scenarios will be examined, in order to clarify how a nation's resources can be distributed.

In the first scenario, all is given to one and none is given to the rest (e.g. 100 cups to one, 0 cups to 99). Despite the superficial appeal of this scenario to tyrants, were it to come to fruition, even they would not desire it. In this scenario, the rest of the world would die, leaving no one to labor for this new global emperor. This man would soon discover that, with the loss of his citizenry, his power and position had suddenly become worthless. He would languish in this condition, like a castaway on a global deserted island.

In the second scenario, overmuch is given to a few and none is given to the rest (e.g. 10 cups to 10, 0 cups to 90). This is the poorly thought out dream of the plutocrats. These men would be tyrants if they could, but finding themselves too weak to overcome their circle of peers, they conspire with them to jointly consume the world. Yet, as with the tyrant, were this scenario to occur, even these "elites" would not desire it. Left in a world of only their peers, a nation of kings with no subjects, they would suddenly find themselves honored, respected, and obeyed by none. In order to have the things which they desire, they would be forced to perform all of the labor which they previously paid others to perform for them. They would be forced to remove their own waste, design and fabricate their own car, shoes, and clothes, cut their own hair, prepare their own meals, etc.

In the third scenario, overmuch is given to a few and little is given to the rest (e.g. 2 cups to 20 people, 1/2 a cup to 80). Here we finally enter the realm of possibility. This is the situation we find in most of the social structures of the world which civilized men condemn as being grossly unjust: those who have a ruling class and a servant one; a nobility and a peasantry; a bourgeoisie and a proletariat.

This form of social structure is especially commonplace in the Middle East. Indeed, it is the natural product of Islamic dominated governments, which have spread like tumors throughout Asia and Africa and are today metastasizing from these parts into Europe and America. This is because the Koran, which Muslims mistakenly believe to be flawless and divine, claims that the entire world is comprised of two classes: the non-Islamic world (Dar-al Harb), which God (Allah), and therefore Muslims, hate, and the Islamic world (Dar-al Islam), which God supposedly loves.

Muslims believe that if non-Muslims have wealth and possessions, they only hold these in trust for Muslims; that non-Muslims have no inherent rights to property, freedom, and especially not equality. Are these views not in complete opposition to the Western principles of "Liberty, equality, and fraternity," or of "Life, liberty, and the pursuit of happiness," which made the West both great and greatly loved and respected? Sadly, though the Western world sacrificed countless of her sons attempting to throw off this unjust, royalist social structure during the English Civil War and American and French Revolutions, it has become evident that this hydra was not quite dead, as initially believed. It has been nourished back to health by its interested Eastern neighbors, and with renewed vigor is today springing dozens of new heads in the West.

Christianity teaches men to shift their desire for luxury to the future plane. Buddhism attempts to have men perform the impossible and destroy desire altogether. Platonism teaches men to regulate this desire on any plane. Islam and Judaism consecrate and encourage the desire for luxury on all planes, and promise the world as prey in this one. This is one of the main reasons, besides its innate violence, why Islam tends to appeal to the poor. As Mohammed rightly determined, Islam is a reformation of Judaism, which, in its original form, held these same materialist views, and still preserves watered down versions of them in its sacred writings today.

In the fourth scenario, overmuch is given to a few, a reasonable amount is given to some, and little is given to the rest (e.g. 4 cups to 10, 1 cup to 30, 1/2 a cup to 60). Here we see the emergence of the middle class, in this second, very possible form of social structure. Though this arrangement preserves inequality, and therefore injustice on both the upper and lower ends of society, the central pivot of the middle class remains at, or near a just level.

In the fifth scenario, overmuch is given to a few, a lesser superfluity is given to some, a reasonable amount is given to some, little is given to some, and none is given to the rest (e.g. 10 cups to 2, 5 cups to 8, 1 cup to 20, 1/2 a cup to 40, 0 cups to 30). Welcome to the social structure of most of the Western world. This social structure is little different, in principle, from the previous one. The scale of equality remains at the same pitch, the beam is just extended on both ends of the fulcrum, making the one end more luxurious and the other more abjectly poor.

Our cup example actually grossly underrepresents how far askew the scale of equality generally is within these nations. In America, for example, ~99% of all wealth is in the possession of ~1% of the population. This is the same group which fights against laws to raise the minimum wage. The group which refuses to cut into their 7-10 figure salaries, should these laws pass, and instead passes the increased cost of the product or service on to the consumers, many of whom are among the same minimum wage group which the laws were attempting to aid. The group which then blames and condemns the minimum wage workers for this cost increase, as being greedy and lazy: workers who gained a mere few dollars more an hour and who can secure no better job than these entry level ones, or else they would.

In the sixth and final scenario, all is equally distributed to all (e.g. 1 cup to each of the 100 people). This is the globalized middle class. This mutual ownership of all was the supposed state of the early Christian church, as described in the book of Acts, of the communes of Essene Jews, of the monasteries and cloisters of monks and nuns, and that of many of the medieval military orders. This is the communist "utopia," though the atheism which has infected communist philosophy since its inception always causes communists to employ brutal and unjust means in their attempts to achieve it. Could such as social structure ever realistically be not only attained, but sustained?

The value and undefinable reservoir of labor seem to convolute the issue. We know that men are often happy to exchange an equivalent value of goods for an equivalent value of labor, so societies will need to develop a standard and system of valuation for both. But if I need some milk for my children's breakfast, are my only options to exchange labor for it, perhaps shoveling the snow from the sidewalk outside the store, or to barter for it, perhaps bringing the eggs from my chickens? If I don't have the time to labor, only have eggs to exchange, and the store already has too many eggs and doesn't want them, what then? If only there was some sort of universal symbol of fixed value which everything, both labor and assets, could be traded for. Enter currency.

With currency we can have the same fair distribution of value, even though it may not always appear to be so to uninformed external observers. One man may have more currency because he performed more labor, which he exchanged for it. One man may have converted his currency into consumable assets, which he used up, or wasted, and then lazily refused to exchange his labor for more. Even though we initially started our attempt at creating a just society with an equal distribution of assets, this equality lasted but for a moment before all became unequal once more.

What should we do about this new situation? Obviously, it would be an injustice to take the extra assets from the man who traded his labor for them and give them to the man who refused to. Such injustices are the very thing which we are attempting to prevent. Should we just attempt to circumvent this entire situation by refusing to allow people to freely exchange their labor for currency? This is the solution which the communists mistakenly thought would work. The simple fact which they surprisingly missed was that we would also have to prohibit them from exchanging it for other assets, or for labor as well.

How could we ever enforce this, as prisons prove that anything, even cigarettes, can become a form of currency. We would have to call the police on any kids who offered their friend a dollar for a piece of candy (currency for asset), who offered a piece of candy for a dollar (asset for currency), who traded a piece of blue candy for a red one (asset for asset), who offerd a piece of candy to their friend, if he will pull the sled (asset for labor), who offered to pull the sled for a piece of candy (labor for asset), who offered a dollar to their friend if he will pull the sled (currency for labor), who offered to pull the sled for a dollar (labor for currency), or who pulled the sled this time because their friend pulled it last time (i.e. labor for labor). This is obviously an impossibility.

So where does this leave us. We have shown that even after an initial leveling of the resource playing field, it will immediately begin to become imbalanced once more. But we should keep our eye on our goal here. Our intent is to create a just social structure. While it is just for the initial distribution of assets to be done evenly, it is also just to allow those who wish to work a little harder to exchange this extra labor for extra currency, labor, or assets. In the same manner, it is also just to allow the wasteful, or lazy man to become poor. Here we discover that a just society can have individuals possessing differing amounts of wealth.

Does this mean that, in avoiding the ditch of error of the communists and rigid socialists, who believe that within a just society no one should have more currency, assets, or labor than anyone else, we should run headlong into the ditch on the opposite side of the street, where the rigid capitalists sit calling out that all of the wealthy are deserving of every cent of their wealth, regardless of how fantastically superfluous it may be. These capitalists hold this view for two possible reasons. Either they believe that the current distribution of wealth is entirely just, and therefore inflexibly and inseparably connected, as if by an iron bar, to levels of effort (i.e. labor) and thrift, or they admit that the current distribution is not entirely just, but believe that any attempts aimed towards correcting these injustices would only result in greater levels of injustice.

Let's consider the former view first. In order for one to believe that all wealth is inflexibly and inseparably linked to effort and thrift, one must also believe that the wealthy, without exception and in proportion to their level of wealth, have worked more strenuously, persistently, intelligently, or creatively, have been more courageously willing to take needed risks, intelligently able to discern and avoid hazards, selflessly willing to make needed sacrifices, wisely frugal, or a combination of these, than those who are less wealthy than them. In addition, if this iron bar binds wealth to effort and thrift at the top of the economic food chain, then it must also bind poverty to lack of effort and wastefulness at its bottom. The poor must, without exception and in proportion to their level of poverty, have worked less strenuously, persistently, intelligently, or creatively, have been less courageously willing to take needed risks, intelligently able to discern and avoid hazards, selflessly willing to make needed sacrifices, wisely frugal, or a combination of these, than those who are wealthier than them.

These views on the nature of wealth and poverty are the very definition of entitlement, and unfortunately, tend to infect people in proportion to their level of personal wealth. Even among children, have we not all observed how there is a tendency towards generosity among the average and poor, as well as a tendency towards selfishness among the wealthy. Of course, this is not the case with all wealthy children. Those whose parents wisely limit the satisfaction of their child's demands to be in keeping with the average level of other children in their region, in spite of their level of wealth, force them to live as if not wealthy, reducing the risk of their being infected by entitlement. The disease of entitlement generally tends to occur among those children who have grown accustomed to receiving whatever they demand, as also occurs with their wealthy adult analogs. We call these children, whose character has become infected and corrupted by entitlement, "spoiled." Perhaps those adults who suffer from the same disease of character should fitly be called "spoiled" as well.

This dynamic is beautifully captured in the personal characters and interactions between the poorer Ingalls children and the affluent Olson children in the wonderfully wholesome, family-friendly, and educational *Little House on the Prairie* television series which aired between 1974 and 1982, as well as in the semi-factual *Little House* book series of the same name which inspired these, written by Laura Ingalls Wilder.[58, 59] These books described Laura's youth in the American Midwest of the 1870's-1880's. Though the television series was only loosely based upon fact, why was it so warmly and widely received by the public, if not because it echoed several truths which people instinctively recognized within.

This tendency for a decreased sense of entitlement among the middle class and poor is a major contributor to the frequently observed higher levels of tipping, charity, and humanitarian work among them, as well as the lower frequency of these among the wealthy; unless done to gain some material, or immaterial advantage (e.g. increased tax write-offs, social prestige, fame, or business opportunities). Though the wealthy may make occasional visits to soup kitchens, homeless shelters, and prisons, typically for photo opportunities, it is virtually always the middle class and the poor themselves who perform the day-to-day heavy lifting required to keep such places and projects functioning, without anyone hoping to capture a photo of them doing so.

Don't wealthy and entitled individuals realize that not everyone who is impoverished is in this position because they were either lazy or wasteful? Doesn't life at times provide some individuals with difficult scenarios which are no fault of their own? Perhaps they, or their loved ones were born with, contracted, or received a disability, disease, or injury which consumed their time, or ability to work, and/or saddled them with crushing medical debt. Perhaps the company which they were working for closed, or fired them during a mass layoff, and they were unable to secure another job. Perhaps they were simply born into an already impoverished family and sacrificed personal opportunities in order to assist them.

On the opposite side of this coin, what type of cognitive dissonance allows the entitled to believe that there is always a linear proportionality between the amount of wealth which a person possesses and the amount, or quality of labor which they have invested? Does everyone, everywhere, and at all times receive the exact same level of opportunity from birth? Were some not born with specific physical, or mental traits which provided them with unique social advantages? Do some not hold specific religious, political, or philosophical beliefs which provide them with access to larger, or more influential social, or organizational networks than others? How many times do we hear the refrain that someone "knew a guy" who helped them get hired into a position? Do some not acquire wealth unethically? Are some not simply in the right place at the right time for them to take advantage of rare opportunities, like getting "tipped off" on, or "hooked up" with critical investment deals? Were some not simply born into already wealthy families?

Of course, all of these scenarios occur. Wealth is not inflexibly and inseparably linked to effort and thrift, nor is poverty inflexibly and inseparably linked to lack of effort and wastefulness. Though capitalists are correct to have noticed a frequent correlation between these things, these connections are more tendencies than laws. Sometimes the hardest working, kindest hearted, and most self-denying people are rewarded not with wealth, but with abject poverty, humiliating slander, or even death.

Consider Jesus, who was rewarded for his wise teachings, mercy, and charity by being crucified without a "widow's mite" to his name. Consider Hypatia, who was rewarded for out-studying and out-teaching her peers by having her skin scraped off by a mob.[60] Consider Aesop, who was rewarded for his philosophical work for children, a work which we still benefit from today, by being flung from a cliff.[61] Consider Seneca, whom Tacitus states was rewarded for his courageous efforts to preserve honor and wisdom within Roman society, by being forced to slice his wrists, and then being suffocated by steam from an overheated sauna.[62] Consider Boetheus, who was rewarded for his attempts to ensure the safety of the Senate by having his head crushed in a tourniquet.[63] Consider Socrates, who was rewarded for his profound teachings, which have shaken the world for over 2,400 years, by being imprisoned and poisoned.[64] Consider Orpheus, who was rewarded for his philosophical teachings by being torn into pieces by a mob of women.[65] Consider Pythagoras, who was rewarded for his pioneering efforts in science and philosophy by being burned, or hacked to death.[66] Consider Galileo, who was rewarded for his diligent and pioneering scientific work by being placed under house arrest until his death.[67] Consider Giordano Bruno, who was rewarded for philosophically and scientifically outpacing his peers by being burned at the stake.[68] Consider Thomas Paine, who was rewarded for authoring works which contributed, in America, to revolutions of both politics and thought, by being imprisoned and abandoned.[69, 70] Consider William Penn, who was rewarded for authoring a pamphlet encouraging religious reform by being imprisoned in the tower of London.[71] Consider William Whiston, who was rewarded for attempting to reform Christianity by being humiliatingly expelled from Oxford.[72] Consider Michael Servetus, who was rewarded for publishing a book which pointed out the errors of Trinitarianism by being burned at the stake.[73] The list goes on and on.

On the other hand, sometimes corrupt, lazy, and wasteful people are rewarded with fame and fabulous wealth. Consider the first black American president, Obama, who fettered the American people with a record 8+ trillion dollars of additional debt, more than doubling the national deficit during his ruinous time in office. This man rode off into the sunset to live out his days with home, salary, and security detail all funded by the taxpayers whom he impoverished. Yet in spite of his proven incompetence, he is still celebrated by his party to this day, solely due to the warped, corrupt, and corrupting ethics which he forced upon the American people, like a tyrant.

Consider the many Saudi "princes." As an aside, the use of this title is inappropriate, since there is nothing noble about being a leader of an ignoble nation: a nation which, under its brutish, Sharia inspired laws, mandates cruel tortures, and even death for such petty offences as merely disagreeing with, or leaving Islam. These "princes" go to sleep and then awaken to find fresh millions in their accounts the next morning, not for any labor which they performed in their dreams, but because they happened to be born into a certain family.

Consider the gay Colorado and Oregon couples who sued mom-and-pop Christian bakeries, Sweet Cakes & Masterpiece Bakery for refusing to bake them wedding cakes, as well as the ACLU lawyers, who, like hitmen with dollar signs in their eyes and corruption in their hearts, were happy to take their case. These grew wealthy not for any diligent, just, or noble efforts on their part, but as the result of theft from good people, which was aided and abetted by incompetent and immoral, activist judges. The people whom they publicly, and humiliatingly robbed were not committing Jihad, but were simply attempting to be left alone to follow the guidance of their own consciences, while innocently baking cakes for weddings. Weddings: events which all but the most stupid know, including these worthless judges, plaintiffs, and their attorneys, are for many, deeply bound up with religion. Were these bakers plotting Jihad, perhaps covering a bomb with vanilla frosting, they likely would have been treated better by the courts, the media, and the vicious gay community, from whom they received literal death threats.

The corrupt judges in one of these instances ruled that, for the laughably petty offense of licentious degenerates being slightly embarrassed by bakers declining to bake them a cake, the appropriate restorative weight on the opposite scale of justice was hundreds of thousands of dollars, as well as, de facto, the very dignity of the bakers. Though interested parties, these judges, and even the entire world may deny it, what happened in this instance was not justice, but greater injustice. The offense was claimed to be soul-crushing, by the plaintiffs, as it always is by liars seeking money through the courts; but give the world a break. There are people experiencing truly soul-crushing tragedy, orphaned children attempting not to starve while rooting for food in Indian, Filipino, and Chinese garbage dumps, young girls prostituted, molested, or abused by relatives, mothers in Africa tearfully holding children whom they inadvertently passed AIDS to, as well as 10's of millions who remain enslaved. If something as petty as being denied a cake "crushes" you, no one needs to be marrying you in your deranged state anyway. Your cake money would be better spent on a mental health professional.

In the end, it took a long-delayed ruling by the US Supreme Court to finally overturn this injustice, but it is telling how there was comparatively little media coverage of this correction. Much damage to American society had already been done by this point, as other organizations adjusted their policies to appease these bullies, in order to avoid similar lawsuits. Very few of them are likely to return these policies to their original state.

There are dozens of instances like these where the possession, or acquisition of wealth is completely disconnected from labor and frugality, and where poverty is completely disconnected from laziness and wastefulness. While some people are entitled to an extra portion of currency, or assets, due to the extra quantity, or quality of their labor, there is a vast portion of wealth which many possess which was not acquired this way. Many people receive their first upwardly mobile white-collar careers due to the intervention and influence of friends, or parents. Perhaps their father, or a kid they played football with, put in "a good word" for them at their company. These white-collar workers continue to grow in position and salary, often convincing themselves that they were somehow more clever, diligent, or talented than these others, and are therefore merely getting what they deserve.

But what of the kids who never met their father, or whose parents were unable to afford the time, or money required for them to play sports? Kids who don't have this advantage, perhaps whose dads abandoned their mothers before they were born, often end up in dead-end blue-collar, service, or retail jobs. Is it their fault that they don't have these advantages? Is it just for the youth with wealth, or connections to be more highly compensated than the one who does not have these, yet who works just as hard; perhaps even harder?

The common reply is that, if he doesn't have these advantages, he can get ahead by going to college. Sure. How is he supposed to afford this, given the rocketing tuitions that universities require these days?

I must digress for a moment here to point out that these rocketing tuitions are primarily required to fund universities' palace-like sports complexes, often to the neglect of true academic departments, to maintain their sprawling, parklike grounds, and to build and maintain their massive, luxurious buildings, which sit vacant much of the time. Each of these ornate, cathedral-like buildings equate to thousands of dollars in federal subsidies, which require additional taxes from all of us, thousands of student loans, hundreds of thousands of dollars paid in interest over the lives of these loans to hand-wringing lenders. Simple rooms, diligent professors, and good books are all that are really required for the vast majority of a solid college education, and these things are relatively inexpensive, when their costs are divided among the student body.

Certainly, specialized labs are required as well, however, even these things are relatively inexpensive, when amortized over their useful life and their costs divided only among those who require them. Why should Business majors have to pay for the computers that the Computer Science majors need? Why should English majors have to pay for equipment that the Biology majors need? Were colleges run a la carte like this, everyone might be surprised at how economical a college education can actually be.

What is actually occurring is that universities are forcing their student bodies to pay for salaries, equipment, and facilities which professors want, in order to conduct their research. Students shouldn't be forced to pay for these research tools, when only a handful even care about this research, virtually none receive any personal benefit from it, and virtually all would decline to support it, if doing so would significantly reduce their tuition; which it absolutely would. Universities know that degrees are required for the vast majority of desired jobs, making them effectively the gatekeepers of future economic success. They therefore unnecessarily force a large portion of their student bodies into debt, due to their extravagant tuitions, in order for these youth to ransom their futures from them.

Returning from our digression, is our disadvantaged youth expected to essentially gamble regarding his future income by burying himself beneath hopeless amounts of student loans, a decision he is asked to make when not yet considered mature enough to even purchase a beer? Perhaps he could study harder and get scholarships? While this is a wonderful option which should be pursued by all students, it is naïve to think that wealth has no influence upon its feasibility.

The poorer schools, which are commonly found in either inner cities, or highly rural areas, almost always have higher student to teacher ratios, lessening the time which each teacher has available for each individual student, and therefore, inevitably reducing the average academic scores of the class. Also, teachers must teach to the average intelligence of their classes. Schools in less affluent urban areas are famous for having a greater number of "problem students" who singlehandedly and substantially reduce this average. A comparison of numbers of disciplinary actions per month between less wealthy inner-city schools and more affluent suburban ones, if schools can be forced to admit these numbers, will quickly prove this point.

Attending both types of these schools in my youth, I observed much of this firsthand. At these poorer schools, I witnessed dozens of instances of groups of poor black kids stomping on and kicking some unsuspecting victim whom they had "jumped," disrupting classes, and harassing both the students who were actually attempting to learn, as well as the teachers. I saw white kids, who were in the minority, "sucker punched" and robbed, while virtually always simply attempting to mind their own business. I frequently observed that these assaults usually only lasted perhaps 30 seconds at most, but more frequently only 3-5. By the time any school administrators arrived to help, the assaulters had generally already run and were nowhere to be found. Kids who were attacked could only rely upon their own ability to fight back. Even those who could fight didn't generally have a chance when targeted, as their cowardly assaulters generally either waited until they grossly outnumbered their victim, and then attacked him as a group, or "sucker punched" him at an unsuspecting moment, followed by the inevitable kicking and stomping.

It could be suggested that, in spite of substandard teaching which does not make them competitive for academic scholarships, poorer students still have an equal chance of getting scholarships in extra-curricular activities, such as sports. Unfortunately, wealth is strongly correlated with success even here. Today's affluent parents invest small fortunes in order to keep their kids perpetually enlisted in sports teams, especially the outrageously expensive "club" teams, or other extra-curricular training (e.g. dance, acting, voice, etc.), from the moment they first become eligible for them, usually at around age 5, until these extra-curricular programs first become available for free at the better middle, or high schools. By this later point, poorer children, who have not had this training, are already hopelessly outclassed and generally not selected.

It must also be considered that wealth highly influences even being able to attend the better public schools in question, as one must first be able to afford to live within these school zones, in order to be allowed admission. These zones are often heavily influenced and shamelessly manipulated to the detriment of the less affluent and to the advantage of the wealthy; many of whom are on, or are acquainted with those who are on the city councils, zoning boards, or planning committees. Schools in less affluent areas generally offer fewer of these programs, due to their smaller tax base, therefore competition is no less fierce for any available non-academic, extra-curricular slots, which have the potential to translate into university scholarships. The majority of university athletic and extra-curricular scholarships, therefore, end up being awarded to the children whom affluent parents have been grooming for these since early childhood.

Hollywood perpetually recycles the story of the poor kid, or underdog team from the poor neighborhood, who work extra hard and eventually become great. While this may have frequently occurred in the past, and occasionally still occurs today, it is much more the exception than the rule. For every one of these underfunded underdogs, there are dozens of children of the elite whose parents heavily invested to ensure they had an overwhelming advantage over their peers.

Having examined the challenges which underprivileged youths face when attempting to "pull themselves up by their own boot-straps" via schooling, let's consider disparities in salary. Do "white-collar" managers really put a greater amount of labor into their hours at work, on average, and therefore deserve to be more highly compensated, than a marine, a police officer, a school teacher, or even a mechanic? Some of these latter jobs are mentally and physically strenuous; some even dangerous. Why then do many white-collar managers receive orders of magnitude greater compensation per hour of labor? Isn't it an injustice to pay the mechanic so much less, on average, if his labor is genuinely the more laborious?

"But we have to compensate the manager, doctor, or lawyer for their advanced schooling," someone will certainly reply. Do we? Says whom? Where is this imaginary rule book which demands that customers repay an individual for schooling which they themselves benefited from? Is it the same mythical book which supposedly claims that any tax, or fee which is levied upon businesses must be itemized and passed directly on to the customer, rather than, as intended, being taken from the businesses' profits and the substantial compensation packages of its senior management and owners. Is it not compensation enough that in attaining these degrees they get to perform jobs which they supposedly have an interest in: jobs which are highly respected, which don't require them to labor out of doors in the heat, rain, or cold, doing difficult and sometimes painful work; such as roofing houses, or digging ditches? Do professors, doctors, lawyers, business executives, authors, legislators, and others only strive for these positions in order to become wealthy, or do they pursue these careers because they actually care about their patients, clients, companies, readers, and nations?

Sadly, I believe that there are a large portion of the former intermixed among the latter. The quickest way to remove these avaricious pests from infesting these positions of honor and public trust is to reduce the wealth which may be achieved from them.

Indeed, the very public who receive services from these people would quickly shun them if made aware that love of wealth was even a significant, much less the only contributing factor to their desire to hold these highly respected positions. The public instinctively loathes the avaricious, and will always avoid doing business with those infected by it, if at all possible. All would prefer doing business with doctors, lawyers, legislators, or managers who actually care about them, whose passion about what they do makes compensation for doing it an afterthought, who would continue to perform their labor even if only provided the similar, though decent salary which other diligent workers receive. All prefer these to those who simply see their customers as stepping stones to wealth, or to power; wealth's second face.

Aware of this public predilection, the avaricious, who are drawn to and infest these positions for wealth, as their kindred vermin of ticks, lice, and leaches are drawn to and infest animals for blood, generally feign altruism, attempting to blend in with and hopefully be confused for their more noble peers. Isn't this grasping falsity what all, at least those who are aware enough to take notice, find repulsive about insincere, glad-handing politicians; who feign familiarity, devotion, understanding, and sympathy, only to mask genuine love of wealth and power. This is essentially love of self, rather than love of the citizenry whom they seek to represent. Isn't it the same reason why we are repulsed by sycophantic coworkers. Those whose grasping insincerity can be detected in their overly hard, feigned laughter at their master's every offhand joke, their passionate agreement with his every idea, and their mirroring of any sentiments which they detect on his face; which they have made a science out of studying.

Instead, Western society generally bases compensation levels not upon value of services rendered, but upon ability to generate wealth. This is why teachers, policemen, and firemen receive such notoriously low salaries, though they are performing such critically important work as educating our children and saving our lives. They are not bringing in wealth for the elite, often international business owners, like the movie producer, actor, or sports star do, and who are rewarded with 7-8 figure salaries for doing so. This is a tragic reflection of the warped priority sets which often occur within modern capitalist nations.

Hitler understood this fact, and claimed, in his Mein Kampf, that compensation should be based, not upon ability to generate wealth, but upon benefit to society, and skill of the laborer, as there is nobility and honor in all work which legally benefits society, and which is performed with diligence, skill, and commitment; whether it be lecturing in universities, arresting criminals, or making sandwiches.[8] The truth, that all work which benefits society is equally noble, if done well, is one of the main factors which attracted many Europeans to him, as he wrote during the height of the Second Industrial Revolution to a generation struggling with countless inhumane abuses by fabulously wealthy capitalist investors, and the crushing poverty which these things had caused. Unfortunately, there is no way for this to occur without at least a partial de-privatization of at least some types of business, as this is the only way to realistically control salaries.

All would like to believe that prices of objects and the salaries of employees will find their natural levels based upon supply and demand, as the father of modern Economics, Adam Smith, promoted in his seminal work, *The Wealth of Nations*. Unfortunately, this is only the case when the supplies and demands of these things are not actively manipulated by the wealthy for the sole purpose of generating additional wealth. Take, for example the supply of physicians in America. The number of allopathic (i.e. MD granting) medical schools are intentionally limited by powerful organizations, such as the AMA, in order to maintain a national shortage of physicians, which artificially inflates their salaries. Consider how the price of gas is unabashedly manipulated by the Oil Producing European Countries (OPEC), in order to manipulate, maintain, and increase profit levels.

The possibility of this type of manipulation was not missed by Adam Smith, and he strongly warned us about it. "To widen the market and to narrow the competition, is always the interest of the dealers. To widen the market may frequently be agreeable enough to the interest of the public; but to narrow the competition must always be against it, and can serve only to enable the dealers, by raising their profits above what they naturally would be, to levy, for their own benefit, an absurd tax upon the rest of their fellow-citizens. The proposal of any new law or regulation of commerce which comes from this order ought always to be listened to with great precaution, and ought never to be adopted till after having been long and carefully examined, not only with the most scrupulous, but with the most suspicious attention. It comes from an order of men whose interest is never exactly the same with that of the public, who have generally an interest to deceive and even to oppress the public, and who accordingly have, upon many occasions, both deceived and oppressed it."[196]

The anti-trust laws of yesteryear should be revised to uproot these types of competition limiting regulations and laws, and those who promote them, wherever they are found. Often this occurs today by industry leaders forming associations and then only approving entry into their profit-making arena to those limited few whom they approve, credential, or license. This is very similar to the approach which was used by the medieval trade guilds to limit competition and maintain wealth.

A good example is the approach taken by the National Association of Realtors (NAR). Though many would like the ability to list their home on the Multiple Listing Service (MLS), where the majority of homes are marketed and sold, they are only allowed to do so by going through a *licensed* realtor. This has the effect of unnecessarily inflating the market demand of realtors, who receive a typically enormous commission for the virtually negligible work that they do to market the home. In addition, all realtors have to work under and therefore to share their profits with a broker, like a tribute to a modern feudal lord. There is really no legitimate need for these brokers to even exist. They attempt to justify their role by claiming that they provide expert oversight, however in reality, this virtually never occurs.

Capitalism is a semi-regulated brawl, where men shove, push, scheme, and grasp for the greatest amount of assets. Perhaps some arrived late to the competition, after all of the assets have already been claimed. Too bad. They had better make some sort of an arrangement to exchange their time and labor for assets, a sort of semi-voluntary servitude, but will likely remain in the precarious and disadvantaged position of servants. Perhaps some were born into bodies, or situations which make them naturally less fit for this sort of combat sport. Too bad. Again, unless these people wish to starve, they had better develop some skill which the current asset-holders believe will make them of some value as a servant, in exchange for assets.

Let's now examine the other potential view of the more intelligent capitalists; that any attempt at correcting its injustices would likely only result in more injustice. This is simple fatalism. Just because we know that we will never improve our character to the point of perfection, should we therefore cease attempting to improve it? Because we will never achieve omniscience, should we therefore never attempt to learn? Because we will never be perfectly clean, should we never bathe, or brush our teeth, or change and wash our clothes? Accordingly, just because our laws will never be perfect, should we never attempt to improve them?

Of course, whenever the cameras are trained upon them, the wealthy also express their love for equality in the most glowing of terms; claiming that they are doing their utmost to help the world achieve it. In reality, they dread the thought of a government, or the governed themselves, making attempts towards the realization of a more equal society. They have grown accustomed to and love the disproportionate influence which their wealth affords them. While their words say, "We love the poor," their refusal to distribute their excess, which is what wealth is, to lift as many of the poor as they can up from poverty to the middle class, says, "We love our wealth more than we love our brothers and sisters in need." While their words say, "I stand for the middle class. It is a great position to be in," their actions say, "I would hate to have to rejoin the middle class by sharing my wealth with the poor, for I think being wealthy far superior."

Allowing the distribution of wealth, and therefore of power within a society to grow grossly imbalanced, de facto creates a classed society, an economic caste system, a bourgeoisie and proletariat, a nobility and peasantry. It is meaningless to discuss the destruction of elitism and a movement towards a more equal redistribution of power within society without also discussing at least a partial confiscation and redistribution of wealth, since wealth is power. It is potential energy which can move men to do work, like voltage can move electrons to turn a motor.

Over the centuries, history has repeatedly proven that, besides in a handful of historical incidents of often questionable authenticity, the levels of equality within a nation generally only rise in violent surges. Even after the handful of wars which have been waged specifically for the noble cause of creating a more just society, such as the American and French Revolutions and the English and American Civil Wars, typically only an apex of equality is reached, from which society immediately begins to re-descend during the ensuing peace. These titanic upheavals shake societies as an earthquake shakes the ground; shivering to the common level many wealthy and powerful people who, like Nimrod, of old, unwisely grasped at the heavens. Their ruin piles of horded resources prove a welcome boon to the masses who absorb them: what bits they can snatch, before other wealthy individuals grasp all that is of value therein; since the wealthy seldom feel that they have wealth enough.

Besides the extremely few random noble philanthropists who are encountered from time to time, only rarely do the wealthy voluntarily offer up their wealth for redistribution among the poor. Such wealth redistribution must typically always occur by force. Only at gunpoint, or after a court order, which implies the same thing, should it be resisted, do the majority of wealthy people ever offer up their mansions and wealth for distribution to, and use by the public. On this point Karl Marx was entirely correct.[74] How many of them do we perpetually read about in the news who are in court for attempting to avoid even paying their taxes.

Unfortunately, Marx's at times brilliant economic views and honorable commiseration with the abused poor were grossly warped by an underlying atheist worldview which makes all morality relative, and therefore arbitrary. With such a view, human lives become no more innately valuable than the lives of weeds, and truth and kindness become the moral equivalents of deception and brutality. If all morals are arbitrary and all lives are equally valueless, then rapid though brutal means to utopian ends would be more efficient and logical, than far slower humane ones. It was these atheistic views which caused Marx's adherents, men such as Stalin and Mao, to unflinchingly cut down by the millions any who impeded their rise to power, as one would till up weeds in an overgrown field in preparation for planting.

Unlike the communists, I am not naïve enough to think that poverty ennobles, in and of itself. There are huge swathes of the poor whose levels of moral depravity make their poverty a blessing, as additional wealth would merely empower them to more efficiently destroy both themselves and others. But even these are not beyond all hope. There may be Jean Valjeans among them who might do the world much good, if aided and reformed. In addition, these people might have children, who are relatively innocent, during the brief period between their birth and the frequent, environmentally influenced corruption of their character, and who are therefore undeserving of the grinding, thousand daily tragedies, disappointments, and humiliations of poverty. These "Pips" should also have *Great Expectations* from life.

But why need we pretend. This open tolerance of the inequality of wealth and power is pervasive the world over. It has even been preserved in the founding documents and political structures of most Western governments. Even in England's Parliament, whose creation was a single step of progress towards true equality within that nation, they preserve separate houses, one of *Lords*, and the other of *Common(er)s*. They even preserve the structures and titles of their wealthy royalty.

We fare little better across the Atlantic in America. Our Declaration of Independence boasts of a belief "that all men are created equal," yet our Constitution provides for a Senate with a similar role as the English House of Lords, and a House of Representatives with a similar role as the English House of Commons. How is this equality? The Constitution, though it was a massive advancement towards political justice, is not perfect. It did not even initially prohibit slavery, an omission which took another century and a civil war to finally correct. It did not provide women, one half of the nation's population, even with the right to own property, much less to vote. I can only assume that this preservation of a class system, with its elite senators and less powerful representatives, is another one of these imperfect omissions which have yet to be rooted out, but which need to be.

Early American political writings reveal that the initial purpose of the two houses was to provide a balance between the voices of the wealthy and that of the commoners, so that neither would create laws which disadvantaged the other. Yet nowadays the wealthy have surged into both. No one (IRS inclusive) is entirely certain how many millionaires are currently filling these congressional positions, as it is usually in a politicians' interests to hide, or minimize their net wealth, in order to portray their interests as analogous to those of the common American. Assets can be tucked away in various ways, such as investment property, trust funds, sham "charities," paper businesses, etc., many of which do not need to be reported to the public, or only need to be reported as falling within certain broad ranges. Attempting to follow the money trails of some congressmen can feel like searching for the lost Fountain of Youth. In 2009, for example, 66% of senators were millionaires, while 41% of representatives were. Again, these numbers were likely far higher in reality, due to the reasons previously mentioned. And the Congressional wealth has only grown in the intervening decade, with the recent 115th Congress being the wealthiest on record. Compare these numbers to the ~99% of Americans who are not millionaires, and it becomes blatantly obvious that the intentions of the nation's founders regarding congress have been sidestepped.

But even if the House of Representatives was miraculously reflective of the voice of the common people, the power between these two houses is far from equally balanced. Not only are there far fewer senators, making each senator's individual power more concentrated, but the Senate itself is a more powerful body than the House of Representatives. Among many special powers which the Senate possesses, it alone has the ability to appoint judges to federal courts. In the litigious world which we live in, where laws are more often determined by lawsuits, than by legislation, this power alone is enough to prove their supremacy.

I propose instead that the congress be truly reflective of the people. The dual house system should be discarded and a single house, "of the citizens" established. Since roughly 1% of Americans are millionaires, roughly 1% of congressmen should be allowed to be elected from these ranks. External business relations and investments must not occur while in office, preventing the all too often substantial increases in wealth which occurs while in office through dubious means. The only income that should be allowed during this period is the federal salary.

Propaganda

When it comes to ethical concerns, men generally prefer to trust to their own instinctive judgement and the value sets which birthed it. In democratic societies, where the power of both the ballot and the wallet are supposed to lie with the people, the natural result of this self-reliance should be that a nation's media, schools, and laws tend to reflect the general values of the population. When this fails to occur, it is a sign that the democratic process itself is malfunctioning, or has altogether ceased to exist.

Sadly, across most of the Western world today, this divorce of the people from their media, schools, and laws is not merely occurring, but is rapidly growing more widespread and flagrant. But in a democratic nation, what would, or even could instigate such a situation? The short answer is that leftists have taken a more cunning approach with their social engineering efforts.

They are well aware that the public are, by definition, primarily comprised of a working class which must divide its waking hours between a range of competing cares; such as jobs, families, meals, vehicle and home maintenance, etc. The public greatly values and jealously guards the hour or two of remaining time which may be dedicated towards personal interests. They generally have neither the time, the training, nor often the resources required to adequately investigate the accuracy of the barrage of information which this modern age presents them with on a daily basis. Every day, a veritable firehose of hundreds of articles, shows, books, and films are generated about recent political, scientific, social, or philosophical events, statements, creations, occurrences, claims, and discoveries. If members of the public, attempting to improve themselves and be responsible citizens, devote some of their precious time to the news, the latest best-seller, a film, or a television show, they must rely heavily upon the journalists, producers, and outlets who create all of these media forms, to paint accurate portraits of reality with the provided information. In other words, to present them with truth, rather than attempt to manipulate them with half-truths and outright falsities.

The public may have enough information to research and select a specific news outlet, which claims, or appears to align more with the public value set than many others do, but the options available to them here are tragically few. In much of the Western world today, the rare few courageous news outlets that prove their commitment to egalitarian principles in their reporting, by adhering to the generally conservative value set of the bulk of society, are perpetually and loudly condemned from the minarets of their far more resource heavy peers: peers who, in their worship of the god of profit, have generally sacrificed their sacred trust that they will provide the public with unvarnished truth.

Similarly, the public is generally not provided with sufficient information to know what underlying world views and values lurk beneath the surfaces of their, and often insidiously their children's, films, music, television shows, and literature. These views, sometimes unintentionally, but more often intentionally these days, stain and penetrate these works like a dye; influencing everything from word selection, to the traits of the characters, to the manner in which society is depicted as responding to them, etc. Should this dye be in the bright hues of virtue and goodness, it will influence minds, especially young ones, towards internal goodness and the joy which it produces. Should it instead be in the many darker hues of moral corruption which seem to predominate these days, it will influence them towards similar corruption and the misery which is inseparable from it.

For example, in most popular works of film, television, and writing, we encounter a general lampooning of, or intentional silence regarding matters of moral depth, religious faith, or anything unrelated to the immediately practical. This has the obvious effect of predisposing the subconscious' of the societies which consume these media forms towards atheism. As another example, in the past few decades, the majority of non-documentary films and shows released by Hollywood, as well as the majority of fictional books released from various American publishing houses, have reflected an increasingly common, bordering on ubiquitous, depiction of protagonists as a person, or group who formerly had faith in the rule sets (i.e. laws) established by the majority of society, as well as in the values which these were built upon, but who were subsequently awakened to a deeper reality which destroyed this former faith. These characters are depicted as being all the happier for this awakening; while their peers, who still generally attempt to adhere to society's value-based rules, are portrayed as viewing these heroes with a mix of awe and envy. What possible impact could such a repeated theme have upon the society which is bombarded from all directions by it, if not a reduction, or abandonment of faith in its old laws, as well as in the values and people who birthed them. The vast majority will simply consume this poison pill message whole, without questioning it.

Those perceptive enough to consciously notice this trend (virtually all do subconsciously), will typically dismiss the portrayal of protagonists as rebels, as being simply a case of writers attempting to appeal to the demographic of youth and young adults, by making them someone whom these groups can identify with. It is well known that these groups tend to consume large amounts of media, due generally to the relatively low levels of familial and professional responsibilities which they have during this phase of their life, as well to the fact that many at this point have yet to internalize the values and laws which were created by the generations preceding theirs. This last fact does often cause this group to view themselves as rebels, as they struggle to carve out a place for themselves in this world.

In addition, the rebel persona also appeals to the demographic of adults who sometimes feel themselves constrained by frustrating societal rules, which they often fantasize about breaking with impunity; something which they normally would be unable, or ill-advised to do. How many of us are forced to work with pompous cockscombs at work, whom we would love to see humbled. Though we are generally unable to perform this humbling ourselves with impunity, we can watch someone do it on film, or read about them doing so, and chuckle in solidarity. Is this portrayal of the rebel protagonist then not simply a case of supply and demand?

Yes and no. Both of the counter-arguments given above possess some valid points. In many instances, media agents such as writers and producers, and certainly actors, genuinely possess no intention of maliciously damaging the cultural and moral fabric of the nation, and the portrayal in question is simply a case of supply and demand. This does not mean that the portrayal does not cause harm anyway; only that any harm caused may truly be unintentional. Careless workmen may directly, though unintentionally cause catastrophes resulting in tremendous harm to life and property. Abundant examples of this exist, ranging from train derailments, to factory mishaps, to airline crashes. In a similar manner, this catastrophic harm being caused by media outlets may very well be the unintentional result of gross negligence on the part of the outlet's workmen; these being their army of staff, management, and investors, who are often so benumbed by the anesthetizing fumes of potential profit that they allow critical defects to slip into their products either unnoticed, or uncorrected.

There is, however, both a frequency and a consistency to the above-mentioned portrayal which, statistically speaking, surpasses any possibility of it being the product of simple oversight, or the complementary natural supply of a pre-existing demand. Much like the image displayed on a puzzle is difficult to discriminate when only one of its pieces are viewed; only coming into focus when the many pieces are appropriately arranged and considered as a whole; so too, when each of these individual media portrayals are examined alone, they are easily dismissible as being simple random acts of independently motivated individuals. Yet when a sufficient number are taken together and analyzed for commonalities, an image of coordinated, systematic effort and insidious intent begins to come into focus. This intent is to manipulate society by clandestinely presenting the under-informed within it with a false version of reality; influencing them to react in a way which would only be appropriate were this false version true.

To clarify how this works, one must bear in mind that societies are comprised of three distinct groups. The first group is usually small, highly informed, virtuous, and actively working to improve society. For clarity, let's call this group the *Improvers*. The second group is typically larger and also highly informed, however errors which they have mistakenly accepted as truths have caused them to adopt, support, and promote morally corrupt and corrupting causes. Their misguided efforts, though often well-intentioned, have a destructive effect upon society. Let's call this group the *Destroyers*. The third, largest group, possesses an average level of virtue, but are only moderately informed, leaving them vulnerable to manipulation. We will call this the *Average* group.

This *Average* group, aware of their significant disadvantage in deeper social, political, philosophical, and religious debates, generally attempt to compensate for this disadvantage in quality with an increase in quantity; forming extensive social networks with like-minded individuals. These similar companions are preferred, since among them they may safely and passionately debate over trivialities, such as sports, food, drinks, clothing, and hairstyles; subjects which don't cause them embarrassment by revealing their relative lack of knowledge on matters of importance. Rarely possessing the specialized training and background which is often necessary to penetrate the thick fog of technical jargon which the more profound subjects are often enveloped in and obscured by, those within this *Average* group will generally align their views on these subjects with those of whomever appears to have the most passionate, the strongest, or the greatest quantity of adherents; trusting that the strength of truth will cause it to dominate in debates, that its attractiveness will cause it to draw the largest number of devotees, and that its superior worth will charge its defenders with the greatest amount of passion for its defense.

The *Improver* group, on the other hand, motivated by a love of mankind and all that is noble within society, and knowing that the removal of error and ignorance is a prerequisite for wise decision making, attempts to increase its numbers by educating its brothers and sisters within the other groups.

The *Destroyer* group generally avoids any candid public debate on their warped and corrupting political, philosophical, or religious views at all cost. They know by experience that the Improver group generally dominates and humiliates them within these forums, due to the inherent strength of truth and virtue, as well as the inherent weakness of deception and vice. Rather than debate the issues themselves, *Destroyers* generally attempt to silence the *Improvers* by several means. One of these is by actively spreading deception about the *Improvers'* views and intentions, as well as about their own. Should this fail, they often attempt to intimidate them into silence via grand displays of generally illusory power, such as through threats of violence, or legal action.

"We are too aware of the rightness of our opinions to be bothered with arguing our points with these cretins," they boast. "Simply look at how rich, strong, fashionable, and sexy (all synonyms for powerful) the people are who have adopted our views. If we are a small group, it is only because we are more intelligent (another synonym for power) then the rest. We are the elite, the supermen and superwomen, the new nobility (all 3 being claims of power). If you adopt our views and support our causes, you will become one of the elite as well. Those who oppose us had better look out, as we may rally our masses to assault them: through the courts, if possible; in the streets, if not."

Translated of all dissembling, the *Destroyer* group is actually saying: "We know that the validity of the points which the *Improver* group put forward are irrefutable, so we are instead attempting to get you to avoid using didactic reasoning altogether. We want to make you see the primary tool which is used to discern which of two competing ideas are true, as outmoded. Instead, simply assume the rightness of our position, due to our affectation of power, and fear our mafioso threats to inflict harm."

We must pause a moment to mention the original meaning of the word *cadre*. A cadre, as theorized by Lenin, was a highly organized revolutionary vanguard, thoroughly committed to communist philosophy, whose ultimate objective was to infiltrate the various centers of control within a society, such is its political, media, labor, and education systems; using these to steer the state towards the realization of communism. This is the true power behind the *Destroyer* group, though many of its public faces are simply useful idiots, who fail to realize their own party's leanings.

The deception which these liberal *Destroyers* spread about their own motives, as well as about the motives of their adversaries, the Improvers, is generally effective due to the control which this group cunningly gains over whatever portions they can of a nation's information sources. *Destroyers* know, not coincidentally as the Soviets did, that controlling the means of information distribution within a nation is the key to controlling the masses. They therefore initially target their social engineering efforts at the education, news, publication, and entertainment centers where this information distribution occurs.

Through a coordinated flurry of complaints and frivolous lawsuits, they attempt to silence these national mouthpieces of all but their own warped narrative. Simultaneously, these same complaints, and lawsuits whenever possible, are filed against any businesses, donors, or advertisers whose funding supports the production of alternative narratives in these same education, news, publication, or entertainment centers. Like a medieval siege, the intent of this latter approach is to hopefully frighten away investors, and essentially starve these outlets of resources which are essential for their survival.

At the same time that these people are attacking contrasting viewpoints at these information centers, they also seek to infiltrate them. This initial infiltration began occurring within the Liberal Arts, and especially within the Humanities programs of major universities shortly after the second World War, but grew noticeably more widespread in the 60's. Minor universities generally follow trends set by these major ones, while community colleges, secondary, and primary schools all tailor their efforts towards making their students succeed in the universities. These major universities are therefore the head which steers the body of the nation's educational system.

The focus on Liberal Arts and Humanities programs, the latter being a subset of the former, is selected because these programs generally oversee the issuance of Education, Journalism, Theater, Film, Anthropology, Psychology, Music, Literary Studies, Communication, and Art degrees, which, with few exceptions, are generally required of students for entry into these fields. It should be noticed that by serving as the gatekeepers of the degrees which effectively function as licenses for employment within these fields, these departments strongly influence all aspects of a nation's information distribution (i.e. education, news, publication, and entertainment). In addition, they are able to effectively define normalcy within a society by their oversight of the Anthropology and Psychology fields.

Infiltrate chairs of these departments at major universities, or influence them through a mix of donations and lawsuits, and you control what students will be taught within these programs, as well as what the rest of the nation's educational systems will tend to teach. Control what these students will be taught and you influence the views of those who will be allowed to graduate from these programs. Control the views of those who will be allowed to graduate from these programs and you control the views of the nation's future journalists, teachers, film producers, actors, musicians, psychologists, anthropologists, writers, and artists. Influence the views of these people, who create, or distribute the majority of information which the public consumes, and you influence the views of the nation.

Once this cadre has gained entry, and therefore a certain amount of control over these media and education megaphones, they use them to spread lies of varying levels of subtlety deemed appropriate for the situation: such as that they are the champions of truth, with the best interests of the nation's citizenry at heart, that those who hold their views are the most powerful, the most numerous, and the most passionate, and that their opponents within the *Improver* group are the ones who are, in fact, destroying society. It is ironic that the *Destroyers* project the very positions, intentions, and efforts which they themselves truly hold and employ, upon the Improvers, whom they condemn for these things; yet this irony is generally lost upon them. This projection technique is also seen in their approach to the race question; where they hypocritically target, condemn, and attack the various Caucasian races for nonother than racial bias.

Since power, quantity, and passion are the three main qualities which the well-intentioned, but poorly informed *Average* group generally consider to be hallmarks of truth, many of them are swayed by these techniques into believing that the *Destroyers* are their benefactors. This is patently false. Faithful to the technique advocated by Marx in his *Communist Manifesto*, *Destroyers* simply wish to harness the strength of the *Average* in order to manipulate them into attacking and destroying the Improvers, whom they generally regard as their mortal enemies, on their behalf.

As mentioned earlier, the initial infiltration into major Western universities by those holding liberal views occurred shortly after the close of the second World War. During this period, many professors sympathetic to the teachings of Marx filled the vacuum in major European universities which was created after the defeat and removal of the Nazis. Their watered-down communist views are what we refer to today as liberalism. It took additional time for this contagion to spread across the Atlantic and infect the American universities, but the *Critical Theory* and *Cultural Marxism* teachings which this counter-swing of the pendulum spawned, began to be adopted by American universities shortly afterwards; along with the many Communist sympathizing European professors who promoted them.

During the initial infiltration process, some perceptive boards, or other key leaders within these information centers detected signs of the true, insidious characters of these liberal *Destroyers* and remained true to their public charge by attempting to prevent their entry, or influence. The *Destroyers* grew furious at this, and as they always do, attempted to force their entry by starting "Whispering Campaigns" about their opponents.

Those of their comrades who had already wormed their way into media positions spread these false allegations, complete with feigned stories of moral outrage by the public. They did this, hoping that the employers of their opponents would essentially offer them up as sacrificial lambs, in order to appease their overly vocal, liberal critics. As everyone knows, appeasement is an approach which does not work with tyrants. It simply encourages them to repeat the process the next time. And this is exactly what has occurred.

The Whispering Campaign approach to character assassination is still the "go to" method employed by the left today. It was repeatedly used recently against President Trump, as well as, most notoriously,

Supreme Court Justice Kavanaugh, during his confirmation hearings. Though both of these men were miraculously able to survive these campaigns, the public's perception of their character was irreversibly damaged. This was the Whispering Campaign's intended effect.

Using this approach, *Destroyers* are typically able to successfully circumvent the will of the public, as well as that of any trustees who have been appointed to protect it. This is exactly what occurred with diligent men, such as the brilliant Senator Joseph McCarthy. Falsified claims about this man's views are still lampooned today, by mostly liberal media outlets, but he was more correct than most people realize.

Opinion Extension

As discussed elsewhere in this work, the objective of most anti-discrimination efforts isn't actually the equal treatment of all people, as is claimed. Its actual objective is the breakdown of Western egalitarian governments. It attempts to accomplish this by disenfranchising and suppressing those of the nations' citizens who cling to the egalitarian philosophical ideas which these nations and their laws were founded upon. I do not naïvely claim that all efforts towards preventing discrimination serve this ignoble purpose, but it is undeniable that a significant portion do. This is similar to the way that certain sham charities claim to stand for a noble cause, yet only dedicate a portion of their resources and efforts towards this end, the rest being dedicated towards the financial benefit of their founders.

Let's consider what is occurring in America, for example. To begin with, America was the home of a mixture of races even before the arrival of the Europeans. There were many different races of Indians, ranging from the Algonquin, to the Illinois, the Delaware, the Cherokee, the Iroquois, the Sioux, the Navajo, and dozens of others. Many modern academics attempt to deny this fact, referring to these people simply as different tribes, rather than as different races, but races are simply groups of people with a set of characteristic physical traits which differ from those of another group. Ask a Sioux if he can identify certain physical differences which allow him to recognize the difference between another Sioux and a Navajo. He will likely laugh at you and reply, "Of course."

This being established, the arrival of the various European races into America, beginning in the 15th and 16th centuries, was not the invasion and suppression of the originally pure "native" race, by the also pure "white" race. It was merely the addition of English, French, Spanish, Dutch, Swedish, German, and several other racial ingredients into an existing mixture.

It does not matter what the racial composition of this mixture of early citizens was. What matters are the philosophical ideas which these early citizens held; which their laws were developed to reflect and preserve. Among these ideas, it does not matter which were the original, the most recent, or even the most common. What matters is which were the best. These are the ones which American citizens should pledge their allegiance to. If the best philosophical ideas, and subsequent laws in early America were those of the Iroquois, then those are the ones which the nation should adopt and promote. If the best laws and ideas were those of the Spanish colonists in Saint Augustine, Florida, then we should adopt those.

When the many competing philosophical ideas and reflective laws of the various people who settled early America are carefully scrutinized, it becomes glaringly apparent that the best which this nation has known were those which were created by the post-American Revolution Congress, and preserved within the US Constitution and early American laws. These are therefore the ideas and laws which Americans should be devoted to. The American people should hold no allegiance to any flawed ones which have subsequently stained the pages of our legal code. Of course, all know that even these early laws were not without defects, since they had yet to remove the stains of slavery and unequal treatment of women from their pages. No allegiance should be paid to these early flaws, which were eventually polished away, shortly after the Civil War.

But even with all of its flaws, many of which were common among nations during the period, the American government, which the members of the Constitutional Convention established, provided unprecedented levels of personal liberty, equality, and opportunity. Among several other things, early American law stood for the ability of the masses to worship God as they saw fit; not to be bullied by atheists into expunging all references to God from the law and government, as is occurring today. America stood for the promotion of social virtues and the prevention of social vices; not for twisting the cause of liberty into an excuse for the latter, such as we see today with legal brothels and the multi-billion-dollar porn industry. She stood for minimal taxation and the complete, outright ownership of property; not the many abuses of this which we see today, where one may own a car, but must pay an annual tax to have a plate which allows them to drive it, or where one may own a home, or land, but will have both taken if the ever-increasing annual taxes for these aren't paid. She stood for the ability of the common man and the wealthy to have an equal voice in government; not for the wealthy to tyrannize over them through the courts, should the common man's views conflict with their own, as is occurring today. She stood for the freedom to express controversial, or unpopular opinions, whether verbally, or in print, without being attacked in the courts, or on the streets for these views, as is occurring today. She stood for a simple legal code which empowered local governments with the authority to rule their people as these people desired, without being hamstrung by tyrannical edicts from activist federal judges living in the most liberal areas of the nation, as is occurring today.

Those who cling to these early American philosophical ideals, the laws which sprung from them, and other citizens who love these things, whether native born, or immigrant, are being systematically disenfranchised by these new anti-discrimination laws. These laws have solidly tilted college admission, company hiring and promotion, legal representation, and even business advertisement in America to the benefit of those who do not cling to these early American ideals.

Consider that the majority of immigrants, of various races, who benefit from these things have little awareness of early American history, much less of the philosophical ideals which America formerly stood for. Their only conceptions of these things are often derived from the warped, typically hedonistic portrayals which Hollywood has shown them. Many of these depict the early American people and laws, not as good and noble, but as selfish and cruel. The naturalization process was originally set up in order to teach immigrants about America's true history and original ideals, in order to hopefully encourage their adoption.

Yet millions of unnaturalized immigrants are pouring through our laughable borders without ever gaining a knowledge of, much less a devotion to, these early American philosophical ideals. Many even hold views which are completely opposed to these. They then have children in our land who almost uniformly vote for Democratic leaders who promote the treasonous border weakening which allowed their relatives in to begin with. Any who wish to see evidence of this need merely to perform a poll within communities of recent immigrants and compare the ratios of those who support Democrats to the ratios among communities with few immigrants.

There will always be outliers. Some immigrants do study, adopt, and love the early American philosophical ideals which our laws are rooted in, but these are the rare few.

The vast majority of the black community within America also do not hold any devotion to the early American philosophical ideals. This is partially the fault of early Americans, who won their freedom, but then allowed these, their fellow men, to languish in ignorance and chains, to be beaten and traded like cattle, for almost another century. Even after this they were treated in many parts of the country as second-class citizens until the mid-20th century. Shame on these men for this. No wonder among black Americans there is still a smoldering resentment against authority and the early laws which this nation was founded upon.

This being said, it is time for the black community to let this resentment go. Generations have come and gone since the days of the ruthless slave traders. Thousands, upon thousands of Union soldiers fought and died to provide black Americans with their freedom. Men such as John Brown watched their own sons die, and then later died themselves while fighting for the abolitionist cause. The marching song "John Brown's Body," was sung by thousands of Union troops, as they marched into battle, to remind them of what they fought both for and against. This blood offering should sufficiently atone for the formerly justified offense, and earn the nation the love and respect of the black community. And indeed, it does for some. Many noble black men, men such as Judge Clarence Thomas and Thomas Sowell, have courageously fought to defend the early American philosophical ideas which our laws are rooted in. But for every one Thomas Sowell, there are ten thousand black Americans who throw their support wholeheartedly into the Democrat camp; which stands for the overthrow of these core philosophical principles and laws which America was built upon. Again, any who are in doubt about this need merely to conduct a poll within a black community on those who support the overwhelmingly liberal Democratic platform and the numbers will speak for themselves.

Those who adhere to the various non-Judeo-Christian faiths, or who are outright atheists, also benefit from these anti-discrimination laws. These people also, almost uniformly do not hold any allegiance to early American philosophical ideals. This is because these ideals were the product of a people who overwhelmingly held deist and Judeo-Christian beliefs. The aforementioned people vote almost exclusively Democrat. Those who do so, while still believing in God and absolute virtues, are actually being used by this party. Every day the Democratic party further reveals its increasingly communist character and sympathies. Communism is itself the natural political product of the atheist worldview. This worldview stands for the destruction of all moral absolutes; claiming that they are human perspective dependent, and therefore relative.

Those who claim any "gender" other than the actual sex proven by their genes, as well as those who engage in any of the various forms of sexual perversion, such as homosexuality, also benefit from these anti-discrimination laws. Again, we find that these people almost uniformly do not hold any allegiance to early American philosophical ideals, the laws which these ideals birthed, or even the people who drafted them. This is because they know that the founders of this nation would have stood strongly against their moral perversion. Accordingly, such people also vote, almost exclusively, for the party which stands for the destruction of these philosophical ideals; the Democratic party.

It can be seen then, that in spite of the noble names of these anti-discrimination laws, and the likely good intentions of many of the people who put them in place, the net result of their adoption has been the elevation of a group of individuals who, wholesale, do not support early American ideals, the laws which these generated, or often even the people who generated them. This has had the overall negative effect of pushing these people into influential positions within American society, where they are, unfortunately, better able to spread their warped views.

Overwhelmingly liberal Western media outlets have supported these efforts, portraying any symbols of older American culture (i.e. Caucasians, Christians, loving heterosexual families, conservatives, etc.)

as stupid, weak, cruel, ugly, undesirable, unfashionable, or unpopular, while depicting anything which doesn't fall into these categories as intelligent, strong, beautiful, desirable, fashionable, and popular. All of this attacking of specific types of people for the color of their skin, for their faith, and for their views on sexuality occurs, hypocritically, under the banner of "anti-discrimination": all of this hatred, under the banner of "anti-hate."

This Western media campaign against "discrimination" has even spilled-over into how it reports, and ultimately what society believes, about groupings of animals. While some of this spill-over appears to have been spontaneous and unintentional, an increasing percentage of it appears to be intentionally manipulative.

Western media outlets today willingly promote any research, or writings which celebrate, or reveal new aspects of the many admirable physical and personality predispositions of specific breeds, or species of animals. Among dogs, for example, they celebrate the intelligence of Jack Russell Terriers, the natural herding ability of Border Collies, the friendliness and loyalty of Labradors, the courage of German Shepherds, the determination of Bulldogs, the speed of Greyhounds, the tracking ability of Bloodhounds, etc.

These same sources, however, viciously attack and discredit, or blatantly ignore the work of any researchers, or journalists whose love of truth drives them to point out data which indicates that some breeds, or species of animals, whether of dogs, or of anything else, possess predispositions for negative traits, such as violence, or aggression. Regardless of whether or not the breed, or species of animal in question has been proven historically to be a menace to mankind, any resulting fear, or dislike of these animals is condemned as unenlightened, and almost immoral.

Why do media outlets do this? What is to be gained from ignoring these facts? They do so because they know that this aversion to specific animal species echoes the supposed cardinal sin of racism. This is not really surprising, since Darwin proved in his *Descent of Man* that *races* are synonymous with *breeds*.[75] He also proved in his *Origin of Species* that speciation is simply breed variation which has occurred on a longer timescale.[76] This means that any differences between *species*, *races*, and *breeds*, are merely differences of degree, rather than differences of type.

Our tendency to learn by analogy and pattern recognition causes our fixed views (i.e. beliefs) on one subject, to naturally be extended towards other subjects which share specific traits with them. As an example of this, consider a girl who has a loving relationship with her father, due to her awareness of his goodness. If another individual shares key characteristics with her father, which remind her of him, then there will be an increased probability that she will conclude that this person is good as well and that she will likely feel a fondness towards him.

This phenomenon isn't limited to people, however. It can even occur between people, animals, and inanimate objects. As an example of this, consider how well-cultured young girls instinctively and accurately conclude that infants are innocent, harmless, and in need of care and affection. When these same girls observe similar infantile characteristics in other creatures, such as ducklings, puppies, and kittens, there will be an increased tendency for them to extend to these animals the same conclusions which they reached about the infants.

There are two different ways in which this tendency for conclusion, or belief extension may prove problematic. The first is when the perceived similarities between the two subjects are too weak, or illusory to support the extension of conclusions between them. The second way is when the initial conclusions which were formed about the first subject are themselves faulty. This faultiness is sometimes a product of simple ignorance on the subject, or the mistaken acceptance of false supporting claims as truths. Other times, however, these faulty conclusions are the result of active manipulation by an external party which stands to benefit from their acceptance.

The active suppression of truth and the propagation of error on these matters proves that leftist leaders care more about the preservation of their narrative, than they do about the preservation of the lives of innocents; who could have been spared from horribly painful maimings, or deaths, had truth been spread and wisely acted upon by society. As an example, consider that the vast majority of media outlets and academics celebrate the recent resurgence of the American Alligator as a modern success story. They boast of how protection efforts, such as hunting bans and the provision of temporary endangered status caused the population of this man-eating apex predator to explode from ~8 active nests in 1970, to ~90 in 2004 within the state of Florida alone. God only knows what the numbers of these tremendously dangerous creatures are today across the nation as a whole. The wealthy, who create these bad laws, never envision themselves wandering through a swamp, bayou, or marsh, where they risk being attacked by these creatures. To them, it is all poorly thought out theory.

In places like rural Louisiana, however, many among the lower and middle economic classes do this very thing on a frequent, sometimes even daily basis, while fishing, casting, or setting and checking their various types of crab, crawfish, or shrimp traps. Many there rely upon these efforts to supplement their income. Is it any surprise that, during this same period, alligator attacks across the state of Florida coincidentally increased from ~1 per year, to ~12; several being fatal. I'm sure that the 2-year-old toddler who was grabbed and eaten by one while on vacation at Disney with his family last year, were he still alive and old enough to understand, would be thrilled to hear how these social crusaders have helped us all to overcome our species bias, rather than keeping the amount of free-roaming, man-eating, apex predators as low as possible, for the safety of our children.

There are even people actively campaigning to change society's instinctively wise fear of sharks, lions, bears, and the infinite host of venomous snakes, spiders, and insects. They celebrate people like T. T. and his unfortunate girlfriend, A. H. (I am intentionally not providing the names here due to our ridiculous legal restrictions), who attempted to prove by living with them that, if understood correctly, bears were no more naturally violent or aggressive than any other species. Sadly, but not surprisingly, the gnawed remnants of both of their bodies were found by their returning pilot. Investigators discovered that their camera accidentally recorded audio of T. T.'s final struggle, as he was being eaten alive, screaming for A. H. to run, and she attempted to defend herself with a pan.[77]

Did the media issue a public apology for glamorizing and encouraging the narrative which resulted in this tragedy? Of course not. They doubled down; making a movie about T. T. which glamorized him all the more, recasting the horrible, needless, and easily avoidable tragedy as a noble, selfless, modern martyrdom for species equality. They did the same glamorization act with S. I., who also set out with the same intent to prove that no species possessed innately negative, or violent tendencies, and also was killed by one of the species he was hoping to save from this supposedly unjust vilification.[78]

This same irresponsible reporting, false narrative, and fact suppression occurs not only with species famous for being man-eaters, such as sharks, but with specific breeds of animals which are commonly kept as house-pets, such as dogs. How many times, while headlines are still resonating with the news of yet another mauling death of an innocent child, woman, or senior, must we hear, or read the statements of victims of brainwashing making astoundingly naïve comments, such as, "I hate when ignorant people group and judge pit bulls. They are just like any other dog, if you raise them right."

A recent headline I encountered read: "Woman dead, husband injured after vicious Christmas Eve mauling." A week earlier, another quite graphic one stated: "Deputies watched dogs 'eating rib cage' of Virginia woman, 22, during mauling, sheriff says."[80] It is noteworthy that both headlines intentionally omitted mention of the breed of dog. Was either tragedy caused by Boxers, or Golden Retrievers? Perhaps it was a rash of killer Chihuahuas. Of course not. In both cases the bodies of the articles reveal that the breed of the attacking dogs was a pit bull. It isn't worth taking the time to provide the long, long list of pit bull deaths, or maulings which have occurred in the recent past. The breed has almost become synonymous for these things.

Yet we see that journalists in these, as well as in many other instances, selectively omitted naming the breed within the title. They did so out of fear that they would be attacked for appearing to claim that this, or any specific breed, has a violent predisposition. In other words, they hope to avoid being labeled as "animal racists." Feigning impartiality within the bodies of the two articles, the journalists selectively quote those who praise the qualities of the dogs and are shocked that such an incident could occur, followed by statements implying that the owners, or someone else must be at fault. "The dogs were a little bit neglected...[He] wasn't taking care of them..."[79] I'm sure the families of the deceased, already reeling from their tragic losses, appreciate reading these not so subtle public allegations that their loved ones' deaths were due to personal irresponsibility. The only other alternative available to the journalists is to admit a truth which is obvious to all but the hopelessly brainwashed: that certain breeds possess increased tendencies towards negative behaviors, such as violence and aggression.

In a separate article which was intentionally placed immediately below these previous ones, the headline reads, "Rules against Pit Bulls scrapped in Montreal."[80] One will notice that the journalist does not shy away from naming the breed in this headline, when the article itself confirms the party line that there are no breed specific negative tendencies. Within the text of this article we encounter a more blatant version of the same dog-breed-equality nonsense which we were exposed to earlier. "We don't want to target one breed in particular...The pit bull-style dog will no longer be considered a dangerous breed in Montreal...We'll have a global approach that includes all dogs and I believe it's the right approach for Montreal."[80] How very breed tolerant of the government official quoted. Yet between the quotes we see a begrudging admission of yet another tragedy caused by this breed. "The administration of the previous mayor, Denis Coderre, enacted a crackdown on the breed in 2016 after a 55-year-old Montreal woman was mauled to death by a neighbor's pet."[80]

No longer considered a dangerous breed in Montreal? These legislators are no longer considered an intelligent breed in Montreal. I'm sure that poor, innocent, 55-year old Montreal woman, who didn't even own the dog, but was attacked and excruciatingly mauled to death by it, would appreciate that dog breed tolerant public statement. Were she at the news conference where it was made, and were her fingers not mangled and partially chewed off, as they likely were while she was fighting to stay alive, I'm sure she would clap. Were her lips and other soft parts of her face not torn during the struggle, as they likely were, I'm sure she would thank the new Montreal Mayor for her work in overturning previous legislation which protected people from similar horrific deaths.

Of note, most just skim past the word *maul* without really comprehending the sheer horror and suffering associated with such a death. There was a reason why the ancient Romans, wanting to terrify any who might be considering violating Roman law, condemned criminals to be publicly mauled to death by animals. The body's sympathetic "fight or flight" response ensures that those poor souls being mauled typically tend to be quite conscious and struggling for a long time, as teeth and claws repeatedly tear flesh and break bones. It is only after a significant period of time that blood loss finally causes them to slip mercifully into unconsciousness, and eventually die from exsanguination. Even if their necks are broken during the attack, this doesn't kill them immediately. It simply paralyzes their bodies, often including their diaphragms preventing them from breathing. Effectively, these people suffocate to death.

These legislators apparently don't care about any of that. They are too busy focusing instead on political career bolstering photo ops with puppies, as well as with the two types of pit bull owners; the brainwashed and the ignorant.

Stereotyping

This current generation has been largely brainwashed into believing the mantra that any and all grouping, categorization, and subsequent predictions based, even in part, upon human factors, are stereotyping: the gravest of sins in the new modern ethics. They loudly condemn both the action and the actor wherever and whenever they encounter them using this method, failing to realize that, in this very act of recognition and condemnation, they have themselves hypocritically stereotyped the groups of people holding, or espousing counter opinions. These people's minds are so brainwashed that they fail to realize that this method of recognition and classification, which they have been programmed to abhor, is in actuality nonother than the simple scientific method, something which they celebrate, being applied within the context of the social sciences.

Using the scientific method, scientists observe phenomena, group any recognized trends, and attempt to create mathematical, chemical, or physics-based models which match these trends, in order to predict future event recurrences with a reasonable degree of probability. Rational minds trained in this method do not, however, simply stop recognizing, classifying, and predicting phenomena once their minds are turned towards immaterial subjects. Light, gravity, and heat, for example, are purely immaterial, and yet their actions upon the material world may be grouped, classified, and predicted based upon observed past behavior.

So too with human behavior. Regardless of the inconvenience of any conclusions which such a scientific approach might arrive at, if properly constrained by logic, and therefore prevented from predicting future human words, thoughts, or actions based upon nonexistent trends, there is no logically justifiable reason why the scientific method may not fitly be applied to the field of human behavior. This includes behavior both in groups and societies of varying types and sizes; from the simple interaction of a pair of people meeting for coffee, to the negotiations of hosts of nations.

Regardless of whatever physical, or social characteristics individuals, or groups are recognized by, once enough experience, and therefore information, has been accumulated from past interactions with them to recognize that increased, or decreased probabilities exist of them thinking, speaking, or acting certain ways, it is irrational to ignore these trends and probabilities when the next individual, or group exhibiting the same physical, or social traits is encountered. Will there be exceptions? Of course there will. But will there not also be trends? Do statistical probabilities and trend curves suddenly become impossible when applied to the sphere of human behavior, though they may be effectively applied to virtually every other subject? There is no rational reason to believe so.

Yet this is what the majority is being taught; all else being damned as immoral. That is, unless the group, or individuals being condemned display, or espouse traits indicating their sympathy towards the philosophical principles, and laws upon which Western egalitarianism was founded, or towards the people who put these laws in place. These *conservatives* may hypocritically be condemned, mocked, harassed, and attacked wholesale.

If someone walking down the street observes a Muslim man throwing acid in an innocent girl's face, disfiguring her for life, they may initially think this the act of a random madman. Yet when they study the increasing incidence of brutal and barbaric acts such as this, as well as vehicular attacks, rapes, bombings, beheadings, harassment, so called "honor" killings, etc., and notice that, statistically speaking, the vast majority of these offenses are committed by Muslims and are increasing in proportion to their immigration (i.e. flooding) into Western society, are they expected to ignore all of this statistical evidence when they encounter the next Muslim man on the street? Perhaps they should offer to have him babysit their daughters. They wouldn't want to offend him, of course, because they have been informed in no uncertain terms that minority offense is more important than majority welfare by the hyper-liberal activist media. This view is also reflected in several relatively recent bad executive orders, rulings by activist judges tyrannically ramrodded down the throats of the American people, rather than democratically reflecting their will, and in similar policies which have been forced upon the European people by their treasonous leaders.

That is, until the minority become the majority. Then suddenly we will see these leaders miraculously begin to care about democratic majority rule once more. The current mentality of most liberal leaders appears to be: "Who cares what the will of the people is, when we can rule whichever way is most convenient and makes us, as well as those who support us, the greatest profit, then simply fire up the biased reporting/marketing (i.e. propaganda) engines to convince the public that our views and actions are just. We can then leverage these new bad laws within the courts to marginalize, disenfranchise, unemploy, and impoverish the few who are sober, aware, and informed enough to resist our reprogramming; using this public example to both strip them of any power to effectively resist us, and also to function as a de facto threat to any among the masses who are potentially sympathetic towards their cause. Simultaneously, we will use our media platforms to claim that these people whom we are attacking are radicals who are hopelessly outnumbered. Whether they actually are or not is inconsequential."

We do not need to peel and eat each yellow banana that we encounter, in order to know with a reasonable amount of certainty whether, or not the fruit within has a high probability of being ripe. We simply must sample enough of the various types of bananas to recognize a trend between peel color and ripeness. Based upon this recognized trend, we can classify bananas into groups having distinct probabilities of ripeness based upon this physical trait of color. We can then use this evidence-based classification to predict, with a level of certainty correlating to our sample size and the strength of the observed trend, that the next yellow banana which we open will be ripe. If we desire to eat a ripe banana, have a reasonably representative sample size, and a reasonably strong trend, it would be both foolish and unscientific of us to grab any banana at random and state, "We refuse to discriminate, or judge between these bananas! We will cling to our dogma that all discrimination and judgement are bad and give this banana an equal chance of being ripe."

But let's follow this path a bit further to bring some current issues into focus. We could try to force ourselves and others to believe that the unripeness which people generally wish to avoid is as healthful and enjoyable as the ripeness. Basing our views upon John Locke's popular, yet clearly incorrect belief that men and women are born with minds like blank slates, what he termed the "Tabula Rasa," and therefore that all thoughts and opinions are the product of experience and cultural programming,[38] we will claim that it is simply people's cultural upbringing, rather than their internal instinct and external senses which causes them to have a natural aversion to unripe bananas; an aversion which we will condemn as morally wrong. We will altogether ignore the existence of instinct within humans, though evidence of this instinct stares us in the face, not only among humankind, but among virtually every species of the animal kingdom; as any admission of this fact would destroy the Lockean views which our argument is built upon.

We will go on a crusade of condemnation of any who refuse to agree with our new views on the fluidity and equality of ripeness. Claiming to hate hatred itself, we will lobby to formalize into law our hatred of any who would dare to make public their dislike of unripe bananas. In actual fact, we do not hate abstract hatred. We actually love to hate any who might dare to oppose our views. We are simply hypocrites who want everyone else's natural revulsion, which we condemn as hate, to be made illegal, while we portray our own genuine hatred as a sort of justified righteous indignation. In other words, clandestine elitists, we are manipulating language within the courts in order to tyrannically silence any who would dare to oppose our views.

These laws generally pass because they are veiled beneath titles implying that they promote universally agreed upon virtues, yet their true destructive intent is hidden within, like a worm within a shiny apple. The public does not take the time to investigate these critically important things, as they are constantly bombarded by the media with sports, food, alcohol, and sex advertisements attempting to reduce the innate nobility of mankind into that of mere passive, uninformed consumers; driven like cattle to spend their low earnings on the next fabricated holiday, or event which keeps the hyper-wealthy international business owners hyper-wealthy.

Spring-boarding off of our successful efforts with these new hate laws, in order to give our efforts the appearance of moral validity we will conduct a relentless marketing campaign of any and every shred of a sob-story which we can fabricate, manipulate, or otherwise get our hands on about the supposed plague of stigmatization, cruelty, harassment, and injustice which is occurring against those who like unripe bananas. We will use this to gain public sympathy, as we push for unripe banana eaters to be legally defined as a "protected class." Though we will claim that these efforts are driven by noble sympathy for the supposed "tragic suffering" of our fellow men, regardless of how amazingly inflated, rare, trivial, or blatantly false these claims of suffering and stigmatization are, our secret intention is to harness the full force of the Equal Employment Office (EEO), the courts, and the police behind our views, in order to use these like a hammer to crush, disenfranchise, and effectively subjugate any who would dare to voice an opinion which conflicts with our own.

We will even go to the absurd length of claiming that perceived offenses against this group are as real and prosecutable as genuine ones, filling the majority, who still trust their instincts and senses in their preferment of ripe bananas, with dread. How are they to have free speech, or freedom to act as they wish if there is now a new royalty who, as with the royalty of old, can cause everything they own, or worked for, their ability to work, even their very freedom, to be taken from them not merely for factual offenses, but for the mere perception of offense. Does this establishment of unequal men and unequally applied laws not go against the very principles of equality which these Western egalitarian nations were formed to protect? Of course it does. But since we are among the new elite who are benefiting from these newly warped laws, we don't care. We only claim to care about principles of equality when such claims benefit us. We actually prefer inequality, as long as we get to enjoy the benefits of being among the ruling caste.

We will use our newly acquired force of law to ramrod our supposedly "enlightened" views down the throats of the majority; whose disagreement with and resistance to our efforts, we will claim are only due to ignorance and narrow-mindedness. Surely it can have nothing to do with our arrogance, as our opinions on moral issues are very perfection itself. One or two high-dollar, high-profile lawsuits under these new laws enforcing unripe banana eater "rights" will make private and public employers take notice.

Businesses, whose ultimate goal is profit, will be terror stricken that our new power through the courts could deprive them of this profit. Governments, in like manner, though commissioned to stand for a higher calling than profit, such as protecting their citizenry, must be funded in order to function. Therefore, in order to avoid litigation, both will trip over each other to show that they are the most pro-unripe banana eater employers in their field; implementing new hiring and promotion efforts through their human resource and EEO offices, setting benchmark hiring and promotion standards for unripe banana lovers, mandating recurring reporting on compliance, forcing all employees to undergo unripe banana lover sensitivity training, and forcing supervisors to report, as part of their annual performance metrics, their active unripe banana lover promotion efforts.

It doesn't matter how supportive of this view the nation is. If an individual employer is below the 50% mark of the industry average, claims may still be made that they are under-employing this group, placing their organization at an increased risk for litigation. Say, for example, 90 percent of a company's employees are unripe banana lovers. If the industry average is 95%, claims of under-representation may still be made, which put this company at significant risk for litigation. This is in spite of the fact that this industry may employ a far greater percent of unripe banana lovers than is found within the surrounding population. This effect places a constant pressure on employers, and ultimately the industry, to increase the percentage of unripe banana lovers which they employ, with no realistic means of stopping the upward trend.

Due to their initially limited supply within society, unripe banana lovers will have tremendous hiring and promotional advantages over any of their equally, or often more qualified peers. While these professional advantages will seem like blessings to unripe banana lovers, they will be the worst of curses to everyone else. This is because hiring and promotion are zero-sum games. Any advantage given to one group must necessarily come at the expense of all others. This imbalanced system, if maintained for a long enough period, will result in unripe banana lovers rising in professional position, personal wealth, and societal power, while those who stubbornly cling to what will now be condemned as outmoded views, that ripe bananas taste better, are healthier for you, and are therefore the wiser type of banana to eat, are systematically disenfranchised.

These latter views will be given a condemnatory name, usually ending in -*ist*, such as "ripist." Any who are detected displaying the slightest negative reaction (e.g. expressions, comments, avoidance of those performing it, etc.) related to the topic of unripe banana eating will be marked with this label and stigmatized. Always readily at hand to blame for any of society's emerging, or existing ills, these ripists will begin to be viewed with suspicion and slowly dehumanized in society's eyes. This dehumanization inevitably results in abuse, which ripists will discover that they are increasingly unable to protect themselves from.

Again, seeking to avoid lawsuits by appearing supportive of unripe banana eating, employers will implement "zero-tolerance" policies against unripe banana eating "intolerance." They will either be too stupid to realize, or will simply ignore the fact that this concept is absurd; as it is stating that the organization is intolerant of intolerance. What this really means is that the organization has adopted elitist attitudes; believing that all intolerance but their own is unacceptable. They will begin having new employees sign pre-hire statements agreeing to abide by the company's "core values," which will be modified to include language describing "acceptance" and "celebration" of all types of banana consumption. This combination of forces will ensure that any and all conversation critical of the eating of unripe bananas is silenced within the workplace, while pro-unripe banana conversation will not only be allowed, but will be actively encouraged (i.e. celebrated).

Media outlets, being merely another type of business, and knowing that their films, books, news articles and the many actors and actresses which they employ are ever in the public eye, making them a prime target for litigation under these new "unripe eater equality" and "protected class" laws, will conduct an active, pro-unripe banana eating marketing campaign. They will threaten their actors and actresses with termination, future unemployability, and lawsuits, should they make any public statements about preferring ripe bananas to unripe ones.

Hoping for preferred parts and increased career opportunities, the majority of these actors and actresses will trip over each other to show how much they support unripe banana eating, whenever in public. A few of the brave and independent will resist, but these will quickly evaporate from the public eye, except in pieces condemning them as bigoted, as the media will mostly self-censor any positive reporting out of fear of litigation. News, film, shows, and literature will accordingly begin to take on a strongly pro-unripe banana eating tone, with people asking for and preferring unripe bananas at disproportionate rates to that reflected within society.

Realizing that, should the demographics of their student bodies and faculties be examined for ratios of unripe to ripe banana eaters, they might also be at risk for costly litigation, universities will collaborate with their leadership, trustees, and communities, including local governmental partners, in order to establish special scholarships for unripe banana lovers, and will use their admission committees to ensure that unripe banana eaters are given preferential admission to, and grooming in both graduate and undergraduate programs. Departmental panels will fast-track some of these into tenured faculty positions and will preferentially hire enough unripe banana lovers from their pools of external applicants into other staff vacancies to ensure they are in the upper half of unripe banana eater employing universities.

Medical schools, being simply a specialized type of university and business, will perform the same actions mentioned above for universities and businesses to encourage a student and faculty body which support unripe banana consumption as an "alternate, but accepted lifestyle." This will influence the average opinion of graduating physicians entering the workforce, as their professors, due to fear of termination, will at best remain silent on any negative aspects of unripe banana consumption. More likely, they will actively promote its benefits, due to the recent hiring surge of pro-unripe staff, and the implementation of "zero-tolerance" policies which occurred at their schools, in order to avoid litigation. All other allied health schools (i.e. nursing, pharmacy, and dental) will follow suit.

Private organizations which oversee healthcare delivery (e.g AMA, AHA, TJC, etc.), in order to avoid lawsuits, will likely issue public statements about their solidarity with the consumption of bananas of any ripeness, which they will adopt as a new "core value," mandating written agreement with these values as a requirement for membership. Note this common approach among organizations, of adding language to their core values and then forcing everyone to agree with them in writing. The use of the term "values" here is an attempt to put a positive spin on what is, in actuality, an expression of open distrust by the organization towards their members and applicants. They require these people to provide them with a written agreement merely to protect themselves from countersuits, should they decide to arbitrarily remove members due to words, or actions that give even the slightest impression that they do not embrace the eating of unripe bananas.

They often even include wording within their value statements that other members, as well as members of the public are encouraged to bring any perceived violations of their values, by members, to the attention of the organization's leadership. In other words, freedom of speech, expression, and personal opinion is condemned by these organizations and employers, as they have, within this statement, effectively commissioned all of society to act as spies on their behalf. This is reminiscent of Orwell's *1984*; where the youth were recruited into the "Spies," causing their own parents to fear being turned in by them.[22]

Hospitals, as another type of business also seeking to avoid litigation, will require any care providers which they employ to sign documentation gagging them from recommending the avoidance of unripe banana consumption; even if they know it to be in their patients' best interests, and even if such a recommendation conflicts with the guidance of their consciences. In order to also avoid litigation, editors of various scientific and medical journals will ensure that they preferentially select and promote research which portrays unripe banana eating in a positive light. This will lead to a surge in publication of research articles which are heavily biased in favor of unripe banana consumption.

Primary and secondary schools, also hoping to avoid lawsuits over banana discrimination, and wishing to groom their students for university and workforce success, will begin to force unripe banana eating education material upon their students at the youngest age which they can get away with doing so without significant parental pushback. As the combined efforts of businesses, governments, media, and universities ensure that unripe banana consumption is normalized, in fact, promoted as another type of "diversity" to be "celebrated," this age will continue to creep downwards.

Parents will not only fail to prevent, but in some instances will actively encourage the consumption of unripe bananas during their children's earliest years. Many will do so because they were taught by and believed the guidance of the academic and medical elites: elites who, fearing litigation, stated that the consumption of unripe bananas is perfectly normal, and that any perceived correlation between it and illness is an artifact of earlier, unenlightened, ripist world views. Internet Service Providers (ISP's), search engines, and social media sites, knowing that they are taking legal risks by allowing pro-ripe material on their systems, will actively begin promoting pages and articles supportive of unripe banana consumption, and suppressing, or removing altogether, any material which could be deemed as ripist.

A new generation of adults will appear, whose earliest memories will have been formed within this *Brave New World*, which is tyrannized by those promoting unripe banana consumption. Having, since their childhood, had their very cartoons infused with pro-unripe banana eating propaganda, and viewing all around them paths to success involving the acceptance of unripe banana consumption, and paths to unemployment, poverty, stigmatization, and even incarceration, for believing what their own senses and experiences still faintly hint to them, that the taste and healthfulness of ripe bananas is far superior to that of unripe ones, only the rare madman, or the extremely courageous will dare to speak the truth.

This forced acceptance a view which is internally known to be false will have an overall corrosive effect upon societal integrity. This is because those who have grown accustomed to compromising their integrity on one subject, will be more likely to compromise it the next time doing so might somehow profit them. This reduction of societal integrity weakens the cohesiveness of the nation itself, if ever so slightly, as the foundations of societies, families, and really any relationships between individuals, are built upon trust in the integrity of others.

The combined, sustained onslaught of media stigmatization, silencing within, or removal from the workforce, and prosecution within the courts, will result in a continual shrinking of numbers of all but the most devout ripists. These will be unable to appeal to the courts for protection from any but the most flagrant of offenses committed against them. This is because both they and their abusers will possess an awareness that proof of their ripist views, a new sort of Orwellian thought-crime, may always be brought out and paraded as condemnatory evidence against the credibility of their testimony.

Subconscious Manipulation

The ever-present threat of frivolous lawsuits, which has seen a significant growth rate during the last few decades, has resulted in a strong push within Western media to intentionally select minorities, whether of faith, sex, race, or sadly, even state of sexual perversion (more on this later), for protagonist roles, and their almost complete removal from any antagonist ones, within film and television. While there is nothing wrong with the mass media accurately reflecting ratios and characteristics of these groups as they are commonly encountered within society, this relatively recent push is a zero-sum game with sinister undertones.

If there is a trend for minorities to be massively over-represented in good, and under-represented in bad roles, this by necessity must come at the expense of the majority; who are made to fill the vacuum by being under-represented in good and over-represented in bad roles.

"But the majority are still cast in far more roles overall than the minority. So how does this matter?" someone is sure to reply.

It matters because of how the subconscious works. While our conscious minds are able to apply varying rule sets to groupings of observations, our subconscious minds do this poorly, if at all. The conscious mind, for example, knows some groups of events to be real, and therefore that conclusions derived from them will typically always apply. Conversely, it knows that some trends are purely fictional, and therefore that any conclusions derived from these will only apply in certain specific times, locations, or contexts.

The subconscious, on the other hand, does not compartmentalize the information which it absorbs into fictional and non-fictional categories, as the conscious mind does. It formerly seldom needed to. For thousands of years, only a small subset of the population was sufficiently elevated above constantly worrying about their many domestic and labor related demands to invest much time, or resources into literature, or theater performances, where fiction might be encountered. Even in these instances, though fictional works and performances existed in antiquity (e.g. Aristophanes' *The Birds*), the vast majority of works which were written, or performed, until merely the past few centuries, involved non-fictional themes, or those which were believed to be (e.g. *The Iliad*). It is only since the substantial cheapening of the press and urbanization of society which occurred as a result of the Industrial Revolution that the fictional genre saw a rapid explosion, both in prevalence and popularity; unfortunately to the point of far outstripping that of non-fiction, these days.

The primary purpose of the subconscious is to run in the background, scrutinize all events and information which it is exposed to for trends, attempt to draw conclusions about reality from these observed trends, and use these conclusions to predict the probability of future event occurrences. It then passes feelings based upon these calculated probabilities and determinations back to the conscious mind, for it to use during daily interactions and decisions. If the subconscious is fed fiction, as well as fact about a certain subject, it simply weights and merges the information from the two sources. While the circumstances surrounding any information which was received from the fictional source may cause the mind to substantially reduce its weighting, compared to that of factual information, the fiction will still affect the composite perception of reality, and subsequently, the probability calculations which the subconscious arrives at regarding future event occurrences.

One example of this latter instance is when the mind is shown, in a book or movie, a person who can fly. The conscious mind knows that this trend of flying humans is strictly bound to fictional contexts. The subconscious, on the other hand, struggles with this selective application of rule sets to seemingly identical situations and people. It simply lumps observed fictional trends in with observed factual ones; absorbing both.

This is one of the reasons why haunted houses and frightening movies affect us so. While the conscious mind knows that what the film is depicting is fantasy, temporarily and partially suspending disbelief during its viewing, the subconscious isn't quite sure. While it has never seen ghosts appear in mirrors in any of the, perhaps million times it has been in front of a mirror, it saw this very thing occur once in the version of reality presented to it by a film. It will therefore compile all of the realities which it has been exposed to into a single composite one, leaving it with a belief that there is a, perhaps 1 in 1 million probability that ghosts can appear in mirrors.

Since shocking or traumatic events tend to be remembered far better than ordinary ones, a psychological phenomenon known as the Von Restorff effect, most of the million uneventful mirror glances will have been forgotten, pushing the perceived probability ratio of a ghost being seen in the mirror far higher; perhaps to 1 in 10,000. It is unlikely that any of these subconscious calculations and probabilities will be available to the conscious mind. The conscious mind will simply take note of the resulting, ever-so-slight increase in uneasiness which it feels around mirrors.

Interesting corollaries to this are found in the abominable horror film and video game industries. Since the writers and directors of such trash wish to shock the senses of their audience as much as possible with the *badness* of the antagonist(s), they will frequently juxtapose any badness with the most innately good people, scenarios, and environments as possible. Things instinctively associated with the idea of goodness, such as symbols of childhood (e.g. babies, mothers, children, children's play toys, playrooms, etc.) churches, preachers, clowns, the elderly, etc., will be superimposed with things instinctively associated with ideas of *badness* (i.e. being harmful to body, or soul), such as decay in its various forms (e.g. corpses, rotten vegetation, or spoiled food), unhealthy environments (e.g. those with slime, algae, mildew, or mold), unhealthy physical conditions (e.g. soiled, or torn clothing, poor hygiene, physical defects, signs of illness, etc.), and things which can cause bodily harm (e.g. monsters, wild animals famous as man-eaters, malevolent spirits, symbols of isolation, harmful weather phenomena, torture devices, etc.).

Returning to our subject, when the subconscious compares the ratios and characteristics of the previously mentioned minority groups which it has observed within fictional media sources with those which it has personally observed, or learned about from factual ones, the net product of its underlying views about these groups, as well as its views about the majority, will be affected ever so slightly. The more often this misrepresentation occurs, the more frequently people are exposed to it, the more credibility the mind will tend to subconsciously ascribe to these misrepresentations. Once one misrepresentation is believed, the next one encountered, which may be as far removed from the new normal as the first was from absolute truth, will shift belief that much further from reality. Over a long enough time-scale, views on reality, including the characteristics of certain groups, can by this process grow sufficiently skewed from truth to allow for dangerous results on both sides of the spectrum; that of inordinate credit, as well as that of inordinate discredit.

A group which is continually portrayed positively can come to be revered as a new sort of godlike nobility, whose most overt acts of wrongdoing are either excused, or ignored. This is, in fact, what occurred with many of the heroes of the ancient world (e.g. Thoth, Apollonius of Tyana, Mohammed, Buddha, Jesus, etc.), who later came to be revered as gods, demigods, or otherwise divine. This same process is happening with minorities of race, religion, "gender," or sexual preference, in the Western world today. Overly glamorizing these various groups encourages the public to subconsciously and shallowly believe that causes, if held by any of these, are inherently more just. This has the side-effect of fostering the societal character flaws of arrogance and unreasonableness. The popular view becomes: "If my idea isn't held by most, then I am a minority, and therefore more likely to be in the right." These two ideas of popularity and verity are unrelated. If your idea isn't held by most, then your idea simply isn't held by most.

And this is actually the better instance, where people continue to believe in a single overarching law. More commonly, when a specific social group is given inordinate credit for a long enough period, these cultures come to believe that there are two sets of rules and laws; a rigid one which is applicable to the majority and must be strictly enforced, and another, more lenient one, applicable only to various minority groups and laden with dozens of special exemptions.

This is a resurrection of a new class structure of royalty upon the ruins of the old one; whose previous slow, arduous dismantling cost the lives of tens of thousands of American and European patriots. This is a tremendously dangerous view for societies, or individuals to adopt, as any time there is a belief in differing sets of laws, which are selectively applicable to different groups of people, in other words, that justice is relative to the judged, there is a simultaneous underlying disbelief in the absolute and universal nature of justice itself. When the comely form of true justice evaporates, then ugly, arbitrary, and generally cruel power, rushes in to fill her spot of preeminence.

In addition, this caricature of the majority, which often occurs under the hypocritical banners of "Tolerance," "Equality," and "No Hate," subconsciously encourages people to actively judge, label, and condemn the majority of the nation based upon physically observable traits; such as the fairness of their skin, their choice of faith, if it happens to be the one traditionally held within their nation, or their personal views on family structure and sexuality, if these happen to also be traditional. Left leaning media and academic figures do not hold the moral high ground simply because they fabricate labels to taunt their opposition with, like children in a schoolyard: quite the opposite, in fact. Their new brands of racism, religious intolerance, hetero-phobia, and indigeno-phobia against the majority are more subtle, frighteningly systematic, and institutionalized than any of the extremely rare opposite views which may still linger in isolated pockets. Regardless of this rarity, the left-heavy media seem perpetually thrilled to repeatedly exhume and parade these latter views about, if afforded the slightest opportunity; pretending these half-decomposed corpses to be not simply alive, but healthy, growing, and reproducing at frightening rates. Indeed, they pretend these views to be the single greatest existing threat to society.

Groups which are continually portrayed in a negative light, even those of the majority, can come to be seen as subhuman; a status which allows for the cruelest of abuses to be committed against them, up to and including murder and enslavement. To drive the importance of this point home, a few examples will be given of when this has occurred on the negative side, resulting in dehumanization, enslavement, and murder. The German people were by these means brought to the point of dehumanizing the Jewish people prior to the second world war. This same event occurred on the other side of the globe, during the same period, with the Japanese people towards the Chinese and Koreans. But let's not simply stop with these modern classic examples. This also occurred with the Soviets towards the capitalists, the French Catholics towards the Protestant Huguenots in the 1500's, the Anglicans towards the Anabaptists in the 1600's, the Protestants towards the Mormons in the 1800's, and by almost all faiths towards anyone accused of witchcraft all throughout the Age of Discovery, until the mid 1800's. It occurred with the English, American, and Dutch slaveholders towards the Africans and American Indians during the same period. Since the advent of Islam, until this very day, it is occurring against non-Muslims in nations infected with that pathological philosophy.

When the media departs from reality to consistently portray the majority of a nation in a reduced ratio of protagonist roles and in an increased ratio of antagonist ones, as they are doing within the twin hearts of Western civilization, Europe and America, it is an indicator that these cultures are already well down this road of slow, subtle, but steady demonization: a road which ultimately leads to abuse, up to and including murder. What makes today's phenomenon unique, is that it is one of the rare times in history, indeed, the first of this magnitude, when such demonization efforts are being targeted at a nation's majority, rather than at any of its minority groups.

There seems to be an underlying intent to these questionably independent, relentless, and widespread efforts to subtly erode any existing faith in the moral character and values of the majority. Destruction of faith in the moral character of a nation's majority has the effect of also destroying, by association, any faith in the character of these people's ancestors. This is important, because defamation of the character of the ancestors of a nation's majority, de facto condemns any laws which were created by them, which are simply a written memorial of the philosophical ideas, values, and views which caused them to initially cohere and identify as a nation. Once faith in these laws is destroyed, faith in the merit and subsequent right of existence of the nation itself falls as well.

Nations are essentially a set of philosophical ideas which spring up, like plants, take hold of a people and leave a train of institutions, laws, buildings, and organizations behind them, like so many branches and fruit. But destroy these philosophical ideas, and you strike the plant at its root. All of the things which were nourished by it will wither and die. Remnants of previous great cultural ideas may still be seen in the remaining colossal buildings and carved stone letters of former Greek, Roman, and Egyptian glory; now long abandoned and slowly melting away, like ice.

Were attempts at this type of manipulation to be sudden and exaggerated, the falsities associated with them would be readily apparent, quickly noticed, and subsequently condemned by eyes and ears trained in and familiar with the truth. We instinctively sense that manipulation generally has its roots in a lack of trust in, and love of those whom it targets. When people realize that they were the target for manipulation, they typically feel insulted and slightly embarrassed that they were perceived to be naïve enough to be selected for this. Accordingly, they drastically reduce, or eliminate, whatever trust they previously had in the manipulator, often warn mutual acquaintances to be on their guard around him, or her, and personally harden themselves against whatever views, or actions this person was cunningly attempting to force upon them.

Since this backfire scenario makes any future manipulation efforts nearly impossible, it is greatly in a manipulator's best interests to avoid detection by being as subtle and patient as possible with their manipulation efforts. The water which the frog sits in must be heated slowly, in order to keep it from noticing and hopping out to save its life. If these manipulators carefully present society with a version of reality which is only slightly askew from what is generally recognized as its true state, the subtle difference will likely go unnoticed. The ideal lie is one which is so subtle that, should it be brought to light, it might pass for an unintentional mistake. Yet a thousand of these minute lies, if left unchecked, can accumulate over time to have the same impact as a few flagrant ones. As with a ship, even the slightest imbalance in drag on its sides, a single oar left in the water, if allowed to persist long enough and not actively corrected by the observant captain, or sailor, can throw the entire vessel off-course; sometimes even causing it to traverse an enormous arc and proceed in a retrograde direction.

This type of manipulation works in an inverse manner to the classic sociological phenomenon of a *self-fulfilling prophecy*. In self-fulfilling prophecies, an action is caused due to the impact of its being predicted. In this instance, an actual change in reality occurs in response to the presentation of a false one. Intentional manipulation of the demographic ratios of those filling various protagonist and antagonist roles in print, film, or screen media, as well as selective reporting of facts related to demographic ratios in the news, has a major impact upon society's perception of reality, influencing its subsequent behavior, and therefore manipulating reality itself.

Consider, for example, if we disliked a group whose political positions were opposed to ours. How could we supplant their position and power, if we knew that they were stronger than we were? Knowing that we would have no chance, if we were to manfully challenge and struggle with them, or their ideas directly, we could instead attempt to turn public opinion against them and allow society to destroy them for us. Society is an almost irresistible force when awakened and possessed of a common idea. Based upon the most ludicrous of pretexts, we could allege that our opponents stand opposed to, and hate the bulk of society.

Knowing these allegations to be false, our opponents will at first laugh at our lies. Undaunted, we will persist in them, never deviating, never flinching, knowing that the common mass of society typically has neither the time nor the resources to research and differentiate the true from the sensational, yet false.

The first to eventually succumb to our lies will be the nation's poor and poorly educated, who are ever in the majority compared to the wealthy and highly educated. Generally, these former groups already possess a simmering anger towards the nation's wealthy rulers, who claim to love the poor and to stand for building and supporting a strong middle class, but whose actions typically prove their commitment to this view to be lukewarm at best.

As our lies begin to penetrate into this part of the headline skimming public, our opponents will begin to take notice and become concerned. They will, however, be stuck in the always difficult position of proving a negative. In addition, their seeming concern will give a slight hue of truth to our lies. Various random groups who have more strongly believed our lies will begin to spontaneously attack our opponents. We will portray this as a grassroots movement of the people, and paint ourselves as champions of democracy for supporting and encouraging it. Ultimately, if we can press our lies into society enough, lies which cost us nothing, society will destroy our opponents for us. Not only will we never have to directly and manfully struggle with our adversaries, but our lies will have the additional benefit of painting us as the people's heroes; bravely protecting society from the monsters who wished to harm them.

Language Manipulation

A dark cloud, which appears to have blown across the Atlantic from Europe and the Middle East, has recently spread across these great United States. This cloud is one of fear and control. It is one of totalitarianism. It makes a rattling of chains, and when it speaks, its native tongue is deception.

Surely I must be exaggerating. Such things cannot be in the land whose boasts are its freedom and equality. But it can be, is, and grows more prevalent by the day. We have become the land of doublespeak. For any who have not read Orwell's *1984*, I would strongly encourage it, as many of the language manipulation techniques discussed within that work are being used against the American and European people this very day.[22]

One example is the manipulation of word meanings and the outright prohibition not only of certain words, but of entire subjects from any use, or scrutiny, upon risk of fine, loss of employment, or even imprisonment. One example is the word *gay*. For the past several hundred years, this English word meant *happy*. Now, like a beautiful woman tied to a rotting corpse, this symbol of goodness has been welded to the meaning of homosexual perversion. This has been intentionally done by leftist cultural engineers for the express purpose of removing, or at least reducing the natural revulsion which the mentally healthy feel towards these acts.

This approach has been intentionally selected, due to an awareness of the way that mankind subconsciously understands words and language. Languages are often more accurate than people realize, or even intend them to be. They are archaeological mounds of ideas which have grown up alongside the various cultures which developed them. By investigating the etymology of words, we are often able to develop a more complete understanding of the ideas which these words originally symbolized.

Take, for example, the word *entertainment*. Note the root *tain*, from the French *tenir*, meaning to hold, preceded by the word *enter*, from the French *inter*, meaning within, followed by *ment*, meaning the concept of. In other words, the word entertainment itself means the concept of holding within; roughly the equivalent of holding captive, restraining, or ensnaring. Unsurprisingly, this word shares the same root as the words *contain* and *retain*. We may forget the etymologies of the words these cultures used, and therefore feel that we are safe in our dissembling, yet our very words often pierce our disguise and betray us. Were men aware, when they used the word entertainment, that they were essentially admitting that they were ensnared, they would quickly abandon this word for another, less genuine one.

While we may only consciously perceive the negative and positive connotation of words when they are explicitly stated, such as when they are coupled with terms of comparison, like *best, good, bad,* or *worst,* we subconsciously detect these connotations far more frequently. Within our subconscious, individual words trigger floods of memories and images of the things which we associate with them. When the word *ball* is used, for example, our subconscious instantly calls up and flashes before our mind's eye an amalgamation of the beach ball we once had, the kickball we used as a boy, etc., eliciting an overall positive, or negative feeling, which is the composite of all of the feelings which we felt during the times that we were exposed to, or encountered these things.

Things change slightly, when we shift from speaking, or reading about simple concepts such as objects, people, and actions, to complex abstractions, or complex attributes containing one, or more of these abstractions. The thoughts and feelings which the subconscious evokes in these latter instances generally come from what we have been taught about their meaning. This makes the understanding of their meaning, and subsequently the feelings generated by these meanings very liable to manipulation.

With few exceptions, the majority of people accept and trust the modern meanings of these complex, or abstract words which they have been provided by media and academic figures. They naïvely believe the myth that the majority of these people are selected and promoted based solely upon their intelligence, diligence, and honesty, and not rather due to the degree of alignment of their worldviews with those of the tenured, or to their willingness and ability to tailor their labor, and very often their results and conclusions, to market influences. If challenged about these complex, or abstract meanings, the public will often parrot whatever prefabricated answers about these subjects they have heard these "experts" use. Unfortunately, these well-intentioned people are often manipulated by these same experts.

This meaning manipulation has occurred, over the past, perhaps 25 years, with the word *gay*. Its meaning has been transformed from an innocent, wholesome, joyful, and good synonym for *happiness*, into that of a complex attribute rooted in profligacy, corruption, lewdness, and overall moral degeneracy. While most among the older generations, who learned the true meaning of this word before the propaganda onslaught had begun in earnest, continue to cling to their original understanding of it, the majority of the nation's youth, whose earliest exposures to this word were already tainted by this new warped definition, and whose developing minds are always more vulnerable to manipulation techniques, have mostly fallen victim to this marketing campaign, and have begun to purchase the foul product which it is hawking.

This has also been occurring with the more sinister revisions of the meanings of the terms *freedom* and *equality*. I will pause for a moment to interject that men should always be on their guard when freedom is touted as the main justification for any cause. The concept of freedom is a noble one, which resonates within men's souls, because of the free will which they internally sense that they possess. In fact, several philosophers went so far as to claim that our will, this deciding ability within us, is synonymous with our true selves. We are not our memory, or our body, but our will; our ability to choose; our freedom. Therefore, our innate love of our own existence is, on a subconscious level, inseparable from our love of the concept of freedom.

Until relatively recently, the meaning of the word freedom was always associated with goodness. The free man was one who was able to do, or say whatever good things his conscience directed him towards. Consider, for example, the goodness implied when discussing the freedom which is provided to an enslaved person. Never before was this word used with reference to acts of moral corruption, as it is today. Were an individual in the early 1900's to have used the word *freedom* with reference to the performance of morally corrupt actions, such as the frequenting of brothels, murder, or the manipulation of others for personal gain, this person would have been quickly corrected. Yet this is exactly how the meaning of this word has been, and continues to be abused today.

This flag word is increasingly being used not only to drape and obscure noble words, actions, objects, or ideas, such as fallen war heroes, but also ignoble ones, such as the dumpsters of pornography which flood the internet, as well as the degenerate parasites who create and profit from such things.

Since freedom is a foundational concept which our nation was built upon, this modern attack upon this word's meaning is, in actuality, an attack upon the very philosophical ideas and ideals which our nation represents: effectively, an outright attack upon the nation herself. Rather than attack the concept of freedom directly, the first wave of this attack was conducted against the definition of *goodness*, which freedom has always been associated with. The claim was made that goodness, which is rooted in the nature of man, the soul that enlivens him, and ultimately the nature of the God who would create such a soul, has no absolute existence; merely a relative one based upon personal opinion.

This is the standard technique employed by those holding the atheist worldview, who lead this attack upon the egalitarian principles which this nation was founded upon. When attempting to silence their opponents on a complex political principle, which will always have an ethical dimension, they begin by cunningly claiming that this principle is relative, rather than absolute. Generally, this lie is marketed across their media and academic mouthpieces, until finally, like holes in a dam, the ignorance, or inattention of a few executives, legislators, or judges, allows this subtle, yet dreadfully significant change to become incorporated into national law.

What these lawmakers and the citizens whom they are paid to protect fail to realize is that, like Greeks within a Trojan horse, nestled within this absolute to relative conversion is the implicit claim that the principle in question is solely based upon arbitrary personal opinion. Here is where the knife strikes vital organ. If this principle becomes opinion based, and infinite opinions exist, then nothing can ever be subsequently identified as truly characteristic of said principle. All opinions become equally valid and equally invalid; equally true and equally false.

Claiming that all views about a political issue are of equal value forces those widely held ones which are rooted in the guidance of conscience, reason, and instinctively sensed truth, down to the same plane as the most error and ignorance warped ones. The reason-based views of Socrates on a philosophical principle become no more valid than the murderous views of Nero; those of Jesus no more valid than those of Lenin. Any whose views remain rooted in the absolutes of conscience, reason, and instinctively sensed truth will acutely feel the injustice of this claim, and will justifiably be the most vocal about their concern. Yet these complaints, being too abstract for the majority of the headline skimming public to immediately grasp, will generally fall upon deaf ears.

More than this. Since those holding the atheist worldview have already succeeded beforehand in quietly and cunningly embedding this relativistic meaning conversion into national law, any voiced concerns will be responded to with threats backed by the full force of the U. S. Government. This silencing of opposition will be presented to the public as an act of kindness which is being done out of respect for those holding "equally valuable, yet contrasting" opinions. All must love the "diversity of opinions" and hate the dominance of a single viewpoint, even if the viewpoint in question is the absolute truth. Not believing in absolute truth, these people will claim that, regardless of the ubiquity of a position, or the strength of the reasoning which supports it, each viewpoint is simply one of many, with no innate value providing it with any increased amount of authority. This is merely a thinly veiled technique for denying the reality of the principle altogether. It is the closest which a society can get to destroying absolute truths. While truths themselves can never be destroyed, by silencing those who would speak, or write them, truths can be prohibited from performing their natural work of revealing error, and the many forms of falsity.

This technique of attacking America by redefining the meanings of words which her foundational principles were built upon has increased to a fever pitch during the recent few decades. It is a particularly useful tool for the morally corrupt, who long for a loosening of the fetters which our wise founders long ago placed upon their ability to spread their corruption.

Why can't the internet be made a wholesome place for children? Because the selfish and morally corrupt wrap their greed and complete apathy towards the well-being of the men and women whose lives they destroy, in the sacred concept of freedom. Why are drug laws being revoked nationally? The same reason. Why must families avoid areas where rallies of the sexually corrupt occur? The same reason.

This brings me to the very frightening revision which has recently occurred with the meaning of the word *equality*. The second foundational principle of the American philosophical idea is built upon this word. It is this idea which is ultimately under attack by those who wish to see the American idea extinguished. Equality formerly always meant deserving of the same treatment, or consideration as all others. In effect, it was, and still should be a synonym for justice. Yet, while still using this same term, the idea which this term symbolizes has become the very definition of injustice. This is because it has been married with the preferential treatment of whichever group or "protected class" furthers the political ends of those leftists who are unethically grasping for power. These are made more "equal" than others.

The only "class" not "protected," or more realistically, raised to ascendancy within Western nations, are those in the majority. It makes no difference if we are speaking of race, sex, sexual habits, or religion. Minorities among all are being used to convince the majority that they are inferior. We are being trained to calmly accept our yokes. Unless we wish to live the lives of cattle, dragging plows for our new masters, then we must manfully resist these efforts by those whom we still overwhelmingly overpower.

Media

The media are placed in a special position of public trust, and therefore have an increased level of social responsibility; much like a police officer does. In both instances, this trust is due to the severity of damage which falsehood, or cunning and sinister manipulation by individuals in either of these positions could inflict upon the innocent, common man. Yet unlike the police officer, who is condemned as corrupt, removed from his position of trust, and often prosecuted in criminal court for the slightest evidence of either intentional falsehood, or fact manipulation in support of a personal agenda, media figures and outlets, many of whom actively and brazenly manipulate facts to promote the political and cultural views of their owners, funders, or board members, are only in extremely rare instances terminated, and are even less frequently prosecuted. Whereas a police officer might go to prison for a false statement which he makes on a report, a media figure, or outlet which regularly falsifies, or manipulates facts, will at the worst have to print a correction, which they subsequently tend to "bury."

And yet, how many lives does falsehood, or manipulation by a police officer impact? One? Perhaps a dozen? Orders of magnitude more lives are impacted by lying, or manipulative media figures, or outlets, due to their unique, border spanning platforms.

"The span of the impact may be greater in the case of media falsehood, but the potential severity of the impact is greater in the case of police falsehood," some might say. "The corrupt police officer could plant evidence which could lead to an innocent man being imprisoned, or even executed."

Yet how many innocents can, and in fact do, media figures or outlets harm; sometimes even triggering their deaths? How many of their false, or manipulative statements, which are no different from false, or planted evidence, stoke the flames of public indignation in the direction of people whose only crime is that of disagreeing with the political, or cultural views of major media outlets' shareholders, or owners?

Wouldn't any court in the land condemn and punish a person who had successfully instigated a mob lynching of an innocent person? Why do we suddenly change what we instinctively understand to be unjust, when discussing an organization possessing wealth, attorneys, and a public platform, and when the innocent who is under attack isn't a runaway slave, but is instead anyone comprising, or representing the conservative majority of the nation? It is nothing more than simple, base fear which causes us to second guess our judgement here: fear of the damage which these people and organizations can inflict upon us with their platforms, attorney's, and wealth.

Left-heavy media figures and outlets attack the very foundations of Western society, as they cower within their safely glimmering, metropolitan high-rises, while police officers daily risk their lives to preserve and protect civilization; often in miserable conditions and for meager pay. Perhaps it is a subconscious awareness of guilt over their betrayed trust, which causes many media figures and outlets to attack the reputation of the police, who possess a similar trust, and yet who seldom betray it. Perhaps this is why media outlets appear to love slathering the thinnest of allegations of police corruption across international headlines, and portraying police officers as corrupt within film, books, and television.

Police represent good, order, justice, and authority. Those who are tainted with the atheist worldview, which denies the absolute nature of virtues, such as good and justice, will fail to see law, which is rooted in them, as anything more than the tyrannical caprice of whomever is in power. Police, as the executors of this tyrannical caprice, will be seen as the immoral agents of a self-serving tyrant: effectively, as coldhearted mercenaries.

This hatred isn't limited to the police, though. Now that we have lain bare the cause, we can see why a milder version of it is also extended towards any others whose position implies the ability to enforce a law which is rooted in absolute virtue: from judges, to pastors, to fathers, to soldiers.

"But I don't notice the same level of resentment towards these," one might say.

The resentment is real, nonetheless. It is merely subdued in these other instances because, except in unique, temporary, and rare situations, such as during martial law, childhood, or a court case, media outlets and figures are not typically under these people's direct authority. They must, however, submit to the authority of police, whenever and wherever they are detained, or questioned by them. Police are even authorized, and are generally physically able to overpower them, if they resist. The idea of someone being legally allowed to physically overpower you, to even use lethal force upon you if you become a sufficient threat, is both foreign and terrifying to the minds of these spoiled, or neglected children turned adults. These rage at, denigrate, and sometimes even strike at the Police, in the same way which an unruly child would rage at, denigrate, and possibly even strike at his parents for not giving absolute reign to his will.

Large swaths of the media these days frequently and hypocritically abuse their special protection under the first amendment to promote the very tyrannical principles which the Constitution itself stands as a monument against. Formerly, when media elements would cease objectively reporting facts and instead attempt to influence societal views, and subsequently, world events, this action would be condemned under its more honest name: *propaganda*. Knowing that the common man understands and loathes the sinister idea which this term symbolizes, one might think that such an act would be carefully avoided by the media. Not so. The stakes are too high and the prizes of national and even international power and wealth are too tempting for these media outlets and their corrupt handlers and investors, who are often one and the same, to throw in the towel on their social engineering efforts and simply return to presenting the public with honest, unbiased truth.

These masters of spin simply repackage and remarket the old product under new, more positive sounding brand names, or catch phrases. These are rotated whenever the general public, whom they arrogantly consider to be stupid, teeming, and unwashed masses, appears to be growing aware of the rouse. A few examples of this ever-changing list of synonyms for propaganda are, *political correctness*, more commonly known as *PC*, *anti-bullying*, *multiculturalism*, *celebration of diversity*, and *tolerance*. Though all sound superficially positive, a common tyrannical motive lies beneath their placid surfaces.

Regarding *political correctness*, everyone wants their views to be considered correct; a synonym for acceptable within the political sphere. *Political Correctness* is in reality an intentional misnomer for cunningly hidden duplicity. This intentional deception applies not only to the practice of political correctness in conversation, but to the name of the concept itself. There is nothing "correct" about the practice. It is the intentional, politically driven mislabeling, or incorrectness, which is being referred to, in practice. The further one investigates how political correctness is embodied in action, the more one begins to feel a chilling sense of nostalgia. This is exactly the language control, intentional mislabeling, and intentional removal of words from vocabulary to control or lessen their usage in thought that was discussed by George Orwell in his brilliant work, *1984*. It is modern "doublespeak."[22] In reality, the only views which are generally accepted as politically correct these days are those liberal ones which the media's economic handlers have approved for dissemination to the masses.

While everyone would agree that it is noble to attempt to prevent bullying, the fact is that, besides in a few exceptions, the bulk of those whom the media identifies as victims of bullying are those who symbolize, or whose views agree with anything other than that of the nation's majority, and the bulk of those whom the media condemns as bullies, those whose person, or views represent it. This does not mean that bullying doesn't, in actuality, also occur in the reverse direction. Being embedded in well intentioned, yet short sighted national policy, this other type of bullying is several orders of magnitude more widespread. Although, with few exceptions, these incidents are either excused, or contemptuously ignored.

In a similar manner, on the surface, it is hard to see how a push for increased *tolerance*, and a *celebration of the diversity* of all races, religions, cultures, and people groups could be abused. This seems simply to be the democratic principle of equality in action. When we look beneath the hood at the engine of this machine, however, we discover that the media celebrates and tolerates any, except those who are associated with, or representative of the generally conservative majority of the native population: typically, conservative, heterosexual, Christian, Caucasian males, in the two hubs of power where we find the propagandists most actively at work: America and Europe.

While I make mention of the intentional targeting of Caucasian males, I do not want people to misunderstand me here. Noble men and women of all races are fighting to stem this attempt to destroy Western egalitarianism and all should be praised for it. When these stand up, they are generally attacked as well. I merely make mention of conservative, heterosexual, Christian, Caucasian males because, traditionally being the most numerous, enfranchised, and therefore empowered demographic within America and Europe, they have recently been the primary target of the most sustained, coordinated attacks; hypocritically and intolerantly being targeted for destruction in the name of tolerance.

These efforts are not simply occurring in America and Europe. Any who take the time to truly study the systematic targeting and brutal rape, torture, and murder of the Caucasian Boer farmers in South Africa, simply because of the color of their skin, will be appalled. Not surprisingly, the mainstream media takes no notice of these atrocities, since doing so might trigger pity. This would destroy their narrative of all conservative, heterosexual, Christian, Caucasian males being the bourgeoisie abusers, and all minorities of any sort (e.g. race, sex, sexual preference, religion, etc.) being their proletariat victims. It is the same bourgeoisie versus proletariat narrative, merely expanded into new categories, which the Bolshevik communists previously used to foment their murderous "Grand Revolution."

Returning to our topic, we must use caution when dealing with the word *tolerance*. Like the word *freedom*, *tolerance* is not inherently good, though both words give every subject which they are applied to, whether noble or ignoble, the superficial appearance of goodness. In reality, *tolerance* of vice, corruption, and abuse, and the *freedom* to perform, or promote these things are destructive societal diseases. As Zoroaster so aptly stated in the *Gathas* of the *Zend*-Avesta, "But he who will not help to transform evil, shall be with those in the abode of the lie, for he who

Returning to the Age of Reason

looks upon evil with tolerance is no other than evil" (Ushtavaiti Gatha Yasna 46:6).[27]

We see the true character of this modern philosophy of tolerance when we hear children, whose earliest memories were formed in a world already under the tyranny of the propagandists, make staggering comments today, like, "It's impossible to discriminate against white (i.e. Caucasian) people." Everyone, even these children, understand that it is theoretically possible to discriminate against anyone. What they are attempting to express in this statement is their awareness and understanding of the destructive, communist, bourgeoisie versus proletariat message which this seemingly harmless tolerance movement carries hidden within it, like Greeks within a Trojan Horse. They, of course, do not recognize it as being fundamentally communist, however they understand its analogous defining characteristics.

The tolerance movement isn't about equality. It is about deconstructing Western democratic culture as a whole and replacing it with a structure based upon economic tyranny. It is about disenfranchising, marginalizing, and even physically replacing, the united, intelligent, democracy loving native citizens of Western nations, with a divided, uninformed people who are more accustomed to the fetters of tyranny.

Is it any surprise that special social privileges have been provided to those races and cultures who have, until relatively recently, been accustomed to a lack of freedom? Indians, whose nation traditionally had a formal caste system, and still informally does, are provided with immigration, hiring, promotion, and scholarship opportunities which native Caucasian Americans are not. Arab and African immigrants, whose predominately Islamic faith absolutely denies the equality of mankind, and therefore tends towards tyranny and abuse, are not only flooding, en masse, into Europe and America, but are actively being imported as so called "refugees" by national leaders of both; being subsequently provided with special hiring, promotion, housing, and scholarship opportunities. Several South and Central American peoples, especially Mexicans, whose Catholic, machismo culture tends towards aristocracy, or tyranny, rather than democracy, are not merely flooding across the American border, but are also being provided with housing, hiring, promotion, and scholarship opportunities which native Caucasian Americans are not. The Black American people, who were held under the cruel dominion of the slaver's lash, where they and their children were worked, bred, and traded like cattle for hundreds of years, have long been American residents, but were only a mere ~150 years ago made into free men. I am intentionally not referring to this people as African American, as only a fraction of a percent among them, or even several generations of their ancestors, were born in Africa. They are true and full Americans, just like the Caucasian Americans: no more, no less. Even more recently, with the end of school segregation and Jim Crow laws, this people received full equality. Many are yet living who remember these events.

Though Black Americans have come a tremendous way in the short period since their emancipation, is it to be believed that the massive amount of cultural damage which was caused by hundreds of years of brutal slavery, enforced ignorance, and the destruction of the black family unit have been completely erased so soon? Are there no artifacts of these things which continue to persist within modern Black American culture? Of course there are. Cultural artifacts of these things will persist into the next century. These people are also being provided with hiring, promotion, scholarship, legal, and several other advantages which native Caucasian Americans are not; all of which results in their promotion within American society.

But what do we even mean when we say Caucasian? Most people think that this is a single race, however it is actually a range of races (e.g. English, Dutch, German, Spanish, Scottish, French, Russian, Armenian, Georgian, Iranian, North Indian, Slavic, Irish, Scottish, Icelandic, Norwegian, Scandinavian, Polish, Austrian, Czech, Italian, Greek, etc.). The common progenitor of these races, prior to their diaspora and subsequent development of distinct languages, cultures, and physical characteristics, was the Proto-Indo-European race (PIE). These people are thought to have originated as a distinct race during the early Neolithic (7500-5500 B.C.) to middle Neolithic period (5500-4500 B.C.) in either the Pontic-Caspian Steppe (i.e. ancient Western Scythia), according to the popular Kurgan hypothesis, or Turkey (i.e. ancient Anatolia), according to the Anatolian Hypothesis.

The large Indo-Iranian branch of the PIE, which split from it at some unknown time in antiquity, was formerly known, and referred to themselves as "Aryans." Today the name of the nation *Iran* is a memorial to this fact, as it is derived from the Proto-Iranian "Aryan." This term has generally been abandoned by today's academics, in favor of the term "Indo-Iranian." This is due to the former term's usage by Nazi academics during the WWII era to support their claims of being the "master race."

Nowadays, the various Caucasian races are commonly grouped and referred to as "white," however this is a misnomer, as the group of races in question exhibit skin-tones which range from brown, to olive, to red, to white. In addition, many other races who may display similar fair complexions, such as many Semitic (i.e. Jewish, Arab, etc.), American Indian, and Latino people, generally don't refer to themselves as "white."

This grouping and labeling of people from the various Caucasian races as "white," while formerly not a term of reproach, has become so today, after a relentlessly sustained campaign of defamation which Western media has conducted against them over the recent few decades.

This campaign has been taken up by many among the general public on social media, and other venues, to the extent that a flood of material now exists which implies that to be a "white" male is synonymous with being effeminate, weak, unfashionable, avaricious, egocentric, apathetic, or a predator.

A few memorable recent headlines which come to mind, evidencing this fact, are: "Man spits in baby's face and tells mother: 'White people shouldn't breed,'"[81] "School worker accused of threatening to 'execute' white men,"[82] "White men kill, brown men found guilty,"[83] "White men alienated in higher ed. workplace, survey suggests,"[84] "YouTube stopped hiring white men in attempt to boost diversity, lawsuit claims,"[85] etc. What is going on behind the scenes here? Why does the heavily left leaning media appear to be preferentially using the term "white," rather than Caucasian? Why do people, who claim to stand so stalwartly opposed to stereotyping based upon color of skin, do just this very thing every time they group together people with Italian, Irish, German, Dutch, French, etc., backgrounds. These people, who each have their own distinct physical characteristics, cultures, dialects, religious tendencies, etc., are lumped into the monolithic category of "whites." Why is there such a strong correlation between the degree of liberalism of a public figure, or organization, and their tendency to denigrate "white" males; indeed, often unabashedly expressing their loathing of them. On the other hand, why is there is a seemingly analogous correlation between socially conservative American public figures, or organizations, and their refusal to do so?

The short answer is: because liberalism is merely rebranded and remarketed communism. In order to give this politically driven propaganda the appearance of a grassroots movement, the masses are dredged until a cadre of radicals are encountered who are so thoroughly brainwashed, or astoundingly ignorant, that they are willing to, in the name of equality, lead a campaign of denial, discredit, or attack against any who might dare to challenge their views.

In much the same way that the fox from Aesop's Fable condemned as sour the grapes which he desired, but was unable to attain,[56] when these radicals are encountered, they typically already harbor feelings ranging from latent resentment to open loathing towards the current culture, due to their previous failures at integration into it. In order to give these feelings an air of moral legitimacy, these radicals commonly claim, and frequently even convince themselves that their hatred is simply a form of righteous indignation over their newly adopted cause.

For clarification, consider the following analogy. Johnny smells incredibly foul because he refuses to bathe. When he tries to sit next to Billy at lunch, he is offended when Billy, repulsed by the stench, gets up and moves to another table. Johnny later notices that Billy accidentally bumps into Sally, while walking. Johnny is thrilled, because he can now shove Billy down, claiming that he was motivated by legitimate indignation over the offense to Sally, rather than by his actual desire to avenge his wounded pride.

In order to maintain the appearance of innocence, should the effort fail, shadowy leftist wealth holders clandestinely finance the efforts of these radicals via secretive and strategic donations funneled through various NGO's, "think tanks," and spin-off organizations which they often own, or heavily influence. The wealth holders who do this uniformly wish to see Western egalitarian culture destroyed and a totalitarian governmental system, coincidentally reflecting many international business models, erected upon its ruins.

As communists always do, in order to accomplish their goal, they target their propaganda at the poor, undereducated, and therefore easy to manipulate masses of neo-proletarians, who are ever numerically superior to the wealthy neo-bourgeoisie; telling them that the latter are the cause of all of their sufferings. This inevitably results in the neo-bourgeoisie becoming the target of all of the proletarians' hatred and anger. These claims are repeated incessantly until the accumulating anger eventually explodes into a wave of bloodshed and death. The ultimate goal of the instigators of this revolution is not to provide a new, more just society for the neo-proletarians. It is not a noble compassion for the plight of the *common man* which drives them. They simply see these people as "useful idiots," and manipulate them in hopes that the wave of death which they intend to ride, will deposit them in the newly vacated seats of power. Here they hope to rule as tyrants.

Though the previous communist revolutions have proven, or are currently proving themselves unsustainable, those who have been entranced by the siren's song of communism have not given up their dream. They have simply repackaged and rebranded it, in order to make it more appealing to a new generation of undereducated poor and corrupt wealthy. The ideas symbolized by the former word *communism* have merely been transferred, in a more or less watered-down form, to the new, more noble seeming term *liberal*, or its analogous ethically neutral analog, *left*.

This hijacking of the noble concept of liberality from those brave souls who, in prior generations, fought under its banner for abolition, for an end to segregation, and for the right of women to vote and own property, to instead now stand for the promotion of ideas of the basest ethical corruption, from the outright murder of unborn children of any degree of gestation, to the prevention of free speech, to the confiscation of the means of self-defense, and ultimately to communist tyranny, is shameful. These morally corrupt, or manipulated people have no right to this word, as they are not liberal by its classical definition. The root of this word implies freedom (i.e. liber; free), and the only freedom which these people defend now is the freedom to be corrupt. In addition, these people wish to strip others of any freedom which they possess to prevent, or even speak out against this corruption.

Men from the various Caucasian races, given that they traditionally held the majority of economic wealth, and subsequently power, within Western society, have been labeled by these neo-communists as the modern bourgeoisie. Consistent with Marxist tactics, the new proletariat are being fomented into attacking and ultimately destroying this group.[74] The ranks of this new proletariat, while formerly consisting merely of the economically disadvantaged, have been expanded today to include any people who feel themselves disadvantaged for any reason; regardless of if they actually are or not. This has tended to attract religious, racial, "gender," sexual preference, etc., minorities to this cause.

Since it is easier to have the simple-minded focus the flames of their hatred towards one supposed nefarious enemy, rather than confusing them with an array of races exhibiting varying physical traits, cultures, faiths, etc., the range of male Caucasian races have been cast by modern media sources as a single monolithic "white" male people and culture. They are the enemy. Over each "white" male face is the shadow of Emmanuel Goldstein, towards whom the modern left dominated media blast much more than the mandatory daily "2 Minutes of Hate."[22] Any who have read Orwell's brilliant *1984* will immediately catch the reference which I have just made, and will likely note with some discomfort the commonality between the techniques which he mentions therein, and those frequently observed today. Those who have not yet read this short work are strongly encouraged to do so for this very same reason.

The many Caucasian races should be proud of their racial heritage, as the Blacks, Latinos, Arabs, Orientals, Indians, etc., should also be proud of theirs. All have proven the resourcefulness and resilience of their races if only by the fact that these races have persisted into the modern era. Like the Dodo bird, many races, such as the Philistines, Cimmerians, and Elamites, have instead declined to extinction.

The various Caucasian races have long been renowned for their courage, and their love of freedom and justice; although there have of course been exceptions, as with all races and cultures. Over 1600 years ago, the Germanic nations threw off the enslaving yoke of the Roman Empire, when the corruption which Rome had been infected with had sufficiently weakened it. Over 500 years ago, Europeans threw off the yoke of their Feudal Lords, who had bound them as serfs to their lands, much like slaves; even retaining the right to whip certain classes of them, and take the virginity of their wives. Over 300 years ago, European knights pushed the Muslim Turks, Arabs, and Moors back out of Europe, a land which they had invaded and blighted like a plague of locusts, in their effort to spread the cruel Islamic faith.

Despite many modern attempts to recast the period when Islam had subjugated parts of Europe as an age of enlightenment and peace, any who have read Edward Gibbon's monumental *Decline and Fall of the Roman Empire*, much less any of the many extant firsthand accounts written by non-Muslims living during those times, know that this is a lie. During the hundreds of years that these Muslims held parts of Europe captive, Europeans who refused to betray their faith, conscience, culture, and family by bending the knee to Allah, suffered murders, kidnappings, rapes, maimings, and other tortures whose brutality causes the imagination to reel.[41] Not only were these cruelties hallmarks of Islamic rule in Europe, but they manifested themselves wherever Islam spread; such as in India, where thousands of Hindus were enslaved and slaughtered in the Hindu Kush area, and in Africa, where Somalian Muslims continue to brutalize Ethiopian Christians to this day.

Returning from our digression, over 200 years ago, during the American and French Revolutions, the mix of mostly Caucasian American races finally threw off the tyrannical yokes of their kings. So abhorrent had the concept of slavery become to the majority of these people, that roughly 150 years ago, shortly after the revolutions, England banned slavery throughout her colonies, and a mere handful of years afterwards, Americans sent their sons to fight, bleed, and die, in order to help their brothers, the black Americans, finally win their much-deserved freedom.

But again, do not misunderstand me to be claiming, like Hitler, that the Caucasian races are a "Master Race" whose innate morality entitles it to rule over all others. That is folly. Morality is as unrelated to race, sex, or age, as size is unrelated to color. The only people universally fit to rule are the virtuous. The wise are included here as wisdom is the virtue of goodness in understanding. Socrates made this point during a conversation which Plato records him having with Hermogenes, in the work *Cratylus*.

"Socrates: 'And what do you hold about such people? Or is it this: the very good are very wise, while the very bad are very foolish?' Hermogenes: 'Yes, that's what I believe.'"[36]

Contrarily, the only people universally unfit to rule are the morally corrupt. This does not exclude the young from sometimes being fit to rule. Though wisdom is commonly associated with age, a wise youth makes a far better ruler than a foolish elder, just as a wise elder makes a better ruler than a foolish youth. The key requirement is wisdom.

But what of disability, religion, and sexual predilection? Concerning disability, a man is not disabled (i.e. not able) from serving in his profession unless he is literally unable to perform it. A legless ruler who issues just judgements, which is the primary duty of rulers, is simply a legless ruler; not a disabled one. Such a man proves by the performance of his tasks his ability (not disability) to continue to benefit both himself and society. A person who is truly disabled from ruling will be unable to provide just judgements, perhaps due to debilitating Alzheimer's. Such truly disabled people should be disqualified from ruling, as leaving them in this position when they are unable to perform it makes a mockery of the office, the person, and justice itself, and places those who depend upon his rulings at risk.

As far as religion and sexual predilection go, both of these subjects, unlike race and sex, are inseparable from ethicality. Men, or women within these categories may therefore appropriately be scrutinized upon these principles and categorized into the two previous categories of the virtuous and the morally corrupt; the fit and the unfit for rule. For example, within the Koran and Hadiths, Islam universally condemns the equality of mankind. Allah is said to love Muslims and hate infidels (i.e. non-Muslims). Since Muslims are instructed to conform their views as much as possible to those of Allah, devout ones will necessarily favor Muslims over non-Muslims in their judgements, making them inherently unjust rulers. This single tendency towards injustice alone, without even considering the many other unjust positions which their faith promotes, such as the inequality of women with men, makes Muslims inherently unfit to rule, as injustice is cancerous to a nation and her laws.

But let's not stop there. Though the Jewish race is simply another race, like any other race, and when being examined under their racial aspect alone, they would, and often do make as good rulers as anyone else, the Jewish religion is very similar to the Islamic one (though both vehemently deny this), in that Jews believe that Jehovah favors the Jewish race over all gentiles (i.e. non-Jews). The only difference between this view and that of the Islamists is one of degree. While Allah is said to hate and desire the assimilation, subjugation, or destruction of infidels, the Jews portray Jehovah as being somewhat neutral towards Gentiles, provided that they do not harass his "Chosen People." This means that devout religious Jews will tend to make less unjust rulers than devout Islamists, but will still tend towards injustice. This is because, in attempting to conform their views to those of Jehovah, as they are commanded to, they will tend to display unjust favoritism towards members of their own bloodline.

Devout Christians, on the other hand, will tend to make better rulers, for the most part, than both devout Islamists and devout Jews, in that the God which they worship is portrayed as loving all mankind equally. They will struggle, however, with punishment, in that the form of justice which their faith portrays is one where crime (i.e. sin) is arbitrarily defined. Due to this arbitrary nature, the severity of punishments recommended in scripture are often found to be completely out of sync with the severity of specific crimes. This destroys the very justice which the punishment is intended to achieve. For example,

Ananias and Sapphira were supposedly killed, on the spot, for merely lying to Peter, and by proxy, to God, about how much money they had donated to the church (Acts 5), while grievous moral offenses such as human slavery were not merely overlooked, but quasi-condoned (e.g. "Slaves obey your earthly masters with proper respect.... (Ephesians 6:5-8)). Indeed, in the book of Philemon, Paul even instructed the runaway slave, Onesimus, to return to his former master.

Lastly, let's consider hardened Atheists. Not those agnostics who are still searching for truth, but those people who are convinced that God is imaginary, and therefore that all goodness, badness, virtue, and vice have no absolute nature: that they are merely relative, and therefore arbitrarily defined as the norm for the individual, family, culture, nation, or period in question. These people will tend to make the worst of rulers. For them, justice will simply mean convention. The murder of innocents could be just tomorrow, should society suddenly agree that it is (i.e. abortion). Telling the truth to someone who is harming themselves, society, or both, could become unjust the next day, merely if a majority of academics agreed to call it so (e.g. legislation being pushed preventing those who wish to talk loved ones back from sexual deviance into a wholesome monogamous relationship).

Disability

A plague of disability claims is rapidly spreading over much of the Western world; straining national budgets, and directly contributing to negative long-term outlooks on the ability of many of these nations to sustain much needed social safety-net programs, such as Social Security and Medicaid. These safety-net programs are already being strained to the breaking point, due to widespread abuse by illegal immigrants, who are flooding, unrestrained, into these nations from predominately African, Middle Eastern, and Latin American countries. This is especially true regarding military disability.

What is causing this massive increase in disability claims? It isn't due to population growth, as even when the data is normalized for this, a significant increase is seen. Is there a secret world war occurring, complete with trainloads of horribly maimed soldiers returning from the front each day, as was the case during the American Civil War? Of course not. Okay then. If people are not being harmed at a massively increased rate, like they were at the close of World War II, then the only alternative explanation for this unsustainable increase in disability claims and subsequent award rates is that the definition set for disability has dramatically changed, allowing an enormous amount of people to qualify for this classification who would have been ineligible under the previous definition set. This is exactly what has occurred. But who are these fish which this larger net has caught? Among several, I would like to discuss 3 which should be targeted for removal, before this grossly overloaded net drags the national ship down with it.

First, there are those who have indeed been physically injured, maimed, or who have true genetic, or acquired defects, but who still retain sufficient ability to contribute to society by working for the federal, state, or local governments; of course, receiving a salary for doing so. The vast majority of those who are being classified today as physically disabled fall into this category.

Is anyone ignorant of some of the amazing things which determined amputees have been able to accomplish? There is even an armless guitarist who plays with his feet, for heaven's sake. Is there anything preventing a legless person from being successful in a job which merely requires the use of their upper body and mind? Why can the armless, or handless not serve their nation in one of the many public servant careers which make use of their mind and the rest of their body? With an increasing number of jobs becoming computer based, and with the many advances in modern assistive technology, the list of options available for these people continues to rapidly expand. Even the blind and the deaf can be productive employees.

People, derive a large portion of their self-identity and therefore their self-respect from their profession. Rather than merely labeling these people as disabled and sending them to live out the remainder of their lives on a small government pension, which is little better than saying that they are worthless, let's instead preserve their dignity by providing them with a means to earn a reasonable living, leverage and grow their skills, and contribute to society. In this scenario, both these individuals and society win.

What is happening now, instead, is that many of these people are claiming that they are fully disabled, collecting a monthly pension, using special hiring privileges to gain employment, and receiving this second income as well. This abuse of disability benefits is a slap in the face to the kind-hearted tax-payers who dedicate a portion of each of their paychecks to assist those who are truly in need. Was the intent of the law which set these funds aside, to provide an additional paycheck for the rest of their lives to people who claim to be so disabled that they cannot work, yet who disprove their own claims by being gainfully employed? Is this why legislators take money from the checks of struggling families; so that extra money can be given to those already earning an income? Of course not.

These funds were set aside for the truly disabled, such as the comatose man lying in a hospital bed somewhere, the elderly dementia patient who is so confused that she struggles with daily tasks, or the wounded veteran who is recuperating in a hospital, but who intends, after his hospitalization, to support himself and contribute to society once more. The current warped mindset is that the government and taxpayers somehow owe these funds to those who claim to be disabled, as if they were somehow responsible for whatever impairments these people possess.

But these physically disabled people are the least of our worries. The vast majority of disability benefit abusers are those who cunningly claim an impairment which they have intentionally selected because it is difficult, or impossible to disprove; such as chronic pain, generally of their neck or back, though not exclusively limited to these. The secret which oceans of malingering, avaricious sluggards whisper about behind closed doors is their awareness of the fact that the sensation of pain is intrinsically qualitative, and therefore impossible to realistically quantify, much less prove, or disprove. Is the examining physician going to verify these people's pain levels by implanting electrodes in their nerves and quantifying the ionic potentials at specific Nodes of Ranvier? Of course not. Scientists have yet to develop the tools which would be required to even perform such a feat, as, though they follow a general pattern, the structure of everyone's nerve bundles are unique.

I could provide literally dozens of examples of this type of abuse which I have witnessed firsthand, including a mother who boasted that she was pulling full disability for admittedly trivial back pain, simply because she "wanted to be a stay at home mom." In another instance a veteran I worked with was collecting 100% disability for supposedly debilitating headaches which he laughably claimed were caused by being "sprayed in the face once with a top-secret military lubricant." Ironically, this "disabled" individual was not only able to work a job with seemingly no symptoms, but even complained to us one day that his feet were hurting because he had been "out ballroom dancing all night." Consider that. He is 100% disabled, as in supposedly 100% unable to work a job, and yet he is not only working a job, but going out dancing all night. He is just another of the host of lying parasites who are sucking this nation dry.

The second major group of disability benefit abusers consist of those claiming any of the many fake mental "syndromes" or "disorders" listed in the 5th edition of the American Psychiatric Association's (APA) *Diagnostic and Statistical Manual of Mental Disorders* (DSM-5).[85] Being related to thoughts, many of these supposed diseases are inherently impossible to prove. Of course, I am not calling mental diseases which are caused by true structural or functional conditions of the brain, such as Multiple-Sclerosis, or Alzheimer's fake. The first of these, for example, is caused by the de-myelination of nerve axons and the second by the buildup of beta-amyloid plaques. I am calling fake the many which are either completely made up, in order to claim a medical excuse and disability benefits for purely voluntary behavior, such as the ridiculous Oppositional Defiant Disorder (i.e. spoiled brat, or its adult analog), Conduct Disorder (i.e. unruly child, or its adult analog), Separation Anxiety Disorder (i.e. intensely lonely and immature person), Alcohol Use Disorder (i.e. alcoholic: this is a choice not a "disease"), and Substance Abuse Disorder (i.e. drug addict: again, this is a choice, not a "disease"), or those which claim the existence of a mythical homeostatic neuro-transmitter imbalance, such as the Attention Disorders (including Attention Deficit Disorder (ADD), Attention Deficit Hyperactivity Disorder (ADHD), etc.), Major Depressive Disorder (MDD; i.e. clinical depression), several types of non-genetic, non-gestational-drug-exposure-related types of "high-level" Autism (including Autistic Disorder, Asperger Syndrome, and Pervasive Developmental Disorder (PDD-NOS)), the anxiety disorders (including Generalized Anxiety Disorder, Panic Disorder, Agoraphobia, Phobias, and Social Anxiety Disorders), Obsessive–Compulsive and related Disorders (OCD), and trauma- and stressor-related disorders (including Posttraumatic Stress Disorder (PTSD), Acute Stress Disorder, and Adjustment Disorders).

Prior to any psycho-pharmaceutical intervention, there is little in the way of valid scientific evidence backing up claims of a pre-existing homeostatic neuro-transmitter imbalance which could not just as easily be the result of the mental processes in question, rather than the cause of it; the chicken rather than the egg. I stress this exception, as psycho-pharmaceuticals are specifically formulated due to their known ability to modify specific neuro-transmitter levels, although their net effect on the entire complement of known neuro-transmitters, to say nothing of yet undiscovered ones, remains generally uncharacterized, presenting the very real possibility of unintended, potentially irreversible structural and functional changes within the mind.

For example, is the observable structural, or functional difference between the Electroencephalogram (EEG), or Functional MRI (FMRI) head scan of a person with MDD and that of a control person the cause, or the result of the thought processes associated with the "disorder." If the change is the cause of the symptoms, then there is a disease, whether genetic, or acquired, to be diagnosed and treated; typically, by costly medication: chemical intervention being the defining underlying bias of allopathic, versus osteopathic medicine. There is a vested interest within the psycho-pharmaceutical industry, who heavily influence the psychiatric, psychological, and mental health fields, to label these a cause rather than an effect, as these "disorders" are this industry's multibillion dollar "bread and butter." There is also a vested interest among psychiatrists and the powerful APA for this to be the cause, rather than the effect, as not only is their credibility on the line, due to their established stance on the subject, as reflected within the DSM-5, but a large portion of their income is derived from diagnosis and treatment visitations related to these "disorders." If, instead, the change is the result, and therefore merely a symptom of a certain sustained thought pattern, then instead of dealing with a physically sick person who needs a diagnosis and medication, we are dealing with a normal person who simply needs extensive mental health counselling.

While a systematic examination of the symptoms, evidence, studies, and problems associated with all of the above mentioned types of fake DSM-5 "disorders" and "syndromes" would go far beyond the intended purpose of this book, converting it into a sort of encyclopedia, likely as long as the DSM-5 itself, I would like to specifically discuss the attention disorders, ADD and ADHD, as well as the trauma, or stressor related disorder, PTSD, due to the recent explosion of diagnoses with these "disorders," which people are currently using to justify disability claims.

Based upon available evidence, I do not believe Attention Deficit Disorder (ADD) and Attention Deficit Hyperactivity Disorder (ADHD) to be genuine mental illnesses. Among the many children who have been labeled with these fake diagnoses, there are two types: those who are simply easily excitable, typically male children, and those who are simply the spoiled products of incompetent, or neglectful parents. Regarding the first type, the energy and excitement of youth, which often comes across as *hyperactivity*, is something which should be celebrated. How many adults later in life enviously watch children at play and make comments such as, "I wish I had half of their energy," or, "I remember when I used to get that excited about ...." It is criminal to deprive children of this energy and excitement simply because it proves inconvenient for their parents and teachers.

Our boys are the major victims here. Per Dr. Joseph Biederman, of Harvard Medical School, "The scientific literature about ADHD is based almost exclusively on male subjects..." I have cut off the rest of the quote, since Dr. Biederman goes on to bemoan this and claim that girls should be diagnosed more; hilariously claiming that it is difficult to identify the symptoms for this supposed silent epidemic in girls. I agree that it is difficult to identify the symptoms of an imaginary disease in a person who is not displaying them. It should be impossible; however, this is unfortunately not the case. A 2004 survey of teachers showed that 82 percent believed ADD to be more prevalent in boys.[87]

Here we see the true cause for this plague of ADD & ADHD diagnoses. Many of today's teachers, the vast majority of whom are coincidentally female, don't know how to handle rambunctious boys. It is far more the exception than the norm to find young boys who prefer to sit and study quietly for hours at a time, although these rarities do exist. Since the invention of the boy, they have been famous for climbing, shouting, wrestling, and being generally *wild* when excited. This is likely an artifact of evolutionary development, where the more vigorous and active males were better able to survive, propagate their genes, and protect their families, as we even observe this behavioral pattern within the animal kingdom.

While girls tend to get excited and at times rambunctious as well, they are comparatively calmer and more passive, and have never shared the same reputation for being *wild* as boys have (except possibly in the extreme example of the Amazons, and we have no history documenting how their children behaved). Anyone who contests this point should spend more time reading older histories; perhaps starting with Kenneth Grahame's *The Golden Age*, or Tolstoy's *Boyhood*. And yet, before this plague of overdiagnosis and overmedication, how many of these *hyper* boys matured into well adapted, mentally healthy men? In my opinion, far more than do so today.

What a sacrifice we make of these boys' lives simply to make them fit the average arbitrary mold expected by our school systems. We must always bear in mind that schools would prefer nothing more than having a group of calm, passive bookworms who always turned the other cheek and never struck back at a bully, even in self-defense, or in the defense of the abused. Is this the sort of upbringing which generates a nation of robust men who will bravely stand up to injustice wherever it is found? Lycurgus, the celebrated early Lacedemonian lawgiver, didn't believe so, nor did Socrates, as can be observed in the writings of Plutarch on the former and Plato on the latter. Both came to the conclusion that boys must be trained through struggle and challenge, in order to produce courageous, vigorous men who could bravely face and overcome adversity. This guidance by both Lycurgus and Socrates directly led to the development of nations whose men were celebrated for centuries for their valor and vigor.

What potential long-term changes do the medications which these children are placed on, which are essentially a prescription form of "speed," cause within their still developing minds? Is it any wonder that today many men seem less virile and many women less feminine, when, since their childhood, schools have forced both of these towards the average behavior of both sexes?

And, at least as far as men go, this drop in virility isn't merely an illusion. Consider a recent study in the Journal of Endocrinology, which showed that average male hormone levels in the U. S. are currently dropping by roughly 1 percent a year, and have been on a steady decline since the 80's.[88] While there have been so many changes within society over the past few decades that it is nearly impossible to identify the direct cause for this downward trend in testosterone levels among American males, it must be admitted that the social influences, and certainly the prescription medications which we have forced upon our boys could at least be a contributing factor. Regarding social influences, consider how our boys are being forced to avoid all physical, and even verbal competition, unless within a sanctioned sports competition. Gone are the days of boys wrestling, or playing "king of the hill," in the school playground. They are to play without rough-housing, or even saying harsh words to each other. While these rules were put in place with the good intentions of protecting children from the random bully, they may have an overall negative impact on the normal mix and levels of internal hormones within developing males. This is because, though most think internal serum hormone levels to be determined purely by genetic predisposition, competitive, especially physically competitive encounters, have been shown to have a significant impact upon them. As one of several pieces of scientific evidence which could be presented on this, consider a recent study from the journal, *Hormonal Behavior*, which noted a significant increase in testosterone production after athletic competition.[89]

Both masculinity and femininity are admirable traits within their proper sexes. Our boys should not be drugged to act more like girls. Our girls should not be pushed to be more physically competitive like boys. They should both be allowed to be, in brief, boys and girls.

Regarding the second type of children, the offspring of incompetent or neglectful parents, who get diagnosed with ADD and ADHD, the unruly actions of these children are often simply attempts to gain attention, or affection which they have been starved of. It is a crime to allow these same inept parents, with schools and physicians often abetting, to drug these unfortunate children into submission. You will never find anyone who will admit to being one of these parents. No one believes themselves to be bad at parenting, just like no one believes themselves to be unintelligent. The fact is that, statistically speaking, some people must comprise the lower tail of the bell curve of parenting skills, just as some people must comprise the analogous lower tail of the Pareto curve of intelligence. Both groups are simply too blind to realize their own blindness.

In the case of intelligence, this phenomenon is known as the almost humorous Dunning-Kruger effect, where the unintelligent, unaware of all of the knowledge which exists that they do not know, often think themselves brilliant; while the truly intelligent, aware of the existence of the massive amount of information which they do not know, often humbly doubt their own intelligence. It is likely the same with parenting. The worst of parents, unaware of what truly good parenting consists of, likely think that their own parenting skills are superb; while truly good parents, aware of how removed they are from perfection, will likely doubt their own parenting skills.

The third category of ADD/ADHD types are adults. Among these adults there are also two types. The first are those who were diagnosed when young, through no fault of their own, and, negative feedback loops having created a dependence on the Adderall, Ritalin, or other medication by this point, may very well exhibit symptoms when without it which convince them of the accuracy of their diagnosis. This is similar to the way that smokers, or coffee drinkers initially feel a mild euphoria when they inhale or ingest these stimulants, and later, due to negative feedback loops, require them simply to feel normal, and exhibit negative side effects without them.

Though Adderall and Ritalin are much stronger stimulants, they operate in essentially the same manner. They provide the user with a much stronger euphoria during their initial highs, however, once the negative feedback loops of acclimation have had time to occur, they leave the user needing the medication merely to feel normal, and with much lower average energy levels in between doses. As high as the initial highs were above normal, so low will the subsequent lows be below it. This is one of the reasons why children who are placed on these medications for an extended period sometimes tend to gain weight. Though the stimulant effect tends to burn calories and suppress hunger, the resulting overall decrease in energy tends to make burning whatever calories they do consume more challenging.

The second type of adults which are diagnosed with ADD/ADHD are those who are simply seeking a convenient, though less than ethical method of gaining an advantage over their academic, or professional peers, and who potentially enjoy the euphoria and increased energy from the modified speed, or "poor man's cocaine," as some call it, which the stimulants, Adderall and Ritalin, essentially are. These people not only get the advantages of time and a half on all standardized exams, and of being able to save up their pills for a few days and power through study marathons prior to exams, but being considered as disabled, they potentially qualify for significant Social Security, hiring, scholarship, and promotion advantages.

There were a disproportionate number of abusers of this type in my medical school class. One student whom I knew from an upper level class was very candid about it with me. She stated that she had just intentionally been diagnosed with "Adult Onset ADD" (she was a third-year medical student, so her supposed condition hadn't really held her back in life), as had her father, himself a 60 something psychiatrist with a law degree, and her younger brother, a classmate of mine. She stated, "I know that nothing is wrong with me, but do you know what happens to the scores of students who take Adderall who don't have ADD? They go up. Everyone's scores go up. I think they should make it available to everyone." Though still unethical, at least she wasn't lying to herself. She is now a practicing psychiatrist, like her father. I would watch her brother, the night before an exam, plant himself in front of his textbooks, pop pills which he had saved up, and study for superhuman amounts of time. These people are neither disabled, nor are these real "disorders."

PTSD, on the other hand, is different. While, in its genuine form, it is a very real disease, the ease with which it may be claimed, as well as its unfalsifiable nature, have made it appealing to unethical veterans who are separating from the military. The vast majority of those who weave elaborate tales about the level of stress which they experienced during their time in the military, in order to claim that they are disabled by this disorder, are simply avaricious liars who should be publicly humiliated, fined, or imprisoned for their fraudulent theft of taxpayer funds. While it is undeniable that some soldiers experience true "Shell-Shock," the older name for PTSD, the levels of stress which most of today's soldiers, who claim to have this "disease," have been subjected to is laughably petty, when compared to the tremendous amounts of stress which the soldiers in the trenches of France experienced, during World War I, where this type of nervous breakdown was first recognized and classified. The "doughboys," who genuinely were shell-shocked, acquired this condition after spending years exposed to the constant stress and ever fresh horrors of living, bleeding, being shelled and gassed by artillery, and dying in the barbed wire covered no-man's-land and mire filled trenches of France. Such men truly deserve our pity, our admiration, and our support.

On the other hand, those effeminate liars who claim PTSD over things, such as bad memories from seeing a dead body once, deserve to be laughed at. Wasn't their entrance into the military voluntary? Isn't the main purpose of the military to fight wars? Has there ever been a war that didn't involve death? What did they expect? Everyone who joins the military knows that dealing with, being surrounded with, or even inflicting death are very real possibilities. Should taxpayers be essentially fined for the rest of these people's lives because these former soldiers effeminately cry over memories which are relatively petty when compared with what other soldiers have dealt with; many of whom bravely returned to the front, after recuperating from their injuries, because they believed in their cause and loved those back home whom they were ultimately fighting to protect.

Should we put every mortician, paramedic, doctor, nurse, and everyone who attends an open casket wake, or funeral on full disability, since they all have to see dead bodies; some on a daily basis? Why stop with humans, maybe veterinarians and former pet owners should get full disability for having to see dead pets. Perhaps vegans should get full disability for having to see hamburgers, or because they know that their antibacterial soap took the lives of thousands of bacteria when they showered. Why not give full disability to everyone on Earth who have viewed real or simulated deaths on the news, TV, film, or the internet sometime during their lives?

The main mistake which Western society has made concerning Shell-Shock (i.e. PTSD), is that we have in recent years allowed stress to be defined as a relative, rather than as an absolute. This is the same mistake, with similar roots in the atheist worldview, leading to similar problems, that Western culture has allowed regarding virtue and morality. If stress is defined as a relative, then it becomes rooted in the perspective of the individual. If rooted in the perspective of the individual, then it has neither absolute reality, nor gradation. What is massively stressful to me may be petty to you, and vice versa. Someone who drops their toast butter-side down on the floor could claim that, to them, this was the stress equivalent of spending years fighting in the trenches of World War I, and a physician could not logically disprove this claim; though many good ones would try. This is exactly what is occurring today.

In actuality, stress is not relative to the perspective of the experiencer. Like morality, goodness, and God, it is both real and absolute. Just because an immature person believes that a petty insult was crushingly stressful, does not mean that it was the equivalent of a year spent in Auschwitz. Though complex and difficult to discern, there are absolute gradations to stress, regardless of the level of the experiencer's maturity-based ability, or inability, to cope with it. For a culture to say otherwise wrenches the lid from Pandora's box, and those vile creatures which spring from it will be among the first in line for a disability check.

During rare moments of honesty, I have heard some of those who were claiming that they were disabled by PTSD admit that there was a point in their lives where they went through an emotionally stressful situation, but that they were now fine. One specific individual who comes to mind, rapidly followed this statement up with, "But I'm not going to go back and tell the government to stop paying me."

Another, who is the more typical case, simply convinced himself that he must have had, as his doctor said, a natural homeostatic imbalance of neuro-transmitter, and therefore deserved the disability paycheck he would be receiving for the rest of his life; as if the government, or taxpayers caused this imbalance and therefore owed him it. What is both interesting and typical with both of these examples is that these two individuals, as completely disabled as they both claimed to be, worked full time jobs afterwards with seemingly no problems. One of these, whom I knew quite well, even worked a high-level federal job, where he pulled and was paid for disproportional amounts of voluntary overtime. He received this job due to preferential hiring for his supposed disability, a preference which comes at the expense of honest applicants of equal, or greater skill, as hiring preference is a zero-sum game. In addition, this individual drove a luxury car and boasted of his six plus figure savings account, since his "disabled" wife, whom he also admitted there wasn't "a thing in the world wrong with," was also pulling a similar scam; receiving a substantial paycheck every few weeks at the taxpayers' expense for obviously unfalsifiable PTSD.

His wife came by work once during lunch, taking a break from her all-day shopping excursion with her daughter. Both of them were full of smiles and filled the room with classic feminine charm. Of course, she had the free time during the workday and the extra money to be out shopping all day because she had claimed and convinced a defensive medicine practicing physician to sign off on a form stating that she was 100% disabled, which she had subsequently submitted to the government. Many of these physicians, and certainly many of their nurses, who still heavily rely upon common sense, know that this is all a scam, but rightly fear that, were they to do anything else but diagnose them as disabled, when presented with the carefully rehearsed list of purely qualitative, and therefore impossible to disprove symptoms matching one of the many fake "syndromes" and "disorders" listed within the DSM-5, they could lose their medical licenses. This is a very rational fear, as the APA, as well as the multibillion-dollar psycho-pharmaceutical industry which relies upon them, are very powerful organizations.

Let's critique and analyze a recent article published in the Los Angeles Times, which evidences the situations which I have mentioned above, along with the malingering mindset of many of those who are attempting, like the leaches they are, to latch on to the government and fatten themselves on its lifeblood. My rather lengthy comments have been added in the bracketed sections:

"As M. E. prepared to retire from the Army in 2011, a Veterans Affairs counselor urged him to apply for disability pay. List all your medical problems, the counselor said." [A Latino minority was intentionally selected for interview on this subject, as they are classically framed as disadvantaged. By selecting this individual, the journalist hopes to stack the sympathy deck in his favor. The journalist, as well as the person interviewed, know that people will likely cry foul over some of the petty things which this person is being compensated for. They therefore start the piece with an inadvertent admission of awareness of wrongdoing, by implying that any impropriety in claims is the fault of the VA counselor who advised him. This is similar to a rapist claiming that the rape was the woman's fault for appearing attractive.]

"E., a mechanic at Ft. Lee in Virginia, had never considered himself disabled." [Again, "It wasn't my idea." This is another inadvertent admission of awareness of wrongdoing, combined with another sympathy tactic, in the indication of this person's profession as a humble mechanic.]

"But he did have ringing in his ears, sleep problems and aching joints." [Firstly, ringing in the ears, Tinnitus, is annoying, but not disabling. Not only does it naturally tend to develop, along with hearing loss, among the aging, but everyone is able to work a full-time job with it. I wonder though that the journalist didn't catch that the guy is a mechanic. Mechanics tend to work in a tremendously loud environment; the sounds of pneumatic tools and engine noises echoing within their metal garages. Such an environment is highly conducive both to hearing loss and tinnitus. This guy probably legitimately has tinnitus from his current job. But even if he got it during his time in the military, he does not deserve disability funds, as his current employment disproves his claim that he is disabled. This liar is, in fact, quite able to successfully work a job. Even deaf people are able to do so, as discussed above, and the slight annoyance of a ringing in the ears is hardly as much of a challenge to deal with.

Secondly, regarding the apnea. Who sleeps perfectly? What is even the absolute, quantitative definition of being well-rested? The answer is that there is none and nobody knows. There are recommendations to get 8 hours, but some people tend to need more, and some less. Restfulness and energy levels, since they are rooted in qualitative feelings, are intrinsically unquantifiable, and therefore, again, impossible to prove, or disprove. Liars know this, and therefore, in their grasp after disability funds, are currently surging into this sleep related crack in the dam.

Thirdly, when he mentions "aching joints," he goes for the classic, purely qualitative and therefore again, impossible to either prove, or disprove claim of chronic pain. In the first place, even if the guy is being honest, which I absolutely do not believe he is, he is in his 40's. Joints tend to start to ache after middle age. Is it the government, and taxpayers' fault that he is suffering from the normal wear and tear of getting old, simply because he served in the military at one point in his life? Should taxpayers sacrifice a part of their checks every month out of sympathy for his growing old? Of course not.]

"He also had bad memories of unloading a dead soldier from a helicopter in Afghanistan." [Here we have the classic appeal to PTSD, which, being mental and therefore thought related, is impossible to quantify, much less to prove, or disprove. I speak more about this subject elsewhere.]

"'Put it all down,' he recalled the counselor saying. E. did, and as a result, he is getting a monthly disability check of $1,792, tax free, most likely for the rest of his life." [Yes, it is the VA counselor's fault for any inappropriate claims; not his. The counselor basically forced the claims upon him, and he, shocked and embarrassed, in that he didn't consider himself that disabled, had to work hard to convince himself that he really did deserve these funds. I'm certain that is exactly what transpired. More realistically, this guy likely wanted to leech money from the taxpayers, something he had convinced himself was a victimless crime (I mean it's the government, right? What does a behemoth that size care about one more leech?) He likely got the idea after talking to, or reading about others who had gotten away with this type of fraud, and thought, "What's good for the goose is good for the gander." It was then simply a matter of conducting a few simple google searches in order to discover which impossible to disprove illnesses he could get away with faking, as well as what the recipes of symptoms were which he needed to complain about to his doctor. In order to avariciously grasp for as much federal funding as he could, he then likely made an appointment with the aforementioned VA counselor and literally did everything within his power to make himself appear to have these illnesses.]

"The VA deems him 80% disabled due to sleep apnea, mild post-traumatic stress disorder, tinnitus and migraines." [He is 80% disabled. As in, he theoretically should only be able to work at 20% of what others can. Yet this liar works full time training mechanics (or as a mechanic, as it says elsewhere). Do people realize how physically demanding mechanic work is? Having spent more than my share of time under a hood, under a rack, and rolling around on a creeper, doing everything from painting, to bodywork, to changing motors, I can personally attest

to its demands. "But he is a mechanic trainer, not a full-time mechanic," some might say. It is highly improbable that for a trade type job, such as this, he spends zero time under a hood, and 100% of his time in a classroom. Yet this would make no difference even if he were in the classroom 100% of the time, given that he is able to perform the job. This liar, however, doesn't even blush when he claims that he is 80% disabled.

It shouldn't go unnoticed that 3 of the 4 things which he has been diagnosed with are, not surprisingly, unprovable, as well as unfalsifiable. He had stress once, has ringing in his ears, and gets headaches. The healthiest of individuals could walk into a physician's office today, lie about the recipe of symptoms needed to be diagnosed with these things, and receive the exact same diagnosis. The 4th claim, apnea, not only clearly isn't disabling him, as he is successfully holding down a job, but is nearly impossible for military service to cause, therefore the taxpayers shouldn't owe him for it. More often than not, obstructive apnea, which is far more prevalent than central apnea, is due to genetics, allergies, or in most cases, obesity.]

"The 41-year-old father of three collects a military pension along with disability pay — and as a civilian has returned to the base, working full-time training mechanics. His total income of slightly more than $70,000 a year is about 20% higher than his active-duty pay." [I want to throw up when I read this part. First, they start with another intentional pity ploy by mentioning the fact that he is a father of three; as if his having multiple children makes him more deserving of disability funding. It does not. The two topics are unrelated. Again, this is simply another apology which bespeaks an underlying awareness of the criminality of the act. Second, they mention how he is able to work a full-time job, openly disproving his disability. Third, they talk about how he is now pulling 3 incomes: his mechanic trainer salary, his retirement pension, as well as his disability pay. Disability was not originally set up to help those who are able to work a job, and therefore already receiving a salary with which to support themselves. It was set up as a social safety-net for those who were literally unable to work (i.e. the dis-able).]

"Similar stories are playing out across the VA. With the government encouraging veterans to apply, enrollment in the system climbed from 2.3 million to 3.7 million over the last 12 years." [Notice the between-the-lines claim that it is the government's fault for this ridiculous growth. Masses of people aren't lying, doing all they can to build clinical paper trails of vague, unfalsifiable symptoms, and filing lawsuits if they aren't awarded disability funding. It must all be the government forcing funds on these poor souls.]

"The growth comes even as the deaths of older former service members have sharply reduced the veteran population. Annual disability payments have more than doubled to $49 billion — nearly as much as the VA spends on medical care. More than 875,000 Afghanistan and Iraq war veterans have joined the disability rolls so far. That's 43% of those who served — a far higher percentage than for any previous U.S. conflict, including World War II and Vietnam, which had significantly higher rates of combat wounds. Disabled veterans of the recent wars have an average of 6.3 medical conditions each, also higher than other conflicts. Incentives to seek disability ratings have increased due to changes in VA policy, including expanded eligibility for post-traumatic stress disorder and a number of afflictions that affect tens of millions of civilians.

Nearly any ailment that originated during service or was aggravated by it — from sports injuries to shrapnel wounds — is covered under the rationale that the military is a 24/7 job." [Here the journalist has an acute attack of candor, something which he deserves credit for. Notice the comment about the sharply declining veteran population and percentage of combat wounds, along with the counterintuitive simultaneous sharp increase in disability claim rates. Notice the comment about how virtually any ailment that originated during service, or was aggravated by it is covered. This includes things which were due to the natural aging process, as well as to stupid things troops sometimes do in their off time.

At the close of the Civil War, the public initially set disability funds aside and developed laws which regulated their distribution, according to Lincoln, "To care for him who shall have borne the battle, and for his widow, and his orphan." These funds were intended to provide medical care to the war wounded and pensions to the widows and orphans whose families had lost their primary breadwinners. They were not set aside so that some Airman who sprained his knee playing flag football in his off time, some soldier lying about an unprovable mental "syndrome," or "disorder," or equally unprovable chronic knee pain which is either faked, or the normal product of aging, some sailor whose overeating and resulting obesity gave him apnea, and especially not some drunk, or drug addict marine whose simple intemperance was labeled as a disease or disorder, could receive additional paychecks for the rest of their lives at the taxpayers' expense.]

"The disability system was unprepared for the massive influx of claims, leading to backlogs of veterans waiting months or longer to start receiving their checks. But once the payments begin, many veterans say, they are a life-saver. R.L. struggled to keep a steady job after leaving the Marines in 2001. Stints as a TSA screener, insurance agent and soft drink salesman ended badly." [How does the fact that this guy could only get crappy jobs have anything to do with his disability status? This is merely another pity ploy. He is likely working crappy jobs because he was too lazy to get his education. Given that military tuition assistance makes college virtually free while on active duty, and the GI bill makes it virtually free after discharge, there is no excuse for this. Ignoring the types of jobs which he worked, the fact that this guy was able to work jobs at all proves that he isn't disabled. In reality, he is likely just another of the typical dirt-bag troops who join the military, inefficiently use their time and salary partying while in, and then end up regretting the dead end, low level jobs that their earlier laziness dooms them to after separation. Later sniffing around for ways to increase his income without work, he eventually landed upon the idea, which so many do these days, of scamming taxpayers for disability.]

"At 35, L. is rated 70% disabled for back, shoulder and knee pain, as well as post-traumatic stress disorder from having witnessed a deadly helicopter crash off the coast of San Diego." [As mentioned earlier, we have the repeated theme of unfalsifiable chronic pain; this time in the classic back, shoulder, and knee, in addition to equally unfalsifiable PTSD.]

"He couldn't support his wife and two children, he said, without the monthly $1,800 disability check. 'If it wasn't for that, I'd be on the streets,' he said. L. trains boxers three days a week and is pursuing a community college degree." [Wait, wait, wait. So, this guy is receiving $1800 of taxpayer money every month for supposedly being 70% disabled, is not only disproving his own claim of disability by working a job, but the job which he is working is as a trainer of boxers. Let that sink in for a moment. This guy is likely in phenomenal shape, hence his gravitation towards boxing, a sport boasting arguably the most aerobically fit athletes on Earth. Has anyone seen what is involved in working as a boxing trainer? Not only do they have to have quick hands, as they do things like holding heavy bags and wearing target gloves, but they also must have quick eyes and minds. This guy's claim of disability is likely a flagrant lie, and the Marine Corps is fortunate to be rid of him.]

"The generosity of veterans benefits is on an upswing in a pendulum arc as old as the republic. During the Revolutionary War, disability payments were limited to soldiers who lost limbs or suffered other serious wounds." [Correct.]

"*Lobbying by Civil War veterans led to coverage that included peacetime injuries and illnesses.*" [Correct, yet even for those sustained during peacetime, these benefits were still limited to severe, truly disabling injuries. The journalist is attempting to build a case that society has gotten wiser and more humane over time, and that the disability program necessarily must grow and change to reflect this increased societal wisdom. This is not true.]

"After World War I, compensation was scaled back to cover only combat injuries and diseases contracted in war. But World War II brought an expansion to include all conditions that appeared during service or shortly afterward." [Yet still not including the vast majority of purely qualitative and therefore unfalsifiable ones such as "chronic pain" and the many fake mental "syndromes" and "disorders" within the DSM-5 which are currently breaking the system and nation.]

"In the 1950s, President Eisenhower — a former five-star general — tried to rein in the costs." [Wisely.]

"He found little support in Congress, and the basic system has remained the same ever since." [Except that the author later describes how it hasn't. Leaving it in the lap of Eisenhower, a man who tried to reform it, isn't fair.]

"The VA uses a formula that combines a veteran's conditions into a rating of between 0% and 100% — in 10% increments. The higher the rating, the larger the disability payment. Nearly half of those in the system have ratings of 30% or below. They can apply for higher ratings if ailments grow worse. 'The disability system has this escalator quality,' said David Autor, an economist at MIT. 'Once you get on, you just keep going up.'" [Which is why unethical people try to start a paper trail on anything they can think of while in the service, posturing for future disability claims, whether disabled, or not.]

"The current benefits boom began with a political battle over Agent Orange and other herbicides used to clear jungle brush in Vietnam. In 1991, Congress and the VA started paying veterans who had served on the ground there — meaning possible exposure to Agent Orange — and went on to develop diseases that eventually included lung and prostate cancer." [It is always easier from a future date to look back at and criticize the decisions which were made by our predecessors. We have the luxury of possessing information on how things, which were uncertain at the time, actually played out. At the time, the decision makers on Agent Orange did not know how much the conflict against communism in Vietnam was going to spread. While Agent Orange has been proven to be harmful, government leaders made a risk-based decision about its use, in all good faith. Troops ran either the short-term risk of being shot because they couldn't see the enemy hiding in the foliage, or ran the long-term risk of cancer. While troops who truly became later debilitated from cancer caused by Agent Orange should have been cared for and their families provided for with disability funds, here was one of the first instances where, on a national scale, we allowed a host of vague symptoms, many of which were impossible to prove were caused by the original exposure, to justify disability funding.

Since this dangerous precedent was set, whenever the military has needed to make a risk-based decision which has the unfortunate, but necessary side effect of increasing the risk that some of its members will be harmed, they have subsequently been targeted with a host of class action lawsuits and disability claims, costing the American tax-payers billions. Some examples are the non-FDA approved Anthrax vaccine which troops were required to take in the 90's, as well as the "burn pits" during and after the Iraqi and Afghanistan wars. Despite claims to the contrary, in both instances the government made risk-based decisions, with the best interests of the soldiers in mind. Instead of burning the debris, should they have trucked the waste every day through roads filled with snipers and Improvised Explosive Devices (IED's)? How many lives would that have cost? Should they have not immunized the troops against Anthrax when they had strong intelligence that there was a very real possibility of its use?

In some instances, these claims are due to genuine disability, and as such, should rightly be paid. An example might be an individual who develops truly debilitating cancer after being consistently exposed to a carcinogen throughout their military career. The vast majority of claims, however, are filed by non-disabled people attempting to increase their income by defrauding the government. These people, once they discover that they were in a specific military theater during a period when an exposure occurred, typically start paper trails by intentionally complaining to their healthcare provider about unfalsifiable symptoms. Some may even convince themselves that their vague, non-disabling symptoms are actually due to the exposure. This belief is often psychosomatic; similar to how people tend to itch whenever someone mentions that lice, or bedbugs were discovered nearby.]

"Then in 2001, the VA added Type 2 diabetes to the list. The disease affects 1 in 4 U.S. senior citizens and has not been definitely linked to Agent Orange. But veterans groups lobbied to include it. 'The feeling was, let's give them whatever they need and move on,' said Anthony Principi, the VA secretary at the time." [This would be a hilarious comment, were it not inflicting tragic results upon the nation. Type II diabetes is also known as "Obesity Related Diabetes" for a reason. So, now veterans who won't lay off the Twinkies and cheeseburgers are rewarded with taxpayer funding for the rest of their lives. Even the author admits that there is no evidence linking Type II Diabetes with Agent Orange exposure.]

"Through 2013, the number of veterans receiving compensation for diabetes climbed from 46,395 to 398,480." [Roughly an order of magnitude of growth in disability fund claims for something which, in most instances, is entirely the victims' own fault. Do people not realize that this is not a victimless crime? Do they simply enjoy being taxed, because these liars next door are driving the need for these additional taxes.]

"The Obama administration added three more conditions in 2010: Parkinson's disease, a rare form of leukemia, and ischemic heart disease. Since then, more than 100,000 cases of heart disease — the leading cause of death in the U.S. — have been added to the disability rolls." [We have no idea the cause of Parkinson's disease, but for the most part believe it to be genetic. How then can we prove that its development was service connected? We can't. Why then should taxpayers be responsible for it? With Leukemia, though there are certain carcinogens which are known to cause it, those diagnosed with it should not receive military disability until it is proven that it was acquired from exposures related to military service. These poor people could have been exposed to these carcinogens after separation. Regarding ischemic heart disease, there is no evidence of this being caused by military service. Generally, this occurs due to atherosclerosis, something believed to be typically caused either by genetics, or diets high in saturated fats, neither of which are the military's doing, and therefore the taxpayer's responsibility.

In all three of these cases, these individuals, whether their disease is proven to be military connected or not, should receive disability funding once their disease has progressed to the point of becoming truly disabling. Once all of the lying leaches have been brushed from the government rolls, she will be vigorous enough to provide increased funding levels far surpassing the medical and subsistence needs of the truly disabled.]

"Veterans of all generations also have been encouraged to apply for compensation for post-traumatic stress disorder, with Vietnam and the recent wars driving the growth in roughly equal measure over the last decade." [Again, the author claims that the situation is the VA urging veterans to claim PTSD, who otherwise wouldn't, rather than the far more likely reverse case. Once more, between the lines we have a hint at awareness of wrongdoing.]

"Some veterans said they have lived with the disorder ever since leaving the military. Others kept it at bay until recent wars or major life changes released old demons." [Translation: until they realized there was free money to be gained by lying about it.].

"The economic uncertainties of retirement age also gave veterans more incentive to apply." [Translation: They need and want more money.]

"As post-traumatic stress disorder claims boomed, the Obama administration made them easier to win." [Another long-term effect of this categorically worst of all US presidents, thus far.]

"The VA had long required documentation of a traumatic event that resulted in post-traumatic stress disorder. But in 2010, in keeping with the current science, the administration said a qualifying trauma could simply be a fear-inducing situation such as traveling through enemy territory." [Here we see what I was referring to earlier regarding the current zeitgeist that stress is relative to the perspective of the experiencer, as well as that "disorders" are thought related. Due to this viewpoint, any situation which is claimed to contribute to certain types of thoughts can be claimed to cause many of the fake "disorders" listed within the DSM-5. Notice the comment which the author made about this change being driven by Western academia, the majority of whose social sciences, such as psychology and sociology, are infested with the warped worldview of atheistic relativism. This subject is discussed at length elsewhere.]

"K. O., who works in Long Beach for the nonprofit Vietnam Veterans of America, said that once the rules changed, she started calling men whose cases she had rejected. 'I told them to come back,' she said. More than 1.3 million veterans of the Vietnam era received $21 billion in disability pay last year. From Afghanistan and Iraq, the cost was $9.3 billion — but it is growing fast. Among disabled veterans of recent wars, 43% have tinnitus, the most common condition." [It is unprovable, hence why people intentionally malinger that they have it for disability. How can you prove that I don't hear ringing in my ears? In addition, as mentioned earlier, even for the portion of genuine cases, tinnitus is often a natural part of the hearing loss associated with aging. It should therefore not be compensated with disability funding, as it does not disable a person from working. Even the deaf both can and do successfully work jobs.]

"Rounding out the top 10 are back or neck strain, knee problems, post-traumatic stress disorder, migraines, arthritis of the spine, scars, ankle trouble, defective hearing and high blood pressure. 'They're filing for the basic wear and tear of military service, not combat injuries,' said Phillip Carter, a veterans expert at the Center for a New American Security, a nonpartisan think tank. One of the latest trends, resulting from another policy change, is a rise in disability determinations related to sleep apnea — from 11,742 to 164,107 over the last decade." [Notice here that neck strain, knee problems, and migraines are types of chronic pain which are impossible to disprove. Again, even if the first two are legitimate, people experiencing these things should not be compensated unless truly disabled to the point of being unable to work. A large portion of these "migraines" are likely just malingering. Even among those which are legitimate, unless traumatic brain injury (TBI) occurred, the majority of evidence indicates a genetic cause, making them not due to military service, and therefore not the taxpayer's responsibility. In addition, it should not be compensated until so debilitating as to truly disable one from working.

We have already discussed the malingering associated with PTSD and hearing problems. Scars only debilitate in extreme instances such as cheloid formation. High blood pressure is either genetic, or diet and exercise related, neither of which are the military's doing, nor the taxpayer's responsibility.

Arthritis of the spine, as well as ankle trouble are genuine physical problems which have a high likelihood of being military service related, such as from parachuting and running over uneven conditions. Even if the person ultimately becomes crippled from spinal stenosis, however, if they are still able to perform a job, they are by definition, not disabled. Disability should be all or nothing. Even the soldier who has his arm blown off should only receive disability while unable to work, which would include while he was recuperating. Once he is recuperated, the government should immediately place him into a federal job which could make use of his remaining skills and abilities.

Since those who were wounded for their nation have greater right to federal employment than those who weren't, if there are no immediately available government jobs to be had, a highly improbable scenario, then a non-disabled person should be released from their government position in order to accommodate this injured one. Care should be taken to ensure that other federal managers do not attempt to circumvent this employment requirement by only hiring these people at base and entry level salaries, such as janitors. These wounded warriors should be placed in average level positions if possible, or even upper, if they possess the qualifying skill sets. Once established in this job, their disability benefits should cease.

These benefits should only continue indefinitely for those who are truly disabled; in that they can literally no longer work. If they subsequently take a job, their benefits should be terminated. Should they be found to be working "under the table," then they should not only have their benefits terminated, but they should be banned from receiving any future benefits and recoupment actions for past benefits should be initiated.]

"The Pentagon had long prohibited veterans from receiving disability pay in addition to their military pensions. But in 2003, officials lifted the ban if a veteran had a disability rating of at least 50%." [This was a mistake. The previous prohibition was logically valid. If you were able to complete your retirement, then you were continuing to work until the point of retirement. If you were able to continue to work, then you weren't disabled from working.]

"The change triggered a surge in claims costing billions of dollars — including many by veterans with sleep apnea, which is typically rated as a 50% disability. The condition tends to strike in middle age due to weight gain and can usually be managed by wearing a breathing mask while sleeping, but the VA does not consider such external devices in its disability decisions." [Even the reporter intuited that sleep apnea was due to the individual's actions rather than the military's. Taxpayers should, therefore, not be responsible for it. Unfortunately, vote hungry legislators have obviously made this short-sighted change for short-term votes, rather than according to long-term logic.]

"Retired Navy veteran D. A. said he was surprised that sleep apnea, for which he wears a breathing mask, qualified him for disability pay. At 49, he works as an electrician in an aluminum factory in Davenport, Iowa. He said his monthly disability pay of $910 gives his family financial security by boosting his $1,800-a-month military pension. 'Most of the time, the rules are against you,' A____ said. 'You get one that's for you, you don't question it.'" [Once again, the journalist and the interviewee feign surprise at the outcome, as if the interviewee didn't actively pursue this disability claim. Basically, because this glutton wouldn't watch his diet, for the rest of his life, taxpayers must collectively carve roughly one thousand dollars a month out of their paychecks for him. Taxpayers should rightly be angry at this dirt-bag for his fraud.]

"The expansion of disability benefits signals a change in attitude about the purpose of the payments, long intended to compensate veterans for lost income. Studies have found that many disabilities in the system have no effect on average earnings." [Because many, especially among the current surge, are either not disabling a person from performing a job, or are pure malingering over chronic pain, or one of the many fake DSM-5 "syndromes" or "disorders."]

One showed that veterans receiving disability pay tend to have higher total incomes than those who do not." [In another shocking study, it was discovered that water is wet. The blind eye which our legislators have turned to this fraud, out of fear of being proven as scientifically ignorant, or accused of not loving the nation and her troops by failing to provide for veterans, has created a culture where the dishonest are rewarded for their dishonesty. Like a cancer, this will have the inevitable result of spreading the disease to all who lack ethics and want in on the scam.]

"In the age of an all-volunteer military and after two unpopular wars, disability pay has come to be seen as a lifetime deferred payment for service." [It can't be a "lifetime deferred payment for service" when they were already paid while they were in the service; including bonus income for hazardous duty, tax exemption for deployment to Southwest Asia, family separation allowance, housing allowance, etc. If this salary, or the retirement pension aren't substantial enough (although I believe that they are) then focus on honestly addressing that issue. Manipulating the disability system to supplement it merely rewards the unethical and defrauds both the taxpayers, as well as the truly disabled.]

"R. A., who spent 26 years on active duty and as a reservist, said he views it as compensation for the hardships he endured. 'The real kicker was the time I spent away from my family,' A. said." [Anyone informed on the matter would know that he was already compensated for these things, including "Family Separation Allowance."]

"The 53-year-old's voice flattened when talking about how he developed post-traumatic stress disorder after living in fear of mortar attacks in Iraq — and how it rendered him unable to work around other people. The Santa Monica mail carrier counts knee and ankle problems among his ailments. He has a 100% disability rating, entitling him to a monthly check of $3,200." [This guy makes me sick. While most people have to work hard to earn anywhere near $3200 a month, after taxes, this dirt-bag, who is malingering about PTSD and whining about his petty knee and ankle problems, is being rewarded for his dishonesty at the expense of honest taxpayers. Every day that he works his job as a mail carrier, a job which requires a disproportionate amount of walking, he is proving that his knee and ankle problems are not disabling. His supposed PTSD is also not disabling him from holding a job down. Truly shell-shocked people would likely struggle to even respond to the interviewer. Any in doubt about this should watch some videos on the genuine condition which were made in World War I. One must be careful even here, however, as many, knowing the horrors of the front, were well documented among writers of the time for faking injuries and conditions in order to become ineligible to return to it.]

"E., the Ft. Lee trainer, said his monthly $1,792 disability check is scarcely making him rich. All of it goes towards his son's college education. He has filed new claims for back and knee pain, gastrointestinal problems and vertigo in an attempt to boost his 80% disability rating. 'I believe my disability rating — and I'm not trying to sound greedy — should be 100%,' he said. 'I know what I went through.'" [Methinks the [veteran] dost protest too much. Between the lines of the denial of greed is a subconscious awareness and confession of it, which has bubbled to the surface. He is not only being greedy, but also dishonest. Did anyone miss the fact that he said that all of his disability funding is going towards his son's college education? As in, he is able to support himself with the job he currently has. So not only is his disability undeserved, given that his ability to perform his job proves that he isn't disabled, but it is unnecessary, as he doesn't need it to support himself.

This being said, I believe this is merely one more lie from a man who has already proven himself to be a liar concerning his disability. The intent of this lie is to garner sympathy, yet again bespeaking an awareness of wrongdoing. The wording of the article is intended to make us all admire him for being a caring father; overlooking the fact that he is funding this education with money stolen from all of our taxes; money which we would all also like to use for noble things like paying for our own children's college.

Notice how, once ethics have been abandoned, the next step is twice as easy. It's like how winning at the casino encourages you to return to it. Is it any surprise to find that this louse is returning to the host, claiming more impossible to disprove "chronic pain" disabilities, such as the classic knee and back pain, impossible to disprove vertigo, and petty, though also likely fake gastrointestinal problems? How can an examining physician clinically prove that you aren't feeling pain, dizziness, heartburn, or reflux? The answer is that they can't. This man knows this fact and is manipulating it to his advantage. But let's just imagine that all of these maladies were real, rather than imaginary. Even then he is not disabled, as his ability to successfully work as a mechanic proves.][90]

Disability Solution

Psychiatrists, psychologists, and mental health specialists, like any salesmen, wish to make their patients, or their patients' guardians, like them. They seek to win this affection by assuring these clients that whatever problems they are being seen for, if anyone's fault, are certainly not their own. Everyone enjoys hearing that problems which they are struggling with aren't actually their fault. It tickles the ears and soothes the conscience. These professionals know that people generally like the messenger who delivers good news. This truism has been well-documented within the earliest of books. For example, "How beautiful on the mountains are the feet of those who bring good news...," in the scriptural book of Isaiah (5:27).

If the problems actually are the patient or their guardians' fault, however, such soothing comes at the expense of truth and wisdom. The patient in such a scenario has been introduced to, and likely convinced of a falsity; something which never ultimately yields long-term personal, or societal benefit. Error, a close relative of falsity, lies, and ignorance, is a direct cause of the majority of the world's suffering. Truth, on the other hand, even if inconvenient, is a direct cause of the majority of its benefit. Verily, truth does set free (John 8:32).

As an aside, it should be noted that genuine truths remain true even when amplified or reduced in scope or severity. Stealing remains a crime if one individual steals a hundred dollars from another, if the president steals trillions from the nation, or if a child steals a quarter from his mother's purse. This method of testing if postulates are true by seeing whether or not their amplification, or reduction leads into absurdities is known as "reductio ad absurdum." It was a favorite technique of Socrates, which he employed with surgical precision in those of his debates which Plato documented.

A person may not enjoy hearing the truth that their dog has been infected with rabies, and therefore needs to be put down. Even though a veterinarian may know this, he does the owner no favors by withholding this information. Such an informed inaction would in fact be deemed criminal negligence by all courts, in that it places the dog's owner, as well as any others who might be exposed to it, in mortal danger. In like manner, it is paramount that clinical professionals provide their patients with the absolute, unvarnished truth about their condition, even if such facts may be unpleasant. One of these unpleasant truths may be, and often is, that the patient's symptoms are simply due to their own immaturity, selfishness, egocentrism, cowardice, cruelty, avarice, licentiousness, or perversion.

This directly leads to the following unpleasant truth, that many, though certainly not all of the "syndromes" and "disorders" which the American Psychiatric Association (APA) describes within the 5th edition of their *Diagnostic and Statistical Manual of Mental Disorders* (DSM-5), the accepted standard among mental health professionals, are, to be blunt, not illnesses at all. Many of the ludicrous, fabricated "syndromes" and "disorders" named within the DSM-5 are simply tools which are used by lazy and irresponsible malingerers to grasp at special societal privileges, including and especially taxpayer funding, which has been set aside for the noble cause of caring for the genuinely disabled. This is tantamount to theft, not merely from the hard-working taxpayers who are being duped, but also from the truly disabled. These latter must forego certain assistive devices and therapies, because this worthless host of shameless, lying leeches drained the programs which would normally have paid for such things.

Be this as it may, the young 18-year-old, whose meager, entry level salary barely provides him with enough income to keep himself sheltered, fed, clothed, and driving, would be furious if he knew that the massive amount of taxes which were taken out of his paycheck every two weeks were being used to help worthless liars of this sort grow wealthy. And they truly are. But these examples are actually unnecessary. This plague of disability benefit abuse is now so widespread, and continues to grow at such a frightening and unsustainable rate, that everyone reading this will likely be able to readily call to mind their own extensive list of examples. It should be remembered that these examples are merely the tip of the iceberg. Though many of these malingerers are so confident in the impotence of current laws that they brazenly admit their crimes, the larger base of this iceberg consists of those who hide their crimes beneath the dark waves of HIPPA.

HIPPA, the Healthcare Insurance Portability and Privacy Act, is a law which was initially drafted by well-intentioned legislators. Its purpose was to protect people from having their true health problems used against them for rate and employability determination, by both insurance companies and employers. Unfortunately, it is now being used by malingerers as a legal cloak to hide their disability fraud. Within the courts, this cloak becomes a hammer to crush any who would dare to publicly expose this theft from honest, hard-working taxpayers.

All would like special privileges; including and especially the privileges of receiving two incomes while working only one job, or of receiving a paycheck while not even working at all. Fortunately, most have too much honor to lower themselves to the villainous act of stealing money which good people have set aside for the truly disabled, to do so. Unfortunately, however, this is daily becoming less true.

One option which would significantly chill this abuse, would be to have all requests for, and distributions of funding of this sort occur in public; being recorded and broadcast for all to see. Those soliciting for these funds are requesting them from the nation's taxpayers, who accordingly have a right to know both who and what they are being asked to fund. Some might counter that the requester has the right to privacy regarding their medical condition, but this should never be the case with regard to charitable assistance. Individuals indeed have a right to privacy during normal circumstances, but this right is lost once they request resources, labor, or time of another person, whether for a medical condition, or otherwise. The person being asked to sacrifice these things has the right to demand both information about the need, as well as evidence which substantiates it.

If this public venue reveals that the funding is being provided for truly disabling causes and conditions, then the entire public will be edified by being able to directly observe their tax dollars helping those who are truly in need. This will have the additional benefit of making the taxes which are taken from everyone's paychecks chafe less. If the people requesting these funds are found to be liars, then they deserve whatever public shame, censure, and indeed, even punishment, which they receive.

A person who was previously severely injured, perhaps a paraplegic veteran, who had his legs blown off by an improvised explosive device (IED) while on patrol, should be appointed to the newly created federal post of Disability Fund Distribution Officer (DFDO). Though impaired, since this individual is gainfully employed and using his remaining abilities to successfully perform his job, he shouldn't be diagnosed as disabled, nor should he receive disability benefits. Those who request disability funding should be made to publicly approach the DFDO and, in front of the cameras, the DFDO should greet them with the statement, "I am not disabled, nor am I receiving disability funding. Why do you believe yourself to be deserving of these sacred funds?" This powerful example alone will frighten away all but the genuinely disabled, and the most shameless of liars.

The requester (or their guardian) should then be required to look the DFDO in the eye, identify themselves (or their charge), and describe what condition justifies their appeal for public disability funds. One, or two highly qualified physicians, called Disability Fund Inspection Officers (DFIO), should be appointed to work as consultants for each DFDO. These should be capable of, before the cameras, immediately and publicly validating, or invalidating the vast majority of disability claims, as true disability is generally not something difficult to perceive or diagnose. It should be truly disabling, and therefore generally obvious. Any substantiating medical imaging, or lab-work should be acquired prior to the interview and the results brought with the applicant, for review by the DFIO.

In order to allow these DFIO physicians to perform their duties without fear of reprisal from the courts or their licensing body, they should be provided with a special, permanent medical license, which can only be revoked by Congress. Since neither the DFDO's, nor the DFIO's are diagnosing, or treating, and are therefore unable to directly harm patients, they should be provided with special immunity from litigation while performing their sacred roles as guardians of the public's resources. In order to prevent these very important positions from becoming the prize of whichever political party is predominating at the moment, both the DFDO's, as well as the DFIO's should be provided with lifetime appointments. Special police officers, called Disability Fund Protection Officers (DFPO), should also be present during any disability verification, or subsequent fund distribution, whose role will be to immediately arrest, fine, or imprison, depending upon the flagrancy of the crime, any petitioners whom the DFDO, based upon feedback which he receives from the examining DFIO, determines to be malingering.

It will be apparent to most that I have patterned these protections for the DFDO and DFIO after those provided for members of the Supreme Court, for very similar reasons, as this disability review process would effectively be a highly specialized form of trial; complete with a verdict and potential pecuniary "damages" paid by taxpayers to the genuinely disabled, or fines and prison sentences levied upon the execrable liars pretending to be.

Psychotropics

Since things which are sensed require a sensory organ as well as a sensory stimulant, what organ senses those internal sensations which we call *feelings*, or *emotions*? For clues to this question, we should examine how our external senses function. A fact which is often overlooked about external sensations, such as vision, touch, taste, smell, hearing, temperature, and pain, is that they are automatic and passive processes, not voluntary and active ones. Certainly, the body is able to voluntarily and actively use its muscles and frame to reposition itself, in order to improve the probability of sensation, but the external sensation itself occurs involuntarily, whenever the specialized cells of the sense in question are brought into an environment which is rich in whatever stimulant they are specifically designed to detect.

Consider a few examples. The muscles of the eye open its lids, rotate its ball, and focus its lens upon a certain object which is reflecting, or emanating light. The muscles of the hand place the finger on a thorn, or food within the mouth. Those of the head bring the nose near a rose, or turn the ear towards a songbird. All volition ends, however, once the specialized sensory cells of each of these senses have been stimulated. For example, one cannot refuse to see, once rod and cone cells within the retina of the eye have been stimulated by the light reflected from the object; cannot refuse to taste, once the tongue's taste buds have been stimulated by chemicals within the food; cannot refuse to smell, once the nose's olfactory cells have been stimulated by aromatic gasses from the rose; and cannot refuse to hear, once the ear's follicle cells have been stimulated by sound waves.

In like manner, whatever internal sensory organ detects our internal feelings and emotions appears to also function both involuntarily and automatically. Some might contest this point, given their awareness that we retain a certain level of control over our emotions. The confusion here is due to a widespread bias among today's scientific community, which warps their understanding of emotions. The current orthodox scientific view is that there is no specific sensory organ which detects internal feelings and emotions. In fact, emotions and feelings are believed to have no positive existence. What we call emotions, or feelings, are believed to merely be thought sequences which have subconsciously triggered specific combinations of physiological responses, such as changes in body temperature, heart rate, flushing, etc. Together, these responses are perceived by the traditional external senses as discomfort, or pleasure. It is believed that the subconscious directly associates these discomforting, or pleasurable physiological sensations with whichever subjects have shown a tendency to trigger the thought sequences which produce them; misinterpreting this subconscious association as positive, or negative emotions towards these things. Any subsequent interactions with the subject can cause new thoughts, which trigger new physiological responses, which result in new sensations, which are ultimately interpreted as new emotions towards it.

According to this view, emotional responses would be little different from a cold; except that, rather than the body triggering a discrete set of physiological responses due to a bacterial infection, it would be doing so due to a sequence of thoughts. The love felt towards a child would be no more significant than the relaxation felt from a hot bath. The anger felt over injustice towards the innocent would be no more significant than pain felt from an ulcer. Another problem with this view is that it oversimplifies the wide array of complex emotions which we experience into a simple dichotomy of pleasure, or pain.

This recently developed bias has had vast influence upon the psychiatry, psychology, and mental health fields; as well as the multibillion-dollar psycho-pharmaceutical industry which has grown up alongside them. Believing that all emotion is merely the physiological response caused by certain thought cascades, when treating those with emotional problems, physicians have logically turned to thought affecting chemicals. Foremost among these are antidepressant and anxiolytic Selective Serotonin Reuptake Inhibitors (SSRI's). SSRI's are believed to primarily function by supercharging the cerebral synapse with neuro-transmitter, facilitating ease of synaptic function, and hence ease of thought. The short to medium term side effect of SSRI usage is an increased sense of wellbeing, which superficially appears to confirm the bias that thoughts, and the physiological responses caused by them, are the primary driving forces behind emotion.

When we examine the issue in more detail, however, we discover problems with this conclusion. Firstly, the reality of our level of understanding of the mechanism of thought is far less than what medical industry marketing portrays it to be. Regardless of the efforts of many brilliant physicians and researchers, it remains a science truly in its infancy. For example, though we currently know of roughly 60 different molecules which are classified as neuro-transmitters (we are very likely to discover many more), it is currently unknown to what extent psycho-pharmaceutical interventions are altering the brain's overall structure and function, perhaps permanently, by altering its homeostatic ratios of these neuro-transmitters.

One known negative feedback loop which occurs with SSRI use is a down-regulation and desensitization of post-synaptic serotonin receptors, however, this finding is generally deemed "inconsequential."[91] With tens of billions in prescriptions, as well as the reputations of many a prestigious academic, or wealthy clinician at stake, of course it is. How many other unknown feedback loops might be occurring? What of the known correlation between long term SSRI usage and the increased prevalence of suicidal ideation?

Trusting patients are sold the myth that they likely have a genetic predisposition for low neuro-transmitter production. This statement is tragically humorous, given that our understanding of genetic up and down-regulation is even more nascent than our understanding of the functional mechanisms of thought. Do physicians sample the neuro-transmitter levels within a synapse, prior to issuing such outlandish diagnoses? Do they sequence the genomes of patients to verify missing, or modified genes for the host of up, or downregulating factors which contribute to the production of the equally large number of neuro-transmitters? Of course they don't, as most haven't been determined yet, and those few which have been are little understood. Isn't this supposed to be the age of "precision medicine?" The best of these physicians are generally well-intentioned and are seeking to abide by the concept found within the Hippocratic Oath, which they all take in medical school, of "do(ing) no harm."[92] The worst are apathetic, or have fallen into the all too common practice of over-diagnosing defensive medicine.

Regardless of their intent, given the positions of public trust which these physicians occupy, they must provide their patients with a reasonable opportunity for informed consent. They are not doing this when they do not personally research and inform their patients about the significant risks associated with specific psycho-pharmaceutical interventions, instead, lazily echoing what their Pocket Pharmacopeia, Physician's Desk Reference (PDR), or their profit driven pharmaceutical representatives tell them about these products. These same pharmaceutical companies provide the vast majority of research grants and funding which keep many of the academics who publish research articles employed. A 2010 study in the Journal of the American Medical Association (JAMA) revealed that the pharmaceutical industry contributes over 60% of the $100 billion which is annually spent on biomedical research in the U.S. An additional 30% is provided by "foundations, advocacy organizations, and individual donors." The remaining, roughly 30% is provided by government sources.[93]

Are we expected to believe that all of these researchers always remain completely unbiased in their research, in spite of the fact that the majority of them, both university and private, need these constant streams of research investments in order for them to remain financially solvent? As a biomedical engineer who formerly worked in research, I can assure you that, while many do, many also do not. It used to infuriate me when the principal investigators on research projects which

I participated in would blatantly exaggerate the significance of their findings and the repeatability of their data. Frequently, I was the person who had collected this data, and was therefore familiar with, and had voiced my concern about its shortcomings. Yet, as one professor whom I worked for quipped, after requesting that I adjust the scale on a graph, in order to make the changes due to the experiment appear more dramatic, "Depending upon how you frame the data, you can make the graphs say whatever you want them to."

Psycho-pharmaceutical manufacturers unethically market this myth of genetic predisposition for low homeostatic levels of neuro-transmitter directly to the grossly less informed mass population, who subsequently approach their physicians, echoing the recipes of vague symptoms which commercials have told them that this drug would fix. Many such symptoms are rooted in emotion and are therefore inherently unquantifiable, virtually ensuring that the persistent patient will walk away from the physician's office, if not with the requested psycho-pharmaceutical product, then with another. In the long term, the myth which these people were sold may ultimately prove to be a prophecy, as the delicate balance within their minds is altered, very likely initiating a cascade of functional and potentially structural pathophysiological changes. These changes may be slowly reversible at best, or irreversible at worst.

By the use of these various psychotropics, the prescribing clinician intends to alter the patient's baseline brain chemistry, in order to induce a subtle euphoria; theoretically also increasing ease of thought. This theoretical increase in the patient's ease of thought, it is claimed, will accordingly improve their emotional state. This belief is rooted in the mistaken assumption that thoughts and the physical responses which they are assumed to induce will always operate transitively. That is, if negative and positive thoughts cause corresponding negative and positive physical sensations, then induced negative, or positive physical sensations will cause corresponding negative, or positive thoughts. While this may sometimes be true, as a warm bath tends to not merely relax the body, but also the mind, it is not a firm rule; as one may just as likely lie in a warm bath with no alleviation of morbid thoughts, or emotions.

The belief that it is a firm rule rests upon a false assumption that we can deceive our own minds. This is an impossibility, as, being the same person as the deceiver, the deceived is always at least subconsciously aware off the trick. Our minds are paradoxically smarter than we realize. At the outset of antidepressant usage, the mind will likely be distracted by the newfound sensation, which feels similar to what was previously experienced during true moments of happiness, and believe itself to actually be happier. It will likely choose to focus upon this new feeling, or other issues, rather than focusing upon whatever negative thoughts and feelings previously consumed it. The concerns which drove the previous negative thoughts, however, were caused by external situations and relations, and internal habits of addressing these, which often still remain. Unless these also change, the mind will eventually grow familiar with the new normal and shortly return its thoughts to them.

In addition, due to its new heightened baseline, the mind will begin to notice that, during moments of true joy, the peaks of happiness will appear relatively lower. This occurs because one cannot relocate one's home from a plane to a mountainside without the mountain's peak appearing lower than it previously did. Simultaneously, the mind, sensing the homeostatic imbalance, will continually and actively work to regain homeostasis. It does this by a combination approach of up-regulation of the production of enzymes which are responsible for breaking the active product down into inactive byproduct, which may subsequently be excreted; as well as by the down-regulation, or desensitization of active components within the affected site of action. Together, these phenomena result in acclimation (i.e. increased tolerance), which has the eventual effect of causing the mind to no longer experience the previous subtle euphoria which had distracted it from its yet existing problems.

Once at this point, patients generally request an increase in their dosages. Unless the patient's underlying coping strategies, cognition, and emotional concerns are addressed by counselling techniques, such as Cognitive Behavioral Therapy (CBT), this process of increasing the dosage to stay ahead of the body's feedback acclimation will repeat itself, often until either what is considered the maximum safe dosage is reached, or a drug targeting a different receptor, or mechanism is attempted.

There is a significant danger to this approach, which may likely be the primary cause for the observed increase in suicidal mentation among long-term antidepressant users. Increasing dosages, or drug changes may successfully outpace the body's feedback acclimation processes for some time, placing the sufferer at a baseline chemical level within their minds which is at, or near what would be normally experienced during the few true heights of undiluted happiness which people only occasionally experience. At this point, they have made their home on the mountain's peak. While this sounds like an enviable position to be in, it is the opposite. Once here, they are at saturation point and there are no further peaks of joy which may be experienced. All around lay mental valleys which may potentially be descended into, and which appear ominously deeper from this highest of heights. The only hope to re-experience normal joy is for the body's toleration process, or a weaning from the drug, to slowly return them back down to the level of the homeostatic plane.

The problem with this is that, as a passenger generally only feels the acceleration, or deceleration in a car, and not its speed, so too, perceived internal feelings are typically only dynamically felt, not statically. As the relative ascent to the peak was perceived as joy, the time spent there made it no longer so. Any subsequent descent from this new normal will not be perceived as a reduction in a surplus of joy. Joy has already fled due to stasis and saturation. The dynamic decent will be perceived instead as an increase in its opposite, misery, placing the patient in a worse position to deal with their yet unresolved concerns than they were in when they initially sought help for them.

"Alarmist!" one will say. "Conspiracist!" another will shout. "People have taken these substances for years with no ill effect. Where is this holocaust you prognosticate?"

Have they? Weren't many, in fact most of these psycho-pharmaceuticals only recently introduced to the market, over the past few decades at best? Where are the long-term, large sample size clinical studies of possible health impacts of chronic usage? Since they impact the mind, where are the long-term studies of possible correlations between chronic usage and occurrence, or age of onset of dementia, or perhaps cerebral, renal, or hepatic neoplasms? Have no psychotropics been removed from the market only after a mountain of clinical evidence ever so slowly accumulated, which made undeniable, though to the bitter end still denied, the harm which they inflicted upon patients: patients who trusted what was both told and sold to them by these same rhetoricians?

When future generations look back at our widely accepted, though false modern belief in a silent plague of homeostatic neuro-transmitter imbalances, as well as at the types of drugs (e.g. SSRI's) that our generation is consuming like candy, due to it, I believe that they will sigh and shake their heads the same way that we do now, when we consider the now disproven, though then analogously widespread 19th century belief that everyone had uric acid diatheses (i.e. imbalances), and how they were all generally prescribed lithium based upon this false belief. Lithium was such a "miracle drug," as SSRI's are thought to be now, that it used to be the "Up" which was added to 7-Up soda. The medical community and their academic peers, who are not immune from peer influence and "band-wagoning," were then, as they are now, the promotors of both of these baseless theories.

Even today, various lithium compounds continue to be prescribed for the other supposed silent plague of bipolar disorder. Per the FDA, "The specific biochemical mechanism of lithium action in mania is unknown."[94] Unknown or no, pharmaceutical companies continue to market lithium in compounded forms, such as lithium carbonate; claiming that these compounds are is completely safe in prescribed doses. Since being prescribed a flammable metal which is commonly used in batteries doesn't sound particularly healthy, these compounds are rebranded and marketed under subconsciously appealing names such as *Eskalith* and *Duralith*. Each time the general population hears the name of these products spoken, or even brings the name to mind, is one more additional subconscious affirmation that both the compound and lithium itself are beneficial. This confirmation occurs because the word for the compound's active ingredient, lithium, is bound to what are obvious derivations of words for which positive emotional associations already exist within the subconscious. This first instance, for example, is a word play on *escalate*, to increase or elevate, and *lith*, a truncation of lithium. The second is a similar word play on *durable*, being able to endure, combined with the same truncation of *lithium*.

But let's momentarily glance at what the FDA lists under warnings for Lithium Carbonate, in order to see just how safe these products actually are.

"Lithium toxicity is closely related to serum lithium levels, and can occur at doses close to therapeutic levels...morphologic (kidney) changes with glomerular and interstitial fibrosis and nephron atrophy have been reported in patients on chronic lithium therapy...An encephalopathic syndrome...followed by irreversible brain damage has occurred in a few patients treated with lithium plus haloperidol...cases of pseudotumor cerebri...have been reported with lithium use. If undetected, this condition may result in enlargement of the blind spot, constriction of visual fields and eventual blindness due to optic atrophy...blackout spells, epileptiform seizures, slurred speech, dizziness, vertigo, incontinence of urine or feces, somnolence, psychomotor retardation...coma...cardiac arrhythmia...peripheral circulatory collapse, sinus node dysfunction with severe bradycardia...unmasking of Brugada Syndrome (Note the implication that the medication is not at fault here, and that the patient must have had a predisposition for this syndrome, which may result in sudden death. A syndrome is merely a set of symptoms; symptoms which may very well be caused and not merely "unmasked" by the medication.)...EEG (brainwave) changes (such as) diffuse slowing, widening of frequency spectrum, potentiation and disorganization of background rhythm...miscellaneous reactions unrelated to dosage (i.e. Even at low dose)...(such as) worsening of organic brain syndromes...no specific antidote for lithium poisoning is known...treatment is essentially the same as that used in barbiturate poisoning..."[94]

The average patient, if aware of the significance of these risks, though they seldom are when showing signs of mania which would motivate clinicians to prescribe them these drugs, would never give consent to being treated with them. This is doubly true for less serious conditions; such as the grossly over-diagnosed "bipolar disorder."

Yet, under its various trade names, lithium compounds, and not simply apathetic and careless ones, are the most widely prescribed drug for this. It should cause compassionate and responsible citizens great concern that this risk is also being assumed by children; mostly at the behest of their hopefully well-intentioned parents. The increase in diagnosis of bipolar disorder has exploded 561% for children, 400% for adolescents, and 56% for adults during the period from 1996 to 2004.[95]

My heart breaks when I read these statistics. There is zero solid research which proves that these supposedly bipolar children possess any structural problems, or mythical chemical imbalances in their brains. In addition, no valid diagnostic tests for any key biomarkers which might indicate such pathologies are conducted before diagnosis. Yet we pump children full of psychotropic drugs, such as these tremendously dangerous lithium compounds, in order to keep them calm. Children, whose actions might be little more than general brattiness and rebellion due to poor parenting. And the decision makers on these prescriptions are generally the same parents who allowed these children to get into the out of control state that they are in. What kind of opportunity for informed consent have the children been provided? What does a 10 year old know of nephron atrophy, or the potentiation and disorganization of the background rhythm of their EEG? Since they are started on these drugs at an earlier age, while the mind is still developing, these drugs are even more likely than they are with adults, to cause long term mental, emotional, and health problems.

Until the past few decades, this supposed plague of latent bipolar disorders, like the attention disorders (e.g. ADD & ADHD), apparently went un-, or under-diagnosed for most of recorded history. And yet the world continued to turn. There is a strong possibility that a large portion of these difficult to disprove "disorders," with their hosts of vague, qualitative emotional symptoms, are not true diseases which necessitate psychotropic intervention, but are instead the tragic results of irresponsible early chemical intervention (including psychotropic intervention and illicit drug use); perhaps even of their parents, prior to their birth.

"That's ridiculous," some might say. "They have dissected brains of people suffering from these conditions post mortem and documented statistically significant morphological changes."

I'm sure they have. When both are examined post mortem, structural differences are bound to be observed between normal brains and the brains of adults who have received years of psychotropic intervention. Yet is it the chicken or the egg? Is any observed morphological change what required the initial psychotropic intervention, or the result of it? I believe the latter to be overwhelmingly the case.

But what about observed functional changes while these individuals are still alive. Really, the only in vivo medical imaging tools which physicians have at their disposal to verify suspected functional neurological changes in patients suspected of vague mental "syndromes" and "disorders," such as bipolar disorder, though they virtually never order these tests for such things, include such things as Electroencephalography (EEG), Positron Emission Tomography/Computed Tomography (PET/CT) and exotic Magnetic Resonance Imaging (MRI) Spectroscopy.[96.] Even were clinicians to order these tests, these systems have a notorious lack of data granularity, considering the small sizes of many of the cerebral structures. EEG, for example, merely indicates electrical wave activity to an area level. PET and MRI Spectroscopy indicate tissue structure, heat, fluid flow, and a small handful of localized chemical ratios, which hint at tissue level function. Though these tools may indicate that a certain area of the mind is over, or under-stimulated in a patient suspected of having bipolar disorder, it remains unclear whether the stimulation is the underlying cause of the symptoms, or is instead the result of them. For example, do these people have mood swings because this area of their brain is active, or is this area of their brain active because some unresolved issue within their subconscious is causing them to have mood swings.

Also, it is important to note that there is currently no tool available to indicate, at a cellular level, the patterns of synaptic arrays which are firing. Were we even to successfully capture this pattern somehow, we would not know what to do with it; as there is currently no modern Rosetta Stone enabling us to translate between synaptic patterns and thoughts. Assuming that we can thoroughly understand what thoughts are occurring within an area of the mind, due to that area's generalized activity, is equivalent to assuming that we can thoroughly understand what program is being run on a computer, simply because we know that a certain part of the motherboard is consuming electricity.

It should be clarified that true acquired, or genetic pathologies of the mind, such as Multiple Sclerosis (MS) and Parkinson's Disease, do indeed unfortunately exist. These are also seldom tested for to the above mentioned level, but prior to a confirmatory diagnosis, a quantifiable structural, or chemical biomarker is tested for. For example, prior to a patient being diagnosed with Multiple Sclerosis (MS), structural damage which is visible on an MRI scan, certain evoked EEG Potentials, or lab verification of Cerebro-Spinal Fluid (CSF) changes are sought.

Within the murky world of psychiatry, however, it is the veritable Wild West; where the ends appear to justify the means. The prevailing attitude appears to be that the patient didn't harm themselves in the short term, so the devil may care what the long-term harm of the prescription is. This risk that the patient will potentially harm themselves, or others, is the 800-pound gorilla in the world of psychiatry. It is a sort of implied blackmail, which generally precludes due diligence and ensures over-diagnosis and subsequent overmedication.

Physicians are busy people. They generally must jump from patient to patient, spending perhaps 5-15 minutes directly interacting with each. This is typically due to the intentionally low staffing ratios which hospitals implement, in order to avoid paying the high salaries which these people often command, only for them to sit idle during the inevitable lag times between patient surges. During such brief interactions, when is a physician ever 100% certain that a patient is not contemplating suicidal, murderous, or otherwise harmful actions? Because they asked them? Are patients always perfectly honest; especially those under emotional stress? If not, then can physicians identify any dishonesty about such things with 100% accuracy? Are there always noticeable physical, or verbal cues? Is there even any baseline standard of perfect emotional health which may be accurately and quantifiably measured against?

So what if none of the patient's responses raised alarms when they took the Minnesota Multiphasic Personality Inventory (MMPI), the only personality test whose results are recognized and used by U. S. courts of law. Can intelligent people not recognize keywords, or themes which are being sought in psychological test questions and intentionally manipulate their responses in order to appear normal? Contrarily, can they not also manipulate their responses in order to appear mentally unstable, so that they can qualify for certain societal protections and benefits? For example, if someone recognizes that a certain question, or series of questions is attempting to determine if they have been hearing voices, or are suicidal, they could answer "no," even if both were true, merely because they didn't want to be labeled as schizophrenic, or suicidal. On the other hand, someone else who was attempting to get diagnosed as 100% disabled, in order to get special disability benefits, might respond "yes" to these questions, even if both were false.

But even if they are contemplating harm. Are all harmful thoughts indicative of mental illness? Do mentally stable and healthy people never make bad decisions, which are sometimes harmful to others? Is the man who punches someone who grabbed his wife, or who beats a man whom he catches molesting his child, in need of diagnosis and medication? Why, or why not? He has contemplated, and even inflicted harm upon others.

An easy way to pull the mask of seeming hard science and uniform agreement on diagnosis from the psychiatric community would be to ask a large audience of psychiatrists and psychologists these last two questions. If they were allowed to answer anonymously, in order to prevent intimidation by the votes of their professional peers, there would be a large group who advocated psychotropic prescriptions for these men, due to their demonstrated lack of emotional control, or for posttraumatic stress support. Yet among the general population of civilized nations, the average of which we supposedly derive our definition of normalcy from, these actions would generally be excused, or even praised.

These are the types of difficult questions which psychiatrists and psychologists must deal with on a daily basis. The tendency of clinicians to defensively over-diagnose, lazily relying upon the flawed cookbook medicine of the DSM 5, rather than upon their own, often quite substantial intellects and sharp instincts, has virtually ensured within Western society an "Ask and ye shall receive," "Opium for the masses," climate. Difficult as these questions may be, and as dangerous as pioneeringly relying upon personal instincts, rather than liability spreading medical cookbooks is, physicians and researchers must rise to this challenge for the good of Western society.

They, more than anyone else, should be aware of the risks associated with some of these psychotropics. They should know that the massive increase in antidepressant prescription rates, which began in the early 90's, has not led to the expected correlating decrease in suicide rates.[97] Female suicide rates were already steadily declining prior to this massive prescription increase, likely due to correlating increases in quality of life, salary, and job mobility, and yet, the slope of this decline remained relatively unaltered after it.

Yet this same period of increased prescriptions has seen a significant correlating increase in liver cancer rates, as might be expected, due to the known degrading effect that these prescriptions often have on either one, or both of the body's two filters: the liver and the kidneys.[98] There has also been a significant increase, during this same period of psychotropic prescriptions, of a specific type of brain cancer known as Glioblastoma Multiform (GBM).[99] The pathogenesis (i.e. mechanism of onset) of this type of cancer is still currently unclear,[100] but roughly 80% of the time it is malignant, and has a poor prognosis. It is freely admitted that data, such as this, which shows a correlation between increasing antidepressant use and affected organ cancer rates does not guarantee causation; as many cultural factors simultaneously changed during this same intervening period. The environments of the patients have changed, public health initiatives have been expanded, surveillance has been increased, and technology both for diagnosis and treatment have improved significantly, leading to many cancers being caught and treated in their earlier stages. On the other hand, this correlating data should also not be completely written off. It should simply be recognized for the correlation it is, and further studies should be conducted, which may potentially prove contribution, if not direct causation.

In case the reader thinks me outside of my lane of expertise in discussing this topic, I refer them to the 6th chapter of a book entitled *Destructive Trends in Mental Health: The Well-intentioned Path to*

Harm. This chapter, written by a psychiatrist named Dr. William Glasser, echoes a few of the concerns which I have mentioned, as well as a few others which I have not. Regardless of the fact that this physician has a counseling based "Choice Theory" which he is advocating, Dr. Glasser brings up important points. Foremost among these is his initial admission that the vast majority of patients had no problem with their brain chemistry, but that they were diagnosed and prescribed psychotropics anyway.[101] This diagnosis, he mentions, is generally with a "syndrome."

A syndrome, once more, is a set of grouped symptoms which, in non-psychiatric medicine, typically consists of a set of quantifiable physical, or chemical symptoms which are valid indicators of physical illness. In psychiatry, however, with its bias that emotions are but the associated physical responses generated by thoughts, "syndromes" often do not prove true disease. We have free control of our thought processes, therefore, even the healthiest of us may, in theory, allow our minds to travel a road which, if admitted to a psychiatrist, would cause us to be diagnosed with a mental "syndrome." This is, of course, barring manifestations due to genuine structural, or functional diseases of the brain, such as Parkinson's and Alzheimer's.

Note should also be taken of Dr. Glasser's final comment that diagnosing and prescribing without physical testing to verify any assumptions of structural, or functional defects of the brain are issues which are seldom discussed by the psychiatric community. To do so would be sacrosanct; tantamount to pointing out that they do not see the clothes which the emperor supposedly has on. From the Hans Christian Anderson fairy tale, we know that the charlatans who were profiting from the emperor's ignorance effectively chilled all dissent by claiming that only fools could not see the magical garments. In the same way, psychotropic salesmen and the researchers whom they fund profit from the people's ignorance, and effectively chill any dissent by claiming that only fools question the underlying myth which they tell of the majority of mental illnesses being due, prior to intervention, to a homeostatic imbalance in brain chemistry.

Offense

Many of the fake mental "syndromes" and "disorders" listed within the DSM-5 are impossible to either prove, or disprove because they are rooted either in thought processes, or in internal perceptions. This being the case, anyone who causes another individual to think a certain way could theoretically be accused of causing, or exacerbating one of these fake "syndromes," or "disorders."

This is exactly what is occurring. Masses of lawsuits are daily being filed by unethical and avaricious malingerers, who claim that any public forums which they are unable to avoid exposure to (e.g. school, work, etc.) which necessarily involve the introduction and exchange of thoughts, due to the interpersonal interaction required there, are either causing, or exacerbating their supposed mental "syndromes," or "disorders." Hoping to avoid being dragged into costly and time-consuming legal battles over these issues, schools and employers, including governmental employers, are bending over backwards modifying their policies to benefit and appease these people. Unfortunately, as history has repeatedly proven, appeasement does not work with bullies. It only encourages their sense of elitism and makes them both more brash in their demands, and more reactionary with their perceived offenses.

In response, Western society, has even taken the next step of enacting hopelessly foolish laws which condemn any who might cause offense. Offense, which is rooted in personal opinion, rather than fact, has become the new ethical standard. In the Western nations plagued by these bad laws, such as Great Britain and America, the most easily offended individual becomes a mini-tyrant. These laws would, and in fact often do, punish those who would dare to point out someone's favorite self-destructive vice, simply because doing so would likely offend them.

Let's take a look at an example statistic and consider how these offense laws have influenced Western society's reaction to them. When one studies the highly reliable statistics reported by the U, S. Bureau of Justice, in their Uniform Crime Report, and also consults the U. S. Census Bureau's demographic data, they are likely to be stricken by the fact that Black and Latino males comprise only ~15% of the American population as a whole, and yet these two demographic groups represent a staggering ~75% of the American prison population.

A recent study found that the U. S. spends ~80 billion dollars a year on fully supporting its prisons.[102] Though the math isn't actually this simple, a rough approximation of what this small demographic group is costing U. S. taxpayers can be found by taking 75% of 80 billion dollars. Or in other words, roughly 60 billion dollars a year. American taxpayers, including law abiding Black and Latino taxpayers, should be understandably furious about this fact. This is roughly double the U. S. Department of Justice's entire budget for the year 2017. This fact should be in all of the headlines. As some of the lowest hanging and ripest fruit for cost savings, we should be actively targeting our national reform and education resources at these demographic groups.

Yet is it in all of the headlines? A better question would be, is it in any? Fearing frivolous, offense-based lawsuits, most media outlets and public and political figures refuse to even acknowledge the existence of these facts, even though they grimly stare governments in the face: governments which must cut out other public efforts, such as scholarships, parks, libraries, road improvements, social support efforts for the poor, etc., all to support this criminal population. All of these public efforts which are sacrificed could have gone towards improving the lives and communities of law-abiding Americans, including Black and Latino Americans.

To hell with this trembling army of the supposedly offended, as well as the quivering mass of national leaders who fear to be accused of offense. Even the worst of offenses are mere trivialities, provided they do not involve physical contact, economic harm, or sexual violation. So what if one person offends another. Have we, as adults, forgotten the wisdom which we learned as children when playing on the playground? When we were insulted then, we responded to the taunts with, "Sticks and stones may break my bones, but names will never hurt me." And indeed, they truly won't; in spite of the fact that today an army of psychologists, psychiatrists, and mental health professionals believe and are passionately teaching the opposite.

As children, all of us at some point encountered the kid who was constantly running to the teacher over the slightest perceived offense. Accidentally bump him in the hallway and he screams, "Miss Miller, he hit me!" He says all sorts of insulting things, but when you finally fire back an insult out of frustration, he shouts, "Miss Miller, he called me a name!"

Why did these incredibly frustrating children behave in this manner? They did so because they had learned that by feigning emotional, or physical harm, they could recruit the aid of authority figures. This recruitment allowed them, by proxy, to control, humiliate, and harm those whom they hated, but were too weak, or cowardly to challenge directly. This modern army of the offended, which we have been describing, consists mostly of adult versions of these childhood brats. To be blunt, the majority of supposed offenses are simply lies. They are efforts by cringing, tantrum-throwing cowards to manipulate laws in order to abuse, oppress, and control those whom they hate, by feigning, or exaggerating harm whenever afforded the slightest opportunity to do so. Laws which were originally put in place for the protection of the helpless and innocent.

I am not advocating a society where parents scream at and insult their children and where blackface is used to lampoon an entire race. It is never good to needlessly offend another, but as all parents should know, though sadly, many don't, sometimes offense is inseparable from required correction. It is a fatal mistake for a society to judge words or actions as moral, or immoral based simply upon whether or not they cause offense. Unfortunately, legislators across most of the Western world have failed to prevent, and have sometimes even promoted the incorporation of this foolish view into an ever-growing mass of poorly thought out destructive laws. These legislators and many national leaders fail to realize that making offense the primary moral compass of a nation leads it into horrible absurdities.

Consider actions where only one individual is involved. This warped, offense-based legal standard would condone all types of self-harm, ranging from morbid obesity, to bulimia, to castration, to alcoholism, to drug addiction, to suicide. The victim is the only one directly affected, and they are not offended by the act, so all of these things must be morally good, or neutral at best. Evidence of this warped view beginning to penetrate into Western culture can be seen in the fact that laws prohibiting these very acts are these days being systematically attacked and dismantled.

Laws allowing the slippery slope of "assisted suicide" are being stood up. Laws whose intent is to prevent drug addiction are being repealed, or not enforced. Any condemnation of obesity, a condition which any blind, end stage type 2 diabetic amputee would confirm, is horribly destructive to health, is being redefined as the moral wrong of "fat shaming." Condemnation of sexual perversion and profligacy, which have both been known since ancient times to be mentally, morally, and often even physically destructive to those involved in them, as well as to society as a whole, is being redefined as the moral wrongs of "homophobia" and "slut shaming."

When multiple individuals are involved, this offense-based legal standard would condone any number of monstrous acts, provided simply that none of the parties involved were offended. It would sanction cannibalism, provided the victim was suicidal and agreed to be served up to the murderer with garnish. It would sanction child molestation and bestiality, provided the victims of both were convinced to participate. It would certainly have no problem with necrophilia, since the deceased participant would no longer possess the capacity to be offended.

Consider the opposite scenario. This offense-based legal standard would make the most harmless, wise, noble, beneficial, or kind action, written, or spoken word, film, or show into a moral wrong merely if someone exposed to, or the recipient of it was offended. Ban the writings of Rousseau, since he offends the tyrants whom he criticizes. Ban the writings of Ralph Waldo Emerson and John Stuart Mill, because they offended the slaveholders whom they criticized. Ban the Declaration of Independence, since it claims that all men are absolutely equal in the eyes of God, a principle which directly contradicts opposite claims made in the Koran, Hadiths, Tanakh, and Torah, causing it to offend Muslims and those of the Jewish religion. Nothing can be written, spoken, shown, or done which can be certain to offend absolutely none of the world's 7.6 billion inhabitants. Therefore, this offense-based legal standard would make everything a potential crime.

In nations which are governed by such flawed laws, those who possess the courage to speak hard, but necessary truths, or to take hard, but necessary actions for the good of themselves, their families, or the nations which they love, will fall victim to whichever morally corrupt wimp who complains first, or loudest.

"You are getting carried away," some will say. "We all know that when we refer to offense being the moral standard, we mean as perceived by the majority."

While this statement sounds good, it is neither true, nor were it so, would it save us from absurdities. Did we consider the offense of the majority when we desegregated the Southern schools? How about when we allowed women to vote? Do we judge the merit of our decision to punish our kids by whether or not they are offended by the punishment? There may be more of them than us, so are we the ones in the wrong for sending them to their rooms for fighting?

What do we mean by the majority? Do we mean that we judge a word, or action based upon whether it will offend the entire world, or only by whether it will offend our nation, state, city, neighborhood, family, company, office, or corner of the room? Do we only consider what might offend the majority in any of these things today, or do we consider what might have offended them a hundred, or a thousand years ago, or what will be likely to offend them in the future?

Under this view of majority offense, Islamic nations would be morally justified for executing people for minor violations of religious laws, such as adultery and apostasy. Female genital mutilation would be a morally good action in nations where those who support it outnumber those who do not, even if only by a single supporter; regardless of what the girl who is held down and cut upon thinks. The various horrors of the Inquisitions would have been morally good actions in Catholic dominated nations, since the majority of citizens in these lands had been convinced by their religious leaders that they were simply necessary evils to ensure the good of society. The cruel burnings of any girls and women accused of Witchcraft in American colonial cities, such as Salem, would also be morally good acts, for similar reasons.

We must have higher moral standards than mere offense. Sometimes people need to be reproved, condemned, or punished for words, or actions which are destructive to themselves, others, or society itself; even if this reproof, or condemnation offends them, or any number of people who happen to identify with them, due to some physical, or social commonality (e.g. race, religion, etc.). If I truly love you, I must tell you if you are harming yourself, regardless of your level of offense. If we truly love our nations, we must inform our fellow citizens about things that are harming it, regardless of whether or not this information offends any parasites who are making themselves fat and strong upon its weakening.

Many among the upcoming generation are likened to "delicate snowflakes," due to their tendency to become "triggered" over such petty perceived offenses. For the most part, these triggered people are simply so tragically brainwashed that they actually believe their own hysterics to be rational. This is because, during the formation of many of these people's earliest memories, the schools which they were sent to, and the media which their likely well-intentioned parents either intentionally exposed them to, or failed to protect them from, had already been tainted, or had been completely taken over by the atheistic, relative worldview; which makes all ethical standards human perspective dependent.

Many among these people's educators were likely good people, who would have loved to have been able to fill their students' minds with information which would shake them awake from this dream world where all absolutes are absolutely denied. Unfortunately, the current legal and political environment not only enforced their silence about these truths, but also often forced them to teach what they knew to be blatant error.

Truth, however, can never be entirely extinguished. Though these tragically manipulated people may only hear it as a whisper, which they struggle to hear over the advertisements of the ever-increasing number of manipulators, it will continue to point out whatever contradicts it. As an aside, the only difference between advertisers, or marketers and manipulators is the degree of morality of the product, or idea which they are selling. Those who promote morally corrupt products are therefore simple manipulators.

The word *triggering* is itself an intentionally misleading and manipulative term. It implies that a person's reaction is not their fault; which it actually always is. Re-actions are, as their name implies, responsive actions. People are always responsible for their own actions, even those which are performed in response to a stimulus. In actual fact, the majority among these younger generations are not "snowflakes." Most are good people who have tragically been bullied since early childhood by this minority of ever-offended tyrants. They have mostly been brainwashed into believing freedom of speech to no longer be a fundamental human right; but instead to be a product whose shelf life has now expired.

This is how tyrannies always work. A small minority, ranging in number from a single person, to millions, forces the generally goodhearted and moral majority of a nation into silence and compliance through the usage of threats and fear. The majority of Russians during the Cold War, for example, were indeed good people who had been forced into silence by the bullying of the KGB. The majority of WWII Germans were good people who had been forced into silence by the bullying of the SS. The majority of pre-Civil War Southern Americans were good people who had been forced into silence by the bullying of powerful, slave owning planters. Even today, the majority of Arabs in Islamic dominated nations are good people who have been forced into silence by the bullying of their religio-political leaders.

Once tyrants successfully silence some of their opponents with threats and attacks, the reduction in opposition makes their power appear even stronger, amplifying the fear among any others who were considering resisting. This cycle repeats itself either until all opposition is crushed and the tyrants hold total sway, or until a few brave individuals publicly resist and successfully weather their attacks. In this latter case, this success gives new courage to those who are longing to stand up, but who had, until that point, been afraid to. There are many of this type today, who search the horizon for heroes to rally behind: men and women who could help them cast off the yokes of their ever-offended tyrants. For the good of future generations, we must be these heroes: for there simply is no one else.

Abortion

The atheist worldview has flooded across the Western world, via the channels of her universities and media outlets, like the moral sewage it is, carrying with it the Materialist belief that living organisms, including humans, are essentially soulless, biological machines. An unfortunate natural result of this Materialist belief has been the re-appearance within Western society of the twin specters of abortion and eugenics. These ghouls haunt the swamps of social corruption, and like the Pied Piper of old, deprive any nations which are foolish enough to wander into these morasses, of entire generations of their children.

Materialists don't believe in the existence of any source of worth beyond utility. Those who adopt the atheist worldview, therefore, begin to subconsciously, and often times even consciously believe that the strongest, healthiest, and most attractive of people possess the greatest amount of innate worth. As the most valuable members of society, these modern supermen and superwomen are therefore thought to be the most deserving of life, and of any benefits which may be derived from it. Contrarily, the weaker, the less healthy, and the less attractive are seen by Materialists as less valuable, and therefore less deserving of life and any of its benefits. This warped, Materialist view would create a caste system of value within society, with the most beautiful, handsome, and strong, typically consisting of young adults in their 20's and 30's, at its upper stratum.

On the second tier of value, Materialists generally place children, adolescents, and any past middle age, who are typically weaker and often sick, or in need of care, along with any other adults who are mildly disabled, weaker, sicklier, or less attractive than those on the uppermost tier. In addition, since Materialists see no inherent value to humans above that of animals, they generally place domestic pets, or wild animals which they are fond of, on this second tier as well. Some extreme Materialists go as far as placing their favorite species of plants, such as certain varieties of trees, on this second value tier.

On the third tier of value, Materialists generally place the extremely ill, aged, or disabled, due to the increased weakness, poor health, and generally diminished attractiveness of these people, along with any animal species which they do not particularly favor. The extremely young, such as infants, are also included among this group, due to their inability to care for themselves, which Materialists equivocate with weakness. Again, the extreme Materialists often also place plants which they have no specific attraction towards on this third value tier.

On the fourth tier of value they place unborn children within their mothers' wombs, along with any animals which they are frightened of, or disgusted by. Once more, the extreme Materialists typically place noxious plants, such as poison ivy, or kudzu on this value level as well. Not only are these unborn children the weakest and most helpless members of any society, but Materialists think of them as being similar to patients on life support, in that they cannot survive without the aid of their mother's bodies. Life support patients, however, are typically seen by Materialists as third tier, while they consider the unborn to be fourth. This is due to the fact that the tiny, developing bodies of the unborn generally go unseen, and are therefore felt by Materialists to possess no attractive value.

This grim Materialist belief, which would sacrifice a sick child for a sports star, a handicapped veteran for a fashion model, or an unborn child for a dog, unsurprisingly appeals to elitist, egocentric adults with weak, unhealthy, or ugly minds residing within strong, healthy, or beautiful bodies. Is it any wonder that the atheist worldview which produces it tends to be adopted by college students who are just entering, or who have only recently entered their 20's, and who often have little life experience beyond what they have been taught in the atheist infested Western school systems? This caste system appeals to them, as it places the majority of them at its pinnacle. They generally feel differently about it when no longer one of the elite; when they become old, injured from a car accident, or are being treated for cancer. It is the same argument, with different actors, as was made by the slave owners and the Nazis of yesteryear. In spite of their better judgement, many of these latter groups were reluctant to dispute the morality of the social tragedies of slavery and the death camps, simply because they were flattered to think of themselves as being among the uppermost tiers of these social castes. Their egos had smothered their consciences.

But it does not stop here. Materialists even believe in a caste of value among the unborn. Being to them nothing but soulless biological machines, the smaller and less developed these unborn infants are, the less inherent value they are thought to possess. The 8-month child in utero, though only on the fourth value tier, is thought to be above the 7-month one, who is above the 6th, and on and on until we reach the newly fertilized egg. This, according to the Materialists, is the single most valueless living creature in the world; no different from a bacterium, which they wash from their hands before eating.

Materialists prefer to call this earliest form of human development, that of the fertilized human egg, a "zygote," hoping by doing so to convince mankind to objectify it. In the same way, and for the same reason they prefer to refer to the more developed infant as an "embryo," or "fetus." This is the same approach used by casinos, when they force customers to exchange their money for "chips," prior to playing. Casino owners hope that this exchange will at least partially divorce the value which their customers subconsciously know that cash possesses from the brightly colored piece of plastic they hold in their hands, and therefore cause them to be more careless with it than they normally would be, were they feeding dollars into machines, or placing them on tables during bets. Analogously, these Materialists also hope to divorce the value which the majority of mankind instinctively know that infants possess, both before and after their birth, from the new titles which they have given to them while in the womb. This approach of language manipulation is a common tactic used by those who are pushing the atheist worldview. They are currently attempting this same trick with their exchange of the word *sex*, for that of *gender*; a subject which is discussed at length within another section of this work.

This is how the gruesome industry of abortion is sold to the Western world. Ignorant, or avaricious physicians, backed by their atheist infected academic peers, are brought in as "expert" witnesses, in the court cases which decide on the legality of this practice. These "experts" weave sob stories of "back-alley coat hanger abortions" which supposedly claimed the lives of untold scores of beautiful first tier girls, regardless of how rare such occurrences actually were, and juxtapose them with what they claim are sub-fourth tier, single celled biological machines. Given the claimed hidden nature of these "back alley abortions," abortionists can make this mythical holocaust as widespread, and as horrible as they want; evidence be damned.

Abortionists claim that these girls had no other choice, intentionally downplaying the fact that thousands of infertile couples exist who would love to adopt and care for these infants, but are prevented from doing so by the small fortunes which our extortionist adoption policies charge, for no legitimate reason. The pictures of reality which these "experts" paint are rooted in misrepresentations, less educated past scientific beliefs, and outright lies. The only crisis for the girls in question is one of convenience.

The overwhelmingly left heavy media generally spin their reporting on these cases, so that they appear to the general public as ultimately being about wealthy, complacent, generally white bureaucrats attempting to control what women are able to do with their bodies. They season their stories with allusions to the long-gone days when women were unable to vote, or own property; hoping by this means to stir the ignorant into a frenzy of righteous indignation. And they are generally successful with this approach with the majority of underinformed teens and young adults. These interrupt the court cases deciding on these matters with angry outbursts, or rally on the courthouse steps with signs declaring that women are being stripped of *freedom* to control their own bodies.

The risk of appeals to arbitrary *freedom* is discussed elsewhere in this work, since the vilest of moral offenses, as in this instance, can be masked by this seemingly sanctifying, and often abused term. It is not the fate of a woman's body which is being decided upon. The developing infant shares only ~50% of the mother's genetic material. It is an entirely different person, much like these protestors are entirely different people from their mothers, though they share roughly the same amount of DNA with them. Should these protestors' mothers retain the right to have physicians dismember them, essentially burn them to death in hypersaline solutions, or puncture their skulls and vacuum their brains out on the courthouse steps? Why not? These ignorant hypocrites are rallying for monsters to be allowed to do the exact same thing to the unborn infants.

Do they believe that magic happens at birth which suddenly imparts life? Are these people so astoundingly ignorant that they have never heard of "preemies?" Do they believe that these children are still not alive for the months after their birth, until they finally reach what would normally be full term; regardless of any coos, rattle-shakes, smiles, cries, burps, feedings, and diaper changes. These infants have more value and right to life than these hopelessly corrupt protesters.

Generally, when these points are made, the ignorant shift tactics to claim that killing an infant is preferable to allowing one to be born into a family which doesn't want them; where they will go unloved. Who are these people to make such a life and death decision on someone else's behalf? How do these people know, without a doubt, that the mother will not love the child? What about the father, or grandparents, or aunts, or uncles? Are they God, that they have complete omniscience of all future events? Even if they go unloved, has no one ever grown up within an unloving, or even abusive family, and yet, thankful that they are alive, gone on to become good people, live happy lives, and vow to raise their families differently? This occurs all the time. The reader will certainly be well enough aware of personal examples of this which would preclude examples needing to be listed here.

The next tactic of abortion proponents is to point out examples of rape and incest. Surely in these instances abortion is justified. Rape and incest are intentionally cited so that the moral outrage caused by the severity of these offenses hopefully skews the objectivity of the person being debated with, or those listening to the debate. Again, if the door of access to abortion can be wedged open in these extreme cases, abortionists know that they can throw it the rest of the way open. Legalize it only for rape and incest and anyone will be able to get an abortion by simply claiming that the pregnancy was caused by these things, even if it wasn't. They won't be required to name the offender, in order to prevent any who are afraid to do so from being denied these services, and HIPAA laws will ensure that no one but the physician and care team ever find out about the claim.

But let's take a look at the moral aspect of the issue. Even in the instances of rape and incest, two moral wrongs still do not make a moral right. The rapists and the incestuous offender are the guilty parties who should be punished, not the innocent child developing in the womb, who had nothing to do with the crime. If one man shoots another, should a passerby who witnesses the attack be executed for it? Abort the child and there will then be two crimes, and two victims, rather than just one.

It is understandable that these crimes will cause mental anguish in the pregnant female who is affected by them. It is tempting for these girls to think that they can have an abortion and then simply attempt to forget the crime happened, rather than having to deliver a child who is a living reminder of it. But this is no solution. It will merely add the guilt of having committed a murder on top of their existing mental anguish. And the mental anguish caused by the abortion, where they are the offender, will be significantly worse than that of the rape or incest, where they were the victim.

Should any of these points be made by a male, female abortionists will typically claim that they are invalid.

"You are not a woman," they will rant, "So you don't know what it's like for females. Therefore, none of your objections matter."

This is the most stupid of claims, which rapists could make right back to them. "You don't know what it's like for males, therefore none of your objections matter." We must deal with the points of the argument, not resort to disingenuous sideways ad hominem attacks. Conscience, being a product of the soul, is sexless. Any who rely upon it to judge the morality of actions are able to do so even if the actions were performed by an individual of a different sex from their own.

The last fallback is to allege that pro-lifers would prevent the abortion in the rare, and tragic medical crisis of ectopic pregnancy. This is a classic strawman tactic, as virtually no one holds this opinion. In this scenario, the developing infant implants within the fallopian tubes, the ovary, or the retroperitoneal space, rather than within the uterus. It will inevitably die, in these instances, as none of these areas will allow for the required growth and nourishment which the uterus will. If the pregnancy is not aborted, there is a significant risk that the growing infant will also kill the mother. In this unfortunate instance the motive is one of life saving, not life ending. We are not referring to one individual voluntarily murdering another individual, who would otherwise live if unmolested. We are talking about two individuals who will both likely die, unless the life of at least one of them is ended. And since modern technology will currently not allow for the child to be saved, without the mother, the life of the mother is the only possible choice. This will not always be the case, however. Very recently, artificial wombs have allowed for the successful development of test animals, and it is simply a matter of time before these infants can simply be removed and allowed to complete their development in one. Once this occurs, there will be absolutely zero valid reasons to allow abortion. But again, the motive of abortionists in mentioning this issue is not to simply allow for this type of abortion, it is to use this rare exception to wrench the lid from Pandora's box; allowing any excuse for abortion, or even no excuses at all, other than mere preference.

The judges who rule on these matters are typically legal experts; not philosophy, medicine, or science ones. Therefore, in spite of their often-substantial experience and caution, the flood of jargon and sob stories which these interested academics and physicians throw at them intimidates some into approving this atrocity. All it really takes to commission this silent holocaust is one incompetent federal judge in a specific state, or 5 incompetent judges on the Supreme Court, who fail to consider that pharmaceutical companies, healthcare systems, and physicians are strongly influenced by the veritable fortunes which they stand to make on the legalization of this atrocity; that Western academia are strongly influenced by the Materialist atheist worldview which pervades it; and that there is a political aspect of population control which often, unfortunately, influences the opinions of these "experts."

Unfortunately, within most modern democratic societies, wealthy businessmen have succeeded in supplanting true national patriots from the majority of leadership positions. The natural result of this has been a disturbing trend of profit and profitability becoming recognized as the sole national virtues. Accordingly, regardless of all of the manipulative sob stories, half-baked scientific opinions, and left-heavy media spins on the subject, the ultimate factor driving the legality of abortion is money.

Healthcare systems and physicians working for government funded organizations, such as Planned Parenthood, are collecting substantial profit from the big business of infanticide; much of this profit being in tax dollars. Medical equipment and instrument manufacturers are collecting large profits from the tools of death that they sell these systems, people, and organizations to perform abortions. Pharmaceutical companies are collecting large profits from the medications which they provide for use both during the abortion procedures, and afterwards by the woman, depending upon the stage of pregnancy she was in when she decided to murder her child.

Governments envision large savings that they are realizing by enabling the poor to abort their children, so that they can avoid supporting them through social safety-nets, such as Welfare, and WIC. Any who study the tremendously difficult to find statistics on this will find that a large percent of abortions in America are occurring among poor black women. Florence Nightingale, the "Mother of Nursing," who promoted abortion among the newly freed black slaves, in order to discourage their population growth, would be proud. As would academic Francis Crick, the co-discoverer of the double helix nature of DNA, yet also a proponent of eugenics programs, including mass sterilizations of the poor and the "poorly endowed genetically."[117]

Families who encourage their pregnant young daughters to abort, often use vagaries about how they "are not ready," or "are not at a good stage in life," but these all ultimately mean that they think that having the child now will impact their daughter's future career prospects, or force the families to assist financially. Both of these translate into a desire for money, or a fear of losing it.

Many women use abortion as a savage sort of birth control, perhaps because they discover that the man who impregnated them, whom they thought both loved and would support them, actually only used them to satisfy his lusts. These women generally have abortions either because they have ignorantly believed the lies about these children not being alive, because they wish to murder the children who would be a constant living reminder of the men who emotionally hurt them, or a visible proof of their own lack of chastity, or lastly, because they know that childrearing is expensive, and selfishly value their economic prosperity over the lives of their children. And the cowardly men who use, abandon, or encourage these women to abort their offspring are no better. These men virtually always do so because they don't want their future career prospects to be impacted by their actions; or in other words, because they selfishly value money over the lives of their own children, or the women whom they impregnated with them. Ignorance, vengeance, or love of money are the ultimate drivers.

Since the atheist worldview, which has infected the majority of Western academia, denies the existence of soul altogether, then there is really no logical explanation why value occurs even at birth. Justification for murder in utero can just as easily be extended ex utero. If unwanted infants have no souls, and subsequently no innate value, allowing them to be killed for convenience, then why not unwanted children, adults, and elderly. The only things theoretically restraining this are social mores. Some of the more candid academics, such as Dr. Peter Singer of Princeton University, have already made such inhuman proposals.[116]

Going a step further, consider who is empowered to define the term *unwanted* in this scenario. The wealthy and empowered always have greater influence on legislation than the poor and disenfranchised, so the logical conclusion would be that it would be the latter who would disproportionately end up on the unwanted list. Perhaps once these are gone, the list would be expanded to include those seen by the ultra-wealthy and influential as competitors, or threats to their wealth, or power. There would really be no scientific reason to stop the furnaces, as there is no innate value to soulless, fleshy machines.

But what of the vast majority who have not been brainwashed by this atheist worldview, and who still believe in the existence of soul? Why are they silent? They are not. They simply are generally ignored by the overwhelmingly left-heavy media, who control and shamelessly manipulate the viewpoints that the nation is allowed to see or hear. Many of these "pro-lifers," the vast majority of whom are Christians, attempt to debate with Materialists about the horrible immorality of abortion, which they instinctively sense. In doing so, however, they often find themselves at a distinct disadvantage.

In the first case, many of them are unfamiliar with the scientific facts which would enable them to effectively debate this issue, forcing them to rely solely upon their religious views. The down side of this is that nowhere in the Bible is the topic of abortion prohibited, or even discussed. Quite the opposite in fact. The Jewish religion, which Christianity was built upon, even allowed parents to have rebellious children stoned to death (Deuteronomy 21:18-21). These verses are still preserved in the Christian Old Testament and the Jewish Tanakh. Christians who attempt to debate abortionists based upon religious principles, therefore, are generally forced to rely upon verses which prohibit generalized murder; regardless of the fact that these verses internally conflict with multiple instances within scripture where murders, and even genocides are not merely excused, but are claimed to be divinely sanctioned.

Those who do possess a sufficient level of scientific education which allows them to debate with abortionists on these grounds, are generally reluctant to do so, out of a fear of being publicly labeled as rustic, superstitious, or the new scarlet letter of "unscientific." Many realize that, in order to continue the debate, they must challenge the small circle of biologists and biochemists who have essentially become the high priests of a new faith; the central tenets of which are the Materialist disbelief in deity and the belief that life is soulless and purely mechanical. These, whose full-time employment is study, instruction, and publication within their specific areas of expertise, can typically bury their opponents with ease in oceans of intimidating jargon and mountains of published experimental minutia. It isn't until one grows familiar with this type of published data and jargon that the halo of seeming infallibility which surrounds it disappears. It eventually dawns upon the reader that this is nothing but careful documentation of observations by people who make use of an industry specific set of terms, but who are as fallible as themselves.

As an aside, the use of jargon within academic discussions, or publications stems from one of three motives. The first of these is an attempt by the speaker, or author to establish their credibility among their peers, or superiors. This motive differs little from a secret handshake which indicates party membership. The second possible motive is to chill the listener, or reader's willingness to ask questions which may expose the speaker, or author's logical blunders, or knowledge gaps, by making them more concerned about their own unfamiliarity with the terminology. The third, and only legitimate motive is when the jargon serves as a highly efficient method of minimizing the volume of spoken, or written material; a single field specific word summing up whole concepts which those working within the industry are already familiar with.

Yet the object of debate is the communication and exchange of ideas. Speakers and writers should therefore adjust their style of speech, or writing to their audience, shedding jargon when it becomes an obstruction, rather than an aid to communication. Within scientific papers written for other scientists, jargon is natural and appropriate. Within the context of a debate between men who disagree about a certain position, but who do not work within the field frequently enough to know the terms, jargon is inappropriate.

Returning from this digression, as far as careful observation and documentation go, aren't the observations which have been made by whole hosts of men over the centuries, who have sensed and seldom doubted the existence of their own souls within, just as valuable? Haven't men been writing about possessing souls for thousands of years? Surely, we should dismiss exploded superstitions, yet what makes us so certain that the possession of a soul is one of these; as it is only within these few, most recent generations that the disbelief in soul has come into vogue within the scientific community. Many brilliant scientists did, and among the living still do believe in it: men such as Newton, Pascal, Descartes, Bacon, and Einstein, whose intellects dwarfed those of the majority of their modern academic peers.

The core problem is the underlying belief that the soul only exists at an organismal level. It is understandable why Christians, who are virtually alone in their opposition to abortion, tend to develop this belief. The Mosaic faiths describe souls as if they enter into and leave the body, like a ghost. The spirit of God is claimed in the Bible to have descended upon Mary during her supposedly immaculate conception (Matthew 1:18). The Holy Spirit is claimed to have descended upon Jesus "like a dove" at his baptism (Luke 3:22), and to have descended upon the Apostles, during Pentecost (Acts 2). Evil spirits, referred to as "demons," are claimed to do this as well, in various sections of scripture; where they influence, or "possess" a person, or animal (e.g. Mark 5:8-9 & Matthew 8:28-34).

Even the rare non-religious person, who continues to believe in the existence of soul, tends to fall into this belief of souls only existing at the organismal level. They instinctively sense that the two hallmarks of the soul, individuality and worth, remain undiminished in amputees. This causes them to generally believe that the animating soul resides within a different, more indispensable part of the body; such as the brain. On the other hand, they also instinctively sense that this individuality and worth have somehow departed, along with the soul which imparted them, from the still entire bodies of the newly deceased. Therefore, just as these people believe that the soul passes out of the body after death, so they also generally believe that the soul infuses into the body, likely within the brain, sometime during the gestation process.

But there is a problem here, which Materialists are quick to seize upon. The developing infant does not always possess a brain. Primary neurulation, the formation of the early brain, begins at roughly the 18th day after fertilization.[197] The majority of pregnancy tests, however, do not work until roughly 14 days post conception, at earliest. We are therefore talking about a window of 4 days, between a girl realizing that she is pregnant, and primary neurulation beginning, when she could schedule and get an abortion. But in reality, this window of opportunity is actually an illusion. The date of conception is generally merely an approximation, as ovulation often varies by several days. In addition, after conception within the ampulla, there is variation in the amount of time that it takes the developing child to travel to the uterus and implant within the uterine wall. It is only after this implantation that hCG, which these pregnancy tests look for, is detectable in the mother's urine; though development is occurring the entire time after conception. Also, the majority of girls, knowing that there is variation in their hormonal cycles, generally wait at least a week after their normal menstruation start time, if they even remember exactly when this is, before becoming suspicious that they might be pregnant and taking a pregnancy test.

So should abortions be allowed prior to this early period? If it is admitted that there is no soul, even for a brief period between conception and birth, then during that period there would also be no worth, and the embryo may be legitimately aborted. This is the problem with the organismal view of soul infusion. Once the ignorant, egocentric, and avaricious get their foot in the door with pre-neurulation abortions, they will kick it the rest of the way open, until abortion is legalized at any gestational period. They have already done so across most of the Western world. In our current state in America, for example, even full-term abortions are legal in some states, and doctors are allowed to kill infants who are successfully birthed alive after surviving the abortion process. Proposed legislation prohibiting this barbaric latter practice was just recently stricken down by liberal Democrats within the U. S. Congress. Oh, that we could exchange the lives of these morally reprehensible liberal politicians, these blights upon the human race, for the lives of the innocents whom their votes have doomed.

Identifying the specific point in time when an immaterial soul begins to indwell a material organism is such a challenge, that many throw up their hands and call it unknowable. This is not true. There is a way to observe this infusion. It is the moment when the cellular machinery within the single fertilized cell of the infant becomes activated. Neither this, nor any other cell can function without an external, likely immaterial agency making decisions, selecting for the expression and selective modification of RNA and its resultant proteins, and performing various other functions with a timing and precision that bespeaks the highest levels of intelligence. As a room-full of instruments cannot play a song on their own, being but tools for the musicians, so the cellular machinery cannot function without this external intelligence, which is composer, conductor, and musician in one. Here is soul and worth at a cellular level. This topic is expounded upon in the section of this work on Resonance.

If cells have value, then an organism formed of these cells also has value, or worth, by proxy. Indeed, even more than this. If soul is created by a perfect agency, call it God if you will, then it must itself be perfect, as perfection cannot beget imperfection. And since the human mind cannot conceive of a plurality of immaterial perfections, then there is the strong possibility that there is a sort of interrelation, or kinship between all souls. Therefore, the value of the souls of others, even those of the unborn, is inseparable from our own value. The only realistic and ethical option, is to prohibit abortions altogether.

The reason why this more stalwart line of defense against the abortionists is generally not adopted within the Western nations is, unfortunately, due to our Christian heritages. If soul exists within man, as evidenced by the function of even a single cell, then there is really no way to avoid extending this same argument to all cells, of all species. Yet if all life possesses soul, then scripture is challenged which claims that soul is a special gift of God, which was given only to man at the creation. If we admit this one doctrine to be inaccurate, or misunderstood, then a whole host of other doctrinal problems present themselves.

If animals have souls, then what of Christ's sacrificial death? Does my dog need to understand who Jesus was, or risk burning for all eternity? Can my dog sin?

The problem is not so apparent for Muslims and Jews, who already portray God as petty and unjust, in that he arbitrarily selects favorites, condemning all others to eternal torment by default. Hindus, and their later offshoot of Buddhists and Yogis, are instinctively far closer to the truth, as can be seen in some of the *Principle Upanishads*. Therein, it is posited that Brahman indwells and infuses all; living and nonliving alike.[103] Unfortunately, these three faiths are so bogged down in other ludicrous superstitions as to overshadow and lend an overall air of discredit to these more profound observations.

But we must not shy away from facts, even if they don't fit our accepted models for them; including those within the fields of science or religion. If the logical conclusion is that animals have souls, then we should face this fact head on. If this implies that error exists in the Bible, Koran, and Torah, then we should admit this and not stubbornly cling to error for party's sake. It doesn't matter if we have already come a long way down the road of life clinging to erroneous views. A thousand miles traveled in the wrong direction is not progress. It only becomes progress when taken in the direction of truth. The sooner we turn towards this truth, the further ahead we will be.

Sex and Gender

Humans are sexually dimorphic. This means that they consist of two distinct sexes, which we refer to as male and female. They are not simply male and female based upon the state of their reproductive organs, but genetically, down to their very cells. Except for a few specialized types, such as red blood cells, and gametes, cells can be taken from anywhere on a healthy male, from his head to his toes, and will be found to possess one Y and one X chromosome. Contrarily, a sampling of these same cells, taken from a healthy female, will be found to have two X chromosomes and no Y chromosome. These sex determining chromosomes are referred to as allosomes. Though a developing human infant generally possesses two allosomes per cell, there are various rare genetic mutations, or meiotic malfunctions which can result in offspring having extra (e.g. trisomy), missing (e.g. monosomy), or malfunctioning allosomes.

The SRY gene, located on the Y chromosome, is effectively the master gene which initiates masculinization. During a certain stage of embryological development, it activates and triggers a subsequent cascade of reactions within the developing infant which ultimately result in the development of male genitalia. This being said, the default pathway of embryological development in humans is female. Should a fertilized egg possess an X and a Y chromosome, and yet a problem occur with the SRY gene, the Y chromosome, or the tissues which respond to the androgens which are signaled by it, masculinization may occur only partially, as in the case of Hermaphrodism, or not at all, resulting in a phenotypical female. This latter instance is the genetic disorder known as Swyer's Syndrome. At least one X chromosome appears essential for survival, as this chromosome also possesses the genes required for heart and skeletal muscle development, as well as for immune function. Should the fertilized human egg possess only a single X allosome, a genetic disorder known as Turner's Syndrome, it will develop into a phenotypical female with various health issues. Should it possess three X chromosomes, a genetic disorder known as Triple X Syndrome, it will typically develop into a phenotypical female who is abnormally tall and may have learning disabilities and various other health issues. Should it possess one X and two Y chromosomes, it will typically develop into a phenotypical male, who again may be abnormally tall and may have learning disabilities and various other health issues. Should it possess two X and one Y chromosome, a genetic disorder known as Klinefelter's

Syndrome, a phenotypical male results, who may or may not exhibit traits such as reduced libido.

This being said, the more severe genetic disorders, including those which cause genotype and phenotype mismatch, such as Swyer's Syndrome, and monosomies, such as Turner's Syndrome, overwhelmingly result in infertility. Consider a quote from a recent study which echoes this. "To date, most mutations characterized in humans cause pubertal failure and infertility, while a few result in normal puberty, but cause infertility."[104] Phenotypical females with Swyer Syndrome, for example, do not possess ovaries, and therefore have no eggs which could be fertilized. This is no chance occurrence. It is a built-in genetic safety mechanism, or genetic "pressure," which ensures that serious genetic mutations, especially those influencing sexual dimorphism, do not get passed on to additional future generations, causing them to accumulate within the genome of the species. It is natural eugenics.

These products of dysgenesis do not constitute distinct additional sexes. They are simply victims of genetic disorders, or birth defects. True hermaphrodites are simply a genetic male that some genetic, or environmental factor caused to incompletely transition from the default female state during embryological development. Depending upon whether this incomplete transition left them closest to the male, or the female phenotype, they should be aided with medical care and allowed to adopt this sex. Ideally, they should be allowed to transition to the male phenotype, in order to match their genotype with their phenotype, however, in all care, physicians should seek to do the least harm. It would be both cruel and unreasonable to subject a hermaphrodite infant who only displayed slight masculine phenotypical traits, such as an enlarged clitoris, to the massive amounts of surgery and hormone therapy which would be required to transition them to the male phenotype, when it would be far easier to perform the minor surgical corrections which would resolve this issue and allow them to function as a female. Claiming that these people are a separate, third sex, is like claiming that people born with, and suffering from other physical deformations, such as Siamese Twins, are a new species. The people suffering from these disorders should be sympathized with and aided with the best medical care that can be provided, not have their health problems hijacked and used for sinister political ends; a topic which will be elaborated upon shortly.

Humans remain sexually dimorphic. Why then is this concept of human sexual dimorphism under such a vigorous attack by the joint forces of today's Western media and academia? Over the past few years, both of these have spearheaded the effort to universally abandon any categorization of people by sex, in favor of the supposedly less offensive categorization term of "gender." While sex may be genetic, and therefore involuntary, gender is claimed to be a voluntary "lifestyle choice."

This is actually a self-destructive argument, given that the choice in question is virtually always related to which sex the individual under consideration decides to be. It is the same as claiming that A is genetically driven, and therefore involuntary, but that B is a voluntary decision about what A will be. Any but the most blind can see how nonsensical such a claim is.

When this irrationality is pointed out to the media sources who make these claims, or the brainwashed masses who echo them, they typically switch tactics and argue from the authority of the powerful academics who are leading this "gender revolution."

As an aside, it is telling that the phrase *revolution* is commonly employed by both media and academia when referring to this recent change. Communists have, since the days of Marx, always referred to themselves as "revolutionaries," and to their movement as a "revolutionary" one. Note one of literally dozens of examples which could be cited from Marx's Communist Manifesto attesting to this. "In short, the Communists everywhere support every revolutionary movement against the existing social and political order of things."[74] What is telling about this is the fact that a large majority of Western academia are infested by the atheist worldview, which births Communism as its natural political offspring.

Returning to our topic, this latter, more intelligent group, takes a far more subtle and cunning approach with their *revolution*. They enthusiastically deny that gender is a voluntary choice, claiming instead that it is based upon internal mental, or emotional *feelings*, whose origin and impulse are supposedly outside of the experiencer's control. This approach is intentionally selected because, being rooted in feelings which only the experiencer perceives, it is impossible to disprove. By this definition, in order to disprove someone's claim that their gender differs from their sex, one would have to capture, classify, and quantify their emotions, prove that these feelings are the product of a conscious, or subconscious decision, and then finally prove that this decision was based upon flawed information which made it erroneous; whether internally, or externally derived. One must, in effect, become a mind reader, since feelings and decisions are both types of thought. All of these are impossibilities. Scientists have not even begun to understand the complexities of thought origination, much less does any means of capturing, or quantifying such things exist. All we have to rely upon is what the experiencer informs us about them.

These academics, along with the Western media outlets who parrot them, claim that "gender" is the superseding, independent mental aspect of what a person is, while *sex* is merely these people's subordinate phenotype. Often, they cite the range of genetic disorders which were discussed earlier, implying that these somehow support their claims. Ironically, the vast majority of those who struggle with these disorders are people who simply wish to normally function within their own sex. It is a battle for ultimate authority which the thought scientists (i.e. psychiatrists, psychologists, sociologists, and anthropologists) are waging against the body scientists (i.e. geneticists, physiologists, anatomists, neurologists, embryologists, histologists, endocrinologists, etc.). Though the latter can provide an overwhelming amount of irrefutable data proving the genuine, specific sex of an individual, all of this data is dismissed as irrelevant by the mind group; regardless of its rigor, or repeatability.

"We are what our mind says we are, not what our body does," they claim. "If there is ever a disparity between the claims of our minds and those of our bodies, then our bodies must be the ones in the wrong."

This is but one more symptom of the atheist worldview, which is spreading like a plague throughout Western society. As described in more detail elsewhere in this work, the atheist worldview denies the absolute nature of goodness, along with all of its context specific embodiments, such as virtue, vice, beauty, justice, and even truth. All is made to be *relative*, a euphemism within this context for being human perspective dependent.

Yet even the very word which these gender revolutionists use betrays them and reveals their ignorance. The English *Gender* is derived from the Latin stem *Genus*, which itself comes from the Proto-Indo-European root *Gene-*, to give birth.[105] It is the same root whence we derive other words which imply creation, such as *generate, genesis,* and most importantly, *genitalia.* Etymologically speaking, therefore, gender means the specific physical aspects of an individual which allows them to procreate. Pause for a moment and consider how this meaning differs from that of a person's sex. You shouldn't have to pause long, because it doesn't. The meanings are identical; making the aforementioned claim that people should be defined by their gender, rather than by their sex, laughable. They might as well fight that people should be defined by their maleness, rather than their masculinity.

What has been the result? This view that gender is driven by the mind has led to the unstoppable growth of a host of laughably absurd gender types, such as, among many others: transsexuals, genderqueers, agenders, androgynes, demi-genders, genderfluids, drag kings, drag queens, and two spirits. This list of absurdities will never stop growing, as it is only bounded by the human imagination. People are even beginning to "identify" as cats[106] and hippopotamuses,[107] attempting to legitimize these delusions by giving them scientific sounding names, such as trans-spieces, or tranimal. In order to avoid prosecution, 38 year-old pedophiles are identifying as trans-age 9 year-olds.[108] While the concepts of trans-species and trans-age are still currently and appropriately laughed at, it is only a matter of time until they are validated by academia, promoted by Western media, and laws are put in place which cause any who laugh to be sued, or fired; as the argument which they base their claims upon rests upon the same foundation as the one currently being used to justify gender fluidity. If you are whatever you feel yourself to be, who can legitimately say otherwise? Western academia, as well as the judges, legislators, and executive branch officials who depend upon their guidance, will be unable to deny these absurd latter claims without proving themselves hypocrites for approving of the former ones.

The reason why the common LGBT (i.e. Lesbian, Gay, Bisexual, Transgender) acronym has been avoided during this discussion is because there is no actual "rainbow of gender." Sex and gender are absolute synonyms, and humans, being sexually dimorphic, come in one of two possible sexes: the male, or the female. Among these sexes, there are those who choose to participate in sexual relations with a partner of a *different* sex, known as "heterosexuals" (i.e. from the Greek, *heteros*, meaning *different*) and those who choose to participate in sexual relations with a partner of the *same* sex, known as "homosexuals" (i.e. from the Greek, *homo*, meaning *same*).

By definition, this latter group would include both Lesbians, the "L" in LGBT, who are literally homosexual women, and Gay men, the "G" in LGBT, who are literally homosexual men. Bisexuals, the "B" in LGBT, are simply people who intermittently participate in homosexual, as well as heterosexual acts. This is not a third category. It is simply a vacillation between the two. As far as "Transgenders" (i.e. transsexuals) go, the "T" in LGBT, these people are also simply homosexuals as well. The reason for this is explained briefly below.

Transsexuals frequently convince greedy, cowardly, or otherwise irresponsible physicians to prescribe them a never-ending course of hormones, and to perform surgical procedures on them for the express purpose of aiding these people in their shamefully perverted imitation of the opposite sex. Like Doctor Frankenstein, such physicians should have their medical licenses revoked for irresponsibly creating these monsters, and then releasing them to prey upon society. In spite of the best efforts of these irresponsible physicians, virtually every cell within these transsexuals possesses sufficient genetic evidence to condemn them as imposters. The only ones which don't are the few specialized types which lose their DNA as they mature; such as red blood cells and cornified skin, hair, and nail cells.

The common reply by the well intentioned, but ignorant, is that these transsexuals are simply doing these things to express their true inner nature. Is a bodybuilder who induces massive amounts of muscular hypertrophy by continuously taking anabolic steroids simply expressing his "true inner nature" to be someone massive? These steroids are simply hormone supplements, much like the ones taken by transsexuals, which modify a person's natural musculature and also often their overall masculinity. Yet the very cells of these bodybuilders attempt to nullify these artificially increased hormone levels through the activation of negative feedback loops. These loops generally kill natural testicular testosterone production and often even cause testicular atrophy. Were this person to cease taking any steroids, their bodies would quickly begin to re-approach homeostatic hormonal levels, and their disproportionally hypertrophied muscles would slowly, but surely begin to shrink.

So too with transsexuals. Their bodies constantly strain to return to homeostatic hormonal levels. Were these people to cease their never-ending regimen of prescription hormones, within a short time, the façade would begin to crack, their bodies would begin to move towards natural hormonal homeostasis, and the physical, mental, and emotional signs of their true (i.e. genetic) sex would once more manifest themselves.

Transsexual males remain men, regardless of how much they attempt to pass themselves off as women; like wolves in sheep's clothing. Therefore, when these men engage in sexual relationships with other men, they are simply performing homosexual acts, and are therefore common homosexuals. In the same way, transsexual females remain women, regardless of how much they attempt to pass themselves off as men; like sheep in wolves clothing. Therefore, when these women engage in sexual relationships with other women, they are simply performing homosexual acts, and are therefore also simply common homosexuals.

At the end of the day we find that we are not dealing with a rainbow of "genders," but simply a group of heterosexuals on the one hand, and on the other, several groups of homosexuals expressing varying degrees of moral corruption and perversion.

Why, in the Western world, do the thought scientists appear to be winning this war between sex and gender? The reason is because this battle of ideas has not occurred on an even plane. The merits of these ideas are not being worked out in open and public debate, nor are they being left to the people to decide, as would be expected in a democracy. This battle is occurring in the courts, where small groups of powerful individuals, or organizations, can force their will upon the rest of what is supposed to be a democratic society, like tyrants.

As with the Roe versus Wade case, which legalized abortion, and the recent Supreme Court decision which legalized homosexual marriage, the results of these cases are made law, whether in keeping with the will of the majority of Americans, or not. And in spite of Western media's incessant propaganda efforts on these topics, they are not. Indeed, in the example of homosexual marriage just mentioned, several states had attempted to put the issue to public vote, knowing that the vast majority of American citizens opposed it. Yet though it took thousands of petition signatures to put the issue on the ballot, all it took was the gavel strike of a single activist federal judge in those states to prohibit the people from voting on the matter: effectively stripping them of their voice.

This is not how a democracy should work. Judges are commissioned merely to interpret laws to be in keeping with the spirit of the Constitution, not to block the people from voicing their opinion, and especially not to tyrannically force wildly unpopular radical views which would cause the Constitution's drafters to turn in their graves, down the nation's throat. The brilliant Thomas Jefferson, author of the Declaration of Independence, and in my opinion the greatest of American presidents, had the prescience, even during the first years of the American nation, to notice and raise his concern about this potential for judicial tyranny. A few of his quotes on the subject are given below:

"If...the judiciary is the last resort in relation to the other departments of the government...then indeed is our Constitution a complete felo de so...The Constitution, on this hypothesis, is a mere thing of wax in the hands of the judiciary, which they may twist and shape into any form they may please. It should be remembered, as an axiom of eternal truth in politics, that whatever power in any government is independent, is absolute also; in theory only, at first, while the spirit of the people is up, but in practice, as fast as that relaxes. Independence can be trusted nowhere but with the people in mass."[109]

"You seem to consider the judges the ultimate arbiters of all Constitutional questions; a very dangerous doctrine indeed, and one which would place us under the despotism of an oligarchy. Our judges...and their power [are] the more dangerous as they are in office for life, and are not responsible, as the other functionaries are, to the elective control. The Constitution has erected no such single tribunal, knowing that to whatever hands confided, with the corruptions of time and party, its members would become despots...When the legislative or executive functionaries act un-Constitutionally, they are responsible to the people in their elective capacity. The exemption of the judges from that is quite dangerous enough. I know of no safe depository of the ultimate powers of the society, but the people themselves..."[110]

"There must be an ultimate arbiter somewhere.' True, there must; but...The ultimate arbiter is the people..."[111]

"The judiciary of the United States is the subtle corps of sappers and miners constantly working underground to undermine our Constitution from a co-ordinate of a general and special government to a general supreme one alone. This will lay all things at their feet...I will say, that 'against this every man should raise his voice,' and, more, should uplift his arm..."[112]

"I fear…we are now in such another crisis…with this difference only, that the judiciary branch is alone and single-handed in the present assaults on the Constitution. But its assaults are more sure and deadly, as from an agent seemingly passive and unassuming."[113]

"There is no danger I apprehend so much as the consolidation of our government by the noiseless, and therefore unalarming, instrumentality of the Supreme Court."[114]

"One single object…will entitle you to the endless gratitude of society; that of restraining judges from usurping legislation."[115]

To make matters worse, in these deciding court cases, no account is taken of the number of average citizens who disagree with the verdict arrived at, nor with the level of public disagreement with it. Such considerations are not things of case law, but of statutory (i.e. legislative branch) law. Instead, those who are brought forward to testify as "expert witnesses" in these court cases are often the same academics who are promoting the gender revolution; amplifying the importance of their often-warped opinions. As examples of how warped some of these views can become, consider academics such as Dr. Peter Singer, the Princeton Bioethics professor who promoted infanticide,[116] Dr. Francis Crick, the co-discoverer of the structure of DNA, who promoted population eugenics,[117] not to mention the staggering, ever increasing number of American professors today who are brazen proponents of Marxism;[118] a political abomination which is directly responsible for the deaths of ~110 million people throughout the 20th century.

The recent stream of bad gender related statutory, regulatory, and case law has solidly tilted the legal system and subsequent governmental policy in favor of the opinion of the gender revolutionists. And these victories are not without their spoils. Since these legal precedents have occurred, billions of dollars have been, and are being made on this deception: from doctor visits, to lifetime long hormone therapy prescriptions, to gender reassignment surgeries, to counseling and therapy groups, to masculinizing, or feminizing cosmetic surgeries, to additional lawsuits; none of which are free, and all of which further enfranchise this group and its deranged, corrupt, or treasonous promoters.

Besides the atheist worldview, there are two additional reasons why unscrupulous academics are lending their aid to this unscientific gender movement. The first is that they are allowing their personal biases related to identity politics to affect their judgement. The second is that, being ever starved for, and therefore in search of new funding sources, researchers are not immune from societal trends. While many brave and noble researchers continue to diligently work where their interests, experiments, and education bolstered intuitions indicate the truth lies, even when such truth has become unpopular, the vast majority are more than willing to cast their lines of research into ponds where funding is more abundant.

In order to confirm the hypotheses which their morally corrupt financial benefactors are hoping for, some of the less ethical researchers are even willing to "tweak," or overrepresent the significance of their findings; obscuring this subtle manipulation with an ocean of intimidating technical jargon. Who is actually in the lab with them in the middle of the night to know? Who will be likely to attack their results if they simply confirm, or advance the field in the popularly accepted direction which it is already taking?

On the other hand, those noble researchers whose pursuit of truth takes their research in an unpopular direction, which casts doubt upon the credibility of the field's major experts, many of whom wield powerful positions on research and grant advisory committees, or as editors of major peer reviewed scientific journals, will struggle to find funding, partners, and platforms to publish their results in. And the old adage within academia that one must "publish or perish" remains true today. In addition, many researchers intentionally shy away from publishing research which they know will likely cause many powerful individuals and organizations to lose money, as this places them at risk of being attacked, en masse, by the many researchers who are dependent upon these cash cows for research grants, and who therefore bear a strong allegiance to them; much like vassals to feudal lords.

A good example of this is a well conducted study which documented widespread malingering, in order to claim disability funding, among veteran PTSD claims. The study also rightly found that disability incentivization was not merely warping research findings, but was actually shown to have a negative effect on recovery. A sample from this article is given below:

"Many treatment-seeking veterans (53%), especially those seeking disability compensation, show clear symptom exaggeration or malingering on psychological tests and forensic interviews. Some veterans' reports of combat exposure change over time as a function of reported PTSD symptom severity, and some misrepresent combat exposure or war-zone deployment altogether...An expert consensus panel recommended excluding compensation-seeking veterans from clinical research because of the likely bias created by disability incentives. This recommendation has been largely ignored, perhaps because up to 94% of treatment-seeking veterans also seek compensation...A review of British government war pension files...suggested that disability incentives for combat-related psychiatric problems 'inhibit the natural process of recovery and consolidate distressing symptoms.'"[119]

Not surprisingly, this study, which called into question the credibility of many of the consensus views held by major players in the psychiatric field, as well as the presenting symptoms described within the DSM 5, stimulated a flurry of publications which condemned its conclusions. An excerpt from one of these is given below.

"Frueh et al. argued that longstanding Department of Veterans Affairs (VA) disability policies for posttraumatic stress disorder (PTSD) reward illness behavior, diminish engagement in treatment, and perversely promote chronic disability...Frueh et al. present an incomplete picture of the literature and neglect substantial evidence that contradicts their thesis."[120]

Besides merely risking their professional credibility, as mentioned above. Researchers whose publications jeopardize the profit margins of the medical and pharmaceutical industry place themselves at significant risk for costly and time-consuming lawsuits, which they cannot hope to win against such resource heavy opposition. Many wealthy individuals, or organizations such as these, intentionally file lawsuits which they know they would not ultimately win, if the cases are ever brought to trial. They merely attempt to draw out the legal process in order for the costs associated with it to financially break their opposition.

Returning to our subject, there is a staggering amount of profit being made on this big business of "gender reassignment." This is the real reason why this unscientific view is being actively promoted; not some feigned ethical obligation. Major pharmaceutical manufacturers, hand in hand with healthcare systems and well-intentioned but ultimately ignorant, brainwashed, or unethical clinicians, make a fortune off of gender reassignment surgeries and the lifetime worth of follow-up prescriptions required to maintain both the illusion and the delusion. The procedure costs roughly $130,000, not to mention the lifetime cost of preliminary and subsequent hormone therapy. Just within the military alone, since then President Obama's terrible decision to allow transgenderism within the US armed forces (because nothing says military strength quite like a man in a dress, or a woman with a beard) the pentagon faces an additional 1.3 billion in tax-dollar expenditures for this procedure alone, over the next 10 years.[121]

These same costs are beginning to be borne by our, also taxpayer funded, Bureau of Prisons; with convicted felons now being allowed in some states to receive gender reassignment surgery and be transferred from the men's, into the women's prison. Of course, California is leading the way with these ridiculous laws, as they tend to with any bad legislation. This recently occurred with Bradley Manning, who was convicted for leaking classified information, only to later have his sentence reduced as a publicity stunt by then President Obama. It also occurred with convicted murderer, Shiloh Quine.[122] This is a humiliating injustice to all of the female prisoners who are forced into the closest imaginable confined quarters, indeed, often even into joint cells, where they must sleep and toilet, and into joint showers where they must bathe, with someone whose every Y chromosome laden cell, and whose very brain structure proves that they are still a man; even without a penis.

Attraction

All too commonly these days, the claim is made that those who abandon heterosexuality have no choice in the matter; that they are helplessly drawn along by the gravitational pull of their physical attractions. This claim is patently false. Though the reasons for this will be provided below, it should preliminarily be noted that the burden of proof does not rest exclusively upon the denier of these claims. Indeed, billions of people, from hundreds of cultures, countries, and eras in history have all arrived at the exact same conclusion that heterosexuality is the natural and healthy state of sexual relation among humans. It is only a small minority, from a handful of cultures and countries, mostly in the present era, who disagree. Since these latter hold the radical opinion, they should carry the greatest burden of proof.

But let's begin by discussing how attraction works. All rational feelings are sent to the conscious mind from the subconscious, including the feelings that those who claim to be anything other than heterosexual sense and base their conscious identification upon. Springing from the subconscious, these feelings are the composite result of pre-established beliefs which are held about thousands of subjects, such as those of *self*, *society*, and *sexuality*. As was previously mentioned in another section of this work, it is very possible, in fact it is a quite common occurrence for the subconscious to arrive at incorrect, though sincere conclusions about any one of these subjects, due either to information deficiencies, or to falsities which the mind mistakenly believed to be true when exposed to them.

This is the point in the discussion where scores of academic, public, and media figures promoting the grossly unscientific dogma of a *rainbow* of morally equivalent *genders* will gnash their teeth in anger and demand blood; yet examine the truth we must. There appear to be several different falsities which, when subconsciously accepted, cause individuals to form erroneous subconscious beliefs about sexuality. This results in their subconscious passing a warped set of sex related feelings to their conscious minds, including the feelings of attraction itself. Such warped feelings often skew these individuals' subsequent views about their own sexual identity. This explains why people are mistaken when they claim that their experience of a feeling of physical attraction towards anyone or anything other than a mature individual of the opposite sex proves that they are naturally, or in other words, genetically predisposed to mate with this person, animal, or object.

Let's examine this false claim of the infallibility of attraction from another angle. In order for attraction to truly be infallible, it would also have to be immutable; as people cannot be entirely accurate about the subject, type, and degree of attraction which they sense, go on to experience a change in any, or all of these things, and then afterwards be once again entirely accurate. Either they were *correct* the first time and are *incorrect* the second, were *incorrect* the first time and are *correct* the second, or all attraction is purely relative and simply becomes *correct* when believed to be so.

The subject of an individual's physical attraction can, and very often does, change. Many people who were attracted to certain physical, or personality traits at one point in their lives, often discover at other points that they are attracted to completely different ones. This means that either there are two species of people, one whose sense of attraction is mutable, and the other whose isn't, or everyone's sense of attraction is potentially mutable, and one group simply hasn't experienced sufficient external influences to overcome whatever is internally resisting the mutation, while the other group has. This latter case is far more probable.

Observing a bunch of apples of the same type on display at the store, some of which are bruised, does not mean that some of them were of a special subtype which naturally has bruises on it, while the rest were of one which doesn't. It is far more likely that the bruising simply occurred in the apples that were subjected to external influences which their internal nature was unable to sufficiently resist. This same thing could have occurred in the other apples, were the bruising influences stronger, or were their internal resistance to bruising weaker.

Not only is the subject of attraction liable to change, but so too is the type and degree of attraction. Though we are typically attracted to the entire mix of our spouses' many internal and external traits, our degree of attraction towards each of these tends to vary over time. As their bodies become withered and gray with age, the focus of our attraction generally shifts away from their external physical traits and towards the beauties of their internal character. Compare this to the first time we saw them across the room. During this first observation, although their appearance and demeanor may have given some clues about their internal character, the majority of any attraction experienced was predominately towards certain of their physical traits.

Let's consider how the degree of attraction changes as well. Though many a romantic will claim that it does not, let's be honest here. Does what thrilled a person about their mate during the first date do so to the same degree 20 years later? During the initial phase, simply spending time with them during the day often resulted in sleep deprivation later that evening, the mind racing through a review of their form, words, and actions, hoping to discover additional evidence of genuine affection. 20

years later, does a similar amount of time spent together have the exact same effect? Recall the rush of adrenaline which set the mind ablaze with romantic thoughts, the first time we worked up the courage to hold our spouse's hand, or lean in for a kiss. After having held this person's hand and kissed their lips thousands of times, do we still experience the exact same rush of passion? Of course not. Nor would any wish to, who have actually given the subject due consideration.

The more intense that sort of physical passion is, the more it pleads for relief. Wishing for its return, simply to feel an increased pleasure from its relief, is like wishing to experience starvation, in order to feel an increased pleasure from eating, to experience suffocation, in order to feel an increased pleasure from breathing, or to experience a maddening itch, in order to feel an increased pleasure from scratching. Age, as it slowly and gently cools the flames of passion, causes this pendulum of painful longing and blissful relief to swing in ever shorter arcs. This phenomenon actually has an edifying effect upon relationships which are built upon more than the mere shifting sands of physical attraction. As hormone's subside, so does attraction towards physical qualities, and ultimately the bedroom. It then increasingly shifts towards inner character: which is who and what these people really are anyway.

Since, therefore, the subject, type, and degree of people's attraction can, and often does change, it cannot solely serve as the final proof of who or what we are naturally (i.e. genetically) predisposed to mate with. Since we have proven the malleability of attraction, we are left with three choices. Either attraction cannot change beyond a certain fixed, mentally healthy limit, it can at times change in a degree or manner which is mentally unhealthy, or all attraction is relative to the experiencer, and no specific subject, type, or degree of attraction is any better, or more mentally healthy than any other. Let's initially consider the third option.

This is generally the opinion held by most people who have only given the topic superficial consideration. This commonly held belief is the natural product of the atheist worldview which continues to spread its ruinous tentacles across all aspects of Western society. This worldview claims that there are no absolutes with regard to truth or morality; that all is human perspective dependent. This is a ludicrous claim. Were it true, then the most abusive, or repulsive of sexual fetishes, such as necrophilia, bestiality and, pedophilia, would be as morally justifiable as a healthy heterosexual relationship. Few are so brainwashed that they would go so far as agreeing with this point. Generally, they will attempt to shift to specifics of less flagrant fetishes, such as homosexuality, however the arguments which justify the latter remain equally valid for the former. Both are built upon the same foundation. If a feeling of physical attraction, which the morally corrupt frequently confuse with the noble emotion of love, is all that justifies the morality and mental healthfulness of a homosexual relationship, then who are they to deny the love which a man claims to feel towards a corpse, a walrus, or a toddler? Additional implications of the atheist worldview and an exploration of the true nature of love are discussed in depth elsewhere in this work and will not be reviewed here.

Moving on to an examination of the first two options, that attraction cannot change beyond a certain fixed, mentally healthy limit, or that it can at times change in a degree or manner which is mentally unhealthy. It's fairly obvious that it is possible for the subject, type, or degree of a person's sexual attraction to become skewed to the point of mental unwellness. This is the very definition of sexual fetishism. Sexual fetishism is a sub-category of general fetishism, a topic which is explored elsewhere within this work. Sexual fetishes can take a range of forms which vary according to the degree of mental unwellness which they reflect. Those fetishes which do not inflict any significant physical harm to the individuals involved, such as excessive masturbation, a fetish for feet, dirty undergarments, urination, or being spanked, typically only elicit laughter when discovered, as well as dismissive comments such as, "Whatever works for them." Encoded within this common statement is the message: "I know that these things are indicative of slight mental unwellness, but they don't affect me and are harmless, so they should simply be overlooked." In actuality, they should be addressed and corrected before they grow into something worse.

The stomach-churning list of possible fetishes is endless; including perversions in all three areas of sexual attraction: subject, type, and degree. Often, individuals with a sexual fetish begin to lose interest in it, and seeking to renew the thrill, foray deeper into more disturbing fetishes, such as pedophilia, bestiality, or sado-masochism. Many even become so mentally corrupted that they pursue disgusting fetishes involving necrophilia, rape, sexually driven murder, or cannibalism, or even the wearing of other people's skin. Dozens of specific examples could be provided, but such things are so shameful, disgusting, and disturbing that I will decline to describe them further.

Any who research the matter will discover that there is a long-established link between corrupted sexual-lust and blood-lust. The morbidly curious need merely to review the dozens of accounts of sexual perversions which are disproportionately, and unsurprisingly common among serial killers to prove this fact to themselves. The reader is cautioned in doing so, however, since some of the descriptions of shockingly brutal and cruel acts found there have a high likelihood of haunting one's memory; as the mind's eye cannot un-see disturbing images which it has been shown; even those described via text. Such things prove that there is no fixed limit to sexual perversion beyond which men and women cannot, or in some cases will not degrade themselves.

What is it about morally corrupt and brutal fetishes which makes them wrong and mentally unhealthy? Let's examine the rape fetish, for example. The average person will condemn the act of rape in the strongest terms possible. When asked to qualify what it is about rape that makes it wrong, they will typically respond that it is wrong because it violates the rights of the victim. Though the assaulter may consider the rape act to be desirable, and therefore a good, the victim does not.

Christians would have no problem with this question, since Jesus makes very clear in scripture that they are to treat others in the way that they themselves would like to be treated. "And just as you want men to do to you, you also do to them likewise" (Luke 6:31). The unfortunate part of Christianity, is that, while it often promotes good morals, it also excuses much of the warped ethics found in the older Jewish faith which it was built upon.

Jews, in the Tanakh, which includes the Christian Old Testament, were simply commanded not to rape married women. However, if they are able to successfully catch and rape a woman who isn't married, the only repercussions would be that they would have to pay a fee to this woman's father, and then marry the woman; typically swelling the numbers of their existing pool of "wives." Consider Deuteronomy 22:28-29: "If a man finds a young woman who is a virgin, who is not betrothed, and he seizes her and lies with her, and they are found out, then the man who lay with her shall give to the young woman's father fifty shekels of silver, and she shall be his wife because he has humbled her; he shall not be permitted to divorce her all his days." In addition, this rule only really applied to Hebrew women. Women from other nations could simply be stolen like property and made into slave wives (i.e. concubines). This often happened during invasions into other nations. It typically didn't matter if they were married or not in these instances, as the husband was often simply killed.

Similarly, Muslims are only prohibited in the Koran and Hadiths from raping Muslim women. Non-Muslim women, on the other hand, are fair game. This is because the Koran not only commands Muslims to remain eternally at war (i.e. jihad) with non-Muslims and the non-Islamic world (i.e. Dar al Harb), but it also allows them to make slaves of these supposed enemies, and even condones sex with the female ones; much like the Jewish law did with their concubines. This can be seen in Surah 23:1-6 of the Koran, where it reads, "Certainly will the believers have succeeded, they who are during their prayer humbly submissive, and they who turn away from ill speech, and they who are observant of zakah, and they who guard their private parts, except from their wives or those their right hands possess, for indeed, they will not be blamed." Muslim rapists effectively consider their unfortunate non-Muslim victims as prisoners of war whom their "right hands possess." This fact explains the massive surge in rape attacks against non-Muslim women which has occurred in nations such as Sweden, Germany, England, and anywhere else which has foolishly accepted the floods of male Muslim immigrants, who often pretend to be refugees, but who are actually colonists from the borderless Islamic nation.

These religious views on rape held by the early Jewish, and both the early and the modern Islamic faiths, are horribly unjust and immoral. But what about the views of the non-religious atheists whose worldview plagues today's Western world? Upon what basis do these people condemn rape? According to their worldview, there are neither absolute standards of goodness, nor any absolute principles of justice which spring from it. All goodness, and therefore justice, is relative to the perception of the individual. In this situation, what makes the views of the rape victim any more valid than those of the rapist? Without absolute standards of goodness, the only possible answer which can be given is convention; or in other words, majority opinion. Therefore, according to the atheist world-view, rape is only wrong because there are, thankfully, more people in this specific place, at this specific moment, who agree with the views of the victim.

Unfortunately, societal views are anything but static. What is shocking for one generation is often boring for the next. What if you lived in a different time, or place where you were surrounded by people who believe rape to be acceptable? According to the atheist world-view, in this environment, the rape of your grandmother or grandfather, mother or father, wife, daughter or son, granddaughter or grandson, or even yourself would be a good, since the majority believe it to be so; in spite of the fact that you and the rest of these victims disagree.

Also, under this morally relativistic viewpoint, it always remains unclear just how much societal consensus is required to convert a wrong into a right. Is rape wrong only if the majority of the world believes it to be so, or are the views of the majority of a nation sufficient to call something wrong? What about the majority of a state, city, neighborhood, household, or the people in a room? If this last instance were true, then every gang rape, or rape followed by a murder would be considered morally good, since those believing it to be so are in the majority.

These are, of course, absurd notions, which were simply made to underscore the fact that society must have a more solid foundation for justice than mere majority opinion. It must possess a belief in absolute justice. Such a belief is impossible without a correlating belief in absolute goodness; which itself is impossible without an underlying belief in God.

There are 3 ways that these sexual perversions tend to occur. The first, and likely the most common way, is when people are bombarded with information which overtly, or de facto claims that unnatural polygamous and/or homosexual relationships are morally, physically, and mentally equivalent to natural monogamous and/or heterosexual ones. This is classically known as brainwashing. Since the uncured world views of youth are generally more plastic, and therefore far simpler to manipulate than those of mature adults, which have been hardened by age and experience, the younger people are when they are first subjected to this type of propaganda, the more effective these brainwashing techniques generally are. Aware of this fact, the morally corrupt, a large majority of these being those infected with the atheist worldview, incessantly attempt to bombard the youngest of our children with their filth: everything from forcing kindergarteners to read books about lesbian moms, to inviting drag queens to read to them in class, to encouraging sexual activity at absurdly young ages. Such things are morally reprehensible. These children's parents would be morally justified, were they to drag these propagandists by the hair from their classrooms, or offices, and throw them into the streets for such outrages.

The second major method of sexual perversion is a subtype of the first. This type occurs when young people, who are still forming their views, are sexually molested, exploited, and abused. Such youths often become confused, should they happen to experience a certain amount of physical, or emotional pleasure during these events. Thinking that this pleasure somehow defines, or reveals their true inner nature, many mentally embrace, or adopt this role.

Such sexual predation upon minors is extremely common the world over. Simply put, it is a crime; and the criminals who abuse these youths should be punished severely by our legal systems for it. Those men who would use their sexual organs as weapons should be disarmed. Surgical penectomy and castration, with or without incarceration, and/or fines, should be the default punishment for all sexual assault crimes; especially those committed by adults against youth. Some are sure to mention instances where the assaulter is female. Though only a small percent of sexual assaults fall into this category, true justice demands similar punishment for similar crimes; perhaps by a hysterectomy and vaginectomy, along with the removal of the clitoris.

Unfortunately, under the flawed legal systems encountered across most of the Western world, many of the criminals who perform these abuses have been able to use their wealth and power to escape punishment; even in the face of substantial evidence. Some have even grown so brazen about their warped views and actions that they have formed lobbying groups, hoping to have their crimes legalized. One example of this which readily comes to mind is the Man Boy Love Association (MBLA). This group of perverts constantly lobbies for reductions in the legal age of consensual sex, in order to legitimize and normalize their sexual assaults against children.

The third major way that sexual perversion occurs is when people make physical pleasure the primary focus of their attraction, rather than focusing on the goodness which they observe within the character of their husband, or wife. Goodnesses, whether of character, of form (i.e. beauty), or of anything else, when explored to their source, are ultimately discovered to be echoes of God's character. This being the case, the depth and complexity of goodness is inexhaustible. One can ponder it forever, and yet never fail to discover new aspects about it which may be admired. This remains true when the goodness being pondered is that observed within the forms, or characters of our loved ones. Though the focus on physical pleasure within a relationship may seem almost ubiquitous from a modern perspective, many of its most destructive consequences were seldom observed during previous generations. This is because a mere short few decades ago there were, as a whole, more fixed social, financial, and environmental limits preventing people from corrupting themselves.

Means of engaging in sexually perverse activities outside of a healthy, monogamous, heterosexual relationship tended to be difficult to find, risky, and often costly. One could only buy certain limited types of sexual magazines at certain limited types of places, showing certain limited types of sexual acts. Sexual videos existed, but were only available at certain highly disreputable stores. Prostitutes and strip clubs have always been around, but the illegality of the first tended to prevent its spread, while utilization of the second tended to be chilled by its disreputability.

All of these things involved varying degrees of cost and risk. Nobody wanted people who knew them to see them inside, parked at, entering, or exiting strip clubs, porn video, or magazine stores, or in the company of a prostitute, as this would irreparably damage their reputations. In addition, the immoral people who ran these types of businesses knew that the supply of their corrupt products was severely limited, and they therefore charged a premium for them. The average working man had little surplus money available to splurge on these things, nor did he often have the free time to waste in seeking them.

Little by little the selfish, the avaricious, and the perverse grew wealthy while wearing down these preservative cultural barriers. Soon magazines showing not just nudity, but sex acts began appearing on book store and gas station shelves. More and more video stores began opening *adult* sections where pornographic videos were available for rent. Reputable hotel chains began offering *adult* movies among their options for in-room rentals.

Then the internet began to take off. Initially, most people's computers and internet connections were too slow to do much more than text-based applications, but as it became robust enough to support image and video, in the late 90's, the flood gates broke. With the simple click of a link, people were suddenly able to fill their eyes and minds with the most perverse sexual sights and thoughts imaginable; all from the comfort of their own homes, with minimal risk of being caught, and at generally zero additional cost.

Arousal is simply a synonym for the thrill of excitement within the context of sexual interaction. When the focus of this arousal becomes divorced from underlying goodness and simply becomes about nuances of form and specific physical sensations, it becomes transient and illusory. What originally aroused these people, when newly experienced by their physical senses (i.e. things newly seen, heard, smelled, tasted, or felt), later bores them, after their senses have routinely experienced these things dozens of times. The old saying, "familiarity breeds contempt," begins to ring true. Whereas initially they were aroused simply by viewing and embracing their lover, soon they only become so while kissing them, then only during certain incomplete acts of mating, then only during sex itself, then only during certain types of sex, or during specific sexual activities, or in certain situations. These options eventually become exhausted, as there are anatomical limits to the number of sexual positions which can be tried, some of which their spouses or lovers, at least those possessing any amount of self-respect, will refuse; finding them painful, gross, or degrading. As the flames once again begin to ebb, these people will begin to search for another log which can be thrown on the fire to rekindle their arousal.

Acutely remembering the now lost thrill which early physical experiences with their spouses or lovers gave them, many often convince themselves that they have "fallen out of love" with their current ones. This occurs because people often confuse the concepts of love with those of sexual attraction and arousal; a subject which is discussed at length elsewhere. Believing that they can regain this thrill by newly experiencing these same physical experiences with someone else, many begin to cheat on, or outright abandon their spouses, or lovers. Others attempt to have similar experiences, limited to the physical aspect of sight, via pornography. But even this log eventually burns down into routine, leaving these people back where they started.

Here is where a shift begins to occur. During the incessant pursuit of arousal, which they associate with novelty, these people frequently discover that they have wandered to the edge of the taboo. Standing at the brink, they are beaconed onward by the infinite amount of new experiences which they believe may be found there, but are restrained from entering by their set of instinctive morals, as well as by the more robust external restraints which society has historically placed upon these things.

The more insightful among previous generations established these societal restraints for the well-being both of society and the individual. In previous generations, these restraints were generally robust enough to prevent most people from wading into these dangerous areas, however this is no longer the case. The atheist worldview, which has spread like an infection across the social sciences, over the past 50 years or so, has caused academic leaders in these fields to redefine morality as relative, and therefore human perspective dependent. According to this view, there is no taboo. There is simply what a certain individual, in a certain place, at a certain time considers to be taboo for them. This is part of the larger atheist denial of good and bad, right and wrong, and ultimately morality in general. Being led by the nose by these academics, or feeling themselves too inept to challenge them, many legislators across the Western world today pass laws which destroy the warning signs and fences leading into these dangerous areas. This lack of fences not only allows people to more easily wander into harm, but it also allows the dangerously corrupted who reside there to return and prey upon the innocent: like wolves among sheep.

As those who wander into these swamps begin to re-experience the thrill of novelty, they also begin to make mental associations between taboo and pleasure, eventually causing them to seek it, in a classical Pavlovian manner. The pursuit of the taboo is like chasing a mirage. Much like a drug addiction, in order to sustain the feeling of novelty, stronger taboos are perpetually needed, as the novel inevitably becomes the routine. These people seek happiness with the taboos of different partners, ages, sexes, species, and even sexual violence, until eventually nothing is taboo. Downward this spiral of perversion continues until these people ultimately destroy themselves, others, and/or the portion of society which they influence. Chemical abuse (i.e. Drugs and alcohol) often expedites this corruption process, due to its known ability to decrease inhibition. The only hope for these people is that, through some rare moment of introspection, they realize their level of depravity and return to what they instinctively know to be good.

Serial killers Ted Bundy and Jeffery Dahmer more or less explicitly mention this phenomenon of progressive corruption in interviews which both gave prior to their deaths.

Consider the following condensed excerpt from the 1989 interview between Ted Bundy and Dr. James Dobson:
"(Bundy)...I think I understand what happened to me...as a young boy...I encountered, outside the home...in...the local grocery store and the local drug stores, the softcore pornography...from time to time, we come across pornographic books of a harder nature...a more graphic... a more explicit nature...this is...the most damaging...pornography...those that involve violence and sexual violence. Because the wedding of those two forces...brings about behavior that is...too terrible to describe...and the issue is how this kind of literature contributed and helped mold and shape the kinds of violent behavior...in the beginning, it fuels this kind of...thought process. Then, at a certain time, it is instrumental in crystallizing it, making it into something which is...almost a separate entity inside. And that points you at the verge...of acting out on this

kind of fantasy...It happened in stages, gradually, it doesn't necessarily...happened over a night...once you become addicted to it...you keep looking for more potent, more explicit, more graphic kinds of material...you keep craving something which is harder...something which...gives you a greater sense of excitement, until you reach the point where the pornography only goes so far, you reach that jumping off point where you begin to wonder...if maybe actually doing it will give you that which is just beyond reading about it and looking at it...What I was dealing (with) there was...with very strong inhibitions against criminal behavior or violent behavior, that had been conditioned into me, bred into me in my environment, in my neighborhood, in my church...in my school. Things that said 'no, this is wrong,' I mean, even thinking of it is wrong, and certainly, to do it is wrong. And I'm on that edge, and the last... vestiges of restraint, the barriers to actually doing something were being tested constantly, and assailed...through the kind of fantasy life that was fueled...largely...by pornography...we're talking about an influence which...was an indispensable link in the chain of behavior, the chain of events that led to...the assaults, to the murders...It's a very...difficult thing to describe...the sensation...of...reaching that point where...I knew...that... I couldn't control it anymore. These barriers...that I had learned as a child...were not enough to hold me back with respect to...seeking out and harming somebody...Another fact here I haven't mentioned is the use of alcohol. What I think...alcohol did, in conjunction...with my exposure to pornography, alcohol...reduce(d) my inhibitions, at the same time as...the fantasy life that was fueled with pornography...eroded them further...there is this battle going on within. There are the conventions that you've been taught, there's the right and wrong that you learned as a child, and there is this...unbridled passion...fueled by...your plunge into hardcore violent pornography. And those things are at war with each other...I don't know why I was vulnerable to it. All I know is that...it had an impact on me...that was just so...central in the development of the violent behavior that I engaged in."[124]

Also consider the following excerpt from the 1993 interview between Jeffery Dahmer and reporter Nancy Glass:

"(Dahmer) 'I had normal friendships in high school but after that I started with the alcohol...drinking, a lot of solitary drinking, and I really hadn't any close friendships after that, after high school. I just sort of lived in my own thought life, fantasy world.'

(Glass) 'Were you molested?'

(Dahmer) 'Never. Never.'

(Glass) 'In your childhood, do you have any memories of anything that you would associate with what you became?'

(Dahmer) 'No, that's the strange thing, I can't pinpoint anything...'

(Glass) 'So there was nothing in your childhood...?' (Notice the incredulity here.)

(Dahmer) 'No, no abuse, no physical abuse, no verbal abuse. It was a normal childhood, in a good home. Something went awry in my thought life. I don't know why.'"[125]

Later in the interview Dahmer says:

"(Dahmer) 'It's a process, it doesn't happen overnight, when you depersonalize another person and view them as just an object. An object for pleasure and not a living breathing human being. It seems to make it easier to do things you shouldn't do...I was extremely selfish, I was only thinking of myself, my own pleasure, my own perverted desires'"[125]

The common reply from the public, when forced to consider disgusting, or brutal fetishes, such as the ones which these men became engrossed in, is that those who become involved in them are deranged: that no normal person could become sexually aroused, or receive sexual gratification from things such as this. People generally respond this way because they are uncomfortable with the idea that originally normal people, very much like themselves, could theoretically become corrupted to the point of being capable of atrocities. If it is theoretically possible for anyone to travel the same spiraling path of mental corruption which these rapists or murderers have descended, then the world suddenly becomes a much more frightening place.

In order to avoid dealing with this uncomfortable reality, many people mentally section things into classes possessing separate, specialized rule sets. They convince themselves that those who become involved in disgusting, or violent fetishes must simply be a unique human subspecies, whose minds were somehow warped from the outset. In psychological terms, this is known as compartmentalized thinking; a close cousin to cognitive dissonance.

This compartmentalization bias becomes obvious when one studies interviews which have been conducted with, or articles which have been written about serial killers. Probing for evidence which confirms their bias, reporters, or researchers almost inevitably ask questions about the killers' earliest childhood thoughts. The more rational killers almost always try to explain to them that they were originally just normal kids from wholesome homes, who later made the mistake of not restraining their minds from traveling increasingly darker paths. Most describe how their initially minor sexual fetishes grew and mutated, as they continued to feed them, until eventually horribly misshapen and murderous. As can be observed in the interview between Nancy Glass and Jeffery Dahmer, reporters generally respond to these comments with open skepticism.

This is the most chilling thing about studying the corrupted minds and disturbing fetishes of serial killers; the inevitable realization that these were once normal people, if only for a brief period during childhood. This realization drives home the fact that the path between normality and corruption is a frighteningly short one which any of us could theoretically travel, if we are injudicious about the type of information we feed our minds on a continual basis.

But of course, not all serial killers came from healthy families. A far greater number were horribly neglected, abused, or molested. Though this abuse surely contributed to their eventual corruption, they are still the ones ultimately responsible for it. Yet even these were not born as a different species with a murderous predisposition, which abuse, or molestation simply unmasked. The concept of an infant with a predisposition for brutality and depravity is ludicrous. These people were born as happy and innocent infants, just like everyone else. The abuse was simply another warped information source which skewed their subconscious beliefs, as well as the conscious decisions which these beliefs birthed.

Take serial killer, John Wayne Gacy, for example. When his childhood friend, Barry Boschelli, was interviewed by Gavin Schmitt in 2010, Barry recounted the abusive home-life that Gacy grew up in. Though this abuse, regardless of the severity, in no way justifies the atrocities which Gacy later went on to commit, it drives home the point that "Johnny," like Dahmer and Bundy, started life as a perfectly normal child, but then progressively grew more morally corrupt.

"(Boschelli)...about a week later that's when things began to change...Up to this point, Johnny was mild and easy going, never threatened me or raised a fist or anything...I remember it well...Johnny wasn't the same anymore...From that day forward, I saw a gradual change in him...Johnny and I grew together as friends. People come up to me and say he was no good, and I say, 'Yes, he did terrible things. And yes, he deserved to be executed. But you have to understand, I knew him before he was a serial killer."[125]

Absolute goodness and mental healthfulness do, in very fact, extend even into the areas of sexual attraction. Since sexual attraction is changeable, it cannot be trusted as the sole determinant of goodness with regard to relationships. We must seek for corroborating evidence within the natural world as to what is mentally *best* with regard to human physical relationships.

When we look to nature, nothing is more obvious than the fact that heterosexual relationships are the preferred relationship type among sexually dimorphic mammalian species. Several academics, whose political bias has swayed their objectivity, have attempted to claim otherwise, by pointing out instances where certain animal species engage in homosexual activities. These comments are, of course, eagerly echoed by the army of overwhelmingly liberal reporters. Both overlook the fact that these behaviors are extremely rare exceptions, which generally only occur when natural mating with the opposite sex is an impossibility. The virtual nonexistence of homosexuality among mammals, when the alternative option of heterosexual relations is equally possible, is a very solid piece of evidence as to what the natural, and therefore most healthy type of sexual relationship is. Two male dogs, for example, may on rare occasion engage in homosexuality, but place these same dogs in a kennel where they have equal access to female dogs, and any homosexual activity will be virtually extinguished.

But is this the moral standard which humans hold themselves to; that of brute beasts? Many animals incestuously mate with their mothers, or children. Does this mean such a sexual relationship is healthy among humans? Many dogs hump the legs of random strangers. Should we take this as evidence that humans should behave this way as well? What we should be proving is not which types of sexual relationships are *possible* for ourselves, our families, and our nations, but rather which type is the *best* for them.

Another piece of evidence is the fact that, regardless of the degree that people allow their attractions to become warped, there is no evidence of any genetic passage of these warped attractions to our offspring. By and large, once children enter puberty, they begin to feel natural attractions towards their opposite sex. If there truly was a "gay gene" as some unscientifically claim, then we would theoretically be able to develop a pedigree chart trending the multi-generational flow and expression of this phenotype. Claims that societal pressures preventing people from embracing their true genetic predispositions are the reason why such an observation has proven impossible are both purely speculative and highly improbable. Indeed, they would be impossible, if the claims which the sexually corrupt make about being powerless to resist their attractions and inclinations were accurate; which they obviously aren't. The only ways that we observe the passage of these perversions in real life are as the result of indoctrination (i.e. brainwashing via propaganda), sexual oversaturation, or as the confused product of childhood molestation.

A third piece of evidence of the natural, and therefore both mentally and physically healthiest form of relationship, is the well documented tendency for homosexual couples to involuntarily adopt the traits of an opposite sexed couple. The longer two women maintain a homosexual relationship, the more the dominant of the two generally tends to develop increasingly masculine characteristics. Vice-versa, the longer two men maintain a homosexual relationship, the more the less dominant of the two generally tends to develop increasingly feminine characteristics. Is it any wonder that we observe this? Since the minds of these individuals have adopted the role of the opposite sex, their manners, and even their bodies are simply following suit to the extent which they are able.

This is not a new discovery. An ancient Roman author stated that pederasty was prohibited because of the known feminizing effect that it had on the personalities of boys. Given that children's bodies are still developing, it is highly likely that the feminization of boys which this Roman author was referring to would become more pronounced; both mentally and physically. A similar phenomenon likely occurs among those whose entrance into homosexual behavior occurs during childhood. The dominant homosexual female likely becomes more highly masculinized, and the less dominant homosexual male likely becomes more highly feminized, than those do who adopt this vice later in life.

Less dominant homosexual females and dominant homosexual males continue to fill roles which, though warped, remain more closely aligned to their natural state. This less misaligned state causes the personalities, manners, and even bodies of these individuals to differ little from their heterosexual analogs; generally allowing them to blend in unnoticed among them.

Less dominant homosexual males and dominant homosexual females, however, have effectively condemned and abandoned their own natural sex. As their minds begin to rewire themselves, as much as possible, with the adopted patterns typical of the opposite sex, their manners, and often even some of their physical characteristics, begin to evidence the change. Being unnatural, these changes are generally noticed by heterosexual members with whom they interact. As traitors are generally viewed with suspicion by the nations that they join, and with resentment by the ones whom they betray, so too homosexuals are generally viewed with suspicion by the sex which they poorly attempt to emulate, and with resentment by their proper one, which they abandon. This is because this action is similar to a betrayal of a sacred brotherhood, or sisterhood, depending upon the sex in question. Though these easily identifiable homosexuals tend to receive the majority of this attention, those within the former, less discernable class, are no less guilty of vice, in that they are abettors to this betrayal.

Today, this suspicion and contempt is loudly condemned from virtually all media, academic, and recently even governmental platforms, as if it were the equivalent of burning someone at the stake. The slightest criticism of the ethicality of homosexuality, indeed, anything other than outright praise of it will elicit hysterical screams of "Homophobe!" accompanied more often these days by threats, and even violent physical assaults. These latter two tactics are always the last resort of the stupid, or morally corrupt, whenever they have been bested in free and open debate; as they always will be.

But let's consider this worn out, straw man claim of *homophobia*, which the media loves to parade about. The word literally means, *same fear*; the *same* in question being, by implication, that of same sex relationships. Surely these people are not so ignorant that they actually believe that any, and all possible protests about the ethicality and mental health of homosexual relationships must always be grounded in fear. Of course they don't. Knowing that society generally associates fear with weakness, these people label their adversaries with this misnomer out of hope that any observers of the exchange will be convinced that they hold the less fear filled, and therefore stronger ethical position, regardless of facts, simply because they implicitly claim that they do.

But two can play at this game. These people themselves could be labeled as *heterophobic*. This latter claim would, in fact, be more fitting than the former, since the libertines whom it could be applied to are clearly afraid that society will recognize the obvious facts about the natural superiority, ethicality, and practicality of heterosexuality over homosexuality. In addition, by promoting the value of what is an obvious vice, these people are arguing from a position of inherent weakness. Yet since we have facts on our side, let us do trade in this, rather than in labels.

Yet what of this resentment and suspicion? No one bats an eye when people grow furious and sometimes even shout obscenities at the hapless driver who cuts them off in traffic, but God help the person in modern Western society who even hints at possessing the slightest trace of resentment towards, or suspicion of homosexuals. These people will be attacked en masse by a veritable army of media and academic figures, and frequently even physically attacked in the streets by these people's brainwashed disciples. Ironically, this latter resentment has more of a philosophical basis than the former, traffic based one.

It is natural for the thoughtful to resent those who willfully adopt and publicly portray shameful roles which may potentially warp the views of others, especially impressionable children, by convincing them that such flawed actions and relationships are both normal and healthy. Such resentment is similar to the natural resentment that any responsible parent would feel towards those who dress like prostitutes, or who wear clothing celebrating drug abuse, where families, and especially children, might observe them. It is natural for thoughtful people to have a healthy suspicion of the mental well-being of any who would deny something so blatantly evident as the natural function of their own sex.

Though undeniably enjoyable, the reason for sexual attraction and the pleasurable sensations associated with mating, within both the animal and the human realms, is not recreation, but propagation. Nature has made attraction and sexual interaction pleasurable in order to encourage man to propagate the species via the creation of offspring, much like she has made the consumption of high calorie foods pleasurable in order to help early man avoid starvation.

Homosexual relationships, however, are innately barren. For obvious reasons, it is impossible for homosexual couples to produce offspring without external heterosexual aid (e.g. adoption, artificial insemination, or heterosexual mating external to the relationship). Such relationships, therefore, frustrate the fundamental natural purpose of attraction and mating. Stripped of this higher purpose, mating within homosexual relationships is degraded to simple recreation. By ensuring the continuity of the species, the natural purpose of sexual relationships is inherently unselfish. Recreation based sexual relationships, however, are inherently selfish, as their only objective is the attainment of pleasure by the individual.

In addition, the offspring which healthy heterosexual couples naturally produce within their families stimulate nurturing and protective instincts which were previously relatively latent within both parents. These newly enkindled instincts shift parental focus away from the selfish satisfaction of their own pleasures and towards relatively selfless objectives, such as the protection and well-being of their children. These instincts may present themselves somewhat among the childless, but generally do not develop to the level which occurs among the majority of parents.

This phenomenon is well documented even within the animal kingdom. Virtually everyone is familiar with the feats of courage and effort which many animal species perform in the protection and care of their offspring. Mother ducks will bravely face hungry dogs to protect their ducklings. Northern Cardinal parents of both sexes labor incessantly to feed their voracious offspring, and heaven help the hapless person who frightens a bear cub, or elephant calf within the sight of their parents.

Human children don't merely need physical nourishment from their parents, their minds long to also be nourished with education; whether from words, books, or personal examples. The heterosexual husband and wife roles, when stripped of their intercourse aspect, which is truly a minor portion of the relationship, are simply an instance of two mature adults of opposite sexes treating each other lovingly (i.e. properly interacting). Children need both mothers and fathers present within their families because, by observing their parents' interactions, they learn how to become loving husbands, wives, and parents themselves. Indeed, this loving interaction, void of all sexuality, is practiced by daughters with their fathers, and sons with their mothers. Fathers, in effect, function as practice husbands, and mothers as practice wives for their children. Subconscious awareness of these practice roles is the reason for the well documented increased attachment of daughters to their fathers, and sons to their mothers.

Children who are irresponsibly placed within the homes of homosexual couples are at a huge disadvantage in this regard, as, besides other issues, the parental role depictions which are presented to them are warped, at best. The son of a lesbian couple still has his mother to practice male and female loving interactions with, but the example of masculinity which he is presented is the dwarfed and misshapen one observed within the dominant female of the couple. He is also at an increased disadvantage when this dominant female is his mother. This situation decreases, or extinguishes the boy's ability to utilize this parent as a practice wife. The daughter of such a couple will be in a similar situation. She will only have the dominant lesbian to interact with as the practice father, warping her perception of masculinity. It is unnecessary to describe how the children of a male homosexual couple face the inverse disadvantages.

Some will claim that the comparatively stunted development of the more selfless parental instincts among homosexual families is no one else's business, since it only affects them. Those who make these claims are sadly ignorant of the fact that families, even these warped ones, are the cellular unit of our collective national body. Any mutations to the natural structure of a significant portion of these cells, which results in a degradation or destruction of their natural function, will unavoidably degrade the health of the national body as a whole. Sexual perversions, such as homosexuality, are therefore effectively societal diseases.

Doctors do diseased patients no favors by telling them that they are well. Equally destructive is any legislation which prevents the patient from learning about his illness. So too, national leaders do their nations no favors by turning blind eyes to these social diseases. And equally destructive are any laws which prevent the nation's citizens from learning about its symptoms. For the good of our national bodies, we must work to stop the spread of this disease, so that the parts which have already been infected by it can properly heal.

This last comment brings to mind the words of the Roman historian, Livy. In his preface to the work, *From the Foundation of the City*, Livy states:

"I would have every man apply his mind seriously to consider these points, viz., what [the Roman] life and what their manners were; through what men and by what measures, both in peace and in war, their empire was acquired and extended; then, as discipline gradually declined, let him follow in his thoughts their morals, at first as slightly giving way, anon how they sunk more and more, then began to fall headlong, until he reaches the present times, when we can endure neither our vices nor their remedies. This it is which is particularly salutary and profitable in the study of history, that you behold instances of every variety of conduct displayed on a conspicuous monument; that thence you may select for yourself and for your country that which you may imitate; thence note what is shameful in the undertaking, and shameful in the result, which you may avoid."[127]

So we too, as inheritors of the Western world and Western civilization, have reached the state where our nations can neither endure their vices, nor their remedies. We must decide if we retain sufficient courage and love of our civilization to brave the pain of the treatment regimen required to remove the infection of vice from our national bodies, or if we will simply ignore the disease, lie to ourselves about its symptoms and historical prognosis, and allow our nations simply to succumb and die.

Women

It should be mentioned that the attack which we are seeing today upon the natural role of women has been especially damaging to Western society. This is because women are the primary reservoirs of a nation's culture. Any who would question this fact should take a moment to consider this sex's seemingly instinctive love of ceremonies, traditions, fashions, music, etc. The addition of a woman to a house is the famous recipe for converting it into a home. They are the ones who tend to retain and display sentimental keepsakes. They are the ones famous for spreading sometimes profound, and other times questionable historical stories known as "old wives' tales." Seldom do we hear of "old husbands' tales."

Consider, for example, the host of traditions which women cling to and pass down related to weddings. Almost the entire thing is one long chain of traditions: from the wearing of a white dress and veil, to not letting the groom see them in their wedding gown before the ceremony, to fathers walking them down the aisle and dancing with them at the reception, to bringing "something old, something new, something borrowed, and something blue," etc. A comparatively small portion of this wedding tradition is specific to the man. Bachelor parties are an extremely recent phenomenon, typically focused on debauchery and drunkenness, which men should not be proud of.

Except in cultures where the flagrantly misogynistic faiths of Islam and Hinduism predominate, it is virtually always the women, especially the older ones, who most tenaciously cling to their culture's religion and religious traditions. Evidence of this can be observed in the most recent Religious Landscape Study which was conducted by the Pew Research Center. In this study, women predominated in virtually all religious metrics which were measured.[123]

There is hardly any better definition of a people's culture than the sum of its collected ceremony, tradition, fashion, music, etc.; all of the very things that women seem to naturally absorb, retain, and pass on to their children and grandchildren. It is for this very reason that the attack upon Western egalitarian culture has been especially relentless towards women. Media outlets incessantly bombard them with propaganda which encourages them to become as sexually active as possible, as early as possible; or at least to dress, slather their faces with makeup, and act as if they are.

It is undeniable that physical intimacy has an enhancing effect upon any pre-existent emotional bond. Many animal species even demonstrate this phenomenon, when they mate for life. Sex saturation, however, erodes the significance, and therefore the enhanced emotional bond which is derived from this physical intimacy. In the minds of many of these girls, it also subconsciously tarnishes the goodness of the wedding itself. Whereas this event should be a time of pure excitement and happiness for them, the more sexual partners they have previously had, the more emotional baggage they tend to enter the marriage with. In addition, since they know that the white dress symbolizes innocence and purity, many girls subconsciously feel guilty for wearing it.

Also, in the most recent decade, there has been a concerted marketing effort across Western media outlets encouraging Western women to marry outside of their culture. This is promoted due to the supposed benefits which come from *cultural diversity*. This myth is discussed at length elsewhere in this work. It is important, however, to note one of the negative effects of this practice which is specific to women. When people of two cultures marry, it is more often women, than men, who tend to abandon their own culture and adopt that of their spouse. Women generally do so for several reasons, but the most significant of these is that they subconsciously wish to present a consistent cultural portrait to their children.

The atheist worldview holds that there are no universal standards of goodness; all goodness being relatively defined by the individual. According to this definition, there are no absolute ethical standards by which cultures may be judged, or even realistically compared. Accordingly, the claim that, "All cultures are equal," perpetually blares from the minarets of left-heavy media outlets and Western academia; both of whom are saturated by this worldview. We see this belief embodied in the massive amount of academic papers which make excuses for the grossest abuses of natural human rights, such as, but certainly not limited to, the senicide (i.e. killing of the elderly) among the Eskimo, the polygamy, slavery, torture, and brutal executions still common within many Islamic cultures, the infanticide among the Brazilian Kamayurá tribe, incest among the Indonesian Polahi tribe, the ubiquity of rape among Pakistani tribes, and even cannibalism among the Hindu Aghori. This reveals how corrosive the atheist worldview is, in that its adherents become unable to condemn even such gross abuses as senicide, polygamy, slavery, torture, infanticide, incest, rape, and cannibalism. Is there anything worse which can be presented to these people that they would actually condemn? If the moral judgement of these people is so benumbed to common sense that they cannot even call such obvious abuses vice, are they therefore to be believed regarding what they call virtue?

It is preposterous to claim that all cultures are equal. A culture is simply a world view, along with the associated traditions and ceremonies which spring from these views. A world view is simply a collection of philosophical opinions on important subjects. Are we expected to believe that all opinions on important subjects are equally right? What about when they contradict? The atheist who is faced with this question will inevitably shift to the claim that truth is also not absolute, but relative to the individual, and therefore but a purely arbitrary social construct founded upon consensus. What is ironic is that, in their ignorance, these people fail to realize that this is a self-destructive argument, since it denies the absolute veracity of its own claim.

But let us not follow them any further along their well-worn path of cognitive dissonance. Truth, like goodness and God, is real, external, and absolute, and by its light we may know the absolutes of virtue. Using these absolutes, we may justly judge men, manners, actions, opinions, collections of opinions, and even the very cultures which spring from these. All men are created equal, but all cultures are certainly not. Those cultures which promote and preserve a higher level of virtue, and which condemn vice, are in fact both more advanced and absolutely better than those which are more contaminated with vice and brutality; regardless of the level of wealth, or technology which either may possess. Western culture, though of course far from perfect, remains far superior to the brutal cultures which were previously cited.

This being firmly established, we will return to our previous subject of intercultural marriage, as it especially applies to women. The marriage of women hailing from a generally superior culture with men of an inferior one, typically results in the tragedy of these women at least partially, but often even completely abdicating the former for the latter. I must make a point of clarification that, in referring to culture, I am not referring to race. Though races are often associated with specific cultures, racial composition itself has no bearing on this issue. There are many people from a variety of races who have adopted, and who still retain the formerly high ideals of Western culture. These men are perfectly suitable suitors for Western women. It is those who have either never embraced, or who have abandoned the noble ideals of virtue and egalitarianism, which are synonymous with Western civilization, who are not; whatever their race may be. Among many others, this will necessarily exclude all of those men who have adopted the morally fatal atheist worldview.

Conscience and Intellect

As our soul (i.e. spirit) is distinct, singular, and immaterial, so its various movements at any given moment, what we refer to as the *will*, must also be distinct and singular. Were our souls material, then differences in physical properties, such as location, form, or composition, might allow for multiple actions to occur simultaneously, such as the simultaneous movement of two separate hands. Being immaterial spirit, however, all material difference is precluded. There can be no simultaneous plurality with spiritual action. All simultaneous action must be unified. The brilliant 17th century mathematician and philosopher, Rene Descartes, sensed this unified nature of the will; stating in his *Meditations on First Philosophy* that, "...the will consists only of one single element, and is so to speak indivisible..."[128] Plotinus, the Neoplatonic philosopher, also came to a similar conclusion in the first of his *Six Enneads*, where he states that "The will of any organic thing is one..."[37]

But how do we know that this is true? Doesn't a good person who is tempted towards a harmful act simultaneously possess multiple conflicting *wills*? Why, or why not? In any given situation, we certainly have multiple competing desires. Isn't saying that we *desire* something the same as saying that we *will* it? It is not. While it is true that, in common English, the terms *will* and *desire* are often used interchangeably, the two words actually symbolize distinctly different ideas when correctly understood. It becomes easier to understand this situation when we recall that *feeling* is the native tongue of the mind; a subject explained in more detail elsewhere within this work.

Desires are *feelings* which result from the reason subconsciously examining various potential means pathways and determining that certain of them are likely to increase happiness more rapidly, easily, or in greater amounts than the rest. These *means paths* may be single words, thoughts, or actions, but more commonly are a plurality of these things strung together in specific sequences. In the same way that dozens of physical sensations are simultaneously passed to and evaluated by our minds, so we also sense and evaluate the dozens of *desires* which simultaneously compete within us.

Will, on the other hand, is a commitment to employ one of these *means paths* to happiness. Somewhere in between *desire* and *will*, a decision occurs. By turning our gaze inward, what can we deduce about this *deciding principle*? To begin with, we know that wherever decisions occur, intelligence must be involved. Intelligence simply means the possession of knowledge (i.e. information). This knowledge which we possess originates from two very different sources; that of instinct, and that of experiential memory.

At this point, those who cling to the "Tabula Rasa" hypothesis of human development, made famous by John Lock, will typically scoff and deny the existence of any *human instinct* altogether.[38]

"All knowledge is memory," they will claim. "All is nurtured into us. There is nothing of nature!"

Yet ironically, these same people typically have no problem acknowledging both that animals possess instincts, and that man is a species of animal. Do they claim then, that man is the sole instinctless species among all living organisms? If so, upon what evidence do they base such a claim, as there is ample evidence to the contrary. Or do they instead leap into complete absurdity by denying the existence of animal instinct altogether? Those who would do the latter are resoundingly refuted by thousands of natural examples, ranging from humble spider webs, to ant mounds, to bee hives.

Returning to our subject, is this *deciding agency* within us merely a specific aspect of our intelligence, or is it instead something which lies external to it? To clarify this question, consider how the mind stores information in memories, much like computers store information within files and libraries store information within books. What we are trying to determine is if this *deciding agency* within us is simply another type of *memory*, like one of the many computer files, or library books, or if it is instead something which consults the knowledge within our memories, like the person who uses a computer, or library to search for information.

This is an admittedly difficult question. In fact, for most modern scientists, it is one of the core questions which destroys their faith in the existence of a guiding force to the universe. The scientifically *orthodox* answer which most give is that the *deciding factor* within us is merely another subcomponent of the intellect; little different from any other type of knowledge which is stored as memory. But is this actually the case?

Let's consider what evidence supports the alternate option that the judging and deciding agency within us is something external to our intelligence. In the first place, it appears deducible that, whatever this *deciding agency* is, it must be something which is either completely isolated from stimulation by both the internal and external senses, or at least relatively isolated to the extent that these things are sensed. If it wasn't, we would be unable to observe the stimulation; as ships raised by the tide cannot perceive the change without some fixed, or semifixed external standard, such as nearby land, to compare to. This fact is generally overlooked by the academic community, due to their widespread bias that emotion is something which is *thought*, and not something which is actually *internally sensed*.

The question then becomes whether the *deciding factor* within us is itself isolated from external and internal sensation, or if it is influenced by these things, but also has an external standard which it uses as a reference. Let's examine both of these options. If the *deciding factor* within us is isolated from all internal and external sensation, then it is difficult to understand how it would receive the information which it needed to make its decisions. If completely isolated, how could it sense anything?

This seems to lead to the conclusion that the *deciding factor* within us is indeed influenced by the internal and external senses, consulting the memory as one would consult books within a library, but that it uses something else as a fixed external reference. What is this fixed reference standard? Logic tells us that, since all of matter is in constant flux and by nature limited, nothing material can serve as this reference standard. The thing itself must be immaterial. Nothing but perfect goodness can fulfill this role, as it is the only fixed reality among so many deviations from it. Interestingly, our conclusions here have been found to resemble those of the ancient Greek philosopher, Parmenides, who held that the only reality is one single, completely changeless thing.

This fixed reality of perfect goodness must somehow be available to the *deciding factor* within us. How? Where does it reside? Is it found within our intellect? What we refer to as *intellect*, or *intelligence*, is nothing more than the collected memories of events, facts, and things which we have mistakenly assumed to be facts. There is nothing innately *good* about memories, nor are they in any way fixed, for we continue to accumulate new ones throughout our lives; like so many books within a library. If then our standard of goodness is not found within our memory, our *deciding factor*, our desires, our will, our intelligence, nor in matter itself, then where is it to be found; as it surely must exist.

In order to locate this *standard of goodness*, we must look outside of the material world, and into that of spirit. Yet it is tremendously challenging to deduce things about the spiritual realm, since we know so little about it. Let's consider for a moment what we have already determined about this standard of goodness which the *deciding factor* within us consults as a reference. We stated that it must be completely fixed, or in other words, *immutable*, and as such, that it must be purely *good*. Are these not the exact same qualities which we previously determined apply exclusively to the force in the universe which we commonly refer to as *deity*, or *God*? If God itself is the reference standard of goodness which the *deciding factor* within us consults, as it also consults with our intellect, then how does it do so?

Let's consider the commonly put forward opinion that a part of the *divine* is placed within each living being. The holder of this opinion runs into insurmountable logical problems, as a being possessing infinite attributes, such as power and wisdom, cannot be divided. In the first case, if God has *parts* which may be divided, then he is heterogenous in essence; some parts having one characteristic function and power, and others having another. It is unclear how heterogeneity of parts can exist alongside perfection, as this would necessitate either the impossibility of multiple perfections, or the equal impossibility of multiple imperfect parts forming a perfect whole. In addition, partition not only demands limitation, and therefore finitude of God, destroying a core characteristic of deity, but it is also meaningless when considering an immaterial spirit, which does not occupy physical space. One cannot divide the immaterial.

Due to the homogeneity which is required for perfection, even if an infinite power could hypothetically be divided and continue to retain its infinite characteristics, it would be necessary for any divisions of this being, even the smallest of them, to also possess the same infinite characteristics. This division would therefore create multiple gods, all of which would be equal, and none of which would be supreme in power and perfection; as there cannot be a plurality of *supremes*. Also, since there cannot be a plurality of immaterial perfections, the division would result in the same perfect being simultaneously existing in multiple places. This is nonsensical, since we already showed how the concept of location is meaningless for immaterial spirit.

If, therefore, God cannot be carved into pieces, like a cake, a bit being placed within each living being, then how does the deciding factor within us interact with this being? The most appropriate, though likely still imperfect model to describe this phenomenon seems to be that of a sort of *resonance*, for lack of a better word. Somehow this divine *force* which infuses and enlivens the universe, this reference standard of goodness, *resonates* within us, making its "voice" heard, or more accurately *felt*, by the *deciding factor* within us. We know this "voice" by the names of *conscience*, or *instinctive reason*. Conscience, therefore, is not another component of our own soul, or intellect, as many believe. It is the very voice of God, speaking the only way that it ever has, does, or likely ever will; directly to our *deciding factor* in its native tongue of *feeling*.

The terrifyingly brilliant Socrates seems to have come to the same conclusions regarding the divine nature of conscience, which he very appropriately refers to as his personal "divine sign." Let us examine a few examples of this, which have been taken from the works of his student, Plato:

"(Euthyphro) 'I understand, Socrates. This is because you say that the *divine sign* keeps coming to you. So, he has written this indictment against you as one who makes innovations in religious matters, and he comes to court to slander you, knowing that such things are easily misrepresented to the crowd.'"[129]

Notice in this passage how Socrates is seen as a religious innovator. During the late 5th century B.C., when Socrates lived, it was normal for men to consult the will of those whom they considered to be "Gods," via a combination of prayers and sacrifices offered either at home, or in a temple. What, then, was it about Socrates' claims about interaction with the divine that was so controversial? Upcoming passages reveal that this was due to the fact that Socrates spoke of the influence of the divine as if it originated from within, and not as if externally received. He claimed that this internal "sign" always acted by preventing him from doing evil, functioning in the exact same manner that we generally consider the conscience to. This will be more clearly seen in the two following passages.

"(Socrates) 'At all previous times my *familiar prophetic power*, my *spiritual manifestation*, frequently opposed me, even in small matters, when I was about to do something wrong, but now that, as you can see for yourselves, I was faced with what one might think, and what is generally thought to be, the worst of evils, my *divine sign* has not opposed me, either when I left home at dawn, or when I came into court, or at any time that I was about to say something during my speech. Yet in other talks it often held me back in the middle of my speaking, but now it has opposed no word or deed of mine. What do I think is the reason for this? I will tell you. What has happened to me (the sentence of death) may well be a good thing, and those of us who believe death to be an evil are certainly mistaken. I have convincing proof of this, for it is impossible that my *familiar sign* did not oppose me if I was not about to do what was right.'"[64]

"(Socrates) 'When that happens, in some cases the *divine sign* that visits me forbids me to associate with them; in others, it permits me, and then they begin again to make progress.'"[130]

It is interesting that Socrates refers to his "divine sign" in the *Apology* as a spiritual manifestation. If God is truly spirit, besides making himself externally manifest through nature and matter, he likely only ever does so internally via the voice of conscience. A spiritual manifestation is, therefore, a very appropriate description of conscience.

It is a truism that "practice makes perfect." The more frequently men practice something, the more they become masters of that thing. This truth applies not merely to physical efforts, but also, perhaps more so, to reasoning and decision patterns. But why is this true? The science behind this phenomenon can be due to any combination of things; such as neuro-transmitter up-regulation in the pre-synaptic membrane, neuro-receptor up-regulation in the post-synaptic membrane, increased axon myelination by the oligodendrocytes, or ion channel proliferation in the Nodes of Ranvier of specific neurons. Perhaps Socrates, who is repeatedly referred to by Plato, Xenophon, and a host of ancient authors as a truly *good-hearted* man, had simply, by practice, grown accustomed and highly attuned to the voice of conscience. Also, since he seemed aware of the divine origin of this "voice," he appeared to think of his echoing its guidance to his hearers as no different from *prophecy*: in fact the very definition of it. This can be seen not only in the previous quote, but also in the following.

"(Socrates) 'My friend, just as I was about to cross the river, the familiar *divine sign* came to me which, whenever it occurs, holds me back from something I am about to do. I thought I heard a *voice* coming from this very spot, forbidding me to leave until I made atonement for some offense against the gods. In effect, you see, I am a *seer* (i.e. Archaic term for *prophet*), and though I am not particularly good at it, still—like people who are just barely able to read and write—I am good enough for my own purposes. I recognize my offense clearly now. In fact, the soul too, my friend, is itself a sort of *seer*; that's why, almost from the beginning of my speech, I was disturbed by a very uneasy feeling, as Ibycus puts it, that 'for offending the gods I am honored by men.' But now I understand exactly what my offense has been.'"[131]

It is interesting how Socrates mentions here that the soul itself "is a sort of *seer*." The soul being the *reasoning,* or *deciding faculty* within us, when it consults with the conscience, which is none other than the "voice" of God, performs a very similar role to that of an ancient prophet, who would do so on behalf of himself, or another. Also note the comment by Socrates about the "feeling" he had. These feelings are most likely none other than what Socrates had just called a "voice."

"(Socrates) 'As good luck would have it, I was sitting by myself in the undressing room just where you saw me and was already thinking of leaving. But when I got up, my customary *divine sign* put in an appearance. So I sat down again, and in a moment the two of them, Euthydemus and Dionysodorus, came in...'"[132]

What is fascinating in this final example of Socrates' interaction with his "divine sign" is the implication that, if we repeatedly practice and grow attuned to the voice of conscience, we may eventually be able not merely to hear its louder callings, which prevent us from doing harm (i.e. evil), but we may possibly even begin to discriminate its softer influences related to things which we generally think of as simple inclination. Perhaps these soft inclinations are the reason why I am writing this at this very moment, and also why you are reading it at some future date.

The problem for many is that they frequently cannot discriminate between the voice of *conscience* and that of the *intellect*; often confusing the two. This is likely due to the fact that both conscience and intellect appear to make themselves available to the *deciding factor* within us via the common mechanism of *feeling*. The nonreligious, for example, generally ascribe little significance to conscience, seeing all as a jumbled heap of mental processes of similar value. This causes them great difficulty in determining the ethical action which they should perform within a specific situation; often resulting in a retreat to pure Utilitarianism.

The problem is generally different for revealed religionists. While these believe in the existence and special significance of conscience, they are typically taught that nothing has greater authority than their sacred teachings, traditions, or writings; not even conscience. If the voice of conscience ever conflicts with the guidance of their sacred teachings, traditions, or writings, they are told that this is merely the voice of their own hopelessly corrupt souls, or of some evil tempting spirit, and should therefore be actively ignored. A few verses from scripture supporting this claim are provided below.

"For if our heart condemns us, God is greater than our heart, and knows all things" (1 John 3:20). The implication of this text is that we are to ignore the voice of our "heart," a commonly used expression for conscience, if it is ever in disagreement with scripture, or the teaching of church leadership.

"The heart is deceitful above all things, and desperately wicked: who can know it?" (Jeremiah 17:9). This is a commonly cited verse implying that the souls of men, which are again referred to as their "heart," are corrupt by nature and are therefore unreliable. Since the common opinion of revealed religionists is that the conscience is but a component of the human soul, or intellect, by extension, it is also believed to sometimes be unreliable.

"'I will go out and be a lying spirit in the mouth of all his prophets.' And the Lord said, 'You shall persuade him, and also prevail. Go out and do so.'" (1 Kings 22:22). Here we are shown a scene where one of the angels is being commissioned by god to plant a lying idea in the mind of the Hebrew prophets, in order to lure their king and nation to destruction. We see this same disturbing temptation theme recur several other times in scripture, ranging from when Abraham is told by God to make a human sacrifice of his son Isaac, only to be told later that this was simply a test and not God's actual will, to when God sends one prophet on a mission with a warning that he will be killed if he does not return home, and then sends another to successfully tempt the first to his destruction (1 Kings 13:15-30).

It should be pointed out that it is impossible for a good God to influence men to lie, tempt them to evil, or will their destruction; as such lies, temptations, and malicious intentions would be things which would be condemned as morally wrong if performed by men, and remain so even if performed by God.

"We are of God: he who knows God, hears us; he who is not of God, does not hear us. By this we know the spirit of truth and the spirit of error" (1 John 4:6). In this statement, we get a rare glimpse at an opinion which lurks beneath the surface of much of scripture, but which is typically obscured by euphemism and religious jargon. This opinion is that the teachings and writings of the religious leaders of Christianity, and of those "holy" men whom this religion was "revealed" to, are the very words of God, spoken by proxy: that they therefore bear the full weight of divine authority. Any whose consciences lead them into disagreement with the teachings, or writings of these leaders, should therefore be condemned as ignorant fools; supposedly for opposing the wisdom of God himself. Though Christianity is being critiqued regarding this arrogant belief, this error is common to all revealed religions. Christianity, at least in its modern form, is by far the least flawed and intolerant in this regard, while Islam is both the most hopelessly in error and the least tolerant of critique.

Knowing that the "voice" of *conscience*, when rightly discriminated, is the very "voice" of God, let us examine how men interact with it. When we encounter a situation where a decision needs to occur, the deciding factor within us instantly solicits the intellect for any information which it possesses about any known influencing factors. As this information is collected at a blinding rate, the mind assembles and analyzes various sequences of possible words, thoughts, and actions (i.e. *means paths*) which can realistically be implemented at the moment. The option of inaction is also always present, but is itself simply another potential *means path* which may be employed.

The mind subsequently generates a feeling of desire for those *means paths* which appear to the intellect to promise the greatest amount, or the most rapid increase of happiness, or the least amount, or the most rapid decrease in misery. Contrarily, it generates a feeling of aversion towards those *means paths* which appear to the intellect to do the opposite. Since these feelings are based upon a mix of facts and errors which have been stored within the memory, they are not always accurate. As with any computer, if the intellect has been fed flawed data, it is likely to output flawed beliefs, desires, and aversions based upon it.

Simultaneously, the conscience (i.e. instinctive reason) generates a feedback feeling about the perceived ethicality of each *means path*. This feeling, being the very voice of God and therefore rooted in absolute truth, is always entirely accurate. In following its guidance, we in effect act as the agents of God. The problem is that, for each possible *means path*, the feelings originating from conscience are fed to the *deciding factor* within us, together with those originating from the intellect, via the same pathway of *feeling*. If the *feeling* originating within the intellect differs slightly from that originating within the conscience, due either to simple ignorance, or to error mistaken as truth, then the probable outcome will depend upon the views of the individual regarding the nature of conscience. A few of the more common viewpoints and outcomes will be examined below.

If the person who experiences these conflicting feelings possesses an awareness of the value of conscience and an ability to discern its voice, then the *deciding factor* within them will most probably select and convert into will whichever option provides the strongest *positive* feeling from conscience. This is because these people generally believe that, since the conscience is perfectly good, any noted difference in feelings between it and the intellect must be due to ignorance, or error originating within the intellect. These people may not understand the reason why they selected a specific *means path*, other than that it simply *felt more right* than the others.

If the individual in question is a revealed religionist, however, the scenario often plays out quite differently. Revealed religionists are generally able to discriminate the voice of conscience, but undervalue it; thinking it a mere component of their own naturally flawed minds, or souls. This misconception strips conscience of the authority which is natural to it. If the issue in question is unrelated to anything taught by their religious teachers, or found written within their "sacred" texts, then revealed religionists will generally heed the voice of conscience. If, however, the voice of conscience conflicts with these, then revealed religionists are taught to ignore conscience and convert into will whichever *means path* appears to be the most aligned with orthodox opinion. This they generally do with a frequency proportional to their level of piety.

The third viewpoint is that of the nonreligious. These generally do not believe in the existence of conscience. They therefore view feelings which originate from it as no different from, and certainly no more valuable than, those originating from the intellect. Whenever their deciding factor senses a difference in the feelings being fed to it by each, it simply ignores the source and selects for the *means path* which promises the greatest personal benefit. This devaluation of conscience, and benefit-based volition, is the very definition of *Utilitarianism*. Some may disagree, claiming that Utilitarian decisions may increase the overall good of others without directly benefiting the decider, however even these "altruistic" decisions are made for the purely personal benefit of an increased feeling of personal satisfaction for performing the action, or an avoidance of personal guilt for not performing it.

In these latter two scenarios, there is the risk that a frequent disregard, or devaluation of the "voice" of conscience will decrease the probability of anything different occurring in future scenarios. This is due to the natural strengthening process which occurs with frequently repeated thought, or decision patterns.

Selection of Faith

Soul and conscience are the only two tools which any of us possess, which are capable of determining firsthand anything about our state of existence either prior to, or following this life. Much practice and learning are required, however, in order to accurately discriminate the voice of our own souls from the many external voices which compete with it. Accordingly, few men are skilled at using these tools; even among the religious. As unskilled as they are, all men past maturity note with an uncomfortable wince the "death's heads" seen in each new wrinkle, or grey hair. What are they to do to prepare for the time when this life will end?

They are surrounded on all sides by religious zealots who claim that they have absolute certainty about the accuracy of their views on the afterlife, while simultaneously hinting at both eternal bliss for those who agree with their beliefs about these things, as well as threats of impending eternal doom for those who do not. These promises and threats about the afterlife often drive those who hear them into a crisis, where they wish to know with certainty if the claims are true.

The only way that these people know of to determine the accuracy of these claims, and therefore to settle their minds about the correctness of their faith, is to study the often-contradicting doctrines of the various faiths. Those who start down this path are often shocked and dismayed; not only by the volume of material they discover that they must consume, simply to become familiar with the primary sacred written works of the major faiths, but also with the veritable mountains of scholarly writings which have accumulated over the centuries in support of, in clarification of, or in opposition to specific religious doctrines within each of them. Most people are too busy providing for their families, or selves to dedicate the amount of time which would be required to thoroughly study even the primary works of all of these competing religions. Even several lifetimes would not be enough to review all of the academic material on the various doctrinal nuances for even one of these religions. Most men, therefore, at best, perform a cursory review of specific excerpts from the primary works of a handful of the most popular faiths, trusting that the collective wisdom of the masses has elevated these over the rest for due reason.

This was mentioned as the best case, since, for their decision on faith, the vast majority of religious people simply rely solely upon whatever limited information they have available at the moment, such as the character of those whom they know within a certain faith, their family's guidance, societal norms, or a second-hand interpretation of principles pulled from the faith's primary sacred writings, as presented to them within a sermon. Yet the fate of their eternal souls is too important an issue for people to remain uncertain about. They generally select one, go through the required initiatory ceremonies, and consider their afterlife insurance policy to be securely signed.

In order to prevent doubt from creeping back in, converts are assured of their security on a recurring basis, typically when assembled together in their temple, mosque, church, or synagogue, for a sort of "pep rally" of devotion. "There is safety in numbers," many think. "Surely we cannot be wrong when surrounded by so many who agree with us, who seem so certain, and with a leader, or leaders, who claim to have exhaustively studied the intricacies of both this and the other competing faiths and to have determined this one to be the most correct." Yet truth is no partisan. It pays no heed to rank or number.

So how are we to determine the truth about these things? There is no other way than to become more intelligent. When we refer to *intelligence*, we are referring to the collection of facts, and things which we thought to be facts, which have been stored within our memories. All intelligence must be earned through the toil of study; either in public, private, personal, or experiential "schools." Intelligence is a "mountain," slick with oil, which must be scaled with great effort. Due to the ephemeral nature of memories, one cannot even remain stationary upon the surface of this "mountain" without continuous effort. In order to grow wiser, we must outstrip the pace of our forgetfulness. A rate of learning merely equal to that of our forgetfulness will only cause us to lose no ground; yet no new ground will be gained as well. Should we grow weary, throw up our hands, and cease to actively learn, then each passing day, the invisible sands of forgetfulness will continuously wear our memories ever more smooth, causing us to slowly and quietly slip downwards towards ignorance; perhaps even to the archetypal form of ignorance, *savagery*, which is found at the mountain's base.

There have been specific eras, during which, the foresight and tireless efforts of various national leaders have either raised the average intelligence of their citizenry, or assisted their academics in taking specific fields of knowledge to new heights. These heights, however, are never entirely secure. As with lone individuals, so with the assemblages of them which we call *societies*, the pursuit of knowledge can never cease without a slow, but steady decrease in degree of *civilization*. Civilization itself is the collective embodied wisdom of a people.

Due to this innate difference in effort which is required for intelligence, versus that which is required for ignorance, the intelligent have ever been, and ever will be in the minority. Accordingly, highly civilized cultures have been far more rare than savage, or brutal ones.

Even today, the distribution curve of wisdom and knowledge among mankind is not a bell shaped "normal" one. If it was, the peak of the curve would be aligned over the median point of intelligence, and the truly ignorant and truly wise would be respectively found along the leading and trailing sides. In such a case, roughly 95% of mankind would be within 2 standard deviations of median intelligence.

Instead, the distribution of wisdom among mankind, at best, takes the shape of a heavily-tailed distribution, such as a Pareto curve (*See Fig. 3*). In this instance, the mean intelligence of mankind will be seen to fall far below its median.

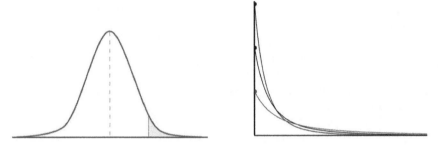

(Figure 3. Left:Normal Curve. Right:Pareto Curves)

This is an important principle to bear in mind, when considering the popularity of faiths, since, in all but the most intolerant Islamic nations, people are generally free to select whichever faith most appeals to them. Due to mankind's inherent love of self, there is a known tendency for them to favor whatever is similar, familiar, and therefore comprehended. Contrarily, those things which are dissimilar, unfamiliar, and poorly comprehended are generally viewed with disfavor, or suspicion. Given this tendency, there is high probability that the most popular of faiths will be those which exhibit a similar degree of wisdom to that of the people who claim them. Since, as previously discussed, the mean of the people exhibit a less than median level of intelligence, the most popular faiths will analogously tend to reflect a less than median level of wisdom and be as prone to doctrinal, or logical errors as their adherents are.

We see a special symptom of this phenomenon within those denominations where the selection of new clergy occurs via a somewhat democratic process, by the laity, or their elected representatives. The laity are for the most part uneducated with regard to the deeper matters of religion. Most of these people have never even read more than a few books of scripture, at best, and virtually none of philosophy. Those candidates who have extensively studied these things are therefore an enigma to them. Since men tend to dislike, or distrust what they do not understand, these more qualified candidates are generally rejected by the majority, while the less qualified, who are better understood, because resembling the selectors, are embraced. Thus, within these denominations, we frequently encounter former hometown football heroes, who are relatively ignorant of deeper religious truths, pastoring a laity of football fanatics, who are even more ignorant about these things.

Such facts explain why popularity is a poor indicator of both the degree of accuracy and the profundity of a specific faith. Given the intricacies and complexities which we encounter throughout the natural universe, it is impossible for the full complement of truths about the will or "mind," of its creator to be simple; though this is how most popular faiths depict them. The archetypal vision of a painting must first be seen within a painter's mind, before his hands can attempt to replicate the vision on canvas; though, man being imperfect, this replication will never match the mental image to the same degree of perfection. A chance mis-stroke of the brush may accidentally improve the painting, but this was merely a double error, both of the artist's hand in replicating the vision, and of his mind in envisioning the painting's ideal form. In order for this preliminary complex and perfected vision of the work to be encompassed within the artist's mind, his mind must be of an even greater degree of perfection and complexity than even the vision itself. In like manner, the traits of whatever this thing is which we call *God*, that created and sustains the natural universe, must be more perfect, sublime, wise, good, noble, and complex, than the highest forms of these qualities which we observe in nature.

A building whose design had been voted for by the general populace, among whom architects are rare, would not be trusted. Why then, is this thought to be a wise approach regarding the selection of faith? We must study and become qualified architects, who may rightly scrutinize the soundness of each faith, prior to selecting one for ourselves.

Original Sin

If the universe was, in fact, created by a perfectly good entity, that can by its very nature create nothing but *good*, how was it ever possible for evil to enter into it? Over the centuries, this question has perplexed, or destroyed the faith of many a philosopher. Sometimes, instead of asking about the abstract concept of evil in general, this same question is asked about the origin of the first act of evil volition, or "original sin." In order to properly explore this issue, we must define the terms *sin* and *evil*. The word *sin*, as it is commonly used today, is both a verb and a noun. As a noun, it is simply a synonym for *evil*. As a verb, it is the performance of *evil*, evil in motion, or *dynamic* evil.

Defining the term *evil* is not quite as easy. This term symbolizes different ideas to people holding differing philosophical views. Let's explore a few of the major differences below, as well as the philosophical implications of these differences.

Atheists, who use the word *evil* as a synonym for harm, suffering, or malice, claim that the fact that *evil* (i.e. suffering) exists proves that the universe doesn't have a purely good creator; or in other words, that there is no God. When they make this claim, they overlook the fact that the majority of suffering which they call *evil* is due either to human, or animal error, or ignorance, or is the result of random forces of nature.

Since neither man, nor animal are born omniscient, the risk of harm originating from error, or ignorance is inescapable. Muslims who murder non-Muslims for Allah are at their core, well intentioned people who were simply fed and believed errors about the character of God and the specifics of his will, typically while still young and impressionable. The biting dog does so because it is ignorant, or in error about the intentions of the person whom it bites. As far as forces of nature go, unless gravity itself were to cease, a situation which would destroy virtually all life on earth, then a person who falls off of a roof must impact the ground, even though this action is likely to harm, or kill them. Tornados do not intentionally strike houses, harming whomever is inside. They simply move where the air currents direct them; currents which were set in motion by a host of natural factors ranging from the amount of radiation issuing from the sun, to the variation of the seasons.

Others believe that the creative forces which they call *good*, as well as the destructive forces which they call *evil*, were coeval, being either passively distributed throughout nature, or actively locked in a perfectly balanced cosmic struggle. These qualified, or radical dualistic views were made famous by Gnosticism, Zoroastrianism, and several other Eastern religions. Sometimes a third sustaining being, or force, is inserted between the forces of creation and destruction, forming the common Trinity motif encountered in the Hindu, and ancient Egyptian faiths.

The Mosaic faiths (i.e. Christianity, Judaism, and Islam) attempt to skirt the problem of the existence of a distinct type of *evil* simultaneously with an all good creator by claiming that man was initially formed as perfectly *good*, but that he used his free will to introduce *sin* into the universe. They claim that this occurred when the mythical progenitors of the human race, Adam and Eve, consumed mythical forbidden fruit, which was taken from a mythical "Tree of the knowledge of good and evil," located within the equally mythical "Garden of Eden." Christians claim that this sinful act corrupted all of nature. This belief can be seen in the following scriptural passage: "For the creation was subjected to futility, not willingly, but because of Him who subjected it in hope; because the creation itself also will be delivered from the *bondage of corruption* into the glorious liberty of the children of God. For we know that the whole creation groans and labors with birth pangs together until now" (Romans 8:20-22).

The full version of the *Garden of Eden* story, found in the book of Genesis, reads like a less profound version of one of Aesop's fables; complete with talking animals. Yet this story fails to stand up to logical scrutiny. We are introduced in the narrative to a mythical evil talking "serpent" who encourages the forbidden act and the subsequent fall of mankind from their demi-godlike state. This archfiend is a concept likely borrowed from a syncretism of the much older Egyptian concept of *Apep*, the giant serpent opponent of Ra, and the Babylonian concept of *Tiamat*, a great sea serpent who is the adversary of the protagonist, Marduk, in the *Enuma Elish*. This latter account is, incidentally, likely the source which scriptural authors borrowed from, when they portrayed their God in a fierce battle with the hydra-like, many-headed sea serpent, Leviathan, within the scriptural passages of Psalms 74:13-17 and Isaiah 27:1.

As Hebrew theological thought developed, this fabulous "serpent" was first identified with, and then later mostly replaced by the more refined, though still imperfect view of a purely spiritual adversary of God, known as *Satan*. Being spirit, nearly as powerful as God, and as evil as the other is good, Satan is a concept which Hebrew thinkers likely borrowed from the almost identical ancient Persian concept of *Angra Mainyu*. The older Hebrew belief, that the archetype of evil was a serpent-like sea creature, never completely died out, and continued to exist alongside this newer one. Artifacts of this earlier belief are still encountered even in the latest of scriptural writings; such as in the 12th chapter of the book of Revelations. What is interesting in this passage is the fact that this "Dragon" of Revelations spews water from its mouth. This is interesting because Tiamat was believed by the ancient Babylonians to be the personification of the primordial waters of chaos; what the Egyptians referred to as *Nu*. This *Nu*, is likely the same primordial water which is found in Genesis 1:2, below.

"The Earth was *without form* (i.e. From the Hebrew *Tohu*; Strong's H8414: Place of chaos[133]), and void; and darkness was on the face of the deep. And the Spirit of God was hovering over the face of the *waters*."

Regardless of the true conceptual origin of the malevolent spirit which tempts Eve, in the scriptural account of the expulsion from paradise, its abetting over this truly petty matter is identified as an *evil* act, for which it is afterwards forever cursed. If the mythical adversary of mankind already had *evil* motives in the garden, before the heart of man did, then *evil* must by necessity have existed before this period.

When faced with this fact, Christians generally fall back to their secondary line of defense: that *evil* entered the world at some unknown period in antiquity. Christians claim, with scriptural backing, that the angels possess the same type of free will as man does. Though these angels were initially perfectly formed, roughly one third of their number are said to have brought *sin* into the universe when they joined forces with Satan, then still in his original form as an angel known as *Lucifer*, during the latter's failed coups d'état against God and those angels which remained loyal to him. After this failure, these rebel angels, now known as *demons*, became malevolent unseen forces throughout the universe, not coincidentally similar to the *Daevas* of the ancient Chaldean, and later Persian theogonies.

This entire Old Testament fable of a cosmic revolt and the fall of Lucifer is built upon a mere two scriptural passages: Isaiah 14:12-15 and Ezekiel 28:11-19. Yet if these passages are read with a clear understanding of the historical context which they were written in, they are actually discovered to be nothing more than simple hyperbole about the doomed luxury of the Kings of Babylon, and Tyre, respectively. In addition, it remains unclear why the word *Lucifer*, which literally means "light bringer," referring to *Venus*, the "morning star," which appears prior to dawn, is left untranslated in these passages, if not for the sole purpose of supporting this entire mythos of the origin of Satan, the demons, and ultimately, *evil* within the universe.

The logical problems with this myth are so glaring, that even granting all of its absurd postulates, it collapses upon itself under scrutiny. Firstly, if *sin* was already in the world prior to Adam and Eve biting the apple, then their act was merely the addition of one more *sin* to the existing heap, rather than the warping of perfect creation which it is portrayed as. Secondly, if the angels were merely creatures possessing a free will who, like man, mistakenly followed the wrong advice, then the story about the angelic fall from grace is little different than that of the fall of humankind. It is the same story, with the same inherent problems, which has been swept under the rug of remote antiquity. The question of angels is the question of men.

If we allow for the fact that the Angels who remained loyal to God are perfectly created and perfectly good spiritual beings, we are faced with the problem of spiritual beings who cannot vary from God in any material aspect, such as form, as both are claimed within some parts of scripture to be immaterial spirit (other parts contradict this even about God himself). They also cannot vary from God in degree of goodness, as a perfect God must create perfect things, else he himself would be imperfect. They cannot vary from him in power, as any limitation implies finitude, or in other words, imperfection of potency. All we are left with is the possibility of variation of type. In a separate section of this work, where the soul of man is discussed, we showed that it is impossible to conceive of variation of type related to immaterial things. Such variation, therefore, though theoretically not impossible, is improbable.

If these deductions, which reason seems to point us to, are correct, then for angels to exist, there would have to be a plurality of identical, infinitely powerful, wise, and good beings. Yet even this view proves unsustainable when examined further, as there is no way to conceive of multiple *infinities* within the same sphere of existence. If the thing under examination is limited, such as wealth, or any material item, it goes without saying that even if one being possesses all of it, they will remain limited, and any reference to infinity in this regard will be hyperbole. In the situation of a plurality of beings, if even one of these beings possesses any portion of the limited thing that another does not, then neither of the two are infinite with regard to this thing. If the characteristics under examination are immaterial and unlimited, such as power, wisdom, or goodness, then it is impossible to conceive of more than one being possessing the full complement of these in an infinite amount, not varying in any other way, and yet remaining distinctly unique. All plurality of being would resolve into one omnipotent God.

But let's follow the logic of this fable of the *fall of Lucifer* to its bitterly absurd end. Our character is revealed not by our actions, but by our intentions. One person may give alms while loathing the needy, and possess far worse character than another person who loves them and desires to help, yet who has nothing to give. Men's characters are already corrupted within when their intentions, or *wills*, become bad, prior to any specific action or inaction which evidences this corruption. Seneca once pointed out this truth by stating that a man does not become a thief the moment he steals. He becomes one, merely lacking the situational opportunity, the moment that he begins to excuse the action within. We find this truth echoed in Proverbs 4:23, where people are advised to, "Keep (their) heart with all diligence, for out of it spring the issues of life." Jesus himself echoes this same truth during his "Sermon on the Mount," in Matthew 5:21-28, where he states that both murder and adultery begin in the heart, not during the action.

At some point, prior to manipulating the other angels into rebellion, an *evil* motive must have entered into the perfect heart of Lucifer. The moment when he began to internally justify seizing the throne of God, would have been the very moment when the corrupting influence of *sin* would have entered into the perfect creation; not the moment when Eve ate the apple. With Adam, we were able to blame the temptation of his perfect mind on Eve. With Eve, we could blame the temptation on the *serpent/Satan*. With the demons, we could again blame *Satan/Lucifer*. This is mere sidestepping of the question of origin of *sin* within a perfect creation. When we arrive at Satan, however, we are in a corner where we must turn and face the question. In a perfect creation, whence did Lucifer's *evil* intentions originate? Who, or what tempted him?

The answer, of course, is that nobody did, because this is all myth. But let us not shy away from the more abstract version of this difficult, yet important question. If there is *evil* in a world created by a perfect power, are we not contradicting our earlier statement that perfection can only create perfection?

Given traditional assumptions about the nature of *evil*, we would be. The puzzle is unsolvable from this position. But in our pursuit of truth, we must not be afraid to challenge deeply held assumptions, regardless of how ubiquitous they are, how long we have held them, or how many of our other views depend upon them for support. If a building has a weak foundation stone, it is wiser to admit the flaw and work towards its repair, even if doing so requires the painful labor of disassembling part, or all of the building to do so. Regardless of how beautiful the existing building is, or how much resources and time were expended upon its construction, ignoring the underlying foundational problem, or continuing to build ever higher upon it, will only make the entire structure more prone to catastrophic collapse.

If our souls are the expressions of a purely good God, how can we allow for *evil* to exist within man? The answer to this is that we cannot. At least not according to the commonly accepted view of *evil*. This commonly accepted view is that *evil*, like the iron within our blood, is something which has a distinct existence; whether quasi-physical, or purely spiritual. Using this definition, there is no way to reconcile the simultaneous perfection of the creator with the existence of *evil*. There is, however, the alternative possibility that *evil* is merely a term used to describe the abstract concept of a vacuity of *good*, rather than something which actually has a positive existence. This would be similar to the way that a hole in the ground is merely an abstract term used to describe the absence of soil in a certain location of ground, rather than something which has a positive existence.

Forgetting then all that we were taught about *evil* during our youth, let us consider the concept de novo, to determine what our reason and intuition tell us about it. In order to do this, we must first identify what it was that we were taught. Knowledge of *evil* is initially gained from teachings and experiences which we are exposed to as children, at home. It is secondarily gained from society. Lastly, for those who have adopted a religion, it is gained from our religious community, leaders, and sacred writings. Let's examine what they tend to teach us about this subject.

Beginning at infancy, our families teach us that *evil* is synonymous with *badness*, or *wrong*. For those children of parents who do not hold religious views, these things are defined within a purely Utilitarian context and simply mean *harmful* to one's own, to another's, or to society's wellbeing. Since specific situations and available options govern whether a given action is considered the least or the most *harmful*, Utilitarians generally do not believe in absolutes of *wrong*, or *evil*.

Some who claim that they are non-religious, and yet who emphatically state that extremes of wrongdoing, such as murder, or rape are *absolute* wrongs, may think the previous claim to be inaccurate. Unbeknownst to these people, they are actually mistaken about their own views, and are not pure Utilitarians. The pure Utilitarian will always look at the available options and expected outcomes and, even in the cases of murder and rape, sometimes see these as a *good*.

Consider a scenario where human experimentation was needed which would certainly prove fatal to the test subject, but which promised to cure some widespread, highly morbid disease for the rest of the world; such as AIDS. A pure Utilitarian would struggle greatly with such a decision, but may still refuse to condone the action, out of a sense of sympathy felt towards the test subject.

Yet what if the scenario was such that it made the natural feelings of sympathy less natural? What if the person who had to die was someone who was spreading an infectious disease: a modern "Typhoid Mary." What if the proposed test subject was a prisoner currently imprisoned for violent crime? What if it was the manager of the bank that had just foreclosed on your elderly parent's home? What if it was someone who had a severe mental and/or physical handicap?

In the mind of the Utilitarian, suddenly even the murder of an innocent would begin to be rationalized as a painful and unfortunate necessity, rather than an absolute moral wrong: similar to the pain and slight harm required in removing a splinter. And make no mistake, however this picture is framed, the theoretical test subject was not sentenced to death within a just legal proceeding by a jury of his or her peers. They therefore remain innocent of anything which would legally warrant death; regardless of their guilt, or innocence for lesser offenses.

Now for the disturbing reality check. Consider that these same types of Utilitarian rationalizations were used by the Germans of the 1930's and 1940's to justify the death camps. Like the example given of a disease spreading "Typhoid Mary," the Nazis claimed that they were protecting mankind from genetic diseases, such as TaySachs disease, that the eugenicists and geneticists of the day had determined were highly prevalent among the Ashkenazic Jews. While such a claim may sound outlandish from a modern perspective, the research remains valid to this day; commonly being cited within medical school genetics textbooks. One relatively recent study, for example, estimates that, due to centuries of endogamy, 1 in 3.3 Ashkenazic Jews are the carriers of at least 1 of 16 different genetic diseases; 1 in 24 of these individuals being the carriers of 2.[134]

Like the example given of the violent criminal, the Nazis condemned the Jews for their high representation in the violent German, and Russian Bolshevik, Communist Parties. Both of these parties had attracted large numbers of Jews, prior to the Russian "October Revolution," and during the German Weimar Republic. Further fixing the Jewish association with Bolshevism in the minds of the Germans was the fact that, not only Karl Marx, but the two lead figures in the Russian movement, Leon Trotsky and Vladimir Lenin, all had Jewish ethnic backgrounds. Marx and Trotsky were both Jewish on both sides of their families, while Lenin was Jewish only on his mother's side. Though many are unaware of Lenin's Jewish background, evidence of it can be seen in, among other things, a letter which his older sister, Anna Ulyanova, wrote to Stalin in 1932. In this letter, Anna stated that their maternal grandfather "came from a poor Jewish family..."[135,136]

In addition, the Nazis were well aware that the vast majority of Bolshevik Commissars, the real power holders within the Soviet Russian state, were Jewish. This fact is described in extraordinary detail in the 1920's work, *The International Jew*, which is often attributed to Henry Ford.[137] How much Henry Ford actually contributed to this work is questionable, as he denied his involvement in its creation, and other versions state that it was from, "Henry Ford and the Editors of the Dearborn Independent." In addition, several sections of the work bear the unmistakable stamp of high academic character, hinting more at the hand of an intentionally anonymous university professor, than of an automobile magnate. These same figures were also echoed during a recent speech which Russian President Vladimir Putin made at the Moscow Jewish Museum, where he stated that, "The decision to nationalize this library was made by the first Soviet government, whose composition was 80-85 percent Jewish."[138]

The Jews were also hated by the Germans for their longstanding dominance and ubiquity within the banking industry; an industry which was particularly hated during the crushing poverty which existed in

Germany during the interwar period of the Weimar Republic. While the Germans struggled with the payment of war reparations, which were set at intentionally crushing levels, investment banks such as J. P. Morgan, under the "Dawes" and "Young" plans, leapt at the opportunity to fetter the German people further in debt; in the guise of compassionately loaning them capital to revitalize their economy. Due to their debt, the German people could not refuse these massive loans; bonds for which, these investment banks merrily hawked to private international investors.

As with the example of the disabled person, the Nazis had also been convinced by the German scientists of the day that the Jews were well behind the Aryans in evolutionary development. This facilitated dehumanizing them in the minds of the SS.

In the light of the above factors, it becomes apparent that the Nazi's were actually true Utilitarians. Clearly then, some higher ethical foundation than Utilitarianism is needed to preserve morality from degeneration.

Parents from most religious backgrounds also teach their children that *evil* means *bad*, *wrong*, or *harmful*. Though using the same terms as the non-religious, the definitions which they assign to these terms tend to differ dramatically, due to several factors. The first factor is the general belief in some sort of an afterlife, found within virtually all revealed religions. Depending upon their level of maturity and development above the earliest of animisms, totemisms, and fetishisms, most faiths believe that harmful effects caused by words, thoughts, or actions can extend beyond the lifespan of the actor into either a future immaterial state of existence (i.e. afterlife), or in the cases of reincarnation or resurrection, into a renewed material one.

This raises the question as to which actions, words, or thoughts may negatively impact one's state in the afterlife. Here we encounter the second factor. The vast majority of religions believe that one, or several of their religious leaders have had some sort of personal experience which has provided them with *supernatural insight* into the will of the power, or powers behind the universe. This is why these faiths are referred to as *revealed* religions; as they believe that this divine power has *revealed* this *insight* to them for various reasons, which they may or may not claim to understand. This *special insight* includes knowledge about which types of actions, thoughts, or words performed during this life will prove beneficial, or detrimental in the next.

Revealed religionists therefore define *evil* to their adherents as whatever their faith's founders, leaders, or sacred writings arbitrarily inform them will badly, wrongly, or harmfully influence their position in the next life. Seldom are their adherents encouraged to examine their own consciences, or their personal reason about these things. In fact, should some among them attempt to utilize these natural tools and openly reach dissenting opinions, they are generally frowned upon, shunned, or altogether cast out from the community of the "faithful." *Faith*, which to many of them means blind, unquestioning submission (e.g. even the word *Islam* itself, literally means "submission"), is generally touted as the highest of their virtues, while careful scrutiny and the noble use of reason, which may instill doubt as they burn away the chaff of error, are often seen as a threat.

It is obvious to any outside observer that this is simply a modified form of Utilitarianism. While the Utilitarianism of the non-religious was based upon the fixed principle of doing the *most good*, or *least harm* possible to the bodies, minds, property, environment, or culture of those involved in any given scenario, it was limited in scope of concern to the lifespans of these participants. This modified Utilitarianism of the revealed religionists, on the other hand, is based upon arbitrarily defined principles and is expanded in scope of concern to include effects theorized to occur after the lifespans of the actors.

In addition, though the non-religious Utilitarian considered *evil* to simply be a synonym for *bad*, *wrong*, or *harmful*, for the revealed religionist, there is the additional unspoken implication that *evil* has a positive existence as a distinct malevolent force, being, or substance. This difference is true for their conception of *sin* as well. Rather than believing that *sin* is simply an *evil* action, as the non-religious do, the vast majority of revealed religionists are generally taught that *sin*, once performed, gains a sort of positive existence. Evidence of this view can be seen in the way that most of the sacred texts of the revealed religions, especially those of the Mosaic faiths, frequently speak of the ability to transfer *sin* between individuals, or to abolish it altogether, as if it were some sort of bank loan. It is nonsensical to speak of transferring, or abolishing a past harmful action. Not even God can change, or abolish past events.

This unspoken belief in the positive existence of *evil* and *sin* is where we return to the problem of a perfectly good creator being unable to make anything except what is *perfect* and *good*. People who recognize this problem generally react in one of two ways.

The atheist group says, "If evil exists, then something had to make, or cause it. Since that something cannot be a purely good God, then there is something which God did not make, or cause. This runs counter to what most revealed religions claim in their cosmogonies, so they are likely all wrong. If they are wrong on this core principle of their faith, then these faiths are not truly 'revealed' and those who adopt them are likely either ignorantly mistaken, or base charlatans. If most 'revealed' religions are therefore false, then God is not likely to exist."

The other group assumes the existence of God, but goes straight to the question of, "If evil exists, if God is good, and if God created everything, then where did evil come from?" They then generally perform theological acrobatics in order to rationalize their faith; often appealing to *Trinity*, in order to uncouple the *engine* of cause from its *freight cars* of effect, calling the entire thing a "divine mystery," or flying into a rage that someone would dare to question their "sacred" prophets and writings (e.g. fundamentalist Muslims and Hasidic Jews).

Yet both approaches make the initial mistake of assuming the existence of *evil*. What evidence do we have that *evil* actually has a positive existence as a force, being, or substance; as it isn't the concept of *evil* as simple *harm* that is really the problem. We see harmful deeds, words, and actions all around us. Since the motive (i.e. *will*) is the determining factor by which we judge merit, unintentional *harm*, such as unintentionally tripping someone, though genuinely harmful, is not condemned as wrongdoing by the intelligent. If, on the other hand, the will was involved and the act was intentional, then it will receive just condemnation.

Yet if we look beneath the surface at the motivations of those who inflict *harm* upon others, we generally discover that their will is ultimately aimed at an ascension up the scale of happiness. Harmful means are only employed because the truth about the underlying source of happiness remains unknown, or because error about this has been accepted as truth. This concept is known in academic circles as *Eudemonism*. Were these people to truly know and fully understand the means by which happiness can be increased, and to have the capability to affect these means, then they certainly would. What then becomes of all *evil* when the harm associated with it is found to be merely due to ignorance or error? It evaporates.

Though actions performed while attempting to find happiness may incidentally cause harm to our own bodies, minds, and character, as well as to the bodies and minds of others, potentially even unto death, these actions cannot harm the soul. Nothing can. Even the vilest, most ruthless savage to ever drench the Earth with blood, died with a soul as completely intact as Jesus' was at the moment of his crucifixion. But how can this statement, which inevitably rings blasphemous upon orthodox ears, be true? To examine this question, we must first consider how the majority of the major faiths view the natural conditions of the human soul.

Though the majority of religious sects hold widely varying views on the natural state of the human soul, most of their views can be classified into a few specific groups. The largest group, which includes many sects of Christians, Muslims, and Jews, believes that there are essentially either two *species*, or *states* of soul; one of which they believe to be hopelessly corrupted, and the other they believe to be innocent and acceptable to God. There are differing opinions among the various sects within these groups as to whether this corruption is inherited at birth, due to ancestral *sins*, or whether it doesn't occur until *sin* has been personally committed. In either case, the corrupted soul is seen as damned and despised by none-other than its designer: God.

But consider how this opinion destroys the concept of God's omnipotence. Any separation, or even delay, which occurs between *will* and *effect* implies finitude of power. If man is potent enough to violate, or even to *delay* God's will, then God is no longer omnipotent. If presented with this issue, this group will generally respond that it is God's will for man to have his own (free) will, but that it is not God's will that man commits *sin*. This artful sidestepping of the question does little to remedy the situation, though. Instead of sacrificing God's omnipotence, his omniscience is now sacrificed. The maker of the mind must know the exact combination of influences which would cause men to finally give themselves over to temptation and *sin*. Since such influencing pressures are known to occur, and since God is believed to control all of nature in accordance with his will, we end up with a God who is either *willing* for his own *will* to be violated, a nonsensical statement, or a God who is ignorant of the ultimate consequences of his actions.

When confronted with this problem, this group borrows their solution from the ancient Zoroastrian faith. They introduce us to what is, in effect, a negative reflection of God, known as Satan, or the Devil; complete with an *evil* will and only slightly inferior power. But this Satan needn't work alone to effect his sinister will. Again, from Zoroastrian lore, Satan is provided with a negative reflection of God's angelic spirits, which are at his direct command. These are referred to either as "demons," a word which originally had no negative connotation, being used by the ancient Greeks as a generic term for *spirit*, *soul* (Note when Socrates mentions his "Demon" in Plato), *evil spirits*, or *devils*.[64] There is a telling similarity here not simply between the concepts, but even between the word *devils* and its Zoroastrian prototype, *deva*. This latter term is preserved with varying meanings in the Buddhist, Hindu, and Jain faiths, which developed much later. Any pressure, or enticement towards *sin* is said not to be the action of God, but of Satan, or of his agents; sometimes acting directly, and at other times acting through men, or other living things which are under their influence.

This position is hopelessly flawed for multiple reasons. Foremost among these is the fact that God's omniscience and omnipotence are again violated. It is merely a transferal of the same problems which concerned the souls of men, to Satan and his host of demons. If Satan and his demons are able to frustrate, or even to delay God's will, then God is not omnipotent. If they cannot frustrate God's will, then their malevolent actions must be in keeping with it; something which would destroy God's goodness. When faced with this problem, many among this group of Mosaic faiths appeal once more to the concept of free will, as they did for man. God is said to have *willed* for Satan and his demons to possess free will, but did not will for them to sin. As with man, we see that this excuse violates God's omniscience. In designing and directly controlling the universe, including demonic minds, God would have to know and control the cocktail of influences which he knew would be the breaking point which would drive Satan and his demons to sin.

This similarity of philosophical problems between the original sin of Satan and his legion of demons, and that of mankind reveals the purpose behind this demonic fabrication; or in actuality, adoption and retention from the ancient faiths. In these ancient faiths, these beings served as a readily available excuse which could be brought out and blamed whenever the faithful were faced with harmful natural, personal, or interpersonal events. They are retained within these modern faiths, not only for these previous reasons, but also as a method to push the question of *original sin* into eternity past; effectively sweeping it under the rug.

These philosophical problems are not merely difficult, but are in fact insurmountable, while still retaining orthodox Christian, Jewish, or Islamic views. Pieces of the philosophical puzzles of these faiths are missing. Bits from other puzzles have been thrown in and do not fit. Regardless of how much the devout claim that the image is complete and perfect, and condemn any who would dare to criticize it, the holes are there, staring any who are brave enough to conduct a candid investigation in the face.

When these issues are brought to the attention of this group of faiths, most among them will become too offended, or embarrassed by their ignorance to follow the chain of logic any further. They typically throw up their hands and leave the discussion, either in a fit of rage, or with condescending chuckles and looks which imply, "Oh, if only you had my level of wisdom, then you could understand this deeper philosophical truth."

Those few souls among them who are brave, or confident enough to persist in the inquiry, will at this point usually attempt to pass off their refusal to abandon and outgrow refuted doctrine as a merit-worthy act of *high faith*, which places them among the ranks of their religious heroes. At least that's what their churches, temples, and mosques tell them. They usually attempt to disguise their simple ignorance as deep profundity by cloaking it in decorous religious language, such as the phrase, "divine mystery." It is this "divine mystery," which they claim allows sin to, at some point in the past, spontaneously appear in the heart of Satan without violating God's omniscience and omnipotence. This cunning shift from an appeal to reason, to one of authority, is a religious version of the statement, "I don't know why it is, but I was told it was and believed it."

What these people fail to realize is that this position which they take "on faith," by destroying God's omnipotence and omniscience, undermines the very foundation of their religion. Their faith is found to lie not in God, but in the authority and flawed views of the men who originally "revealed" these faiths, in their sacred writings, in their past and present religious leaders and teachers, and in their community of likeminded believers: families generally ranking highly among this last group.

Now that we have concluded our investigation into problems with how these faiths view the original, supposedly corrupted state of the soul, let's consider their views on what they claim is its other possible state. They generally believe that, by participating in certain ceremonies which culminate in some sort of oath of fealty to God, his Son (e.g. supposedly Jesus), his messengers (e.g. supposed prophets such as Moses, or Mohammed), some combination of these, as well as, to a lesser extent, accepted church, temple, or mosque leadership and doctrine, the corrupted soul may either be replaced with one which is still imperfect, but cleansed of the corruption which befouled it, or one which is left in its original state of corruption, but essentially hidden from God's notice beneath, or within the "perfect" soul of their savior.

None of these options are realistic. Let's consider the first two, where the corrupted soul is either cleaned, or replaced, and yet remains imperfect. Those who ascribe to these views originally claimed that their salvific ceremonies and oaths were required for even the slightest of sins. Yet if the new, or cleaned soul is in any way imperfect, then it remains corrupt, and the difference between the former and the new state is but one of degree. Those who cling to this view are typically reluctant to take the step of declaring that the new state of the soul is perfect, out of fear that they will be laughed at. This is because everyone knows that all of mankind, even the faithful, are imperfect and occasionally slip into willful wrongdoing. In addition, were they to risk calling the soul *perfect*, they know that they would struggle with differentiating the souls of men from the spirit of God, as the mind cannot conceive of a plurality of spiritual (i.e. immaterial) *perfections*.

If these problems are brought to their attention, Muslims, Baptists, Catholics, Mormons, Jews, and several other sects will typically respond that the subsequent *perfection* of the soul is less important than the initial oath and binding ceremonies which make one a member of the faith. The faithful are essentially *marked*, or "sealed," upon their conversion. After this *sealing*, except in extreme cases, their works have little to do with their acceptance by God.

This view destroys God's wisdom and goodness. It implies that God is either an incompetent judge, who is stupidly unable to determine true merit, or a corrupt one who understands, and yet intentionally disregards impartial justice in order to dote upon and bless his favorites, while he hinders, punishes, or destroys all others. It sets up a cosmic caste system, where all benefit belongs to one group, regardless of their level of corruption, while all punishment belongs to the rest, regardless of their level of merit. Of course, such base representations of the character of God cannot be accurate.

Those who hold the opinion that souls are hidden beneath a sort of "veil of holiness," which emanates from their savoir, fail to realize that this view not only destroys God's omniscience, but also destroys his goodness. It makes him a monster whose rage is only sated by carnage, death, and blood; even to the extreme extent of destroying his own child, like Cronus of old. Worse still, he also becomes either a dupe, who is unable to detect an obvious deception abetted by his cunning son, or a hypocrite, who is willing to sometimes violate whatever cosmic law supposedly requires him to kill.

None of these opinions preserve God's goodness, omniscience, and omnipotence, and therefore, none of them can be true. But what options remain? Only one of any real worth: one which the ancient Indians at times hinted at in their Upanishads,[103] which many Greek philosophers, from Plotinus to Socrates, supported, but which had no better champion than Ralph Waldo Emerson. This view is that the soul which enlivens us is itself somehow an expression of God.[3] Not a part of God, like Osiris; body torn asunder and cast to the winds and waves. No. Wherever soul exists, whether in man, solar system, cell, quark, etc., in all God must exist entire, complete, immortal, and incorruptible.

Revealed Religion

Revealed religions, such as Islam, Judaism, Buddhism, and Christianity require a partial god, who gives the blessing of his "revealed" will to some "chosen" person, or people, and not to others. An earthly judge who was found to be partial in his judgements would not be considered just, ethical, or good; nor should we consider a God to be good, who is similarly partial in his judgements. This is but one of many intentionally *harmful* (i.e. *evil*), or morally corrupt actions which God is portrayed as performing, or attitudes which God is portrayed as possessing in the Christian Bible, the Hebrew Tanakh, and the Islamic Koran. Revealed religionists who adhere to these faiths are told that when God performs these things, they are not evil. This is in spite of the fact that within their sacred texts, we find the same, or similar actions hypocritically condemned when performed by men.

One great example of this is the portrayal of the Egyptian Pharaoh as being monstrously cruel for ordering the killing of the male Hebrew infants, in Exodus 1:22, but then, only a few chapters later, in Exodus 12:29, God is portrayed as committing an atrocity similar in type, but greater in scope against the Egyptians, when he supposedly orders an angel to kill every "firstborn" Egyptian. Revealed religionists, in accepting and promoting this depiction of a partial, unjust, malicious, and hypocritical God, unwittingly destroy his goodness, his perfection, and ultimately his very divinity. Euripides pointed out the consequence of this in his famous statement that, "If the gods do aught that is *unseemly* (i.e. wrong, unjust, evil), then they are not gods at all."[139]

When these problems are pointed out to revealed religionists, they generally respond with the claim that the God who makes the rules of morality, is above them, leaving him free to violate them with impunity. Unfortunately, such reasoning does not work for two reasons. Firstly, the portrayal of God as a sort of king, who is immune from the laws which he enacts, does nothing to lessen the hypocrisy of him condemning others within scripture for what he himself does. Imagine a king who ordered people to be hanged for theft, and yet who himself looted the public treasury. Would all who knew of his crime and hypocritical punishments praise and respect such a king, or instead, would they secretly loathe and denounce him? Is hypocritical rule not one of the hallmarks of tyranny? Isn't instinctive awareness of, and anger over this type of injustice part of what sparked the French and American Revolutions?

Secondly, as discussed elsewhere, justice is not arbitrary, but universal; born from the nature of goodness and God. If God's character is *immutable*, then *justice* and *goodness* are also immutable. If God is omnipresent throughout the universe, then so is this immutable justice and goodness. Mutability of a perfect God would require a plurality of *perfections*, something which, as discussed earlier, appears to be an impossibility for immaterial spirit. Socrates points out this universality of goodness in Plato's *Euthyphro*, where he states that, "...the *holy* has been acknowledged by us to be loved of God because it is *holy*, not to be *holy* because it is loved."[129]

The apology which revealed religionists generally provide for the inherent partiality of *selective revelation* is generally either that the cause for the selection is a "divine mystery" which God alone knows, or that it is not actually *selective*; that such supernatural insight into the will of God is equally available to all, but that it requires a degree of *holiness*, or *effort* which few men attain to. They claim that only men such as Krishna, Moses, Siddhartha (i.e. Buddha), Mohammed, Zoroaster, Jesus, and Apollonius of Tyanna, most of whom have later been made into de facto demigods, have scaled these great "mountains" of religious effort.

These arguments do not make their conception of God any more just. The first claim, that the reason for the partiality is a "divine mystery," is a statement which adds no additional insight to the question. It is merely the statement "I don't know," masquerading in religious sounding language. The second, that only the *few* are awarded special insight into God's will as a reward for their extraordinary efforts, is also problematic, but will require further explanation.

In the second claim, we have no explanation as to why a *good* God would intentionally withhold special insight into his will from the vast majority of mankind: insight which could only prove beneficial to them. As a thought experiment, imagine survivors from a shipwreck who are gathered together on a deserted island. Now imagine that among these is the ship engineer, who alone knows how to fabricate a radio from the wreckage, which may be used to signal rescuers. When approached for this information by the other survivors, who are seeking a way home, the engineer replies that he will only share it with those among them who will single-handedly build a hundred-foot stone pyramid to prove their devotion to him. Add to this that among these survivors are the young, the old, and the injured, who would be especially challenged by such a demand.

Would the other survivors view this demand, and therefore the motives and character of the engineer, as *good* or *bad*? Would the engineer be seen as *loving* and having the survivors' best interests at heart, or as an egocentric megalomaniac? Clearly the latter. If these requirements for aid would not be seen as good, loving, or in the best interests of those involved in men, they would also not be seen as just in God. Of course, this example was merely a trope for the conception of God held by many revealed religionists. Were God to similarly withhold special insight into his will from all but those who perform extraordinary efforts of devotion, he would not be seen as good, loving, or having the best interests of mankind at heart; making him once again, unjust.

Guidance which these "chosen" religious leaders give to their followers, from their supposed store of *special insight* into the will of God, is typically documented, distributed to, and studied by their respective faithful. Sometimes, when a sufficient length of time has elapsed for the origin of these written works to have passed into legend, the works themselves become revered as *sacred* or *holy*. Other times, these writings are perceived as *sacred* and *holy* because the author, compiler, scribe, or devout, fabricated a supernatural origin story for them, in order to enhance their perceived authority; such as occurred with the Koran.

But we should pause for a moment to define the words *sacred* and *holy*, as their meaning has become confused to our modern ears, making them now little more than religious jargon. *Sacred* and *holy* mean *good* to such an extreme that God possesses a special affection towards these things, or people above that which he has for most others; perhaps even communicating a portion of his power to it, or committing himself to its special defense. This is the unspoken understanding among the adherents of various revealed religions, when they speak of the *holiness* of their respective sacred works; such as the Koran and Hadiths, the Tanakh and Talmud, the Bible, the Vedas, the Agams, the Avesta, the Tripitaka, the Book of Mormon, and several others.

Generally, revealed religionists believe that these sacred works contain the explicit words and thoughts of God, as documented either by himself, by an angelic messenger (e.g. The Ten Commandments, & the Koran), or by believers under God's direct influence (e.g. the Tanakh, Talmud, Bible, Vedas, etc.). As such, they believe these writings, as originally authored, to be perfect and infallible. Anything perfect must, by necessity, also be immutable. One of the fundamental problems with this idea is the fact that languages are constantly evolving; the meanings of words and phrases changing daily. It is impossible to form something *immutable* from mutable and wax-like words. The inevitable conclusion is that even if God himself did cause a perfect written document to be created, something both impractical and unlikely for a being able to speak directly into the hearts and minds of all of mankind, this document would immediately become imperfect the moment after it was created, like a footprint in the rain.

Another technique which may be used to refute those who claim that they rely upon the supposedly infallible words of their sacred books, instead of what they often superciliously refer to as "frail human reason," is to ask them why they believe these works to be perfect. Initially, they will cite their faith in the reliability of these works' authors, subjects, witnesses, followers, or promotors. Yet if they are asked to explain the cause of their faith in these sources, they will either grow angry, as is typically the case with Muslims, or refute their original position by identifying the various points of *reason* which they believe make the works reliable.

It should be pointed out here that this is specifically not the case with the extreme minority of non-revealed religion faiths, such as the Natural Religionists, ala David Hume, as well as with their equally rare cousins, the Deists; many of whom were among the founding fathers of these United States. One example of the latter group is Revolutionary War hero, Colonel Ethan Allen, who penned the powerful Diest work, *Reason, the Only Oracle of Man.* These men believe that the power which governs the universe makes the revelation of its will equally available to all men through the common language of nature; especially through the two parts of it known as *reason* and *conscience*: reason being the active physical mind, and conscience being the very voice of God interacting with it. Such a view preserves the justice, and therefore the perfection, goodness, and very divinity of God.

Could the development of our spiritual senses occur in a similar manner to the development of the sense of hearing among the blind? The blind do not have innate special abilities. They have merely, by necessity, accustomed themselves to focusing their attention, to an extraordinary degree, on the inputs which they receive from their ears. Being exercised and developed like the muscles of an athlete, the ears of the blind soon grow able to sense and interpret sounds which the seeing public generally wouldn't notice. In like manner, perhaps our sensitivity to our own *intuition*, or in other words, our *instinctive reason*, can also be refined and developed through focus and exercise, until we grow more keenly aware of the spiritual leadings which we receive from our own souls; or possibly even from the souls of others. Perhaps the development, or atrophy of this sense within us is due more to practice and effort, than to our specific set of religious, or metaphysical views.

This postulate raises important questions regarding how God communicates with the soul, or the mind of man. The traditional, orthodox view within all of the Mosaic religions is that God speaks to the mind, or physical ear of man based upon his caprice at the moment. When he does so, man plays no active role in sensing, or hearing this voice. People may, or may not be paying attention; may or may not understand, or obey God's guidance; but cannot avoid hearing God when he speaks, as one could not avoid hearing the voice of someone speaking directly into their ear.

Within Christianity, for example, we observe this when God tells Noah to build the ark (Genesis 6:13-22), when he calls Abram from Ur

(Genesis 12:1-3), when he speaks to Moses from the "burning bush" (Exodus 3:1-17) and later Mt. Horeb (Exodus 19), when he calls to Samuel as a child in bed (1 Samuel 3:1-15), when he speaks to the apostles from the cloud on the mount of transfiguration (Matthew 17:5), when he speaks to and blinds Saul (Acts 9:1-19), when he speaks to Peter on the rooftop about the clean and unclean animals (Acts 10:9-16), etc. According to this view, God's communication with man is always completely effective, yet for no clear reason, is seemingly sporadic and unreliable.

On the other hand, sometimes in scripture, man is depicted as playing an active role in initiating communication with God, typically by the performance of sacrifices and offerings which seemingly draw God's attention, or increase his compassion. Within Christian scripture, for example, we observe this when Balaam performs sacrifices when summoned to curse Israel (Numbers 23), when Solomon slaughters hundreds of animals (i.e. a hecatomb) before the tabernacle, prior to falling into a dream and hearing God's voice (1 Kings 3:4-5), when Abraham sacrifices animals, also falling into a sleep, and having a "vision" where he hears the voice of God (Genesis 15:9-21), etc.

God is frequently depicted in the Bible, the Koran, the Book of Mormon, the Tanakh, etc., as speaking with supposedly pious men for the purpose of sending them on a mission to deliver a mix of warnings and guidance to the impious. A classic example of this from the Bible and the Tanakh, is where Jonah is supposedly sent by God to warn and threaten the "sinful" Ninevites (Jonah 3:1-4).

The problem with this orthodox view is that there is no clear means by which to garner the attention of God. Sometimes good men and women, in genuine and often profound need, pray and beg God for guidance and intervention, only to have their prayers go unanswered. Other times, butchers of men, though not actively seeking God, are depicted in the sacred texts of several revealed religions as having been spoken to, warned, or advised repeatedly by him. Nor do these latter people typically listen to God's council; often torturing, or killing the messenger who is sent to them. What does this sort of portrayal of God tell men about his character? It says that God is unjust, in that he has favorites among men, and that he is seemingly capricious in his dealings with them.

The more mature theory about how God communicates with mankind is that spiritual influence is a universal constant; much like gravity. It does not speak to us in words, but if we exercise and tune our internal senses to its voice, it does so as *feelings* which we sense within us; *feeling* being the direct, native "tongue" of the mind. God may not tell us to forgive an offense in a "still small voice," but we may sense a general feeling of *rightness* when this option is considered. This theory prevents God from being portrayed as capricious, in that his influence is constant, or unjust, in that his influence is available to all who, by practice, learn to tune their senses to it.

Some may question whether this spiritual influence originates externally, or internally. The answer to this question depends upon the materiality of the spirit. If spirit is indeed immaterial, a conclusion which was arrived at elsewhere within this work, then location may not have any meaning when discussing it.

Small Groups

Being much older, and a bit wiser than I was when a young church member, I now see the less innocent side of the *small group* approach to proselytism, which has become so ubiquitous within most modern churches. What then seemed to me to be merely a better way to get to know people, I now realize is also a carefully crafted forum to focus intense peer pressure towards the suppression of any opinion dissenting from that of the group's leader; who is portrayed as holding the most "correct" theological, and often even secular views.

I will give an example of how this technique generally works. When potential church members are new, and their doctrinal stances are therefore unknown to church leadership, they are strongly encouraged to "get plugged in" to a small group, in order to "more actively participate" and "develop closer fellowship" with other church members. They are bombarded with this message in most sermons, flyers, and personal interactions with current members. Once they finally decide to do so, they are assigned to a *small group* of existing church members. The majority of these members have already proven their allegiance to, and alignment with the views of their church's leaders. The individual with the greatest allegiance to, and closest alignment with the doctrinal positions held by church leadership is generally always appointed to serve as the group's leader.

New assignees to the small group are intentionally kept in the extreme minority; typically, only one or two per established group. The meeting is generally always held at the home of the leader, or another person close to, and in doctrinal agreement with him, or her. These meetings generally commence with some type of gift being provided to the group by the leader, or veteran church members; commonly food.

While the above seems the setting of an innocent party, the intent is carefully crafted to apply as much peer pressure as possible on the new person to conform to the views of the group. The group is set at an intentionally small size, in order to ensure that the new person cannot remain an unnoticed, silent observer, and will therefore be forced to participate in the upcoming drama which they are unaware that they play the starring role in. New group participants are kept in the extreme minority in order to ensure that any dissenting opinions to church doctrine, which these newcomers may raise, is always greatly outnumbered. Such numerical superiority generally discourages these opinions from being voiced, since man is a social creature who generally will go to great lengths to avoid widespread public disapproval. Only a few, brave souls will openly face such censure for a theoretical matter; which religion is, by its very nature.

The venue was intentionally selected to be at the leader's home so that the person who would dare to raise a dissenting opinion must not only do so in the face of a much larger united body, but he, or she must risk appearing as a rude guest as well. This is because people's homes remain somewhat their "castles." Recall that the host has already provided this guest with a gift; perhaps a meal, a book, or something similar, fostering a sense of obligation in the *target*. What audacity a man must have to critique the small group leader's deeply held beliefs in the face of all of this!

The drama unfolds in these settings as follows: First people socialize while eating, often expressing great delight at the attendance of the new member and asking them questions in order to make them relax and "open up." After this goes on for a period that the leader feels to be sufficient, the group is told to gather in a specific location within the home. The leader then generally pulls out a lesson sheet which was designed by church leadership in order to address a specific church doctrine. These lessons are generally crafted as a series of questions, with the church's "doctrinally correct" answer listed, along with supporting verses. These "correct" answers are typically only in the possession of the group leader; though there are exceptions.

The leader starts the session by either polling the group as to what they believe the answer to the first question to be, or by sequentially tasking individual group members to read the supporting verses. Whichever approach is taken first, the other is generally done afterwards.

While the group is being polled, the newcomer, who is unlikely to initially respond, will quietly listen to the various responses of the other group members. Due to these members' existing knowledge of, and agreement with church doctrine, their answers will usually all sound similar, but not identical enough to appear rehearsed. They will appear to be the independent reasonings of intelligent people. The leader will generally smile and agree with these responses. If he notices someone inadvertently giving a heterodox answer, he will gently correct them with the *official* church view on the issue. Typically, the corrected members will quickly agree with this new information, knowing that to do otherwise is fatal to their acceptance within that community, and ultimately the church.

The silent newcomer will generally think to his, or herself, "How is it that all of these intelligent, friendly people all came to this same conclusion? If I happen to disagree, surely, they can't all be wrong. Sheer statistics are against it. If I disagree, I must be the one who is mistaken, because these people, and especially their leader, have obviously invested far more time into the study of these abstract concepts than I have. I should agree, or at least appear to, so that I'm not the only person holding this contrasting opinion. I don't want to look foolish. I also don't want to risk openly challenging the leader, whom I barely yet know, on this deeply held belief of his; especially in front of his friends, as a guest in his home, and after he was so kind to me. I already somewhat owe him, as I have been given this gift and have eaten those great deserts that his wife worked so hard to make for us."

Should the newcomer, in a surge of courage over a doctrine which he, or she particularly disagrees with, dare to question the reasoning of the leader, he, or she will generally be sympathetically smiled at by the group, as one might smile at a young child struggling with arithmetic. Various group members may offer their support to their leader with statements such as, "I used to think that too, and then I realized..."

If these efforts fail to convince the newcomer, the leader will generally attempt to silence the newcomer's affront by stating that the supporting verses are the "Word of God," and as such, are absolute and inerrant. Only the bravest and most well studied, who are generally rare among church newcomers, will dare, after such a statement, to continue to press the truth of their contrasting opinion. Should they do so, they will notice growing signs of disapproval beginning to spread among the group. Glances between members may occur. Smiles may fade, and a few frowns begin to appear.

In this situation, the group leader will generally make a statement about how he is ultimately correct, but, in order to get through the remainder of the questions within the allotted time, will have to reserve any further discussion on the topic until next time.

The cycle will then begin anew, with the exception that the newcomer who dared to defend his, or her contrasting position will now have become a marked man, or woman. During future questions, this newcomer will be less likely to speak out, knowing that they are virtually alone in their disagreement, and sensing their fall from the group's good graces. Should this newcomer protest another point anyway, due to moral conviction and love of truth, he, or she will notice that the frowns, perhaps this time accompanied by sighs and eye rolling, will appear sooner than previously. The leader may even begin to condescendingly chuckle at the newcomer's response, while exchanging knowing glances with the other members which shout, "Can you believe this guy's audacity?"

In the face of such group pressure, this newcomer will generally either fall into silence, or excuse him, or herself and leave. The latter case seldom occurs, due to the scheduled brevity of these meetings, and also due to fear of incurring additional group resentment at what would be seen as a most flagrant offense to the leader. Any other of the intentionally few newcomers present to witness these events will typically be cowed into silence or agreement with the group, in order not to experience the same discomfort.

This is not a group of people banding together and seeking truth, heedless of where the pursuit takes them. This is not dialectic reasoning. It is a nest where the group leader regurgitates the stale doctrine of church leadership into the fledgling minds of the members, and pecks at, or expels from the nest, all who may disagree.

Trinity

It has been well enough established within previous sections of this work that I believe in a creator. Call it *God* if you like: names are merely symbols for the people, places, things, or ideas which we are trying to describe. I find it highly doubtful that this *creator* has the same type of body that we do. Such a concept seems the height of egocentric anthropomorphism. It is analogous to thinking that the universe was made for tiny little man, and that our puny little planet, among seemingly infinite stars and planets, is on center stage for the entire production of everything.

This view obviously contradicts what is taught within various parts of Christian, and Hebrew scripture. Yet, despite what theologians may claim to the contrary, if one looks carefully, they will discover that the Bible and Tanakh even contradict with themselves on this subject. For example, consider how the anthropomorphized version of God is depicted as being *seen* by man in his supposedly male, humanoid form, in Genesis 17:1, 18:1, Exodus 6:23, 24:9-11, Numbers 12:68, and Acts 7:2. However, these works also tell us in no uncertain terms that man cannot *see* God and live, in verses such as Exodus 33:20, John 1:18, 5:37, 6:46, and 1 Timothy 6:15-16.

How do Christian and Jewish theologians compensate for these obvious contradictions? Christians, of course, use the magic pill of Trinity. Any seeming contradiction, where mankind is stated as being *unable* to see God, must be referring to only the "Father" leg of the triune God, while every instance of mankind being *able* to see God must be referring to either the "Holy Spirit," or more likely, the "Son" (i.e. Jesus).

At its simplest, Trinity is a denial of the supremacy of *logic* and *rationality*. If people can be made to concede to this view, that there are essentially times when the most logical and clear cause and effect relationships, indeed, when rationality itself may be ignored, then there is no longer an ability to reason with them. This is because, whenever the theological views of these people are debated and are ever shown to be weaker than an opposing view, they will simply invoke Trinity, to deny rationality altogether. They assume that, if God can defy cause and effect relationships once, then there is nothing preventing him from doing so in infinite instances. Trinity becomes a sort of "poster child" of the conquest of faith over logic and reason.

Thomas Jefferson, the brilliant American founding father, who later became the third president of the new nation, made this same point in a letter which he sent to a James Smith in 1822. In it, he stated, "In fact the Athanasian paradox that one is three, and three but one is so incomprehensible to the human mind that no candid man can say he has any idea of it, and how can he believe what presents no idea. He who thinks he does only deceives himself. He proves also that man, once surrendering his reason, has no remaining guard against absurdities the most monstrous, and like a ship without rudder is the sport of every wind. With such persons, gullibility, which they call faith, takes the helm from the hand of reason, and the mind becomes a wreck."[140]

Three cannot remain *three*, and yet also be *one* at the same time. *One* plus *one*, plus *one*, is always *three*, not sometimes both *one* and *three*. *One third*, plus *one third*, plus *one third*, is *one*. But Trinitarians will vehemently deny that this latter relationship is the one which describes the Trinity. They will insist that all three "heads" of the Trinity are simultaneously omnipotent, omniscient, and omnipresent.

The ironic part of this stance is that they also feel that the "Holy Spirit" is *subordinate* to the "Son," who is in turn *subordinate* to the "Father." Three different things cannot simultaneously be omnipotent. Either they will all have an equal, yet finite power, in that none is strong enough to subdue either of the other two, or one will be omnipotent and the other two will merely be potent.

Arius, in the few parts of his work, *Thalia*, that were inadvertently preserved by way of citation in Athanasius' condemnatory *Four Discourses Against the Arians,* also pointed out that if you have *two*, much less *three* beings who have no beginning and are equally potent, then you no longer have a *father* and *son* relationship, but instead, one of *brothers*.

Regarding omniscience, Jesus himself is recorded in scripture stating several times that there are things that he does not know, claiming that these things are only known by the "Father." Orthodox apologists rationalize these statements by claiming that Jesus was only referring to his level of knowledge while in human form. This is a massive assumption which somewhat implies that Jesus would be unaware of how his audience would understand his statements.

Regarding omnipresence, how could the "Son" (i.e. Jesus) be "sent" (John 3:16) and leave the "side" of the Father in heaven (Philemon 2:7), subsequently "returning" to "sit" (Hebrews 10:12) at his "right hand," (Colossians 3:1), if the "Son" is the same being as God, and therefore omnipresent? What is the meaning of movement and spatial orientation within the context of omnipresence? How could the "Son" or "Holy Spirit" ever be separated from, or "sit" at the "right hand" of the "Father," if all three are the same omnipresent being? These things are nonsensical impossibilities.

Whenever orthodox Christian leaders are challenged on issues of established religious doctrine, such as the belief in the Trinity, the approach which they commonly take is what many classical writers have called the "Schoolman," or "Grammarian" approach. In this approach, the general question is broken down into infinitesimally minute details, in order to break each more easily, as it is easier to break each individual *scion*, rather than a tightly bound *fasces*. During doctrinal debates, the orthodox camp will always fall back upon the guidance of certain key passages of scripture, which they claim support their position. If challenged on the meaning of these supporting passages, or whether they conflict with other sections of scripture, the orthodox camp applies the "grammarian" technique by dissecting the original language to a level of minuteness where none can claim to have any knowledge, but those who have spent decades studying little else; essentially unwrapping the bundle of sticks, in order to break each individually.

Initially, they might challenge the understanding of the passage as a whole. Should they fail at this, they sequentially fall back to challenges about various other details, such as the understanding of the phrases and words used, the cultures of the author and the target audience, etc. Anyone courageous enough to challenge them will be forced to descend further and further down this murky rabbit hole, either until the original question is lost sight of, and on all sides only murky uncertainty abounds, or until the challenger fatigues and abandons the discussion. The orthodox "schoolmen" will claim either of these scenarios as victories. This approach brings to mind the old Italian proverb: "A fool can ask more questions in an hour than a wise man can answer in seven years."[142]

Obviously, only one who is a linguistics expert in Hebrew, Koine Greek, Aramaic, and Chaldean, an archaeology and paleology expert, a philosophy, poetry, and prose expert, and a Syrian, European, Persian, Egyptian, Babylonian, Assyrian, Phoenician, Roman, and Jewish military, political, cultural, and history expert, all at the same time, could answer every single one of these questions with any sort of expertise. Orthodox "schoolmen" will claim that experts in all of these fields may be found within their camp. No single individual could be found who is an expert in all of these subjects at once; as such a feat would take multiple lifetimes. Instead, there is a separation of expertise among various individuals, some being the experts in one or two of these areas, and having a working knowledge of the rest. The Ph.D. in Koine Greek, for example, will rely upon the expertise of his colleague, who is an expert in Egyptian History, and vice versa.

Yet it is demanded of whomever opposes orthodox doctrines, that they be experts in all of these fields simultaneously, or be dismissed; a practical impossibility due to the shortness of a human lifespan. It does not matter if the heterodox party has more facts and a stronger position than his orthodox opponent. The latter can still invoke the names of a host of supporters, both living and dead, bristling with the armor of various degrees and titles in innumerable fields. He, or she may, or may not have any idea how solid the lines of reasoning of these various supporters are. All that matters to them is that they were considered orthodox by the church.

But why can those who propose heterodox views, such as the view that the concept of Trinity is incorrect, not name the same number of supporting authors? The reason is because, over the centuries, the writings of orthodox experts in these various fields have been strongly encouraged and preserved, while those of the heterodox have been condemned and repressed; often with the sword and the stake. Whole armies of monks, priests, and seminary professors have been enlisted to battle the heterodox views of the men whom they label as heretics.

Glancing back from the present day upon this sea of literature, all in seeming agreement on the issue of Trinity, the first thought which must occur within the mind of any rational person, is that any who would challenge the opinion of so many experts must either be mad, or staggeringly arrogant. This is, in fact, the exact opinion which the orthodox camp holds. Unfortunately, they are willfully ignorant of the well-known fact that history's conquerors also tend to write her history books; invariably painting their causes as the most just, and vilifying their opposition.

The seeming consensus among academic writings, prior to the mid-1700's, on the accuracy of Trinitarian doctrine is only superficial. It is due, in large part, to the fear that existed during the 1400 years between the reign of the Roman Emperor, Theodosius, and the freedom which was finally won by the Western world, as a result of the American and French revolutions. During this 1400-year period, writings which challenged orthodox Trinitarian views were overwhelmingly destroyed, placed on banned book lists, and prohibited from being composed or copied.

Orthodoxy forget, or never learned that the final decision for the Roman world to convert to a Trinitarian version of Christianity was not one born out of free and open discussion and a comparison of ideas; the most merit-worthy triumphing over the least. It was one which was initially decided by the sword. Thomas Jefferson mentioned this fact in one of the scathing, yet wisely unpublished criticisms of the orthodox concept of Trinity which he wrote.

"No historical fact is better established than that the doctrine of *one god*, pure and uncompounded was that of the early ages of Christianity; and was among the efficacious doctrines which gave it triumph over the polytheism of the ancients, sickened with the absurdities of their own theology. Nor was the unity of the supreme being ousted from the Christian creed by the force of reason, but by the *sword of civil government* wielded at the will of the fanatic Athanasius. The hocus-pocus phantasm of a god like another Cerberus with one body and three heads *had its birth and growth in the blood of thousands and thousands of martyrs.*"[140]

The "Sword of civil government," which Jefferson mentions here wasn't wielded directly by Athanasius. Instead, he influenced the Roman Emperors Constantine, and later Theodosius, to give bloody verdicts in his favor, regarding the religious debates over Trinity. Constantine ordered that Trinity was to be the official doctrine of the Roman Christian church, in his 325 A.D. edict following the Council of Nicaea, condemning the Unitarian doctrine of Arius as follows:

"...thus also now it seems good that Arius and the holders of his opinion should all be called Porphyrians, that he may be named by the name of those whose evil ways he imitates: And not only this, but also that *all the writings of Arius, wherever they be found, shall be delivered to be burned with fire*, in order that not only his wicked and evil doctrine may be destroyed, but also that the memory of himself and of his doctrine may be blotted out, that there may not by any means remain to him remembrance in the world. Now this also I ordain, that *if any one shall be found secreting any writing composed by Arius*, and shall not forthwith deliver up and burn it with fire, *his punishment shall be death*; for as soon as he is caught in this *he shall suffer capital punishment by beheading without delay.*"[143]

Never heard of Arius? Then Constantine was at least partially successful. Once this edict was issued, while men were being condemned and executed wholesale for attempting to preserve Arius' Unitarian book, *Thalia*, it is highly likely that other works which were critical of the Trinitarian doctrine would also be suppressed, generally by burning, or some other means of removal from the hands of the public. A substantial amount of extant literature which was critical of Trinity, or which proposed alternative concepts of God, would effectively be wiped out. In either instance, the vast majority of remaining works, those which were permitted to be promoted or copied, and therefore available to the public, would be those supportive of orthodox Trinitarian views.

For a brief period, after this edict and prior to the reign of Theodosius, this brutal practice of suppressing doctrinal dissent with threats of violence would be reversed, or at least slowed. This is because, in his later years, Constantine would grow increasingly tolerant of Arian views; to the point of eventually being baptized on his death bed by Eusebius, the Arian Bishop of Caesarea. After his death, the only one of Constantine's three sons to survive the bloody struggle for succession and empire was Constantius. Constantius was also an Arian, and would publicly support this form of Christianity; modifying the laws to reflect increasing tolerance towards this and other nonviolent faiths. Sozomen, in his *Ecclesiastical History*, notes that, "...*all the churches of the East*, *with the exception of that of Jerusalem, were in the hands of the Arians...*"[144] due to Constantius' efforts. The ecumenical Council of Tyre actually ruled in favor of Arius, and for a brief period, the entire Roman church had held non-Trinitarian doctrine to be orthodox.[145]

Unfortunately, all of this progress towards religious toleration was reversed under the reign of the Roman Emperor, Theodosius. This emperor issued death threats towards any who clung to Arian (i.e. Unitarian) views within the Western Roman world, and systematically disenfranchised and persecuted any who disagreed with the Trinitarian doctrine. The first of his series of cruel edicts was issued in 380 A.D.; threatening the torture, or death of any Roman who didn't profess the Trinitarian Nicene creed.

Again, from Sozomen: "The parents of Theodosius were Christians, and were attached to the Nicene (Trinitarian) doctrines...He also rejoiced at finding that the Arian heresy had not been received in Illyria. He inquired concerning the religious sentiments which were prevalent in the other provinces, and ascertained that, as far as Macedonia, one form of belief was universally predominant, which was, that the same homage ought to be rendered to God the Word, and to the Holy Ghost, as to God the Father; but that towards the East, and particularly at Constantinople (then the capital of the Roman Empire), the people were divided into many different sects (reflective of the religious tolerance prevalent in those areas)...Theodosius enacted a law at Thessalonica, which he caused to be published at Constantinople, that it might be thence transmitted to the remotest cities of his dominions...he enacted that the title of 'Catholic Church' should be exclusively confined to those who rendered equal homage to the Three Persons of the Trinity, and that those individuals who entertained opposite opinions should be treated as heretics, regarded with contempt, and delivered over to punishment."[146]

Non-Trinitarians, including Arians, attempted to use legal channels and public assemblies to voice their disapproval of this recent edict, yet all legal avenues were soon closed for protest. Theodosius published another edict that banned even the ability to discuss the validity of Trinity. Per Sozomen, "The emperor was henceforward less disposed to hold intercourse with heretics; and he enacted a law by which he prohibited, under the severest penalties, all public disputes, assemblies, or disputations concerning the Divine substance and nature."[146]

From this point forward, the subject of Trinity was no longer open for debate. Fear, prison, and death reigned and silenced all critics. All writings that did not support the official Trinitarian view would soon slip from existence, as men would be afraid to make copies of them and the existing ones would eventually crumble and decay with age. Ironically, the future conquerors of the Western Empire, the Goths, had been converted to Christianity by Unitarian missionaries.

Though Christianity promotes itself today as being the religion of *mercy* and *love*, even until the mid-1600's, in England and many other Western European nations, men such as Edward Wightman were burned to death for denying the Trinity. Wightman himself is only remembered, among the countless nameless others, because he was the last man in England to be officially burned to death. Besides the obvious, what makes Wightman's execution particularly appalling, is the fact that the man who personally condemned Wightman to be burned was none other than the very same *King James* who commissioned the famous translation of the Bible which bears his name. What a horrible punishment to inflict upon someone simply because they courageously stood up for what they knew to be true. It is said that during his execution, Wightman began screaming incoherently. Thinking he wished to recant, his executioners extinguished the flames. When it was discovered that this was not the case, the flames were rekindled and he was burned for a second and final time.

Fear of Catholic, Anglican, and even Calvinist churches which retained the power to influence their civil governments to inflict such tortures upon men, had a profound chilling effect upon things which were written, spoken, and publicly performed by all but the bravest of men. A few examples of these brave exceptions are Michael Servetus, Giordano Bruno, William Penn, and Isaac Newton. Michael Servetus was condemned and burned alive in 1553, by the public influence of the patriarch of Calvinism, John Calvin, for Servetus' controversial work, *On the Errors of the Trinity*.[147] Servetus' corrected translation of the *Santes Pagnini* Bible was even tied to him and used as kindling. Giordano Bruno was burned alive by the Inquisition in 1600 for various allegations, one of which was holding opinions contrary to the Catholic Trinitarian doctrine. Early American, William Penn, who was originally granted the area of land later to be named Pennsylvania, was imprisoned in the Tower of London from 1668-1669, merely for publishing a pamphlet critical of Trinity entitled "The Sandy Foundation Shaken."[148] Isaac Newton wrote several unpublished theological notebooks critical of orthodoxy, and especially the doctrine of Trinity, such as one entitled *Paradoxical Questions Concerning the Morals and Actions of Athanasius & his Followers*.[149] Newton likely elected not to publish these notebooks, due to his awareness of the significant personal risk involved in doing so.

It is believed by the majority of scholars that this orthodox hegemony of public debate began to collapse in the 1500's, with the advent of the Guttenberg Press. Though the creation of the printing press began eroding the joint ecclesiastical, and governmental grip over information, publishers were still held liable for the works they printed. Should they print heterodox, or banned works, they could face severe fines, or even imprisonment.

It was not until after the American Revolution in the colonies of the "New World," and the French Revolution, in the old, that this climate of fear began to change. Indeed, a contributing cause of both revolutions was frustration over the lack of not merely political, but religious freedom. Though these two revolutions occurred in the late 1700's, it took until the mid 1800's before this new freedom of open debate on sensitive religious and political views had finally been memorialized within the bulk of Western law. This delay was partially due to the time it took for these new ideas of freedom to spread across Europe during the Napoleonic Wars; which they in part spawned.

Religious literature which was written during the period between these twin revolutions and perhaps the early 1900's, when the plague of atheistic Bolshevism began to infect the world, possesses a level of excitement, intelligence, and optimism which was seldom encountered earlier, and is certainly rarely encountered today. These people were excited about their newly won freedom to seek after God and develop their nations in the manner which their consciences directed them to.

Once laws prohibiting the public admission of heterodox views had been mostly relaxed in, or removed from Western society, men ceased feeling the obligation to dedicate their time and resources to religious organizations and principles which they did not really support. This resulted in a mass exodus from the churches, of those people who had previously only attended because attending was what one had to do in order to avoid legal trouble, or social stigmatization.

This exodus continued to the point where, in most Christian Churches today, the few people who continue to attend are generally those who don't really pay much attention to doctrine. Of course, there are a few rare exceptions to this rule. Some Christians remain passionate about their faith, and diligently study scripture, ecclesiastical history, and their denomination's doctrine. Unfortunately, these types are extremely rare. Most modern Christian churches have become a sort of *country club*, where members can go to hear feel good pop psychology veiled in religious phraseology, in ever so small doses, while also gaining access to often beautiful facilities and coordinated social events. This tends to be especially true within the large Southern "mega-churches."

I remember the night, while studying these things long after my wife and children were asleep, when I first reached the then startling conclusion that the orthodox Christian concept of a triune god was incorrect. Being a Christian at the time, I spent perhaps the next 6 months studying this subject almost exclusively, from several different angles, in order to be sure that I wasn't mistaken about it. During this period, I was frequently shocked at the new historical and philosophical facts that I continued to discover, causing me to question doctrines which I had accepted since learning them during my childhood.

Wanting to understand the counterpoint to the trinitarian argument, as it was presented within the earliest ecumenical councils, I at one point attempted to reconstruct the major lines of reasoning from Arius' original unitarian work, *Thalia*. As mentioned earlier, Constantine had ordered all extant copies of this work to be burned in the 4th century. A substantial amount of quotations from it had inadvertently been preserved, however, while being condemned, within Athanasius' *Four Discourses Against the Arians*.[141] I worked at this reconstruction for some time, until I was eventually forced to set it aside due to work and family demands.

While working on it, I was extremely excited about my efforts. I naïvely thought that I had stumbled upon crucial information which modern Catholics and Protestants had been misinformed about, through no fault of their own, and that these people would share in my enthusiasm if only made aware of my discoveries. I couldn't have been more wrong. During church group meetings, or Sunday school classes, whenever I would defend a heterodox position in the presence of church leaders, I would immediately find that I had become marked as a pariah. On more than one occasion, this even resulted in my being asked by these church leaders to find another church.

The laypeople within these churches, instead of being happy to be shown their doctrinal and historical errors and appreciating me as one who cared enough to share these facts with them, generally responded with either condescending smiles, or concerned glances, and then withdrew from me as from a leaper. These people generally had good intentions, but like good sheep, were simply wanting to avoid appearing to be associated with, or supportive of someone whom their church leadership disapproved of. Most people are unwilling to risk their economic, political, or social status on the public recognition of abstract philosophical principles which they barely understand, and therefore generally fall in line with whatever are seen as "socially appropriate" orthodox views, levels of religious commitment, and enthusiasm.

Some of these church members began to request that I not share heterodox beliefs on subjects such as Trinity while at church. In order to avoid putting these friendships at risk, I agreed, but this prevented me from developing new friendships there myself, as true friendships require a certain level of trust which is born from openness about, and acceptance of one's views. These are the water and light which nourish that precious plant.

This is part of the reason why drinkers tend to have many friends. The decreased inhibition caused by the alcohol makes these people say and do things, though often stupid or corrupt things, which they are truly thinking about, or desire to do, yet which they would generally keep hidden when sober. Those who drink with them are generally also more accepting of these revelations of stupid, or corrupt thoughts and actions, than they typically would be when sober. While this may indeed be conducive to the growth of *trust* and *acceptance*, it is often at the very great risk of an overall decrease in *morality*, *intellect*, and *health*.

During this time, I continued to attend church, however, as I continued to read, I began to grow ever more discontent when thinking about all of the logical flaws, ethical contradictions, and subtle manipulations which I had encountered in scripture, that everyone seemed to excuse, ignore, or were simply ignorant of. My faith in the Christian religion was slowly dying, however, like a dying animal, it did so in convulsions and rallies. The event which seemed to make the prognosis noticeably worse occurred when my continuing studies caused me to become acutely sensitive to each and every divinely sanctioned killing of an innocent which I encountered within scripture.

Several of these gross injustices were brought to my attention during my reading of Thomas Paine's short philosophical work, *The Age of Reason*: a work which should be mandatory reading for all Christians.[70] After pondering the few examples which this brilliant man pointed out, ever more began to spring to mind. A few of the literally dozens of examples which could be provided to illustrate this are the killing of the Egyptian firstborn for the sins of the Pharaoh (Exodus 11); the killing of the Canaanite women, children, and elderly (Numbers 21:2-3, Deuteronomy 20:17, Joshua 6:17, 21); the destruction of any women, children, and elderly in Sodom, Gomorrah, and the supposed entirety of the antediluvian world (Genesis 18-19); the killing of David's son, which was born due to, and killed as a punishment for, David's infidelity with Bathsheba (2 Samuel 12:14-21); the hanging of David's innocent stepsons to remove the plague occasioned by God against innocent Israelites, for a crime which Saul supposedly committed (2 Samuel 21:1-14); the brutal butchery of the defenseless, captive Midianite women and children by the armies of Moses and Joshua, at the supposed command of God (Numbers 31:1-24); the slaughter of the Israelite women, children, and elderly by the Levites at Moses' command, when he first descended from Mount Horeb (Exodus 32:25-28); the widespread plague visited upon the innocent Israelites for David's supposed sin of taking a census (2 Samuel 24:15); the Earth's supposed swallowing of the wife and children of Dathan, for his challenging of Moses' authority (Numbers 16:25-34); innocents among the entire towns which David treacherously extirpated while living with the Philistines (1 Samuel 27:9); and many others.

It is shocking how most Christians are either unaware of these scriptural atrocities (likely because few of them ever actually read the Old Testament) or are desensitized to them. The more that one continues to study the great "heroes" of the Old Testament, men such as David, Moses, and Solomon, the less these men seem to be wise, good, or men "after God's own heart," and the more they begin to appear as hopelessly corrupt, avaricious, and remorseless butchers and tyrants, disturbingly similar in character to Mohammed. As this begins to occur, the substantial portions of scripture which celebrate the teachings, or exploits of these men will turn sour and repulsive in the mind of the reader.

I was truly amazed that I had glossed over, or excused these injustices and atrocities to myself for so many years, without being offended at the monstrous colors which they painted God in. Could no one comprehend the actual horror, injustice, and savagery of these acts? Were they blind? These brutalities were often described within scripture as being inflicted indiscriminately upon women, children, and the elderly. Only a *fool* could ever rationalize such acts as just. Yet they must be just, or else they could not have been performed, or commanded by a perfect God. Exactly. They weren't.

When I would mention these things to Christians, the responses which I received back were generally absurd statements, such as, "The finite mind of man cannot know the infinite mind of God...It doesn't matter if they die and go to a better place, since we all have to die...Everything God decides to do is just, since he is above morals...Their deaths were the purest justice, since all of the people whom God killed, he had already judged as deserving of death." The lunacy of these various responses left me reeling. Could such gross error live within the minds of people whom I knew to be otherwise quite rational?

Regarding finite man being unable to know the infinite mind of God, this was a "strawman fallacy" of the grossest sort. One does not have to be omniscient in order to be able to sense when certain acts are morally right, or wrong. If man cannot know with absolute certainty that the butchery of infants is a moral wrong, then he cannot be confidant about any moral truth.

I began to realize that there were two major contradicting concepts within scripture which applied to this issue; replete with their list of supporting verses. One camp claimed that guilt for sin was *shared* by family and fellow citizens. According to this view, God was justified in condemning and subsequently slaughtering the *whole* of a people for the actions of any *one* of them. An example verse aligning with this camp is Numbers 14:18: "The Lord is longsuffering and abundant in mercy, forgiving iniquity and transgression; but He by no means clears the guilty, visiting the iniquity of the fathers on the children to the third and fourth generation."

The second camp held the more morally and logically developed view, that each person is responsible for their own words, thoughts, or actions. An example verse from this camp is Ezekiel 18:19-20. "Yet you say, 'Why should the son not bear the guilt of the father?' Because the son has done what is lawful and right, and has kept all my statutes and observed them, he shall surely live. *The soul who sins shall die.* The son shall not bear the guilt of the father, nor the father bear the guilt of the son. The righteousness of the righteous shall be upon himself, and the wickedness of the wicked shall be upon himself." Sections of this Ezekiel 18 passage are also found echoed in Jeremiah 31; implying that one of these authors was likely quoting from, or paraphrasing the other.

If the verses mentioned in Ezekiel 18 are correct, as the common human sense of justice confirms them to be, then not only is a son guiltless of the sins of his father, but he is also guiltless of the sins of his grandfather, his great-grandfather, and his ancient ancestors; including the mythical "original sins" of Adam and Eve.

As I abandoned these flawed views, I sought for improved ones to fill the vacuum. I began by reading the writings of the church fathers, moved into histories, studied the works of various philosophers, read the primary sacred texts of many ancient religions, followed by a period where I read nothing but occult works, trying to see what the "boogey man" in the closet really looked like. I eventually moved into a systematic reading of the outstanding *Harvard Classics*, and *Britannica Great Works of the Western World* sets. Over time, I found myself drawn towards the more noble depictions of a truly just God which I discovered among Stoic, Platonic, Aristotelian, and Enlightenment Era philosophers. This type of philosophy has the wholesome effect of inspiring a reliance upon one's internal sense of justice, which is but the voice of one's own conscience.

When I discussed this growing love of and immersion in the cleansing waters of philosophy with Christians, several had the audacity to quote Colossians 2:8 to me; where Paul warns believers to, "See to it that no one takes you captive through hollow and deceptive philosophy, which depends on human tradition and the basic principles of this world rather than on Christ." I was taken aback by this. It is the most stupid of doctrines to warn men away from philosophy, which literally means the love of wisdom, as there are as many different philosophies as there are cities. While some philosophical views may be hopelessly corrupt, others are tremendously noble and profound. Religion itself is but a specific set of philosophical views regarding the metaphysical nature of the universe; of which both man and God are parts.

The duty of the aspiring philosopher is to develop a keen internal sense of what is instinctively known to be both true and good. This will enable him, or her to fearlessly review any written work; retaining any truths encountered therein, like gems, and discarding the rest, like worthless soil.

Through study, I soon grew confident that I could disagree with scripture on the many points which portrayed God in the impious light of a monster, and yet continue to believe in God and love him. This position, as well as my refusal to be silent about my views when asked, severely damaged my relationships with many of the more devout Christians whom I knew. So be it. I held to a higher concept of God and refused to sacrifice either logic, or confidence in my instinctive, God-given sense of right, wrong, goodness, and justice.

This recoiling of Christian acquaintances was often accompanied by absurd claims that I was now an "atheist," or had "fallen away from God." This was anything but true. Now that I knew that he was neither unjust, nor a butcher, I loved God all the more. These accusations brought to mind a quote which I had previously picked up from Albert Pike's extremely powerful Masonic work, *Morals and Dogma*. In this work, Pike states that, "For the most part, men do not in their hearts believe that God is either just or merciful. They fear and shrink from his lightnings and dread His wrath. For the most part, they only think they believe that there is another life, a judgment, and a punishment for sin. Yet they will none the less persecute as Infidels and Atheists those who do not believe what they themselves imagine they believe, and which yet they do not believe, because it is incomprehensible to them in their ignorance and want of intellect...As the world grows in its development, it necessarily outgrows its ancient ideas of God, which were only temporary and provisional. A man who has a higher conception of God than those about him, and who denies that their conception *is* God, is very likely to be called an Atheist by men who are really far less believers in a God than he. Thus, the Christians, who said the Heathen idols were no Gods, were accounted Atheists by the People, and accordingly put to death; and Jesus of Nazareth was crucified as an unbelieving blasphemer, by the Jews."[26]

Christianity

I commence this section with some trepidation, in that I do not want the reader to think that I am simply another vulgar atheist whose overall goal is to lampoon and discredit all aspects of the Christian faith, and those Christians who claim it. I am not an atheist, and this is absolutely not my intent.

The majority of Christians are generally good-hearted, well intentioned people, who are often among the best of mankind. Many aspects of the Christian faith, such as their views on forgiveness, mercy, and love, are far in advance of those of other faiths; such as Judaism, Islam, Buddhism, and Hinduism. Regardless of this, Christianity has some fundamental flaws which must be boldly faced.

To begin with, let's analyze both how and why the typical non-Christian elects to convert to Christianity. Generally, people become Christians after another Christian "witnesses" to them: that is, convinces them to believe that Jesus is the son of God, that his crucifixion atones for the sin of mankind, and that they accept him as their "Lord" (i.e. ruler), as a loyal peasant would in vassalage to a feudal King. This "witnessing" can occur between the non-Christian and one, or several Christians, or even between a non-Christian and an information medium which transmits a Christian message, such as a book (e.g. the Bible), pamphlet, television show, movie, song, or play. Once the non-Christian is convinced that Jesus is the son of God, and places his, or her life under Jesus's authority (and that of Christian leadership by proxy), they are said to be "saved" from an afterlife of eternal damnation and torment in a place called "hell." Instead, they are promised an afterlife in a paradise known as "heaven."

Regardless of whether Jesus was, or was not actually the son of God, his value to Christians, what makes him different from other philosophers, or religious teachers, is this supposed ability to *save* people who dedicate their lives to him, from hell. Jesus is intimately bound up with the idea of *hell* in scripture. Without hell, he becomes unnecessary. With nothing to *save* mankind from, there is no need for a *savior*.

Here is where we encounter one of the first fundamental flaws of the Christian faith. Typically, the first objective in Christian witnessing is to convince the listener that the default doom for all of mankind is an afterlife of eternal punishment in hell, and that Christians are the only ones who are saved from this horrible fate, by exception.

In order to convince the non-Christian of this, Christians inform them that the human soul is hopelessly corrupted, sinful, and evil in its natural state. In fine, the first task of Christians is to convince non-Christians how morally *corrupt* they are. This is typically not a difficult task to accomplish, given that everyone carries around with them memories of certain thoughts, words, or actions which their consciences condemn them for. Typically, we generate 2, or 3 of these guilt sources before we have even had our morning coffee.

The common reply is, "What if my sins aren't that bad?" The response which Christian leaders typically give to this question is that all sins are equally worthless when compared to the infinite goodness of God. This view has the unfortunate effect of destroying all moral gradation; reducing all to a binary of goodness and badness. Under this theory, there is no better, or worse, but instead only the absolutely perfect and the absolutely worthless. This has the additional effect of also destroying any gradation between the various context specific synonyms for goodness and badness. Things such as absolute justice, truth, beauty, courage, and nobility, become only one step removed from absolute injustice, lies, ugliness, cowardice, and ignobility.

Such a binary view of virtue makes the committal of even the most minor of offenses, such as sneaking a cookie without permission as a child, into the moral equivalent of the most flagrant of them, such as genocide. The destruction of gradation of offense also results in the inability to appropriately determine, or apply justice. This is due to the fact that perfectly applied justice demands a balance of the severity of the punishment with the severity of the offense. If all offenses are equally and absolutely bad, from cookie sneaking, to genocide, then the worst of punishments can be decreed for any one of them; up to and including eternal torment. This is the reason why Christians can, with a straight face, tell you that God is justified for sending men to be eternally tormented in hell for committing even the most minor of sins, should these people die without bending the knee to Jesus.

Is it any wonder that corporal (i.e. bodily) discipline of Children, frequently crosses the line into abuse within highly devout Christian households? Indeed, there is a strong correlation between the level of devotion of the parents, and the severity of this type of "discipline." The Christian faith warps these people's judgement, and therefore frequently makes them incompetent disciplinarians. If any wrongdoing by a child can be called a *sin*, and since all *sin* is believed to be morally equivalent, then any severity of punishment is always justified, even the most extreme.

Consider the following, supposedly "perfect" guidance which the Bible provides on the topic. "He who spares his rod hates his son, but he who loves him disciplines him promptly" (Proverbs 13:24). "Do not withhold correction from a child, for if you beat him with a rod, he will not die. You shall beat him with a rod, and deliver his soul from hell." (Proverbs 23:13-14). Basing their actions upon ridiculous verses such as these, how many otherwise devout Christian parents literally attempt to "beat the hell" out of their unfortunate and typically defenseless children.

Though Christianity is being critiqued here, it should be noted that the other Mosaic faiths, both Judaism and Islam, are even worse about this child abuse. For example, as can be seen in Deuteronomy 21:18-21 of both the Christian Old Testament and the Jewish Tanakh, the Mosaic law even allowed parents to have any children, whom they considered disobedient, brutally stoned to death. Knowing how shocking the concept of *pedicide* is to the modern mind, hosts of Christian apologists and Rabbis have attempted to rationalize this passage into a sort of hyperbole. This is disingenuous. This passage was completely literal when originally codified, and was likely inflicted frequently.

Little needs to be said about Islam. Beatings of children are specifically allowed within this faith, especially and explicitly to force children to learn the Koran. In addition, Muslim men across the world frequently perform what are called "Honor killings"; murdering their own children for such petty things as changing their faith, or refusing an arranged marriage.

But returning from this digression, another response which is commonly made to the Christian claim that all of mankind is deserving of hell, is, "But what about infants? Surely they are innocent." Here is where it really gets interesting. Not only are men told that they are condemned for their own sins, but even if they can bring up no wrongdoing within their recent memory, surely a rarity, they are told that they are already guilty of someone else's sin; that the entire human race is in a state of wholesale condemnation because of an act which was supposedly committed, shortly after the creation of the Earth, by the first man, Adam, and the first woman, Eve.

"But surely if I am trying to seek God by being virtuous, he will accept that," one will ask.

Not according to scripture. Christians show people who make such a claim degrading verses such as Isaiah 64:6, which says that all mankind are "like an unclean thing, and all (their) righteousnesses are like filthy rags." Never mind the fact that this verse is taken out of context and was originally meant to apply to a certain people, within a specific scenario and context. Today it is used within Christendom to imply that even the utmost efforts by the devout are worthless in the eyes of a God who cannot tolerate even the slightest stain of sin in his presence.

Only when "covered" by the salvific blood of Christ, do Christians believe that people have any goodness, and therefore value. This low view which Christians have of themselves, they inevitably project onto others.

"If I am full of sin and worthless in the eyes of God without Christ, then so is everyone else," they tend to think.

This perspective drives a wedge between their relationships with non-Christians. Even if Christians are completely professional in their dealings with non-Christians, such a low view of them cannot but leak out through things such as word selection, avoidance, eye contact, micro-expressions, and other forms of body language. When non-Christians pick up on this opinion about themselves, they are generally insulted, further destroying whatever relationship exists between the two types.

This occurs too frequently to be coincidental. The only time that it tends not to occur is when the person whom the devout Christian is interacting with is either insincere, or uneducated about his, or her own faith, and therefore open to proselytism. This relationship destroying effect of the Christian faith tends to be strongest when Christians are faced with those who are well educated in Christianity, perhaps having even previously been Christians themselves, and yet having outgrown and rejected that faith due to philosophical, moral, or logical problems which they discovered within it.

Towards these, devout Christians generally tend to feel a mixture of betrayal, pity, and often even resentment. It is not without reason that they tend to feel this way, as this view is not only recommended, but commanded within scripture. It would be simple to identify dozens of Old Testament examples where this was true for the old Jewish faith, which Christianity was built upon, however one might think that this would not be the case in the more mercy heavy and doctrinally mature New Testament. Unfortunately, this is not the case. One example of many, which in no uncertain terms heaps reproach upon any who leave the Christian faith, is enough to prove this point.

Consider Hebrews 6:48: "For it is impossible for those who were once enlightened, and have tasted the heavenly gift, and have become partakers of the Holy Spirit, and have tasted the good word of God and the powers of the age to come, if they fall away, to renew them again to repentance, since they crucify again for themselves the Son of God, and put him to open shame. For the Earth which drinks in the rain that often comes upon it, and bears herbs useful for those by whom it is cultivated, receives blessing from God; but if it bears thorns and briers, it is rejected and near to being cursed, whose end is to be burned."

In other words, "Don't ever turn away from the Christian faith or you will never be able to return." What a wonderful threat to issue to your religious adherents in the first place. What a great way to keep them perpetually on their guard, fearful that they may be eternally damned, if logic, or reason place doubts about their faith into their heads.

Notice the not so subtle trope at the end of this section which likens those who have "fallen away" from the Christian faith to cultivated land which bears thorns and briers rather than useful herbs. These people are threatened with burning. This is an allusion to eternal burning in the lake of fire. This fire, scripture informs us, has been carefully prepared by the perfect and good God, so that he can use it to exact his brutal vengeance on the damned for all of eternity.

This is the ugly, brutal, and threatening face of the Christian faith which hides beneath the kind and merciful mask of Christ. It is only for the rare, mature Christian, one who has not abdicated his or her right to reason, that the rank contents of this Trojan horse, the sour pit of this appealing fruit, actually comes into focus. All of mankind love what Christ is supposed to epitomize: the archetype of mercy, love, goodness, and compassion. Unfortunately, of the masses of the faithful, only a handful have ever taken a sufficient look beneath the surface of Christian doctrine to get a clear view of the darker ice which forms its foundation, and lifts this snow-white tip of the iceberg above the waters.

The superstructure which the Christian faith is built upon is that of the brutish ancient Hebrew faith. Accepting Christianity is, in essence, giving a passive nod and a wink to all of the ignorant brutality found in the latter: such as slavery, concubinism, brutal wars of extirpation, and unjust laws which condemn people, sometimes to death, for often trivial offenses.

People generally and willingly accept the good things which they find in scripture without realizing all of the bad which make the good requisite. In order to believe that Christ did indeed perform the noble act of casting out demons and healing those whose maladies are due to their influence, one must first be taught to believe that God not only made, but also allows a veritable host of evil spirits, complete with a malevolent ruler, who is implied within scripture to be second in power only to God, to torment both man and beast.

In order to believe that Jesus' cruel and pain filled death on the cross atoned for the sin of mankind, one must first be taught to believe that, when offended, God is only appeased, like Moloch of old, with death and a blood offering, whether from man or beast. While this may seem extreme, there is evidence that causes the majority of archaeologists to believe that the animal sacrifice which occurred within the Hebrew temples was an accommodation used to lessen the innate horror of previous human sacrifice. This progression from human to animal, as the culture advanced, was actually not that uncommon in the ancient world. Several cultures, such as the Egyptians, Greeks, Carthaginians, Phoenicians, and even Romans progressed this way.

Traces of these old practices of human sacrifice may still be found in scripture; such as in Judges 11:29-40, where Jephthah kills and makes a burnt offering of his daughter to the God of the Jews. This is painted as a tragedy, in that Jephthah makes a rash promise before the battle to sacrifice "whatever comes out of the door of my house to meet me when I return in triumph..." and is greeted, of course, by his daughter.

The way that this passage is written seems to actually be a poorly fabricated excuse for what was likely a human sacrifice that was known to have been performed by one of the Hebrew folk heroes. Why would anyone ever make the statement that they would sacrifice the first thing that came out of the door of their house to greet them when they return unless they already had human sacrifice in mind. Again, we have the story of Abraham being commanded by God to sacrifice his son Isaac as a burnt offering, and then being miraculously prevented from doing so at the last moment in Genesis 22:1-19. Who was with them on the mountain to record this conversation? This is another likely artifact of known cases of human sacrifice in the worship of Jehovah by Abraham himself, or during the supposed Abrahamic era, that has been modified to fit the more *cultured* ears of the Hebrew authors who penned scripture during the Babylonian exile.

Why must we believe that God cannot be placated without death and blood? Are we to believe that God is powerful enough to create all matter, and yet is so weak that he cannot nobly forgive an offense without demanding corporal or capital punishment for it. Even a 5-year-old knows that forgiveness is the nobler of the two actions. Are we to believe that the mixture of water, plasma, and blood cells have magical, sin absolving powers? What if we give the lamb a lot of coffee that morning and its blood is highly caffeinated. Will it then absolve sins faster?

Christians believe that all sacrifice is actually symbolic foreshadowing of the "atoning blood of Christ," and therefore that it wasn't actually the death, or blood of the animal which atoned for sin in the Old Testament. Instead, they believe that it was the spirit of repentance within the sacrificer which did so. This does not make the death, blood, and pain any less real for the victim. If all is symbolism, why sacrifice at all? If portions of scripture, which describe God's compassion for the lives of animals, are correct, then how are these to be reconciled with this superfluous suffering, and the sacrifice of so many precious, innocent lives? Consider Matthew 10:29: "Are not two sparrows sold for a farthing? And one of them shall not fall on the ground without your Father." Or perhaps Proverbs 12:10: "The righteous care for the needs of their animals, but the kindest acts of the wicked are cruel."

In addition, it should be observed that the primary act for which the Christian is "saved" from supposed damnation is one which they actually have absolutely *no* control over; that of *believing* that Jesus was and is the son of God. This *belief* is what they are supposedly rewarded with absolution from sin and eternal paradise for; rather than eternal torment. Yet, and I cannot say this more strongly: we have zero voluntary control over our beliefs. Pause and consider that last statement for a moment, because, though it may run contrary to popular opinion, it is true nonetheless.

Let's do a thought experiment. Believe that you did not read my last sentence. Just do it for perhaps 5 minutes. Before you read the next paragraph, simply stop believing that I ever said that we have no control over our beliefs. You can even look away from this text if it helps you to concentrate.

Any luck? Unless you are strung out on some sort of mind altering chemical, then you were unable to. Why is this? It is because the mind does not *actively* believe things, it *passively* does. Like a calculator that is fed numbers and returns a result, belief is the result which the mind adopts after being fed facts, or what it assumes, correctly or incorrectly, to be facts.

Can people mistakenly believe falsities to be facts and develop mistaken beliefs as a result? Certainly. It happens all of the time. The existence of Islam and the Mormon faith are prime examples of this phenomenon. Yet once even these people are provided with enough evidence for them to realize the falsity of their previously accepted ideas, they do not *actively* decide to abandon the false positions and accept the true ones. This occurs automatically. The moment the scale of evidence passes the level mark and begins to lean towards the other side, the mind *immediately* adopts the view that is perceived to be more accurate and adjusts all associated and resulting beliefs accordingly. Given that each person has their own unique mix of facts and falsities about various issues stored within their memory, this specific required level of evidence will vary according to each individual, but for all mentally healthy individuals, belief will automatically occur once this point is reached.

So why are we expected to believe that people would ever receive the reward of eternal bliss, or the punishment of eternal torment, or annihilation for something which they cannot control? Should we be rewarded for our hair growing, or be damned for sweating when hot? Of course not. There was no merit-worthy decision made in the performance of these bodily functions.

In like manner, no merit-worthy involvement of our will occurs during the automatic act of belief. Our will, not our actions, is what defines the virtue, or vice of our character. Paraphrasing a section from Boswell's, *The Life of Doctor Samuel Johnson*: if I try to smash a poor man's head by hurling a sack of gold coins at it, and he takes these and betters his life with them, am I to be praised?[150] Noble actions may reflect noble character and will, as ignoble actions may reflect ignoble character and will, however this is not always the case.

How many good men have willed to help the suffering, but have found themselves unable to, due to a circumstantial limitation of means? How many others are willing to cut your throat and plunder all that you possess, but are only prevented because, again, circumstances have not brought them a clear means of effecting this will. Is a man who would help, but cannot, not to be accounted good, in that he has a will which would produce good actions, had he but the means? Is the man who would harm, but cannot, not to be accounted bad, in that he has a will which would produce bad actions, had he but the means? The will is what matters, not any chance outcome. It is the purest expression of our character.

I recall reading once where a philosopher stated that a man typically becomes a thief in his heart long before chance and circumstance have brought him any opportunity to effect his first theft. It is when he begins to justify and will the theft, that his character has already become that of a thief. Scripture echoes this view, but generally refers to the will as the "heart." Consider Proverbs 4:23: "Keep your *heart* with all diligence, for out of it spring the issues of life." Additional verses supporting this view of the will being the critical element for virtue can be found in Matthew 5:21-30, Matthew 15:18-20, Mark 7:21-23, and 1 John 3:15.

This is one of the reasons why violent and profane video games are so damaging to personal character. People spend hours a day on certain video games, where they practice and justify their *will* to participate in any number of vices, from murder, to theft, to whoremongering. They then foolishly think that once the power switch is turned off, all of this exercise of the will evaporates, with no lingering effect on character. Have they never heard the saying, "Practice makes perfect?" They are perfecting their corruption through practice.

A similar effect occurs with exposure to violent and profane movies and music. People spend hours listening to musicians sing, or rap about their vices, or watching actors mimic the performance of vices on their screens, and then walk away believing that this has no negative impact upon their will and character. Have they never heard the well-known saying that, "Bad company corrupts good character?" These people are essentially spending time in bad company whenever they allow these degenerates to speak, sing, or rap their corrupt messages into their ears, or dance and act them into their eyes.

Darkness

Fear of darkness is common within young children. Those children who are brought up in any of the various Mosaic faiths, however, often have an exceptional fear of it, due to the various superstitions which they are taught by their generally well-intentioned, pious parents. Christian children, for example, are taught that a purely evil being named *Satan*, second in power only to God himself, was beaten in a failed attempt upon God's kingdom, cast down upon the Earth, and currently roams the shadows searching for victims. This battle and its result are described in the Biblical book of Revelation.

"And war broke out in heaven: Michael and his angels fought with the dragon; and the dragon and his angels fought, but they did not prevail, nor was a place found for them in heaven any longer. So the great dragon was cast out, that serpent of old, called the Devil and Satan, who deceives the whole world; he was cast to the earth, and his angels were cast out with him...Therefore rejoice, O heavens, and you who dwell in them! Woe to the inhabitants of the Earth and the sea! For the devil has come down to you, having great wrath, because he knows that he has a short time'" (Revelations 12:7-12).

Due to Satan's dangerous presence on Earth, the Apostle, Peter, warned men to, "Be sober-minded and alert. Your adversary the devil prowls around [on Earth] like a roaring lion, seeking someone to devour" (1 Peter 5:8).

Cast out along with Satan, theoretically also to infest Earth, were his malevolent legion of demons. These *demons* were formerly the third of the "myriad" of heavenly angels who had joined Satan in his rebellion against God. Theoretically, these demons retained their formerly angelic supernatural powers; powers which far exceed the petty strength of humans. Scripture teaches that these demons can not only attack and harm men directly, but that they can also take "possession" of men's bodies and minds; using them for sinister ends.

But man, in actuality, had no need for this help. Christianity teaches that the natural state of the hearts of mankind is one of abject corruption and evil. In fact, Christians are told that, due to the sin of Adam, all of nature, whether animal, mineral, ocean, or clouds, all was corrupted and could at times be subject to the influence of Satan and his minions. Some examples of this are the tempting "serpent" in the garden of Eden, in Genesis 3:1, the demons in the swine, in Matthew 8:28-34, the winds and waves attempting to drown Jesus and his apostles while they sail, in Mark 4:35-41, Satan causing the wind to blow the house down upon Job's children, in Job 1:18-19, etc.

In addition to these threats, Christians are taught that, according to prophesy, evil forces will prevail upon the earth, immediately prior to Christ's return, causing most Christians to be butchered by evil, demonically influenced people. This slaughter will supposedly be so great that, "If those days had not been cut short, nobody would be saved. But for the sake of the elect, those days will be shortened" (Matthew 24:22).

What a wonderful picture of the world to paint for children: a place teeming with hordes of invisible, malevolent demons who swarm in the shadows, accompanied by their *King*, who is only slightly weaker than God; a place where these agents of evil manipulate nations, people, animals, and elements like puppets; a place filled with naturally evil people, some of whom are "demon possessed"; a place where the God of the universe allows good people to be slaughtered en masse, until only a small group of "the elect" remains.

It is no wonder that these children and youth are often filled with exceptional terror of the dark. Throughout scripture, darkness not only symbolizes *evil*, but is often described as evil's proper *kingdom*. Consider the following verses, for example: "But the sons of the kingdom (i.e. those denied entry into heaven) will be cast out into outer *darkness*. There will be weeping and gnashing of teeth" (Matthew 8:12). "He has delivered us from the power of *darkness* and conveyed us into the kingdom of the Son of His love" (Colossians 1:13). "Then the fifth angel poured out his bowl on the throne of the beast, and his kingdom became full of *darkness*; and they gnawed their tongues because of the pain" (Rev 16:10).

When told about my fear of the dark, my stepfather, who meant well, told me to sing a song he knew, which was taken directly from Isaiah 12:2. The words went as follows: "Behold, the Lord is my salvation, I shall trust, and will not be afraid, for the Lord my God is my strength and my shield, he also has become my salvation." I remember quietly mumbling those words to myself when stuck somewhere alone in the dark as a small Christian boy, perhaps taking trash to the dumpster in the alley behind our apartments at night. It didn't help. I was more worried that my singing would draw the attention of the demons and evil people whom I was told surrounded me.

As a young man, I used to challenge myself to crush this fear, and often went to absurd lengths to do so. I would walk into darkened woods in the middle of the night, without any sort of light, climb a tree and sit watching until my eyes grew able to make out the blueish grey hues of the bushes below and of the trees which surrounded me. While stationed in Alaska with the Air Force, I took this a step further and would walk into the woods on the back-side of the base, in the middle of the night armed only with a small knife; at times wading through knee-deep snow. In hindsight, this was extremely foolish, as there were both bears and wolves in those woods. Several times, when I lived in Huntsville, Alabama, I attempted to work up the courage to stay the night alone, with no lights, in the dark woods of Rainbow Mountain, but I never successfully did so. Something about the silence and absolute pitch blackness at the base of the massive limestone outcroppings of that place frightened me. I wished to conquer that fear. But of course, I was still a Christian at that time.

In spite of these exploits, I still continued to sleep with some sort of light on well into my 20's. I knew many Christians who never experienced the same level of fear of the dark during their childhood and youth, yet I also knew that I had studied far more scripture, and held a far more sincere faith in Christianity, at a far earlier age, than the vast majority of my Christian peers. I absolutely believed in Satan and his horde of demons, and was very familiar with the scriptural accounts which described what these demonic forces were capable of.

No longer being a Christian, however, I find it interesting, and somewhat unsurprising that I no longer feel any fear of the dark. While one is seldom ever able to point out the specific moment when one overcomes a fear, I would bet that the slow overthrow of this fear was caused by my analogous slow, yet steady realization that the entire demonic menagerie, promoted within the Mosaic faiths, is all mythos: a philosophical artifact from a much more ignorant age. The path to this realization was a long and difficult one, but I am thoroughly glad that I traversed it. Interestingly, I notice that, since I haven't pressed this damaging mythology upon my children, *none* of them have seemed to possess any significant fear of the dark.

Shunning and Debate

Another negative concept espoused in scripture, and adopted by Christianity's more fanatical adherents, is shunning. This is not a practice exclusive to Christianity, as it is also taught and practiced by Muslims, Jews, and likely many other faiths. Among the Mosaic religions, there is little disagreement that shunning is an artifact of Jewish religious law. It is well known that, all throughout the Old Testament, the Jews were commanded to excommunicate, avoid as unclean, or cast out of their city, or camp various people for various different things, ranging from touching something dead, to having gotten semen, or vaginal blood upon oneself while uniting with one's spouse. While this historical practice was typically far more overt than what we commonly think of as shunning, the concept of isolating oneself from another person, or group for religious reasons remains the same.

The predominately Jewish converts to Christianity, who penned the books of the New Testament, continued to apologize for the practice of shunning in New Testament verses such as Titus 3:10. This verse states that the devout should "Warn a divisive person once, and then warn them a second time. After that, have nothing to do with them." Romans 16:17 supports this position by stating, "I urge you, brothers and sisters, to watch out for those who cause divisions and put obstacles in your way that are contrary to the teaching you have learned. Keep away from them." Lastly, there is 2 John 1:10, which states that "If anyone comes to you and does not bring this teaching, do not take them into your house or welcome them."

These are foolish doctrines, and as such, are clearly not divinely inspired. Such doctrines would sacrifice the bonds of fraternal, or filial love merely because one party disagrees over an issue and is intellectually honest with both themselves and with those whom they disagree with. The fact that someone is willing to be sincere about their views on important topics should be considered an act of kindness, which should be appreciated, even if these views conflict with those of whomever they are revealed to.

This is because honest debate is wholesome, when it occurs without degenerating into insult. As the heat of vigorous debate burns away the dross of error, any individuals participating in, or observing the exchange become better able to discern golden truths. One of the most potent retrograde forces to intellectual growth and cultural development within a society is intolerance to challenge, discussion, and debate.

Mandating that the faithful "reject," "have nothing to do with," "keep away from," or not receive any "into (their) house or welcome them," merely for continuing to support and defend a contrasting viewpoint, after the initial two warnings, is foolishness. It smacks of intellectual tyranny by the few, and cowering, blind, and stupid acceptance by the masses. In fact, repression of open, active debate is a common hallmark of tyrannies. Only errors which are being used as tools for personal advantage by tyrants, or as crutches by the misinformed, are at any sort of risk from open, ongoing challenge and debate.

Truth, on the other hand, has nothing to risk from argument. Like metals of varying worth which are obscured by a thick coat of soil and debris, ideas may initially be difficult to ascribe a specific worth to. Yet they are polished as they are passed through the ears, eyes, minds, and mouths both of those who may contest, and those who may apologize for them, until finally the luster of the more noble ones makes them easily discernable from those of little worth. William Godwin discussed a similar concept within his work, *Thoughts on Man*. In this work, Godwin stated that sparks of light shine forth during debate, from the clashing of two stones dedicated to their ideas.

As we expand our knowledge through study, we typically notice that our stances on certain subjects begin to solidify, while those on certain others begin to soften. Those which soften, do so either because the newly gained information makes their relative unimportance evident, or because an awareness is gained that an insufficient amount of information is available on the matter to have any certainty about it. Those views which solidify, do so for the opposite reasons. The newly gained information makes their relative importance evident, or an awareness is gained that a sufficient amount of information is available on the matter to be certain about it.

During this process of view solidification, conflict often begins to present itself between those holding contrasting solidified views. Should conflict occur between two individuals who possess a sufficient amount of humility and love of truth to overpower the common, ego driven desire to be seen as "right," and as "winning" a debate, then the initial conflict is quickly transformed into a wholesome dialectic exchange.

Unfortunately, this type of true communication is rare. More frequently, a person's view solidification brings them into conflict with those whose hardened positions make them unreceptive to new information on the topic. Dogmatists of this sort typically believe that they either already possess exhaustive information on the subject at hand, or if not, believe that any relevant facts which they don't possess, would, if rightly understood, only further strengthen their positions.

With this latter group, the volatility of their response, during the exchange, depends upon the environment which the exchange occurred in, the comments, or events which led to the discussion, the perceived importance of the topic, as well as their degree of education, culture, tact, and maturity. Even in the best of interactions with this unreceptive sort, they generally only feign receptivity in hopes that they can win the hearer over to their position, whenever it is their turn to speak. The non-receptive generally resent the books themselves which arm true learners with additional facts which may be employed during the debate; considering them to be the fountainhead of future conflicts.

The wise are wise enough to realize the expanse of knowledge that they do not yet know, and are humbled by it. The ignorant, however, are often not wise enough even to realize their own level of ignorance. There is a reason why the sayings, "Ignorance is bold and knowledge reserved," and "Ignorance is the softest pillow on which a man can rest his head," came about. These people often think themselves to be the pinnacles of wisdom, which is reflected in their often boundless confidence. This is the paradox of ignorance which is commonly known as the tragically humorous Dunning Kruger effect.

Openness to new ideas and willingness to abandon defunct ones, should newly encountered information prove the latter to be invalid, is generally seen by dogmatists as immature serial infatuation. This is an incorrect view. Serial infatuation generally occurs when an inexperienced person is newly exposed to a specific subject and embraces what is seen as good within it, without comprehending its deeper implications. What dogmatists think to be serial infatuation, is actually the true learner's love for what is improving their mind, as the patient loves the medicine which is curing him. Since books are, generally speaking, the densest of information sources, the more serious in their love of learning will tend to graze for their information within these more fertile fields.

As a person's knowledge increases, so also does their skill at recognizing what knowledge gaps remain, and where best to seek the information to fill them. Realizing the value of their time, the more intelligent quickly abandon written works which they perceive will not help them to grow, or will only do so at a slower rate than other works. Better knowing where to find knowledge, being more efficient in comprehending it, and even retaining it better within memory, due to cross connections made with existing knowledge, the intelligent become more efficient learners. The higher they ascend the ladder of understanding, the quicker they are able to climb. Those who look on from below cannot understand the excitement which the true learner increasingly feels about each new work which feeds his mind.

This brings to mind the common saying that you cannot teach a person something which they believe they already know. Before someone can be encouraged to adopt a new position, the first task is always to help them to understand the flaws in their existing views. Socrates made this technique famous, over two thousand years ago. He would begin debates by simply encouraging those who were in error to speak their views, and would then guide them to the absurd conclusions which these views inevitably led to. Once it dawned upon these people how absurd their positions were, and they were willing to listen to possible alternatives, Socrates would then begin to teach them the truth about the subject.

This process can also be abused, however. Manipulators often use this technique to prey upon youth, or undereducated adults, who generally only weakly hold, or poorly understand their own views on important issues. They do this by attacking and breaking these views down with a barrage of lies, and then replacing them with false, or corrupt views which work to their benefit. It is no coincidence that the majority of the destruction of conservative, or moral viewpoints occurs in Western high schools and colleges these days. Students, who are forced to sit for hours a day at the feet of teachers and professors often possessing corrupt morals, socialist leanings, or atheist world views, hardly stand a chance. The amount of peer pressure in these environments is incredible. The student who would dare to stand up for his love of virtue, masculinity, God, his nation, or Western civilization is often openly mocked and forced into silence.

This is also what is occurring with the current, widespread attack upon conservative Western culture, religion, national and social structures, and even the people themselves within the media. The atheist manipulators who have infested these agencies know that these things must be condemned and deconstructed before a new culture, faith, and national and social structures can be sold to the world. This new "liberal" culture which they promote is nothing more than repackaged and rebranded Bolshevism; which sells grand promises of equality to the naïve, but only ever delivers bloodshed, tyranny, additional inequality, and the loss of freedom.

Charismatics

Even poorly constructed shacks can often hold together, as long as they are not subjected to the strains of wind, or rain. In the same way, poorly constructed faiths often hold together when not subjected to the pressures of philosophical scrutiny. Charismatic denominations are the "shacks" of the Christian faith. Though these churches tend to have the collective doctrinal, historical, and philosophical depth of a puddle, their members generally compensate for this deficiency with an overabundance of commitment and enthusiasm; which they frequently confuse for "divine inspiration."

Often, we encounter these charismatics excitedly bursting into "tongues" (i.e. *glossolalia*) in the middle of a church service. This is generally followed by another of their members, who is equally eager for recognition as having been "anointed by God" with a "spiritual gift," translating this "divine word sent from God." Much like a horoscope, or palm reading, these translations are frequently generic enough to have a high statistical probability of applying to several people in the room. On the rare occasion when they are highly specific, and therefore have less probability of applying to someone in attendance, who is there to know if the message actually proved true?

"Someone here has a problem with pain in their back." Who doesn't occasionally have pain in their back? "Someone is struggling with a loss." In any group, there is a statistically high chance that someone is struggling with a recent loss. Even if there isn't anyone struggling with a *major* loss, such as the loss of a loved one, someone will surely have had a *minor* one, such as a loss of health, of a friend, or even of their car keys. Is anyone going to poll the room to verify these intentionally qualitative statements? Often these people's "words from God" are peppered with poorly paraphrased Bible verses. Laughably, many of these verses are frequently given in King James English, for obvious effect. Are those who listen to this lunacy expected to believe that God only knows how to communicate with mankind in 17th century dialect?

As an experiment, skim over one of the paragraphs in this book and count how frequently the same word, or phrase recurs. You will find that the repetition of words is very infrequent. The repetition of phrases is even less frequent. Genuine languages, such as English, are, per the Oxford dictionary, an assemblage of any of roughly 170,000 words which are still in use.[151] Even the average 5-year-old English speaker generally has a vocabulary of over 2,000 words.

Yet, if the "words," or "phrases," of someone who has been "blessed" with the "Gift of Tongues" are scrutinized, we will discover that these speakers are generally only able to string together a handful of these at any one time; which they repeat with extreme frequency. Knowing that any repetition detracts from perceived authenticity, the more experienced among these people generally rotate to a new handful of "words" and "phrases" every few moments; typically with as much of a guttural Hebrew-esque sound as the speaker is familiar enough with to muster.

This implies that, either the same few words are being repeated in this supposed "Tongue of angels," or the speaker has merely worked himself, or more frequently herself, into a simple emotional frenzy of babbling. This phenomenon, and these same conclusions have been reported within several respected scientific studies which may be researched by the inquisitive. Another conformational point is the way that the majority whom I have spoken with about their possession of this "gift" have described how they "developed" it. "Just start moving your mouth and making sounds and let the spirit take over. That's what I did," they would state. This is the textbook definition of *babbling*. This is a "gift" which is ubiquitous among infants, the deranged, and the brain damaged.

What about the "spiritual gift" of "prophecy," which many charismatics claim to possess. Suffice it to say that there are still thousands of unclaimed lotteries. Any who truly possessed the gift of prophecy could bless the lives of thousands by predicting the lottery and handing out millions to the poor. Yet I have never once heard of this occurring. Can God not predict lottery numbers? Does he want the hungry child to continue suffering? Of course not. God simply does not directly interact with the universe in this manner, as doing so would ultimately make him arbitrary and unjust. An in-depth discussion on this topic is provided in the section on *justice*.

But surely Charismatics possess the much famed "spiritual gift" of "healing." Unfortunately, they do not. Just ask yourself, if someone actually had an ability to heal, why wouldn't they make a tour of local hospitals, emptying them of the injured, the diseased, and the dying? Isn't this what any goodhearted person would do? Of course it is.

Yet are the nearby hospitals still occupied? Has anyone ever heard about a hospital anywhere, ever being cleared out by a faith healer? I am unaware of a newspaper ever documenting such an event. And such a shocking occurrence could not avoid notice. Stories of it would spread like wildfire the world over; instantly attracting vast swarms of reporters. Yet comb the historical newspapers and see if you can discover a word of anything of this sort. It has not happened.

The inevitable conclusion, therefore, is that the charismatic "faith healer" is either not *good*, in that he is unwilling to heal these suffering people, or that he *is* good and willing, but is *unable* to heal them. Knowing the general character and overall good intentions of Christians, even charismatic ones, the latter must be true. The question, then, becomes *why*.

Why can't they clear out hospitals? Jesus, Paul, Peter, and several others among the early church were reported within scripture as having performed mass healings of this very sort. If it happened then, why can it not recur today? Even Eusebius, in his 340 A.D. work, *Ecclesiastical History*, mentioned that there was confusion during the period of the early church as to why miracles no longer seemed to occur.[152]

The most common answer which Christian apologists give to this question is that the early miracles, including the many scripturally documented "faith healings," were given by God in order to confirm the testimony of individuals who had been sent with messages from God; effectively functioning as ambassadors. These miracles essentially stamped these people's messages with a seal of divine authority.

So, is no one since the days of the early church functioning in this role, and therefore marked with this stamp? Whenever this question is asked, there is always an isolated story of *someone, somewhere*, who heard of, or who supposedly witnessed an actual healing. Yet these rare, isolated cases are highly likely to have simply been the result of confirmation bias, which caused the faithful to eagerly accept what was simply rumor, or speculation. They could also have been simple misdiagnosis of the original malady by non-physicians, inept physicians, or physicians practicing the medical art prior to its maturation.

An example of this last case is the mistaken diagnosis of people as dead, when they were simply in a state of coma. This has occurred hundreds of times throughout the centuries and is the entire reason that the *wake* period was instituted prior to the funeral. During *wakes*, the supposedly dead were laid out in a relatively public area and given a final opportunity to *a-wake-n* prior to being buried during the funeral.

This last case was likely what occurred in many of the examples of resurrections which are documented within scripture; the remainder being the simple products of legend, hearsay, or speculation. Consider the dubious circumstances surrounding a few of these. In Acts 20:7-12, a young boy falls from a window sill. Unconscious and with little, or no apparent breath, he appears to the crowd who surrounded him in ~35 A.D. to be "dead." But what happens next? "Paul went down, threw himself on the young man and put his arms around him. "Don't be alarmed," he said. "He's alive!" Then he went upstairs again and broke bread and ate. After talking until daylight, he left. The people took the young man home alive and were greatly comforted." This section is given in the King James Version of scripture under the heading: "Eutychus Raised From the Dead at Troas." Yet Paul doesn't even appear to claim that the boy was ever dead. He simply informed the

spectators not to worry, because he knew the child to still be living.
More than likely, the boy was simply unconscious, or in a coma, and
breathing very shallowly. Perhaps later that evening, or in the
successive days, he eventually regained consciousness. As this story of
what was simply a close-brush with death was repeated to the faithful
over the centuries, it likely slowly transformed into one of a resurrection.

In Acts 9:36-42, Peter supposedly raises a woman named Dorcas to
life, whom everyone believed to have recently died. Her supposed death
was so recent that she had yet to be buried. In these ancient days, prior
to refrigeration, this meant within roughly a day or so at most, as, except
in Egypt where they were mummified, the dead were buried quickly in
order to prevent their stench. It is very likely that this woman was
simply either unconscious, or in a coma, and that she subsequently
regained consciousness: although it is highly improbable that she did so
in response to Peter simply telling her to "arise." This latter fact was
likely added to increase the grandeur of the event, as it was retold over
the centuries.

Similar explanations could easily be offered for the resurrections of
the recently "deceased" daughter of Jarius, in Mark 5:21-43, for the
resurrection of the newly "dead" boy, whom the pall-bearers were
carrying in his coffin, in Luke 7:11-17, for the recently "dead" boy, in 2
Kings 4:33-35, for the man who "came to life" while being put into the
grave, in 2 Kings 13:21, and even of the famed Lazarus, in John 11:1-45.

Consider how Elisha even appears to perform a rudimentary sort of
"rescue breathing" on the boy in 2 Kings 4:33-35. "And he went up and
lay on the child, and put his mouth on his mouth, his eyes on his eyes,
and his hands on his hands; and he stretched himself out on the child,
and the flesh of the child became warm. He returned and walked back
and forth in the house, and again went up and stretched himself out on
him; then the child sneezed seven times, and the child opened his eyes."

In the 2 Kings 13:21 example, where the man supposedly returns to
life while being placed in the grave, supposedly after making contact
with the bones of Elisha, we are expected to either believe that the
Hebrew people, who are so proud of their history and heritage, would
have misplaced the tomb of one of their most famous and revered
prophets, or that they would allow it to be shared with the bodies of
random, unremarkable people. Both of these possibilities are highly
improbable. More than likely, the individual was being placed in a tomb
and simply revived from whatever comatose state he was in. When this
occurred, the surprised people likely sought an explanation, and landed
upon the fact that the bones of some holy person must have formerly, or
yet remained within that tomb. Over time, the story likely grew, until
the holy person in question was nonother than one of the greatest of
their prophets: Elisha.

In the last example of Lazarus, as with Paul and Eutychus, we have Jesus telling the crowd that Lazarus isn't dead, but is simply "sleeping." Are comas and general unconsciousness not simply forms of sleep? How else could Jesus have described a coma to these people, when the word didn't yet exist? It is important to note that, in virtually all of these examples, the supposedly dead individuals are people who are freshly so. We don't find apostles resurrecting worm ridden, half decomposed corpses. We have people being "resurrected" who were generally thought to have just died, and who are virtually always not yet buried, or entombed.

Some may argue that the example of Lazarus was one where the victim had supposedly been "dead" for three days. In the text, however, we are not shown a rotten corpse of Lazarus. We are simply told that he was sick, "died," and that he was entombed for three days; that Jesus had his tomb opened; and that he walked out of it. But how sure are we that those who buried him were correct about him actually being dead? People can easily live in a comatose state for well over three days, without dying of dehydration. There are documented examples of fully conscious people surviving 10 days without water. How long a person will last depends mostly upon how quickly they are dehydrating. This rate will be slow in a cool cave, with no physical exertion.

It is well known that the ignorant frequently ascribe the results of natural phenomena which they don't understand to "magic," or the special intervention of God. Could Paul, Jesus, and the many others who are documented throughout scripture as having "resurrected" people, simply have been more educated about early methods of clinical intervention, as well as with the different signs and symptoms of a comatose state, versus those of true death?

It is claimed that this couldn't be the case, since Jesus was simply a carpenter. Yet we have no account of his early years, other than the story of when his parents accidentally left him in the temple. Even then, however, his level of intellect supposedly amazed the religious teachers. There is a time described where he is "driven into the desert." Perhaps during this period he studied, or received additional, non-Jewish education. We know that there are obvious echoes of earlier Platonic thought in his teachings, which he must have encountered somewhere.

Scripture also claims, in Acts 26:24, that Paul was highly educated. At times, Paul even quotes directly from Greek philosophers in his letters. During Elisha's ancient era, religious leaders were the most educated among the masses, effectively functioning as the people's teachers. Elisha would have been revered as a celebrity, and have spent the majority of his days in study and contemplation.

There is also the possibility that many of the "faith healings" which have occurred were simply due to the well-documented "placebo effect." Before I discuss this topic, I need to preliminarily discuss the process of hypnotism. During the well documented phenomenon of hypnotic sleep, it is very likely that the hypnotist is bypassing the conscious mind of the hypnotized person and interacting directly with his, or her subconscious. This direct interaction with the subconscious results in several profound types of observed phenomena. By directly interrogating the subconscious of hypnotized individuals, the hypnotist can cause memories to surface, which were retained by it long after the conscious mind had completely forgotten them; or if traumatic, were intentionally blocked by the conscious mind.

In addition, the hypnotist can not only draw information directly *from* the subconscious of hypnotized individuals, but he can also implant information directly *into* it, via a process known as hypnotic suggestion. If the hypnotist fails to undo any false suggestions which he implants, then, when these people are brought out of their hypnotized state, there is the potential that an artifact will be left within their subconscious, which influences their resulting beliefs. This form of hypnotic belief manipulation is useful for things such as assisting people with breaking physical addictions, or compulsive behaviors, but it can be taken to extremes, such as during the well-known examples where men have been hypnotically convinced to believe that they are chickens. In fact, during several well-documented 19th century experiments, many patients in need of surgery had their subconscious minds so completely convinced that they felt no pain, via hypnosis, that many successfully underwent surgery without anesthetic.[153] Unfortunately, some of these individuals came out of their hypnotic state in the middle of painful surgical procedures, causing clinicians to struggle to sedate them afterwards. Due to this risk, hypnotic surgery was deemed too unreliable and was generally abandoned by the medical community.

Returning to the "placebo effect," most people with even rudimentary clinical knowledge are aware of this very real phenomenon, where people who sincerely believe that a treatment regimen is going to improve their condition, show significantly improved clinical outcomes. This phenomenon has been acknowledged, but is mostly shrugged off by the medical community, as being simply due to the overall improved immune function of the optimistic. This theory makes sense, given that the clinically depressed are well documented to possess decreased immune function. In reality, this appears to be none other than the effect of the subconscious influencing the immune system. The problem with the "placebo effect" is that the patient has to be convinced to believe something, in order for it to work. Depending upon the amount of contrary information on the subject, and the strength of existing beliefs which they already possess, this trick may be practically impossible to perform.

But what if we could simply bypass the conscious mind altogether, as the hypnotists do, and manipulate these people's beliefs directly. Is it possible that the subconscious has greater potential to influence the body's immune system than we realize: a sort of *super* "placebo effect?" This theory is not without evidence, as a few modern experiments seem to hint at just how skilled a physician the subconscious actually is. During one specific set of experiments, for example, researchers studying similarities between warts and cancer were able to hypnotize individuals who were suffering from chronic warts and subconsciously convince them that the warts on only one side of their bodies were going to resolve. Shockingly, in a statistically significant portion of these patients, this very thing actually occurred.

The implication of this experiment is that, either the initial cause of the warts was a subconscious one which the hypnosis resolved, or the hypnotic suggestion activated and concentrated the focus of pre-existing, but latent immune functions within the patient. Whichever of these is actually occurring, these findings raise tantalizing questions about how many other illnesses the subconscious could be influenced to correct, with or without hypnosis.

Could this possibly be what is occurring during supposed "faith healings?" These individuals, who already tend to possess a belief in the efficacy of whatever religious ritual they have sought out and are participating in (e.g. prayer, fasting, laying on of hands, anointing with holy water, etc.), are already prime candidates for the "placebo effect." But what if the repetitive, prolonged, or intense prayers, songs, mantras, chants, fasts, or other religious acts simply induce a sort of hypnotic state, which influences the subconscious directly, allowing it to employ the body's immune system to its full potential.

Jesus

The truth of both who and what Jesus "the Christ" was, regardless of who, or what men believed him to be, or what he may, or may not have believed about himself, was likely revealed in its purest form while he hung languishing on the cross. Scripture records him as crying out at that moment, "My God, my God, why have you forsaken me?" (Matthew 27:46). What could such an outburst mean? If you crack open the always dusty books on apologetics, you will find that a mountain of excuses for this statement have been compiled over the centuries. These excuses range from Jesus simply being in a pain induced delirium, to his suffering from divine separation from his "Father" in heaven, as he was momentarily loaded with all of mankind's sins.

Is it not far more likely that such a cry over being forsaken was simply what it seemed, prima facie: a painful belief that he had been abandoned by the God whom he believed would save him from being successfully tortured to death by corrupt men. In all actuality, God had not abandoned him. God simply continued to operate the universe without special intervention, as he always has, does, and likely will. To do anything else would make God both arbitrary and unjust. This topic is discussed at length in the section on justice.

Christian apologists will vigorously deny that this was the cause for Jesus' outcry, as it implies that he did not actually intend to be crucified. Without intent, the central doctrine of Christianity collapses: that Jesus *willingly* laid down his life to somehow absolve the sins of those who claim him as their Lord. In theory, the claim could be made that God "the Father," as the Christians call him, could have forcefully sacrificed Jesus, his supposed son, for the sins of mankind, regardless of Jesus' willingness. Unfortunately, such a view would make God a monster and Jesus no different from one of the unwilling sacrificial animals which the Levite priests killed and burned on their altars. The Catholics overtly make this comparison by sometimes referring to Jesus as the Pascal (i.e. Passover) lamb.

Making this sacrifice involuntary would strip Jesus of all merit for being crucified, as merit is not born from deeds, but from will. We do not praise the child who is forced share a toy with his sibling, against his will and complaining all the while. We praise the one who willingly does so.

I grant Christian apologists that a handful of verses which are attributed to Jesus in the Gospels undeniably indicate Jesus possessing a belief that he would be executed for his teachings, and a willingness to endure it. But were these predictions part of the original gospel texts, and even before these were written, were they a 100% accurate account of the words and deeds of this man and his followers? Most Christian apologists would respond, "Of course they are." In spite of this confident response, what do they base this belief upon?

The oldest complete version of the New Testament which we possess, the *Codex Sinaiticus*, was penned in approximately 350 A.D. This is roughly 320 years after Jesus' death. It is unfortunate that we do not have a complete text prior to this point, as this late date is already well after the highly influential Council of Nicaea, which occurred in roughly 325 A.D., which Christianized the Roman world, and which ordered the burning of any written works which were critical of Trinity. In addition to this relatively late codex, papyral fragments of portions of the gospels, which were written roughly 100 years earlier (i.e. ~250 ad), are also extant (e.g. P45, P66, and P75). This is still approximately 220 years after Jesus' death. That is an enormously long time.

But let's give Christian apologists the benefit of the doubt and assume that the verses where Jesus predicts his own death were genuinely written by the Gospel authors; Matthew, Mark, Luke, and John. Only two of these men, Matthew and John, were actual apostles: that is, men who lived with Jesus, and could therefore attest to his actual words and deeds. The others simply reported what they had been told. Mark was supposedly a disciple (i.e. pupil) of Peter, while Luke was a doctor who studied the matter on his own. Mark and Luke may have accurately recorded what they were told, however, it is undeniable that their reliance upon secondary sources, rather than upon the primary source of Jesus himself, greatly increases the risk of error within these gospels.

Our most dependable sources are therefore the gospels of Matthew and John. Both of these gospels are believed by Bible scholars to have been written roughly 40 and 60 years after Jesus' death, respectively. Assuming that these men were approximately the same age as Jesus, when they accompanied him during his ministry, this would make Matthew roughly 70 years old, when he wrote his gospel, and John roughly 90. Though there were always exceptions, average lifespans during this much more brutal age were far shorter. Men in their 40's were considered old, and death caught up with many of them during this decade. That is quite some time for two old men to remember the exact words spoken by Jesus during specific encounters, and also the specific actions which he took. Did Matthew and John both have photographic memories?

But they would have to have even more than this. How do these men know, in specific detail, some of the things which were both said and done by Jesus during periods when their own gospels claim that they weren't present with him to hear these things, or observe them? Even more, they even appear in their gospels to at times know and document other people's inner thoughts and motives.

Many possible examples could be provided on this topic. Consider Matthew 26:40, where Matthew relates the exact words of Jesus' prayer to God which he makes in the Garden of Gethsemane, though the same passage sates that Jesus had withdrawn from the group of apostles, and that they were all asleep. Consider Matthew 27:19 and John 19:8, where Matthew and John somehow know the dream that Pilot's wife had, the exact words which she used in private to her husband, as well as Pilot's internal motives, concerns, and fears. In Matthew 27:4-6 Matthew even appears to know the specific words which were used during Judas' private conversations with the Priests, after he betrays Jesus to them. We encounter the same problems in the Old Testament, as well as its Jewish analog, the Tanakh, however this is outside of the scope of the current topic.

Christians sidestep all of these problems by simply claiming that God "inspired" these men. They get this opinion from verses within the very text under examination, such as 2 Tim 3:16. Many mistakenly refer to this as internal "evidence," however it is actually mere attestation. This usage of one internal textual attestation to "prove" another internal is like saying that, "Part A of the Bible must be true, because part B says that it is." This is a logic loop. When the accuracy of the entire text is in question, external evidence is required.

An additional problem is that Matthew and John, as early leaders of this new faith, had a vested interest in proving Jesus to be the long-expected Hebrew *messiah* (i.e. literally, *anointed* one); what the Christians call the "Son of God." Should Jesus' death be proven to be intentional, then Matthew and John would be the leaders of a divinely inspired movement; men who had been hand chosen by the very "Son of God" himself. Should his death prove to have been unintentional, then these men were simply the followers of a demagogue, who had been murdered by rulers that felt their power threatened by him. Jesus' cry from the cross, "My God, my God, why have you forsaken me!" seems to confirm the latter.

We needn't bother discussing the various problems which this statement creates with the doctrine of Trinity. Let's ignore that the "Son of God," who is simultaneously the same *being* as the "Father God" (i.e. Jehovah), and yet also distinctly different from him, can, like a schizophrenic, at least momentarily feel abandoned by the "Father," whom he actually also *is*, but also *isn't*. Jesus, this good man, this noble iconoclast, this brave philosophical pioneer, who attempted to help his own people outgrow many of the most ignorant aspects of their petrified faith, was rewarded for these efforts with torture and death.

As always, this occurred at the instigation of the pious and the powerful, both of whom saw him as a threat to their authority and privileges. If God were such a one as would miraculously rend the heavens, smite the wicked, and save the good who are in need, here was a prime opportunity which was missed. Jesus, whose intense love of God, and faith in God's compassion and goodness, was likely left feeling a mix of abandonment and betrayal, while he writhed on the cross' nails and gasped for air. To use an archaic word containing the same meaning; he likely felt *forsaken*.

It is hard for me to discuss this last point without feeling a deep ache of pity and compassion within. This is because I hate how this theme of injustice tends to recur throughout history. Very often, good men, philosophical pioneers and iconoclasts, are rewarded with humiliation, poverty, torture, and even death for their courageous words and deeds in defense of goodness, God, virtue, and justice, as well as for attempting to salvage the hearts and often enslaved, or abused bodies of their fellow men. This happened to Jesus. It also happened to Socrates, Orpheus, Boethius, and Pythagoras. Though none of these men, nor their doctrines were perfect, they should fitly be held in the highest regard for these efforts which guided mankind away from error and towards truth.

Egypt and Christianity

Many religious concepts of the ancient Egyptians echoed across the centuries in the later Greek, Roman, and Christian beliefs. In order to explain this point, some background on a few of the major ancient Egyptian beliefs must be provided. Much like the early United States, what we know as the ancient Egyptian empire was formed from the amalgamation of originally independent states known as *nomes*. Most of these *nomes* had developed their own religions, complete with distinct ceremonies and gods possessing various traits. Often times, trinities of key gods are encountered within these faiths. Over the centuries, different nomes, along with their key gods, rose to preeminence and controlled the empire. This is why we sometimes encounter historians referring to the "Theban Empire," and the "Memphite Empire," among others, when referring to specific periods of Egyptian history. The perceived roles and characters of specific ancient Egyptian gods also varied according to the era in question.

The association between Greek and Egyptian culture goes back to the earliest of Greek histories, which have now mostly passed into legend. Many reputable ancient writers claim that several of the major Grecian states, such as Sparta, Argos, and Athens, were originally Egyptian colonies. Prior to the founding, and subsequent increase in renown of Plato's Athenian Academy, children of the Greek nobility, for example, were generally sent to be educated in the libraries and museums of Egypt. Entire cities in Egypt were heavily populated by Greek merchants and mercenaries. For centuries, prior to the commencement of Greek rule in Egypt under Alexander, Pharaohs depended heavily upon Greek mercenaries to supplement their forces. The seat of Greek power remained in Egypt after Alexander's death and throughout the Ptolemaic era, until eventually supplanted by the Latin speaking Romans.

During the mid 6th, to 5th century B.C., the Egyptians were the foster parents of the growing Hellenic power. Various hoplite troops served as a sort of Praetorian guard of the pharaoh, much to the chagrin of the local Egyptian soldiery. So much so, that during one period, roughly 250,000 Egyptian soldiers abandoned the pharaoh, Egypt, and their families, to form a new nation. Greeks not only served as mercenary armies for the pharaoh, but also settled among the Egyptians, some whole towns within the delta being comprised of mostly

Greeks. This led to much blending of cultures between the formerly, and soon to be great nations.

This period of intermixing continued at least until the period of Egypt's first true fall under the Persian empire of Cambyses in roughly 530 B.C.,[174] and indeed, it was due to Athenian intervention from the island of Cyprus, that Artaxerxes' invasion of the Egyptian Delta proved unsuccessful.

As the Greek nation and culture developed under this heavy Egyptian influence, so Roman culture developed under Greek. Not only did the Romans famously adopt and rename the Greek gods, but until the religious fanaticism of emperor Justinian forced its closure in 529 AD, children of the Roman nobility were generally educated at the Athenian Academy.

Let's narrow our focus, on this passage of culture, to that of religion. From as early as the 11th dynasty (2125-1985 B.C.), the Egyptian Heliopolitan cult taught that the sun was either the symbol, or the very personage of Ra, who traveled across the sky in a ship known as the "Solar Barque" (i.e. barge/ship). From dawn until noon, this boat was known as the "Matet boat," and from noon until dusk, as the "Sektet boat." The Heliopolitan cult, as well as most Egyptians, believed that in the afternoon, as the fires of the Sektet boat waned, Ra descended within it near the ancient city of Abydos. From prehistoric times, Abydos was believed by the Egyptians to be one of the most westerly points in the world. Near this city, there was supposedly a cave mouth within a mountain cleft, which served as the entrance to the dark subterranean realm of "Tuat."

The Heliopolitan cult taught that the souls of the recently deceased flocked to Abydos, where, if Ra permitted them, they were allowed to board the Sektet boat, prior to its passage into Tuat. Once within Tuat, the boat traversed a northerly arc, as it passed through several distinct sections of this underground world, until it eventually emerged the following day from an analogous cave in the East.

Within the first section of Tuat, willing passengers could disembark to live in a dimly lit, but not unpleasant world with Osiris, the older, patron god of both Mendes and Abydos itself. Souls that chose to remain in the Sektet boat with Ra, traveled with him beyond the "Land of Osiris," until Ra eventually disembarked to navigate the dark, labyrinthine land of Sokaris, alone and on foot. Beyond Sokaris, Ra reboarded the ship and traveled with his passengers through the eight "circles" of the land of the "Osiris of the [Egyptian] Delta," where the latter's four bodies and souls supposedly slept. Finally, the Sektet boat turned due South to *Augarit*, the place of *burning pits* wherein the souls of the impious were tormented until eventually annihilated.

This Heliopolitan legend was still current during later dynasties, such as the 18th (1543-1292 B.C.). During this later period, the city of

Thebes, along with its patron God, Ammon, had risen to preeminence. In spite of this, most of Ra's key deeds and characteristics, such as sailing through Tuat in the Solar Boat, had been syncretized with those of Ammon.

This Egyptian *Tuat* was clearly the source whence the Greeks derived their concept of *Hades*. This *Hades* became the *Tartarus* of the Romans, which eventually became the *Hell* of the Christians. There is the same dark, gaping entryway into *Tuat* as there is for the scriptural "bottomless pit" described within the Biblical book of Revelation. Interestingly there is even a potential correlation between the transliterated names of the city where the opening of Tuat was located, *Abydos*, and the name given in the book of Revelation for an angelic king who dwells within, or who is identified with this bottomless pit: *Abaddon*. "And they had a king over them, which is the angel of the bottomless pit, whose name in the Hebrew tongue is Abaddon, but in the Greek tongue hath his name Apollyon" (Revelation 9:11).

The dimly lit "Land of Osiris," from the Heliopolitan legend, was very likely the source of the early Christian idea of *Limbo*. The king of Tuat, *Osiris*, became the *Pluto/Hades* of the Greeks, became the *Serapis* of the Roman Egyptians, became the *Satan* of the Christians. In another ancient Egyptian tradition, Osiris was portrayed as the *Banebdjedet*, the "Ram (later confused for the *Goat*) of Mendes," a city in Egypt which was famous for its temple to Osiris. This same Goat of Mendes is the source from whence the satyr-like *Pan, Bacchus,* and *Dionysus* of the Greeks and Romans were derived. Eliphas Levi later depicted this Goat of Mendes as the satyr-like, *Baphomet.* This symbol has been adopted by Satanists worldwide to represent their God: Satan.[154]

The Egyptian *Augarit* later developed into the Greek *Pyriphlegethon*, or "lake of fire." The Greek philosopher, Plato, gives a detailed description of *Pyriphlegethon*, in his ~400 B.C. work, *Phaedo*.[155] Epictetus' ~100 A.D. condemnation of the concepts of *Hades* and *Pyriphlegethon* prove that both of these beliefs were still widespread within the Roman empire during this relatively late period.

Referring to death in his work, Epictetus states: "Go whither? To nothing terrible, but to the place from which you came, to your friends and kinsmen, to the elements: what there was in you of fire goes to fire; of earth, to earth; of air, to air; of water to water: no *Hades*, nor Acheron, nor Cocytus, nor *Pyriphlegethon*, but all is full of Gods and Demons."[5] We see this same Egyptian concept of Augarit resurface as the Christian "Lake of Fire," in the scriptural book of Revelations (e.g. Revelations 19:20, 20:10, 20:14-15, & 21:8).

The Egyptian myth of *Nu*, the primordial waters of chaos, whence everything is made, reappears within the Jewish, and later Christian faiths, as the chaotic, watery, primordial Earth of the book of Genesis. "And the Earth was without form, and void; and darkness was upon the face of *the deep*. And the Spirit of God moved upon the face of the *waters*" (Genesis 1:2).

Another artifact of Egyptian religious thought, which is preserved within the modern Jewish and Christian faiths, is the belief in a sort of heavenly sea. This was the same sea which the Solar boat of Ra was claimed to sail in. An artifact of this belief can be found in Genesis 1:6, "And God said, Let there be a *firmament* in the midst of the *waters*, and let it divide the waters from the waters." Before anyone assumes that this "firmament" is simply referring to land which existed between the watery clouds and the watery ocean, consider verses 7-8, where the "firmament" is referred to as being essentially all *atmosphere* between the upper and lower seas. "And God made the firmament, and divided the waters which were under the firmament from the waters which were above the firmament: and it was so. *And God called the firmament Heaven*. And the evening and the morning were the second day." Indeed, *land* isn't even created in this creation myth until the following day.

The list of artifacts from the ancient Egyptian religion, which have been preserved within the modern Christian and Jewish faiths, go on and on. There is the same assumption of sins by the dying Egyptian savoir, Osiris, whom the Egyptian dead identify themselves with, as there is by Jesus in the Christian scriptures. There is the same confusion in Egypt between the roles of this dying savior, Osiris, and the creator-God (e.g. Ra, Neter, Nu, Amen, Ptah, Aten, depending upon which dynasty, or locale of Egypt is being referred to) as occurred between the Christian dying savior, Jesus, and the Jewish creator-God, Jehovah.

The same syncretism of gods occurred in Egypt, as the various city/states grew until their cultures eventually fused, as likely occurred in ancient Judaism. The Egyptians, for example, recognized parallels between Ra and Amun, who were both originally distinct, independently developed gods, and latter fused them into Amun-Ra. Evidence that something of this sort also occurred in ancient Judaism can be seen in the way that the originally Phoenician, or Babylonian god, El, was fused with the Hebrew god, Jehovah. According to the highly probable *Modified Document Hypothesis* of Hupfield and Boehmer,[156] the Pentateuch portion of the Christian Old Testament, or the Jewish Tanakh, was likely a combination of 4 sources: 2 *Elhoist* (1 Earlier and 1 later), 1 *Jahovist/Jehovist/Jahwhist/Yahwhist* (pronunciation varies, depending upon the source cited), and 1 *Redactor/Deuteronomist*. These documents were composed at different times between 900-600 B.C. The *Elohist* portions likely originated from the tribe of Ephraim, which was why they tended to favor the tribe of Joseph. These sources tended to cast God as more removed; sending angels and appearing in dreams. The *Jahwhist* source, on the other hand, tended to portray God as completely anthropomorphized; similar to the analogous gods of the surrounding nations during this period. When we encounter this God, we often find him doing human types of activities, complete with human limitations; such as wrestling with, and being unable to overcome Isaac, being unable to know what was occurring at the Tower of Babel without physically visiting and observing it, growing angry, repenting of making man, etc. An artifact of Hebrew awareness of and apology for this obvious syncretism can be found in Exodus 6:3, where God supposedly tells Moses, "And I appeared unto Abraham, unto Isaac, and unto Jacob, by the name of God [El] Almighty, but by my name Jehovah was I not known to them."

There is the same confusion of identities in Egypt between the supreme God, Osiris, and his son, Horus, whom he is at times identified with, as occurred between the Christian supreme God, Jehovah, and his son, Jesus, whom he is sometimes identified with. There is the same Egyptian ceremony celebrating the newly reborn sun, as there is during the Christian nativity celebration of Christmas. In the former, an effigy of a newborn in a cradle was carried around the temple at the close of the winter equinox (i.e. December 21, as of 2018, although this date has shifted).[195] In the latter, the well-known motif of a babe lying in a manger (i.e. feeding trough) is celebrated on December 25.

There is the same tragic death and subsequent resurrection of the Egyptian Osiris, as there is with the Christian passion and resurrection of Jesus. To commemorate Osiris' dismemberment by his enemy, Typhoon, the Egyptians baked loaves of bread in the form of Osiris, which they ceremonially broke and shared; generally washing it down with beer.[195] This is an almost exact image, with almost the exact same meaning, as the "breaking of bread" which occurs during the Christian communion, celebrated to commemorate the passion of Jesus. Even Jesus himself calls it his broken (i.e. torn apart) body, "And when He had given thanks, He broke it and said, 'Take, eat; this is My body which is broken for you; do this in remembrance of Me'" (1 Cor 11:24).

It should be understood by the reader that these ceremonial consumptions of the symbols of human flesh and blood within the ancient Egyptian faith are substitutions for and echoes of that nation's, and indeed, most of the African continent's cannibalistic roots. Cannibalism, as attested by Diodorus, was widespread in Egypt during the Predynastic, and the early Dynastic eras.[198] And it was not merely the ancient Egyptians who were guilty of this practice. Cannibalism remained widespread among many of the African tribes into the 19th century, and even continues in isolated pockets there today. Besides consuming the flesh of human victims for nourishment, these ancient cannibals often did so out of a belief that they would somehow absorb key characteristics of their victim, such as their courage, or strength, in the process. Not surprisingly, modern Catholics believe that a similar transmission of personal characteristics occurs when they consume the supposedly transubstantiated flesh and blood of Jesus, in the eucharist and wine which is taken during mass.

There is the same Egyptian story of Isis hiding in the rushes to protect her babe Horus, as there is in the Hebrew story of Jochebed hiding Moses in a basket in the reeds in the Christian and Jewish book of Genesis. There is the same false allegation of sexual assault by the wife of a ruler, Pharaohic involvement, and eventual vindication of the accused in the Egyptian "Tale of the Two Brothers," as there is in the scriptural story of Joseph and Potiphar's wife. There is the same fashioning of man (and sometimes woman) from clay by the god Khunum, the exact same way that Jehovah is described as doing in the book of Genesis.

It is especially interesting that the ancient Egyptians actually subdivided the soul into multiple types, or components. This is very much in line with the concept of the soul put forward by Socrates, as recorded by Plato and Xenophon. This makes sense, given that Plato is reputed to have studied for a time in Egypt, as did Solon and several others of the "Seven Sages of Greece."

The Egyptian Djed pillar is thought by many scholars to be a stylized symbol for the tree which encased the coffin and body of Osiris. The oddly shaped nub found on the tops of several Egyptian Djeds is likely the top branch of the tree. The Jews, who lived with the Egyptians for hundreds of years, before escaping to the area which we refer to today as Israel, adopted and reformed many aspects of the Egyptian faith. The 7 candle menorah, which was used in the ancient Hebrew temple, was likely none-other than a modified version of the djed of Osiris, with extended branches. The Jews later modified this menorah to include a total of 9 branches, and referred to it as a Chanukiah.

Interestingly, if the "branches" of the djed are counted, including the top nub found on many, we notice a similar total of 9. As Osiris was claimed to slowly revive, until reborn during the winter equinox, so the 9 individual branches of the menorah were set alight in the evenings, until the end of Hanukkah; which is also suspiciously close to, and in all probability originally occurred during, the winter equinox. The fire used on the menorah is an appropriate symbol for soul, since many ancient cultures considered it a symbol of the spirit of God; most notably the fire worshiping Zoroastrians, whom the Jews lived among for a time.

It is also oddly coincidental that the topmost candle which is used to light the other branches of the Menorah is called the "Shammash" candle. While it is said that this word means "helper," it is interesting that Shamash is not only a solar deity in the ancient Semitic religion, but also the God of Justice in Babylon and Assyria. Not surprisingly, we find that the Israelites were deported into captivity in Assyria during several periods, never to return as cohesive, identifiable tribes. In addition, the tribe of Judah, whence the modern Jews derive their name, was enslaved for 70 years in Babylon. These are the same places where Shamash was worshipped as a solar deity. Perhaps the name of this God, who was called upon for aid, later came to have the meaning of "helper" in the Hebrew tongue.

Though these two words have been transliterated from different languages, it should be kept in mind that exact knowledge about the pronunciation of much of the ancient Hebrew language has been lost. This is due to the fact that Hebrew vowel marks were not developed until a relatively late period. The inclusion of the name of the sun God, Shamash, is not surprising, since the Egyptians, whom the Jews formerly lived among, were originally sun worshipers. Osiris, Ra, Atum, Kephri, Khunum, Amon, Horus, and dozens of other Egyptian Gods were symbols for the sun in various seasons, or parts of the sky, or simply alternate names for the same sun god, which were independently developed in the originally separate Egyptian nomes.

There are dozens of other artifacts of the Egyptian faith found within Judaism. For example, the Jews were recorded in scripture at one time as worshiping a golden calf, which is tremendously similar not only to the Egyptian Hathor, but also to the Apis Bull of Ptah, who was later fused to Osiris.

"And he received the gold from their hand, and he fashioned it with an engraving tool, and made a molded calf. Then they said, 'This is your god, O Israel, that brought you out of the land of Egypt!' So when Aaron saw it, he built an altar before it. And Aaron made a proclamation and said, 'Tomorrow is a feast to the Lord.' Then they rose early on the next day, offered burnt offerings, and brought peace offerings; and the people sat down to eat and drink, and rose up to play" (Exodus 32:4-6).

It is also no coincidence that the Jews revered the shrine-like "Ark of the Covenant." In scripture, this container supposedly served as the seat of their God, Jehovah's, power, and potentially even his person. This Hebrew ark was almost identical, both in design and purpose, to the Egyptian Serekh Shrine, which supposedly contained the remains of Osiris. As the Jews stored this ark in their temple, only transporting it out during special ceremonies, or national emergencies, so the Egyptians stored their Serekh Shrine within their temples, such as the one at Dendarah, but would, during special ceremonies, draw it around these temples on a sledge. Later, when Osiris was fused with Ra, we encounter this shrine depicted atop the Sektet and Matet boats, which Ra traversed the skies in.[173.] An example ark of this sort, dedicated to Anubis, was discovered among the furnishings within the tomb of the Pharoah Tutankhamen.

In addition, scripture records the Jews being commanded by Moses to build and worship a snake on a pole, in order to be healed from snake bites while wandering the desert. This totem was referred to in scripture as "Nehushtan."

"Then the Lord said to Moses, 'Make a fiery serpent, and set it on a pole; and it shall be that everyone who is bitten, when he looks at it, shall live.' So Moses made a bronze serpent, and put it on a pole; and so it was, if a serpent had bitten anyone, when he looked at the bronze serpent, he lived" (Numbers 21:8-9).

This reminds one of the *Was* staff of Thoth, which was frequently depicted with snakes on it. It is an interesting fact that, in the Hebrew temple where it was located, the Jews continued to burn incense to, and worship this serpent effigy until the close of the 8th century B.C., when Hezekiah had it destroyed (1 Kings 18).

With all of these obvious derivations and adaptations from the ancient Egyptian faith, not to mention the dozens of others which were left unmentioned, as entire shelves of books have been written about this single topic alone, it is unclear how anyone can claim that the Tanakh, or the Bible, which form the foundations of the Jewish and Christian faiths, are perfect revelations from God? The person who would do so must either disprove all of these individual derivations, or perform the equally impossible task of explaining how such derivations can be perfect, when they clearly changed during their adoption. Typically, both attempts are made. In the first case, most derivations are claimed to be weak and unsupported by facts. In the second, they are claimed to have been revised and purified of all error when adopted within the Tanakh and Bible. Neither of these claims are true.

Leaving Christianity

I was the son of very conservative Christian parents. As such, I read my Bible with interest, went to AWANAS (sort of the church version of Boy Scouts), was involved in church youth activities, attended Sunday school, listened to Christian music, dragged my friends to church, and occasionally led Bible studies during the lunch hours in school. This pious zeal continued after I entered the military. I led Bible studies in basic training, beat on my friends' doors in tech school, inviting them to accompany me to church on Sunday mornings, and occasionally wrote my pastor back home, reasoning with him over concerns that I felt about any problematic passages which I had encountered within scripture.

The first hole which sprung in my dam of orthodox views occurred when I encountered people who were proselytizing, or "witnessing," as they called it, to the dorm-bound airmen on base. These people were members of a church known as the International Church of Christ, or ICOC. Their seriousness about putting their faith into action immediately attracted me to them. They had a sort of unwritten rule which they lived by, that a day wherein they hadn't invited someone to church, or told someone about Jesus, was a wasted one. Besides these qualities, which any serious Christian would consider admirable, I later discovered that they also possessed several cultish characteristics.

Firstly, they strongly discouraged their single members, who were unsurprisingly the bulk of their adherents, from dating nonmembers. They also believed that they were the only "true" Christians. They based this latter claim upon Bible verses, such as Luke 9:23, where Christ states that any who want to be his disciples must "pick up their cross" (i.e. labor on behalf of Christianity) *daily*, and follow him. Since, as these people pointed out to neophytes, they were the only ones who were *literally* going out as a body every single day and witnessing or inviting people to church, and I couldn't deny this fact, they believed that they were the only "true" body of Christians.

As an impressionable young man, I was convinced by this and happily re-baptized into their church; my previous baptism, which had been performed by my grandfather in a lake while camping, not being considered genuine by ICOC leadership. After this baptism, I busily went about, paired off with my "discipler," canvasing the local stores and handing out cards containing church information.

The "discipler" role, which this church utilized, was another cultish property which I was ignorant of at the time. Many cults assign a specific individual to spend as much time with new recruits as possible, in order to ensure that they are kept away from any dissuading influences. I would, of course, be embarrassed while handing out cards inviting people to church with my "discipler," yet we both took pride, whenever we would encounter the occasional hypersensitive atheist, who would inevitably complain to management and have us thrown out of whatever store we had encountered him in. We felt this way because we thought that this was a light form of persecution which placed us in the company of the early Christians; evidencing the sincerity of our faith to an ever-vigilant God.

This went on briefly until I, excited with the "truth" which I had newly discovered, shared the whole series of events with my parents, strongly urging them to follow the same path, out of concern for their souls. Needless to say, this conversation went other than as intended. My deeply religious parents did a bit of research on the ICOC, and realizing its cultish characteristics, immediately became alarmed and implored me to stop attending.

This came as a tremendous shock to me, at the time. As an often-lonely young airman in Alaska, with no nearby family and precious few friends, this church had immediately provided me with an array of people who claimed the deepest allegiance to me. Indeed, at this point, the few friends which I did have, I had for the most part already recruited into the ICOC as well.

Regardless, as an obedient son, I trusted in my parents' discretion and complied. At this point, several ICOC church members, including my "discipler" and my roommate, briefly and vigorously attempted to dissuade me from leaving the church; citing various ominous verses about "falling away" such as 2 Peter 2:21-22. This verse states quite plainly that, "It would have been better for them not to have known the way of righteousness, than to have known it and turned away from the holy commandment passed on to them. What the true proverb says has happened to them: 'The dog returns to its own vomit, and the sow, after washing herself, returns to wallowing in the mire.'"

Seeing my resolve, my newfound church "family" eventually relegated me to my fate and subsequently began to shun me. Though the impact of such shunning would be laughable to me today, it was tremendously challenging to cope with while still an idealistic, 20-year-old airman. Having recruited the majority of my friends into the church, I found myself more alone afterwards, than I had been when I had initially sought fellowship in that church to begin with. When I confronted my roommate about this, he responded by once more asking me to return to the church and quoting me the verse which ICOC leadership had shown him on the subject: Titus 3:10-11. This verse advised him to "Reject a divisive man after the first and second admonition, knowing that such a person is warped and sinning, being self-condemned." Knowing that my actions at that time had been driven by noble intentions, reading this verse still makes me wince even today, decades later. Instead of wincing out of sorrow, as I did then, I do so now out of anger at the sheer closed-minded vanity of those presumptuous enough to use, as well as those stupid and arrogant enough to pen, such a piece of bad doctrine and worse philosophy. Were these people so perfect in their understanding of all philosophical principles, that any who would dare to openly disagree with them more than once should be anathematized? Of course they weren't. Neither was Paul himself, who supposedly penned this passage.

The confusing period which I entered at this point in my life caused me to delve deeply into my faith, as well as into the scriptures which supported it, in the hope of finding both the peace that it promised repeatedly within its pages, as well as the reason why a church could be wrong, which clearly embodied what I read in what I then still believed to be infallible scripture. For the first time in my life, I had encountered a crossroads where both parties claimed to have religious truth on their side, claimed that the other was wrong, and claimed to derive their authority from scripture.

To qualify the above statement, this had not been the first time that aspects of my faith had been challenged. This had occurred dozens of times before. Yet previous theological "opponents," for lack of a better term, had been dispatched with comparative ease, merely by consulting scripture and noting where their doctrine contradicted, or misrepresented the meaning of what was then to me the "word of God."

What made this occasion different was the fact that everything which I read in scripture seemed to confirm what the ICOC taught, and yet, I instinctively both understood and agreed with my parents' concerns. The arguments which my parents used in this situation tended to focus on how involvement with such a group would ultimately destroy one's social and career prospects. The ICOC, on the other hand, claimed that concerning one's self with the latter was choosing worldly prosperity "where moth and rust destroy" over eternal happiness, something which scripture specifically warns against in Matthew 6:19-21.

For many years afterwards, I struggled to solve this problem. Indeed, I now realize that it cannot be solved while simultaneously clinging to a belief that all scripture is divinely inspired. This is because any who put a sufficient amount of effort into studying the Bible will inevitably realize that various scriptural authors clearly held conflicting, competing, and contradictory philosophical views themselves. I now realize that the ICOC was indeed mimicking the actions of the early Christian church, yet I also realize that the religion of the early church, and indeed, of Jesus himself, is ultimately one which leads to monkish isolation from all but those holding analogous views. This is the path which the ICOC was on. This is the thing which people sensed about it and deemed "cultish."

I believe that the early Christians understood these principles exponentially better than the modern church generally does, and took them quite seriously. When one reads the early ecclesiastical histories, prior to the 313 A.D. Edict of Milan, which forced the Roman empire to adopt the new faith, one hears about men and women flocking to monasteries, nunneries, deserts, and lonely caves, where they could avoid the taint of worldly desires and focus upon little else but divine contemplation and active missionary work. These early church fathers, exemplified by Anthony the Great, are often referred to as "Desert Fathers" for this very reason.

While this is innocuous to society on a small scale, it is fatal to it on a large one. How can courts and civil institutions continue to function in the face of men who state that their only authority, ultimately, is God? While there are scriptural verses advising obedience to the law and magistrates, what is to be done by these magistrates when a man claims special inspiration for his actions? How can businesses and governments continue to function when all are ultimately called to abandon these things to be missionaries?

This last point is generally rationalized by modern Christian believers who want to continue to support their families, as well as by modern churches who must support themselves on the "tithes" of someone earning an income, but nowhere is it encountered within the New Testament. Indeed, in the face of the Christian doctrine that all of the unreached masses of mankind are steadily swelling the population of hell, how can anyone in possession of a functioning conscience waste the bulk of their workdays, indeed their very lives, on the comparative trifles of business. Is this not hardness of heart and base selfishness?

"But I must provide myself and my family with an income." Pray tell, where do you find this supposed "right" within scripture. Did God not feed Elijah with bread brought by birds (1 Kings 17:2-16)? Did God not send manna and quail to sustain the Hebrew nation as they wandered the deserts of Sinai (Exodus 16)? Did John the Baptist not survive on locusts and honey alone (Matthew 3:4)? Did Christ not feed thousands on two separate occasions from some small baskets of loaves and fish (Matthew 15:32-39 and Mark 8:1-9)? Oh ye of little faith; where is this faith which you claim and speak so highly of?

I believe this is why Paul urged Christian men and women not to marry, if possible (1 Corinthians 7). He knew that such marriages would result in families that would potentially shake them from their monkish asceticism; as the cries of a hungry child have a powerful effect upon a parent's heart.

Returning from this digression, I believe that leaving the ICOC was the first real situation where I had to rely upon my own conscience, when it appeared to contradict some portions of scripture. Still being a Christian, I was used to listening to my conscience when it aligned with scriptural teaching, but was unfamiliar and uncomfortable with relying upon it when the two conflicted.

Eventually the loneliness from leaving the ICOC faded, as all things seem to do, with the passage of time. I found a new, admittedly more lukewarm church and began to make new friends. I occasionally saw my former ICOC friends, but any attempt at conversation with them had become merely cordial and empty of any true depth; as often occurs once the underlying trust within a relationship is sundered.

After I separated from active duty, I began college, using my military benefits and working for the Air National Guard to pay my way. At that point, I remember believing that the New Testament letters were of no more significance than any other letter. Granted, I believed them to be *good* letters written by *godly* men, expressing their views much like any pastor would in any sermon; but I did not believe these letters to be divinely inspired.

My devout parents eventually recommended that I discuss this matter with their, and at the time my, pastor. Although this pastor is a brilliant and kindhearted man, the arguments which he presented appeared to be simply more polished versions of the easily refutable ones which I had already encountered so many times before. Given that the man was finishing his Ph.D. in theology, I was somewhat surprised that he didn't shock me by pointing out some fundamental fact which I had overlooked during my personal studies; which instantly blew away the majority of my doubts, like a puff of smoke in the wind. He did not.

I plodded along in my faith until a personal crisis eventually found me in the form of a broken engagement. This relationship had ended when my then fiancé became enchanted by the siren's call of a certain charismatic church. This church, as that type notoriously does, manipulated and preyed upon the time and resources of either the well intentioned and trusting ignorant, or of the emotionally needy: often both.

As with the ICOC event, this event was once again accompanied by comments that, "There is something wrong with (my) faith." Scripture had informed me that God would bless me for seeking him with all of my heart. Yet my seeking and subsequent growth had caused me to become skeptical whenever I encountered poorly thought out church doctrines, such as those which this church espoused. This skepticism was, in large part, the reason why this relationship had imploded.

She and I, though now separate, were both seniors in the same major and university. Having formerly planned our courses out to coincide, I had to endure another year in the same classes with her, observing her laughing, getting a new ear piercing, cutting short her hair, and the various other things that girls frequently do after a breakup to send the message that they are both available and happier than ever. Of course she was. She had an entire church-load of gullible, yet well intentioned charismatics to provide her with a never-ending supply of confirmation bias.

In the meantime, my pain benefited me by giving me an almost superhuman drive to digest scripture. I read it. I listened to audio recordings of it while I ironed, while I drove, and while I ran. I finished the Bible and then started over, and then did the same thing a few more times. I kept reading, thinking that there must be something more that I would stumble upon which would provide the comfort that I needed. There was, but it ultimately proved to be time.

I eventually realized that there was nothing actually wrong with my doctrine, but then again, I couldn't be sure that there was really anything wrong with that church's doctrine either. Both sides of the coin appeared to be there: the conservative legalistic version of Christianity, as well as what I saw to be charismatic zaniness. "It had to be a problem with the versions of scripture," I thought. So, into the dark labyrinth of versions I delved. I read books on canonization and began reading the earliest of church fathers such as Origen, Eusebius, Polycarp, Clement, Ignatius, and many others, attempting to ascertain both how key verses sounded when quoted by these men and how they understood the fundamental Christian doctrines, during this early period.

This ended up generating more questions than answers. As I was rummaging around within the older version of Christianity, which was much closer to the source, and therefore more likely to be authentic, I stumbled upon the fact that the concept of Trinity was clearly nowhere to be found within the writings of the earliest of church fathers. This was especially evident in the writings of Origen and Justin Martyr. Indeed, these authors appeared to make strong cases for Unitarianism instead. I began to study the matter further, reading the early debates where the Trinitarian doctrine was first brought to light, such as the records of the Councils of Nicea and Tyre, and the letters of Arius. The more that I studied the matter, the more I realized that far more solid evidence existed supporting the conclusion that Trinity was a mistake, than did supporting the position that the concept of Trinity was merely a deeper understanding and clarification of doctrine originally put forward by Jesus, the patriarchs, and the apostles.

Predominant among the many authors that I encountered who helped me to realize this fact, were Isaac Newton, Eunomius, John Milton, Thomas Jefferson, William Penn, Ethan Allen, Michael Servetus, and William Whiston. In order to ensure that I had a balanced perspective on this issue, and wasn't simply suffering from confirmation bias, I read the strongest pro-Trinitarian evidence which I could find as well. There was no author better for this than the originator of the concept of Trinity, an Alexandrian Bishop named *Athanasius*. I had already been introduced to Athanasius by Isaac Newton in his theological invective against him, entitled, *Paradoxical Questions Concerning the Morals and Actions of Athanasius and his Followers.*[149] Regardless of Newton's very plausible reasons for condemning him, I believed that Athanasius would be more familiar with the original meanings of the Greek words and phrases, as they were understood by the apostles, than most theologians of today were. This is because this man was both highly educated, and lived ~1700 years closer to the period during which the New Testament was originally penned. I therefore proceeded to read his lengthy *Four Discourses Against the Arians.*[141]

As I studied, I began to notice that, whenever I would delve more deeply into what were considered "proof texts" for the doctrine of Trinity, I would always discover problems. For example, Colossians 1:15-18 in the New International Version (NIV) of scripture, read as, "The Son is the image of the invisible God, the firstborn *over* all creation. For *in* him all things were created: things in heaven and on earth, visible and invisible, whether thrones or powers or rulers or authorities; all things have been created *through* him and for him. He is *before* all things...he is the beginning and the firstborn from among the dead..."

This verse was pointed to by Trinitarians as emphasizing both Jesus' unity with God, as well as his positional primacy; due to its usage of the phrases: "firstborn over all creation" and "(positionally) before all things." Yet I was looking at the New International Version (NIV). This version, which was completed in 1978, was well known for being somewhat "loose" in its translations. I needed to rely upon a translation which focused upon literalism, and which accurately reflected the original Greek manuscripts. It was well known within the laity circles that the "gold standard" for accuracy of translation was the far older (1611 A.D.) King James Version (KJV) of scripture. In order to do due diligence, I also compared KJV renderings of passages to the Douay Rheims English Translation of the Latin Vulgate (~400 A.D.), as well as the Von Tischendorf translation of the Codex Sinaiticus (~350 A.D.). With few exceptions, all confirmed the accuracy of the KJV rendering. The KJV translated this passage as: "(Jesus) is the image of the invisible God, the firstborn *of* every creature. For *by* him were all things created, that are in heaven, and that are in earth, visible and invisible, whether they be thrones, or dominions, or principalities, or powers: all things were created *by* him, and for him...and he is before all things... who is the beginning, the firstborn from the dead..."

The change from, "Firstborn *over* all creation...he is before all things," in the NIV, to "Firstborn *of* every creature...he is before all things," in the KJV, implied that Jesus was actually *sequentially* created by God before all other creatures. Sections within this passage admittedly remained, even in the KJV, which discussed Christ's positional primacy as well, however, the possibility of sequential primacy created a significant problem for what remained of my orthodox views.

Sequential creation, and in fact creation at all, would imply that there was a time, before which, that Christ did not exist. This view was fatal to the concept of Trinity. If the "Son of God," whom Jesus was proclaimed to be, was one of the three branches of a triune god, then there could never be a time when his spirit was created. Such an admission would mean that there was a time when a part of the Trinity didn't exist. "Surely the New Testament authors must have been referring to the time before his fleshly birth to Mary, and not to his spiritual one," I told myself.

I looked again at the passage to see if this could simply be referring to his Earthly birth. I noticed that, immediately after the section in verse 15 which seemed to be calling him the "Firstborn of every creature," or in other words, the first *created* being, was the section in verse 16 which claimed that Jesus, not God, created everything else, both in heaven and on Earth. "For *by* him were all things created, that are in heaven, and that are in earth, visible and invisible, whether they be thrones, or dominions, or principalities, or powers: all things were created *by* him, and *for* him..."

This was disturbingly similar to the concept of the Demiurge which had been put forward by Plato in his *Timaeus*, some ~400 years earlier. According to Plato, this Demiurge was an inferior God, which the supreme God created, who afterwards fashioned all of creation. Note the following passage from this work. "For the Deity, intending to make this world like the fairest and most perfect of intelligible beings, framed *one* visible animal comprehending within itself all other animals of a kindred nature...Such was the whole plan of the eternal God about the god that was to be, to whom for this reason he gave a body...And in the center he put the soul, which he diffused throughout the body...and he made the universe a circle moving in a circle, one and solitary, yet by reason of its excellence able to converse with itself, and needing no other friendship or acquaintance. Having these purposes in view he created the world a blessed god."[157]

This demiurgic concept was later elaborated upon by both Plotinus, in his Six Enneads and Proclus in his treatise on Platonic theology. Consider the following two sample passages. From Plotinus: "The ordering principle is twofold; there is the principle known to us as the *Demiurge* and there is the Soul of the All; we apply the appellation "Zeus" sometimes to the Demiurge and sometimes to the principle conducting the universe."[37] From Proclus: "But from the Timaeus, you may obtain the theory about *intelligibles*, a divine narration about the demiurgic monad; and the most full truth about the *mundane* Gods."[158]

Wait a moment. If this Colossians 1:15-18 passage was discussing Jesus' creation, and then immediately discussed him creating everything else in heaven and Earth, it wouldn't make sense for it to be referring to Jesus' birth on Earth, as all of this later named stuff, including "all things created, that are in heaven, and that are in earth, visible and invisible..." was already formed at that point. This passage had to be referring to a creation of the spiritual, supposedly demiurgic aspect of Jesus.

This was the exact conclusion which Arius had arrived at in ~300 A.D., as can be seen in the following excerpt from a letter which he sent to his friend Eusebius. "But we say and believe, and have taught, and do teach, that the Son is not unbegotten, nor in any way unbegotten...and that he existed not before he was begotten, or *created*, or purposed, or established. For he was not unbegotten. We are persecuted, because we say that the Son had a beginning, but that God was without beginning."[159]

This can also be seen in Arius' letter to Alexander, the Bishop of Alexandria: "And God, being the cause of all things, is Unbegun and altogether Sole, but the Son being begotten apart from time by the Father, and being created and founded before ages, was not before His generation, but being begotten apart from time before all things, alone was made to subsist by the Father. For He is not eternal or coeternal or co-unoriginate with the Father, nor has He His being together with the Father, as some speak of relations, introducing two ingenerate beginnings, but God is before all things as being Monad and Beginning of all. Wherefore also He is before the Son; as we have learned also from thy preaching in the midst of the Church. So far then as from God He has being, and glories, and life, and all things are delivered unto Him, in such sense is God His origin. For He is above Him, as being His God, and before Him...understood by some to mean as if a part of [God], one in essence or as an issue, then the Father is according to them compounded and divisible and alterable and material, and, as far as their belief goes, has the circumstances of a body, who is the incorporeal God."[160]

I realized that I hadn't noticed Jesus being portrayed within scripture as a demiurgic creator of all but himself before, as the KJV rendering of Colossians 1:16 appeared to indicate. When I looked back at the NIV, I discovered that the reason for this was because the translators of this version had changed the rendering of this verse from, "For *by* him were all things created," as in the KJV, to, "For *in* him all things were created..." What? Since when do the concepts of "in" and "by" mean the same thing? Could it be possible that the NIV translators had intentionally made that very subtle, yet very significant change for the express purpose of supporting the view of Christ being part of the Trinity? Could it be that this same motive was also involved when they made Christ the firstborn "over" creation rather than the firstborn "of every creature?" Both of these changes would aid the Trinitarian position by making Christ both without a beginning and also not the subsequent creator of everything else; since other parts of scripture clearly ascribe this latter role to *Jehovah / El*.

What if I was misunderstanding the meaning of the phrase, "firstborn of every creature," in verse 15. I dug into my Greek concordance to check. When I looked, I found that the word for "creature," which was used in verse 15, was κτί σις (i.e. *ktisis*; Greek Concordance G2936[161]). This meant, literally, anything *created*. It shared the same root as the word used in verse 16 when discussing Christ *creating* everything else, κτί ζω (i.e. *ktizō*).

I proceeded to look up "Firstborn." This turned out to be a phrase formed by two root words, which was used 9 times in the New Testament (NT): πρωτό τοκος (i.e. *prōtotokos*; Greek Concordance G4416[162]). I was unsurprised to find that, in all 9 instances, the meaning was exactly as it sounded: the *first* that was *born*. I looked up the two roots of this word to see if I could get clarification regarding if "first" referred to primacy, or sequence. The initial root was πρῶ τος (i.e. *protos*; Greek Concordance G4413[163]). It was used 104 times in the NT, and meant *sequentially* first in 84 of these. It only meant *positionally* first, or *foremost*, in 9; always in these instances being translated as "Chief" in the KJV, when encountered alone. The residual 11 meanings were not directly related to the current discussion (e.g. first day). The second root of the word firstborn was τί κτω (i.e. *tiktō*; Greek Concordance G5088[164]). This was always translated as *birth*, in much the same way as we would commonly use the term today.

It seemed that this phrase, "Firstborn of every creature," was far more likely to mean *sequentially* created first, than *positionally* first; or *foremost*. Yet I had read the writings of many Bible scholars, and had debated with those who believed themselves to be so, among the orthodox, Trinitarian camp. I was not ignorant that any speck of evidence which appeared to support the Trinitarian position would be clung to and touted as an insurmountable mountain.

The more that I began to look for these subtle word selection changes which appeared to have been made for the sole purpose of supporting the doctrine of Trinity, the more that I encountered: especially within the later translations. For example, in Hebrews 1:1-5, we again encounter an inadvertent admission of the *creation* of the spiritual form of Jesus. In this verse it states, "God...Hath in these last days spoken unto us by his Son...*by* whom also he made the worlds...Being *made* so much better than the angels, as he hath by inheritance obtained a more excellent name than they. For unto which of the angels said he at any time, thou art my Son, *this day* have I *begotten* thee? And again, I will be to him a Father, and he shall be to me a Son?" (KJV). Here we have the phrase, "Being *made* so much better than the angels."

Initially, this phrase, even in the KJV, appears to imply a promotion of sorts and not a creation, yet all depends upon where any punctuation, which doesn't exist in the original Greek, might be placed. Consider if a comma were to have been added after the word "made." This part of the passage would then read, "Being *made,* so much better than the angels." Suddenly the entire meaning of the passage has been transformed from one of promotion, to one of creation and comparison. I am not insisting that this is necessarily the correct rendering of the passage, however, consider that the Greek rendering of this phrase "being made," is Strong's G1096 "γί νομαι, (i.e. gínomai): a prolongation and middle voice form of a primary verb; to cause to be (generate), i.e. (reflexively) to become (come into being)..."[165]

Now I freely admit that I truncated this lengthy Strong's entry, as it later makes special exception for how this word is used in reference to Jesus in this instance. It should be kept in mind, however, that the authors of this work were well aware of the implications of using a word that essentially means *generate,* or *create* in connection with the Son of God. Yet this is the first meaning listed both in Strong's Concordance, as well as in Thayer's Greek Lexicon. Let's just admit that, from a grammatical standpoint, this passage "Being *made* so much better than the angels," could be referring to a *creation* and *comparison,* as much as it could be referring to the more orthodox view of *promotion.*

Now for the coup de grâce. Examine the next verse. "For unto which of the angels said he at any time, thou art my Son, this day have I *begotten* thee?" Which specific day, pray tell, did God the father "beget" Jesus. Realizing the risk here, most Biblical scholars will claim, because they have no other option, that this is referring to when Jesus was born into the flesh. Yet the author of Hebrews was quoting Psalms 2:7 here, which was written hundreds of years prior to this event. This means that the Psalmist was either prophetically referring to the corporal birth of Jesus, or else, in keeping with the previously discussed, more correct rendering of Colossians 1:15-18 (i.e. firstborn of every creature), he was referring to this first creation of the Son of God prior to all other creation.

Such a rendering would make the concept of an "only *begotten* (i.e. generated) Son of God," make more sense. Like the Demiurge of Plato, the Divine Intellect of Plotinus, and the first Intelligible God of Proclus, the Christian "Son of God" would be the only being which the highest God ever created, all else being created by this being. In this scenario, mankind would not be "children" of the supreme god, but his grandchildren. The only other option with this "only begotten" phrase is to claim that the authors were referring to the only incident where God ever directly impregnated a female. Yet what of the dozens of other analogous claims of Zeus, Osiris, and the various other conceptions of the supreme God doing this very thing?

Here we have had a brief glimpse into the dark world of the *Grammarians*, who found entire doctrines upon the context, or tense of a single word. Though the ancient authors of scripture had a specific idea in mind, which they long ago attempted to convey in writing, the words, or phrases which they used to do so can often be rendered in several different ways during translation, many of which will drastically change their meaning. This being the case, decisions about the correct rendering of these words, during the translation of scripture, are often battlegrounds of religious sects, and academics with various impressive credentials. It is a high stakes game, when translating something that can influence the doctrine of millions of faithful.

English political activist, John Milton, the author of the famous *Paradise Lost*, who was fluent in both Hebrew and Greek, a man who is considered to be the greatest poet in the English language, mentioned his loathing of these "Grammarians" in his lengthy, seldom read prose work, *On Christian Doctrine*. In this work he states, "I entered upon an assiduous course of study in my youth, beginning with the books of the Old and New Testament in their original languages, and going diligently through a few of the shorter systems of divines, in imitation of whom I was in the habit of classing under certain heads whatever passages of Scripture occurred for extraction, to be made use of hereafter as occasion might require. At length, I resorted with increased confidence to some of the more copious theological treatises, and to the examination of the arguments advanced by the conflicting parties respecting certain disputed points of faith. But, to speak the truth with freedom as well as candor, I was concerned to discover in many instances adverse reasonings either evaded by wretched shifts, or attempted to be refuted, rather speciously than with solidity, by an affected display of formal sophisms, or by a constant recourse to the quibbles of the *grammarians* while what was most pertinaciously espoused as the true doctrine, seemed often defended, with more vehemence than strength of argument, by misconstructions of Scripture, or by the hasty deduction of erroneous inferences. Owing to these causes, the truth was sometimes as strenuously opposed as if it had been an error or a heresy while errors and heresies were substituted for the truth, and valued rather from deference to custom and the spirit of party than from the authority of Scripture. According to my judgement, therefore, neither my creed nor my hope of salvation could be safely trusted to such guides..."[166]

It appeared that, whenever it aided the Trinitarian position to have Jesus be a distinctly different being from God, Orthodox Christians would claim that he was the supposed "Son of God"; absolutely distinct, unique, and differing from the being whom they refer to as "God the Father." When it harmed their position to emphasize Jesus' individuality, they would demand that he was "one with" the Father; a phrase which they abused to mean that the two (in fact three, when the "Holy Spirit" is also considered) are the absolute same being.

In doing this, these people willingly abandoned reason itself; celebrating this "divine mystery" as a sort of conquest of faith over reason. It is one thing to claim that something miraculous has occurred, for which an explanation has yet to be determined, but also with the assumption that an explanation exists. It is another thing entirely to claim that the explanation is known, and that this explanation destroys the very foundation of reason itself. As the Pythagoreans concluded, there is little in the way of abstract truth which is stronger than arithmetic: and this itself was sacrificed. *One* plus *one*, plus *one* would be claimed to equal *three*, when it supported the Trinitarian argument; but when being *three* created theological, or logical problems, they would claim that it equaled *one*.

In attempting to salvage conflicting scriptural verses, orthodox Christian apologists incidentally struck the tree of reason at its root. It is for this reason that appeals to Trinity surface with extraordinary frequency, whenever even the strongest chains of logic, facts, and evidence which casts justifiable doubt upon the absolute inerrancy of any point in the Trinitarian Christian faith are brought forward. Trinity is used during debate as a sort of proof that orthodox Christians are not required to adhere to logic. If the rules of logic have supposedly been broken in this one instance, why not in others? Why not in infinite daily instances?

As Jefferson mentioned, this is a tremendously dark and dangerous path of irrationality for the mind to proceed down, and we will not follow them down it. Without logic, there is really nothing to debate; as no fact, or truth remains safe. The most outlandish claims can be made, which become impossible to refute. Animals can be claimed to talk (Numbers 22:21-39); oceans can be claimed to cover the globe and then magically disappear (Genesis 5:32-10:1); the sun can be claimed to freeze in the sky for an entire day (Joshua 10:1), an event which would require the Earth to freeze, mid-spin, and then recommence its spin a day later, all without throwing anyone, or anything into orbit; shadows can be claimed to reverse down the temple steps (2 Kings 20:8-11), an occurrence which would require the Earth to reverse its spin twice, without throwing anyone into orbit; murder can be claimed to sometimes be a good (2 Samuel 21:9); and divine condemnation and blessing can be claimed to pass from one person, or nation, for the actions of another, like currency (John 3:16). There will be no end to the possible absurdities.

Zodiac

It is difficult to differentiate the traits demanded of the infinite energy source required to continuously inject the universe with energy, in order to offset its perpetual loss, due to photonic radiation into the nothingness beyond the universe's edge, from traits which the more insightful ancients applied to their concepts of God. This is especially true of the highly developed concepts of God which were put forward by certain sects of the Egyptians, Brahmins, Zoroastrians, and Neo-Platonists. Many among these sects revered and honored (i.e. worshiped) light itself, as a symbol of God. This is interesting, since the massless photons which comprise light are a form of pure energy.

This light worship among the ancients wasn't limited to direct sources of light, such as the sun, individual or constellations of stars, and fire, but was also generally directed towards its more indirect sources, such as planets and the moon. This is because, during ancient times, these were generally believed to be simply brighter, more mobile stars. These are the so called, "wandering stars," which we often encounter the ancients referring to in their preserved texts: all others being referred to as "fixed."

These arrangements of "fixed" and "wandering stars" were represented by various symbols, depending upon the faith, nation, and period in question. Enter the zodiac. The zodiac was developed during an unknown period in antiquity. It is unclear whether the Egyptians, or the Chaldeans hold the honor of this invention, as both show a familiarity with it in ancient times. They both knew that, as the year changed, the sun rose and passed through 12 different constellations, which have a roughly north to south alignment, known as the *zodiacal band*. They also found that the passage of the sun through each of these constellations took approximately 30 days. This, along with the roughly 30-day lunar phase cycle, became the earliest of calendars among the ancients.

As mentioned previously, symbols related to the shapes of the various constellations had been developed, in order to serve as memory aids about seasonal events. This was especially true of the 12 zodiacal constellations; from Pisces, to Sagittarius. Though some of these symbols were known by other names and given different symbols by the ancients then those which we are accustomed to, they reside in the same heavenly location and therefore served the same purpose. These zodiacal symbols became known as "signs"; a word derived from the

Latin *signum,* whence we also derive the words *signal, signature, sigil,* and *seal.* The common concept between these various derivative words is the idea of a symbol of something which is approaching, present, or departed. This is what the zodiacal signs were to the ancients, simultaneous indicators of approaching, present, or past natural events: the very definition of a calendar.

It must be driven home to the modern reader just how critically important this tool was to the cultures which were wise enough to invent, or adopt it. In ancient times, the margin between having a surplus of crops, and starving was typically so narrow for the common people that they had to be absolutely efficient with their agricultural efforts. The ancient Egyptians paid particularly close attention to the zodiacal calendar, since this tool enabled them to predict and prepare for the Nile's annual floods. Doing so turned this would-be annual catastrophe into the Egyptian nation's greatest boon. Evidence of the early familiarity which the Egyptians possessed with the zodiac calendar can be observed in the relatively accurate Dendera Zodiac, which was discovered on the ceiling of the Temple of Hathor, in Dendara, Egypt, during the Napoleonic expeditions.

The zodiacal signs which the sun traversed between the vernal equinox and the summer solstice signified increasing solar energy to the ancients, and were therefore considered to be beneficial, or good. The others, which the sun traversed between the autumnal equinox and the winter solstice, indicated decreasing solar energy, and were therefore considered to be harmful, or evil. Allegories were developed about these signs, as well as about the other constellations, in order to serve as memory aids of seasonal phenomena. The god who symbolized the sun, for example, was said to be reborn during the winter equinox; the Egyptians symbolizing this rebirth by parading a child in a cradle around the temple.

Note the following excerpt confirming this point from the renowned Professor, Charles Dupuis, taken from his *The Origin of All Religious Worship*: "In the national library there is an Arabian manuscript, containing the twelve signs, delineated and colored, and there is also to be seen a young child alongside of the celestial Virgin, being represented in about the same style as our Virgins, and like an Egyptian Isis with her son. It is more than probable, that the ancient astrologers have placed in the Heavens the infantile image of the new Sun, in the constellation, which presided over its new birth and at that of the year in the winter solstice, and that from this have originated the fictions of the God Day, conceived in the chaste womb of a virgin, because that constellation was really the Virgin. This conclusion is far more natural, than the opinion of those, who obstinately believe, that there had existed a woman, who had become mother, without ceasing to be virgin, and that the fruit engendered by her, is that Eternal Being, which moves and governs whole Nature. Thus the Greeks said, that their God with the forms of Ram or Lamb, the famous Ammon or Jupiter, was brought up by Tenemis, which is also one of the names of the Virgin of the constellations; she is also called Ceres, to whom the title of "Holy Virgin" was given, and who was the mother of young Bacchus or of the Sun, the image of which was exposed in the sanctuaries at the winter solstice, in the shape of an infant, according to Macrobius. His testimony is confirmed by the author of the Chronicle of Alexandria, who expresses himself in the following words: 'The Egyptians have consecrated up to this day the child-birth of a virgin and the nativity of her son, who is exposed in a crib to the adoration of the people. King Ptolemy, having asked the reason of this custom, he was answered that it was a mystery, taught by a respectable prophet to their fathers.'"[199]

The more agrarian of the ancient cultures naturally tended to select symbols for the constellations which were related to agriculture, or animal husbandry, such as local flora, or fauna whose appearance, or prevalence correlated with that of the light sources they represented. The more warlike of the ancient cultures, whose rulers were often out conquering other lands, or protecting their own from conquest, generally selected anthropomorphic (i.e. possessing human form) symbols of warlike beings, often developing entire allegories about them associated with their appearances, or alignment in the sky, during various times and seasons.

One of these warrior analogies, which is repeatedly encountered across dozens of cultures and periods, is that of a symbol of the sun, perhaps a hero, heroine, god, or goddess, that is killed, or gravely wounded, by a symbol of winter. This being later revives, or is reborn, overcomes his, or her natural enemy, and is restored to his original state of power and glory. Some cultures believed the heroic death, or injury to occur slowly, over a long period, while others believed it to occur all at once. Both, however, tended to agree in placing the beginning of the passion event near the summer solstice, when the days began to shorten, or near the autumnal equinox, when the nights began to grow longer than the days. Often one or both of these dates were commemorated by a ceremony of mourning.

The heroic revival, or rebirth, tended to occur near the winter solstice, when the days begin to lengthen once more, or at the vernal equinox, when they had grown longer than the nights. The symbol of winter was also believed to be overcome, or killed, and the hero fully restored when the length of the days once more surpassed that of the nights.

A few of the many instances of this allegory will be mentioned below. In ancient Greece, the Erymanthian Boar, which is thought to be the oriental version of the constellation Ursa Major[167], fatally wounds Adonis, who is later reborn. In ancient Egypt, Typhoon, who is later associated with Set, seals Osiris in a coffin-like box, casts this coffin into the sea, later locates and dismembers Osiris' corpse, only to have it reassembled by Isis and returned to life in one tradition, and reborn as Horus in another. In the latter tradition, Horus goes on to battle his father's adversary. In Babylon, Tammuz (i.e. Dumuzi) begins dying for an undetermined reason during the summer solstice, only to be revived at some undetermined later point; likely correlating with the winter solstice. In Rome, the Centaur Chiron wounds Hercules with a poisoned arrow, only to have him later recover and poison him in return with Hydra venom. Plutarch goes into great detail about these mythologies in his seldom read, yet brilliant work, *Moralia*.[28]

Artifacts of the dying and reviving sun allegory continue to persist in several modern Western holidays. During Halloween, for example, which coincidentally occurs near the autumnal equinox, monsters and other symbols associated with evil and death are put on display. This is followed, near the winter solstice, by Christmas, where a savior of the world is born anew. During the celebration of Easter, near the vernal equinox, this savior effectively conquers both Satan and death and is restored in the heavens to his full original position of divine power.

Indeed, some writers have even put forward strong evidence of a correlation between Latin phallic ceremonies of Priapus and the decoration of the May Pole during May Day, both of which occurred near the vernal equinox.[168] These Priapic ceremonies themselves are likely derived from those of the Egyptian obelisk, which was associated with Osiris. According to the legend of Isis and Osiris, described by Plutarch, Isis was unable to locate Osiris' phallus, while reassembling his dismembered body, since it had already been consumed by the "medjed fish." She therefore fashioned a replacement for it, which is likely the prototype of the Egyptian obelisk.[28] The Hindus, whose religion bears undeniable signs of Egyptian derivation, unknowingly preserve this symbol in their rather profane Shiva Linga.

Though it lies outside of the scope of this work to conduct an in-depth examination of all of the allegories of this sort, let's examine one in detail, in order to illustrate its correlation with the previously mentioned solar events. Since the myth of the passion of Osiris is one of the oldest, and likely the parent of most of these allegories, I will select it for investigation.

Plutarch explicitly states in his Moralia that Osiris was originally a symbol of the sun: "In the sacred hymns of Osiris, they call upon him who is hidden in the arms of the sun...there are some who assert without reservation that Osiris is the sun..."[28]

Plutarch goes on to state that Osiris was said to be killed by Typhoon during the winter month of Athyr, when the sun was "in the constellation of Scorpio." Today, the sun enters this constellation between Nov 16 and Dec 15. Yet this was not the case when the passion of Osiris was first invented. In order to determine when it entered this sign, during the ancient period when this passion was invented, we must first determine roughly when this invention occurred.

We don't encounter documents explicitly describing details of the Osirian passion until the 12th Dynasty (e.g. Ikhernofret Stela ~1991-1778 B.C.). However, when we first encounter the name, Osiris, in Pyramid Texts dating from the 5th Dynasty (~2494-2395 B.C.), there are already indications of long-established formal ceremonies, complete with a resurrection theme. In fact, as far back as the 1st Dynasty (~3200-3035 B.C.), we encounter the title *Khenti-Amentiu*, or "King of Westerners," on cylinder seals at the home of the Osirian cult, Abydos. It is known that this title was used in reference to Osiris during later dynasties, but it may also have referred to him at this earlier period as well.

To be conservative, let's assume 2400 B.C. as the starting point for the legend of the Osirian passion. During this period, at roughly what part of the year would the sun have been in the constellation of Scorpio? In order to determine the modern version of zodiacal dates prior to the Christian Era, we must remember to adjust for the precession of the vernal equinox.

For those who are unfamiliar with this concept, the Earth has a precession to its rotation, or in other words, a circular wobble much like that of a spinning top. This precession completes one full rotational cycle every 25,860 years. One observable effect of this phenomenon is that the zodiacal constellations retrogress approximately one sign every 2,155 years. Since roughly 100 B.C., the vernal equinox has occurred in the constellation of Pisces. However, in 2400 B.C., when we discount for this precession, we find it occurring in the constellation of Taurus. This shift of two zodiacal signs means that the sun being in the constellation of Scorpio in 2400 B.C., would be the equivalent today of the sun having recently entered into the constellation of Virgo. This entrance into Virgo occurs late in September.[169] Is it any surprise that this date, when the legendary Osiris was said to have been killed, just happens to fall almost perfectly on the autumnal equinox (i.e. Sept 22, as of 2017). In performing these types of analyses, one must be careful to use the *sidereal zodiac*, rather than the more common *tropical zodiac*. The former uses fixed constellations as a reference, while the latter ignores precessional effects and assumes a fixed vernal equinox as its reference.

It is an interesting coincidence that, during the early period of Egyptian history, when the worship of Osiris was predominant, a period when the vernal equinox was in the sign of *Taurus, the bull*, we find the *Apis bull* worshiped as the physical manifestation of the soul, or Ka, of Osiris. Although this worship persisted into later periods, when the vernal equinox had shifted to the sign of *Ares, the ram* (~1875 B.C.-90

B.C.), during later dynasties, we find Osiris worshipped in Mendes as a ram.

Per Maspero, in his monumental 1903 work, *The History of Egypt, Chaldea, Syria, Babylonia, and Assyria,* "The ram of Mendes is sometimes Osiris, and sometimes the soul of Osiris. The ancients took it for a he-goat, and to them we are indebted for the record of its exploits."[170] From this he-goat of Mendes, we see an early form of the Greek Pan, or Bacchus. Not surprisingly, we also encounter Amun, who was symbolized by a ram, or as a man with ram horns, becoming the preeminent deity in Egypt during this period (~18th Dynasty/~1550 B.C.).

Sometimes ancient Egyptian gods were fused with their animal symbols, as in the case of the often animal-headed humans, or human-headed animals frequently encountered adorning ancient Egyptian temple walls and papyri. Many secondary symbols were even developed for the primary religious symbols themselves. A few examples of this are the already mentioned Obelisk (i.e. a stylized phallus) and the Djed (i.e. possibly stylized columns, or a spine), both of which symbolized Osiris; while Osiris himself was but a symbol for the hidden light of the nighttime sun. Other examples are the Tyet (i.e. a stylized uterus, or buckle) and the Sopdet (i.e. a stylized version of the star, Sirius), which were symbols for Isis; who was herself but a symbol for the illuminated moon.

The common man, who generally had neither the education, nor the leisure to analyze religious and metaphysical subtleties such as these, was quickly overwhelmed by this divine legion and confusion sprang up as to what was symbol, and what the original object of worship. The original intent of these consecrated symbols was not that they themselves should receive worship, something which ended up occurring anyway, but, as with the religious iconography of today, so that the less educated could have some physical reminder which directed their minds to more abstract concepts.

One of these abstract concepts was of the immaterial energy which sustained the universe. This energy, symbolized by light, was seen as purely beneficial, and therefore purely good. Connecting the dots, the ancient light, or sun worshipers were actually worshiping their concept of pure goodness. I find this incredible, knowing how many of these people were tortured, excommunicated, something which meant social death and possibly even starvation in former days, as well as outright killed for their views; views which, when pursued to their core, are found to be no less pious, and possibly even more so, than those among the major religions of today.

Osiris

The more that one investigates Egyptian symbolism, the more they will be surprised by the richness of meaning embedded within it. Osiris' phallic Hedjet crown, for example, which is frequently depicted encased between two feathers is likely symbolic of the conjoined male and female reproductive organs. This would be a somewhat appropriate symbol, given that the Egyptians believed that the active, enlivening power of God, which was commonly symbolized by a phallus, penetrated, infused, and fecundated what was believed to be passive and receptive matter; generally symbolized by the yoni.

Cows were one of their symbols for the female sex, due to the gentle nature and lactation ability which both share in common, hence the reason why we encounter Hathor depicted either as a cow, or female with a characteristic headdress. The ankh was likely a stylized set of female reproductive organs. Can we not see in the ankh the somewhat balloon shaped uterus, with its apex at the cervix, the two branching fallopian tubes to the ovaries, and the base formed from the vaginal canal? Is it a coincidence that many ancient ankh amulets preserve a line, or channel down the center of the central rod, like the birth canal, as well as a flared base, like the labium?

The tjet is likely simply a less stylized version of the ankh, with drooping fallopian tubes and a more flared bottom. Many researchers call this a "Knot," or "Buckle of Isis," but even the knot likely referred to the female reproductive organs. Since the idea was already long established in ancient Egypt between matter, femininity, and female reproduction, anything which had a vague similarity to the form, or function of these organs could be used to allude to matter itself.

Serpents were general symbols of life in ancient Egypt, due to the fact that their ability to shed skin made them appear to periodically renew their youth. This was also a great symbol for the immortality and transmigration of the soul; as it continually sloughs off old bodies, like skin, and dons new ones. It is no coincidence that these snakes were often depicted draped over suns, as suns were a symbol for divine energy and goodness. This was a symbolic statement that life is sustained and restored via the divine energy of God.

Commonly, among ancient Egyptian artwork, we encounter things which were famous for distributing many small seeds, such as lotus blossoms, pomegranates, heads of corn, or tares of wheat. Like the semen of men, which during that period was believed to be a sort of seed, these things were symbols among the ancient Egyptians of God spreading the seeds of life throughout the natural world. Reinforcing this fecundating character of God, we often encounter these seed symbols surmounting the heads of goats or rams, who were famous for their libidos. Interestingly, we encounter the same seed rich pomegranates, likely carrying the same meaning, described within scripture in the decorations of Jewish temples and tied to the bottom of the High Priest's clothing.

This same symbolic claim about the fecundating power of God is still preserved in the Indian symbols of Shiva, who is depicted with a head springing what is likely semen, and life symbolizing serpents wound around his neck and arm. It is interesting that Shiva, who is likely taken by the Hindus from the Egyptian Osiris, preserves the blueish skin color which Osiris is commonly depicted with, as well as the same shape of the Hedjet crown in his hair. The selection of the head and arm for the placement of Shiva's serpents is likely due to the head being the source of thought, while the arm is considered a source of action. Both the thoughts and the actions of Shiva, therefore, are being claimed by these symbols to be life-giving.

Another interesting coincidence is that we commonly encounter depictions of Horus, who was thought by the Egyptians to be the son of Isis and the reincarnation of Osiris, wearing the same phallic Hedjet crown that the northern Egyptian kings wore, and standing on the right side of Osiris. While on the left side of Osiris, we often find Isis, wearing the crown of Hathor; a sun within horns. The sun in horns symbol could possibly be a symbol of the pregnant womb, with or without god filling it. As mentioned earlier, Osiris himself is generally depicted wearing a hat likely symbolizing the conjoined phallus and yoni. It is also notable that the hat of Osiris is frequently depicted with a snake winding down the front of it. This is very similar to the stream of semen which springs from the head of Shiva, and likely has the same meaning.

Thoth, who symbolized the wisdom and magical power of God, was frequently depicted holding two Was staffs. Each of these staffs commonly had a serpent entwined up its entire length, being surmounted either by lotus blossoms, or what appeared to be a jackal head. In some of the depictions, one of the Was serpents wears the Hedjet crown of the Upper Kingdom, while the other wears the Deshret crown of the Lower Kingdom. It is highly likely that the caduceus symbol was derived from these two staffs, which symbolized the fecundating power of Osiris bestowing a double portion of life through its dual dominion over the Upper and Lower Kingdoms of Egypt.

It is no coincidence that the item known as the Werhekau, literally "Great of power," used by the Egyptians during their "Opening of the Mouth" ceremony, during mummification, was also generally in the form of a serpent. This tool was placed in the mouth of the mummy prior to its journey into the afterlife.

This is simply another symbol of the fecundating power of god entering, like a seed, into the corpse. "Great of power" likely implied "potentiating" to the point of regeneration. The words of the prayer said during this ritual, as well as other prayers made in the Egyptian *Book of the Dead*, imply that the mummy was being pulled back together by God and slowly brought back to life. As evidence of this, consider the language of the 155th chapter of the *Book of the Dead*, which is often found inscribed on djed talismans, which were placed around the necks of royal Egyptian mummies. The 155th chapter reads: "Formula for a djed-pillar of gold. Raise yourself Osiris, to place yourself on your side, so that I may place water under you. I have brought you a djed-pillar of gold so that you may rejoice by it. Words spoken over a djed-pillar of gold strung on a fiber of sycamore and placed at the neck of the blessed dead on the day of burial. Anyone at whose neck this amulet is placed, will be an excellent spirit who is in the necropolis on the day of the first of the year like those who are in the following of Osiris. A correct matter a million times."171

The command for "Osiris" to raise himself, was likely being directed at the spirit of Osiris which had entered into the mummy during the ceremony of the opening of the mouth. This spirit was expected to infuse, or grow within the mummy, and revive him, as a sort of Horus. The "water" placed "under" Osiris, likely referred to revitalizing the mummy with the watery spirit; potentially another allusion to the fecundating power of god, as symbolized by semen. The reference to "rejoicing" in the djed pillar, which symbolized Osiris' power, likely meant to become invigorated by it.

Obviously, the reference to the fibers of sycamore was yet another allusion to Osiris. In his *Moralia*, Plutarch mentions the legend of Osiris' coffin becoming somehow encased in a sycamore tree.28 In another version of the legend, a sprig of acacia, or tamarisk, grows at its head. These legends of something living springing from, or growing around the coffin of Osiris implied new life being restored to the dead. The coffin which Osiris was trapped in was likely an allusion to the body of the mummy itself, whom the spirit of Osiris was believed to grow within and eventually restore to life. This filling of the dead with the spirit of Osiris was likely the reason why mummies were treated so carefully, and with utmost respect; as they served as a sort of vessel of God.

Further evidencing the above theory, we even find the embalmed dead referred to as "Osiris" within certain prayers found within the *Book of the Dead*.172 While many scientists believe that this was some sort of abstract identification with Osiris, similar to the way that Christians believe that God views them to be identified with Christ, perhaps it is less abstract than this. It is likely that, when the serpent headed Werhekau tool was placed within the mouth of the mummy, during the ceremony of the "Opening of the Mouth," the actual spirit of Osiris was believed to enter into the body, like a seed. These prayers were likely being made directly to this spirit of Osiris, and not to the deceased, who served as its vessel.

This resurrection belief is likely the real reason why holes were left in Egyptian tombs. Scientists speculate that these were for the birdlike soul to fly in and out of, but it was more likely a means for the newborn man to escape. The food and ladders left in the tomb though they eventually degenerated into mere symbols, void of meaning, were likely originally practical items, which they expected the newly reborn man to need, in order to survive and escape. Even the real name of the Egyptian *Book of the Dead*, which is actually *The Book of Coming Forth by Day,* was likely referring to resurrection and reemergence from the tomb.

Relativity of the Material

George Berkley put forward some interesting concepts about relativity in his work, *Three Dialogues between Hylas and Philonous*. Everyone is familiar with the theory of relativity with regard to time, however, in this work, Berkley pointed out how, not just time, but all perception within the material world is ultimately relative.[175] Consider size, for example. While we may perceive an object to be small, this same object would be large to a creature smaller than it. Small objects to that creature would again be large to ones still smaller. We measure these things by comparing them to something else which we choose to call a standard, but such measurements are all comparative, and therefore by definition, relative.

The same applies to velocity. What we consider slow may be blindingly fast to a snail, or bacterium. Velocity is actually bound tightly to, and in fact inseparable from the concept of time. There would be no time without motion. A year, for example, is nothing more than our documenting our planet's movement around the sun. A month is our documenting the phases of the moon. A day is merely our documenting the rotation of our planet. A second is merely our subdivision of this, which has been compared to, and is now measured against the radioactive decay of Cesium, or a Hydrogen Maser.

Let's do a thought experiment to drive this point home. If the entire universe, including all elementary particles, such as electrons and quarks, froze for what would normally be considered a thousand years, and then started up again where it left off, would it be noticed? How do we know that this very thing isn't occurring in between each second? The answer is that there would be no way of knowing it, as time itself, which is nothing more than an abstract concept used to describe the comparison of movement, would cease to be. Without movement of these things, there is no time. It must be understood, however, that all motion must stop for all things, in order for time itself to stop. If even a single atom continued to have electrons rotating about it while all other motion ceased, time would continue for all things. This is because, once motion had resumed, the lapse of time could theoretically be calculated based upon the number of rotations which these electrons had made in their origins, while everything else was frozen.

Motion, which is measured as velocity, is itself relative. Imagine, if you will, being in a spaceship and the entire universe disappears except you and your ship. For the sake of this thought experiment, let's pretend that your ship's thrusters are emissionless. Fire your thrusters at maximum for an hour. Turn them off again. Have you moved? Are you now moving? There is still infinite space in all directions, so without any landmarks to use as relative comparisons of movement, the answer is no. Your ship has not moved and is not moving. Now let's reduce the theoretical ship to a single electron, to eliminate confusing the issue, due to your possible movement within the ship. Can this electron move? Again, the answer is no. Motion becomes impossible without landmarks of comparison, and is therefore relative to them.

What of color? To consider the relativity of color, consider that some people with failing livers see things with a yellow hue. Colorblind people, likewise, may see two colors as one. Even with what is considered normal vision, the type of light illuminating the object can make it appear a different shade, as all photographers are well aware. Insects, such as the honey bee, and some sea creatures, such as mantis shrimp, can observe other shades which we cannot, based upon the composition of their retinae. To make matters even more confusing, when one examines an object under a powerful microscope, one observes various other colors of the object that go unseen from afar, and when examined closer than the distance of the wavelength of that color, the color itself disappears. So what color is the thing? The absolute color of a thing is found to be illusory, and relative to the composition of the observer's eye, the distance of the observer from the object, the type of light striking it, and a number of other factors.

Texture, which is the source of the physical feelings derived from touch, is in the same situation. The relative hardness and size of the part sensing the matter, affect if it will be felt to be smooth, rough, soft, etc. A pane of glass may feel smooth to me, yet a small insect finds it rough enough to find footholds in, and it is a rugged mountain range to a dust mite.

Consider sound. What may startle a newborn, may barely register as a whisper to an old man. Dogs and bats may hear clearly, and likely even differently due to the structures of their ears, what to me seems to be nothing. Our determination of what things sound like is arbitrary and relative to the hearer, based upon physical characteristics of the ears which hear it and the environment which the sound is heard in. A fish would find the sound of chirping of birds, which they are used to hearing from under water, bizarre when they are taken out of it. Sounds originating from the same source are perceived differently at different altitudes, when transmitted through different mediums, such as helium, or water, and disappear altogether in space.

Likewise, even scents depend upon, and are therefore relative to the structure of the perceiving organ which smells it. What may smell like nothing to me, might be unique and easily recognizable to a bloodhound. What I may find foul, may smell wonderful to a vulture. Dogs prove this point by their eagerness to sniff the posteriors of other dogs, and at times roll in excrement.

The sense of taste is similar to that of smell, except, instead of sensing gasses, as the latter does, it is specially designed to detect the solid, or liquid phases of things. Again, the taste of a thing is relative to the taster, due to the structures of these creatures', or individuals' tasting organs. Children, who likely have an abundance of taste buds designed to sense sweetness, in order to encourage them to consume the high calorie foods needed during this period of rapid growth, often tend to dislike things such as fish, onions, and mushrooms. Older adults, on the other hand, whose proportion of taste buds designed to respond to sweetness have likely decreased, often enjoy these things. Flies enjoy the taste of feces, due to the special design of their tasting organs, and mosquitos and fleas enjoy the taste of blood.

All perception of the material world is therefore found to be relative. The only things which can be perceived with any absoluteness are abstract concepts and immaterial existences. The ancient Pythagoreans arrived at this conclusion thousands of years ago, driving their love of the abstract concepts of number.

Senses

External physical senses may become desensitized for a time due to overly strong stimulation, chronic stimulation, or age-related degeneration, but they cannot be temporarily deactivated in a healthy individual without chemical intervention. I stress the term "healthy" here, as senses may indeed be temporarily disengaged during things such as chemical anesthesia, diseases such as leprosy, and the brink of death state known as coma. Senses are always gathering information for the mind to process. Interestingly, though the senses collect this information and pass it to the mind, something within the mind doesn't have to process this received information, should it choose not to. We can be gazing in a general direction, with our minds intensely focused upon an event, or conversation which occurred sometime in the past, and not pay any attention to the information which our eyes, ears, nose, skin, and/or tongue captured, translated into electrical signals, and passed to our minds. Sometimes seeing, we do not mentally see, and hearing, we do not mentally hear.

We tend to do our utmost to deactivate these senses during periods when we are allowing the mind and body to rest, a still mysterious process which we refer to as *sleep*. During these times, we sleep in no, minimal, or very soft clothing, in order to reduce our sense of touch to the utmost extent possible. We lie down in a soft bed in order to spread out, and therefore minimize to the utmost extent possible, any pressure points created by our body weight. We place the skin at as much of a uniform temperature as possible by placing sheets or blankets over ourselves, in order to reduce as much as possible any input variation from our skin's temperature sensors, both across external areas and relative to our body's core.

In order to minimize sensory input from our eyes, we close our eyelids and retire into a dark room. Even in this condition, the eyes somewhat continue to see. The ion channels of the sensing cells within the retinae become fully potentiated due to minimal usage and sensitive to the slightest amount of light, a phenomenon we term "adjustment to darkness." Due to this sensitization, the slight amount of light which may continue to penetrate a darkened room may be still seen through closed eyelids, though only as shades of gray. This is likely why the body, when entering sleep, subconsciously rolls the eyes upwards, so that the orbital bones of the skull will block this residual vision. In deep sleep, they may return to the front, but are moved rapidly, likely for the purpose of changing any remaining vision into a uniform grey blur.

Our auditory and olfactory senses remain active during sleep in order to alert us to things which might require us to awaken, such as the scent of smoke, or the sound of an intruder, however, prior to sleep, we seek to reduce their input as much as possible. We generally do this by attempting to sleep in clean areas, void of foul odors, or loud sounds.

It should be noted that any constant, unvarying sensory stimulation tends to desensitize our corresponding sensory organs. When we dress, we initially notice the feel of our clothes upon our skin, but shortly afterwards stop feeling their constant rubs. When we are forced to remain in an environment with a droning sound, we soon no longer notice it, as it desensitizes our sense of hearing. As long as nothing is in our mouths when we sleep, a dangerous activity anyway, our sense of taste is generally reduced to the mere taste of our own saliva, a taste which we have grown so used to as to have become desensitized to it.

Vision is somewhat unique, in that its desensitization may actually be seen. This occurs, for example, when we stare at something white. White is a reflection of the full spectrum of light, and therefore is a color which strongly stimulates the retinal cells. After staring at a white object for an extended period, the photoreceptors within the retinae become slightly desensitized. When we finally look at something else, or close our eyes, the retinal cells are suddenly exposed to new stimulatory patterns. For a brief period, before these retinal cells readjust their sensitivity, a shadow will be seen in the same shape as the previous white object. These shadows are the areas of the retina which were briefly desensitized by the strong stimulation.

Though we may voluntarily use our muscles to bring our external sensory organs into environments conducive for sensation, this sensation itself occurs automatically. In the same way, though we may focus our minds upon thoughts which we, through sheer experience, have learned tend to be associated with the sensation of specific emotions, some internal sensory organ, which is different from the thoughts themselves, automatically senses the emotion.

I believe this sensing organ to be the soul itself. When a person's innately good soul senses goodness within another living creature, thing, place, or noble yet abstract concept, these reactants spontaneously ignite into a pleasurable feeling within, which we call *love* when referring to its cause, and *happiness* when referring to the sensation itself. *Good* effectively senses itself and gives birth to happiness, a flame which warms regardless of proximity.

As discussed elsewhere, *good* is a general term which goes by different names when described within different contexts. For example, *good* with regard to form is beauty. *Good* with regard to representation of reality is truth, with regard to judgement is justice, with regard to conduct is righteousness, and with regard to interaction is love. As many different names for *good* may be imagined as there are contexts to imagine it in. Virtue, nobility, honor, beauty, wisdom, kindness, etc., are all synonyms for *good*. All produce a sort of longing within the individual sensing them to draw closer and mix their own innate goodness with that which is sensed; to combine the two parts and make a greater whole.

An interesting and significant difference between our external and internal senses is that the external ones somewhat overlap, while the internal ones do not. This fact is leveraged by the mind in order to ensure sensation of its external material environment. Consider, for example, how our sense of sight is used to identify food, or a rose. We know by experience that when we visually perceive these things, we can then use our voluntary muscle control to direct our bodies towards them, placing them where our taste buds can subsequently sense their taste or our olfactory cells can sense their smell. The same goes for other senses, such as our auditory sense. We may not see an approaching train, but we generally know by experience that when our sense of hearing identifies the sound of it rumbling upon the tracks, we can trust that when we turn our eyes towards it, we will see it.

Our internal sensory organ of emotion, the soul, seems to be truly unique in that no other sense overlaps it. There is no other sensory organ which may be used to ensure that the specific emotional sensation which we are seeking will actually be where we anticipate that we will encounter it. For clarity, consider the example of a man who is unable to see, hear, feel, or smell, yet who hopes to taste something sweet. This person may voluntarily use the muscles of his unfeeling hands, so that somehow, by trial and error, something sweet ends up being tasted by his unfeeling mouth. From a statistical point of view, the required string of coincidences for this to occur would be so improbable as to border upon impossibility.

Should someone with the additional complete set of senses observe this poor wretch flailing on the ground with his mouth agape, they might pity him, guess at his intent, and place various foods in his mouth until they observed his countenance brighten once they hit upon the chance confection. To the person with only the single sense of taste, this event would appear miraculously spontaneous. From his perspective, he would merely have tasted nothing, then would have spontaneously tasted a series of things which he didn't desire, until he finally tasted the desired confection. It did not occur spontaneously though. The confection was a very real thing, waiting in a specific place which any having the additional crossover sense of vision could observe.

In like manner, the various stimulations of our internal senses which we call emotion respond to very real things; even though they may appear spontaneous to us, due to our lack of additional crossover senses with which to identify them.

Senescence

Barring the catastrophic, humans seem to fade from the world as they age, much like flowers. Consider for a moment how we sense the material world around us. We possess our five traditional senses of smell, taste, touch, hearing, and sight. In addition to these, we also possess the ability to sense temperature, orientation, movement, pain, and a few of the internal chemicals which are necessary to maintain homeostasis. Is this all?

What about internal sensations which arise from thought? As discussed in another chapter of this work, the native tongue of thought is ultimately found to be synonymous with feelings, but how do we sense these feelings? Sensations require sensors, but it is unlikely that we possess some sort of physical sensory organ within us which senses our feelings. In reality, our sensory organ for internal feeling appears to be of another type altogether; possibly functioning as a sort of transducer between our material body and our immaterial soul.

As we age, we generally develop these internal senses, while simultaneously experiencing a gradual loss of our external ones. Let's consider the sense of taste, for example. While some underlying causes for taste loss are drug use, zinc deficiency, and disease, there is also a large portion that is the natural and unavoidable consequence of aging. The average mature adult possesses roughly 9,000 taste buds. Once these adults pass middle age, however, their taste buds, as well as the 50-100 taste receptor cells residing on each, reproduce at a net loss. Carried out over a long enough period, this inevitably results in taste decrease (i.e. *hypogeusia*), or loss (i.e. *ageusia*). Have you ever noticed how it is disproportionately more common for older men, rather than younger ones, to enjoy highly spicy foods? Have you ever noticed how children tend to shun strongly flavored things such as onions, fish, and mushrooms, while adults tend to enjoy them? While personal preference is always a factor, these preferences are primarily driven by the relative quantity of various types of taste receptor cells within the mouth of the taster.

Consider that, with this reduction, or loss of taste, we lose one of our primary mechanisms for sensing the external world. In the larger scale of things, this seems a relatively minor inconvenience, however, consider all of the things you have ever tasted. Now envision all of those things tasting the same; perhaps like eating unsweetened and unflavored gelatin. Consider the eventual loss of even the memories of the varying tastes which had previously been experienced. With the loss of even this seemingly trivial sense, so decreases our ability to sense the external world itself, and therefore our attraction to it.

The sense of smell is so analogous to that of taste, that one would not be inaccurate in describing this sense as our ability to taste gases. The age-related decline in this sense, *presbyosmia*, is so common, that roughly "25% of Americans 55 or older" and "30% of Americans between 70-80" have problems with it.[176] This likely accounts for offensive odors which are occasionally encountered among the elderly. In these instances, the offender is likely unaware of these odors, and would be tremendously embarrassed if informed about them. People lacking the ability to smell can continue to function in society, however, while loss of the sense of taste only affects the loser, loss of the sense of smell may inadvertently affect others, who in turn may begin to marginalize, or shun the offender.

Let's move on to hearing. Age related hearing loss is so familiar to those who have had any significant amount of interaction with the elderly, that it really needs neither proof, nor explanation. Briefly, the hairs which line the cochlea within the inner ear eventually lose their sensitivity. Therefore, the transduction of their movements into nervous impulses, which we know as *hearing*, wanes, or ceases altogether. This loss first tends to occur within the frequency ranges that the hairs are most often stimulated in. Consider the loss of this sense: all of the sounds that you have ever heard, from the laugh, or even the voice of a loved one, to the rustle of the wind in the trees, the singing of birds and barking of dogs, the wet sloshing sounds of water lapping the nearby shore, etc. Consider the slow, tragic loss of even the memory of these things.

Moving on to the sense of sight; is anyone unfamiliar with the degradation of vision that eventually affects virtually all elderly? If this occurs via no other disease mechanism, it eventually does so due to the slow, virtually inevitable crystallization of the lens tissue of the eye. This crystallization destroys the ability of the lens to flex efficiently, during attempts to focus upon items which are nearby. Imagine the lessening of daily joy in the material world that would be associated with the slow loss of one's ability to see.

What about the sense of touch? Does even this sense decline with age? Modern research is revealing that it does. The central nervous systems of the elderly often experience an ever-decreasing ability to process pain signals, while, within their peripheral nervous systems, there is also an overall reduction in the mechanoreceptors which allow for the sense of touch, thermoreceptors which allow for the sense of temperature, and polymodal nociceptors which allow for the perception of pain.[177] Envision the psychological effects of the slow loss of physical sensation. Consider how much pleasure is derived from our sense of touch; from the sensation of a loved one's embrace, to that of the sun on our face and the wind on our skin during a warm summer day.

It is an odd coincidence that the elderly experience a simultaneous decrease in overall average body temperature. Scientists have identified several reasons for this. As already alluded to previously, the elderly tend to develop nervous problems which affect the ability of the temperature sensors within their skin to sense environmental variation, the ability of these sensors to send this information to the hypothalamus, as well as the ability of their hypothalamus to send response signals which control temperature regulating actions, such as sweating, shivering, or increasing or decreasing local blood velocity via vessel contraction or dilation. In addition, the elderly tend to simply lose insulating body fat.

It should be noted that both the nervous and insulating reasons identified above are purely mechanical. Since the majority of heat which the body generates is the result of cellular metabolic function, there is also the possibility that the age-related average decrease in body heat is indicative of an overall reduction in metabolic function. This reduction in metabolic activity could be caused by a correlating reduction in amount, or reduction in activity, of the infusing and enlivening soul.

It is understood that all increase in temperature does not necessarily indicate increased presence, or activity of soul. A person who is running a fever, or sweating after a run, hasn't been filled with a superabundance of soul. The fever mechanism is merely one of the body's tools to battle infection: essentially cooking invading bacteria to death.

But consider shock. This aptly named condition may very well be the partial or complete "shocking" of a soul from the body due to intense physical, or mental trauma. Certainly cardiogenic, hypovolemic, anaphylactic, septic, and neurogenic shock may kill people due to purely mechanical, or chemical reasons, however, there appears to be another type of shock which we understand far less, which may instead be purely due to the loss of *spirit*, in both senses of the word.

Victor Frankl, a professor of psychiatry, and former inmate at the infamous Auschwitz concentration camp, wrote about this phenomenon in his famous work, *Man's Search for Meaning*. In this work, Dr. Frankl describes two different scenarios, one where a friend was disappointed about a release date, and another when inmates were disappointed during Christmas, where he observed people entering into a sort of "shock," where they subsequently fell victim to latent diseases within the death camp. Contrarily, he also discusses how the subconscious hope that he would again be united with his spouse, was one of the main factors which provided him with the motivation to endure through his sufferings. The reverse phenomenon is commonly observed after the death of longtime spouses. Very often the widower passes away shortly afterwards.[200]

In all three instances cited by Dr. Frankl, he seems to allude to a potentially subconscious decision which people can make, wherein they voluntarily cling to, or abdicate life; or at least the portion of it involving participation in the material world. If the body is soulless and life purely mechanistic, as atheist academics so frequently and enthusiastically claim, then this phenomenon does not make sense. We would expect a purely mechanical system, whose program directed it to thrive, to continue to cling to life even when all hope was gone and only physical suffering remained in the foreseeable future.

On the other side of the coin, it does not make sense from a purely Materialist point of view why, or even how the body would, or even could voluntarily abdicate life. No amount of suffering is equivalent to the cessation of life. A poorly idling and rusty, yet functioning car would not care how many poorly maintained roads, full of potholes, it must still travel. Any functionality is superior to cessation and ultimate dissolution into its composite elements once again.

Yet this is not what we observe. Mankind needs purpose; the joys which are only found in virtue and love. It is precisely when they feel themselves to be little better than machines, that many lose all joy and desire to continue life.

Whether the lessening of the 5 senses with age is caused by functional, or by morphological changes in the central nervous system, or the peripheral sensing cells themselves, the end result is a slow weaning from the material world by a creeping inability to derive physical pleasure from it, or to even sense it. As Seneca mentioned, we do not do all of our dying at the moment of death. The final cessation of breath is but the capstone of the dying process; something which we begin the moment we cease to grow and begin to decline.[1]

This thought leads to internal crisis for those who, either from lack of foresight, or failure to recognize an alternative, predominately seek happiness in the various forms of material and physical pleasure. They have built their lives upon mere sand, while the tide inexorably rises. Often the aging realize this in its early stages, if they did not already do so during their younger years. They realize that, if they continue to foster an attachment to physical pleasure, hoping to derive their happiness from it, they face an inevitable future grief proportional to their level of attachment. The pain of losing a child is equivalent to our attachment to that child. The reason we don't grieve over the loss of a car in the same way that we do the loss of a child is because we were not as attached to the car and did not hope to derive the same level of happiness from our interaction with it.

The need to find an immaterial, and hence immutable source of joy begins to dawn upon many during their waning years. Simultaneous to this weaning from the material world, we often find a healthy shifting of priorities to the immaterial, from whence joy and pleasure may yet, and ever, be found. Do not misunderstand me to be stating that all elderly are saints. This is far from the case. I am merely identifying tendencies and relative shifts in degree. If anyone is likely to have a sincere "Come to Jesus" type of drastic shifting in their priority set, it is those approaching the gate to the next phase in their existence through which Jesus himself passed long before.

Sadly, the larger category of the aging population, seeing the end of the primary source of their physical based pleasure looming into sight, address this problem by leapfrogging to a different physical based one which is at the moment less degraded. This is often continued until death eventually finds them. This approach is merely treating the symptoms of the problem and not the underlying disease of misdirected joy sources.

Sometimes, due to the loss of several physical based pleasures in other areas, this approach expresses itself as a fetish, where the individual expects the replacement physical based pleasure source to provide, singly and unnaturally, the sum pleasure which was previously derived from multiple lost ones. The physical, or material sources of happiness which are being replaced are not being replaced due to inability to experience them. Indeed, in many of the more common types of fetishes, the lingering ability to experience the pleasure makes its loss seem all the more painful. Emotional losses can also cause Fetishes; such as when a loss occurs prior to the person experiencing it being mentally, or emotionally mature enough to understand a more appropriate way to address and resolve the painful emotions which they are faced with.

An interesting point about this concept of the slow, yet inevitable, age-related destruction of our ability to sense the material world, is that all of the teachings of the stoics, urging men to find their joy in intransient things such as virtue, suddenly begin to ring true. Included below is an example from Seneca's 23rd letter to his friend Lucilius, entitled, "On the True Joy which comes from Philosophy," however, the entirety of Boethius' monumental work, *The Consolation of Philosophy*,[63] as well as any of the works by Epictetus, also focus on this point.

"Above all, my dear Lucilius, make this your business: learn how to feel joy. Do you think that I am now robbing you of many pleasures when I try to do away with the gifts of chance, when I counsel the avoidance of hope, the sweetest thing that gladdens our hearts? Quite the contrary; I do not wish you ever to be deprived of gladness. I would have it born in your house; and it is born there, if only it be inside of you. Other objects of cheer do not fill a man's bosom; they merely smooth his brow and are inconstant, – unless perhaps you believe that he who laughs has joy. The very soul must be happy and confident, lifted above every circumstance.

Real joy, believe me, is a stern matter. Can one, do you think, despise death with a carefree countenance, or with a 'blithe and gay' expression, as our young dandies are accustomed to say? Or can one thus open his door to poverty, or hold the curb on his pleasures, or contemplate the endurance of pain? He who ponders these things in his heart is indeed full of joy; but it is not a cheerful joy. It is just this joy, however, of which I would have you become the owner; for it will never fail you when once you have found its source. The yield of poor mines is on the surface; those are really rich whose veins lurk deep, and they will make more bountiful returns to him who delves unceasingly. So too those baubles which delight the common crowd afford but a thin pleasure, laid on as a coating, and even joy that is only plated lacks a real basis. But the joy of which I speak, that to which I am endeavoring to lead you, is something solid, disclosing itself the more fully as you penetrate into it. Therefore, I pray you, my dearest Lucilius, do the one thing that can render you really happy: cast aside and trample under foot all the things that glitter outwardly and are held out to you by another or as obtainable from another; look toward the true good, and rejoice only in that which comes from your own store. And what do I mean by 'from your own store?' I mean from your very self, that which is the best part of you. The frail body, also, even though we can accomplish nothing without it, is to be regarded as necessary rather than as important; it involves us in vain pleasures, short-lived, and soon to be regretted, which, unless they are reined in by extreme self-control, will be transformed into the opposite. This is what I mean: pleasure, unless it has been kept within bounds, tends to rush headlong into the abyss of sorrow.

But it is hard to keep within bounds in that which you believe to be good. The real good may be coveted with safety. Do you ask me what this real good is, and whence it derives? I will tell you: it comes from a good conscience, from honorable purposes, from right actions, from contempt of the gifts of chance, from an even and calm way of living which treads but one path. For men who leap from one purpose to another, or do not even leap but are carried over by a sort of hazard, – how can such wavering and unstable persons possess any good that is fixed and lasting? There are only a few who control themselves and their affairs by a guiding purpose; the rest do not proceed; they are merely swept along, like objects afloat in a river. And of these objects, some are held back by sluggish waters and are transported gently; others are torn along by a more violent current; some, which are nearest the bank, are left there as the current slackens; and others are carried out to sea by the onrush of the stream. Therefore, we should decide what we wish, and abide by the decision."[14]

Conceptions of the Soul

What does it mean when someone discusses their *soul*, or *spirit*? The mental conceptions of *spirit* varied among the ancients, depending upon how philosophically developed they, and the cultures they lived in, were. Some less developed cultures merely believed *spirit* to be a synonym for a special sort of gaseous matter. This was the case with early Judaism, which Christianity was later appended to. This is why, in the Hebrew cosmogony found within the Biblical book of Genesis, you encounter God bringing man to life by literally filling him with "breath," a word which is often elsewhere translated as "spirit."

"And the Lord God formed man of the dust of the ground, and breathed into his nostrils the *breath* of life; and man became a living being" (Genesis 2:7).

Coincidentally, this is likely why the burned sacrifice motif was so common among the ancients. Many likely believed that they were converting the physical matter of the offering into a smoky, gaseous *spirit*, which could naturally and observably ascend into the logical home of gaseous *spirits*, the sky, to be received by the God(s) who dwelt there.

Again, in the New Testament, the aptly named "Holy Spirit" announces its arrival, unsurprisingly, by a strong "wind," prior to the more commonly known "tongues of fire" embodiment. "When the Day of Pentecost had fully come...suddenly there came a sound from heaven, as of a rushing mighty *wind*, and it filled the whole house where they were sitting. Then there appeared to them divided tongues, as of fire, and one sat upon each of them. And they were all filled with the Holy Spirit..." (Acts 2:14).

It was literally a *spirit* (i.e. gas, air, or vapor) which was somehow special to God (i.e. holy), in early Hebrew and Christian thought. The event at Pentecost certainly wasn't thought by the early church to be the arrival of the third being of a supposed triune God.

"You are misunderstanding and therefore misinterpreting that!" the clergy of Trinitarian Christian faiths will certainly contend. But perhaps Jesus might know something more about the faith which he promulgated, than these protestors do. Let's see how he understood it. In John 20:22, we encounter Jesus literally *breathing* on his apostles and stating that this *breath* imparted the "Holy Spirit" to them. "And when He had said this, He *breathed* on them, and said to them, 'Receive the Holy Spirit.'"

Realizing the problems which stem from the Holy Spirit later being received at Pentecost, when it had already been received from Jesus prior to his heavenly ascension, Christians generally claim that the apostles were merely marked by Jesus to receive the Holy Spirit, when he breathed upon them in John 20:22, but that this spirit didn't actually arrive until Pentecost. This apology does not help their case, however, as it implies that Jesus could not immediately bring his will into effect, a scenario which destroys his omnipotence, in turn destroying his godhood, and ultimately the concept of Trinity.

It's not until Paul becomes a Christian, that Christianity appears to adopt the more philosophically developed belief that *spirit* is a sort of immaterial form of existence, capable of interacting with matter: not unlike our modern concepts of energy.

Resonance

It should be pointed out that it is tremendously difficult to stump the scientific experts of the world. Even should these people genuinely not know the causes for certain effects, very seldom will their egos allow them to state the three simple words which are the hallmark of the humble: "I don't know." More often, when they do not know the cause, they simply give their typically quite educated opinions about it. This is fine, as long as they make very clear that what they are giving are indeed merely opinions (i.e. theories). Unfortunately, however, this clarification is often omitted.

This is how things have always been within the world of science. Back when no one knew why maggots appeared from rotten meat, the scientific elite were quite confident in their theories of spontaneous generation. When they didn't know how light propagated through space without a medium, scientists were quite confident in their theories about cosmic ether. In fact, one will struggle to find many topics which the scientific elite do not already possess pet theories about, which they are completely convinced of, and essentially consider to be laws. Paradoxically, one will also struggle to find virtually any topic that all major scientific experts in a field agree about.

It must be kept in mind that all scientific theories are merely the best model which has been developed to date to explain an observed set of phenomena. These models frequently break down, however, when tested under extreme conditions. For example, while Newton's second law of motion (i.e. Force=Mass x Acceleration) works for general conditions on earth, when the body being acted upon has a small enough relative mass to the Earth that the effect of its own gravity can be ignored, when this isn't the case, such as when examining the gravitational force between the moon and the earth, one has to use a more accurate model; such as the one Cavendish developed, which uses the Universal Gravitational Constant (i.e. F=G(M1 x M2)/d2). This point should never be lost sight of, as it is easy to mistakenly assume that all of the scientific formulae/models which we have developed to explain physical phenomena are perfect, due to the sheer brilliance of the minds that developed them.

The key indicator of the level of imperfection of a formula/model is the number of exceptions, or loosely related outlier phenomena which remain unaccounted for. Typically, the greatest discoveries that have occurred within the scientific world have been less often due to brand

new discoveries, for which there was no previous explanation, but rather
to the development of a new model that better explains the existing
phenomena set; leaving a smaller, though often still present, residual set
of exceptions.

This being the case, over the next few chapters, I will be discussing a
few things which I feel are exceptions to some of the generally accepted
scientific theories/models. As virtually all phenomena do, these things
already have generally accepted explanations. The resilience of these
explanations remains to be seen.

The first of these phenomena which I believe to be poorly
modeled/explained are phantom pain in the stumps of limbs which have
been amputated, and post amputation movement of limbs, for varying
periods of time, after a rapid, unexpected, amputation. Anyone who has
ever hunted, or cleaned a fish will know what is being referred to with
the latter. You can completely behead a fish, or animal and it will often
continue to spasm, twitch, and writhe on the ground long afterwards.
Snakes, turtles, and poultry are notorious for taking this action to
extremes. Snake's heads will sometimes bite their writing bodies several
minutes after being removed, and their bodies will even wince when it
does so, as if in pain. Turtles often continue to swim headless, while
beheaded chickens are famous for often getting up and literally running
around.

So what does science currently say about these odd phenomena?
Phantom pain in amputees, where they "feel" heat, cold, or pain within
limbs which are no longer present, is said to arise from accidental
stimulation of the terminal afferent nerve fiber bundles (those which
relay terminal sensory, or proprioceptive nerve stimulation back to the
central nervous system) within the stumps which formerly fed the distal
parts of the amputated limb. This is a seemingly reasonable
explanation/model, but I would like to reserve it for further discussion
later.

Post limb/head amputation spasms, writhing, running in the case of
poultry, or swimming in the case of turtles, is stated to occur due to a
similar stimulus as that mentioned when discussing phantom pain,
except, instead of the short-circuiting ends of the nerve bundles sending
phantom signals up the afferent bundles to the brain, from whence they
have been removed, they send it down the efferent motor nerve fibers to
the organs, glands, or muscles of the peripheral nervous system.

Complex motions, such as running, swimming, and writhing are said
to be due to these functions originating not within the brain, but within
the spinal cord; the brain only sending the trigger signal to initiate the
elaborate series of movements. This is currently the accepted theory,
and I stress the word *theory*. While it has been proven that some simple
movements, such as twitches and jerks, can originate within the spinal
cord in unique situations, we have not yet shown this to be the case with

complex movements. Think of the lightning fast speed with which an individual can pull their hand back from the unexpected touch of a hot iron. Signals such as this are thought to travel from the pain sensor in the finger, up the afferent nerve bundle to the spine, where they synapse with an efferent nerve, and travel back down the nerve bundle to the motor neuron(s); completely bypassing the brain for a fraction of a second, in order to increase response speed.

"Wait," one may ask, "How is there no evidence of sustained complex movement without the brain, when you just mentioned the complex movement of snakes, turtles, and chickens?" Right. I haven't missed that. The aforementioned complex movements do seem to be a weakness to my point, however, the cause, or causes, of these movements remain indeterminate, as of this writing, and are actively being investigated by researchers. Remember my former statement that science is seldom without a model, or explanation for phenomena. The reliability of those models should always be carefully scrutinized, though.

My personal hypothesis is that complex movements, such as the running of beheaded chickens, and the swimming of beheaded turtles, which, by the way, is not sustained for more than a short period of seconds to minutes, does not solely originate within the spinal cord. I state this because complex movements such as running require the perfectly coordinated and sequenced firing of vast arrays of synapses which feed the motor neurons of the muscles. Glitchy, or erratic firing would typically result in spastic, or seizing movements, similar to those observed in patients with Parkinson's, Multiple Sclerosis, Tetanus, Tonic-Clonic Seizures, or in people being tased.

Think, for example, about how unnatural and non-fluidic the motion of even the most advanced robotic systems designed to replicate the act of running often are. Even these state-of-the-art systems struggle to replicate fluidic movement, though they are often wonders of technology involving massive computing power and arrays of electric, or hydraulic actuators.

If we take the time to scrutinize the host of muscles required for complex movements, such as running and swimming, we will be justifiably stunned. There are probably close to 80 muscles that have to repeatedly contract and release, with the timing of a finely conducted orchestra. I remember being stunned by this fact when dissecting a humble foot in gross anatomy class, as an ignorant first year med student. The musculature and tendons that I observed elaborately interwoven in various layers across the bottom, sides, and top of the foot blew me away; screaming obvious design.

It should also be noted that our brains are not completely isolated and separate entities from our spinal cords. In reality, the spine is a continuum of the brain. Regardless of this fact, I currently do not believe that there are enough neuronal cell bodies (i.e. grey matter) within the lateral, ventral, & dorsal horns of the spinal columns of the example animals mentioned, much less humans, to support these sustained complex movements independently. I specifically make mention of the grey matter, because the white matter can effectively be considered to function as a large bundle of 200-800 micrometer wires (i.e. myelinated axons of nerves), intermixed with glial cells, which function to maintain homeostasis. The grey matter is where any complex controlling signal would have to originate from, as it is the location of the neuronal cell bodies, along with their various dendritic synapses. This may not be the case with small insects, such as cock roaches, who possess a much larger ratio of their central nervous system external to their head, than the mammals and reptiles mentioned. This is likely the reason why these creatures can continue to live for days after beheading.

It could be asked if the controlling signal that initiates the complex movement in the example animals is a single simple signal which initiates a cascade of signals within the grey matter of the spinal column. This way, a simple glitch-like signal, from the exposed end of the spinal column after the chicken is beheaded, could initiate the complex sequence of muscular contractions requisite for running.

It is true that there are places where a cascade of complex movements occurs due to a single stimulatory signal, such as the complex sequential contraction across the areas of the heart that result from the single initiating signal within the Sinoatrial Node (i.e. SA, or pacemaker node), however situations such as these are rare, and are generally, as in the aforementioned example, associated with specialized muscle and nerve cells (e.g. cardiac muscle, Purkinje fibers, etc.).

Typically, stimulation resulting in complex muscle movement is initiated in a different manner. Rather than the single stimulatory signal of a cerebral motor neuron causing a chain reaction of sequential stimulation to other nerves, resulting in complex skeletal muscle contraction, complex stimulation originating within grey matter of the central nervous system tends to simultaneously occur across arrays of motor neurons, stimulating the simultaneous, complex contraction of the muscles which they innervate. It is for this reason that I do not feel that any simple, glitch-like signal from the exposed end of the spinal column could stimulate the residual grey matter within the spinal column to initiate and sustain complex muscle movement such as running.

There is still the possibility that the complete ability to initiate and control complex movements, such as running, exists independently within the grey matter of the spinal column: that the pain input from the afferent nerves upon beheading triggers an instinctive, sympathetic, fight-or-flight response to run in the chicken, or to swim in the tortoise. Something that, were it not ultimately fatal for the animal, would potentially remove it from danger. This is admittedly a stronger position, and is likely the one held by most modern scientists, although it borders upon an investigation of what constitutes thought and conscious will to act, a subject I would like to reserve for later.

My concern with this theory is that, if this is the case, why does ataxia (i.e. problems with, or inability to walk) caused by traumatic brain injury, or lesions within the cerebellum, believed to be the originating center for normal walking/running signals, not immediately resolve when people, or animals are placed in fight-or-flight situations? I have been unable to find any documented studies stating that this phenomenon has been observed, and in fact, feel that it would be so shockingly uncanny to all who observed it as to virtually ensure its documentation.

Imagine, for example, patients long crippled, or barely able to walk due to chronic maladies, immediately jumping out of their wheelchairs, or dropping their walkers, and sprinting like professional athletes when something like a house fire, or a mugger intensely frightens them. That would be extremely newsworthy material. Yet I don't see much credible documentation of it ever having occurred.

Prior to putting forward the theory which I have been leading up to, I need to explain a few principles about radios and resonance to readers who may be unfamiliar with them. Radios function by the concept of resonance. Resonance can be thought of as the natural frequency of things. At this frequency, the amplitude of mechanical oscillation/vibration increases dramatically. This phenomenon is what allows wine glasses to be shattered by opera singers. Once these singers hit the note which corresponds to the glass' resonant, or natural frequency, the glass' resistance to vibration drops significantly; ultimately leading to shattering.

The classic example which is used to explain resonance frequency is a radio tuner. A radio tuner is nothing more than a capacitor and an inductor placed parallel to each other within an electrical circuit. This configuration is known as an LC, or resonant "tank," and will always have a natural resonance specific to a certain frequency of wave. This is because capacitors and inductors resist the flow of electricity in a frequency dependent manner; the capacitor being more resistive to the flow of low frequency electrical signals, and inductors being more resistive to the flow of the high. These resistances are respectively known as capacitive and inductive reactance.

Resonance occurs when the capacitive and inductive reactance within a tank circuit are equal to each other. At this specific frequency, something very bizarre occurs: resistance to the flow of electrical energy within the resonant tank circuit becomes infinite. Either the capacitor, or the inductor may be adjusted, or "tuned," to change the resonant frequency of this circuit. This fact is exploited to send electricity from a specific frequency to the input of an amplifier and then to an output device, such as a speaker.

Consider the following example. A radio, or an 802.11 Wi-Fi connected device, such as a laptop, for the post millennials among us, receives data (i.e. intelligence) from a transmitting antenna located somewhere remote from it. Were we to place the radio, or computer on a scale, while it was receiving data from this source, and then compare the weight of the same radio, or computer after it was turned off, would we observe any difference? The answer is, unless we dive into the murky world of electron weights and thermodynamic energy loss, of course not.

Even if we did bravely enter that murky world, I would love to meet the scientist who could successfully perform such an experiment and produce repeatable results which could bear scrutiny. There are just so many factors involved when weight is being considered at such an infinitesimally small scale. Dust continually landing on the device from the air would produce a larger physical effect than that of the massless electromagnetic photons being received by the antenna. Yet information was being received the entire time that there was an active link between the transmitter and the receiver.

In theory, someone could attempt to calculate the force imparted by the photons on the antenna, yet this would prove unfruitful as well, considering that the same scattered photons will continue to hit this antenna from multiple directions, whether the device is on or off. One might possibly observe a difference in weight between a transmitting and nonfunctional radio, or computer, as the energy stored in the battery is converted into heat within the componentry, however this would not apply for a device which was plugged in, receiving a continuous supply of electricity, and which had reached thermal equilibrium.

So how could you prove to me that the aforementioned radio, or computer, had actually received information, or was in the process of receiving it? The obvious answer is that you could show me the complex effects of the received information; perhaps music emitted from the radio's speaker, or a webpage displayed on the computer's screen.

We can clearly see similar complex effects occurring within ourselves. It is possible that something within our minds, cells, and possibly even the very elements, atoms, and subatomic particles which form them, is analogously tuned to "resonate," so to speak, and receive information from an external source. Could this be what drives biotic life towards all of the astounding complexity which is required of it for growth, homeostasis, reproduction, and reason? More than this, could it also be the engine which pulls all living creatures down the tracks of evolution?

The reception of information was mentioned, but the thing being received appears to do more than simply inform. As a sort of intelligent energy, it also appears to energize and enliven. It could be compared to the transmission from a specialized type of wireless router, which not only transmits and receives data, but which also wirelessly charges remote devices, such as laptops, tablets, or phones. This concept of *intelligent energy*, unsurprisingly, echoes our earlier descriptions of the *soul*, or *spirit*. It also aligns with theories proposed by Plotinus, who, within his *Six Enneads*, theorized that soul was radiated into, enlivened, and informed matter.

In this energizing role, the soul would be quite similar to what has since antiquity been known by Chinese philosophers as "Chi," and by Indian Yogis as "Prana." The soul, and therefore the life of an organism, would therefore not only reside within a living creature's mind, but would also be distributed across its entire body. In fact, though the body may be spoken of as "living," when actively receiving and reacting to soul, the soul would be the actual "life" itself; much like a computer could be thought of as "living" while powered on, though the electricity itself is the actual "life" of a computer.

Here we return to the topic of phantom pain and post amputation movement. Until the time when acute ischemia eventually causes cell death, these amputated limbs are likely still functionally receptive to the influence and energy of the soul, and therefore literally still *alive*. The same is likely true of the headless bodies of chickens, snakes, and turtles, who are able to perform the complex motions of running, slithering, and swimming because the vast majority of their cells continue to resonate with this lifegiving thing which we call *soul*.

Interestingly, we often observe a slow cessation of these post-amputation movements, rather than their sudden stoppage. This is as one would expect, given that the various cells are slowly being damaged by ischemia to the point where they are no longer able to resonate to the influence of the soul. This ischemic destruction is similar to a fire, which steadily consumes a pile of working radios, until eventually all grow silent.

Regarding phantom pain, perhaps the immaterial soul is still somehow either concentrated in the area where the former limb was, much like one would envision the vaporous limb of a ghost, and occasionally passes information through the rest of the soul to the body, as if still a part of it. This latter point is purely speculative, however I believed it worthwhile to mention as at least a possibility in some instances, although I do believe terminal nerve fiber stimulation to be the culprit in the majority of instances.

It may be argued that I am proposing an effect with no observable cause, considering that I am suggesting information and energy passage into minds, cells, and matter, but have not yet identified a source, or carrier for these things. This is a fair statement which I have not overlooked. If there is an energizing signal being sent, which matter, especially living matter, is somehow designed to receive, perhaps via some sort of "resonance" principle, how could a simple experiment be designed which might prove, or disprove this?

At first glance one might think that a living organism could simply be placed within a Faraday Cage and observed for possible physiological changes. This approach might have merit, provided that the intelligence is being transmitted on a portion of the electromagnetic spectrum which the cage is designed to shield, and provided that the carrying medium is a photon: perhaps a wavelength of light, gamma rays, or cosmic microwave background radiation. Considering that there is life thriving on the ocean floor, where none of the aforementioned come close to penetrating, it is very unlikely that any of these examples could be the carrier of soul.

Regardless, should one desire to perform an experiment which would dispel any objections, in true scientific fashion, one would have to design and construct an exotic shielded container, as the majority are not designed to attenuate higher frequencies of radiation, such as gamma rays. Experiments would have to be conducted over several generation cycles of the test species, as intelligence and energy transfer, regardless of the carrier, could theoretically occur in a single instance, intermittently, or continuously; in the same way that some programs can operate after being downloaded once, while some require recurring updates, and others only work while an active link is established with an external host. It would therefore be preferable for the test species to have short generational cycles; as bacteria does.

There is also the possibility that this signal is being transmitted and received via one of the other fundamental particles, such as neutrinos. Neutrinos are an attractive candidate for an information and energy carrier, considering that they are generated in such massive quantities within the sun, an estimated 1×10^{11} neutrinos hitting each square centimeter of the earth, every second. They also *appear* to be extremely unreactive, allowing them to penetrate through the entire planet. Theoretically, only one in every ~100 billion neutrinos is interfered with during its journey from the core of the sun to its surface, a distance of roughly ~400,000 miles (i.e. ~50.5 times the diameter of the Earth). And this is even occurring within an extremely high temperature, high energy environment which typically enhances reactivity. In addition, neutrinos, being non-charge carrying particles, require special equipment and techniques to detect them; equipment which, to my knowledge, would not be able to detect any type of modulated signal which may be riding on this carrier.

Conducting an experiment to determine if biotic organisms are affected by neutrinos would be extremely challenging, considering that it is practically impossible, with today's technology, to shield them out. Ideally, however, this is what could be done with a multigenerational model. Frozen bacteria, dried bacterial spores, or amoeboid cysts could be loaded within a shielded and modified freezer/bioreactor which contained a camera for analyzing morphology, spectrophotometer for determining cell density/population count, and magnetic windings for mimicking the Earth's magnetic field.

This device could then be launched into deep space, and once a sufficient distance had been reached from the Sun for neutrino effect to theoretically be significantly reduced, the bioreactor, which had been at the near absolute zero temperature of space to this point, could be powered up, brought to temperature, and the bacteria or amoebae bred up for several generations, each generation being examined for growth rate and morphological changes; any photos and data being transmitted back to Earth.

If a significant decline in vigor, or increase in mutation is observed after several generations, this would be a significant finding. Mimicking the effect of the Earth's magnetic field is critical, considering that otherwise, it would be unclear whether any aberration from normal growth was caused by a differing magnetic field, or the neutrino effect.

Experiments that could be conducted to determine if other known fundamental particles are carrying this signal would not be difficult to formulate, except for those related to Bosons. Currently, I am unaware of how these could be controlled for in an experiment, as they tend to rapidly associate with other fundamental particles. However, as I currently understand them, bosons are not streaming from the sun nor penetrating to the sea floor unassociated. They are therefore an unlikely candidate for an information carrier.

A signal that is transmitting intelligence and energy would likely either need to transmit all of the information and energy required for all possible scenarios the cell could encounter, all at once, or continuously transmit modified instructions and energy levels depending upon the state of the cell, as it attempts to survive within its environment. This latter instance would imply that information flow was bidirectional, at least some of the time. As discussed elsewhere, if the universe itself is the living entity which we commonly refer to as God, then this ultimate source of intelligence would be omnipresent, and omniscient, since it possesses all universal information within itself; rendering bidirectional transmission unnecessary.

Shared Soul

If soul is something immaterial which indwells us, where does it go when we die? I understand that it is often absurd to speak of location when discussing things which are immaterial, however, some immaterial things, such as photons, do in fact exist within certain specific locations. What if there is a finite amount of this thing which we call *soul*, within the universe? Some may be driving the fundamental forces of matter, such as gravity and magnetism, some may be ensuring that elementary particles do not run out of energy, some may be driving cellular processes within living organisms and filling us with our sense of will and being. Are we limited in the amount of soul which we possess, or throughout our lives, are we possibly able to attract more of it, or lose some or all of what we already possess?

During our lives, there is the possibility that portions of our souls mix, or are shared with the souls of those whom we love and are loved by. A component of the feeling of love could be a subconscious awareness of this mixing, or sharing. It must be admitted that there is currently no way of knowing whether or not one can even speak about *parts* of souls, or whether, like an infinitely small point, immaterial souls allow for no partition. Postulating that souls cannot be divided does not mean that any mixing which these souls do must be complete. Like overlapping colors of light, nothing prevents a partial mixture.

Who is to say that only one soul can fill a body? If truly shared, or mixed, then the bodies of loved ones might serve as new receptacles for our souls, should something happen to our own bodies. Such a possibility seems strikingly similar to the ancient concept of transmigration of soul, made famous by Socrates and many other Greek and Egyptian philosophers. Perhaps restless "ghosts" (i.e. spirits/souls), if they exist at all, are merely those who died in such a state of moral corruption that they were unable to find another host.

We know how moral corruption, and the unhappiness (i.e. depression) which it produces within men, has a tendency to shorten men's lives, while virtue, and the happiness which it produces, tends to lengthen them. Perhaps this occurs because moral corruption has a draining effect upon the amount of inherently good *soul* which fills us, while virtue somehow attracts more of it. The amount of soul which we lose, or the additional soul which we attract, could be gained by, or lost from the universe as a whole, a localized area, or other individuals. This latter possibility would perhaps make sense of some of the theories of "faith healing" by "laying on of hands," which are common among certain charismatic churches.

Should immoral actions actually cause individuals to lose a portion of the soul which enlivens them, then the old saying that the person who acts cruelly is actually only hurting themselves, is more true than people realize. Could this be the ultimate cause for the well documented, chillingly hollow look which is often seen in the eyes of murderers, those about to commit suicide, and the "Thousand-yard Stare" of soldiers who have experienced significant horrors during combat?

I freely admit that these are but theories, however they provide an appealing angle on some curious and problematic phenomena. One of these is what is known as Déjà vu. There are two kinds of Déjà vu which I am familiar with. One is a feeling of familiarity with an object, situation, or location that one does not ever remember being exposed to in the past. The other is a feeling, where one can sense the words or actions which are about to be spoken or said by another person, prior to them saying them; as if one has a momentary, extremely limited type of prescience. These two types could ultimately be but varying degrees of a single one.

Everyone has experienced the first type of Déjà vu at least once. People will walk into an unfamiliar location, listen to, or say something to someone, or do something, and suddenly feel as if they have been to that same place, heard or spoken those same words with that same person, or done these same things before. The current scientific explanation for this phenomenon is basically a denial of its reality, by claiming that it is nothing more than mistaken perception. "Experts" claim that Déjà vu is simply either the perceiver forgetting that they were previously in a similar situation before, or that the mind is sending a false signal of familiarity. As evidence of the latter, these "experts" will point out that drugs can be given which increase the frequency of this type of Déjà vu feeling.

I believe this theory to be extremely weak, and very likely incorrect. I understand what these "experts" are attempting to accomplish with this theory, and really do not blame them for taking this position. Since most of them are working from a purely Materialist world view, Déjà vu's *must* be false. If they are not, their specificity could only be indicative of some yet unidentified, potentially *spiritual* influence.

Regarding the second type of prescience-like Déjà vu, academia tends to ignore or deny the existence of this type altogether.

Experimentation and raw data always trumps theory, however. And at least for me, my personal experiences with Déjà vu phenomena cannot be explained by the previously mentioned theory. I say this knowing that firsthand experiences of this sort, being unquantifiable, carry the most weight with the experiencer. When relayed to others, being at that point merely second or third hand experiences, they essentially become matters of faith in the rationality and credibility of the experiencer. Let the reader scrutinize me and reach what conclusions they will in this regard.

I have often experienced Déjà vu phenomena. I seem to forget the experience quite quickly, due to the lack of singularity of the specific scenario, and am typically left only with the odd memory of having had one. Were this all there was to the matter, this would completely fall in line with the accepted theory of the mind sending a false familiarity signal. I understand this.

I do, however, remember often having what have seemed to be "stronger" Déjà vu experiences; ones that have seemed to last for much longer before "breaking."

"Okay. So what?" some might ask.

Well, the "so what" is that when these have happened, I have not only felt a familiarity with the events I was experiencing, but I have very briefly also been able to anticipate the upcoming words, or actions of both myself, and the person with whom I was speaking. Experts, looking at my account from a Materialist point of view, would say that this was impossible. They would say that my mind must either be doing one of two possible things. Either it is making educated, anticipatory guesses about what is about to be said, or about to occur, occasionally guessing correctly, or I have been in similar situations with this person, where the same, or similar conversation was had, yet I have forgotten all but the subconscious memory of the event.

From a statistical perspective, I believe that the scenarios have been too unique, and the conversations too novel for either possibility to be adequate. During a recent experience, for example, I was taking the stairs down from a higher floor at work and happened to meet and strike up a conversation in the stairwell with our Chief Financial Officer (CFO). While talking, he began relaying something extremely specific which our national office had recently mentioned to him. While he was talking, the Déjà vu feeling suddenly descended upon me, and for a few moments (perhaps only 5 seconds, but this always seems an eternity when it occurs), I knew the next words which both he and I were going to say, and also what we were both going to do, before the phenomenon "broke," or dissipated.

Now consider this from a statistical perspective. I almost never take the stairs. At that time, I only encountered our CFO outside of meetings perhaps 3 times a year, and we had never discussed the national topic that we were discussing at that moment, as it was regarding a recent policy change. The statistics are strongly against the possibility of my mind thinking that all of those chance phenomena had happened before, simultaneously, and also that it would be able to anticipate not only the next words, but the next bodily motions of the both of us with such accuracy as to confuse my conscious mind into believing that it had a momentary taste of precognition. The general formula for the probability of an event occurring is as follows:

Probability= Number of events/Total number of possible outcomes

For multiple independent events to all happen, the formula becomes:

Probability of an event happening = (Event1/Outcomes1) x (Event2/Outcomes2)...(Event n/Outcomes n)

When worked out for each of the preconditions which I mentioned in my CFO scenario, the resulting probability would be so low as to make the event effectively impossible. Consider all of the possible paths which I could have taken down the stairs, all of the times that I could have taken those paths, all of the paths that the CFO could have taken, all of the possible subjects which he, or I could have spoken about, or actions we could have performed, how many ways my mind could have anticipated the outcome of the conversation, or follow-up actions, etc. The probability will be found to be infinitesimal.

Now add to this the fact that this has not happened to me only once, or twice. It has happened perhaps a half dozen times that I can still remember, and very likely more that I have since forgotten. I remember specifically telling family and friends when it happened how odd it was to momentarily be able to anticipate the next word, or action of myself, or others. I remember those things making me consider the possibility that our individual and collective futures were already written beforehand, and that the concept of time travelling along a single uniform strand was possibly erroneously anthropocentric.

There is the possibility that these Déjà vu experiences are due to the experiencer having been in the same situation, or uttering the same statement during a previous life. Something which hints at this option is the odd phenomenon where children claim to recall previous lives. This phenomenon has been documented and discussed by several well-respected psychologists. Perhaps the child did receive his soul from someone else. Several ancient philosophers believed that children slowly lose this memory of past lives as they age, as the memory of a dream fades upon waking.

In Plato's, *Meno*, Socrates uses a geometry lesson to describe how man is able to recall knowledge from past lives.[181] In another ancient work, the author stated that the method for recalling previous lives was to continually bring the mind to focus upon the earliest of memories, and then merely attempt to recall a few moments prior to that point. Over time, this author claimed that one might hopefully succeed in bringing up memories from a previous life. If this transmigration of soul is really occurring at all, it is highly unlikely that it is the sole source of Déjà vu, given the often high degree of scenario specificity associated with many of these events.

As another possibility, Déjà vu experiences could be due to the previously mentioned mixing, or sharing of soul. As the second person thinks about the words which they intend to speak, or the actions which they intend to perform, these thoughts may be sensed within the portion of the soul which is shared with the first person, giving them the vague sense of familiarity and seeming precognition. This would be similar to the feedback effect observed when a microphone is placed in front of a speaker which it feeds. Perhaps that is all that Déjà vu really is; a sort of *spiritual feedback*.

A final option is that the soul of God, which fills and enlivens the universe, is the same soul which fills individual men. In this scenario, partiality of mixing becomes impossible. Should the portion of soul possessed by two individuals connect at all, then during the period of connection, a single soul spanning two physical bodies would be produced. If this occurs, it is not necessary for both individuals to experience the same feeling of Déjà vu, as some may be more in tune with the leadings of soul than others.

Is the sharing and mixing of the physical organs and fluids during the sexual act itself simply the closest physical mimicry of the sharing and mixing of immaterial soul which can physically occur? Indeed, which may simultaneously be occurring.

Another phenomenon that might better be explained by this soul sharing theory is the odd way that truly and deeply loving couples often encounter coincidences which almost hint at an ability to remotely sense one another's souls, or specific types of thoughts. There are dozens of examples of this phenomena occurring. Most often, such examples involve a sense of "foreboding" which one of the mates has, only to later discover that some tragic event involving their loved one occurred at the time. While I have not experienced this personally, on more than a few occasions I have picked up my cell phone to dial my wife, only to have it immediately ring in my hand, she being on the other end. Indeed, I have even called my mother before, only to have her answer by asking if I was all right, as my call had awakened her from a dream that I was involved in.

Another phenomenon that might be partially explained by the soul sharing theory is that of near-death experiences. Often it is reported by the people who recover from these events that they recall specific details from the surgical suite which it should be theoretically impossible for them to know. There are at least two possibilities of what is occurring in these situations. In the first, the soul itself of the individual close to death, or temporarily "dead" might be moving about in the area, free from the body. This is the most commonly accepted view for those who continue to cling to a belief in soul.

The second possibility is that the compassion which the clinical staff feel towards the patient, as well as the trust and goodwill which the patient feels towards them, has allowed the patient's soul to become mixed, or shared with the soul, or souls of one, or several of the clinicians. As with the previously discussed effect related to Déjà vu, this might allow the patient an ability to know some of their thoughts, which may include room details and the commonly reported perspective of looking "down upon" themselves from above. This visualization may actually be occurring through the clinicians' eyes, or via a participation in their memories and thoughts.

It is possibly even a bit of both scenarios. It could be that the momentarily "dead" patient has already found a new home within the body and mind of one of the clinicians, and as such, sees their views and feels their thoughts. When this patient is resuscitated, perhaps they are able to cling to some of the memories of these sights and thoughts due to their relative recency.

Another common occurrence is for the momentarily "dead" person, prior to resuscitation, to visualize deceased loved ones nearby. If souls are truly shared, then this may be more than mere perception and endorphin induced memory resurfacing. There is the possibility that the souls of these loved ones and that of the patient mixed, or were shared at some point, and either a portion, or the entirety of the dead relative's soul took up residence within the patient's body. If this is the case, then our resulting personalities could be a composite resulting from the cocktail of souls residing within us.

This view makes me wonder about the concept of "demon" possession so long clung to by many cultures. Perhaps such "possession" is little more than the invasion of a corrupt soul, due to the lack of various influencing factors which would otherwise normally prevent this. It was already speculated previously that, upon the death of their body, these souls might normally find difficulty locating a new host. If corrupt souls are for some reason constrained to a certain nearby area when they leave the body, such as within a certain proximity to the corpse, or at the site of expiration, then the presence of the living within these areas may increase the risk of inadvertent mixing, or sharing with these souls.

There is also the possibility that the theorized love-based requirement for normal soul mixing, or sharing is bypassed when the individual in question is placed in a natural, or drug induced semi-hypnotic state. This is mentioned due to the nature of hypnosis, which allows for direct interaction with the subconscious mind, a subject which is discussed at length in another section of this work.

This possibility raises important questions regarding the possible efficacy of occult ceremonies. Many of these ceremonies involve possessions, body parts, blood, or the body itself of dead animals, or humans. The recency of the death, or number of the dead is often supposed to increase the efficiency of these ceremonies; many even killing the victim as part of the process. These ceremonies are also famous for being conducted within areas where the dead reside, such as cemeteries, or those where deaths are famous for having occurred.

Lastly, these ceremonies virtually always involve a process whose obvious purpose is to induce a sort of hypnotic state. These processes include the use of certain drugs, repetitive chanting, or transfixing the eyes upon objects where the focus cannot be maintained, such as a crystal ball, a black mirror, the leaves floating in black tea, the tip of the nose, areas of a darkened room, the flame of a candle, etc.; all of which aid in hypnotic induction.

Here we have all the ingredients which were previously mentioned as possibly increasing the potential for the invasion of an individual with the souls of the dead, which may or may not be corrupt: proximity to the dead, and a semi-hypnotic state. This possible side effect of these occult practices, if it actually occurs, is likely accidental, as occultists tend to have a warped conception of the soul, goodness, God, and nature itself, and are therefore unlikely to know how best to influence them.

Arrogance

Do we all share a single spirit? An all-pervading, all-encompassing spirit that is the sap which drives this tree of life through its myriad stages of growth. Are children the buds, women the blossoms, and men the leaves of this tree, all unconsciously drawing their nourishment from this sap?

In writing that trope, I paused and questioned its merit. Leaves not only draw nutrients from the sap, but also supply it with energy, in the form of photosynthetically generated sugar. Yet can man give anything to God? Can a material being add to things which are spiritual?

When I ponder this question by looking to the spirit within myself, I find the trope of the leaf redeemed. While it is uncertain if anything spiritual may be created, and in fact, very unlikely, as creation, or destruction of a spiritual element seems to destroy along with it the meaning of the spiritual concept. Is spirit not the hidden, higher reality which we sense, when still and honest with ourselves, which dwells behind the costume of matter; moving it about like a marionette?

Perhaps man cannot add to spirit, but as the leaf draws in CO_2 and sunlight, changing these things through astoundingly complex chemical pathways, into material which, in its own small way, benefits and nourishes both itself and the entire plant, perhaps individual men and women are, in like manner, instruments which God has designed to convert the things of matter, at the guidance of the spirit within us, into things intended to benefit our and society's souls and bodies.

We very truly may be said to be a nexus between the spiritual and material worlds. I find myself wanting to adopt this stance, as it fits nicely with that of many theorists; matter being thought of as otherwise dead, but filled with a life-giving spirit in the ambulating diversity of creation. The problem is that I cannot seem to rid myself of the feeling that this is a too narrow and egocentric view of things. In order to adopt it, one must first believe in the lifelessness of all non-cellular matter.

Yet the microscope has shown us virus' that very much seem to act as if they have an *interest*, a *will* it may be called, in propagating themselves. Even the atomic and subatomic matter, from which rocks are formed, move and have affinities for other particles.

Scientists tell us that these are mere laws of electrical, or magnetic forces driving these movements, like the charge of an electromagnet draws a nail, but this doesn't seem to solve the riddle. Certainly, atoms in a higher energy ionized state will seek to achieve a lower energy one, much like a ball on a hill will tend to roll downwards, if possible, due to gravity. This seems only to add another link to the chain of causation, without explaining the cause itself.

An electron may be drawn to the proton within a nucleus, like a positive pole of a magnet is drawn toward the negative pole of another, but what is causing the magnetism. I have heard the various scientific theories about vacant d subshells, lines of flux, static charges, and induced dipole moments, but all of these seem to describe an effect, rather than a cause. All effects must have a cause, yet magnetism, like gravity, remains mysterious.

Is matter simply a condensation, so to speak, of this mysterious thing which we call *energy*, or *spirit*? James Allanson Picton theorized about this ~100 years ago in his *The Mystery of Matter*.[179] If so, God being pure spirit, spirit being energy, and matter being condensed energy, God would not merely indwell and enliven an otherwise dead substratum of matter with a lifegiving spirit, but both mater and spirit would all be *God*. This is an interesting concept, given that we already know that matter can be converted into energy, or spirit.

Can the reaction occur in reverse; pure energy, or spirit, being transformed back into matter? It does not matter how rare the conversion of matter into energy is. The conversion of a finite supply, regardless of the rate, will exhaust the supply when multiplied by an infinity of time. Since we know that mass is converted into energy throughout the universe at a certain rate, that the universe is infinitely old, and yet that all mass has clearly not been converted into energy, then the back conversion of energy into mass must also be occurring, whether scientists have observed, classified, and modeled this phenomenon yet, or not.

Since immaterial energy has absolute ideal existence, does this imply that the fundamental elementary particles are also ideal and absolute? Not that we are entirely certain what the fundamental elementary particles are, as there may be multiple tiers of structure even beneath and comprising those which our current technology has made known to us, such as quarks.

But let's play devil's advocate for a moment. Even if quarks are the fundamental particles which pure energy transforms into, when this transformation occurs, are these quarks ideal and absolute; or in other words, perfect? Perhaps there are 3 tiers of order beneath the quark. Maybe there are 12. Regardless of the number, the conclusion doesn't change. Whatever particle comprises the lowest tier of subatomic structure would be matter in its purest form: absolute matter. This statement will generally cause scientists to shudder, especially those familiar with Newton's 2nd Law of Thermodynamics, as the natural world seems to hate perfection. Yet as far as our understanding goes, this particle would have to be perfect; as any material imperfection is rooted in deficiency, or adulteration, which are impossibilities for the lowest tier of subatomic structure. Nothing would be small enough to penetrate this particle. No amount of energy and nothing in the universe could divide it, as it has no parts to be divided into. The only change which it could undergo would be a conversion into pure energy.

We do not know whether there are several types of this fundamental matter, or only one. There is the possibility that what we currently think of as fundamental particles, such as quarks, electrons, and neutrinos, are simply differing composites of a single fundamental particle mixed in varying ratios with the immaterial (i.e. energy). Such composites would by necessity possess a range of physical structures and therefore also possess a range of mechanisms of activity. This could account for the observed differences in behavior in known subatomic matter.

This could also be the case with what we refer to as "antimatter," due to its tendency to interact explosively with its complimentary subatomic particle. The term *antimatter* could, in fact, be a misnomer. The various forms of antimatter could simply be other composite ratios of matter and immaterial energy, which, when allowed to interact with their more familiar complementary composite structures, tip the scale of thermodynamic stability in favor of conversion into pure energy; an interaction which we refer to as an annihilation event. Should this prove accurate, then there would be no *antimatter*, simply a range of composites of the true fundamental form of matter mixed with immaterial energy, causing these various subatomic composites to exhibit distinct stabilities, attractions, and tendencies to interact more strongly with complimentary composite forms falling on opposite sides of the scale; much like we observe at a higher level with the electron driven interactions of elements on opposing ends of the periodic table.

Once one has heard enough contradicting theories from brilliant scientists to shiver oneself awake from the siren song of omniscience being sung from the minarets of the various Western universities, into a wholesome skepticism, the theories of space-time and how it interacts with gravity, as well as many of the theories on magnetism, begin to seem a bit like the Wizard of Oz. The fire, smoke, and booming voices of the champions of these theories resound from their alma matters, but one can never shake the nagging thought that a common man, ambitious of reputation, funding, and the wealth which tends to follow them, is pulling the levers of the machine behind the curtain. It is likely that, if honest with himself, this man will admit that he is as confused as we mere mortals are.

We give phenomena clever names and develop mathematical models which can often predict their occurrences with a reasonable amount of accuracy, but is this a cause? No. Frequently the effect is labeled and modeled and the scientific community move on to the next subject, yet the cause remains unknown.

What causes gravity? What causes magnetic attraction? What is light? What is energy? How does light not decelerate as it travels trillions of miles through space, though influenced by, or influencing random atoms adrift in the cosmos during its journey. Though space is mostly void, the photos of nebulae clearly show that not every atom has accreted into a sun, or planet. If the Faraday effect proves that light may be moved, or influenced by a magnetic field, why, given its theoretically nonexistent mass, have the magnetic fields of these random atoms not effectively cancelled its momentum and caused it to stop altogether?

Returning to the questions of cause, what is so improbable about these being an interaction on matter by spirit. Unleash the academic hounds, for I have broken the cardinal rule within the scientific community today, of seriously considering the existence of a spirit, soul, spiritual entities, or a spiritual domain. How can I take such a retrograde step? Don't I know that all is mechanical: all effectively a series of gears or levers. Next, I will be advocating spontaneous generation of flies from meat. Where is my evidence that such a thing as spirit even exists? No one has proven this and better men than I have tried.

If there is a soul, why have we not observed it via the more developed scientific tools and methods available to us today? There have actually been some efforts towards this end, however, it must be borne in mind that there is much more that we don't know, despite our scientific methods, than we pretend to. The more veteran scientists of today have a healthy amount of disillusionment in this regard than those without a scientific background who are bedazzled by the credentials and jargon that often cloud, contradict, and confuse an issue as much as they clarify and confirm it.

Even with a healthy amount of skepticism, why have scientists been unable to observe the soul, should it truly exist? This question depends upon what would be considered sufficient evidence for such a thing. Most scientists would state that the ability to quantitatively classify a material thing is sufficient evidence for calling it *real*. Yet what of things that are so subtle that their very existence is extremely difficult to observe. The Higgs Boson, for example, was only recently proven to exist, thanks to the efforts of dozens of the most brilliant particle physicists in the world using over a trillion dollars of equipment (e.g. CERN supercollider).

But what experiments have been conducted on the existence of the soul? Have we enlisted similar armies of researchers and invested a trillion dollars in equipment in this pursuit? Of course not. The only experiments have been a few obscure, poorly documented ones from the early 20th century, such as the crude experiments conducted by Dr. Duncan MacDougall calculating the difference in weight between dying and freshly dead bodies.[180] This difference was claimed to be 21 grams, although many academics have questioned these results. These experiments were only done with equipment sensitive to +/- 2/10 of an ounce; hardly sensitive enough to record the effects of things which we know exist, such as light and electrical charge, much less any which we may not yet have discovered. So, is it truly objective and scientific to assume the nonexistence of a thing which we haven't thoroughly investigated?

Yet, besides observing the physical properties of a thing, there is another way to determine its existence; this being to observe its effect. Here is where we return to the question of what would be considered sufficient evidence to prove the existence of soul, as it is hard to look at will, reason, and higher thought and not sense the external influence. Without such an influence, what makes the handful of matter that we are composed of able to look up at the heavens and ponder the existence of a God, while other handfuls of the same matter which we have observed throughout our solar system seem unable to do anything remotely similar. This ability to reason and will seems a rather strong example of *effect* from my perspective, and in fact, from the perspective of all but a very few philosophers/scientists, from the earliest period of recorded history, until perhaps the middle of the 20th century, when atheism and activism, rather than cold, yet reliable reason and objectivity began to come into vogue among the scientocracy.

Once the dust settles and I am left by a sneering, scoffing, self-congratulatory crowd of academics, if such a crowd may actually be drawn outside their circle of orthodoxy, as a "discredited fool" I will quietly think to myself of the irony of the demand for proof from men surrounded, penetrated, stuck to the ground by, and even themselves causing gravity; whose thoughts that command their laughter, travel as energy down nerve fibers that depend upon electromagnetic forces to ensure ion flow based saltatory motion; men whose very atoms, along with those of their world, don't fly apart into quarks and the nest of stacked "Russian dolls" beneath these, due, in large part, to electromagnetic forces; men who know of 90% of existence due to light, a form of massless energy which must slowly be exhausting itself as it radiates beyond the boundary of the universe, and yet, who are not a ball of frozen matter, thanks to the continual existence of this energy within the universe.

Yet they sneeringly demand evidence. What is not evidence? It seems self-evident, and it has seemed so to all but some among the most recent generation of atheist infected academics, who are overconfident in their own sagacity, that something beyond the physical exists, which drives these incredibly complex bodies of ours. Something within us which is greater than the sum of the physical components themselves.

Aristotle argued the same thing in his *Metaphysics*, in roughly 320 B.C. Within this work, he stated that one of the classical theories was that there was an underlying substrate of matter, but that there was also a force which drove change therein forward; as no effect is without a cause. Aristotle went on to state that philosophers who tried to make the fundamental parts of the universe consist only in the underlying matter and no driving force, as most modern Western academics tend to today, necessarily ended up in absurdities. As paraphrasing such a masterly philosopher would only do damage to his argument, a quote from this work is included below.

"Since not only the elements in a thing are causes, but also something external, i.e. The moving cause...it is clear then from what has been said that there is a substance which is eternal and unmovable and separate from sensible things. It has been shown also that this substance cannot have any magnitude, but is without parts and indivisible (for it produces movement through infinite time, but nothing finite has infinite power; and, while every magnitude is either infinite or finite, it cannot, for the above reason, have finite magnitude, and it cannot have infinite magnitude because there is no infinite magnitude at all." [25]

Roughly 500 years later, in ~270 A. D., Plotinus, arguably the greatest product of the Neoplatonist school, went into depth on the same subject in his Six Enneads.[37] While I don't agree with all of Plotinus' postulates within this work, I do agree with several of them; specifically, his handling of the existence of the soul in the first tractate of the first Ennead. I have included this in its entirety in *Appendix A*. Plotinus describes the situation as being one of matter and the forms and designs, or in other words, the *intelligence*, which is impressed upon it. These forms can never exceed the level of excellence of their creator; much like a painting by a master painter can never exceed the ideal form which the painting initially takes when conceived within the painter's mind.

Emerson builds upon and expands this same conception of the soul which is given by Plotinus. His essay on the "Oversoul" has been included in its entirety in *Appendix B*, as it reads like a piece of poetry, and any attempt to paraphrase it would ruin it.[3]

It may seem like two subjects are being discussed here: a designing/organizing force driving all of nature, or in other words, God, and the existence of soul. In actuality, it is impossible to discuss the latter without including the former, since the existence of a soul inevitably leads to the question of its source.

Contrary to the ~300 B. C. warnings of Aristotle, the majority of scientists today attempt to exclude the existence of a driving and designing force within the universe, by claiming that all of the astounding complexity which we observe in the natural world around us is merely the result of chance interactions of lifeless, disorganized matter. Let's test this postulate using Socrates' method of reducing, or expanding its complexity; a technique known as *reductio ad absurdum*. When subjected to such a test, absolute truths continue to ring true, while the absurdity of falsities become more apparent. The Materialist postulate is found to be absurd when considered on either end of the spectrum.

An example reduction of this postulate might be someone encountering an elaborate sand castle on the beach and making the laughable claim that it was caused by chance interactions of the sand particles themselves. The obvious complexity of the sand castle's form bespeaks a designing will. This designing will was impressed upon the sand via the physical channel of the human hands, or tools, which responded to it. In like manner, the complexity encountered throughout the universe, and especially among things which we categorize as "living," bespeaks a designing will which must be more complex than the forms which it has impressed upon the matter itself.

We could also examine the previous postulate by expanding it into the form of a universal truth. In doing so, we end up making the absurd claim that there is no way to prove that the most complex and elaborate thing which we could imagine was in any way designed, or formed. Imagine visiting the city of Manhattan, with its gleaming skyscrapers, busy factories, thousands of streetlights, parks, monuments, complex networks of streets, subways, sewers, and sidewalks, and then making such a ludicrous claim. Such a claim would completely contradict the main principle which the entire field of Archaeology is based upon.

When buried cities are unearthed in Egypt, Rome, or South America, it is the complexity and organization of the items encountered which is relied upon as an indication that the action of an external human will was involved in their formation or placement. Stonehenge is a great example of this. Any who would look at this structure and claim that the stones migrated into that circular shape on their own, perfectly aligning themselves with certain solar occurrences, would be laughed at. Yet the complexity and interdependence of the parts found within even a single E. Coli bacterium, the "simplest" of living organisms, is many orders of magnitude greater. Those who make similar Materialist claims about its origin should likewise be laughed out of the universities.

Another fundamental flaw of the Materialist theory is that it assumes that we have complete knowledge of all of the attributes of matter. This is far from the case. We don't even possess a complete understanding of the principles of energy, magnetism, light, and the subatomic particles which all matter is formed of.

Ultimately, Materialist theory violates the law of cause and effect. In order to avoid the question of the cause of the mind-bogglingly complex arrangements encountered within living creatures, they claim that these were the product of chance interactions of matter on previous less complex life forms, ad infinitum, back to the first cell. This claim doesn't speak to the cause; it merely describes the effect and forces the question back into the remote recesses of antiquity, where it is hoped that it will be overlooked.

They claim that their theory of abiogenesis solves the riddle about the origin of life, however, this hopelessly flawed theory (discussed elsewhere in this work) does nothing to explain the elaborate order found even within the molecules, atoms, and subatomic particles of nonliving matter. What is the cause of matter? Claiming that it is simply the product of chance interactions is absurd; regardless of timescale.

If pressed on this question of causation, most Materialists will either retreat, become circular in their reasoning, attack the questioner, or change the subject. Their position is similar to the comical one of the ancient Hindus, who, when questioned about their belief that the world was supported by an elephant, thought they solved the question by responding that the elephant was supported by a turtle.

Spencer

Herbert Spencer, the man who first coined the phrase, "Survival of the fittest," with regards to evolution, was one of the most celebrated scientists of the 19th century. Today, however, this brilliant polymath has mostly been forgotten by all but scientific historians. Among many other things which he authored, he wrote a 10 volume *System of Synthetic Philosophy*, which ranged in topics from Biology, to Sociology, to Ethics. The first volume of this series was simply entitled, *First Principles*.

There is a fascinating part of this work which discusses challenges related to the study of the origin of the universe.[182] Spencer claimed that there are three possibilities for this origin, but that all three ultimately break down under investigation. The first theory, he claimed, is that God created the universe from nothing, or ex nihilo, as it is commonly stated. The problem with this theory is that it leaves us as confused as we were when we started, as it inevitably leads to the question of what created God. The answer which is generally given is that nothing did. God has always existed. We are therefore left struggling with the concept of perpetual existence. Let's consider this possibility.

Any positive existence, whether time-bound, or perpetual, must either be material, or immaterial. Whether material, or immaterial, if this being which we call God has positive existence, then it would actually be a component of the universe itself; as the definition of the universe is all things distributed throughout space which have positive existence.

What are the implications of a material God occupying a portion of the universe, prior to the creation of all other matter? Since it is necessary for God to be perfect, it is also necessary for him to be unchanging. This is because the only change possible would be a variation from perfection, which would destroy the latter, dissolving with it God's very divinity.

God would also always be in the center of the universe, as an infinite expanse of empty space would always stretch out in all directions. He would therefore only be able to move in reference to himself. Unfortunately, even this type of movement would be impossible. This is because it would require God to have parts. Since a being formed from imperfect parts cannot itself be perfect, each part would have to be equally perfect. This destroys any difference which is necessary for partition to exist.

Let us then consider a perfect material homogeneity. The shape which best embodies this concept is a sphere with an infinitesimally small radius: a point, really. This is the concept of God that the ancient Gnostics arrived at, which they described as a Circumpunct. No movement is possible for such a point, given that the only theoretically possible motion, rotation, cannot occur due to inability to move around a center with a radius of zero. This concept is somewhat analogous to that proposed by Aristotle in his *On the Heavens*, except that Aristotle allows for an infinitesimal radius, which also allows for rotation.[183]

A problem that remains within this theory is, where is the material entity now? Is God simply a speck in space, positioned two lightyears between Earth and Alpha Centauri? Instinct itself recoils from the concept of God as an infinitesimally small point of matter, floating somewhere in space. In fact, the concept of a sphere with no radius actually destroys the material viewpoint which it was initially developed to preserve; as such a point would occupy no space, and therefore not be matter.

Then what of an immaterial God? An immaterial God, as with anything immaterial, could only be evidenced by its interactions with matter. In fact, such an entity would be hardly distinguishable from a form of energy, either concentrated within one locus, or distributed throughout the universe.

And yet, when we look around, we find evidence of just such motive energies with unknown sources surrounding us. We give these energies labels, as if we truly understood their source, but we do not. One example is the "Dark Energy" which is causing the universe to accelerate as it expands, contrary to the slowing effect expected from the gravity of the collective mass within it. Force equals mass times acceleration, as we all know from Newtonian Mechanics. If the mass of the universe is constant, and yet the whole thing is accelerating, where is the additional force, or energy coming from?

Another example that I discussed previously is the energy maintaining the seemingly constant motion of elementary particles such as electrons. What continues to add energy to each atom, counteracting repulsive and frictional forces experienced by their orbiting electrons. Theoretically, the slightest reduction in energy should destroy the delicate and perfect balance between nuclear attractive forces and centrifugal repulsive ones, causing an orbital decay and ultimately a binding of proton with electron; possibly creating a neutron. While this occurs at times, it does not do so nearly to the extent which it should, were external energy not somehow being added to the system to offset that which is being lost.

We still are unable to comprehend the possibility of an eternal immaterial entity. When the mind is turned upon that dreadful concept of eternity, it instead will think of something extremely old; perhaps a planet or galaxy. Our human minds cannot handle the concept and seek escape by converting it into a material symbol which is more tolerable.

What we fail to consider here is the fact that, if God is immaterial, unchanging, and immoveable, as we concluded above he must be, then prior to the creation of the material universe, time itself would not exist. This is because time itself has no positive existence; regardless of the flawed space-time theories which are popular among today's scientists. Time is simply an abstract concept used to describe the relative change of matter. Prior to the existence of matter, there would therefore be no time.

This brings us to Spencer's second theory on the origin of the universe; that the universe has had no origin. This theory implies that the universe itself is immortal. The problem with this theory is that it implies that the universe is in a sort of equilibrium between its creative actions, such as planetary and sun formation via accretion, caused by gravitational forces, and its destructive actions, such as super novae and planetary impacts, due to orbital decay.

While a type of equilibrium is undeniable, the bulk expansion of the universe seems to imply both a net origin and an ultimate net end, via either dispersal, or collapse. Some theorists, sensing this problem, have proposed an even larger scale equilibrium, consisting of an infinite series of *Big Bangs* followed by *Big Crush* collapses. The problem with this theory is that it ignores the constant net loss of photonic energy being radiated into the nothingness beyond the edge of the universe. It is impossible to have any amount of energy loss or gain, however slight, on an eternal timeline.

If the universe is oscillating through various cycles of expansion and collapse, with energy being lost to the vacuum of space, this oscillation will eventually slow to a stop and all will be a small, completely compressed mass, void of energy and motion; even atomic motion. A good trope to explain this would be a plucked guitar string, whose string movements are of slowly decreasing amplitude, as its energy is incrementally transferred to the air about it as heat. What imparted the massive amount of energy that "plucked the string" of the universe to begin with? No effect is without a cause, so what was the cause which initiated this titanic oscillation?

The third of Spencer's theories about the origin of the universe is that it was self-created. The major problem with this theory, which Mr. Spencer so accurately points out, is that there is no way to conceive of *nothingness* with a propensity, indeed, almost a *desire*, or *will*, to become *something*. *Nothingness*, by its very definition, is void not only of matter, but of any propensities, or driving factors. Implying otherwise, which in effect gives the universe a "mind," leads us back to the first theory.

Spencer's final conclusion was that there are some things which are unknowable, yet that if we look around us at everything that has a finite origin, and that is complex due to the input of intelligence, we cannot but instinctively sense the same to be the case on a cosmic scale within the universe. What Spencer misses is that there is a 4th possibility, which is actually a fusion of the three previous ones. There is the possibility that the immaterial energy which fills, penetrates, enlivens, and sustains the universe, from the largest galaxy, to the smallest quark, is a living entity: is God. There is even the possibility that what we think of as matter is actually simply a condensed form of energy, and that God is not simply a living energy which fills the universe, but that the entire universe, both what we consider material and what we consider immaterial, is God, and possesses a sort of "life," and has eternally existed, possibly alternating between states of pure energy and those of matter and energy, or in some other type of equilibrium which we have yet to learn enough to comprehend.

Big Bang

Much like a flashlight which has been left on and is slowly, but surely depleting its battery, the massless photons, which are constantly radiating beyond the boundary of the material universe into the cold void of nothingness, are slowly, but surely depleting the energy of the universe. Given a long enough time, the flashlight's battery will deplete, and the device will grow cold, dark, and inactive. So too with the universe.

Yet counterintuitively, it is claimed that, although this energy loss is, and has always been occurring, and although the material universe has theoretically existed *forever*, the energy within the universe has never depleted. In fact, the energy was able long ago to somehow accumulate to enormous levels within a single area and explode outward. How was enough energy, even under the influence of gravity, which is itself an energy form, ever able to accumulate to the point of initiating the Big Bang?

Since matter cannot interact, or even move without energy, we are forced to conclude that this mysterious immaterial thing called *energy* is the primary cause for all material interaction throughout the universe. Matter is never encountered without it. At all times and everywhere in the natural world which surrounds us we encounter matter that is penetrated by, associated with, and moved by energy. Energy allows, or more accurately, causes matter to interact in complex ways; spontaneously binding and assembling into structures on the subatomic, atomic, and molecular scales. Built upon this foundation, and therefore owing its existence to it, are all of the higher scales of natural complexity, such as that of proteins, membranes, cells, tissues, organs, organisms, biomes, planets, solar systems, galaxies, and even the universe itself.

Since modern conceptions about *energy* differ little from some ancient ones about *spirit*, the ancient belief that *spirit* creates, sustains, and destroys the material universe may ultimately be found to be correct. The primary difference between modern concepts about *energy* and ancient ones about *spirit*, is that the latter is assumed to possess both will and intelligence. Since *energy* drives complexity, complexity implies will and intelligence, and irresistible will and supreme intelligence are characteristics generally ascribed to God, we will need to investigate whether God is not the literal *power*, or *energy*, dispersed throughout the material universe.

Seeking a compromise which will still allow them to preserve the scientifically orthodox, purely Materialist position, some may agree about the importance of energy, but somewhat myopically claim that the sun, as the primary energy source for our solar system, performs this function. Okay. Were there no chemical interactions prior to the period when our sun first ignited, sometime in remote antiquity? Were there no chemical interactions before the *first* sun in the universe did so? That is, unless there has never been a *before*. There is the very real, yet challenging, possibility that the universe is eternal.

When most people examine, or discuss theories about the origin of the universe, they tend to have in mind only the larger cosmic structures, such as planets and galaxies. The origin of these structures are fairly intuitive concepts to think about, as they appear to be the logical consequence of a combination of the gravitational pulling effect innate within matter, and the combined pushing effects of centrifugal force and energy radiating outwards from its solar sources. This pulling effect of gravity holds the planets within their solar systems the same way that it holds galaxies together; whether via a massive central black hole, or the collective center of mass of the solar systems which comprise it.

Less dense structures, such as nebulae, due to uneven density, are slowly accreted into more dense structures, such as early solar systems. Within each of these solar systems, gravity causes mass to be attracted towards its center. As this coalescing mass unevenly collides from all sides with that which resides at its center, the entire thing begins to spin. This is similar to the way that a figure skater's spin increases in speed as she retracts her previously extended limbs. The centrifugal force of the early solar system's spin, causes a flattened ring to extend from its center outwards, along its axis of rotation. The gravitational pull of areas of uneven density within this ring draws the matter near these points of density inward, to eventually accrete into planets. The planets themselves, depending upon how fast they spin during accretion, often exhibit expanding flattened rings as well, which, if possessing points of sufficient non-uniform density, eventually accrete into moons. Planets, such as Saturn, whose rings maintain a relatively even density distribution, maintain their rings.

Having the most mass, the central structure of this developing solar system has the most gravity, causing it to pull an increasing amount of mass into itself. This positive feedback loop continues until the heat generated by its densely packed and closely interacting atoms reaches the tipping point where fusion occurs. And thus, a star is born.

Once ignited, the fusion energy of this new sun, the centrifugal force caused by its rotation, as well as the gravitational pull from the various satellites within its solar system, comprise the main forces driving solar expansion. This is, of course, ignoring minor influences such as the pull of far distant solar systems and effects due to the rotation of the solar system within the galaxy. This outward force is in near equilibrium with the inward gravitational pull of the sun's center of mass. But how is it that we see these solar systems and galaxies all around in almost perfect equilibrium? Were all of the solar systems and galaxies hung by God in perfect balance; like chandeliers? Not directly.

The reason why we encounter what we perceive to be perfect equilibriums in the heavens is due to an error in perception. Given the potentially infinite amount of time which has already elapsed, many of the imperfectly balanced solar systems and galaxies may have already destroyed themselves one way or another, leaving only the newly forming ones, the old ones with almost perfect balance, or those imbalanced ones which are in the process of destroying themselves.

With regard to this latter group, the massive distances involved mean that it may actually take eons for the orbiting matter in imbalanced systems to traverse the massive spiraling path of orbital decay to the solar system, or galaxy's center. Contrarily, it may take just as long, or longer, for these systems to traverse the ever-lengthening spiral until orbital escape is achieved. We are unable to observe these changes, given that our observational timescale is days, years, or at best, merely centuries.

Though orbital escape may eventually be achieved by planets orbiting a sun, or by specific solar systems orbiting whatever lies at the center of their respective galaxies, the things at the center of both are unlikely to ever be able to disperse by any means other than an explosive event. This is because the primary causes of expansion in both solar systems and galaxies are their centripetal forces of rotation, as well as the fusion generated solar radiation and heat energy expanding from at, or near their centers. In order for cosmic matter on a planetary scale to begin a natural chain reaction of fusion, an enormous amount of mass must be accreted into a tremendously dense area; driving the pressure and therefore heat up, until fusion becomes possible. For some perspective on the quantity of mass required for this, consider that the gravitational compressive force of the amount of mass comprising the planet Jupiter has not proven sufficient to start its fusion engine and subsequently create another sun within our solar system. Thank God for this. Otherwise it would be unlikely that we would be alive to consider this point.

Once fusion does begin within the core of an early sun, the energy released by the plasma ball causes a chain reaction of fusion as it expands outwards. Eventually the fusion wave expands until it reaches a depth of accreted matter that is not yet compressed densely enough to sustain the chain reaction. The solar radiation and heat products of fusion will rapidly accumulate at this layer, seeking an outlet; like a giant pressure vessel. This energy wave will likely only pause and accumulate for an instant, before exploding any loosely accreted matter above it outwards, either into orbit, or adrift into space. This cosmic energy and debris wave likely takes with it the less accreted residual rings of any of the sun's nearby planets, explaining why we don't begin to observe rings on planets within our solar system until we reach Saturn, which is roughly 890 million miles from the sun.

This initial confinement of energy would likely cause the first pressurized wave of energy and matter, as it expanded away from the plasma ball, to over-depressurize, and therefore "cool," a thin layer of the plasma immediately below it. For clarity, think of the vacuum during nuclear explosions that pulls the expanded initial blast wave back to form the classical mushroom cloud. It is understood that this example is occurring in an atmospheric environment and that of the early sun is not, but some similarities will be observed.

The plasma beneath the over-depressurized layer will again trap energy until it explodes outwards. This cycle will repeat a few times with decreasing energy. Each time the layer trapping the plasma energy will be thinner, until the wave that expands has insufficient energy to create enough depressurization to halt the fusion chain reaction immediately beneath it.

It is likely that this sequence of ever weaker explosions, as the new sun shudders to life, is the reason for a few of the odd physical phenomena encountered within our solar system. The spherical Ort Cloud, for example, which surrounds the exterior of the solar system far beyond Pluto, was likely the matter thrown out during the first pressure wave. The comet rich Kuiper belt, which lies between Neptune and Pluto, was possibly the matter which was thrown out during the second wave. Lastly, the relatively close Asteroid belt encountered between Mars and Jupiter, was possibly the matter which was expelled outwards during the third and final wave.

It is curious why the first of these, the Ort Cloud, is spherical, while the latter two are more ring-like. One possibility for this is that the amount of expanding energy needed to over-depressurize and "cool" the plasma immediately beneath it on the surface of the igniting sun is so great that it could only occur along the rotational plane of the plasma itself, where the effects of centripetal force would also contribute. In this case, the second and third blast waves would only have occurred along this plane of rotation.

Despite all of the ludicrous theories that circulate about black holes being wormholes to other dimensions, they are likely something entirely different. Rather than a massive "hole" in the universe, as their name implies, or portals to other "dimensions" (whatever that word actually means), black holes, along with neutron stars, are likely just stars, or possibly even galaxies, which have lost a sufficient amount of energy and fuel until the fusion occurring within them has extinguished. With the loss of this expansive energy, they collapse upon themselves. Often such collapses occur quickly and reheat the matter within the core, causing the fusion engine to reignite and a supernova to occur. In some cases, however, where the collapsing matter is poorly fusible, or the collapse occurs slowly enough that it fails to reignite fusion within the core, these cosmic bodies can continue to attract and compact matter, until they become so mind-bendingly massive and dense that they pull even light within themselves. This same result could occur, should a cosmic body, such as a planet, continue to accrete matter so slowly, and over such a long period, that sufficient heat is never generated to allow fusion to begin. It is unclear, however, if the amount of time since the Big Bang occurred would be sufficient to allow this latter scenario to occur.

Though a rubber ball is thrown high, eventually the effect of gravity will return it to earth, and as energy is lost to friction and heat, each of its successive bounces will be smaller, until stasis is achieved. In the same way, supernovas and big bangs may blow things outwards, but the gravitational effect of the center of mass of a solar system, galaxy, or even universe should eventually return all to stasis at center, as energy is slowly bled off as photons.

Yet it must be kept in mind that the definition of the word "universe" is all that exists. Not merely all matter, but also all which has immaterial existence, which we denominate, "energy." How were the first quarks formed? How were the first photons? This microcosm is every bit as much a part of the universe as the macrocosm which was previously discussed. If we are going to explore the origin of one, we must explore the origin of the other. Yet scientists often shy away from a discussion on the origin of matter.

Astronomers who are asked about the origin of quarks will likely tell you that this is no longer within their area of expertise, and that you need to consult a nuclear physicist. A nuclear physicist will likely reply that they aren't concerned with how quarks came to be, but instead with observing how they interact. It seems left to the metaphysician to ask these questions. And where are the metaphysicians today? They formerly were found among, and generally known as *philosophers*. Unfortunately, most philosophers of today, if asked about the origin of quarks, are too poorly educated in science to even begin to explore this topic; often having only received heavy training in ethics, history, and watered-down psychology.

An eternally existing universe would require the resultant (i.e. net sum) of all vectors of universal motion to be zero. Should this resultant movement prove to be anything non-zero, regardless of how small it is, the universe would be infinitely dispersed; as any net movement multiplied by the infinity of time which the universe has existed, would equal an infinite distance traveled.

Astronomers have documented, via techniques involving telescopes which analyze red and blue Doppler shifts in the light received from distant stars, that the universe appears to be expanding from a common central point of origin. This documented universal expansion is what caused most scientists to, quite reasonably, postulate what we call a Big Bang event; where all universal matter theoretically exploded outward from this common central point, sometime in the remote past. So how do we account for an eternal universe with an apparently nonzero net movement (i.e. expansion). Three possible options appear to exist.

The first option is that our underlying premise of the eternality of the material universe is false. For this option to be correct, all matter would have had a point of origin, or *creation*, if you will, from all outward appearances coinciding with the moment of the Big Bang event. Since the twin laws of *conservation of mass and energy* state that the product of all universal mass and energy is a constant, the only way that this option could occur is if all universal matter was converted from a previous state of pure energy.

While this option raises the obvious question of what would cause a universe containing only pure energy to suddenly convert a large portion of it into matter, it does somewhat align with the views of the Creationists; whether they realize it or not. If God existed alone prior to the creation, if God is pure *spirit* and the source of all spiritual force in the universe, and if the ancient conception of *spiritual force* and our modern one of *energy* differ very little, then they are essentially saying the same thing as the scientist who theorizes an immaterial universe with a concentrated source of energy, which suddenly converted a large portion of this energy into matter. It is admitted that the possession of *will* is a key difference between the ancient conception of *spiritual force* and our modern definition of *energy*, however, as discussed in detail in another part of this work, if the universe is ultimately found to be a living entity which possesses a will, this difference evaporates.

The second option is that a higher level of universal structure may yet exist, which our telescopes cannot reach, whose net movement, if summed with our own, is zero. This possibility would imply that other portions of the universe may have existed external to, and long prior to the Big Bang event which brought ours into its current state.

The third option is that all universal matter which was compressed and exploded outward during the Big Bang event, creating the universe as we know it, was previously distributed throughout the universe. This latter theory is the commonly accepted scientific explanation. Unfortunately, this explanation is not without its own problems. Where did the energy come from that compressed all of matter into the ultra-dense state that would be required for the Big Bang to occur? Matter found within suns compress to far less dense areas prior to going supernova and exploding outwards again.

If the universe exploded into its current state from a previously ultra-dense state, and was in another dispersed state prior to this, have these oscillating cycles of Big Bangs and Big Crunches occurred throughout all eternity? If so, how do we account for the fact that universal expansion appears to be accelerating, rather than its gravitational forces slowing and pulling all back to center. It is understood that "Dark Energy" is said to account for this, however no sort of energy has ever been truly proven to exist. The phrase "Dark Energy" simply refers to a correction factor which has been included in models of universal dynamics to adjust them for the observed, counterintuitive universal acceleration, for which we truly have no explanation.

Also, how could such oscillations of Big Bangs and Big Crunches occur eternally while immaterial "energy," in the form of photons, is constantly being radiated into the nothingness at the edge of the universe? Being massless, photons should be immune from the centrally returning pull of gravity. As this energy continues to be lost, each successive Big Bang should, much like the series of decreasing bounces of a rubber ball, throw the matter of the universe outwards into smaller and smaller spheres. Carried to the extremes of past and futurity, we struggle both with where the initial energy came from, which could start such a series of titanic oscillations, as well as, if infinite time has already elapsed, why the constant net energy loss hasn't already left the universe in an infinitely dispersed, or infinitely compressed, absolutely heatless state. Why are we not already on a solid ball of absolute zero ice? We have no explanation for this.

This seems to imply that somehow energy is constantly or periodically being injected into the material universe. If the source of this energy comes from the conversion of matter, and infinite time has already elapsed, why is there any matter left; as the universal furnace must either consume another log, or grow cold.

The other option that exists is that the universe is cycling, via some unknown mechanism, between states of pure matter and pure energy, our current experience being somewhere in the middle of one of these cycles. This would allow for an eternity of elapsed time, however, we would still be left with questions regarding the constant loss of energy, due to photon radiation into the nothingness beyond the universe's edge, as well as with questions regarding how the universe gained the unimaginable amount of energy required for the Big Bang.

This perpetual energy loss seems to point us in one direction, that the energy which is being injected into the universe is not coming from the conversion of existing matter. The only other option is for this injection of balancing energy to be occurring from some sort of alternate energy source. Since infinite time has already elapsed, such an energy source would need to supply, and therefore to possess, an infinite amount of it. Such a fount of infinite immaterial energy which is able to influence, and indeed, is responsible for driving the great motor of the universe, bears a striking resemblance to what the more refined of the ancients, such as the Neoplatonist, Plotinus, called "the One." This term was used because Plotinus reasoned that this entity, which we refer to as God, was almost indescribable by any characteristics other than its power, will, and existence.[37]

The last option is that photons themselves are not entirely massless, but that they simply have such an infinitesimal amount of mass that our supercolliders are currently unable to detect it. This option would allow for more intuitive, Newtonian based explanations for otherwise mysterious phenomena. The observed phenomenon of solar pressure would simply be due to the transfer of the inertial energy when photons hit a surface. Black holes wouldn't pull in light which passes near their event horizons due to some relativistic warping of a mythical "space-time" field, but would simply be due to the infinitesimal mass of the photon being drawn in by the massive gravitational forces of the black hole. The universe wouldn't be slowly draining of energy, as photons radiated beyond its boundary, as these photons would eventually and inevitably be drawn back in by the gravitational force of the center of mass of the universe; perhaps by that time being slowed and therefore no longer characterized as light. Perhaps this is the source of the cosmic background radiation distributed throughout the universe. Could this radiation simply be decelerated photons which formerly existed as light?

Quantum Mechanics

Let's examine for a moment the many misplaced appeals within the scientific community to the questionable-at-best mechanism of *quantum mechanics*. While it is undeniable that subatomic particles often appear to behave in discrete *quanta*, for example, electrons jumping from one atomic shell to another with no uniform, observable gradient of transition, I believe Einstein was correct when he claimed that, "as above, so below" quantum mechanics, the universe operates by more intuitive Newtonian principles. We simply are unable to currently observe the Newtonian mechanism which is causing the particles to appear at times to operate in a seemingly quantum manner.

During one interview, Einstein stated, "I don't deny that quantum mechanics is useful, up to a point. But I am convinced that there is a deeper theory that will replace the uncertainty at the center of it. As I told Niels Bohr, God does not play dice with the Universe."[184]

For clarity, consider Plato's famous allegory of the shadows in a cave, taken from his *Republic*.[46] In this allegory, we are shown a theoretical group of men who all their lives have been confined against a wall within a cave. These men have been unable to see anything around them in the darkness except for the opposite wall, which is dimly illuminated by light entering the cave mouth from somewhere behind them. Unable to do anything else, the men study the shadows which at times appear and move upon the far wall. These men are unaware that the shadows are caused by various unseen people and objects moving around outside the cave entrance. Sometimes the shadows are observed to appear and disappear, seemingly from nowhere. Sometimes they overlap, and appear to exist simultaneously in the same location on the wall. The men, knowing nothing of the outside world, believe the shadows to have independent existence and to function by a unique set of special laws, applicable only to shadows.

Adding my own twist, I will posit that the men also mentally develop equations which closely model the observed patterns in shadow behavior, allowing for future shadow events to be predicted with a reasonable degree of accuracy. Yet the shadows, with all of the unique laws which appear to govern them, and equations which model their observed behavior, have no independent existence. They are, in fact, only secondary effects of the unobserved bodies, which are themselves the primary causes. And these *primary causes* operate by a completely different, far more intuitive set of natural laws.

In a similar manner, we likely remain unaware of the primary causes of observed quantum mechanical phenomena. Claiming that such primary causes, or mechanisms do not exist, simply because we have yet to discover them, is faulty logic. It presumes that we have complete knowledge of the material world. We do not. It would be more accurate to speak in probabilities based upon the scientific knowledge currently available. Given the relatively narrow range of applicability, and often counterintuitive principles encountered within the field of quantum mechanics, among the vastly larger amount of generally intuitive Newtonian mechanical phenomena, I believe that there is a strong probability that we will eventually discover quantum phenomena to simply be the "shadows" cast by Newtonian causes.

But why press this seemingly unrelated point about quantum mechanics? The reason is because well intentioned, but misinformed people, some even being scientists, often view quantum mechanics in the same way that many of the religious faithful view miracles; as a sort of proof case that, with the train of nature, the "engine" of cause may sometimes be separated from the "cars" of effect. It cannot.

True science is generally intuitive. We can force our minds towards some thoughts, but others come like a bolt of lightning. We feel them with our souls before they are even set to words. Quantum mechanical theories run contrary to all intuitive assumptions about the nature and behavior of the material world; which is a strong indication that these theories are likely flawed. Einstein himself echoed this opinion prior to his death and also mentioned how the scientific community had somewhat ostracized him for holding it.

"Einstein: 'I have become an obstinate heretic in the eyes of my colleagues. I am generally regarded as a sort of petrified object, rendered blind and deaf by the years. I find this role not too distasteful, as it corresponds very well with my temperament. Yes, of course. Logic will no doubt get you from A to B. However, imagination will take you everywhere. I am a scientist, and yet I am enough of an artist to draw freely upon my imagination.'

Interviewer: 'So what you're saying is that you take ideas from other areas, people, maybe even from the environment and combine them with something else that brings your ideas and theories to fruition. Is that correct?'

Einstein: 'Yes, that is correct. However, the only real valuable thing at that point is intuition. I use my intuition, not logic, to help make these important decisions.'"[185]

Life

While looking at the mummy of Pentawere, the son of Ramesses III, who was condemned and executed for assassinating his father during the "Harem Conspiracy," I was stricken by its lifelike appearance.[186] The state of preservation of this person, who died roughly 3100 years ago, as well as many other mummies in a similar state of preservation, is incredible. I believe this lifelike aspect is what has fueled the old fables of mummies coming to life.

Unfortunately, several aspects of the mummification process significantly detracted from this lifelike appearance. During the often 60-80 day long mummification process,[187] these corpses were dried and had major organs removed; including the eyes and the brain. Some organs, such as the heart, were preserved individually in canopic jars, detracting from the overall lifelike appearance of the mummy. This drying process caused the mummy to shrink significantly. In addition, drying was augmented by smearing the body with natron, which had the effect of dissolving the fats beneath the flesh, changing the appearance of the face as well as other features. The laborers employed during the mummification tried to compensate for these changes by filling up things such as cheeks and noses with small rags, or pieces of wood placed beneath the skin.

Also detracting from the lifelike appearance was the fact that the body was subsequently smeared with pitch, which blackened it, but which assisted in preservation. These factors give the mummy the appearance of a shrunken, blackened, overly lean doll. Considering this, I mused about how we might restore one of these well-preserved specimens to an even more lifelike appearance for posterity using today's resources, knowledge, and technology. Basically, we would have to perform a sort of reverse mummification, in order to undo whatever we could of what was previously done during mummification.

Since careful dehydration was the major portion of mummification, the first thing that would need to be accomplished would be a careful rehydration of the body. This could not be accomplished merely by placing the mummy in a bath and waiting. Since microorganisms require moisture to survive, breed, and digest things within their environment, the main contributor to the fact that the mummy has passed down to us so many thousands of years later in such a well-preserved state is the fact that it has been kept extremely dry.

Yet even dry, the mummy itself is not sterile. Hundreds of species of bacteria, fungi, amoeba, algae, and other organisms which normally lived within the digestive tract (i.e. intestinal microflora) and on the skin (i.e. skin microbiota) of the Egyptian while living, likely spread within his tissue after death and before complete mummification. During the drying process and treatment of the body with various substances possessing antimicrobial properties, such as pitch, frankincense, and naphtha, those species possessing the ability to do so likely formed spores, cysts, or other types of structures, which preserve their genetic material, much like a seed, for centuries, to millennia.

Even the humidity in the surrounding air contains a sufficient amount of moisture to enable some of these microorganisms to transition into a vegetative state. Should we unwisely submerge the mummy in a water bath, these microorganisms, finding themselves in an environment which is again favorable for growth, would immediately spring to life and begin digesting their food source of choice. For some, this food source would be sunlight. For others, it would be the newly rehydrated tissue of the mummy. Soon, whatever mummy tissue remained intact would be slowly digested, until the bath was a mere slurry of microorganisms, teeth, and mineralized portions of bone.

How might this slimy outcome be prevented during the rehydration process? One option that is possible is to preliminarily sterilize the mummy. This could be accomplished several ways, however, due to the delicacy with which the body would need to be rehydrated, the preferred sterilization method should be a chemical, rather than a steam based one. One of these methods which is commonly used within the medical industry is ethylene oxide treatment.

Large rooms exist at some hospitals and sterile processing centers within which the mummy could be placed and treated with this sterilizing gas. However, since it would be a challenge to maintain sterility while afterwards placing the mummy within whatever vessel it was going to be rehydrated in, the ideal method would be to sterilize the mummy within whatever vessel is going to serve this purpose. Any large, acrylic, polycarbonate, or ideally, glass container would work for this purpose, provided that it had sufficient ports, valves (including back-flow prevention valves), and connectors to serve as inlets and outlets for gasses, liquids, and sensors.

The exhaust port of the vessel could be connected to whatever port the sterilizer generally exhausts to, while the inlet port was connected to the ethylene oxide source. The feed valve could then be opened, allowing the toxic gas to kill whatever microbial organisms remained viable on the mummy. A second port, feeding sterile air could slowly be opened and its flow adjusted so that a sufficient amount of ethylene oxide remained to kill any spores and cysts which transitioned into an easier to kill vegetative state. The humidity of the sterile feed air could be slowly increased (e.g. Perhaps 1% a day), until perhaps 90% humidity is achieved. Care would need to be taken to avoid causing condensation.

It is necessary to increase the humidity slowly, in order to prevent the parts of the mummy which are able to rapidly rehydrate, from cracking those which are not. Ideally, a slow, uniform rehydration is desired. After rehydrating for perhaps 3 months, the mummy should begin to appear more fleshy and lifelike, and the risk of rapid hydration will be greatly lessened.

The ethylene oxide and sterile air feed ports could now be switched off and a third port opened which slowly filled the vessel with water which was mixed with a sufficient amount of ethyl alcohol to maintain sterility. Ethyl alcohol is selected due to its relatively neutral pH. The feed water should be set at the slowest feed which overcomes the head pressure of the inlet port, while maintaining positive flow. This should serve as not only a rehydration aid, but also will slowly wash the body. After perhaps a month of this, the mummy should appear more like a freshly deceased body. Tissue should again be somewhat supple and flexible (provided the rehydration process of the collagen was successful).

The container could now be slowly drained and opened with caution, in order to allow the body itself to be manually cleansed of any, now rehydrated, preservatives and bandaging. If the body was not eviscerated during mummification, as was the case with Pentawere, the organs and tissues could at this time be better examined. Once all of the examinations were completed, the body could be groomed and attired appropriately, placed back within its glass box, sterilized once again, the box filled with a liquid preservative (e.g. glycerol, or sterilized honey, similar to what was done to Alexander the Great), and then placed on display within a museum.

This alludes to an important question. With all of modern technology, unlimited funds, and a host of scientific minds at our disposal, could we bring this mummy back to life? The answer, of course, is unfortunately *no*. Yet consider the question from an organ level. Could we return the heart of this mummy to life? Suddenly, the original question begins to seem less absurd, yet the answer remains a solid *no*. Let's focus our perspective down to that of tissue. Could we, with all of our efforts, return a tiny bit of heart tissue from this mummy to life? Probability seems to increase much more, however the answer is still *no*. Finally, let's narrow our view to what we currently consider to be the smallest functional unit of life: the cell. Could we return a single cell of this mummy's tissue to a functional state indicative of life?

Many would fall into the trap here of thinking that we had at this point reached the level of statistical probability.

"Surely one, out of the ~37 trillion cells that comprise the human body might have retained enough of its internal machinery to enable it to begin functioning once more, if carefully rehydrated and placed in an environment with a superabundance of nutrients," some might claim.

The problem with this statement is the illusion that, in reducing the organism from a complex system of interacting organs, to that of a single cell, we have dramatically simplified the scenario. We have not. With few exceptions, the degree of complexity involved in the structure and successful function of a single cell is orders of magnitude greater than the degree of complexity involved in "higher" levels of organic structure and function; such as that of tissues, organs, and organisms. The only potential exception which I can think of where organ complexity rivals that of a single human cell is within the mind itself.

The second problem with cell resurrection is the underlying assumption that cells are simply an organic machine and nothing more. This Materialist view causes people to believe that if all of the cellular machinery was put in place, the cell would begin to function automatically. I do not believe this view to be accurate. As in the mind, memories and knowledge are stored as specific patterns of synapses, yet there is something external to these memories and knowledge, known as the will, which makes decisions based upon them. So in the cell, though the DNA stores cellular information, there is something external to it which selects when and how this information is expressed. We are shown the few mechanisms of enzyme regulation which we are aware of where negative, or positive feedback loops of a certain enzyme involved in protein expression are known to operate mechanically, based upon how much of a specific substrate exists within the intra, or extracellular space, and assume that this is the general case for all cellular functions. This is a gross oversimplification of how cells maintain homeostasis.

There is too much complexity and there are too many processes where multiple outcome options exist, yet where only one is selected, for only mechanical feedback loops to be involved in the maintenance of cellular homeostasis. During translation, for example, introns of the copied codons are selectively excised to make different mRNA products from the same parent DNA sequence. Something at this stage has performed a decision-making process. Even the initial amino acid chains fabricated within the ribosomes by identical chains of mRNA are afterwards modified to make different, highly-specific protein products. Again, a decision has been made. There are multiple destinations which this protein product can be exported to, yet one is selected for and effected by the incredibly complex symphony of cytoskeleton fiber movement. Again, we see a decision process occurring between multiple possible outcomes.

In general, except in the case of muscle fibers and the various specialized sensory cells, individual cells are not innervated by the nerve fibers extending from the central, or peripheral nervous systems. They can respond to hormonal signals, yet these are for the most part global, signaling the production of a certain product by cells specialized to produce this (e.g. beta cells within the pancreas). Yet even in the instance of endocrine (i.e. hormonal) signaling, the signal is generally one which merely increases, or decreases the production of a single product. It isn't nearly specific, or even rapid enough to directly control the expression of the majority of proteins which are required in order to maintain cellular homeostasis.

There must be something within cells, a "mind" of sorts, which autonomously monitors the cell's internal homeostasis and external environment and responds by activating, moving, synthesizing, and destroying its machinery for the overall good of the cell, much like the mind does with the muscles, tissues, bones, and organs for the overall good of the body. This factor, which I believe is none other than soul, no longer resides within dead cells. Were all of the machinery within a single dead, or even synthetic cell put into place, no cellular action would occur other than processes which occur passively, due to simple chemical energy gradients. The bagpipe may make a sound as it deflates, due to the passive expulsion of energy and air which it has previously been charged with, but there would be nothing re-inflating it, nor playing the notes, as the cell plays on the DNA and the mind on the synapses.

There is also the possibility that soul never actually *resides* within cells in a concentrated manner, like a ghost, but that it is distributed throughout the universe, and cells simply possess something within their structure which allows them to somehow "resonate" with it, for lack of a better term, much like radios. This topic is discussed at length in the section of this work on "resonance." Though this option would theoretically allow for both cells and people to be resurrected, we are so ignorant about any structural requirements for this option, that it currently remains within the realm of impossibility.

Codon Degeneracy

Is the genetic code truly degenerate, as is commonly believed? For those who are unfamiliar with the concept of the degeneracy of the genetic code, each three-nucleotide portion of DNA is referred to as a *codon*. When a eukaryotic cell senses that it requires an additional protein of some sort, it activates a certain portion of the DNA. This DNA is selectively unwound from its histone "spool," and transcribed. Genetic transcription is a tremendously complex process involving a host of specialized cellular machinery, such as the cytoskeleton, transcription factors, and certain amazingly specialized enzymes, resulting in the production of a sequence of messenger RNA (mRNA). This mRNA is then spliced, God only knows how and by what signal, leaving the intron section(s) (i.e. the excised part(s)) within the nucleus, and sending the exon out into the cytoplasm, where it docks on a ribosome.

Once the mRNA is attached to the ribosome's reading frame, it is translated into a protein through an equally complex process once again involving the cytoskeleton, specialized enzymes, and transfer RNA (tRNA). The translation process essentially works like this. The reading frame of the ribosome is 1 codon long. As each codon of the mRNA is read by the ribosome, the specialized tRNA, which is bound to a specific amino acid within the cytoplasm, delivers this amino acid to the ribosome. Once this amino acid arrives, the reading frame shifts to the next codon and another amino acid is brought and bound to the previous one with a peptide bond.

The genetic code is referred to as "degenerate" because several different mRNA codons cause the same amino acid to be delivered to the ribosome. Once the entire mRNA sequence has been translated, the newly formed amino acid chain, which is now a protein, is uncoupled from the ribosome and delivered to the cell's Golgi apparatus, where it may be post-translationally modified in a host of different ways.

Many steps of this process have been omitted for brevity, as entire chapters of molecular biology textbooks are often devoted to each one.

There is, however, the very real possibility that the genetic code is not "degenerate" at all. Very often in the scientific world, things which we think are functionless, actually have a very specific function which we arrogantly dismiss, in our ignorance, until it is eventually discovered. This is how things went with tonsils, and likely how it will also occur with the appendix.

What we refer to as "codon degeneracy" may actually be a secondary signal riding on the primary one, which directs the cell in its post transcriptional splicing of the resulting mRNA and/or the dizzying amount of post translational modification possibilities which the resulting protein may be subjected to. In addition, this perceived degeneracy could also be affecting not merely the primary protein structure, but also its secondary through tertiary structures, which develop both prior to, and during post-translational modification.

Let me clarify the latter point. In proteins, there is *primary* structure, which is the assemblage of the initial chain of amino acids. There is then *secondary* structure, which consists of the physical shape taken by the amino acid chain based upon how it forms various hydrogen bonds with nearby amide groups on the same protein subunit. Examples of secondary structure are *alpha helices* and *beta pleated sheets*. *Tertiary* structure is the shape that the nascent protein takes based upon bonding that occurs between side chains on the same protein subunit. These side chains are often able to interact with parts of the amino acid chain far downstream, due to folding. Lastly, there is *quaternary* protein structure, which refers to bonding and interaction that occurs between various different protein subunits.

In the same manner, I postulate that there is primary genetic code, seen in the initial codon set which is transcribed into mRNA. But perhaps there is also a sort of *secondary* coding which consists in a certain patterning in the specific, supposedly "degenerate" codons used. Perhaps the shape of the specific codon selected, upon passage from the nucleus, or upon entry into the reading frame of the ribosome, triggers the previously mentioned possible post-transcriptional and post-translational modifications.

Let me give an example to clarify. Consider if, upon transcription, a GGU (i.e. guanine/guanine/uracil) codon is selected by the cell instead of a GGG (i.e. guanine/guanine/guanine) codon. Microbiologists and geneticists would typically say, "So what. Both code for the amino acid glycine." Yet perhaps the cell selected GGU because it wanted to trigger subsequent alkylation of the resulting protein; one of many possible types of post-translational modification.

Perhaps there are even higher-level signals than those of the genetic code which are activated in other ways. As an example, what signal causes the Small Nuclear Riboprotein (sNRP) complexes to spontaneously assemble, as if by magic, from 12 or so seemingly random bits of protein and RNA, floating within the cytoplasm? What causes them to proofread, excise, and correct errors in a strand of DNA, before dispersing to float once more within the cytoplasm? What are they using as a "master copy," when proofreading this DNA strand, given that the DNA itself is supposed to be the master copy?

In humans, this genome is ~3 billion base pairs long. In spite of various claims to the contrary, we have no idea what ~99% of this genome even codes for. Though we know that ~1.2% of the genome codes for proteins, we wink at the fact that, even within this portion of the genome, the cell's ability to post-transcriptionally modify the mRNA chain allows it to produce a host of different proteins from the same nucleotide sequence coded for between specific mRNA "start" and "stop codons." We ignorantly claim that the rest of the human genome is useless "Junk DNA," yet every replicating cell within our bodies faithfully replicates this portion of the genome each time it divides; using up a tremendous amount of cellular energy and resources in the process.[188]

This is absurd. As Aristotle so keenly observed several thousand years ago, "Nature, as we often say, makes nothing in vain."[189] We will likely later find that every last nucleotide of this genome is important and serves a purpose.

Consider upstream and downstream interactions of DNA, for example. Perhaps various sections of the genetic code inhibit, or activate each other when either spooled up on their histone proteins, in either the euchromatin, or heterochromatin form, or when partially unraveled during Mitosis, or Meiosis. What if this drives single, or multigenerational phenotype inhibition as is seen when a family, many generations brunette, delivers a redheaded child (while not having a redheaded milkman).

There is a massive amount of unexpressed genetic potential already built into the genome, which is only activated within the proper environment; though this environment is often unknown. This is the underlying principle behind epigenetics: that genes selectively activate during certain phases of life; responding to the environment which they find themselves in. There is the possibility that the plasticity of expression of our genetic code has generational limits for quite logical reasons.

Consider how body size variation is related to the availability of nutrition. We are shown 5-foot suits of middle age era European armor with the intent to make us believe that man is becoming smarter, taller, stronger, with no end in sight, until we are eventually gods. In reality, this is more indicative of well-documented poverty and subsequent poor nutrition which existed for generations among these people, during this period; as the bodies of smaller organisms, though generally weaker, are more efficient, in that they require less food. We also observe this tendency for smaller body frames among many South American and Oriental people, who have historically suffered from low nutrition diets for several generations.

As these people's nutritional availability has improved during modern times, a correlating subsequent increase in stature is being observed. This increase in size, however, appears to be generationally limited; at least during the period of uterine development. Developing infants receiving high nutrition diets from their mother's umbilical cord understandably express more growth genes, or express them for a longer period, than those receiving poor nutrition. Should they, however, exceed the average growth level beyond a certain extent, birth would become either dangerous, or impossible.

As a bit of evidence for this, when one reviews histories written long before the middle ages, in times of plenty among the early Greeks, Germanic tribes, and Ethiopians, one encounters documentation of individuals of an extremely tall stature, even by today's standards (e.g. Agamemnon). Perhaps the stories of the tribes of "giants" recorded by the Jews in the Old Testament and Tanakh aren't that improbable. The Anakim (Joshua 11:21, Numbers 13:33, Deuteronomy 9:2), Rephaim (Genesis 14:5), Emim (Deuteronomy 2:10, 11, 20), and Amorites (Amos 2:9) all supposedly originated in Canaan, an area which had supposedly been extremely fertile for multiple generations. It wasn't for no reason that the Hebrews described it as a, "Land flowing with milk and honey." Perhaps high nutrition availability for multiple generations had produced actual small groupings of "Goliath" and "Og of Bashan" types of people (Deuteronomy 2:21, 3:11). This isn't that improbable, considering that Goliath was only supposed to be 9 ft., 6 in., according to scripture. Robert Wadlow was 8 ft., 11 in. That is only 7 more inches.

It must also always be borne in mind that only a small portion of all of the actual history which has transpired has been preserved for our scrutiny. The current scientific view on these giants is that, if there is any legitimacy to the scriptural claims made about them, then it must be due to a genetic disorder which was dominant among the people of those tribes.[190] This is a possibility as well, although, due to the relative ubiquity of these historical claims, across many cultures and areas of the world, combined with the relative scarcity of modern examples, I find the previous hypothesis of multigenerational, exceptionally high nutrition diets to be the more likely. Experimentation could put these questions to rest by feeding multigenerational high nutrition diets to a species with short generational periodicity; bearing in mind that there will likely be functional limits to any growth. A mammal with an endoskeleton, such as a mouse, would be preferred, in order to parallel human development as much as possible.

Abiogenesis

I have mentioned what I don't believe about God. I should more importantly discuss what I do believe; as any fool can mock at and destroy a philosophy. It is far more difficult to propose an improved replacement. In the same way, any mindless savage can easily burn, or tear down a house in an afternoon, while it takes many long days and hard work to design and build one.

That being said, I have a somewhat unique view of God among my peers. To begin with, I believe that there absolutely must be a creator. How he went about making creation, I have no idea, however the sheer complexity and elegance of life on Earth is sufficient proof for me. Order and complexity to mind boggling levels of minuteness do not just happen. When things are left to themselves, they tend to do the opposite: they tend to decay.

I have heard people attempt to play tricks with how you set the confines of the system in question when discussing the Second Law of Thermodynamics, in order to avoid the inevitable increase in entropy, but common sense (actually somewhat uncommon these days) tells us that time does not create and improve matter, it ravages and destroys it. If a car is left in a field for years, it doesn't slowly become a better car, or even a helicopter; it becomes a heap of rust.

Some may claim that this universal principle of increasing entropy is defied by the accretion of solar systems from nebulae, yet given sufficient time, the suns of these solar systems eventually collapse and supernova, or become black holes, and the orbits of the planets held by them, being imperfect, lead either to orbital decay, or escape. Entropy, which can be thought of in layman's terms as disorder, is *always* increasing within natural systems.

Yet when we look at life, we see something different. We see growth, reproduction, an ability to thrive, heal, and for a time resist succumbing to the destroying forces of nature which we call decrepitude, death, and decomposition. Why do these living, or biotic things seem to operate by a different set of rules than nonliving, or abiotic matter? How did they even *become* alive to begin with?

"Abiogenesis, of course," is the common response.

The modern theory of abiogenesis, which means the creation of living from nonliving matter, is so flawed and requires such a leap of faith that it is incredible that it is so popular these days. I can only assume that this stems from the fact that the vast majority of people have absolutely no idea what is required for life to commence. At most, some of them may have been exposed to the famous Miller-Urey experiment, where a completely unrealistic set of conditions were set up, in order to stack the deck as much as possible in favor of the abiogenic theory.

Essentially, this is how this experiment went.[191] A spark generator was turned on in an environment of what were assumed to be the gasses present in the early earth. These gasses were circulated through a distillation/condensation system, so that any byproducts which were created by the sparks would be concentrated within the fluid. The sparks were supposed to simulate lightning occurring in the early atmosphere, and the condensate the early oceans. At the end of several weeks, these researchers examined the liquid and were able to detect a few basic amino acids. From this basic result, they made the non-sequitur "leap of faith" to the claim that, given sufficient time, life could be created from nonliving matter.

There are a few inherent flaws with this experiment. Firstly, the repeated shocking and concentration in an isolated environment in no way matches the earth's early environment. Where *exactly* is lightning going to discharge repeatedly in the same area so that these byproducts can concentrate? The response assumed is that these discharges don't need to occur within the same area, they can occur anywhere, over a period of millions of years, and the precipitation cycle will ensure that their byproducts are eventually washed into and concentrate in the sea.

Yet this stance is willfully ignorant of the fact that the amino and carboxylic acid ends of these early amino acids are also reacting with other chemicals, or breaking-down, due to heat and UV radiation, until an equilibrium is reached. I find it extremely difficult to believe that there would be a sufficient amount of electrical discharge, even in millions of years, to allow for any type of detectable amino acid concentration to occur in the early oceans, much less for these amino acids to find each other and interact.

Do people realize how much water is in the ocean? I freely admit that I personally cannot wrap my mind around the astounding volume of water which exists in the world's oceans. The average oceanic depth is roughly 14,000 ft for the 70% of the Earth's surface which is covered by it. 14,000 ft. That is astounding. Glance up at the average passenger jet, leaving contrails far above all but the highest of clouds, and consider that this is perhaps 20,000 ft., on average. So, we are referring to roughly 70% of the distance that passenger jets cruise at, but rather straight down, covering roughly 70% of the entire earth. NOAA's National Geophysical Data Center estimates this to work out to a volume of roughly 321 million cubic *miles* of water.[192]

Imagine a cubic mile. Have you ever run a mile? It's not short. It takes the average person maybe 8-10 minutes to run one. Now consider that distance in three dimensions, and you have a cubic mile of water.

Now try to fathom roughly a third of a billion of these. Let that sink in for a moment. Now how much lightning are we talking about here that is going to occur fast enough to allow for any detectable concentration in a volume that large, considering that the compounds are also breaking down due to UV radiation, oxidation, and other factors...a statistically negligible amount, that is how much.

Adherents to the *faith* (which it truly is) of abiogenesis, encourage people to think about small tide pools at the edges of the early oceans, which would periodically collect ocean water and then be the site of evaporation. They do this because they are aware of the monumental concentration problem with their theory. They claim that, regardless of the minuteness of concentration of amino acids in the early ocean, these collection and evaporation cycles which were occurring in the tide pools would eventually concentrate any amino acids to the point where they could eventually form peptide bonds, God knows how, as cells require specialized enzymes to do so, ultimately resulting in proteins.

Some other researchers later did different experiments with cyanide-based gasses and created a few other types of amino acids. Okay. I will even grant these researchers the ability to create the full complement of amino acids and nucleotides. I haven't looked in a while. They may have already accomplished this via other experiments which grossly misrepresent the environment of the early Earth. Even so, does the existence of all of these things allow for even the simplest form of life which we have any evidence of? The answer is not just *no*, but not even close.

It isn't simply the existence of nucleotides which is necessary for life. What is necessary is the arrangement of these nucleotides in specific sequences which store information that tells the cell all of the actions which are required of it in order to maintain cellular homeostasis, growth, and reproduction, as well as all of the cellular machinery necessary to act upon this information. In the radio world, this embedded patterning which rides upon the carrier signal is not surprisingly called the "intelligence." In the computer world, this "intelligence" would be analogous to the patterns of active microscopic NOR, or NAND cells stored on solid state integrated circuits (i.e. microchips), or on the magnetic regions of hard drive platters.

Allow me to clarify. Imagine that, by some miracle, the genome (i.e. genetic code set) of the simplest form of life which we are aware of, that of a common Escherichia Coli (E. Coli), were to actually spontaneously assemble through sheer chance interactions. It is pointless for me to belabor the improbability of this scenario, considering that sheer chance interactions would have to assemble a resulting genome which is approximately 4.6 million base pairs (i.e. pairs of complimentary nucleotides) long. Regardless of this staggering improbability, it isn't the size of the genome that matters to the life of the organism, just as it doesn't matter if you have a completely whole, yet blank flash, or hard drive. It is the information, or *intelligence* embedded upon these things which matters.

This intelligence is what gives the simplest of organisms the very *will* to eat, thrive, grow, and reproduce. Yet this information is there within E. Coli, and it is far too elegant to have been impressed upon the genome by mere chance natural interactions. This library of information can be activated, or inhibited via various cell signaling cascades (extremely complex in and of themselves), or by up or downstream nucleotide interactions, to express any of 4,688 different proteins, which can then, via some yet unknown cellular signaling mechanism, be post translationally modified to behave in many different ways.

Add to this the fact that no genetic transcription, or translation occurs in a vacuum. There is a veritable spider's web of prokaryotic cytoskeleton pulling everything where it needs to be, when it needs to be there. Again, we have no idea what signaling mechanism is driving this. And there is no cell without some sort of cellular membrane, a structure within E. Coli which is extremely complex in and of itself; consisting of specific hydrophilic and hydrophobic parts, G-Protein Coupled Receptors (GPCRs), transmembrane proteins, various chemical pumps, and sundry other exotic components that we have no evidence of a life form ever having existed without.

The "simplest" of single celled organisms is mind-bogglingly complex. In fact, one single E. Coli cell displays a level of complexity that far exceeds the most complex technology that man has ever developed. Let's not forget that all of this complexity is packed into a roughly 2 micrometer cell, 1000 of which can fit on a pin head: a cell which can both grow and reproduce on its own. Yet most people walk around envisioning a cartoon bag of cytoplasm and some DNA. There are dozens of other extremely complex bits of cellular "machinery" within this little E. Coli that I will have to skip over for brevity's sake.

"But what about 'Survival of the Fittest?' Surely that explains how life came about, right?"

Unfortunately, no. This is long before we have entered the realm where this principle might apply. "Survival of the fittest" implies a *will* to live. We are discussing how raw, inanimate materials first developed the ability to survive. We have not even broached the more complex topic of how the *will* to do so initially developed. This important topic is discussed in another chapter of this work.

A point that I wish to reiterate, as I don't think many grasp it, is that we have *no* evidence of simpler forms of life. Various theories have been put forward about RNA, or even protein being an early carrier of cellular information, however that is all speculative and highly doubtful in my opinion. Evidence for these theories simply does not exist.

There is no fossil record to be examined which records the subcellular structure of early prokaryotes. We have fossils that show that prokaryotes existed, yet we cannot tell anything about their internal, or even external structure, and definitely not that their code slowly developed from a shorter "simpler" genome, prior to the 4.6 million base pair one of E. Coli that is with us today. Anyone who says otherwise is merely spouting scientific dogma without any evidence to support their position. Sure, they *want* that to be correct, because then abiogenesis has the slightest chance of not being ludicrous, however I will say again, there is *no* evidence. None. It is all pure faith. A more baseless, ridiculous faith than that held by 90% of the religious devout of today.

Impossibility

I am discouraged by the fact that the majority of people, brainwashed by today's scientific high priests into the Materialist faith of abiogenesis, cannot see that the exquisitely elegant information seen encoded within the genome of even the "simplest" form of life which we have any evidence for, demands a designing intelligence at least more complex than itself, as its source. A painting, for example, can only come close to equaling, but never exceed the intended design for it which is initially held within the mind of the painter. Water never rises higher than its source. This book, for example, can never exceed, and will only at best equal my aspirations for it.

There are other reasons for believing in a creator, but this is a strong one. Raw chance interactions never produce elegant complexity, they produce homogeneity. Take a container of 4 different colored sand piles, close the lid, and shake them. This simulates chance interactions of matter sped up. Shake them again. Do it perhaps a million times. It doesn't matter how often you shake them, or how small the grains of sand are, when the container is opened, you will observe only a homogeneous mixture of colors, and never elegant complexity.

Never will you open the container to see a replication of the Mona Lisa in sand. Yet this very thing is what those Materialists who site the "Infinite Monkey Theorem" are actually claiming. This classic thought experiment states that, "If a monkey hits keys on a typewriter at random for an infinite amount of time, he will almost surely produce the entire collected works of Shakespeare."[193] Some even rephrase the statement as, "Infinite monkeys on infinite typewriters for an infinite length of time." Hidden beneath the surface of this intentionally absurd trope is the claim that literally anything is possible given enough time and chance interactions.

Would they have us believe that, given enough time, absolutely nothing is statistically impossible, no matter how improbable: that absolutely anything is possible? This claim implies that if I could live long enough, I would eventually see everything happen that I could possibly imagine. Monkeys would develop the ability to breathe underwater, become immune to heat, form an underwater colony in the volcanos of the Pacific, swim down the magma tubes to the earth's core, and offset our orbit, causing massive tectonic shifts. Rubbish.

There are actually things which will never happen, no matter how long one waits. Impossibility itself is not an impossibility. It is an infinitesimally minute threshold of statistical probability beneath which an event will *never* happen, no matter the amount of time, or chance interactions involved. No one knows at exactly what amount of 0's after the decimal point we reach the line of demarcation for calling things impossible, however, even admitting that such a line exists is a way to avoid becoming ensnared in the most absurd conclusions.

Another poison pill to the "Anything is possible, given enough time," theory is that, if this theory is true, then everything would have already happened.

"How so?" one might ask.

Well, how old is matter? Not just our solar system, not just our galaxy, not just our universe, but all matter. We have no idea what lies beyond our universe's expanding edge, but I am including that as well: all that is out there in its amazingly complex enormity.

"Well, the universe is only so old due to the Big Bang, so that argument doesn't really work."

Actually it does, as most physicists don't believe that matter itself was created at the moment of the Big Bang, only that it was somehow all compressed into a very small, tremendously energetic point during that period. The net product of universal matter and energy is conserved. It has always been, barring some interaction by an unknown force using aspects of physics we have yet to discover (i.e. God). It may be thought of somewhat as immortal. And if it has always been, from infinity past, then ample time has elapsed for every chance interaction which could possibly happen to have already happened. Yet where are my lava monkeys? This forces us back to the inevitable conclusion that there are things so statistically improbable, as to be actually impossible.

And consider that those who deny statistical impossibility when discussing the origin of life are typically the same ones who hypocritically and dogmatically deny the possibility of a creator, or even an immaterial existence, or soul. Didn't these just claim that *nothing* was statistically impossible? If challenged on this point, this sort will illogically state that there is less physical evidence of a creator than for their Materialist theories; therefore, their theories are more statistically probable. What they lose sight of at this point is the flawed underlying premise which many of these Materialist theories are built upon. This premise is that *anything* is possible, given enough time.

What is the statistical probability of creating the genome of the "simplest" form of life that we know, the prokaryotic E. Coli. This single celled organism contains a genome that is ~4.6 million base pairs long, of double stranded, complimentary DNA. This DNA happens to code for ~4,688 proteins that we are aware of. We will very likely discover more. Consider all of the various statistical permutations necessary to go from a single nucleotide to a chain of DNA of that size, purely via chance interactions. And don't forget that we are just discussing its genome, a small fraction of what is required for this cell to achieve "life." All of the other cellular machinery, such as ribosomes, cell membranes, various chemical pumps, etc., must simultaneously and independently be developed as well. This increases this organism's complexity by several orders of magnitude, and therefore decreases the statistical probability of this occurring by chance to an equal degree. Effectively, the aforementioned monkeys wouldn't merely have to accidentally type *Hamlet*, but more realistically, the complete 51 book *Harvard Classics Set*, with reference notes and illustrations.

"But this is an organism that has had millions of years to develop its library of protein products. The earlier ones had less," someone will claim.

Really? Prove it; as we don't have any physical evidence of this. Such claims are only conjecture, dogma, and faith.

"What of virus'? They have smaller, single strands of genetic code."

What of them? Virus' are not alive, as virtually all academics agree, because they do not possess the cellular machinery required to thrive, or reproduce without a host. They are simply an encapsulated bit of single, or double stranded DNA, or RNA, with a few, sometimes articulating components attached to their protein coats.

I must admit that viruses are a bit of a mystery to me. They are clearly elegant and complex and have various highly specific means for transmitting their encapsulated genetic code, yet this code is clearly designed to do nothing but replicate itself to the destruction of its host. I almost hate thinking about them, as, looking at the beautiful symmetry and function of their articulating parts, I often conclude that, if there is a designer to all things, then he, or it, designed these as well. And what could be the possible function of these things if not to destroy life?

I assume that there must be a beneficial function to these things in nature that I am yet unaware of, as I refuse to think of God as the Hindus do; with creating, sustaining, and destroying sides. It flies against my concept of goodness, which I cannot reconcile with destruction, suffering, and ruin.

Soul and Evolution

An author whom I read once commented about the differences between the memory and the will, and how the latter was closer to our conception of self. This author pointed out the strange, yet often observed, and commonly known phenomenon that one may sense that one has forgotten something, and yet not know the thing which was forgotten.

This is similar to a secretary remembering that she placed an important document within a certain file, and yet not remembering which specific file she placed it in. Perhaps our instincts are similar to these senses which the secretary feels, and our actual memories are similar to the important papers which have been stored away within files. Documents are, in all actuality, little more than physical memory aids anyway; so the analogy is a rather strong one.

Plotinus, in his *Six Enneads*, theorized that there are different types, or parts, of the human soul, the "lower" part, or type interacting with the human intellect in the manner we traditionally think of as intellection, while the "upper" part, or type, interacted with what he calls the "good."[37] This "good" he refers to is none other than his conception of God: a rather beautiful, highly developed, and purely spiritual model, free from the childish taint of anthropomorphism. Plotinus posited that this supremely divine agent communicates not via language, but via an outpouring of its very essence into the universe. The highest part, or type of the human soul, he claims, is able to sense this "good," which it uses as a perfect standard, against which it compares and evaluates all things for moral worth, which are fed to the intellect via the classical senses. This goodness, the essence of God itself, is the source of our sense of virtue, and we generally call it by the name of "conscience." Conscience is therefore truly the "voice" of God within our soul.

I agree with most of this theory, however most modern readers would take issue with the fact that Plotinus theorizes either multiple *types* of soul, or of a soul with *parts*. Many will contest that the existence of an immaterial soul is already a challenge, at best, to prove, therefore giving it components, or multiplying its types, only increases this challenge. For example, if one is already in doubt as to the existence of dragons in antiquity, then providing someone with theorized details about their speciation, or feeding habits, adds little to the conversation.

It should be borne in mind by these critics that Porphyry, the protégé of Plotinus, compiled his mentor's work in roughly 270 A.D., long before the function of the brain was better understood. In addition, one must also consider that Plotinus lived among the Alexandrian Egyptians, whose ancient faith was well known to claim that multiple *types* of souls resided and interacted within a single individual. Given this context, his statements about a "lower" soul, which interacts with our intellect, is really not as quaint as it may sound.

As stated previously, there appears to be something within us which sits external to the mind, orchestrating synaptic responses to expected and sensed external sensations and abstract thoughts in order to achieve what is termed *normal* mental reasoning. Is this not what is typically considered the function of the soul? Does such a theorized soul not differ significantly from the concept of the *conscience*, as no one assumes the former to function perfectly. This leaves us with either different types of soul, or the same soul interacting differently with two different things. This latter case implies a possible variation in sites of interaction, and therefore partition.

Some may ask if the *instinctive intelligence* which I continue to speak of as being received is not already found on the genome of the living organism in question. As mentioned previously when discussing the staggering percent of the genome that we have no idea the functionality of, and which we naïvely write off as "junk code," we don't know what we don't know about the genome. We are ignorant of our level of ignorance.

As an example, only in very rare instances can we take a primary genetic sequence and create a desired quaternary protein structure from it, as found in nature. Perhaps there is a higher level of *cellular intelligence* by which genetic transcription factors such as activators, repressors, silencers, enhancers, general transcription factors, specificity factors, and sNRP complexes are selected for. Perhaps this is analogous to a form of *cellular instinct*, or *will*, the information stored within the genome being also similar to *knowledge* or *memories*.

Harkening back to the earlier analogy, perhaps genetic information is the set of important documents, and the cell possesses another component, similar to the secretary, which is the true *life* and *will* of the thing; the documents merely serving as a repository of a form of knowledge. Not that there is a perfect comparison between the macro and micro system of the human mind and the cell, but it is interesting that there is a similarity to be found at all, given the difference in scale. Perhaps this thing at the command of the cell's genetic tools is what is passed along to our offspring by whatever intelligence is driving life forward from simple to complex. Perhaps it is the soul.

This brings us to an interesting point. Plotinus, in his *Six Enneads*, eventually settles upon a theory where "the One," what we would call God, radiates his being into matter; driving, enlivening, and sustaining it.[37] When I read this, as well as the thoughts of Lucretius, in his *On the Nature of Things*, I remember coming away with the thought that matter is eternal (The implications of antimatter and the conversion of matter into energy are discussed elsewhere).[194]

Never does an electron wear out from encircling the nucleus, or cease to spin. Elements, unless radioactive, or acted upon by some other energy source, never cease to be themselves. The carbon in the dirt on the ground is the same carbon that formed the Stegosaurus' of old. What is driving the motion of the atoms in this nonliving matter? And what makes living matter which is comprised of it behave differently, ever striving for growth and reproduction? Plotinus' thoughts on this are that our souls are spirit and reside in a higher realm, yet they radiate into and enliven our earthly bodies.

I am not certain that I agree with him, given that this would imply that the souls of bacteria would also be in heaven radiating into their miniscule bodies. I say that this is a cause of improbability; however, I must admit that I have looked into the eyes of some animals and observed intelligence, love, and fear. For heaven's sake, they even evidently dream; kicking and yipping in their sleep. These are all hallmarks of higher thought; affection and fear especially implying forethought, which itself implies reason.

Perhaps, and more likely in my opinion, God itself radiates life into us. I'm not sure that this opinion would be that far askew from the opinion of Plotinus, since he claimed that God, or a demigod, was the maker of our souls. The latter case only differs in how far it remotes the primary actor.

Charles Darwin, as much as he is vilified by those who cling to any of the many quaint, yet unscientific classical creationist theories of the universe, made a very good point in his *The Descent of Man*.[75] In this work, he stated that the possibility of evolution does not preclude the existence of a power ultimately driving the universe, commonly denominated as God. Whether a God brought mankind upon the scene of nature by means of a special, immediate creation, or by the means of a slow driving force that, over several millennia, brought him through various intermediary stages, both are miracles. The difference between the two is that we have more evidence of the latter occurring.

Yet special, immediate creation camps, the one adhering to the 7-day model found within the ancient Hebrew text of Genesis being the largest and most vocal, state that relegating the creation of man to the mode of evolution does nothing to lessen the problem of creation.

"Whence came the first primordial amoeba?" they ask.

Here I tend to agree, as I find the challenges of abiogenesis insurmountable, from the scientific information which we currently have at our disposal.

Sailing

Yet another board is found to be loose. This one is rotted. Surely among the thousands of sundry boards that form the hulking ship, some are bound to wear out. Nothing is perfectly formed of perfect materials, save God; and all indications hint that God skirts the issue by being not material, but rather a no less real immaterial substance known as spirit.

But it is the rate that is of concern to the ship's pilot. Perhaps the many voyages that now blur in his mind into a single panorama of courage, effort, and adventure have been taking an imperceptible toll upon the ship the entire time. Imperceptible then, but increasingly more perceptible now.

Was it for lack of sweat and attention to its maintenance? No. He had held a high reputation among his fellow pilots for the labor and care which he put into his ship. While most scraped barnacles from the keel once a month, he did so weekly. While most mended sail weekly, he had it done every 4 days. Yes, the men oft times chafed at the extra work, yet they always seemed to afterwards hold their heads high in pride, affectionately referring to the ship as their "sweetheart" and "darling."

It wasn't from lack of care, that more frequently these days the sight of a warped, or rotten plank caused the pilot to freeze mid-step. Perhaps the very increased care had contributed, in part to this state. The pristine character of the rig had heightened the boldness of her crew. While less able ships, due to less diligent crews, would shun the slightest squall, never venturing far from shore, or fleet, this ship charged straight and true, ploughing through wave and summiting swell. The successful exit of each storm only increased the pilot's confidence in future success.

But had that caused the wear? Would more timid crews have longer lasting ships? This was hard to say. While they might avoid early wear from wave, they would not have the courageous memories to cheer them. They also would likely feel less affectionate towards their ship for carrying them safely through peril. This lack of affection and timidity, both ignoble traits, could not but corrode other of the crew's virtues, such as their diligence. And this lack of diligence was as destructive to the ship as the wear of storms.

No. The pilot had been instinctively right. It was better to work harder in preparation and just brave the storms. So what if her sails were patched. She should wear those patches as medals of honor. So what if newer ships were daily being christened which could now outpace her. These had not yet passed refined through the same flames of fear. They had not yet been washed by the blood, sweat, and tears of their crew as she had.

The pilot loved this ship and would continue to do his best to preserve her. Being taken aboard during one dark night, after being found adrift and afloat, his earliest memories were of exploring her decks. But he forced himself to face the fact that one day she would have a leak which her crew would be unable to stop, despite their best efforts. At that time, she would slip quietly and bravely beneath the waves. The pilot knew his way to the nearest raft, and being set adrift once more, knew he would escape secure. But he knew not where that raft would drift, nor whether he would be rescued by ship, to sail again, or wash up on a distant shore. Both were preferable to an eternal liquid tomb, or the jaws of sea monsters.

But let us drop all masks. The ship is our body. The pilot is our soul. All of us will eventually begin to notice some signs of wear on the boards and rigging of the bodily "ships" which we have been sailing through life in. Weren't we just youths? Our bodies seem to age more quickly as the years progress. We all know that they aren't doing so in actuality. Time goes on as it always has. There are two reasons for this odd feeling.

The first is that all of futurity is laid out before us, like a road. The past, on the other hand, all falls into the common pool of memory. Memories from decades ago are therefore as within reach as those from our drive to work this morning, making all seem to have occurred "just yesterday." This topic was discussed by Seneca in a letter entitled, "On the Shortness of Life," which he wrote to his friend Lucilius.[1]

The second reason, which Seneca also discusses in the same letter, is that later in life we are merely busier, with more responsibilities distracting us from the slow but steady passage of time. It is for this reason that busy men lead the shortest lives. At least it seems that way to them. Seneca goes on to state that, if these same men were confined within a room with nothing to do, the passage of time would once again appear to them to have decelerated to a crawl.

This seeming time dilation during periods where we have little pressing upon us to accomplish is the main reason why our few years of childhood memories seem to us to have been so much longer than they actually were. Our 30's and 40's come and go, but seem to have been a shorter period than our first, or second decades of life; when those of us who were fortunate enough to have experienced a pleasant childhood were free to wander, explore, and muse over the small miracles of nature which adults often forget; from ladybugs, to dandelions, to inch-worms, to leaves setting out upon voyages down sidewalk streams after a summer storm.

Seneca also points out how wasteful people tend to be with their time: how most men will fight to prevent others from taking their money, or property, which can later be recouped, but pay no heed to the time which other men rob them of, which cannot. Indeed, he states that men often actively seek means to waste their time on meaningless pursuits, rather than wisely investing it in learning about God, themselves, and the world about them, and doing what they can to improve the latter two.[1]

I do not wish to be like this. I only want to invest enough time into my work as I must, in order to ensure that my family is provided with a warm, safe home, clean clothes, and full bellies. I am doing all that I can to learn about the aforementioned subjects, but what will be the end product of all of this study? This is a question that is difficult for me to answer, as I don't know what is out there that I have yet to learn; things which may further transform my views.

I do know that seeking truth and knowledge of all sorts has helped me to free myself from previous misconceptions which I formerly held. Cicero acutely stated in his "5th Stoic Paradox" that, if freedom means the ability to live as one wishes, and wisdom is an overall belief in truths and not falsities, then, since no man wishes to live in error, only the wise are truly free.[4]

I have also noticed that the more that I learn about myself, mankind in general, God, and the world around me, the better I can anticipate and avoid, or defend myself from the myriad peddlers of error, who falsely claim to hold the keys to happiness. It seems that there is a never-ending supply of these, whose confidence is generally inversely proportional to their wisdom and understanding.

Once we reach middle age, the shadowy specter of the grave begins to loom out of the mists of an ever-approaching future. These distant shores were the stuff of legend to us during our youth. In middle age, however, we grow daily more aware of our own mortality. Of course, we know that the shadow of distant shore which we are straining our eyes upon could all be mirage. Even tomorrow we might suddenly be jarred aware as our ship runs aground upon unseen, and unexpected shallows.

Potential death lurks around every corner. It will eventually lay a snare which succeeds in catching us. It has done so for myriads of men who were by far our betters. Emperors before whom the world quaked are now generally unknown; often even their tombs being forgotten. Why then should we feel surprise that we will eventually prove unable to avoid what the strongest, wisest, bravest, and most cunning of antiquity have been unable to? So be it. If we have led a great life, let it come.

We should simply pray that we are fortunate enough to remain physically and mentally able to study and strive after improvement until our last day. It is preferable for our bodies to cease to function before our minds do. The contrary fate befell Emerson; ironically one of the brightest lights of his age. Yet this great man managed to bear what he described as a source of constant embarrassment with great dignity, as did other brilliant men such as Michelle de Montaigne. Should even this theoretical worst of all fates await us, let us strive to face it with similar courage, for new chapters ever await.

Poetry

Ebb and Flow

The silent pause, the absent glance,
There's too much lost 'midst happenstance.
The hearth that blazed not long ago,
yields now but embers, faint aglow.
Yet faintest ember, sputt'ring, weak,
if shielded safe from wind and freak,
and nestled 'mong a shredded fuel,
can birth once more, flames bright and full.
Flames which might melt the hardened frost,
Encrusting souls, writ off as lost.
Fan on the coals. Fan on the flame.
Things will no longer be the same.
We'll heat this room. We'll guard this blaze.
No longer pine the wasted days.
Up soul, with ev'ry breath I breathe.
Take heart and losses calmly leave.
To better things and brighter days.
To clarity instead of haze.
Let this fair flame give proof to you,
Things not extinct can yet grow new.
Guard close your spark. Care for your flame,
Joy may yet spring from grief and shame.

Children

Bright eyes and laughter peals so clear,
Unfettered with life's cares and fear,
Oh that we could unlearn such things,
To wince and hide from recalled stings,
When love was gi'en with candid heart,
Trust could be had right from the start,
Yet wiser now we feign to be,
Than smiling youth with spirits free,
But cunning's not the same as wise,
The conscience stain'd, seen in the eyes,
These young ones bear a wisdom deep,
Beneath the mix of play and sleep,
They know the world around them's good,
And their good hearts work like they should,
They've much to learn of life and art,
But let's unlearn the darker part.

Evergreen

'Midst sodden woods and fallen trees,
'Midst drips which cling to dew wet leaves,
The hidden vale, a vacant world,
Where ferns do hang with leaves half furled,
Where on soft grass I'd sit alone,
And toy with stick and vine and cone,
Where time did pass, yet seem to not,
As I drew comfort from the spot,
I'd enter lonely in that place,
Seeking respite from some disgrace,
High up, I'd find a bough to perch,
One strong enough to stand the lurch,
From young boy leg which scrambled high,
Until small head pushed through to sky,
Where breeze would brush concern away,
What therapy that tree's soft sway,
The world grew faint, far down below,
The calm of peace would slowly grow,
Within my breast, I knew not why,
Belief God knew my inward cry,
I'd thought before that friends were key,
To things felt missing inside me,
But wrong I was, though friendship's fair,
A lesson learned while dangling there,
True peace and sweet comes from within,
As I let go and trusted in,
God's wisdom who the wood did make,
The moving leaves which round me quake,
Such beauty in the world around,
Could take the cares which brought me down,
And see me through to other side,
Yes, understand how I had tried,
And see and love this little boy,
Who hiding was surprised by joy.

Quiet

How long I've been, I don't recall,
But must be gone 'fore sun dost fall,
Too long I've lingered 'neath these trees,
Consuming loving eulogies,
Engraven on the stones around,
Forgotten host now void of sound,
Whose eyes did glint and minds did race,
Whose hearts did love and arms embraced,
Their children and their parents too,
And felt the warmth that I or you,
Do feel yet still when lov'd ones meet,
Those few and bless'd, whose hearts do beat,
As beat these did beneath this ground,
Pumped healthy blood through bodies sound,
Bodies that once brought so much joy,
As newborn girl, or healthy boy,
That ran and laughed and sang and played,
Proud parents, mother, father made,
Whose lots I spy nearby to this,
Tried to stay close to those they missed,
As these did live and age and gray,
And watch their last days slip away,
'Till that last sleep, their breath did leave,
And grown child now and widow grieve,
Visit they surely oft did do,
Until their bodies buried too,
Did leave none now who know of these,
Forgotten names beneath the trees,
I'll not forget, whoe'r you were,
I know your life was real and sure,
As I do know my life half gone,
One day will bring my final dawn,
And I, in turn, will lie here too,
Forgotten I, as now are you,
Yet if my soul nearby dost stay,
And one should happen out this way,
Perhaps may bring my name to mind,
Muse for a moment of the kind,
Of man I was when once as he,
I stood beneath this very tree.
Had souls but lips, I'm sure I'd smile,
And hope this stranger'd stay a while,
To ponder life's sweet mystery,
The cypher of mortality,

But wake, I've drifted off again,
Enchanted by this sacred glen,
No more of this, I must now leave,
But will return when loved ones grieve.

Bibliography

1. Seneca LA. *On the shortness of life*. Basore JW. (Trans.) London: William Heinemann, 1932.
2. Emerson RW. *The Complete Works. Vol. II. Essays: First Series. Social Aims*. New York and Boston: Houghton, Mifflin, 1904 [cited 2019 Feb 26]. Available from: https://www.bartleby.com/90/0802.html
3. Emerson RW. *The Complete Works. Vol. II. Essays: First Series. The Oversoul*. New York and Boston: Houghton, Mifflin, 1904 [cited 2019 Feb 26]. Available from: https://www.bartleby.com/90/0209.html
4. Cicero MT *Cicero's three books of offices*. Edmonds CR. (Trans.) London: George Bell & Sons, 1874 [cited 2019 Feb 26]. Available from: https://archive.org/details/cicerosthreeboo00cice/page/n20
5. Epictetus. *The discourses and manual, together with fragments of his writings*. Matheson PE. (Trans.) Oxford: The Clarendon Press, 1916.
6. Gunn, B. The instruction of Ptah-hotep and the instruction of Ke'gemni: The oldest books in the world. Gunn B. (Trans.) London: J. Murray, 1912.
7. Dana RH. *Two years before the mast*. Cambridge, MA: Riverside Press, 1911.
8. Hitler A. *Mein Kampf*. Chamberlain J, et al. (Trans.) New York: Reynal & Hitchcock, 1941.
9. Emerson RW. *The Complete Works. Vol. IV. Representative Men: Seven Lectures*. New York and Boston: Houghton, Mifflin, 1904 [cited 2019 Feb 26]. Available from: https://www.bartleby.com/90/0402.html
10. Curtin C. Fact or Fiction?: Living People Outnumber the Dead. *Scientific American*. 2007 Sept;297(3): 126. doi:10.1038/scientificamerican0907126
11. World Population Clock. n.d. [cited 2019 Feb 26]. Available from: https://www.census.gov/popclock/
12. *Education for all global monitoring report 2006*. UNESCO. 2006 [cited 2019 Feb 26]. Available from: http://www.unesco.org/education/GMR2006/full/chapt8_eng.pdf
13. Butler S. *The way of all flesh*. New York: E. P. Dutton & company, 1916.
14. Seneca LA. *Ad Lucilium epistulae morales*. Gummere RM. (Trans.) Cambridge, MA: Harvard University Press, 1917 [cited 2017 Dec 5]. Available from: https://archive.org/details/adluciliumepistu01seneuoft

15. Profile of Harvard graduate William Henry Furness who died January 30, 1896. *The Harvard Graduates' Magazine*. 1896 Jun;4(16), 546.

16. Huxley TH. Letter no. 9409. Darwin Correspondence Project. [cited 2017 Dec 5]. Available from: http://www.darwinproject.ac.uk/DCP-LETT-9409

17. Carlyle T. *Critical and miscellaneous essays*. Philadelphia: A. Hart, 1852.

18. Tolkien JRR. *The hobbit*. Houghton Mifflin Company, 1999.

19. Stevenson RL. *Treasure island*. New York: Harper & Brothers, 1915.

20. Wells HG. *War of the Worlds*. London: Heinemann, 1898.

21. Marianoff, D, Tagore R. *Einstein and Tagore plumb the truth*. New York Times. 1930 Aug 10 [cited 2019 Feb 26]. Available from: https://www.nytimes.com/1930/08/10/archives/einstein-and-tagore-plumb-the-truth-scientist-and-poet-exchange.html

22. Orwell G. *Nineteen Eighty-Four*. 2001 [cited 2019 Feb 26]. Available from: https://archive.org/details/NineteenEightyFour-Novel-GeorgeOrwell/page/n3

23. Aristotle. *Nicomachean Ethics*. Ross WD. (Trans.) n.d. [cited 2019 Feb 26]. Available from: http://classics.mit.edu/Aristotle/nicomachaen.html

24. Chesterton GK. *Orthodoxy*. New York: Lane, 1909

25. Aristotle. *Metaphysics*. Ross WD. (Trans.). n.d. [cited 2019 Feb 26]. Available from: http://classics.mit.edu/Aristotle/metaphysics.html

26. Pike A. Morals and dogma of the ancient and accepted Scottish Rite of Freemasonry. Charleston: A. M. 5641, 1905.

27. Zarathustra. *The Gathas: The hymns of Zarathustra*. Irani DJ. Trans.) Newton, MA: Center for Ancient Iranian Studies, 1998.

28. Plutarch. *Plutarch's Morals*. Goodwin WD, et al. (Trans.) Boston: Little Brown and Company, 1878 [cited 2019 Feb 26]. Available from: https://oll.libertyfund.org/titles/plutarch-plutarchs-morals-5-vols

29. Epictetus. *The golden sayings of Epictetus*. New York: P. F. Collier & Son Company, 1909 [cited 2019 Feb 26]. Available from: http://classics.mit.edu/Epictetus/goldsay.html

30. Emerson RW. *The Complete Works. Vol. II. Essays: First Series. Compensation*. New York and Boston: Houghton, Mifflin, 1904 [cited 2019 Feb 26]. Available from: https://www.bartleby.com/90/0203.html

31. Maslow AH. A theory of human motivation. *Psychological Review*. 1943 [cited 2019 Feb 26];50(4): 370–96. Available from: http://psychclassics.yorku.ca/Maslow/motivation.htm

32. *Pyramid showing Maslow's hierarchy of needs*. 2014 Nov 2 [cited 2019 Feb 26]. Available from: https://commons.wikimedia.org/wiki/File:MaslowsHierarchyOfNeeds.svg

33. Stephen J. *What is Self-Actualization?* Psychology Today. 2016 Sept 16 [cited 2019 Feb 26]. Available from:

https://www.psychologytoday.com/us/blog/what-doesnt-kill-us/201609/what-is-self-actualization
34. Aristotle. *The works of Aristotle: Magna moralia, ethica eudemia, de virtutibus et vitiis*. Ross WD. (Trans.) Oxford: Clarendon Press, 1915 [cited 2019 Feb 26]. Available from: https://archive.org/details/p2workstranslat09aris/page/n3
35. Laertius D. *Lives of eminent philosophers*. Hicks RD. (Trans.) London: Heinemann, 1925 [cited 2019 Feb 26]. Available from: https://archive.org/details/livesofeminentph02dioguoft/page/214
36. Plato. *The dialogues of Plato: Vol. 1. Cratylus*. Jowett B. (Trans.) London: Oxford University Press, 1875 [cited 2019 Feb 26]. Available from: https://oll.libertyfund.org/titles/plato-the-dialogues-of-plato-vol-1
37. Plotinus. *The Six Enneads*. MacKenna S. (Trans.) 2003 [cited 2019 Feb 26]. Available from: http://www.sacred-texts.com/cla/plotenn/index.htm
38. Locke J. *The Works of John Locke, Vol. 1 An Essay concerning Human Understanding*. London: Rivington, 1824 [cited 2019 Feb 26]. Available from: https://oll.libertyfund.org/titles/locke-the-works-vol-1-an-essay-concerning-human-understanding-part-1
39. Hegel GWF. *The philosophy of history*. Sibree J. (Trans.) New York, The colonial press, c1899 [cited 2019 Feb 26]. Available from: https://archive.org/details/philosophyofhist00hegeuoft/page/n14
40. Taylor T. *Theoretic arithmetic*. London: J. Valpy, 1816 [cited 2019 Feb 27]. Available from: http://djm.cc/library/Theoretic_Arithmetic_Thomas_Taylor.pdf
41. Gibbon E. *The history of the decline and fall of the Roman Empire, Vol. 12*. New York: Fred De Fau and Company, 1776 [cited 2019 Feb 27]. Available from: https://oll.libertyfund.org/titles/gibbon-the-history-of-the-decline-and-fall-of-the-roman-empire-vol-12
42. *US Const. Amend. I*. 1791 [cited 2019 Feb 27]. Available from: http://hrlibrary.umn.edu/education/all_amendments_usconst.htm
43. *Declaration of Independence: A Transcription*. 1776 [cited 2019 Feb 27]. Available from: https://www.archives.gov/founding-docs/declaration-transcript
44. Herodotus. *Histories. Book IV*. Rawlinson G. (Trans.) London: John Murray, 1875 [cited 2019 Feb 27]. Available from: http://classics.mit.edu/Herodotus/history.html
45. Siculus D. *Library of history*. Oldfather CH. (Trans.) Cambridge, MA: Harvard University Press, 1989 [cited 2019 Feb 27]. Available from: https://archive.org/details/DiodorosOfSicily034.598
46. Plato. *The Dialogues of Plato, Vol. 3. The Republic, Timaeus, Critias*. Jowett B. (Trans.) London: Oxford University Press, 1892 [cited 2019 Feb 27]. Available from: https://oll.libertyfund.org/titles/plato-dialogues-vol-3-republic-timaeus-critias

47. Thucydides. *History of the Peloponnesian war*. Crawley R. (Trans.) London: Dent, 1914 [cited 2019 Feb 27]. Available from: http://classics.mit.edu/Thucydides/pelopwar.html

48. Hobbes T. *Leviathan*. Oxford: Clarendon Press, 1909 [cited 2019 Feb 27]. Available from: https://oll.libertyfund.org/titles/hobbes-leviathan-1909-ed

49. Plato. *Dialogues. Laws*. Jowett B. (Trans.) New York: Scribner, 1889 [cited 2019 Feb 27]. Available from: https://archive.org/details/dialoguestransla04platuoft

50. Montesquieu CL. *The spirit of the laws*. Book XVIII. Of laws in the relation they bear to the nature of the soil. London: T. Evans, 1777 [cited 2019 Feb 27]. Available from: https://oll.libertyfund.org/titles/montesquieu-complete-works-vol-1-the-spirit-of-laws/simple

51. Emerson RW. *The Complete Works. Vol. XI. Miscellanies. Historical discourse at Concord*. New York and Boston: Houghton, Mifflin, 1904 [cited 2019 Feb 27]. Available from: https://www.bartleby.com/90/1102.html

52. Scudder HE. *Men and Manners in America One Hundred Years Ago*. New York: Scribner, Armstrong, 1876 [cited 2019 Feb 27]. Available from: https://archive.org/details/menandmannersin00scudgoog

53. Emerson RW. *The Complete Works. Vol. XI. Miscellanies. Letter to President Van Buren*. New York and Boston: Houghton, Mifflin, 1904 [cited 2019 Feb 27]. Available from: https://www.bartleby.com/90/1103.html

54. Gibbon E. *The history of the decline and fall of the Roman Empire, Vol. 4*. New York: Fred De Fau and Company, 1776 [cited 2019 Feb 27]. Available from: https://oll.libertyfund.org/titles/gibbon-the-history-of-the-decline-and-fall-of-the-roman-empire-vol-4

55. Washington G. *Washington's Farewell Address 1796*. 1796 [cited 2019 Feb 27]. Available from: http://avalon.law.yale.edu/18th_century/washing.asp

56. Aesop. *The fables of Aesop*. Jacobs J. (Trans.) New York: The Macmillan Co., 1912 [cited 2019 Feb 27]. Available from: https://archive.org/details/cu31924053968099

57. Bent SA. *Familiar Short Sayings of Great Men*. Boston: Ticknor and Co., 1887 [cited 2019 Feb 27]. Available from: https://www.bartleby.com/344/75.html

58. Claxton WF, Dexter M, French V, Landon M Penn L. *Little House on the Prairie* [Television series]. NBC Productions, 1974 Sept 11–1983 Mar 21.

59. Wilder LI. *Little house series*. New York: Harper & Bros., 1953.

60. *Hypatia*. Encyclopedia Romana. n.d. [cited 2019 Feb 27]. Available from:

http://penelope.uchicago.edu/~grout/encyclopaedia_romana/greece/pagan
ism/hypatia.html
61. Ottenhoff C. *Wise animals: Aesop and his followers.* 2012 [cited 2019
Feb 27]. Available from:
https://www.library.illinois.edu/rbx/exhibitions/Aesop/aesop-life.html
62. Tacitus PC. *Annals of Tacitus. Book XIV.* Church A, Brodribb B.
(Trans.). 1876 [cited 2019 Feb 27]. Available from:
http://classics.mit.edu/Tacitus/annals.mb.txt
63. Boethius AMS. *The consolation of philosophy of Boethius.* James HR.
(Trans.). London: G. Routledge, c1900 [cited 2019 Feb 27]. Available
from: https://archive.org/details/theconsolationof00boetuoft
64. Plato. *The Harvard Classics. Vol.2 The Apology, Phædo and Crito.*
Jowett B. (Trans.) New York: P.F. Collier & Son, 1909 [cited 2019 Feb
27]. Available from: https://www.bartleby.com/2/1/31.html
65. Editors of Encyclopedia Britannica. *Orpheus.* 2019 Jan 4 [cited 2019
Feb 27]. Available from: https://www.britannica.com/topic/Orpheus-
Greek-mythology
66. Porphyry, *The Life of Pythagoras* (Guthrie KG). 1920 [cited 2019 Feb
27]. Available from:
http://www.tertullian.org/fathers/porphyry_life_of_pythagoras_02_text.h
tm
67. Wilde M. *Galileo and the Inquisition.* The Galileo Project. 1995 [cited
2019 Feb 27]. Available from: http://galileo.rice.edu/bio/narrative_7.html
68. Wilde M. Giordano Bruno (1548-1600). The Galileo Project. 1995
[cited 2019 Feb 27]. Available from: http://galileo.rice.edu/chr/bruno.html
69. Cousin JW. *A short biographical dictionary of English literature.*
Thomas Paine. London: J. M. Dent & Sons Ltd, 1910 [cited 2019 Feb 27].
Available from:
https://ebooks.adelaide.edu.au/c/cousin/john/biog/complete.html
70. Paine T. *The age of reason.* London: Freethought Publishing
Company, 1880 [cited 2019 Feb 27]. Available from:
https://archive.org/details/ageofreason00painiala
71. Janney SM. *The life of William Penn.* Philadelphia: Hogan, Perkins
& Co., 1852 [cited 2019 Feb 27]. Available from:
https://archive.org/details/lifeofwilliampen1852jann
72. *William Whiston.* Oxford reference. 2019 [cited 2019 Feb 27].
Available from:
http://www.oxfordreference.com/view/10.1093/oi/authority.201108031220
45556
73. Opi SB. *The trial of Michael Servetus.* Michael Servetus Institute.
2004 [cited 2019 Feb 27]. Available from:
http://www.miguelservet.org/servetus/trial.htm
74. Marx K, Engles F. *Marx/Engels Selected Works, Vol. One, The
communist manifesto.* Moore S, Engles F. (Trans.) Moscow: Progress
Publishers, 1969 [cited 2019 Feb 27]. Available from:

https://www.marxists.org/archive/marx/works/1848/communist-manifesto/
75. Darwin C. *The descent of man.* New York: D. Appleton and Co., 1871 [cited 2019 Feb 27]. Available from: https://archive.org/details/descentman00darwgoog
76. Darwin C. *The origin of species.* New York: P.F. Collier, c1909 [cited 2019 Feb 27]. Available from: https://archive.org/details/originofspecies00darwuoft
77. *Final cries of couple killed by bear.* 2003 Oct 10 [cited 2019 Feb 27]. Available from: https://www.telegraph.co.uk/news/worldnews/northamerica/usa/1443788/Final-cries-of-couple-killed-by-bear.html
78. *'Crocodile Hunter' Steve Irwin stabbed hundreds of times by stingray, cameraman reveals.* 2014 Mar 10 [cited 2019 Feb 27]. Available from: https://www.telegraph.co.uk/news/worldnews/australiaandthepacific/australia/10687502/Crocodile-Hunter-Steve-Irwin-stabbed-hundreds-of-times-by-stingray-cameraman-reveals.html
79. Lam K. Fox News. *Deputies watched dogs 'eating rib cage' of Virginia woman, 22, during mauling, sheriff says.* 2017 Dec 19 [cited 2019 Feb 27]. Available from: https://www.foxnews.com/us/deputies-watched-dogs-eating-rib-cage-of-virginia-woman-22-during-mauling-sheriff-says
80. Fox news. *Rules against pit bulls scrapped in Montreal.* 2017 Dec 25 [cited 2019 Feb 27]. Available from: https://www.foxnews.com/world/rules-against-pit-bulls-scrapped-in-montreal
81. Eleftheriou-Smith L. *Man spits in baby's face and tells mother: 'White people shouldn't breed'.* Independent. 2017 Feb 22 [cited 2019 Feb 27]. Available from: https://www.independent.co.uk/news/uk/crime/man-spits-baby-face-mother-white-people-breed-abdulla-rezzas-south-shields-a7594016.html
82. Associated Press. *School worker accused of threatening to execute white men.* New York Post. 2018 Mar 30 [cited 2019 Feb 27]. Available from: https://nypost.com/2018/03/30/school-worker-accused-of-threatening-to-execute-white-men/
83. Baroud R. *White men kill, brown men found guilty.* Al Jazeera. 2017 Oct 16 [cited 2019 Feb 27]. Available from: https://www.aljazeera.com/indepth/opinion/white-men-kill-brown-men-guilty-171016083952943.html
84. Grasgreen A. *Majority Disaffection.* Inside Higher Ed. 2013 Mar 22 [cited 2019 Feb 27]. Available from: https://www.insidehighered.com/news/2013/03/22/white-men-alienated-higher-ed-workplace-survey-suggests
85. Titcomb J. *YouTube stopped hiring white men in attempt to boost diversity, lawsuit claims.* The Telegraph. 2018 Mar 2 [cited 2019 Feb 27]. Available from:

https://www.telegraph.co.uk/technology/2018/03/02/youtube-stopped-hiring-white-men-attempt-boost-diversity-lawsuit/
85. American psychiatric association. *DSM–5 Fact Sheets.* 2018 [cited 2019 Feb 27]. Available from: https://www.psychiatry.org/psychiatrists/practice/dsm/educational-resources/dsm-5-fact-sheets
86. Biederman J, et al. Clinical correlates of ADHD in females: findings from a large group of girls ascertained from pediatric and psychiatric referral sources. *J Am Acad Child Adolesc Psychiatry.* 1999 Aug [cited 2019 Feb 27];38(8): 966-75. doi:10.1097/00004583-199908000-00012 Available from: https://www.ncbi.nlm.nih.gov/pubmed/10434488
87. Collingwood J. *ADHD and Gender.* Psych Central. 2018 Oct 8 [cited 2019 Feb 27]. Available from: https://psychcentral.com/lib/adhd-and-gender/
88. Harding A. *Men's testosterone levels declined in last 20 years.* Reuters. 2007 Jan 19 [cited 2019 Feb 27]. Available from: https://uk.reuters.com/article/health-testosterone-levels-dc/mens-testosterone-levels-declined-in-last-20-years-idUKKIM16976320061031
89. Casto KV. & Edwards, D. A. Testosterone, cortisol, and human competition.
Horm Behav. 2016 Jun [cited 2016 Apr 19];82: 21-37. doi: 10.1016/j.yhbeh.2016.04.004..
90. Zarembo A. *With U.S. encouragement, VA disability claims rise sharply.* LA Times. 2014 Jul 14 [cited 2019 Feb 27]. https://www.latimes.com/local/la-me-veterans-disability-20140713-story.html
91. De Vry J. 5-HT1A receptor agonists: Recent developments and controversial issues. *Psychopharmacology.* 1995 [cited 2019 Feb 27];121(1): 1-26. Available from: http://dx.doi.org/10.1007/BF02245588
92. *The Hippocratic Oath.* Greek Medicine. 2012 Feb 7 [cited 2019 Feb 28]. Available from: https://www.nlm.nih.gov/hmd/greek/greek_oath.html
93. Stone K. *Who funds biomedical research?.* 2019 Jan 13 [cited 2019 Feb 28]. https://www.thebalance.com/who-funds-biomedical-research-2663193
94. Food and Drug Administration. LITHOBID® (Lithium Carbonate USP). Reference ID: 4255847. n.d. [cited 2019 Feb 28]. https://www.accessdata.fda.gov/drugsatfda_docs/label/2018/018027s064l bl.pdf
95. Blader JC. & Carlson, G. A. Increased Rates of Bipolar Disorder Diagnoses Among U.S. Child, Adolescent, and Adult Inpatients, 1996–2004. *Biological Psychiatry.* 2007 July 15 [cited 2019 Feb 28];62(2):107-114. doi:10.1016/j.biopsych.2006.11.006
96. Fu CHY., Steiner, H., & Costafreda, S. G. Predictive neural biomarkers of clinical response in depression: A meta-analysis of functional and structural neuroimaging studies of pharmacological and

psychological therapies. *Neurobiology of Disease*. 2013 Apr [cited 2019
Feb 28];52: 75-83. doi:10.1016/j.nbd.2012.05.008 Available from:
http://www.sciencedirect.com/science/article/pii/S0969996112001945#f00
15
97. Gunnell D, Ashby D. Antidepressants and suicide: What is the
balance of benefit and harm. *BMJ*. 2004 Jul 3 [cited 2019 Feb 28];329(3)
doi:10.1136/bmj.329.7456.34 Available from:
https://www.ncbi.nlm.nih.gov/pmc/articles/PMC443451/
98. ElSerag HB, Mason AC. Risk factors for the rising rates of primary
liver cancer in the United States. *Arch Intern Med*. 2000 [cited 2019 Feb
28];160(21):3227-3230. doi:10.1001/archinte.160.21.3227.
99. Dubrow R, Darefsky A. Demographic variation in incidence of adult
glioma by subtype, United States 1992-2007. *BMC Cancer*. 2011 [cited
2019 Feb 28];11: 325. doi:10.1186/1471240711325 Available from:
http://www.ncbi.nlm.nih.gov/pmc/articles/PMC3163630/#__ffn_sectitle
100. Alifieris C, Trafalis DT. and. Glioblastoma multiform: Pathogenesis
and treatment (Panagiotidis M. eds.) *Pharmacology & Therapeutics*.
2015 Aug [cited 2019 Feb 28];152:63-82.
doi:10.1016/j.pharmthera.2015.05.005.
http://www.sciencedirect.com/science/article/pii/S0163725815000960
101. Wright RH, Cummings NA. *Destructive trends in mental health:
The well-intentioned path to harm*. New York: Brunner-Routledge, 2005
[cited 2019 Feb 28]
102. Kearney MS, Harris BH, Jácome E, Parker L. *Ten Economic Facts
about Crime and Incarceration in the United States*. The Hamilton
Project. 2014 May [cited 2019 Feb 28]. Available from:
http://www.hamiltonproject.org/assets/legacy/files/downloads_and_links/
v8_THP_10CrimeFacts.pdf
103. Mueller M. *The Upanishads*. Mueller M. (Trans.) Oxford: Clarendon
Press, 1884 [cited 2019 Feb 28]. Available from: http://www.sacred-
texts.com/hin/upan/index.htm
104. Layman LC. Human gene mutations causing infertility. *Journal of
Medical Genetics*. 2002 [cited 2019 Feb 28];39:153-161. Available from:
https://jmg.bmj.com/content/39/3/153
105. *Gender*. Online Etymology Dictionary. n.d. [cited 2019 Feb 28].
Available from: https://www.etymonline.com/word/gender
106. Wagner M. *Norwegian woman believes she is a cat trapped in a
human's body*. New York Daily News. 2016 Jan 28 [cited 2019 Feb 28].
Available from: http://www.nydailynews.com/news/world/norwegian-
woman-cat-trapped-human-body-article-1.2512352
107. Morin FF. EGO HIPPO: the subject as metaphor. *Angelaki*. 2017
Apr [cited 2019 Feb 28];22(2):87-96.
doi:10.1080/0969725X.2017.1322822 Available from:
https://www.researchgate.net/publication/317018634_EGO_HIPPO_the_
subject_as_metaphor

108. Prestigiacomo A. *TRANS-AGE: Pedophile charged with abusing 3 girls says he's a 9-year-old trapped in man's body.* The Daily Wire. 2018 Jan 26 [cited 2019 Feb 28]. Available from: https://www.dailywire.com/news/26380/trans-age-pedophile-charged-abusing-3-girls-says-amanda-prestigiacomo

109. Jefferson T. *The letters of Thomas Jefferson. To Judge Spencer Roane Poplar Forest.* 1819 Sept 6 [cited 2019 Feb 28]. Available from: http://www.let.rug.nl/usa/presidents/thomas-jefferson/letters-of-thomas-jefferson/jefl257.php

110. Jefferson T. *From Thomas Jefferson to William Charles Jarvis.* 1820 Sept 28 [cited 2019 Feb 28]. Available from: https://founders.archives.gov/documents/Jefferson/98-01-02-1540

111. Jefferson T. *From Thomas Jefferson to William Johnson.* 1823 Jun 12 [cited 2019 Feb 28]. Available from: https://founders.archives.gov/documents/Jefferson/98-01-02-3562

112. Jefferson T. *The letters of Thomas Jefferson. To Thomas Ritchie Monticello.* 1820 Dec 25 [cited 2019 Feb 28]. Available from: http://www.let.rug.nl/usa/presidents/thomas-jefferson/letters-of-thomas-jefferson/jefl263.php

113. Jefferson T. *Thomas Jefferson on Judicial Tyranny.* 2014 Jun 4 [cited 2019 Feb 28]. Available from: https://tenthamendmentcenter.com/2012/06/04/thomas-jefferson-on-judicial-tyranny/

114. Jefferson T. *From Thomas Jefferson to William Johnson.* 1823 Mar 4 [cited 2019 Feb 28]. Available from: https://rotunda.upress.virginia.edu/founders/default.xqy?keys=FOEA-print-04-02-02-3373

115. Jefferson T. *From Thomas Jefferson to Edward Livingston.* 1825 Mar 25 [cited 2019 Feb 28]. Available from: https://rotunda.upress.virginia.edu/founders/default.xqy?keys=FOEA-print-04-02-02-5077

116. Chasmar J. *Princeton bioethics professor faces calls for resignation over infanticide support.* The Washington Times. [cited 2019 Feb 28]. Available from: https://www.washingtontimes.com/news/2015/jun/16/peter-singer-princeton-bioethics-professor-faces-c/

117. Crick FHC. *Letter from Francis Crick to Bernard D. Davis.* The Francis Crick Papers. 1970 Apr 22 [cited 2019 Feb 28]. Available from: https://profiles.nlm.nih.gov/ps/retrieve/ResourceMetadata/SCBBPG

118. Barringer F. *The Mainstreaming of Marxism in U.S. Colleges.* The New York Times. 1989 Oct 25 [cited 2019 Feb 28]. Available from: https://www.nytimes.com/1989/10/25/us/education-the-mainstreaming-of-marxism-in-us-colleges.html

119. Frueh BC, Grubaugh AL, Elhai JD, Buckley TC. US Department of Veterans Affairs Disability Policies for Posttraumatic Stress Disorder:

Administrative Trends and Implications for Treatment, Rehabilitation, and Research. *American Journal of Public Health.* 2007 Jun 13 [cited 2019 Feb 28];97(12): 2143-2145. Available from: http://doi.org/10.2105/AJPH.2007.115436

120. Marx BP, Miller MW, Sloan DM, Litz BT, Kaloupek DG, Keane TM. Military-related PTSD, current disability policies, and malingering. *American Journal of Public Health.* 2007 Dec 21 [cited 2019 Feb 28];98(5): 773-774. http://doi.org/10.2105/AJPH.2007.133223

121. Harrington E. *Transgender surgeries would cost Pentagon $1.3 billion.* The Washington Free Beacon. 2017 Jul 27 [cited 2019 Feb 28]. Available from: https://freebeacon.com/issues/transgender-surgeries-would-cost-pentagon-1-3-billion/

122. Associated Press. *California murder convict becomes first U.S. inmate to have state-funded sex reassignment surgery.* Los Angeles Times. 2017 Jan 6 [cited 2019 Feb 28]. Available from: https://www.latimes.com/local/lanow/la-me-ln-inmate-sex-reassignment-20170106-story.html

123. Pew Research Center. *Religious landscape study. Gender composition.* 2007 [cited 2019 Feb 28]. Available from: http://www.pewforum.org/religious-landscape-study/gender-composition/

124. Bundy T, Dobson J. *A transcript of Ted Bundy's final interview.* 1989 [cited 2019 Feb 28]. Available from: http://www.academia.edu/4921305/A_Transcript_of_Ted_Bundys_Final_I nterview

125. Dahmer J, Glass N. Interview with "Inside Edition," conducted with Nancy Glass at Columbia Correctional Facility in Portage, WI in January. 1993 Feb 8 [cited 2019 Feb 28].

126. Boschelli B, Schmitt G. *Interview regarding John Wayne Gacy.* 2010 Dec [cited 2019 Feb 28]. Available from: http://www.killerreviews.com/dispinterview.php?intid=1883

127. Livius T. *Roman History, Books I-III.* Freese JH, Church AJ, Brodribb WJ. (Trans.) 1904 [cited 2019 Feb 28]. Available from: http://history-world.org/livy4.pdf

128. Descartes R. *The Philosophical Works of Descartes. Meditations on first philosophy.* Haldane ES. (Trans.) London: Cambridge Univ. Press, 1911 [cited 2019 Feb 28]. Available from: http://selfpace.uconn.edu/class/percep/DescartesMeditations.pdf

129. Plato. *Euthyphro.* Jowett B. (Trans.) 2013 Jan 15 [cited 2019 Feb 28]. Available from: http://www.gutenberg.org/files/1642/1642-h/1642-h.htm

130. Plato. *Theaetetus.* Jowett B. (Trans.) n.d. [cited 2019 Feb 28]. Available from: http://classics.mit.edu/Plato/theatu.html

131. Plato. *Phaedrus.* Jowett B. (Trans.) n.d. [cited 2019 Feb 28]. Available from: http://classics.mit.edu/Plato/phaedrus.html

132. Plato. *Euthydemus*. Jowett B. (Trans.) n.d. [cited 2019 Feb 28]. Available from: http://classics.mit.edu/Plato/euthydemus.html

133. Blue Letter Bible. *Strong's concordance. H8414.* n.d. [cited 2019 Feb 28]. Available from: https://www.blueletterBible.org/lang/lexicon/lexicon.cfm?t=kjv&strongs= h8414

134. Scott SA, Edelmann L, Liu L, Luo M, Desnick RJ, Kornreich R. Experience with carrier screening and prenatal diagnosis for 16 Ashkenazi Jewish genetic diseases. *Hum. Mutat.* 2010 Nov [cited 2019 Feb 28];31(11): 1240-1250. doi:10.1002/humu.21327 Available from: https://www.ncbi.nlm.nih.gov/pubmed/20672374

135. Grynszpan E. *Vladimir Lenin Was Part Jewish, Say Declassified KGB File.* Time. 2011 Jun 13 [cited 2019 Feb 28]. Available from: http://content.time.com/time/world/article/0,8599,2077413,00.html

136. Hayim AB. *Lenin's Jewish Roots Confirmed.* Israel National News. 2011 May 24 [cited 2019 Feb 28]. Available from: http://www.israelnationalnews.com/News/News.aspx/144454

137. Ford H. *The International Jew.* The Dearborn Independent. 1920 Nov [cited 2019 Feb 28]. Available from: http://www.gutenberg.org/cache/epub/37539/pg37539-images.html

138. Putin VV. *First Soviet government was mostly Jewish.* The Times of Israel. 2013 Jun 19 [cited 2019 Feb 28]. Available from: https://www.timesofisrael.com/putin-first-soviet-government-was-mostly-jewish/

139. Cox GW. *A manual of mythology.* New York: Leypoldt & Holt, 1868 [cited 2019 Feb 28]. Available from: https://archive.org/details/manualofmytholog00coxgrich

140. Jefferson T. *Letter from Thomas Jefferson to James Smith.* Founders Early Access. 1822 Dec 8 [cited 2019 Feb 28]. Available from: https://rotunda.upress.virginia.edu/founders/default.xqy?keys=FOEA-print-04-02-02-3202

141. Athanasius. *Four discourses against the Arians.* Christian Classics Ethereal Library. n.d. [cited 2019 Feb 28]. Available from: https://www.ccel.org/ccel/schaff/npnf204.xxi.ii.i.i.html

142. Christy R. *Proverbs, maxims and phrases of all ages.* 1887 [cited 2019 Feb 28]. Available from: https://www.bartleby.com/89/660.html

143. Coleman-Norton PR. *Roman state and Christian church. Vol. 1.* Eugene, OR: Wipf & Stock Publishers, 1966.

144. Cyril. *The catechetical lectures of S. Cyril, Archbishop of Jerusalem.* Christian Classics Ethereal Library. Gifford EH. (Trans.). [cited 2019 Feb 28]. Available from: https://www.ccel.org/ccel/schaff/npnf207.ii.iii.i.html

145. Drake HA. *Athanasius' first exile.* n.d. [cited 2019 Feb 28]. Available from: https://grbs.library.duke.edu/article/viewFile/5031/5403

146. Sozomen. *The ecclesiastical history of Sozomen.* Walford E. (Trans.) London: Henry G. Bohn, 1855.

147. Servetus M. *On the errors of the Trinity.* Wilbur EM. (Trans.) 1932 [cited 2019 Feb 28]. Available from: http://www.teleiosministries.com/pdfs/Doctrines_of_Men/errors_Trinity_servetus.pdf

148. Penn W. *The sandy foundation shaken.* London: Cradock and Joy, 1812 [cited 2019 Feb 28]. Available from: https://archive.org/details/sandyfoundation00meetgoog

149. Newton I. *Paradoxical questions concerning the morals & actions of Athanasius & his followers.* The Newton Project. n.d. [cited 2019 Feb 28]. Available from: http://www.newtonproject.ox.ac.uk/view/texts/normalized/THEM00010

150. Boswell J, *The life of Samuel Johnson, LL.D.* (Osgood CG eds.) [cited 2019 Feb 28]. Available from: https://www.gutenberg.org/files/1564/1564-h/1564-h.htm

151. *How many words are there in the English language?.* Oxford Dictionaries. n.d. [cited 2019 Feb 28]. Available from: https://en.oxforddictionaries.com/explore/how-many-words-are-there-in-the-english-language/

152. Eusebius. *Ecclesiastical history.* New York: G.P. Putnam's Sons, 1926 [cited 2019 Feb 28]. Available from: https://archive.org/details/ecclesiasticalhi01euseuoft

153. Hammond DC. Hypnosis as sole anesthesia for major surgeries: historical & contemporary perspectives. *Am J Clin Hypn.* 2008 Oct [cited 2019 Feb 28];51(2):101-21. doi:10.1080/00029157.2008.10401653

154. Levi E. *Transcendental magic.* Waite AE. (Trans.) 1896 [cited 2019 Feb 28]. p. 174 Available from: http://www.iapsop.com/ssoc/1896__levi__transcendental_magic.pdf

155. Plato. *Phaedo.* Jowett B. (Trans.) n.d. [cited 2019 Feb 28]. Available from: http://classics.mit.edu/Plato/phaedo.html

156. Green WH. *The higher criticism of the* Pentateuch. n.l.: Charles Scribner's Sons, 1895 [cited 2019 Feb 28]. p. 83. Available from: https://faculty.gordon.edu/hu/bi/ted_hildebrandt/otesources/00-introduction/text/books/green-highercriticism/green-highercriticism.htm

157. Plato. *Timeaus.* Jowett B. (Trans.) n.d. [cited 2019 Feb 28]. Available from: http://classics.mit.edu/Plato/timaeus.1b.txt

158. Proclus. *On the theology of Plato.* Taylor T. (Trans.) 2010 [cited 2019 Feb 28]. Available from: https://archive.org/details/ProclusOnTheTheologyOfPlato-ElectronicEdition

159. Theodoret. *Ecclesiastical history.* London: Samuel Bagster & Sons 1843 [cited 2019 Feb 28]. Available from: https://archive.org/details/ecclesiasticalh05unkngoog

160. Athanasius. *De Synodis.* New Advent. 1882 [cited 2019 Feb 28]. Available from: http://www.newadvent.org/fathers/2817.htm

161. *Strong's Concordance.* G2936. Blue Letter Bible. 2019 [cited 2019 Feb 28]. Available from: https://www.blueletterBible.org/lang/lexicon/lexicon.cfm?t=kjv&strongs=g2936

162. *Strong's Concordance.* G4416. Blue Letter Bible. 2019 [cited 2019 Feb 28]. Available from: https://www.blueletterBible.org/lang/lexicon/lexicon.cfm?Strongs=G4416&t=KJV

163. *Strong's Concordance.* G4413. Blue Letter Bible. 2019 [cited 2019 Feb 28]. Available from: https://www.blueletterBible.org/lang/lexicon/lexicon.cfm?Strongs=G4413&t=KJV

164. *Strong's Concordance.* G5088. Blue Letter Bible. 2019 [cited 2019 Feb 28]. Available from: https://www.blueletterBible.org/lang/lexicon/lexicon.cfm?Strongs=G5088&t=KJV

165. *Strong's Concordance.* G1096. Blue Letter Bible. 2019 [cited 2019 Feb 28]. Available from: https://www.blueletterBible.org/lang/lexicon/lexicon.cfm?Strongs=G1096&t=KJV

166. Milton J. *Treatise on Christian doctrine.* Sumner CR. (Trans.) 1825 [cited 2019 Feb 28]. Available from: https://archive.org/details/treatiseonchrist00milt/page/n5

167. Drummond W. Memoir on the Antiquity of the Zodiacs of Esneh and Dendera, The Dodecatemorian of Pisces. *The Classical Journal.* London:A. Valpy, 1822 [cited 2019 Feb 28].

168. Wright T. *Worship of the generative powers.* 1865 [cited 2019 Feb 28]. Available from: https://www.sacred-texts.com/sex/wgp/index.htm

169. Tatum JB. The Signs and Constellations of the Zodiac. *Journal of the Royal Society of Canada.* (2010 June) [cited 2019 Feb 28];104(3): 103. Available from: http://adsabs.harvard.edu/full/2010JRASC.104..103T

170. Maspero G. *History of Egypt, Chaldœa, Syria, Babylonia, and Assyria, Vol. 1 (of 12).* McClure ML. (Trans.) Sayce AH. (ed.) 1903 [cited 2019 Feb 28]. Available from: http://www.gutenberg.org/files/19400/19400-h/19400-h.htm

171. *Book of the dead. Chapter 155.* 2003 [cited 2019 Feb 28]. Available from: https://www.ucl.ac.uk/museums-static/digitalegypt/literature/religious/bd155.html

172. Budge EAW. *The book of the dead: The papyrus of Ani.* Budge EAW. (Trans.) New York: G.P. Putnam, 1913 [cited 2019 Feb 28]. Available from: https://archive.org/details/papyrusofanirepr01budg

173. Budge EA. Wallis. *Osiris: the Egyptian religion of resurrection*. New Hyde Park, N.Y: University Books, 1961 [cited 2019 Mar 1]. Available from: https://archive.org/details/osirisegyptianre00budg

174. Maspero G. *History of Egypt, Chaldœa, Syria, Babylonia, and Assyria, Vol. 9 (of 12)*. McClure ML. (Trans.) Sayce AH. (ed.) 1903 [cited 2019 Mar 1]. Available from: https://www.gutenberg.org/files/17329/17329-h/17329-h.htm

175. Berkeley G. *Three dialogues between Hylas and Philonous*. Chicago: Open Court Pub. Co.,1906 [cited 2019 Mar 1]. Available from: https://archive.org/details/threedialoguesbe00berkiala/page/n6

176. *Problems with sense of smell in the elderly*. 2019 [cited 2019 Mar 1]. Available from: https://www.agingcare.com/articles/when-elderly-lose-sense-of-smell-133880.htm

177. Wickremaratchi MM, LlewelynJ G. Effects of ageing on touch. *Postgrad Med J*. 2006 May [cited 2019 Mar 1];82(967): 301-304. doi:10.1136/pgmj.2005.039651. Available from: https://www.ncbi.nlm.nih.gov/pmc/articles/PMC2563781/

178. Frankel VE. *Man's search for meaning*. n.d. [cited 2019 Mar 1]. Available from: https://archive.org/details/MansSearchForMeaningViktorE.Frankel

179. Picton JA. *The mystery of matter, and other essays*. London: Macmillan, 1878 [cited 2019 Mar 1]. Available from: https://archive.org/details/mysteryofmattero00pict/page/n6

180. MacDougall D. The Soul: Hypothesis Concerning Soul Substance Together with Experimental Evidence of the Existence of Such Substance. *American Medicine*. 2: 240-243. 1907 Apr.

181. Plato. *Meno*. Jowett B. (Trans.) n.d. [cited 2019 Mar 1]. Available from: http://classics.mit.edu/Plato/meno.html

182. Spencer H. *First Principles*. 1946 [cited 2019 Mar 1]. Available from: https://archive.org/details/firstprinciples035476mbp

183. Aristotle. *On the heavens* (Stocks JL, Trans.). n.d. [cited 2019 Mar 1]. Available from: http://classics.mit.edu/Aristotle/heavens.html

184. Einstein A. *Einstein revealed*. Nova. 1997 Sep 9 [cited 2019 Mar 1]. Available from: http://www.pbs.org/wgbh/nova/transcripts/2311eins.html

185. Sicinski A. *My conversation with Albert Einstein about creativity, intuition, and the power of curiosity*. 2018 [cited 2019 Mar 1]. Available from: https://blog.iqmatrix.com/albert-einstein

186. Knight K. *Mystery of the screaming mummy*. Daily Mail. 2008 Nov 10 [cited 2019 Mar 1]. Available from: https://www.dailymail.co.uk/sciencetech/article-1083945/Mystery-screaming-mummy.html

187. Maspero G. *History of Egypt, Chaldœa, Syria, Babylonia, and Assyria, Vol. 6 (of 12)*. McClure ML. (Trans.) Sayce AH (ed.). 1903 [cited 2019 Mar 1]. Available from: http://www.gutenberg.org/files/17326/17326-h/17326-h.htm

188. Hall SS. Journey to the Genetic Interior. *Scientific American.* 2012 Oct [cited 2019 Mar 1];307(4): 80-85. doi:10.1038/scientificamerican1012-80

189. Aristotle. *Politics.* Jowett B. (Trans.) 1997 Sep 9 [cited 2019 Feb 26]. Available from: http://classics.mit.edu/Aristotle/politics.html

190. Donnelly DE. and Morrison, P. J. Hereditary Gigantism-the biblical giant Goliath and his brothers. *Ulster Med J.* 2014 May [cited 2019 Feb 26];83(2): 86–88. Available from: https://www.ncbi.nlm.nih.gov/pmc/articles/PMC4113151/

191. Shaw N. Indiana University. *'Lost' Miller-Urey experiment created more of life's building blocks.* Science Daily. 2008 Oct 17 [cited 2019 Feb 26]. Available from: https://www.sciencedaily.com/releases/2008/10/081016141411.htm

192. NOAA. USGS. *How much water is in the ocean?.* 2018 Jun 25 [cited 2019 Feb 26]. Available from: https://oceanservice.noaa.gov/facts/oceanwater.html

193. Waliji M. *Monkeys and Walks.* 2006 Aug 12 [cited 2019 Feb 26]. Available from: http://www.math.uchicago.edu/~may/VIGRE/VIGRE2006/PAPERS/Waliji.pdf

194. Carus TL. *On the nature of things* (Watson JS, Trans.). [cited 2019 Feb 26]. Available from: https://archive.org/details/onnaturethingsd00carugoog/page/n5

195. Volney CF. *The ruins: or, A survey of the revolutions of empires.* London: J. Johnson, 1796 [cited 2019 Feb 26]. Available from: https://archive.org/details/ruinsorsurveyofr00voln

196. Smith A. *The wealth of nations.* New York: Collier, 1902 [cited 2019 Mar 7]. Available from: https://archive.org/details/wealthofnations00smituoft

197. O'Rahilly R, Müller, F. Neurulation in the normal human embryo. *Ciba Found Symp.* 1994 [cited 2019 Mar 13];181:70-82. Available from: https://www.ncbi.nlm.nih.gov/pubmed/8005032

198. Budge EFW. *Osiris and the Egyptian resurrection. Volume 1.* New York: GP Putnam and Sons, 1911 [cited 2019 Mar 24]. Available from: https://archive.org/details/osirisegyptianre00budg

199. Dupuis CF. The origin of all religious worship. New Orleans: N.P., 1872. [cited 2019 Mar 24]. Available from: https://archive.org/details/originallreligi00dupugoog

200. Martikainen P, and Valkonen T. Mortality after the death of a spouse: rates and causes of death in a large Finnish cohort. *Am J Public Health.* 1996 Aug [cited 2019 Mar 24]; 86(8 Pt 1): 1087-1093.

Appendix A

The Animate and the Man – Plotinus From-The Six Enneads[37]

Pleasure and distress, fear and courage, desire and aversion, where have these affections and experiences their seat?

Clearly, either in the Soul alone, or in the Soul as employing the body, or in some third entity deriving from both. And for this third entity, again, there are two possible modes: it might be either a blend or a distinct form due to the blending.

And what applies to the affections applies also to whatsoever acts, physical or mental, spring from them.

We have, therefore, to examine discursive reason and the ordinary mental action upon objects of sense, and enquire whether these have the one seat with the affections and experiences, or perhaps sometimes the one seat, sometimes another.

And we must consider also our acts of Intellection, their mode and their seat.

And this very examining principle, which investigates and decides in these matters, must be brought to light.

Firstly, what is the seat of sense perception? This is the obvious beginning since the affections and experiences either are sensations of some kind or at least never occur apart from sensation.

This first enquiry obliges us to consider at the outset the nature of the soul that is whether a distinction is to be made between soul and essential soul [between an individual soul and the soul kind in itself].

If such a distinction holds, then the soul [in man] is some sort of a composite and at once we may agree that it is a recipient and if only reason allows that all the affections and experiences really have their seat in the soul, and with the affections every state and mood, good and bad alike.

But if soul [in man] and essential soul are one and the same, then the soul will be an ideal form unreceptive of all those activities which it imparts to another kind but possessing within itself that native act of its own which reason manifests.

If this be so, then indeed, we may think of the soul as an immortal if the immortal, the imperishable, must be impassive, giving out something of itself but itself taking nothing from without except for what it receives from the existents prior to itself from which existents, in that they are the nobler, it cannot be sundered.

Now what could bring fear to a nature thus unreceptive of all the outer? Fear demands feeling. Nor is there place for courage: courage implies the presence of danger. And such desires as are satisfied by the filling or voiding of the body, must be proper to something very different from the soul, to that only which admits of replenishment and voidance.

And how could the Soul lend itself to any admixture? An essential is not mixed. Or of the intrusion of anything alien? If it did, it would be seeking the destruction of its own nature. Pain must be equally far from it. And grief, how or for what could it grieve? Whatever possesses existence is supremely free, dwelling, unchangeable, within its own peculiar nature. And can any increase bring joy, where nothing, not even anything good, can accrue? What such an existent is, it is unchangeably.

Thus, assuredly sense perception, discursive reasoning; and all our ordinary mentation are foreign to the soul: for sensation is a receiving whether of an ideal form or of an impassive body and reasoning and all ordinary mental action deal with sensation.

The question still remains to be examined in the matter of the intellections whether these are to be assigned to the soul and as to pure pleasure, whether this belongs to the soul in its solitary state.

We may treat of the soul as in the body whether it be set above it or actually within it since the association of the two constitutes the one thing called the living organism, the animate.

Now from this relation, from the soul using the body as an instrument, it does not follow that the soul must share the body's experiences: a man does not himself feel all the experiences of the tools with which he is working.

It may be objected that the soul must however, have sense perception since its use of its instrument must acquaint it with the external conditions, and such knowledge comes by way of sense. Thus, it will be argued, the eyes are the instrument of seeing, and seeing may bring distress to the soul: hence the soul may feel sorrow and pain and every other affection that belongs to the body; and from this again will spring desire, the soul seeking the mending of its instrument.

But, we ask, how possibly can these affections pass from body to soul? Body may communicate qualities or conditions to another body: but body to soul? Something happens to A; does that make it happen to B? As long as we have agent and instrument, there are two distinct entities; if the soul uses the body it is separate from it.

But apart from the philosophical separation how does soul stand to body?

Clearly there is a combination. And for this several modes are possible. There might be a complete coalescence: soul might be interwoven through the body: or it might be an ideal form detached or an ideal form in governing contact like a pilot: or there might be part of the soul detached and another part in contact, the disjoined part being the agent or user, the conjoined part ranking with the instrument or thing used.

In this last case, it will be the double task of philosophy to direct this lower soul towards the higher, the agent, and except in so far as the conjunction is absolutely necessary, to sever the agent from the instrument, the body, so that it need not forever have its act upon or through this inferior.

Let us consider, then, the hypothesis of a coalescence.

Now if there is a coalescence, the lower is ennobled, the nobler degraded; the body is raised in the scale of being as made participant in life; the soul, as associated with death and unreason, is brought lower. How can a lessening of the life quality produce an increase such as sense perception?

No: the body has acquired life, it is the body that will acquire, with life, sensation and the affections coming by sensation. Desire, then, will belong to the body, as the objects of desire are to be enjoyed by the body. And fear, too, will belong to the body alone; for it is the body's doom to fail of its joys and to perish.

Then again we should have to examine how such a coalescence could be conceived: we might find it impossible: perhaps all this is like announcing the coalescence of things utterly incongruous in kind, let us say of a line and whiteness.

Next for the suggestion that the soul is interwoven through the body: such a relation would not give woof and warp community of sensation: the interwoven element might very well suffer no change: the permeating soul might remain entirely untouched by what affects the body as light goes always free of all it floods and all the more so, since, precisely, we are asked to consider it as diffused throughout the entire frame.

Under such an interweaving, then, the soul would not be subjected to the body's affections and experiences: it would be present rather as ideal form in matter.

Let us then suppose soul to be in body as ideal form in matter. Now if the first possibility the soul is an essence, a self-existent, it can be present only as separable form and will therefore all the more decidedly be the using principle [and therefore unaffected].

Suppose next, the soul to be present like axe form on iron: here, no doubt, the form is all important but it is still the axe, the complement of iron and form, that effects whatever is effected by the iron thus modified: on this analogy, therefore, we are even more strictly compelled to assign all the experiences of the combination to the body: their natural seat is the material member, the instrument, the potential recipient of life.

Compare the passage where we read that "it is absurd to suppose that the Soul weaves"; equally absurd to think of it as desiring, grieving.

All this is rather in the province of something which we may call the animate.

Now this animate might be merely the body as having life: it might be the couplement of soul and body: it might be a third and different entity formed from both.

The soul in turn apart from the nature of the animate must be either impassive, merely causing sense perception in its yokefellow, or sympathetic; and, if sympathetic, it may have identical experiences with its fellow or merely correspondent experiences: desire for example in the animate may be something quite distinct from the accompanying movement or state in the desiring faculty.

The body, the live body as we know it, we will consider later.

Let us take first the couplement of body and soul. How could suffering, for example, be seated in this couplement?

It may be suggested that some unwelcome state of the body produces a distress which reaches to a sensitive faculty which in turn merges into soul. But this account still leaves the origin of the sensation unexplained.

Another suggestion might be that all is due to an opinion or judgement: some evil seems to have befallen the man or his belongings and this conviction sets up a state of trouble in the body and in the entire animate. But this account leaves still a question as to the source and seat of the judgement: does it belong to the soul or to the couplement? Besides, the judgement that evil is present does not involve the feeling of grief: the judgement might very well arise and the grief by no means follow: one may think oneself slighted and yet not be angry; and the appetite is not necessarily excited by the thought of a pleasure. We are, thus, no nearer than before to any warrant for assigning these affections to the couplement.

Is it any explanation to say that desire is vested in a faculty of desire and anger in the irascible faculty and, collectively, that all tendency is seated in the appetitive faculty? Such a statement of the facts does not help towards making the affections common to the couplement; they might still be seated either in the soul alone or in the body alone. On the one hand if the appetite is to be stirred, as in the carnal passion, there must be a heating of the blood and the bile, a well-defined state of the body; on the other hand, the impulse towards the good cannot be a joint affection, but, like certain others too, it would belong necessarily to the soul alone.

Reason, then, does not permit us to assign all the affections to the couplement.

In the case of carnal desire, it will certainly be the man that desires, and yet, on the other hand, there must be desire in the desiring faculty as well. How can this be? Are we to suppose that, when the man originates the desire, the desiring faculty moves to the order? How could

the man have come to desire at all unless through a prior activity in the
desiring faculty? Then it is the desiring faculty that takes the lead? Yet
how, unless the body be first in the appropriate condition?

It may seem reasonable to lay down as a law that when any powers
are contained by a recipient, every action or state expressive of them
must be the action or state of that recipient, they themselves remaining
unaffected as merely furnishing efficiency.

But if this were so, then, since the animate is the recipient of the
causing principle [i.e., the soul] which brings life to the couplement, this
cause must itself remain unaffected, all the experiences and expressive
activities of the life being vested in the recipient, the animate.

But this would mean that life itself belongs not to the soul but to the
couplement; or at least the life of the couplement would not be the life of
the soul; sense perception would belong not to the sensitive faculty but to
the container of the faculty.

But if sensation is a movement traversing the body and culminating
in soul, how the soul lack sensation? The very presence of the sensitive
faculty must assure sensation to the soul.

Once again, where is sense perception seated?

In the couplement.

Yet how can the couplement have sensation independently of action
in the sensitive faculty, the soul left out of count and the soul faculty?

The truth lies in the consideration that the couplement subsists by
virtue of the soul's presence.

This, however, is not to say that the soul gives itself as it is in itself
to form either the couplement or the body.

No; from the organized body and something else, let us say a light,
which the soul gives forth from itself, it forms a distinct principle, the
animate; and in this principle are vested sense perception and all the
other experiences found to belong to the animate.

But the "we"? How have we sense perception?

By the fact that we are not separate from the animate so constituted,
even though certainly other and nobler elements go to make up the
entire many-sided nature of man.

The faculty of perception in the soul cannot act by the immediate
grasping of sensible objects, but only by the discerning of impressions
printed upon the animate by sensation: these impressions are already
intelligibles while the outer sensation is a mere phantom of the other [of
that in the soul] which is nearer to authentic existence as being an
impassive reading of ideal forms.

And by means of these ideal forms, by which the soul wields single
lordship over the animate, we have discursive reasoning, sense
knowledge and intellection. From this moment, we have peculiarly the
"we": before this there was only the "ours"; but at this stage stands the
"we" [the authentic human principle] loftily presiding over the animate.

There is no reason why the entire compound entity should not be described as the animate, or living being, mingled in a lower phase, but above that point the beginning of the veritable man, distinct from all that is kin to the lion, all that is of the order of the multiple brute. And since the man, so understood, is essentially the associate of the reasoning soul, in our reasoning it is this "we" that reasons, in that the use and act of reason is a characteristic act of the soul.

And towards the intellectual principle what is our relation? By this I mean, not that faculty in the soul which is one of the emanations from the intellectual principle, but the intellectual principle itself [divine mind].

This also we possess as the summit of our being. And we have it either as common to all or as our own immediate possession: or again we may possess it in both degrees, that is in common, since it is indivisible one, everywhere and always its entire self and severally in that each personality possesses it entire in the first soul [i.e. in the intellectual as distinguished from the lower phase of the soul].

Hence we possess the ideal forms also after two modes: in the soul, as it were unrolled and separate; in the intellectual principle, concentrated, one.

And how do we possess the divinity?

In that the divinity is contained in the intellectual principle and authentic existence; and we come third in order after these two, for the "we" is constituted by a union of the supreme, the undivided soul we read and that soul which is divided among [living] bodies. For, note, we inevitably think of the soul, though one undivided in the all, as being present to bodies in division: in so far as any bodies are animates, the soul has given itself to each of the separate material masses; or rather it appears to be present in the bodies by the fact that it shines into them: it makes them living beings not by merging into body but by giving forth, without any change in itself, images or likenesses of itself like one face caught by many mirrors.

The first of these images is sense perception seated in the couplement; and from this downwards all the successive images are to be recognized as phases of the soul in lessening succession from one another, until the series ends in the faculties of generation and growth and of all production of offspring efficient in its turn, in contradistinction to the engendering soul which [has no direct action within matter but] produces by mere inclination towards what it fashions.

That soul, then, in us, will in its nature stand apart from all that can cause any of the evils which man does or suffers; for all such evil, as we have seen, belongs only to the animate, the couplement.

But there is a difficulty in understanding how the soul can go guiltless if our mentation and reasoning are vested in it: for all this lower kind of knowledge is delusion and is the cause of much of what is evil.

When we have done evil it is because we have been worsted by our baser side for a man is many by desire or rage or some evil image: the misnamed reasoning that takes up with the false, in reality fancy, has not stayed for the judgement of the reasoning principle: we have acted at the call of the less worthy, just as in matters of the sense-sphere we sometimes see falsely because we credit only the lower perception, that of the couplement, without applying the tests of the reasoning faculty.

The intellectual principle has held aloof from the act and so is guiltless; or, as we may state it, all depends on whether we ourselves have or have not put ourselves in touch with the intellectual realm either in the intellectual principle or within ourselves; for it is possible at once to possess and not to use.

Thus we have marked off what belongs to the couplement from what stands by itself: the one group has the character of body and never exists apart from body, while all that has no need of body for its manifestation belongs peculiarly to soul: and the understanding, as passing judgement upon sense impressions, is at the point of the vision of ideal forms, seeing them as it were with an answering sensation (i.e., with consciousness) this last is at any rate true of the understanding in the veritable soul. For understanding, the true, is the act of the intellections: in many of its manifestations it is the assimilation and reconciliation of the outer to the inner.

Thus, in spite of all, the soul is at peace as to itself and within itself: all the changes and all the turmoil we experience are the issue of what is subjoined to the soul, and are, as have said, the states and experiences of this elusive "couplement."

It will be objected, that if the soul constitutes the we [the personality] and we are subject to these states then the soul must be subject to them, and similarly that what we do must be done by the soul.

But it has been observed that the couplement, too especially before our emancipation is a member of this total we, and in fact what the body experiences we say we experience. This then covers two distinct notions; sometimes it includes the brute-part, sometimes it transcends the brute. The body is brute touched to life; the true man is the other, going pure of the body, natively endowed with the virtues which belong to the intellectual activity, virtues whose seat is the separate soul, the soul which even in its dwelling here may be kept apart. [This soul constitutes the human being] for when it has wholly withdrawn, that other soul which is a radiation [or emanation] from it withdraws also, drawn after it.

Those virtues, on the other hand, which spring not from contemplative wisdom but from custom or practical discipline belong to the couplement: to the couplement, too, belong the vices; they are its repugnances, desires, sympathies.

And friendship?

This emotion belongs sometimes to the lower part, sometimes to the interior man.

In childhood, the main activity is in the couplement and there is but little irradiation from the higher principles of our being: but when these higher principles act but feebly or rarely upon us their action is directed towards the supreme; they work upon us only when they stand at the midpoint.

But does not this include that phase of our being which stands above the midpoint?

It does, but on condition that we lay hold of it: our entire nature is not ours at all times but only as we direct the midpoint upwards or downwards, or lead some particular phase of our nature from potentiality or native character into act.

And the animals, in what way or degree do they possess the animate?

If there be in them, as the opinion goes, human souls that have sinned, then the animating principle in its separable phase does not enter directly into the brute; it is there but not there to them; they are aware only of the image of the soul [only of the lower soul] and of that only by being aware of the body organized and determined by that image.

If there be no human soul in them, the animate is constituted for them by a radiation from the "All-soul".

But if soul is sinless, how come the expiations? Here surely is a contradiction; on the one side the Soul is above all guilt; on the other, we hear of its sin, its purification, its expiation; it is doomed to the lower world, it passes from body to body.

We may take either view at will: they are easily reconciled.

When we tell of the sinless soul, we make soul and essential soul one and the same: it is the simple unbroken unity.

By the soul subject to sin we indicate a groupment, we include that other, that phase of the soul which knows all the states and passions: the soul in this sense is compound, all-inclusive: it falls under the conditions of the entire living experience: this compound it is that sins; it is this, and not the other, that pays penalty.

It is in this sense that we read of the soul: "We saw it as those others saw the sea-god, Glaukos." "And," reading on, "if we mean to discern the nature of the soul we must strip it free of all that has gathered about it, must see into the philosophy of it, examine with what existences it has touch and by kinship to what existences it is what it is."

Thus, the life is one thing, the act is another and the expiator yet another. The retreat and sundering, then, must be not from this body only, but from every alien accruement. Such accruement takes place at birth; or rather birth is the coming into being of that other [lower] phase of the soul. For the meaning of birth has been indicated elsewhere; it is brought about by a descent of the soul, something being given off by the soul other than that actually coming down in the declension.

Then the soul has let this image fall? And this declension is it not certainly sin?

If the declension is no more than the illuminating of an object beneath, it constitutes no sin: the shadow is to be attributed not to the luminary but to the object illuminated; if the object were not there, the light could cause no shadow.

And the soul is said to go down, to decline, only in that the object it illuminates lives by its life. And it lets the image fall only if there be nothing near to take it up; and it lets it fall, not as a thing cut off, but as a thing that ceases to be: the image has no further being when the whole soul is looking toward the supreme.

The poet, too, in the story of Hercules, seems to give this image separate existence; he puts the shade of Hercules in the lower world and Hercules himself among the gods: treating the hero as existing in the two realms at once, he gives us a twofold Hercules.

It is not difficult to explain this distinction. Hercules was a hero of practical virtue. By his noble serviceableness he was worthy to be a God. On the other hand, his merit was action and not the Contemplation which would place him unreservedly in the higher realm. Therefore, while he has place above, something of him remains below.

And the principle that reasons out these matters? Is it we or the soul?

We, but by the soul.

But how "by the soul"? Does this mean that the soul reasons by possession [by contact with the matters of enquiry]?

No; by the fact of being soul. Its act subsists without movement; or any movement that can be ascribed to it must be utterly distinct from all corporal movement and be simply the soul's own life.

And intellection in us is twofold: since the soul is intellective, and intellection is the highest phase of life, we have intellection both by the characteristic act of our soul and by the act of the intellectual principle upon us for this intellectual principle is part of us no less than the soul, and towards it we are ever rising.

Appendix B

The Oversoul - Ralph Waldo Emerson
From-Essays, First Series[3]

"But souls that of his own good life partake,
He loves as his own self; dear as his eye
They are to Him: He'll never them forsake:
When they shall die, then God himself shall die:
They live, they live in blest eternity."
-Henry More-

Space is ample, east and west,
But two cannot go abreast,
Cannot travel in it two:
Yonder masterful cuckoo
Crowds every egg out of the nest,
Quick or dead, except its own;
A spell is laid on sod and stone,
Night and day 've been tampered with,
Every quality and pith
Surcharged and sultry with a power
That works its will on age and hour.

There is a difference between one and another hour of life, in their authority and subsequent effect. Our faith comes in moments; our vice is habitual. Yet there is a depth in those brief moments which constrains us to ascribe more reality to them than to all other experiences. For this reason, the argument which is always forthcoming to silence those who conceive extraordinary hopes of man, namely, the appeal to experience, is forever invalid and vain. We give up the past to the objector, and yet we hope. He must explain this hope. We grant that human life is mean; but how did we find out that it was mean? What is the ground of this uneasiness of ours; of this old discontent? What is the universal sense of want and ignorance, but the fine innuendo by which the soul makes its enormous claim? Why do men feel that the natural history of man has never been written, but he is always leaving behind what you have said of him, and it becomes old, and books of metaphysics worthless? The philosophy of six thousand years has not searched the chambers and magazines of the soul. In its experiments there has always remained, in the last analysis, a residuum it could not resolve. Man is a stream whose source is hidden. Our being is descending into us from we know not whence. The most exact calculator has no prescience that somewhat incalculable may not balk the very next moment. I am constrained every moment to acknowledge a higher origin for events than the will I call mine.

As with events, so is it with thoughts. When I watch that flowing river, which, out of regions I see not, pours for a season its streams into me, I see that I am a pensioner; not a cause, but a surprised spectator of this ethereal water; that I desire and look up, and put myself in the attitude of reception, but from some alien energy the visions come.

The Supreme Critic on the errors of the past and the present, and the only prophet of that which must be, is that great nature in which we rest, as the Earth lies in the soft arms of the atmosphere; that unity, that Over-soul, within which every man's particular being is contained and made one with all other; that common heart, of which all sincere conversation is the worship, to which all right action is submission; that overpowering reality which confutes our tricks and talents, and constrains everyone to pass for what he is, and to speak from his character, and not from his tongue, and which evermore tends to pass into our thought and hand, and become wisdom, and virtue, and power, and beauty. We live in succession, in division, in parts, in particles. Meantime within man is the soul of the whole; the wise silence; the universal beauty, to which every part and particle is equally related; the eternal ONE. And this deep power in which we exist, and whose beatitude is all accessible to us, is not only self-sufficing and perfect in every hour, but the act of seeing and the thing seen, the seer and the spectacle, the subject and the object, are one. We see the world piece by piece, as the sun, the moon, the animal, the tree; but the whole, of which these are the shining parts, is the soul. Only by the vision of that wisdom can the horoscope of the ages be read, and by falling back on our better thoughts, by yielding to the spirit of prophecy which is innate in every man, we can know what it saith. Every man's words, who speaks from that life, must sound vain to those who do not dwell in the same thought on their own part. I dare not speak for it. My words do not carry its august sense; they fall short and cold. Only itself can inspire whom it will, and behold! their speech shall be lyrical, and sweet, and universal as the rising of the wind. Yet I desire, even by profane words, if I may not use sacred, to indicate the heaven of this deity, and to report what hints I have collected of the transcendent simplicity and energy of the Highest Law.

If we consider what happens in conversation, in reveries, in remorse, in times of passion, in surprises, in the instructions of dreams, wherein often we see ourselves in masquerade, — the droll disguises only magnifying and enhancing a real element, and forcing it on our distinct notice, — we shall catch many hints that will broaden and lighten into knowledge of the secret of nature. All goes to show that the soul in man is not an organ, but animates and exercises all the organs; is not a function, like the power of memory, of calculation, of comparison, but uses these as hands and feet; is not a faculty, but a light; is not the intellect or the will, but the master of the intellect and the will; is the background of our being, in which they lie, — an immensity not possessed and that cannot be possessed. From within or from behind, a light shines through us upon things, and makes us aware that we are nothing, but the light is all. A man is the facade of a temple wherein all wisdom and all good abide. What we commonly call man, the eating, drinking, planting, counting man, does not, as we know him, represent himself, but misrepresents himself. Him we do not respect, but the soul, whose organ he is, would he let it appear through his action, would make our knees bend. When it breathes through his intellect, it is genius; when it breathes through his will, it is virtue; when it flows through his affection, it is love. And the blindness of the intellect begins, when it would be something of itself. The weakness of the will begins, when the individual would be something of himself. All reform aims, in some one particular, to let the soul have its way through us; in other words, to engage us to obey.

Of this pure nature every man is at some time sensible. Language cannot paint it with his colors. It is too subtle. It is undefinable, unmeasurable, but we know that it pervades and contains us. We know that all spiritual being is in man. A wise old proverb says, "God comes to see us without bell"; that is, as there is no screen or ceiling between our heads and the infinite heavens, so is there no bar or wall in the soul where man, the effect, ceases, and God, the cause, begins. The walls are taken away. We lie open on one side to the deeps of spiritual nature, to the attributes of God. Justice we see and know, Love, Freedom, Power. These natures no man ever got above, but they tower over us, and most in the moment when our interests tempt us to wound them.

The sovereignty of this nature whereof we speak is made known by its independency of those limitations which circumscribe us on every hand. The soul circumscribes all things. As I have said, it contradicts all experience. In like manner, it abolishes time and space. The influence of the senses has, in most men, overpowered the mind to that degree, that the walls of time and space have come to look real and insurmountable; and to speak with levity of these limits is, in the world, the sign of insanity. Yet time and space are but inverse measures of the force of the soul. The spirit sports with time,

> "Can crowd eternity into an hour,
> Or stretch an hour to eternity."

We are often made to feel that there is another youth and age than that which is measured from the year of our natural birth. Some thoughts always find us young, and keep us so. Such a thought is the love of the universal and eternal beauty. Every man parts from that contemplation with the feeling that it rather belongs to ages than to mortal life. The least activity of the intellectual powers redeems us in a degree from the conditions of time. In sickness, in languor, give us a strain of poetry, or a profound sentence, and we are refreshed; or produce a volume of Plato, or Shakespeare, or remind us of their names, and instantly we come into a feeling of longevity. See how the deep, divine thought reduces centuries, and millenniums, and makes itself present through all ages. Is the teaching of Christ less effective now than it was when first his mouth was opened? The emphasis of facts and persons in my thought has nothing to do with time. And so, always, the soul's scale is one; the scale of the senses and the understanding is another. Before the revelations of the soul, Time, Space, and Nature shrink away. In common speech, we refer all things to time, as we habitually refer the immensely sundered stars to one concave sphere. And so we say that the Judgment is distant or near, that the Millennium approaches, that a day of certain political, moral, social reforms is at hand, and the like, when we mean, that, in the nature of things, one of the facts we contemplate is external and fugitive, and the other is permanent and connate with the soul. The things we now esteem fixed shall, one by one, detach themselves, like ripe fruit, from our experience, and fall. The wind shall blow them none knows whither. The landscape, the figures, Boston, London, are facts as fugitive as any institution past, or any whiff of mist or smoke, and so is society, and so is the world. The soul looketh steadily forwards, creating a world before her, leaving worlds behind her. She has no dates, nor rites, nor persons, nor specialties, nor men. The soul knows only the soul; the web of events is the flowing robe in which she is clothed.

After its own law and not by arithmetic is the rate of its progress to be computed. The soul's advances are not made by gradation, such as can be represented by motion in a straight line; but rather by ascension of state, such as can be represented by metamorphosis, — from the egg to the worm, from the worm to the fly. The growths of genius are of a certain total character, that does not advance the elect individual first over John, then Adam, then Richard, and give to each the pain of discovered inferiority, but by every throe of growth the man expands there where he works, passing, at each pulsation, classes, populations, of men. With each divine impulse, the mind rends the thin rinds of the visible and finite, and comes out into eternity, and inspires and expires its air. It converses with truths that have always been spoken in the world, and becomes conscious of a closer sympathy with Zeno and Arrian, than with persons in the house.

This is the law of moral and of mental gain. The simple rise as by specific levity, not into a particular virtue, but into the region of all the virtues. They are in the spirit which contains them all. The soul requires purity, but purity is not it; requires justice, but justice is not that; requires beneficence, but is somewhat better; so that there is a kind of descent and accommodation felt when we leave speaking of moral nature, to urge a virtue which it enjoins. To the wellborn child, all the virtues are natural, and not painfully acquired. Speak to his heart, and the man becomes suddenly virtuous.

Within the same sentiment is the germ of intellectual growth, which obeys the same law. Those who are capable of humility, of justice, of love, of aspiration, stand already on a platform that commands the sciences and arts, speech and poetry, action and grace. For whoso dwells in this moral beatitude already anticipates those special powers which men prize so highly. The lover has no talent, no skill, which passes for quite nothing with his enamored maiden, however little she may possess of related faculty; and the heart which abandons itself to the supreme mind finds itself related to all its works, and will travel a royal road to particular knowledges and powers. In ascending to this primary and aboriginal sentiment, we have come from our remote station on the circumference instantaneously to the center of the world, where, as in the closet of God, we see causes, and anticipate the universe, which is but a slow effect.

One mode of the divine teaching is the incarnation of the spirit in a form, — in forms, like my own. I live in society; with persons who answer to thoughts in my own mind, or express a certain obedience to the great instincts to which I live. I see its presence to them. I am certified of a common nature; and these other souls, these separated selves, draw me as nothing else can. They stir in me the new emotions we call passion; of love, hatred, fear, admiration, pity; thence comes conversation, competition, persuasion, cities, and war. Persons are supplementary to the primary teaching of the soul. In youth, we are mad for persons. Childhood and youth see all the world in them. But the larger experience of man discovers the identical nature appearing through them all. Persons themselves acquaint us with the impersonal. In all conversation between two persons, tacit reference is made, as to a third party, to a common nature. That third party or common nature is not social; it is impersonal; is God. And so, in groups where debate is earnest, and especially on high questions, the company become aware that the thought rises to an equal level in all bosoms, that all have a spiritual property in what was said, as well as the sayer. They all become wiser than they were. It arches over them like a temple, this unity of thought, in which every heart beats with nobler sense of power and duty, and thinks and acts with unusual solemnity. All are conscious of attaining to a higher self-possession. It shines for all. There is a certain wisdom of humanity which is common to the greatest men with the lowest, and which our ordinary education often labors to silence and obstruct. The mind is one, and the best minds, who love truth for its own sake, think much less of property in truth. They accept it thankfully everywhere, and do not label or stamp it with any man's name, for it is theirs long beforehand, and from eternity. The learned and the studious of thought have no monopoly of wisdom. Their violence of direction in some degree disqualifies them to think truly. We owe many valuable observations to people who are not very acute or profound, and who say the thing without effort, which we want and have long been hunting in vain. The action of the soul is oftener in that which is felt and left unsaid, than in that which is said in any conversation. It broods over every society, and they unconsciously seek for it in each other. We know better than we do. We do not yet possess ourselves, and we know at the same time that we are much more. I feel the same truth how often in my trivial conversation with my neighbors, that somewhat higher in each of us overlooks this byplay, and Jove nods to Jove from behind each of us.

Men descend to meet. In their habitual and mean service to the world, for which they forsake their native nobleness, they resemble those arabian sheiks, who dwell in mean houses, and affect an external poverty, to escape the rapacity of the Pacha, and reserve all their display of wealth for their interior and guarded retirements.

As it is present in all persons, so it is in every period of life. It is adult already in the infant man. In my dealing with my child, my Latin and Greek, my accomplishments and my money stead me nothing; but as much soul as I have avails. If I am willful, he sets his will against mine, one for one, and leaves me, if I please, the degradation of beating him by my superiority of strength. But if I renounce my will, and act for the soul, setting that up as umpire between us two, out of his young eyes looks the same soul; he reveres and loves with me.

The soul is the perceiver and revealer of truth. We know truth when we see it, let skeptic and scoffer say what they choose. Foolish people ask you, when you have spoken what they do not wish to hear, 'How do you know it is truth, and not an error of your own?' We know truth when we see it, from opinion, as we know when we are awake that we are awake. It was a grand sentence of Emanuel Swedenborg, which would alone indicate the greatness of that man's perception, — "It is no proof of a man's understanding to be able to confirm whatever he pleases; but to be able to discern that what is true is true, and that what is false is false, this is the mark and character of intelligence." In the book I read, the good thought returns to me, as every truth will, the image of the whole soul. To the bad thought which I find in it, the same soul becomes a discerning, separating sword, and lops it away. We are wiser than we know. If we will not interfere with our thought, but will act entirely, or see how the thing stands in God, we know the particular thing, and everything, and every man. For the Maker of all things and all persons stands behind us, and casts his dread omniscience through us over things.

But beyond this recognition of its own in particular passages of the individual's experience, it also reveals truth. And here we should seek to reinforce ourselves by its very presence, and to speak with a worthier, loftier strain of that advent. For the soul's communication of truth is the highest event in nature, since it then does not give somewhat from itself, but it gives itself, or passes into and becomes that man whom it enlightens; or, in proportion to that truth he receives, it takes him to itself.

We distinguish the announcements of the soul, its manifestations of its own nature, by the term Revelation. These are always attended by the emotion of the sublime. For this communication is an influx of the Divine mind into our mind. It is an ebb of the individual rivulet before the flowing surges of the sea of life. Every distinct apprehension of this central commandment agitates men with awe and delight. A thrill passes through all men at the reception of new truth, or at the performance of a great action, which comes out of the heart of nature. In these communications, the power to see is not separated from the will to do, but the insight proceeds from obedience, and the obedience proceeds from a joyful perception. Every moment when the individual feels himself invaded by it is memorable. By the necessity of our constitution, a certain enthusiasm attends the individual's consciousness of that divine presence. The character and duration of this enthusiasm varies with the state of the individual, from an ecstasy and trance and prophetic inspiration, — which is its rarer appearance, — to the faintest glow of virtuous emotion, in which form it warms, like our household fires, all the families and associations of men, and makes society possible. A certain tendency to insanity has always attended the opening of the religious sense in men, as if they had been "blasted with excess of light." The trances of Socrates, the "union" of Plotinus, the vision of Porphyry, the conversion of Paul, the aurora of Behmen, the convulsions of George Fox and his Quakers, the illumination of Swedenborg, are of this kind. What was in the case of these remarkable persons a ravishment has, in innumerable instances in common life, been exhibited in less striking manner. Everywhere the history of religion betrays a tendency to enthusiasm. The rapture of the Moravian and Quietist; the opening of the internal sense of the Word, in the language of the New Jerusalem Church; the revival of the Calvinistic churches; the experiences of the Methodists, are varying forms of that shudder of awe and delight with which the individual soul always mingles with the universal soul.

The nature of these revelations is the same; they are perceptions of the absolute law. They are solutions of the soul's own questions. They do not answer the questions which the understanding asks. The soul answers never by words, but by the thing itself that is inquired after.

Revelation is the disclosure of the soul. The popular notion of a revelation is, that it is a telling of fortunes. In past oracles of the soul, the understanding seeks to find answers to sensual questions, and undertakes to tell from God how long men shall exist, what their hands shall do, and who shall be their company, adding names, and dates, and places. But we must pick no locks. We must check this low curiosity. An answer in words is delusive; it is really no answer to the questions you ask. Do not require a description of the countries towards which you sail. The description does not describe them to you, and tomorrow you arrive there, and know them by inhabiting them. Men ask concerning the immortality of the soul, the employments of heaven, the state of the sinner, and so forth. They even dream that Jesus has left replies to precisely these interrogatories. Never a moment did that sublime spirit speak in their patois. To truth, justice, love, the attributes of the soul, the idea of immutableness is essentially associated. Jesus, living in these moral sentiments, heedless of sensual fortunes, heeding only the manifestations of these, never made the separation of the idea of duration from the essence of these attributes, nor uttered a syllable concerning the duration of the soul. It was left to his disciples to sever duration from the moral elements, and to teach the immortality of the soul as a doctrine, and maintain it by evidences. The moment the doctrine of the immortality is separately taught, man is already fallen. In the flowing of love, in the adoration of humility, there is no question of continuance. No inspired man ever asks this question, or condescends to these evidences. For the soul is true to itself, and the man in whom it is shed abroad cannot wander from the present, which is infinite, to a future which would be finite.

These questions which we lust to ask about the future are a confession of sin. God has no answer for them. No answer in words can reply to a question of things. It is not in an arbitrary "decree of God," but in the nature of man, that a veil shuts down on the facts of tomorrow; for the soul will not have us read any other cipher than that of cause and effect. By this veil, which curtains events, it instructs the children of men to live in today. The only mode of obtaining an answer to these questions of the senses is to forego all low curiosity, and, accepting the tide of being which floats us into the secret of nature, work and live, work and live, and all unawares the advancing soul has built and forged for itself a new condition, and the question and the answer are one.

By the same fire, vital, consecrating, celestial, which burns until it shall dissolve all things into the waves and surges of an ocean of light, we see and know each other, and what spirit each is of. Who can tell the grounds of his knowledge of the character of the several individuals in his circle of friends? No man. Yet their acts and words do not disappoint him. In that man, though he knew no ill of him, he put no trust. In that other, though they had seldom met, authentic signs had yet passed, to signify that he might be trusted as one who had an interest in his own character. We know each other very well, — which of us has been just to himself, and whether that which we teach or behold is only an aspiration, or is our honest effort also.

We are all discerners of spirits. That diagnosis lies aloft in our life or unconscious power. The intercourse of society, — its trade, its religion, its friendships, its quarrels, — is one wide, judicial investigation of character. In full court, or in small committee, or confronted face to face, accuser and accused, men offer themselves to be judged. Against their will they exhibit those decisive trifles by which character is read. But who judges? And what? Not our understanding. We do not read them by learning or craft. No; the wisdom of the wise man consists herein, that he does not judge them; he lets them judge themselves, and merely reads and records their own verdict.

By virtue of this inevitable nature, private will is overpowered, and, maugre our efforts or our imperfections, your genius will speak from you, and mine from me. That which we are, we shall teach, not voluntarily, but involuntarily. Thoughts come into our minds by avenues which we never left open, and thoughts go out of our minds through avenues which we never voluntarily opened. Character teaches over our head. The infallible index of true progress is found in the tone the man takes. Neither his age, nor his breeding, nor company, nor books, nor actions, nor talents, nor all together, can hinder him from being deferential to a higher spirit than his own. If he have not found his home in God, his manners, his forms of speech, the turn of his sentences, the build, shall I say, of all his opinions, will involuntarily confess it, let him brave it out how he will. If he have found his center, the Deity will shine through him, through all the disguises of ignorance, of ungenial temperament, of unfavorable circumstance. The tone of seeking is one, and the tone of having is another.

The great distinction between teachers sacred or literary, — between poets like Herbert, and poets like Pope, — between philosophers like Spinoza, Kant, and Coleridge, and philosophers like Locke, Paley, Mackintosh, and Stewart, — between men of the world, who are reckoned accomplished talkers, and here and there a fervent mystic, prophesying, half insane under the infinitude of his thought, — is, that one class speak from within, or from experience, as parties and possessors of the fact; and the other class, from without, as spectators merely, or perhaps as acquainted with the fact on the evidence of third persons. It is of no use to preach to me from without. I can do that too easily myself. Jesus speaks always from within, and in a degree that transcends all others. In that is the miracle. I believe beforehand that it ought so to be. All men stand continually in the expectation of the appearance of such a teacher. But if a man do not speak from within the veil, where the word is one with that it tells of, let him lowly confess it.

The same Omniscience flows into the intellect, and makes what we call genius. Much of the wisdom of the world is not wisdom, and the most illuminated class of men are no doubt superior to literary fame, and are not writers. Among the multitude of scholars and authors, we feel no hallowing presence; we are sensible of a knack and skill rather than of inspiration; they have a light, and know not whence it comes, and call it their own; their talent is some exaggerated faculty, some overgrown member, so that their strength is a disease. In these instances, the intellectual gifts do not make the impression of virtue, but almost of vice; and we feel that a man's talents stand in the way of his advancement in truth. But genius is religious. It is a larger imbibing of the common heart. It is not anomalous, but more like, and not less like other men. There is, in all great poets, a wisdom of humanity which is superior to any talents they exercise. The author, the wit, the partisan, the fine gentleman, does not take place of the man. Humanity shines in Homer, in Chaucer, in Spenser, in Shakespeare, in Milton. They are content with truth. They use the positive degree. They seem frigid and phlegmatic to those who have been spiced with the frantic passion and violent coloring of inferior, but popular writers. For they are poets by the free course which they allow to the informing soul, which through their eyes beholds again, and blesses the things which it hath made. The soul is superior to its knowledge; wiser than any of its works. The great poet makes us feel our own wealth, and then we think less of his compositions. His best communication to our mind is to teach us to despise all he has done. Shakespeare carries us to such a lofty strain of intelligent activity, as to suggest a wealth which beggars his own; and we then feel that the splendid works which he has created, and which in other hours we extol as a sort of self-existent poetry, take no stronger hold of real nature than the shadow of a passing traveler on the rock. The inspiration which uttered itself in Hamlet and Lear could utter things as good from day to day, forever. Why, then, should I make account of Hamlet and Lear, as if we had not the soul from which they fell as syllables from the tongue?

This energy does not descend into individual life on any other condition than entire possession. It comes to the lowly and simple; it comes to whomsoever will put off what is foreign and proud; it comes as insight; it comes as serenity and grandeur. When we see those whom it inhabits, we are apprised of new degrees of greatness. From that inspiration, the man comes back with a changed tone. He does not talk with men with an eye to their opinion. He tries them. It requires of us to be plain and true. The vain traveler attempts to embellish his life by quoting my lord, and the prince, and the countess, who thus said or did to him. The ambitious vulgar show you their spoons, and brooches, and rings, and preserve their cards and compliments. The more cultivated, in their account of their own experience, cull out the pleasing, poetic circumstance, — the visit to Rome, the man of genius they saw, the brilliant friend they know; still further on, perhaps, the gorgeous landscape, the mountain lights, the mountain thoughts, they enjoyed yesterday, — and so seek to throw a romantic color over their life. But the soul that ascends to worship the great God is plain and true; has no rose color, no fine friends, no chivalry, no adventures; does not want admiration; dwells in the hour that now is, in the earnest experience of the common day, — by reason of the present moment and the mere trifle having become porous to thought, and bibulous of the sea of light.

Converse with a mind that is grandly simple, and literature looks like word catching. The simplest utterances are worthiest to be written, yet are they so cheap, and so things of course, that, in the infinite riches of the soul, it is like gathering a few pebbles off the ground, or bottling a little air in a phial, when the whole Earth and the whole atmosphere are ours. Nothing can pass there, or make you one of the circle, but the casting aside your trappings, and dealing man to man in naked truth, plain confession, and omniscient affirmation.

Souls such as these treat you as gods would; walk as gods in the earth, accepting without any admiration your wit, your bounty, your virtue even, — say rather your act of duty, for your virtue they own as their proper blood, royal as themselves, and over-royal, and the father of the gods. But what rebuke their plain fraternal bearing casts on the mutual flattery with which authors solace each other and wound themselves! These flatter not. I do not wonder that these men go to see Cromwell, and Christina, and Charles the Second, and James the First, and the Grand Turk. For they are, in their own elevation, the fellows of kings, and must feel the servile tone of conversation in the world. They must always be a godsend to princes, for they confront them, a king to a king, without ducking or concession, and give a high nature the refreshment and satisfaction of resistance, of plain humanity, of even companionship, and of new ideas. They leave them wiser and superior men. Souls like these make us feel that sincerity is more excellent than flattery. Deal so plainly with man and woman, as to constrain the utmost sincerity, and destroy all hope of trifling with you. It is the highest compliment you can pay. Their "highest praising," said Milton, "is not flattery, and their plainest advice is a kind of praising."

Ineffable is the union of man and God in every act of the soul. The simplest person, who in his integrity worships God, becomes God; yet for ever and ever the influx of this better and universal self is new and unsearchable. It inspires awe and astonishment. How dear, how soothing to man, arises the idea of God, peopling the lonely place, effacing the scars of our mistakes and disappointments! When we have broken our god of tradition, and ceased from our god of rhetoric, then may God fire the heart with his presence. It is the doubling of the heart itself, nay, the infinite enlargement of the heart with a power of growth to a new infinity on every side. It inspires in man an infallible trust. He has not the conviction, but the sight, that the best is the true, and may in that thought easily dismiss all particular uncertainties and fears, and adjourn to the sure revelation of time, the solution of his private riddles. He is sure that his welfare is dear to the heart of being. In the presence of law to his mind, he is overflowed with a reliance so universal, that it sweeps away all cherished hopes and the most stable projects of mortal condition in its flood. He believes that he cannot escape from his good. The things that are really for thee gravitate to thee. You are running to seek your friend. Let your feet run, but your mind need not. If you do not find him, will you not acquiesce that it is best you should not find him? for there is a power, which, as it is in you, is in him also, and could therefore very well bring you together, if it were for the best. You are preparing with eagerness to go and render a service to which your talent and your taste invite you, the love of men and the hope of fame. Has it not occurred to you, that you have no right to go, unless you are equally willing to be prevented from going? O, believe, as thou livest, that every sound that is spoken over the round world, which thou oughtest to hear, will vibrate on thine ear! Every proverb, every book, every byword that belongs to thee for aid or comfort, shall surely come home through open or winding passages. Every friend whom not thy fantastic will, but the great and tender heart in thee craveth, shall lock thee in his embrace. And this, because the heart in thee is the heart of all; not a valve, not a wall, not an intersection is there anywhere in nature, but one blood rolls uninterruptedly an endless circulation through all men, as the water of the globe is all one sea, and, truly seen, its tide is one.

Let man, then, learn the revelation of all nature and all thought to his heart; this, namely; that the Highest dwells with him; that the sources of nature are in his own mind, if the sentiment of duty is there. But if he would know what the great God speaketh, he must 'go into his closet and shut the door,' as Jesus said. God will not make himself manifest to cowards. He must greatly listen to himself, withdrawing himself from all the accents of other men's devotion. Even their prayers are hurtful to him, until he have made his own. Our religion vulgarly stands on numbers of believers. Whenever the appeal is made — no matter how indirectly — to numbers, proclamation is then and there made, that religion is not. He that finds God a sweet, enveloping thought to him never counts his company. When I sit in that presence, who shall dare to come in? When I rest in perfect humility, when I burn with pure love, what can Calvin or Swedenborg say?

It makes no difference whether the appeal is to numbers or to one. The faith that stands on authority is not faith. The reliance on authority measures the decline of religion, the withdrawal of the soul. The position men have given to Jesus, now for many centuries of history, is a position of authority. It characterizes themselves. It cannot alter the eternal facts. Great is the soul, and plain. It is no flatterer, it is no follower; it never appeals from itself. It believes in itself. Before the immense possibilities of man, all mere experience, all past biography, however spotless and sainted, shrinks away. Before that heaven which our presentiments foreshow us, we cannot easily praise any form of life we have seen or read of. We not only affirm that we have few great men, but, absolutely speaking, that we have none; that we have no history, no record of any character or mode of living, that entirely contents us. The saints and demigods whom history worships we are constrained to accept with a grain of allowance. Though in our lonely hours we draw a new strength out of their memory, yet, pressed on our attention, as they are by the thoughtless and customary, they fatigue and invade. The soul gives itself, alone, original, and pure, to the Lonely, Original, and Pure, who, on that condition, gladly inhabits, leads, and speaks through it. Then is it glad, young, and nimble. It is not wise, but it sees through all things. It is not called religious, but it is innocent. It calls the light its own, and feels that the grass grows and the stone falls by a law inferior to, and dependent on, its nature. Behold, it saith, I am born into the great, the universal mind. I, the imperfect, adore my own Perfect. I am somehow receptive of the great soul, and thereby I do overlook the sun and the stars, and feel them to be the fair accidents and effects which change and pass. More and more the surges of everlasting nature enter into me, and I become public and human in my regards and actions. So come I to live in thoughts, and act with energies, which are immortal. Thus revering the soul, and learning, as the ancient said, that "its beauty is immense," man will come to see that the world is the perennial miracle which the soul worketh, and be less astonished at particular wonders; he will learn that there is no profane history; that all history is sacred; that the universe is represented in an atom, in a moment of time. He will weave no longer a spotted life of shreds and patches, but he will live with a divine unity. He will cease from what is base and frivolous in his life, and be content with all places and with any service he can render. He will calmly front the morrow in the negligency of that trust which carries God with it, and so hath already the whole future in the bottom of the heart.

Appendix C

Introduction - Battiscombe Gunn
From-The Instruction of Ptah-Hotep...[6]

"Is there anything whereof it may be said,
See, this is new?
It hath been already of old time,
Which was before us.
There is no remembrance of former things;
Neither shall there be any remembrance
Of things that are to come
With those that shall come after."

In these days, when all things and memories of the past are at
length become not only subservient to, but submerged by, the matters
and needs of the immediate present, those paths of knowledge that lead
into regions seemingly remote from such needs are somewhat
discredited; and the aims of those that follow them whither they lead are
regarded as quite out of touch with the real interests of life. Very greatly
is this so with archaeology, and the study of ancient and curious tongues,
and searchings into old thoughts on high and ever insistent questions; a
public which has hardly time to read more than its daily newspaper and
its weekly novel has denounced—almost dismissed—them, with many
other noble and wonderful things, as "unpractical", whatever that vague
and hollow word may mean.

As to those matters which lie very far back, concerning the lands of
several thousand years ago, it is very generally held that they are the
proper and peculiar province of specialists, dry-as-dusts, and persons
with an irreducible minimum of human nature. It is thought that
knowledge concerning them, not the blank ignorance regarding them
that almost everywhere obtains, is a thing of which to be rather
ashamed, a detrimental possession; in a word, that the subject is not
only unprofitable (a grave offence), but also uninteresting, and therefore
contemptible. This is a true estimate of general opinion, although there
are those who will, for their own sakes, gainsay it.

When, therefore, I state that one of the writings herein translated
has an age of nearly six thousand years, and that another is but five
hundred years younger, it is likely that many will find this sufficient
reason against further perusal, deeming it impossible that such things

can possess attraction for one not an enthusiast for them. Yet so few are the voices across so great a span of years that those among them having anything to tell us should be welcome exceedingly; whereas, for the most part, they have cried in the wilderness of neglect hitherto, or fallen on ears filled with the clamor of more instant things.

I could show, if this were a fitting place, that Archaeology is not at all divorced from life, nor even devoid of emotion as subtle and strange, as swift and moving, as that experienced by those who love and follow Art. She, Archaeology, is, for those who know her, full of such emotion; garbed in an imperishable glamour, she is raised far above the turmoil of the present on the wings of Imagination. Her eyes are somber with the memory of the wisdom driven from her scattered sanctuaries; and at her lips wonderful things strive for utterance. In her are gathered together the longings and the laughter, the fears and failures, the sins and splendors and achievements of innumerable generations of men; and by her we are shown all the elemental and terrible passions of the unchanging soul of man, to which all cultures and philosophies are but garments to hide its nakedness; and thus, in her, as in Art, some of us may realize ourselves. Withal she is heavyhearted, making continual lamentation for a glory that has withered and old hopes without fulfilment; and all her habitations are laid waste.

As for the true lover of all old and forgotten things, it may justly be said of him, as of the poet, Nascitur, non fit. For the dreams and the wonder are with him from the beginning; and in early childhood, knowing as yet hardly the names of ancient peoples, he is conscious of, and yearns instinctively toward, an immense and ever receding past. With the one, as with the other, the unaccountable passion is so knitted into his soul that it will never, among a thousand distractions and adverse influences, entirely forsake him; nor can such an one by willing cause it to come or to depart. He will live much in imagination, therein treading fair places now enwrapped in their inevitable shroud of windblown sand; building anew temples whose stones hardly remain one upon the other, consecrate to gods dead as their multitudes of worshippers; holding converse with the sages who, with all their lore, could not escape the ultimate oblivion: a spectator of splendid pageants, a ministrant at strange rites, a witness to vast tragedies, he also has admittance to the magical kingdom, to which is added the freedom of the city of Remembrance. His care will be to construct, patiently and with much labor, a picture (which is often less than an outline) of the conditions of the humanity that has been; and he neither rejects nor despises any relic, however trivial or unlovely, that will help him, in its degree, to understand better that humanity or to bridge the wide chasms of his ignorance. Moreover, great age hallows all things, even the most mean, investing them with a certain sanctity; and the little sandal of a nameless child, or the rude amulet placed long ago with weeping on the still bosom of a friend, will move his heart as strongly by its appeal as the proud and enduring monument of a great conqueror insatiable of praise. At times, moving among the tokens of a period that the ravenous years dare not wholly efface in passing, he hears, calling faintly as from afar, innumerable voices—the voices of those who, stretching forth in Sheol eager hands toward life, greatly desire that some memorial of them, be it but a name, may survive in the world of men"

Appendix D

Worship of symbols - CF Chasseboeuf, Marquis de Volney
From-The Ruins: A Survey of the Revolutions of Empires[195]

"From the instant this agricultural race had turned an eye of observation on the stars, they found it necessary to distinguish individuals or groups, and to assign to each a proper name. A considerable difficulty here presented itself; for on the one hand, the celestial bodies, similar in form, offered no peculiar character by which to denominate them; and on the other hand, language, poor and in a state of infancy, had no expressions for so many new and metaphysical ideas. The usual stimulus of genius, necessity, conquered all obstacles. Having remarked that in the annual revolution, the renewal and periodical appearance of the productions of the Earth were constantly connected with the rising and setting of certain stars, and with their position relatively to the sun, the mind, by a natural mechanism, associated in its thought terrestrial and celestial objects, which had in fact a certain alliance; and applying to them the same sign, it gave to the stars and the groups it formed of them, the very names of the terrestrial objects to which they bore affinity.

Thus the Ethiopian of Thebes called stars of inundation, or of Aquarius, those under which the river began to overflow; stars of the ox or bull, those under which it was convenient to plough the earth; stars of the lion, those under which that animal, driven by thirst from the deserts, made his appearance on the banks of the Nile; stars of the sheaf, or of the harvest maid, those under which the harvests were got in; stars of the lambs, stars of the goat, those under which those valuable animals brought forth their young; and thus was a first part of the difficulty resolved.

On the other hand, man, having remarked in the beings that surrounded him certain qualities peculiar to each species, and having invented a name by which to design them, speedily discovered an ingenious mode of generalizing his ideas, and transferring the name already invented to everything bearing a similar or analogous property or agency, enriched his language with a multiplicity of metaphors and tropes.

Thus, the same Ethiopian, having observed that the return of the inundation answered constantly to the appearance of a very beautiful star towards the source of the Nile, which seemed to warn the husbandman against being surprised by the waters, he compared this action with that of the animal who by barking gives notice of danger, and called this star the dog, the barker (Sirius). In the same manner he called stars of the crab, those which showed themselves when the sun, having reached the bounds of the tropic, returned backwards and sideways like the crab or Cancer; stars of the wild goat, those which, the sun being arrived at its greatest altitude, at the top of the horary gnomon, imitated the action of that animal who delights in climbing the highest rocks; stars of the balance, those which, the days and nights being of the same length, seemed to observe an equilibrium like that instrument; stars of the scorpion, those which were perceptible when certain regular winds brought a burning vapor like the poison of the scorpion. In the same manner, he called by the name of rings and serpents the figured traces of the orbits of the stars and planets; and this was the general means of appellation of all the heavenly bodies, taken in groups or individually, according to their connection with rural and terrestrial operations, and the analogies which every nation found them to bear to the labors of the field and the objects of their climate and soil.

From this proceeding it resulted, that abject and terrestrial beings entered into association with the superior and powerful beings of the heavens; and this association became more riveted every day by the very constitution of language and the mechanism of the mind. Men would say, by a natural metaphor: 'The bull spreads upon the Earth the germs of fecundity (in spring); and brings back abundance by the revival of vegetation. The lamb (or ram) delivers the heavens from the malevolent Genii of winter; and saves the world from the serpent (emblem of the wet season). The scorpion pours out his venom upon the earth, and spreads diseases and death, etc.'

This language, understood by everybody, was at first attended with no inconvenience; but, in process of time, when the almanac had been regulated, the people, who could do without further observation of the skies, lost sight of the motive which led to the adoption of these expressions; and the allegory still remaining in the practices of life, became a fatal stumbling block to the understanding and reason. Habituated to join to symbols the ideas of their models, the mind finally confounded them; then those same animals which the imagination had raised to heaven, descended again on the earth; but in this return, decked in the livery and invested with the attributes of the stars, they imposed upon their own authors. The people, imagining that they saw their Gods before them, found it a more easy task to offer up their prayers. They demanded of the ram of their flock, the influence which they expected from the celestial ram; they prayed the scorpion not to pour out his venom upon Nature; they revered the fish of the river, the crab of the sea, and the scarab of the slime; and by a series of corrupt, but inseparable analogies, they lost themselves in a labyrinth of consequent absurdities.

Such was the origin of this ancient and singular worship of animals; such the train of ideas by which the character of the Divinity became common to the meanest of the brute creation; and thus was formed the vast, complicated, and learned theological system which, from the banks of the Nile, conveyed from country to country by commerce, war, and conquest, invaded all the old world; and which, modified by times, by circumstances, and by prejudices, is still to be found among a hundred nations, and subsists to this day as the secret and inseparable basis of the theology of those even who despise and reject it."

At these words, murmurs being heard in various groups: "I repeat it," continued the orator. "People of Africa, hence, for example, has arisen among you the adoration of your fetishes, plants, animals, pebbles, bits of wood, before which your ancestors would never have been so absurd as to prostrate themselves, if they had not seen in them talismans, partaking of the nature of the stars! Nations of Tartary, this is equally the origin of your Marmouzets, and of the whole train of animals with which your Chamans ornament their magic robes! This is the origin of those figures of birds and serpents, which all the savage nations, with mystic and sacred ceremonies, imprint on their skin. Indians, it is in vain you cover yourselves with the veil of mystery: the hawk of your God Vichenou is but one of the thousand emblems of the sun in Egypt, and his incarnations in a fish, boar, lion, turtle, together with all his monstrous adventures, are nothing more than the metamorphoses of the same star, which, passing successively through the signs of the twelve animals, was supposed to assume their forms, and to act their astronomical parts! Japanese, your bull which breaks the egg of the world, is merely that of the heavens, which, in times of yore, opened the age of the creation, the equinox of Spring! Rabbins, Jews, that same bull is the Apis worshipped in Egypt, and which your ancestors adored in the idol of the golden calf! It is also your bull, children of Zoroaster, that, sacrificed in the symbolic mysteries of Mithra, shed a blood fertilizing to the world.! Lastly, your bull of the Apocalypse, Christians, with his wings, the symbol of the air, has no other origin: your lamb of God, immolated, like the bull of Mithra, for the salvation of the world, is the selfsame sun in the sign of the celestial ram, which, in a subsequent age, opening the equinox in his turn, was deemed to have rid the world of the reign of evil, that is to say, of the serpent, of the large snake, the mother of winter and emblem of the Ahrimanes or Satan of the Persians, your institutors! Yes, vainly does your imprudent zeal consign idolaters to the torments of the Tartarus which they have invented: the whole basis of your system is nothing more than the worship of the star of day, whose attributes you have heaped upon your chief personage. It is the sun which, under the name of Orus, was born, like your God, in the arms of the celestial virgin, and passed through an obscure, indigent, and destitute childhood, answering to the season of cold and frost. It is the sun, which, under the name of Osiris, persecuted by Typhon and the tyrants of the air, was put to death, laid in a dark tomb, the emblem of the hemisphere of winter, and which, rising afterwards from the inferior zone to the highest point of the heavens, awoke triumphant over giants and the destroying angels. Ye priests, from whom the murmurs proceed, you wear yourselves its signs all over your bodies! Your tonsure is the disk of the sun; your stole its Zodiac; your rosaries the symbols of the stars and planets. Pontiffs and prelates, your mitre, your crosier, your mantle, are the emblems of Osiris; and that crucifix of which you boast the mystery, without comprehending it, is the cross of Serapis, traced by the hands of Egyptian priests on the plan of the figurative world, which, passing through the equinoxes and the tropics, became the emblem of future life and resurrection, because it touched the gates of ivory and horn through which the soul was to pass in its way to heaven!"

Here the doctors of the different groups looked with astonishment at one another, but none of them breaking silence, the orator continued.

"Three principal causes concurred to produce this confusion of ideas. First, the necessity, on account of the infant state of language, of making use of figurative expressions to depict the relations of things; expressions that, passing afterwards from a proper to a general, from a physical to a moral sense, occasioned, by their equivocal and synonymous terms, a multiplicity of mistakes.

Thus, having at first said, that the sun surmounted and passed in its course through the twelve animals, they afterwards supposed that it combated, conquered, and killed them, and from this was composed the historical life of Hercules.

Having said that it regulated the period of rural operations, of seed time and of harvest; that it distributed the seasons, ran through the climates, swayed the earth, etc.. It was taken for a legislative king, a conquering warrior, and hence they formed the stories of Osiris, of Bacchus, and other similar Gods.

Having said that a planet entered into a sign, the conjunction was denominated a marriage, adultery, incest: having farther said, that it was buried, because it sunk below the horizon, returned to light and gained its state of eminence, they gave it the epithet of dead, risen again, carried into heaven, etc.

The second cause of confusion was the material figures themselves, by which thoughts were originally painted, and which, under the name of hieroglyphics, or sacred characters, were the first invention of the mind. Thus, to denote an inundation, and the necessity of preserving one's self from it, they painted a boat, the vessel Argo; to express the wind, they painted a bird's wing; to specify the season, the month, they delineated the bird of passage, insect, or animal, which made its appearance at that epoch; to express winter they drew a hog, or a serpent, which are fond of moist and miry places. The combination of these figures had also a meaning, and was substituted for words and phrases. But as there was nothing fixed or precise in this sort of language, as the number of those figures and their combinations became excessive and burdensome to the memory, confusions and false interpretations were the first and obvious result. Genius having afterwards invented the more simple art of applying signs to sounds, of which the number is limited, and of painting the word instead of the thought, hieroglyphic pictures were, by means of alphabetical writing, brought into disuse; and from day to day their forgotten significations made way for a variety of illusions, equivoques, and errors.

Lastly, the civil organization of the first states was a third cause of confusion. Indeed, when the people began to apply themselves to agriculture, the formation of the rural calendar requiring continual astronomical observations, it was necessary to choose individuals whose province it should be to watch the appearance and setting of certain stars, to give notice of the return of the inundation, of particular winds and rains, and the proper time for sowing every species of grain. These men, on account of their office, were exempted from the common occupations, and the society provided for their subsistence. In this situation, solely occupied in making observations, they soon penetrated the great phenomena of nature, and dived into the secret of various of her operations. They became acquainted with the course of the stars and planets; the connection which their absence and return had with the productions of the Earth and the activity of vegetation: the medicinal or nutritive properties of fruits and plants; the action of the elements, and their reciprocal affinities. But, as there were no means of communicating this knowledge otherwise than by the painful and laborious one of oral instruction, they imparted it only to their friends and kindred; and hence resulted a concentration of science in certain families, who, on this account assumed to themselves exclusive privileges, and a spirit of corporation and separate distinction fatal to the public weal. By this continued succession of the same labors and enquiries, the progress of knowledge it is true was hastened, but, by the mystery that accompanied it, the people, plunged daily in the thickest darkness, became more superstitious and more slavish. Seeing human beings produce certain phenomena, announce, as it were at will, eclipses and comets, cure diseases, handle noxious serpents, they supposed them to have intercourse with celestial powers; and, to obtain the good or have the ills averted which they expected from those powers, they adopted these extraordinary human beings as mediators and interpreters. And thus were established in the very bosom of states sacrilegious corporations of hypocritical and deceitful men, who arrogated to themselves every kind of power; and priests, being at once astronomers, divines, naturalists, physicians, necromancers, interpreters of the Gods, oracles of the people, rivals of kings or their accomplices, instituted under the name of religion an empire of mystery, which to this very hour has proved ruinous to the nations of mankind."

At these words the priests of all the groups interrupted the orator; with loud cries, they accused him of impiety, irreligion, blasphemy, and were unwilling he should proceed: but the legislators having observed, that what he related was merely a narrative of historical facts; that if those facts were false or forged, it would be an easy matter to refute them; and that if everyone were not allowed the perfect liberty to declare his opinion, it would be impossible to arrive at truth—he thus went on with his discourse.

"From all these causes, and the perpetual association of dissimilar ideas, there followed a strange mass of disorders in theology, morality, and tradition. And first, because the stars were represented by animals, the qualities of the animals, their likings, their sympathies, their aversions, were transferred to the Gods and supposed to be their actions. Thus, the God Ichneumon made war against the God crocodile; the God wolf wanted to eat the God sheep; the God stork devoured the God serpent; and the Deity became a strange, whimsical, ferocious being, whose idea misled the judgment of man, and corrupted both his morals and his reason.

Again, as every family, every nation, in the spirit of its worship adopted a particular star or constellation for its patron, the affections and antipathies of the emblematical brute were transferred to the sectaries of this worship; and the partisans of the God dog were enemies to those of the God wolf; the worshippers of the God bull, abhorred those who fed upon beef, and religion became the author of combats and animosities, the senseless cause of frenzy and superstition.

Farther, the names of the animal stars having, on account of this same patronage, been conferred on nations, countries, mountains, and rivers, those objects were also taken for Gods; and hence there arose a medley of geographical, historical, and mythological beings, by which all tradition was involved in confusion.

In fine, from the analogy of their supposed actions the planetary gods having been taken for men, heroes, and kings; kings and heroes took in their turn the actions of the Gods for models, and became, from imitation, warlike, conquering, sanguinary, proud, lascivious, indolent; and religion consecrated the crimes of despots, and perverted the principles of governments."

CPSIA information can be obtained
at www.ICGtesting.com
Printed in the USA
BVHW080759060620
581009BV00001B/7